W9-AXF-293

CYCLE OF FIRE

Stephen J. Pyne

"Cycle of Fire" is a suite of books that collectively narrate the story of how fire and humanity have interacted to shape the earth. "Cycle" is an apt description of how fire functions in the natural world. Yet "cycle" also bears a mythic connotation: a set of sagas that tell the life of a culture hero. Here that role belongs to fire. Ranging across all continents and over thousands of years, the Cycle shows Earth to be a fire planet in which carbon-based terrestrial life and an oxygen-rich atmosphere have combined to make combustion both elemental and inevitable. Equally, the Cycle reveals humans as fire creatures, alternately dependent upon and threatened by their monopoly over combustion. Fire's possession began humanity's great dialogue with the Earth. "Cycle of Fire" tells, for the first time, that epic story.

"Cycle of Fire" is part of Weyerhaeuer Environmental Books, published by the University of Washington Press under the general editorship of William Cronon. A complete list of Weyerhaeuser Environmental Books appears at the end of this book.

World Fire: The Culture of Fire on Earth (paperback reprint, 1997)

Vestal Fire: An Environmental History, Told through Fire, of Europe and Europe's Encounter with the World

Fire in America: A Cultural History of Wildland and Rural Fire (paperback reprint, 1997)

Burning Bush: A Fire History of Australia (paperback reprint, 1998)

The Ice: A Journey to Antarctica (paperback reprint, 1998)

Vestal Fire

An Environmental History,
Told through Fire, of Europe and
Europe's Encounter with the World

Stephen J. Pyne

Foreword by William Cronon

UNIVERSITY OF WASHINGTON PRESS

Seattle and London

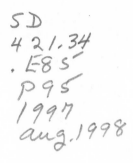

Vestal Fire has been published with the assistance of a grant from the Weyerhaeuser Environmental Books Endowment, established by the Weyerhaeuser Company Foundation, members of the Weyerhaeuser family, and Janet and Jack Creighton.

Library of Congress Cataloging-in-Publication Data

Pyne, Stephen J., 1949–
    Vestal fire : an environmental history, told through fire, of
Europe and Europe's encounter with the world / Stephen J. Pyne ;
foreword by William Cronon.
        p.   cm. — (Cycle of fire)
    Includes bibliographical references (p.   ) and index.
    ISBN 0-295-97596-2 (alk. paper)
    1. Wildfires—Europe.   2. Fires—Europe.   3. Fire ecology—Europe.
4. Wildfires.   5. Fires.   6. Fire ecology.   I. Title.   II. Series: Pyne,
Stephen J. 1949–   Cycle of fire.
    SD421.34.E85P95   1997
    304.2—dc21   97–19032
                                                                          CIP

The paper used in this publication meets the minimum requirements of American National Standard for Information Sciences—Permanence of Paper for Printed Library Materials, ANSI Z39.48-1984.

To

Sonja, Lydia, Molly

Tack så mycket

and

Johann

mit vielen Grußen

CONTENTS

Book 1: ELEMENTS

FOREWORD:
THE SACRED HEARTH
William Cronon

Vestal Fire, simply put, is Stephen Pyne's masterpiece. In it, he offers nothing less than a retelling of all of European history from a vantage point no other historian has ever adopted so consistently before: that of the fire which in Pyne's view burns at the very heart of Western civilization. Fire, he argues, was pivotal throughout the long process of creating Europe as we know it today: employed by early European peoples to clear the continent for agriculture, present always in the march of armies and empires, contained but never fully controlled in the rise of a new urban-industrial order, and fundamental to Europe's eventual colonial expansion to the far corners of the planet. Rarely have such disparate and far-reaching environmental and historical phenomena been brought together between the covers of a single book, and rarely has an author been able to reveal so many unexpected connections by choosing so unusual a lens through which to view some of the most familiar material in human history.

The book is a masterpiece not merely in the sense that it is a great work of scholarly synthesis, but also because Stephen Pyne has been preparing himself to write it for at least the past two decades. When Pyne embarked during the early 1980s on the long journey that would eventually become his multi-volume "Cycle of Fire," his destination was as yet not clear. Beginning with the continent he knew best—North America—he traced the regional variation of fire ecology and management across the different parts of the United States, producing *Fire in America* before he even knew that it might have successors. Because of that book, he received one of the MacArthur Foundation's cele-brated fellowships, enabling him to pursue his personal scholarly passion with a single-mindedness that might not otherwise have been possible. Liberated in this way, Pyne wandered from his home ground of North America, first to the fireless continent of Antarctica to write *The Ice,* and then to Australia to record in *Burning Bush* the story of a landscape ablaze with fire-loving euca-lyptus. Only then did Pyne fully embrace the vision that has since emerged as "Cycle of Fire": a series of books dedicated to retelling our human past as a tale of people and fire cooperating in a shape-shifting but never-ending part-nership to transform the face of the earth. Pyne offered a suggestive and provocative series of sketches for that epic story in his book *World Fire,* but only now, in this latest volume, is the full promise of his original vision finally realized.

Vestal Fire takes its title from the Roman goddess Vesta, keeper of the sacred fire and tender of the sacred hearth on Mount Olympus. The title suggests the core of Pyne's argument: the story of civilization is in fact the story of fire. Between the untamed fire of the wilderness and the seemingly tamed fire of the hearth lies a never-ending dialectic in which human beings struggle to control natural forces and processes that in fact can sometimes be directed but never wholly dominated or contained. From this beginning, Pyne takes us on a complex tour across thousands of years and many hundreds of miles. He begins with climate, topography, and vegetation, carefully tracing the intricate geographical elements that have combined to create the different firescapes of Europe. The crisscrossing vectors that make some parts of the continent hot and others cold, some parts of it wet and others dry, define a broad set of regional boundaries in which Mediterranean fire ecology (and hence fire *culture*) is necessarily very different from that of the boreal north.

Having introduced the natural geography of fire, Pyne casts a long view back in time to examine prehistory, the movements of ancient peoples as they occupied this landscape and shaped it to their own purposes, more often than not employing fire as one of their chief tools in the process. The result is a story of hominid evolution and early cultural history in which fire becomes an ever-present companion to human beings as they proliferate across the European continent and begin to create their different communities in different regional landscapes. With this as an introduction, we are ready to absorb one of Pyne's most important lessons: we will best understand European fire history as an epic narrative in which certain common themes—the use of fire for clearing, its role in maintaining transhumance grazing lands, its contribution to warfare, the importance of accumulating fuel burdens in determining the likelihood of conflagration, and so on—recapitulate but also transform themselves from region to region. The large central section of this book looks in turn at central Europe, the boreal north, the Mediterranean, the Slavic steppes, and the Atlantic west, to demonstrate the profound differences and similarities that have joined and separated the parallel histories of these areas. In each case, fire turns out to be far more central to the evolving landscape and regional culture than one might have realized had one not been in the hands of this unusual guide.

For most authors, this immense geographical and historical survey would have been more than enough to make a book. But not Stephen Pyne. He knows too well that the history of empire gives European fire a significance far beyond Europe itself. And so *Vestal Fire* closes with a remarkable set of chapters on the spread of European fire practices and relationships across the entire planet as an inextricable part of the colonial enterprise. Just as Alfred Crosby once demonstrated in his classic *Ecological Imperialism* that the expansion of Europe is inexplicable without a firm understanding of its biological components, so too does Stephen Pyne now reveal how important fire has been to that same process. It is in these closing chapters that one finally realizes the breathtaking scope of Pyne's intellectual vision, enabling us to see fire as the fundamental force it so clearly has been throughout human history—despite its near invisibility in the work of most other historians. Readers who make their way to the grand conclusion of this long volume will find themselves rewarded with new historical and environmental perspectives that they would be unlikely to gain in any other way.

That said, it is worth adding a word of warning. Fire is not like the human protagonists that occupy center stage in most history books. It possesses great power and it is an almost irresistible agent in shaping the course of events. Although most histories focus almost entirely on the actions of human beings, in this book fire is an actor coequal with the people who try to possess and control it. But it is also an actor without consciousness, an agent whose motives remain inscrutable, a protagonist whose morality we have no plausible way to judge. And so our ordinary human ways of understanding and empathizing with the characters in stories, our strategies for extracting moral meanings from our own past, do not work very well in a book like this one. No simple linear plot line could possibly encompass the protean central character or the wandering, cycling, epic plot line that lie at the heart of *Vestal Fire*.

As a result, the book can be difficult, even frustrating reading for those who like their stories neat and clean, with unambiguous moral lessons and a clear sense of closure to impose Aristotelian order on an otherwise uncertain and chaotic reality. Hidden within this seeming chaos is in fact another important lesson that Stephen Pyne wishes his readers to extract from his long, variegated narrative. It is simply this: like many other parts of nature, the protean demiurge called fire will never deign to be encompassed by the simple stories people might wish to tell of it. Over and over again, our efforts to impose our wills so as to make fire fit the tidy, convenient, orderly world that we ourselves imagine we might prefer to inhabit have ultimately yielded hubris and failure. Instead, fire inhabits an ineluctable dialectic between order and chaos, between human control and the uncertain nature we would work so hard to repress. To recognize this is to learn something profoundly important not just about fire, but about history and nature both.

Readers will therefore get the most from *Vestal Fire* if they shed some of their ordinary expectations about what a work of history should look like. Fires do not burn according to simple linear rules, and this book reflects that complexity. Although it is probably best read from beginning to end, it will also repay—and perhaps repay in different ways—a more wandering approach in which a sampling of places and times that are more familiar becomes an entrée into places and times that are less so. Stephen Pyne is not only a superb scholar but an elegant and playful crafter of images and metaphors and journeys. He rarely takes the direct path to reach the destination toward which he is leading us, but this is because his side tours and digressions are just as interesting as the main path of the burn he is helping us follow. The best policy in reading him, therefore, is simply to trust him to keep moving forward even when the way seems momentarily obscure. His passion for fire and history makes him a most unusual guide, and we are fortunate indeed to have the benefit of his company for the grand tour this book lays out for us.

AUTHOR'S NOTE

How can I answer which is best
Of all the fires that burn?
I have been too often host or guest
At every fire in turn.
—Rudyard Kipling, "The Fires"

Vestal Fire is the fifth volume in the "Cycle of Fire" suite, and the most comprehensive of its narratives. The early Cycle had evolved opportunistically, its volumes a kind of Leatherstocking Tales, written as circumstances had made possible, which is to say, out of sequence, rife with gaps and overlaps, and void of a narrative driver. It fell to *Vestal Fire* to bring historical structure to this sprawl, to serve as a thematic locomotive that might, if successful, pull the other volumes in its train. That the Earth's fire history over the past five hundred years has been influenced profoundly by Europe makes this scheme plausible. The book represents my mature understanding of what a fire history can do and how it can be told. To it I have tried to invest something of Spanish zeal, French clarity, German thoroughness, Russian sweep, Dutch detail, English eccentricity, and (yes) American naïveté.

If the book is to stand alone, as it should, it must revisit some topics contained in previous volumes, even to the point of virtually recycling essays (such as the fire history of Britain) or of retelling in fresh ways the experiences of British imperial forestry, for example, or the histories of European colonization in America and Australia. To the irritated or unimpressed, this will smack of repetition. To those anxious for connections or curious only about Europe, those points of contact should serve as welds and linchpins.

What has ultimately resulted is a literary analogue to a fire-patched landscape, some sites burned intensely, some lightly, some reburned, some missed. My hope is that for history, as for nature, a scene spot-burned or burned erratically is often better than one not burned at all.

Many persons have assisted in this project, knowingly or not, willingly or not.

Special mention first goes to the staff of the Fletcher Library at Arizona State University West, most notably Carol Hammond, Sondra Brough, and Elizabeth Smith. They were invariably efficient and ineffably cheerful, and without their indefatigable labors through interlibrary loans this book would not exist.

Among those who assisted with translation are: Gunilla Oleskog (Swedish); Muriel Osborne and Rex Olpin (French); Henry Telitsyn, Richard McNabb, and Mrs. N. I. Veruigina (Russian); Hannele Mortensen (Finnish); Hartmuth Weismann and Johann Goldammer (German). Without their assistance, I could never have plumbed far into the national literatures that proved so rich in fire references.

A Fulbright Fellowship took me and my family to Sweden for three months. This gave me the opportunity to plunge into Swedish and Finnish material. For their willing assistance (and excellent English) I want to thank Olle Zackrisson, Anders Granström, Lars Östlund, Jonny Schimmel, Marie-Charlotte Nilsen, Gunilla Oleskog, and the rest at the Wallenberg Lab, Sveriges Landbruksuniversitet, Umeå.

Various European and American colleagues have helped with information and travels. I wish to thank, in particular, Ricardo Velez Muñoz, Michael Williams, Alexander Dimitrakopoulos, Johan Goudsblom, Peter Lex, and Louis Trabaud. Cathy Frierson very generously lent me drafts of chapters from her book on the social history of fire in European Russia, and shared information that otherwise would have been beyond my grasp. Three Russian scientists contributed, under contract, some very helpful essays on fire ecology and history: Henry Telitsyn, Nicolas Kurbatsky, and V. V. Furyaev. For a most productive expedition to the Soviet Union, I wish to thank various officials with Avialesookhrana, but especially Nicolai Andreev and Eduard Davydenko. Not least, I wish to thank my companion on those travels—and unfailing source of enthusiasm and references—Johann Georg Goldammer, Europe's outstanding fire ecologist and fellow pyromantic.

Administrators and colleagues at Arizona State University West—the Little Campus That Could—made it possible for me to exploit a MacArthur Fellowship and have encouraged me in my unorthodox pursuits. That a new campus, rising out of the creosote and brittlebush of degraded desert, could support such an endeavor speaks volumes about its determination and future promise.

Onno Brouwer and his colleagues at the University of Wisconsin Cartographic Laboratory made or remade a host of maps with care and clarity. The Lab has my thanks and will earn the gratitude of *Vestal*'s readers.

William Cronon and Simon Schama read the manuscript, Bill at an early stage and Simon at a later one. Both got more than they bargained for, and both have earned my enduring gratitude. Beyond identifying assorted errors and malapropisms, they compelled me to think through the premises of the book. To oversimplify their subtle critiques, Bill urged me to think more pedagogically; Simon, more artistically. Bill sought more explanations and fewer evocations. Simon suggested, in effect, that fire be seen as an art form. Torch could be brush, chisel, mortar: the landscapes it shaped as canvas, statue, building. Something of the complexity and nuance of European experience (and a greater empathy for that experience) could thus replace the book's polemical bias. Valid critiques both; our exchanges have changed some of the tone and style of parts, all for the better. Perhaps I could have done more.

But the book has a different conceit, and *Vestal*'s liabilities are also a measure of its purpose. It was my intention to redirect the narrative core away from humanity per se and into its competition (and symbiosis) with fire. Instead of circling around a human center, the narrative inscribes a kind of ellipse, balancing two foci, humans and nature, their traced and shared circumference a curve of fire. The book begins and ends with fire. That decision placed the text, for better or worse, outside the conventions of traditional genres.

And it placed an even greater burden on the book's context. That context is the "Cycle of Fire" suite. That the Cycle exists in print is due to the vision and good will of William Cronon, editor of the Weyerhaeuser Environmental Books; Donald Ellegood, director emeritus of the University of Washington Press; and Gerard McCauley, my ever-tolerant agent. Special gratitude goes to Julidta Tarver, whose bottomless patience and tact make criticism almost a pleasure to receive, and to Leila Charbonneau, gifted copyeditor, who let me speak in my own voice but smoothed its stuttering and expunged from it many errors and idiocies. I extend to them all my sincerest thanks.

To Sonja, Lydia, and Molly, who reified the hearth fire from an ancient symbol into a living presence, my thanks, and my love.

Stephen J. Pyne
Alpine, Arizona; Glendale, Arizona

Vestal Fire

*An Environmental History, Told through Fire, of
Europe and Europe's Encounter with the World*

Every Greek state had its prytaneum which may be described as the town-hall of the capital. . . . The essential feature of the prytaneum was its hearth. . . . On this hearth there burned a perpetual fire. The prytaneum was sacred to Hestia, the personified goddess of the hearth. . . .

Turning to Italy we at once identify the Latin Vesta with the Greek Hestia. . . .

The question still remains, why was so much importance attached to the maintenance of a perpetual fire? The extinction of this fire at Rome was regarded as the greatest misfortune that could befall the state. . . . That its history goes back to the embryo state of human civilization seems proved by the fact that when the fire chanced to go out it was formally rekindled by the most primitive of all modes of lighting a fire, that of rubbing two sticks against each other.

James George Frazer (1885)

PROLOGUE
Quest for Fire

Before there was Europe, there was fire.

When Europe was little more than a crustal slab amid vast oceans, there was oxygen, spewed first from the seas like foam, baptizing every nook of planetary surface with its reactive chemistry. There were also terrestrial plants, seasonally or at least episodically dried and cured and available for burning. And there was lightning generally and volcanoes locally to spark the brew to life, setting it to simmer over a geologic hearthstone. By the Carboniferous era fossil charcoal made up a significant fraction of the organic sediments that would evolve into the coal beds of Wales and the Ruhr. Once kindled, that fire would never be completely extinguished.

Crustal Europe grew as its continental core smashed into North America and then broke away, welded to Siberia and Africa, ringing that central fire with basins, some of which flooded, and mountains, many of which towered around it like immense reflector stones. Over the eons Europe's biota evolved, vanished, migrated, retreated, fiercely seizing sites exposed by rising mountain, subsiding sea, or receding ice, but always stoking the stony hearth with combustibles. The passage of storms, seasons, and climates acted like a bellows, alternately quelling fire into coals or fanning it into flame. Lightning continued its restless foraging, ever probing for suitable kindling. Eventually fire-wielding humans joined that search, sometimes supplementing and sometimes competing with lightning but always rearranging the biomass that sustained combustion. Their quest became an obsession. They could not live without fire. The manipulation of fire was their biotic niche, an evolutionary charge to their species.

In time, Europe's humans claimed the possession of fire as their own; the fire regimes of Europe were those that they, through deliberation or default, made possible. Europe sought fire, seized it, remade it, nurtured, feared, distrusted, craved, shackled, and unleashed it. As with the rest of its natural endowment, Europe sought above all to domesticate fire, to subject it to the discipline of the garden, to subordinate it to the order of society. Anthropogenic fire replaced natural fire. Fire became a tool, a tamed beast, a sacred symbol, an obedient

3

servant. It knew its place in the social order and kept to it. In truth, civilization was impossible without fire; and the tended fire became Western civilization's most elementary emblem of itself. In their symbiosis, fire and civilization each took on the attributes of the other.

Europe displayed characteristic fire practices much as it exhibited basic literary themes and decorative designs. There were diagnostic European fire regimes just as there were distinctive agricultural fields, city architectures, and economic systems. It is possible to study Europe's fire regimes as one might read its novels, study its paintings, or analyze its political institutions for their cultural revelations. Boreal and mediterranean fire practices were as alike in purpose and as different in form as a Norwegian stave church and a Greek temple. As its population swelled and its agriculture intensified, Europe could less and less imagine a world outside the socially constructed landscape and could conceive of fire within no context other than its service to human society.

There was literally no place in Europe for the primordial fire. It went the way of the auroch, the lion, the mastodon, and the mouflon—extinct, bred to domestication, recorded in art, or nurtured in the social zoos of preserved ritual. The originating fire survived only in ancient ceremonies, like vanished bison recorded on Aurignacian rock art, and it flourished only in times so unsettled that the fabric of society was shredded. Then wildfire reappeared like a monstrous birth, and became a feral force that, savage with the memory of its suppression, revolted violently against its warders. Desired fire belonged on hearth and altar; unwanted fire appeared along the rough fringes of an unraveling society, in the cracks of disintegrating cities, amid the rubble of collapsed civilizations. Intellectual Europe saw fire as an atavism, as disorder and destruction, as nature gripped by delirium tremens. But wild or tame, fire persisted. Humans could neither wholly control it nor live without it. Now here, now there, now quiescently, now violently, Europe burned.

In much of this, Europe was not so different from other continents. Everywhere humans exploited fire, shaped raw terrains into habitats through fire, and countered the wild fire with the domesticated. But Europe's peculiar geography and dense demographics, and the intensity of its agricultural reclamation, gave European fire a special character. Europe's temperate core—not shaped by a well-defined fire season—granted humans an unusual degree of control over fire, and encouraged the belief that fire was, in principle, a strictly human agency, that it was a convenient tool but not an essential process. If fire's importance was instrumental and ceremonial, it could be replaced by less volatile technologies and more modern rites, much as wheat replaced weedy brome and draft oxen replaced wild aurochs. Fire was, so the saying went, a good servant but a bad master.

The keepers of Europe's flame accepted this condition as normative. They distrusted free-burning fire and sought to cultivate it from the landscape and ultimately replace it with the industrial combustion of fossil fuels. Europe came itself to resemble a fire in which a burned-out core smoldered, aglow with random embers, while flames propagated along its perimeter, not only the margins of western Eurasia but that colonial periphery to which Europe carried the torch. The geography and dynamics of fire on the contemporary Earth is largely a consequence of European expansion, the impact of an imperial Europe and an industrial Europe. Europe's fire became as much a standard of reference for fire practices as Greenwich mean time for the world's watches or SI units for global physics.

This, in précis, was the Great Narrative of European fire: nature tamed, fire domesticated, the garden as a metaphor of humanity's relationship to landscape, the vestal flame as a symbol of an anthropogenic fire; the promulgation of these ideals to every niche of Europe, the propagation of European ideas and institutions to every continent. Around this saga mass the Lesser Narratives: institutional stories like the invention of forestry, by which Europe created the means to impose that vision on diverse lands; intellectual stories, the myths and sciences by which Europe interpreted its acts and ambitions; imperial stories, in which Europe projected its influence throughout the globe; the industrial story, through which Europe sought, with renewed Promethean defiance, to transcend fire altogether.

Yet it was never that simple. European society was plural, not singular; and even within each ethnicity and nation-state there were endless quarrels over fire practices. Those who used fire clashed with those who thought about it, peasants disagreed with urbanites, pastoralists with farmers, rulers with servants. More seriously, nature resisted. Only in the temperate center of Europe could the ideal impose itself without chronic rebellion or parody. Instead, the Great Narrative broke into geographic subnarratives. The Mediterranean narrative differed in profound ways from the Boreal, the Atlantic from the Eurasian. A common vision could not impose a common geography. Indeed, the fracturing proliferated, the pieces held by the compulsory grout of social institutions and the willed frame of intellectual conviction. Often the mosaic became a kaleidoscope.

The tendency accelerated as Europe expanded. When imperial Europe ventured beyond the shores of western Eurasia, the narrative splintered into scores of subnarratives, many lost at sea, others hybridized beyond recognition. To its colonies the European fire often seemed contrived and antithetical. Such differences, for example, inform the curious dialogue between Europeans and Americans. Europeans see fire as inextricably social, its presence an outcome of human artifice. Lightning fire is a freak of nature, an aberration, and the episodic return of wildfire an index of social unrest. Americans, by contrast, begin with an axiomatic natural fire and seek to strip away the social context that encumbers its study, like physicists contemplating an ideal frictionless surface. For Europe the sacred fire remains the fire in the hearth. For Americans it is the fire in the wilderness. Europeans are right in that both peoples see fire through the prism of their unique histories. But Americans are right in insisting that fire exists autonomously outside human contrivance.

Eventually industrial Europe sought to reconstruct altogether the fire cosmography it had inherited, one that had grown as complex in its biotic calculations as the equants and epicycles of Ptolemaic astronomy. The burning of fossil hydrocarbons proposed a Copernican revolution for combustion. The Earth's fire history would be recentered. The modernist era would rewrite the future narrative of fire by abstracting fuel from its geologic past. The reconstruction would be as thorough as Le Corbusier's radiant city, as complete as James Joyce's *Finnegans Wake,* as fundamental as the *Principia Mathematica* of Bertrand Russell and Alfred Whitehead. Not only would there be no alternative to anthropogenic fire, but an abstract combustion would banish it to the purgatory of bourgeoisie bric-a-brac. By decree or default, by direct application or indirect influence, Europe's flame would become a vestal fire for the planet. So even as European fire became more, not less, exceptional amid the fire-rich ecosystems of the Earth, it also became more, not less, dominant. Over the last 500 years Europe has refigured the planet's combustion calculus.

But Nature is not so easily reconstructed as city blocks, the plastic arts, and printed texts. It exists apart from humanity. Its fires have a logic and imperative of their own. At best all anthropogenic fire is a hybrid, a dialectic, a pyric double. Europe's fire is no exception.

Europe could not abolish fire, which thrived on its own. Rather, fire remained to challenge the theses Europeans proposed to the natural world, allowing at best a new, metastable synthesis. Above all it endured as a flaming mirror of Europe's—of humanity's—identity: powerful, ironic, confused, compromised, indeterminate, pervasive, insistent. Europe could never overcome the Otherness of fire. It could not remove fire from nature any more than it could extricate itself from fire. Fire had preceded Europe and would survive it, and would, in defiance of theory and hope, impose itself on human Europe. Postmodern Europe found a self-reflexive fire embedded in the texts of its landscapes. Europe could never end its quest for fire by transcending fire.

> *Fire ever doth aspire,*
> *And makes all like itself, turns all to fire.*
> —John Donne,"Eclogue for the
> Marriage of the Earl of Somerset"

BOOK 1: ELEMENTS

He sang how in the mighty Void, the seeds of Earth and of Air and of Ocean, and of Fire—that pure thing—ranged themselves together; and how from these principles all the Elements arose, systematically cohering in the tender globe of the World.
                                    —Vergil, *Sixth Eclogue*

FLAME

*The power of fire, or Flame . . . we designate by some trivial
chemical name, thereby hiding from ourselves the essential
character of wonder that dwells in it as in all things. . . . From
us too no Chemistry, if it had not Stupidity to help it, would hide
that Flame is a wonder. What is Flame?*
—Thomas Carlyle, "Heroes"

Whatever its larger mysteries, fire is a physical process. It is a chemical reaction, not an object. It has no existence apart from the fuel and oxygen that feed it, and the heat that kindles and sustains it. The story of fire is the story of how each of those elements came to be, and how it is they have combined.

There is not one fire but many. Each has its habitat, its traits, its behavior, its ecology. To call something "fire" is like calling an organism a tree or an insect. Because fire depends on life for its existence, it shares in the diversity, complexity, and subtlety of the living world. Oxygen is a by-product of photosynthesis. Fuels are the hydrocarbon hardcopies of living or dead plants. A field guide to fire would distinguish between combustion that smolders in organic soils, flames that soar through long-needled conifers, fires that crackle through brush and stubble. So symbiotic is the alliance that many prescientific peoples considered fire as itself living. Today it might still be regarded as metaorganic. Certainly in any ecological inventory, fire remains elemental.

Fire is exclusively a product of its environment. The history of fire—the explanation of why particular kinds of fires exist in particular places at particular times—is the history of how that environment evolved. How geologic forces created the lithic landscape. How evolution and ecology fashioned a biotic milieu. How climates organized winds, wet and dry seasons, and lightning-laden storms to prepare fuels for burning and to kindle them at appropriate times.

In all this, Europe was exceedingly complex. No single fire could claim dominion over all the habitats of the continent. Distinctive fires clustered, just as field mice and grasses did, into ecological blocs: fire provinces roughly defined by their geologically arranged hearthstones, the size and opaqueness of their climatic flues, and the density and magnitude of the biotic kindling and the available logs. Whatever cultural compositions humans might impose in recent centuries, that primordial order would endure, and would ensure that fire had a genealogy as ancient as Europe's stones, shrubs, and siroccos.

DIAMOND IN THE ROUGH:
A PHYSICAL GEOGRAPHY OF EUROPEAN FIRE

(i)

Europe began as a slab of lithosphere like an immense hearthstone laid on the Precambrian Earth. That continental craton—itself the composite of mountain-building revolutions that occurred between 3,500 and 900 million years ago—stabilized into a resistant shield, the Baltica, one of three major crustal plates that rafted in the vast ocean covering most of Paleozoic Earth.[1]

Over the next 400 million years the Baltica shield grew and fissioned, rose and fell, migrated twice across the equator, crashed, ripped, rotated, and erupted into the geologic matrix that today defines continental Europe. It smashed into Laurentia, the core of North America, to raise the Caledonian Mountains; collided with the Gondwana craton to the south, throwing up the Hercynian ranges like the deep berm of a storm-swept shore; welded to the wandering Siberian shield, a cold fusion traced along the Urals; and absorbed the blows of Asian microplates that rammed across its new eastern rim. By the end of the Paleozoic these blows, and others involving other shields, had hammered them all into the crustal collage of sprawling Pangaea that arced around a vast embayment of the world ocean, the Tethys Sea.

This tectonic union proved unstable, however, and by Jurassic times Pangaea broke up into a widening gyre of ruptured cratons. For Europe the major events were two. North America fissioned off, pulling away to fashion the Atlantic Ocean, trailing islands like so much lithic litter. Meanwhile Gondwana shattered into five major plates, two of which, Africa and India, moved northward, closed the Tethys Sea, and battered the Eurasian platform into a formidable borderland of mountains, volcanoes, plateaus, and basins ranging from the Pyrenees to the Dzhugdzhur Khrebet.

For Europe proper, the collision between Eurasia and Africa created a vast shatter zone in which plates fragmented, warped, thrust, and twisted to shape the Mediterranean Basin, a subcontinental region neither wholly European nor wholly African but a crustal breccia of the two. In time—the opposing forces have not yet ceased—an almost unbroken chain of mountains divided northern from mediterranean Europe. Oceanic crust rode into the Alps, the Balkans, the Anatolian plateau. Volcanoes boiled up from hot spots in southern Italy, Sicily, Malta, and the Aegean. Crust splintered to form Corsica, Sardinia, and the Balearic Islands. With each thrust and parry, Iberia, like the battered gate of a barbican, swung around the hinge of the Pyrenees. The cratonic crust buckled downward to fashion enormous depressions before or behind the ringing mountains that in turn filled to become the Aral, the Caspian, the Black, and the Mediterranean seas. Europe acquired its distinctive, perhaps defining, matrix of lands and seas.

But what geology roughed out, climate refined. Not merely land but water defined Europe's borders; and climate, not solely tectonics, inscribed the boundaries of European existence. The distribution of land and water had historical as well as geographic dimensions. Sea level rose and fell with climatic tides, alternately draining the continental shelves into lowlands or flooding them into shallow seas. The border between land and water was dynamic—sometimes global, sometimes local—as seas deluged old valleys and plains, as soils filled coastlines and bays, as mountains inched upward, and as land, groaning with sediments, subsided under its lithic burden. The ebb and flow of the world ocean determined whether Britain and Ireland were continental highlands or outright islands; whether peripheral basins were littoral lowlands or filled to become the Black, Adriatic, North, White, and Baltic seas; where and how the relics of past shorelines resided, swept inland or outward like enormous sand berms; how, at Gibraltar, the Atlantic and Mediterranean met.[2]

The Mediterranean Basin has sometimes been a blue sea and sometimes a saline hellhole. Over six million years ago Iberia slammed its gate shut while the world ocean dropped. In consequence, the Mediterranean dried into a Death Valley six times the size of California and deeper than Mount Whitney is high. When the Atlantic finally breached the Gibraltan barrier, it cascaded over a two-kilometer fall at a rate ten times that of Niagara. The cycle repeated over and again, ceasing only five million years ago. The solar draining of the Mediterranean, known as the Messinian salinity crisis, dramatically redefined the southern border of Europe. Whether the basin held water or evaporites profoundly influenced the regional climate. Filled, the basin was a mixing bowl; emptied, it was a barrier.[3]

More recently, with the sea full, the drying of the Sahara (in its final stages, 6,000 to 4,000 years ago) has erected a more meaningful border. Lands that once flourished as a savanna stocked with African megafauna from giraffes to gazelles, that knew rivers fetid with hippopotamus and reeds, dried up like a mudcrack. The animals vanished, preserved only in bones and ocher cave paint-

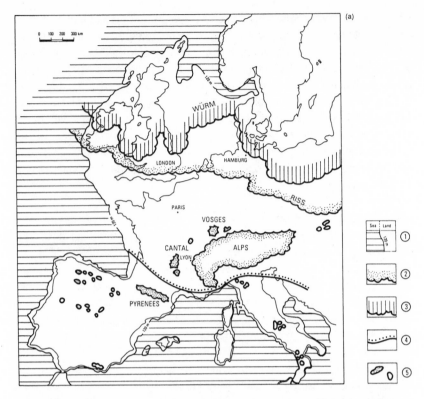

Glaciation: Western Europe's climatic borders. Legend: (1) shoreline; (2) maximum extent of Riss glaciation; (3) maximum extent of Wurm glaciation; (4) extent of periglacial processes; (5) mountain glaciers. (From A. Autran, "Introduction to the Geology of Western and Southern Europe," in *Geology and the Environment in Western Europe*, ed. G. Innes. Oxford: Clarendon Press, 1992. By permission of Oxford University Press)

ings, and were replaced by the camel; rivers sank into sands, fossil reservoirs of once-flourishing wadis; and North Africa joined the Mediterranean melange, part European, part Asian, segregated from sub-Saharan Africa more fully than if its crust had rifted apart or if its stony surface had sunk beneath the Atlantic Ocean.

Climatic forces redrew the northern borders of Europe with equal thoroughness. Glaciation—some seventeen major episodes since the advent of the Pleistocene—scraped out and weighted down the Baltic basin, periodically scoured valleys in the Alps, the Pyrenees, and the Scottish Highlands, redistributed soils, and redefined what land would be available when. The presence of massive ice sheets spread periglacial conditions far beyond its moraines and meltwaters. The enormous mass of ice sopped up water from the world ocean like a sponge, dropping the global shoreline. But what northern Europe gained from continental shelves newly emerged from the ocean, it more than lost to advancing ice. The border of boreal Europe was what the ice made it; that border moved with the ponderous ice sheets. Even after the ice departed, land depressed by the ice masses rebounded upward, and continues to do so, reconfiguring not merely the shorelines and depth of the Baltic but the landed bulk of Finland and Sweden.

Europe became a plexus of peninsulas. West of the Urals the European landmass, like a splintering wedge, breaks into a fractal geometry of peninsulas, shorelines, and barely sundered islands. No other continent—certainly not the rest of Eurasia—has anywhere near the proportion of coastline to landmass characteristic of Europe, or anything like its ratio of water to land. Only southeastern Asia approaches those proportions, and here the comparison fails not only because the trend dissolves into islands outright but because the islands are, geologically speaking, of oceanic origin, not slivers from a splintering continent.

Europe's distinctive fire history reflects this anomalous mix of land and water, or more precisely the peculiar distribution, in space and time, of wet and dry conditions. Fire needed both. It was necessary to grow fuels, and then to prepare them for burning. What mattered was not that a place was wet or dry on average, but the way in which wet and dry conditions interchanged. Wet years in dry climates could build up abnormal levels of fuel, stoking fire where little was normally possible; so, too, dry years in wet regions could ready existing stocks of biomass, normally immune from fire, for burning. The regimen of wet and dry provided the geographic logic behind fire regimes.

(ii)

This peculiar geography of wet and dry conditions allows for a generalized identification of fire provinces. Collectively, they form a rough diamond, with a short axis running north and south, and a long axis east and west. One axis is primarily a gradient of temperature, the other of moisture. Taken together, Europe's fire provinces reside at the center and four apexes—Mediterranean to the south, Boreal to the north, Atlantic to the west, Eurasian to the east, and Central at the core. Each boasts distinctive fire regimes, each supports characteristic fire practices, and each displays a unique fire history.

The most easily identified is Mediterranean Europe. An immense shoreline fringed by mountains, the Mediterranean revolves climatically around two strongly developed seasons: a short, wet winter, and a prolonged, dry summer. Droughts and episodes of intense, dry heat are also frequent. Strong winds, sufficiently notorious to receive local names, spill across mountains. In the summer come the *tramontana* of Catalonia and Italy, the Rhone's *mistral,* the *kham-*

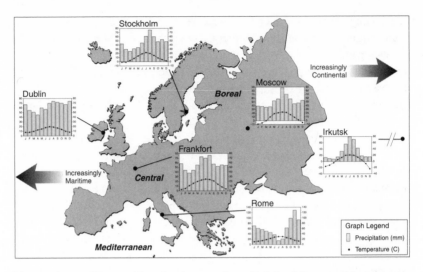

Fire provinces of Europe. Note the absence of a well-defined fire season in temperate Europe. Even where precipitation rises in the summer, it does so proportionally to temperature, since warm air can hold more moisture than cold. Deep in Siberia, Irkutsk displays a continental climate. (University of Wisconsin Cartographic Lab)

sin of Lebanon and Syria, the *sharav* of Israel, the Maghreb's *sirocco,* the *poniente* in Valencia, the *levante* in the Straits of Gibraltar, the *bora* of the Balkans; in the winter, the desiccating *Föhn* winds that blow over the Alps, across the Spanish *meseta,* and along the lee of storm-wracked ranges. Thus every year the summer favors burning, and every few years drought ensures that combustion can be extensive. Then the rains restore the fuels. The phoenix flora is ready to burn again. The opportunities for fire are endless, and the flames seemingly eternal.[4]

The northern complement is boreal Europe, also clustered around an inland sea. But where the Mediterranean Sea tends toward salinity, the Baltic edges into fresh water. Winters are long, cold, and wet; summers short and (comparatively) dry. The prospects for burning, as for other forms of decomposition, are brief. When they occur, fires can erupt with savage, stand-clearing intensity. Large-scale burning requires drought, and that reflects the fluid frontier between maritime influences from the Atlantic and continental influences from the Eurasian landmass. Boreal Europe balances in the tidal zone between them. When—for a month, a year, a decade—wet conditions ebb, then fire advances.

Europe's long axis, from the Atlantic to the Eurasian interior, is a gradient of moisture. Increasingly, land reclaims sea, and a dry climate replaces a wet one. For Atlantic Europe, islands all, maritime climates are the norm, although trade winds and storm patterns often divide the land into a geography of wet windward and drier lee sides. For Eurasian Europe the maritime influences wedge out, narrowing dramatically beyond the Urals. The province's northern border traces the frozen Arctic Ocean; its southern, the monsoon-blocking mountains of central Asia. The greater bulk of land, even where forested, is dry, subject to long cold winters and warm summers. Land and water compete primarily through muskegs, rivers, and thawing permafrost; winter snows are relatively light, and Siberian precipitation falls mostly in summer storms. Only in the Far East, where the summer Asian monsoon swings around the blocking mountains, does the continental climate collapse.

That leaves central Europe, a vast *aurea mediocritas* that sweeps from the Atlantic to the Urals. Its informing geoclimatic facts are the magnitude of its exposure to the Gulf Stream and the absence of intercepting mountains in its long-scoured continental shield. The one projects warm waters from the Caribbean into the North Atlantic, the other means that nothing blocks the prevailing westerlies from transferring that moisture and relative warmth inland in a climatic wedge. Large inland seas frame it north and south. The upshot is that central Europe boasts a temperate climate far north of expected latitudes, and a maritime presence far inland from the nominal shoreline. While seasons exist, there are no annually defined wet and dry periods; instead hot and cold epochs, wet and dry eras slowly fluctuate over the course of decades and centuries.

These provincial boundaries are porous, mobile, and often unstable over time. Northern and southern borders can change with the advance or recession of ice sheet and desert; the frontier between continental and maritime climates swings back and forth as high pressure moves east or west, as storm tracks veer north or south. Winds seep from one province to another. Exceptional times—years without summers, summers of endless rain, seasons crushed by drought—are as vital in shaping the character of a province as the norm. Moreover, if provincial borders divide, they also join; mountains and seas are corridors as well as barriers; select mediterranean flora, for example, have traversed across the southern rim of Europe from Anatolia to the Himalayas.

To this geographic figuration there is an uncanny symmetry. North and south, there is the complementarity of ice and sun, a gradient of temperature; east and west, of land and sea, a gradient of moisture. Central Europe rests at the plump axis of this rough diamond. Viewed one way it is a source, both intellectual and institutional, for European fire practices; the province that, more than others, has determined the means and ends of European fire. Viewed another way, it is a sink for European fire regimes, the burned-out core of a fire that has survived by propagating away. Undeniable, anomalous, powerful, that temperature center remains the unmoved mover of European fire.

New Worlds from Old:
A Biogeography of European Fire

Fuel, oxygen, heat—the indivisible trinity of fire. Life created the first two, and after the appearance of *Homo,* it wrested control over the third from the inorganic physics of lightning. The story of European fire is the story of how Europe's biota created those conditions, and how fire, once kindled, began to interact with the combustibles on which it fed.

Life did more through geologic time than passively raft on crustal cratons, pruned here by frost, there by desiccation, multiplied or obliterated by enfolding mountains. It helped create its own environment. Organisms lived amid other organisms, with the biosphere their primary substrate. But life also broke rock, intercepted water, absorbed and released gases, altered albedo, prompted and retarded erosion, and invented fire. The plants that created fuel also created oxygen and thus closed the Earth's fire triangle. The slow combustion of respiring organisms had its counterpart in the fast combustion of burning ecosystems. The informing conditions for both were identical: photosynthesizing plants.

(i)

A critical transition occurred between the mid-Cambrian and the mid-Devonian. Oxygen from phytoplankton and terrestrial plants filled the atmosphere to the point where carbon dioxide could combust, sedimentation removed sufficient quantities of carbon that might otherwise have bonded with the liberated gas, and plants colonized enough of continental landmasses to propagate free-burning fires.

Oxygen, a toxin, shocked the primitive Earth with its reactivity. In its high-octane forms, it introduced a chemistry of combustion. In early eons, well into the Carboniferous era, oxygen's rate of increase swelled it to 30 percent of total atmospheric gases. Then it dropped, and has oscillated around 21 percent since the end of the Paleozoic. Those figures matter. Laboratory experiments suggest that if oxygen content plummets below 12 percent a fire cannot start, and if it rises above 25 percent a fire will not stop. It is further argued that the persistence of atmospheric oxygen within these limits is an index of biospheric self-regulation and that these biotic checks have kept the planet in balance between respiration and conflagration.[5]

In reality, fuel attributes such as particle size, arrangement, and especially moisture far exceed the partial pressure of oxygen as an influence on fire behavior. There is little conflict; the colonization of the continents by plants coincided with the stabilization of an oxygen atmosphere. By the late Devonian, possibly earlier, fire was possible. By the lower Carboniferous, it had become a permanent presence in Earth's geologic record. For at least the last 400 million years, it has been possible to sustain free-burning fire on any combustible surface touched by the Earth's atmosphere. Across such scales, virtually every environment can burn, and most eventually do.[6]

(ii)

With oxygen stable, the burden of fire history shifted to fuels. These, too, had their evolution. Fire competed for the available biomass with consumers and decomposers. Each turn of the evolutionary screw reconfigured the quantity and arrangement of combustibles; each evolution of fast-combustion fire challenged, in turn, its slow-combustion rivals. By the early Silurian (400 million years ago) sedgy plants had colonized coasts; by late Devonian time (350 million), there were forests stocked with trees over a meter in diameter. By the Carboniferous, rich biomes that were rank with giant club mosses, horsetails, cycads, ginkgoes, and primitive conifers flourished, their ripe residues ossifying over the eons into coal and petroleum. Angiosperms—the flowering plants—emerged during the Cretaceous and rapidly radiated from their Gondwana homeland into dominance everywhere they reached. In the mid-Miocene (ca. 15 million years ago), the early grasses appeared. Each such floral revolution prompted a faunal counterrevolution, and vice versa, so that flowering plants coevolved with pollinating insects, and grasslands developed through an evolutionary dialectic with grazers. And mediating between both, sharing their evolution was fire.[7]

Steadily, as Europe's geophysical matrix firmed up, so did its biogeography. Like other continental cratons, primordial Europe was a biotic ark. Its tectonic migrations reshaped its genetic cargo—sundering, merging with other cratons, purging, and prodding as the lithic life raft passed new latitudes, broke off from common ground, erected new borders, wiped out coastal landscapes, and reforged new ones. By the time Pangaea gathered the errant cratons together, there were characteristic floras for North America and Europe, for Siberia, for China, for Gondwana—evolutionary pedigrees that would persist to the present. There were also terrestrial corridors for the Pangaeic dispersion of emergent plants and animals, the diaspora of the angiosperms being a prime example.

Pangaea's subsequent breakup further segregated Europe's biota. The fragmentation left the pines wholly in Laurasia, the acacias in Gondwana, and the eucalypts in Australia. Among the continents, Eurasia, despite its dominant bulk, held fewer flowering plant families than any other. Though both later fused with it, coefficients of biotic similarity link India and Africa twice as strongly with Australia than with Eurasia. Europe's closest biotic ally is North America, reflecting the ancient geologic unity of Laurasia and the contemporary similarity of climates. Of the six floral kingdoms on Earth, Eurasia and North America constitute one; the remainder reside on the separated arks of fractured Gondwana.

Still, Europe held great biotic reserves. They could assume many forms, and they did, as climatic prompts intensified, as the Pleistocene flickered between glacial and interglacial, as seasonality became more pronounced, as rapid and often violent change became the norm. However elastic, however porous, over time the dominions of Europe's physical geography also came to define its dominant biomes. Each province had its characteristic flora and fauna that stoked the geologic hearth with combustibles. And even as those biomes made fire possible, fire reshaped them as surely as sun, frost, herbivores, and rain.

(iii)

The most critical events were those that occurred during the last two million years. Some 80 percent of the Pleistocene was glacial, the ice-free epochs fleeting and unstable. Under the impress of the tidal ice, Europe's biotic constituents experienced extinction, retreat, recolonization, fragmentation, and reconstitution, not once but over and again.

The conclusion of the final glacial epoch, the Würm (the *primum mobile* of Europe's Holocene history), signaled the onset of a modern climate, and the retreating ice made Europe a virtual *terra nova*. Old World Europe was, paradoxically, as much a new world as the Americas, and certainly newer than Australia and Africa. Considering the relative magnitude of their ice sheets and periglacial penumbras, Europe's renewal was proportionally greater than North America's. Released from its refugia, the biota seized the exposed lands as weeds would a plowed field. The biological recolonization of western Europe was one of the planet's great land rushes, the prelude to a subsequent, human-assisted dispersion throughout the globe.[8]

It was a tough, opportunistic biota, well suited to pioneering. Its repeated climatic heating and quenching had tempered it like steel into a sword. Accustomed to the long rhythms of snow and sun, it adapted to the annual cycle of seasons. That violent climatic history had wiped out many of the returning species or driven them back into hiding, leaving the saving remnant both impoverished and highly selective. Over and again that biotic elect had survived in mountain refugia, while climatic storms blew over it. In North America, species could migrate over broad landscapes. On the narrowing peninsulas and isthmuses that composed western Europe, such flight was not possible; and ice, sea, and mountain squeezed the surviving biota ever tighter in a geophysical vise. No other continent experienced a reformation quite so extensive, certainly none so recently in its evolutionary history.

Between 10,000 and 8,000 years B.P., as the ice sheets withdrew in climatic collapse, long suppressed flora raced to the new lands, each at its own rate, roughly following the path of botanical scout species. Trees congregated in whatever associations could survive, an ecosystem managed like a mining camp. Birch, aspen,

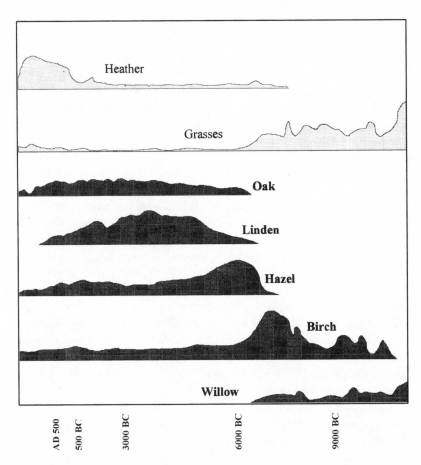

·The Great Migration: Holocene Europe. Successive colonization of Denmark by post-glacial flora. By the Birch period, human influences have become significant. (Redrawn and simplified from Iversen 1967)

and pine—avid pioneers all—led this biotic folk migration, helping to stabilize and maturate the soils, breaking the land for other, less volatile species. The deciduous forests came later. Elm and hazel, untrammeled, expanded over their range in less than 500 years. Oak, linden, alder, and ash advanced more cautiously. Increasingly the biota responded not only to the physical matrix of rock, sand, marsh, loess, and moraines left by the ice but to the presence of other species. Some species thrived together, some did not. Biotic colonizers first conquered, then converted the frontier, and so proclaimed the tragedy of the pioneers who could no longer survive in the land they had so eagerly transformed.

By 8,000 years ago the modern ensemble of biogeographic provinces was evident. Warmer and wetter conditions had driven the steppes east; an ever-green woodland, complete with an understory of tough shrubs and grasses, had colonized the Mediterranean littoral; tundra retired to the cold coast of the Arctic Ocean; the boreal forest advanced from the east and south onto Fenno-scandinavia; and a mixed woodlands, rich in decidious species, an *omnium gatherum* of temperate species, filled central Europe like forty-niners pouring into California. Specialty biomes proliferated, particularly along the margins of sea and mountain—fens, blanket bogs, heath, marshes, alpine nooks, and craggy shore.

Yet these associations were still unsettled. Opportunistic species had grabbed onto newly revealed landscapes, and aggregated into communities of conve-nience. Europe's ecosystems roughly began to assume their modern form. Still, some species lagged and with them the dynamics of the fully stocked woods and marshes. Rising temperatures reached a maximum around 7,000 years ago, and then dropped somewhat to a more or less equilibrium figure around 6,000 years B.P. Sea level stabilized. The contemporary climate arrived, its full biotic baggage yet to come. Spruce, for example, began its major travels only 2,000 years ago, an expansion that is still in progress.

Throughout, there was one species of special note. Early on, hominids joined the boisterous throng that recolonized Europe. *Homo sapiens* was always and everywhere present—a forager along the ice edge, a hunter in periglacial steppes, an opportunist amid birch and pine, a resident within woodlands, a transient visitor to bog and heath and fens. Humans were seizers of disturbed sites who had the capacity to further disturb. Restlessly, compulsively, *Homo* reorganized the biota—adding and subtracting species, reshaping biomes as he did coarse flint into arrowheads; harvesting, pruning, plucking, draining, planting, dig-ging, watering, and through proxy fauna, grazing, browsing, fertilizing, tram-pling; and above all, burning. Alone among the revanchist biota, humans manipulated fire. The rough diamond of Europe they seized, shaped, polished, and set. The fire regimes of Europe were largely the creation of this peregri-nating pyrophile.

FUSAIN AND FLAME:
A NATURAL HISTORY OF EUROPEAN FIRE

(i)

For an evolving Europe, fire became a kind of two-cycle engine, powered by the relative rotation of wet and dry conditions, sparked primarily by lightning. There were other ignition sources—volcanoes, spontaneous combustion in dung-layered caves and sun-dried bogs, perhaps falling rocks (like striking flints) shaken loose by earthquakes, as has happened in the Himalayas and South Africa. But the only spark universal enough to penetrate every province across every geologic period was lightning. The fire regimes of primordial Europe were undoubtedly kindled by lightning.[9]

Not a visitation from an ecological netherworld, lightning hurtled down from thunderstorms, and thus was part of a climatic regime to which the flora—the fuels—had adapted. A biota could adjust to lightning fire as it could to early frosts, summer drought, marshy soils, and high winds. Lightning fire was less a geophysical chisel than a biochemical probe. It dripped on diverse ecological substrates like an electrochemical acid, etching the biota's fire regimes. Some places had many and small fires, others few and large. Some sites experienced fire almost annually, some by decade, some by century. Every storm did not have to kindle fires and every place did not have to burn every year for fire to be ecologically significant. It was not the presence or relative absence of fire that mattered; it was the fire *regime* to which the biota adapted.

Lightning fire persists today, though often hidden by agricultural artifice. Statistics are poor, doubly so since lightning fires generally come in clusters, and are difficult to interpret, since the abnormal years are typically those that do the most biological work. Moreover, how many fires of "unknown origin" in national fire statistics (often the largest category) are caused by lightning is indeterminate. A dry lightning storm arced across the drought-blasted peats of Moscow in 1972; 59 lightning fires staggered the Kärnten Alps in 1988, accounting for 46 percent of Austria's annual fire load; dry lightning kindled a 10,000 hectare fire in Gascony pine plantations in 1990. Between 1985 and 1987, Austria experienced 106 lightning fires, Finland 164, France 160, Greece 113, Italy 84, Turkey 140, and Spain an impressive 971. Most of the starts for Mediterranean countries occurred in mountains. These rates agree broadly with cognates elsewhere in the world: boreal Europe and Russia with Alaska and Canada, Mediterranean Europe (1.6 percent of all fires) with figures for mediterranean-climate lands in southern California, South Africa, and Australia. Central Europe is a virtual vacuum for natural fire.[10]

Where cities replaced forests, and barns great field oaks, lightning preyed on the built landscape, pummeling towers instead of old-growth trees. It may be that the practice of segregating steeples from churches, common in Scandinavia (until the advent of lightning rods), was intended as an architectural firebreak. About 10 percent of the 500–1,000 lightning strikes that rain down on the Netherlands each year result in fires, mostly to unprotected houses, barns, and haystacks. Something like the natural order is revealed only when and where the remorseless grasp of humanity loosens, as it does along the fringes of settlement, within special refugia like parks, during bouts of exceptional weather, and when humans, by choice or compulsion, decamp from a site.[11]

Nature's fire had never left. But, so long as humans claimed the land, it was never allowed to burn freely. Humans controlled that fire by controlling its fuels. And they controlled those fuels—as they controlled Europe's wild flora and fauna—by finding domesticated surrogates. They controlled natural fire with anthropogenic fire.

(ii)

Accordingly, fire suffuses European history from the earliest times. Charcoal was the ink black of the geologic record (*ink,* in fact, derives from the Latin *encaustum* and Greek *enkaustos,* meaning to burn). Nature's economy wrote its ledgers in fire.

It is there, for example, in the dispersed charcoal that saturates kerogen, a bituminous constituent of shale (and estimated to exceed known coal deposits by a factor of 500). It is abundant with the fossil charcoal—*fusain* (*fusinite* in its mineral form)—that laces a noncarbonaceous matrix in Lower Carboniferous strata from Ireland and Scotland. It appears in Devonian-Carboniferous coals from Pennsylvania and Nova Scotia, both formed during periods when North America and Europe had fused, thus confirming fire on their shared landscapes. The Carboniferous coals of central Europe, Britain, and Russia contain 1 to 6 percent fusain, sometimes concentrated into dense lenses. Europe's Jurassic coals harbor abundant fusain, preserving the charred structure of ferns and conifers and even the wings of beetles. Of the total organic fraction contained in Jurassic-Cretaceous oceanic sediments from the north Atlantic, 1 to 10 percent is charcoal. The dramatic border that divides the Cretaceous from the Tertiary, a time of mass extinctions, is a geologic fireline. Along with iridium, an index of a putative extraterrestrial body that impacted the Earth, there are large quantities of fusain, the apparent record of widespread fires, possibly ignited by fiery ejecta. Perhaps 7×10^{16} grams of soot resulted worldwide. Whatever the source, the residual charcoal is there, from Denmark to Spain, vivid testimony to an ancient European Ragnarok. Across that divide, the fires continue. The Tertiary brown coals of the Rhine, formed over a period of 50 million years, are filled with fusain and chocked with charred stumps, with the rhythmic banding of fossil fire and lignite. Sedimentary cores from lakes bear witness that fire accompanied the Holocene reclamation of Europe. By then humans, not nature, set the larger parameters of fire regimes.[12]

There is every reason to believe that fire was not simply present but routine in such places, that fusain commemorated organic matter that had begun with fire—as, following industrial exhumation and combustion, it would end in fire. Laboratory experiments have successfully replicated the patterns preserved in fusinite by burning contemporary analogues of the extinct ferns and trees that combusted long ago. Equally intriguing are analogies to contemporary land-scapes. The coastal marshes of Louisiana, the Florida Everglades, Georgia's Okefenokee Swamp, the Great Dismal Swamp of Virginia—all burn regularly, sometimes with light burns across grass and sedge, sometimes, during droughts, deep into exposed peat, and sometimes kindled by lightning.[13]

True, the analogy fails on specifics. The flora of the Holocene is not the flora of the Carboniferous. But it succeeds in demonstrating that places that accu-mulate organic sediments can burn, and that places that burn adapt to their reg-imen of fires. The fusain that intercalates Europe's coals testifies not only to ancient fires but to an ancient fire ecology, as surely as the charcoal of buried Troy bears witness to a once-thriving civilization, and to a windy height prone to fire and sword.

(iii)

So, throughout, there was fire. It was there when Europe was a stony raft adrift in a Paleozoic ocean; when the Hercynian orogeny downwarped the crust into the fetid wetlands of Carboniferous Europe; during the Pangaeic hegemony and its violent fragmentation; and flickering through geologic eons like a can-dle in the wind as the climatic storms of the Pleistocene blew cold and hot. It left its ashes in watery sediments, released its gases to the atmosphere, branded itself into the genetic heritage of Europe's biota, joined the riotous swarm that recolonized Holocene Europe, and passed to the Promethean hominids who carried it always with them and who nurtured it in an act of mutual domestication. Through them the Holocene reconquest newly stoked, and in places rekindled, a perpetual fire.

Europe's primordial fire was as boisterous and vital as the environmental hearth in which it kindled, propagated, flared, and smoldered. By Holocene times European fire was plural, as complex as the winds, storms, seasons, and droughts that propelled it, as varied as the pine, fir, peat, ling, thatch, oak, steppe grasses, and maquis that fed it, as complicated as the purposes that rubbing sticks, steel and flint, and sulfurous lucifers could conceive. If there was a unity to European fire, it was culturally imposed, and if it is possible to speak of a common flame, it is in the sense that one fire, of a unitary ori-gin, can propagate across valleys and sunbaked mesas, through conifer forests and grain-thick fields, can flash through crackling shrubs and browning grasses, torch thickets of close-packed pine, lightly scorch oaks, smolder in moors, flame through heather.

But with ever firmer grasp, the control over fire passed from nature to human-ity. If climate still dictated how fully the flue might be open and how wet the wood might be, humans split the kindling, fed the hearth, banked the coals, and shielded the slow match of combustion. The complexity of fire's ecology multiplied. Fire became a pervasive medium and a universal catalyst for a vast symbiosis between humans and their surrounding world. With progressive intensiveness, humanity controlled fuels and ignition. The one, in fact, was a means to control the other. The new order of fire passed from lightning to the torch.

TORCH

Tiger! Tiger! burning bright
In the forests of the night

. . .

In what distant deeps or skies
Burnt the fire of thine eyes?
On what wings dare he aspire?
What the hand dare seize the fire?
—William Blake, "The Tiger"

During the early Pleistocene, perhaps 1.6 million years ago, *Homo* erectus evolved among the hominids, and soon thereafter, probably, he captured fire. Lightning now had to compete with hominids for control over combustion. With steadily increasing mastery, the torch, not the lightning bolt, kindled the fire regimes of the Earth. Increasingly Europe's biota reflected that fact. In exploiting fire to reshape the world to its needs, humanity also reshaped the habitats of fire.

The capture of fire defined a unique ecological niche, established a species monopoly, and began to transfer the power of fire from the cloud to the hand. The torch became a universal tool, an enabling device for endless biotic and industrial technologies, a lever to move entire ecosystems, an unquenchable symbol of humanity's aspirations, self-identity, and ironic dominance. Domestication began with anthropogenic fire, the home its defining habitat; agriculture depended on controlled burning as fully as it did on axes and manure; industry was an endless declension of pyrotechnologies. In seizing fire, humanity also accepted its ecological responsibilities, the origins of an environmental ethos.

Origins are obscure. It is not clear whether the baked clay at Chesowanja, Kenya (ca. 1.4 million years ago), or Swartkrans, South Africa, is the remnant of an ancient campfire or a deep-burning log, not known whether *Homo erec-*

tus could make fire or only preserve it (or recapture it if lost), not self-evident that early hominids alone had the capacity for manipulating fire, not known by what paths hominids entered Europe or how the various species and subspecies —*erectus, neanderthalensis, sapiens*—interacted among themselves and mingled their fires. What is clear is that Europe's hominids—alone among the species that swarmed in and out of its lands—possessed fire, that they used it wherever possible to make their world more habitable, and that their power over fire forced change not only on the surrounding environment but on the fireholders themselves.[1]

Some consequences derive from the sheer possession of fire, and some from the monopoly hominids have enjoyed over it. Fire shielded hominids from the cold, it pushed back the night, it warned off predators, it extended the hunter's range and the forager's grasp—driving and attracting grazers, promoting and extinguishing plants. It assisted in toolmaking by hardening wooden spears, quarrying stone, glazing flint; the techniques of drilling, scraping, and striking are the same for making fire as for shaping tools from bone, wood, and stone; tools and torch reacted synergistically, each amplifying the power of the other. Hunting, felling, and gathering altered the array of fuels, making fire more or less potent, while controlled burning greatly magnified the ability to fell trees, clear shrubs, stimulate grasses, drive or draw fauna, and select for or against resident flora. The evolutionary presence of natural fire ensured that the biota could respond to a new ignition source and could assume new regimens of burning. For nearly all environments, fire provided a means of access, and for some, a medium of rapid domination.[2]

Fire could both propagate and concentrate. If the running fire could project power outward, the stationary fire could distill it. Cooking expanded the domain of foodstuffs by making accessible plants that were otherwise inedible or poisonous. In turn, it became a model for the technologies of ceramics and metallurgy. Through broadcast burning it is an apt metaphor for the application of fire throughout extended ecosystems, as humans began cooking the Earth. And some would argue that cooking is also a paradigm for the cultural remaking of the world, the essence of domestication. The tamed fire had to be fed, either by letting it roam in search of new fuels or by bringing new fuels to it.

The tended fire reworked society as fully as the free-burning fire did ecosystems. Around its nurtured flames gathered the family, the tribe, the nation. Over fires, elders told the stories that instructed the young and decided the fate of the group. Through fires, shamans and priests offered sacrifice, intoned for divine help, performed ceremonies of pyromancy, and conducted rites of passage. With mingled fires, couples married and groups sealed treaties. Torch in hand, émigrés departed for new lands. With the torch in mind, intellectuals sought to explain the place of humans in the world, the uniqueness of human destiny.

Universally, fire myths proclaimed that humanity originated from the welter of animal creation only with the acquisition of fire. Although the Philip-pine tarsier will pick up and toy with coals from campsites, raptors in north-ern Australia will drop glowing sticks on grasslands, and nicotine-addicted chimpanzees in the Johannesburg zoo can manipulate glowing cigarettes to keep chain-smoking, it is only humans who possess fire as a species, and, no less vital, all humans possess it. If other species show adaptations to fire, and a few have on occasion manipulated fire, only one came to possess it exclusively. The ecological audacity of this act is staggering: it is as though a single species laid claim to water or land or air.[3]

Controlled fire is everywhere a signature of human presence. The range of such fires inscribed the range of the habitable world. It was anthropogenic fire that mattered most; wild fire belonged with wild animals and wild lands, beyond the pale of human life and understanding. Early fire-carrying hominids sought out those environments most prone to fire, for those were landscapes most amenable to human manipulation. Where fire was possible, humans thrived; where fire was difficult, humans suffered. The residue of fire is as much an artifact of archaeological sites as potsherds and stone points, and not a few times has fire, by charring, preserved the artifactual heritage of ancient human-ity. At virtually every point of contact between early humans and the natural world, fire was present, throwing flames like sparks from a grindstone.

ERRANT FIRE:
THE HOMINID COLONIZATION OF EUROPE

(i)

The Pleistocene passage of anthropogenic fire across Europe is understood poorly. It is likely that Europe, close to Africa, felt early the impress of emi-grating hominids, and that the saga of colonization was repeated as climatic pressures shoved glaciers, raised and lowered sea level, and dried or flooded vast landscapes. Evidence of *Homo erectus* dates from 500,000 to 200,000 B.P., and possibly one million years. Recent excavations at the Menez-Dregan cave in Brittany report a hearth dated at 465,000 (±65,000) years. By then, similar evidence places the hominid throughout southern Asia, China, even Java.[4]

Many of the sites are associated with fire. The Cave of Arago in the French Pyrenees suggests a pattern of seasonal occupation. The celebrated excavations at Torralba, Spain, discovered evidence of fire dating back 400,000 years in a distribution that may testify to fire drives for the hunting of elephants, cattle, horses, deer, and rhinoceroses. The scattered charcoal patches may indicate only temporary cooking sites, common after a kill; or they may record sys-tematic firing to push prey into a boggy gully where hunters could more easily dispatch trapped beasts. Certainly the two uses—hearth and hunt—embrace the dual roles and dual landscapes of anthropogenic fire.

Neanderthals began replacing *Homo erectus* around 250,000 years ago, shortly before the third glacial epoch. Hominids basked in the interglacials and adapted to the returning cold. Fire helped enormously here. The Neanderthal renaissance reached its peak between 70,000 and 30,000 years B.P. Throughout they kept flame alive, stirring the embers of natural fires and kindling their own. Certainly they preserved those flames not only for themselves but for all of Europe's biota, even as harsher climates drove them to huddle in caves, in tents of hide and mastodon bone, and in daub-and-wattle shelters, their fires sustained by burning wood and bone and those fires in turn shielding the firekeepers from the rigors of a full-blown ice age. Certainly anthropogenic fire helped select what flora and fauna would survive the changing climate, toughening the biota as it did the points of wooden spears.

Between 40,000 and 10,000 years ago anatomically modern hominids, *Homo sapiens sapiens,* appeared throughout Europe. The newcomers possessed a more sophisticated technology of stone and bone, probably a more cognitively complex culture, and fire practices that were similar magnitudes of evolution from their predecessors. They could, for example, start fires several ways. They could drill and saw with wood, and strike sparks from iron pyrites—all techniques directly related to their microlithic toolkit. Undoubtedly Cro-Magnons contested with Neanderthals for game, for caves, for the restricted habitats of the waning Pleistocene. No species has shared fire with another, and only reluctantly have human cultures.

Compared to the Neanderthals, with whom they often overlapped, the newcomers were far more numerous, congregated more in river valleys, and hunted select species with singular ruthlessness. One animal dominated—reindeer, red deer, auroch, horse, or ibex, according to regions; reindeer, for example, account for 99 percent of the faunal assemblages found in the Périgord region of southwestern France. The rapid diaspora of this new hominid hunter corresponds, with uncanny fidelity, to a global wave of extinctions. In the end, whether by outright competition or by slow submersion, Neanderthals faded from the scene, another in the long litany of megafauna that apparently melted away before the torch and spear of *Homo sapiens sapiens.* That left only the survivors, an ice age creation but a fire creature, poised to recolonize Holocene Europe and to rekindle its fire regimes.

How this was done is not clear. The fire practices of Upper Paleolithic and Mesolithic Europe are poorly and indirectly preserved. As the environment changed, so did human economies and the fire practices appropriate to them. Perhaps the wisest path is to reconstruct by analogy, which is, in all probability, how humans learned their fire practices in the first place. Hominids did not invent fire; they captured it. So too they did not invent exotic ways of exploiting fire; they imitated nature. Analogy argues strongly that fire accompanied most interactions between new Europe and Europe's new colonists.

Except for the most severely glaciated landscapes (or periglacial margins), there were no prohibitive environments for fire. But all other lands today experience fire according to some regimen. The critical environmental factor was not the differential between hot and cold but the cycling of wet and dry; the sharper the seasonal or secular gradient, the greater the range for burning. Similarly, there are no known peoples, the Eskimo again excepted, who do not burn routinely the landscapes around them, at least in portions as the opportunity arises. Aboriginal peoples have burned in the boreal forests of Canada and Siberia; in the temperate forests of pine and oak, prairies and steppes, mature chestnut woods and rough understory; in mediterranean woodlands, chaparral, and grasses; in tropical savannas, llanos, monsoonal forests, even patches of felled rainforests. Wherever climate allowed a sliver of dryness and wherever pyrophytes salted biomes, humans could drive a wedge of fire to crack open the ecosystem and cook it into more palatable forms. "Wherever primitive man has had the opportunity to turn fire loose on a land, he seems to have done so, from time immemorial," concluded Carl Sauer, "it is only civilized [industrial] societies that have undertaken to stop fires." No one who has studied aboriginal fire anywhere else on the planet has concluded otherwise. There is no reason to believe that the hunting and foraging humans who colonized Holocene Europe behaved any differently.[5]

Probably groups carried fire with them, as did the Fuegans, Andaman Islanders, Australian Aborigines, remote hill tribes of India, and Pygmies. Certainly they had with them the tools and kindling to make fire as necessary, but the most technologically primitive peoples carried fire itself either as a firestick or a slow match, or as coals wrapped in bark or banana leaves. Torches of resinous pine have continued well into modern times. Early Europeans probably nurtured a continuous fire at their premanent settlement, and also rekindled fire whenever they paused, over a kill, at a campsite, or at a break in travel.

Fire assisted all aspects of wrenching or coaxing food from the landscape. For this there were ample precedents in nature. Foragers soon recognized that berries, mushrooms, bracken, edible tubers like camas, and wild grasses flourished best on burned ground, that a light fire exposed acorns and chestnuts, that smoke deadened bees into a stupor that made honey accessible. Fishers recognized that torches attracted fish at night, when they could be easily speared or netted. Hunters saw that evening torches froze deer and geese, that flames could drive ungulates, that the fresh growth sprouting on old burns drew grazers, that fires flushed both elusive prey and dangerous predators from thickets, that burned areas made for easier travel than unburned, that smoke and ash masked the scent of stalking humans, that fire stripped protective covering from burrows and nests. It is likely that hominids had, from their origins, foraged around fires; it was inevitable that, having seized fire, they would apply it in the old ways but to their own purposes, limited only by the receptivity of the land to respond.

Analogies from more recent times abound. Consider hunting. In Africa, hunters in the Sudan and east African veld have used fire to drive elephants into killing grounds probably in ways similar to those used by Europe's early big game hunters to hound mastodon and mammoth. They use fire to attract springbok, gazelles, and other grazers to select sites; they bait traps for rhinos with the succulent growth of patch burns. In Australia, Aborigines drove kangaroo and wallaby, scavenged through burned spinifex for the burrows of marsupial and lizard, and returned to the greening swaths to reclaim more grazers. In North America, indigenes burned for rabbit, bison, wood rats, deer, alligator, muskrats, moose, elk, antelope, even grasshoppers. Fire hunting was a double-barreled blast: there was one harvest during the flaming drive, and a second when the fauna irresistibly returned to the new growth. Regular burning, moreover, retained the desired habitat indefinitely. When Cabeza de Vaca marveled how early sixteenth-century Texas tribes, through judicious burning, "compelled" the animals "to go for food where the Indians want," he spoke equally for peoples in Africa, Asia, South America, and almost certainly for early Holocene Europe. Surely it is no accident that Artemis, the ancient goddess of the hunt—with an ancestry predating the Greeks—held a bow in one hand and a torch in the other.[6]

Controlled fire entered almost every dimension of food gathering. Take, for example, the pre-Columbian cycle of fishing in coastal Virginia, of plant harvesting in California, of hunting on the Great Plains. Fishermen used fire both to fell trees and then to hollow them out to make canoes. They carried fire in the canoe while fishing, at once a source of warmth and a lure of light for drawing fish. Their catch they cooked over flame, smoked for long-term preservation, and stored in baskets, probably woven from thatch or twigs shaped by burning. California gatherers burned patches to promote berries and tubers, fired prairies to assist wild grasses, and underburned mature oaks to help collect acorns. Their food they prepared by cooking; storage baskets they manufactured from branches specially pruned by selective burning; small mammals like rabbits they hunted while burning brushy hillsides and grassy valleys. Bison hunters on the plains also burned regularly. Again, firing was orderly, not promiscuous; specific, not generic. The routine pattern was to burn some distance from settlements in the fall, part of a prewinter hunt to store up pemmican and to force herds to move nearer encampments to secure winter forage. Spring fires then nudged herds to the fall-burned sites, now greening up profusely. For all pre-Columbian peoples, social eating occurred around a fire in longhouse, wickiup, or tepee.[7]

Why should it have been different for proto-Europeans?

(ii)

Still, direct evidence for early European fire remains elusive. Until the Neolithic revolution introduced exotic plants and animals whose pollen and bones lie with preserved charcoal and trace an unequivocal horizon of anthropogenic burning, there are sparse means by which to discriminate between natural and anthropogenic fire. The changes wrought by fire merge with the massive migrations and extinctions of flora and fauna, including humans, set in motion by the waning Pleistocene. If the consequences are difficult to determine precisely, the burden of proof must nonetheless rest on those who would deny anthropogenic fire a prominent role. Why, alone among the known peoples of the planet, would Upper Paleolithic Europeans not use fire as widely as possible? Why would they not exploit fully the most indispensable element of their toolkit?

For Mesolithic times (10,000 to 5,000 years B.P.), there is stronger evidence of anthropogenic-inspired change. By now climate was stabilizing, the big game had vanished, and humans adopted a more mixed economy of seasonal fishing, hunting, and foraging. Ivy and hazel, both valuable for hunting, increase, probably due to selective pressures by humans. Charcoal intercalates with other sediments in such disparate locales as the Apennines and Yorkshire, almost certainly the residue of anthropogenic burning. While hard data are scattered and specific, the economic mosaic closely mimics that of many historically studied peoples elsewhere on Earth, all of whom exploited fire extensively.[8]

Two factors seem to have limited fire's domain. One was climate, in particular the regimen of wet and dry seasons. Where the gradient between wet and dry persisted or sharpened, as in the Mediterranean or the Eurasian interior, there fire flourished, arcing between the seasons like electricity between charged wires; and anthropogenic fire had access to many niches. But the moderate climate of central Europe probably shrank the dominion of free-burning fire as a seasonality based on hot and cold replaced that based on wet and dry. Thus central Europe probably followed the example of tropical Brazil, where a uniformly moist climate promoted the recovery of forest from steppe, rather than the example of the American plains, where the climate allowed anthropogenic fire to resist the climatic pressures to reforest and retained the lands largely in (for humans) more productive grasses. The second factor was the presence of fire-assisting technology. Just as fire could amplify the power of other tools, so mechanical implements and domesticated biotas could counter some climatic effects. Axes could pry open sites otherwise sealed, cattle and sheep could consume as browse the reproduction of new forests. But these reforms had to wait for the firebrands of the Neolithic revolution.

If fire's legacy is elusive or evanescent, so are the other relics of early modern humans in Europe. The cave paintings of Lascaux recreate something of the

Paleolithic hunter's landscape. They were done by torchlight, with red ocher and black manganese dioxide prepared over flame, an art as impossible without controlled burning as the hunting that it depicts. As fire allowed ancient hunters to inscribe their world onto the stone walls of caves, so fire helped them to impress themselves on the biota of the world beyond.

But fire also felt the continued changes, the slow settling of climate, the more stable congregations of plants and animals, an equilibrium of the combustion environment. Always fire had assumed the personality of its human tenders. As early Europeans evolved, so did fire. Like Europe's Paleolithic pioneers, hominid fire wandered, testing trees and scrub, assaying soils, deconstructing landscapes into their signifier species, until eventually coarse colonization ended. Something like permanent settlement succeeded biotic prospecting, and communities replaced wanderlust. Progressively, the forager became the farmer, the hunter the herder, and the errant fire the sedentary fire. Increasingly home was where the hearth was.

> *And first Achates struck from flint a spark,*
> *And caught the fire in leaves, and round it fed*
> *Dry fuel, and on tinder snatched a flame.*
> —Vergil, *Aeneid*, Book I

CULTIVATED FIRE:
THE AGRICULTURAL RECLAMATION OF EUROPE

Anthropogenic fire segregated the wild from the human. By competing with lightning, controlled burning reshaped the frontier between culture and nature, between what humans could reasonably control and what lay beyond their grasp. By compelling humans to tend it, fire restructured human society; it defined the domestic as the place of the hearth. The Neolithic revolution began when, with the tended fire, modern humans undertook their first act of domestication: they domesticated themselves.

As they found ways to propagate that tended fire, humans began to cook the Earth. And as they brought more species within their expanding ring of fire, they restructured whole landscapes. The torch circumscribed the realm of human life. Where fire cast its light, humans could see, however dark; where it radiated heat, they could survive, however cold; where its flames danced, humans congregated, no matter how alien and threatening the world beyond. The domesticated landscape contained those plants and animals that would also gather around the tended fire and, like humans, came to depend on it.

(i)

The process had ample precedents. Controlled burning had already altered land-scapes, selected for species, kept lightning's wildfires at bay as it did bears and wolves. Lightning and humans competed, through fires, over a common reservoir of fuels. What one burned the other could not. The issue was not whether fire would exist, but what regimen of fire would dominate. Typically humans burned outside the primary seasons of lightning fire, just prior to or after the rainy season, not at its onset, thereby dampening lightning's effectiveness. Other practices indirectly affected their competition by manipulating the fuels on which both fed. The extinction of Pleistocene megafauna, mostly high-consumption grazers and browsers like mastodons, probably upset fuel complexes enough to perturb fire regimes just as the introduction or removal of elephants and bison do today.[9]

But domestication evolved into something approximating whole biomes. Once converted from wild to cultivated, the domesticated landscape demanded new fire practices. Just as dogs might share a fireplace with their human masters, so cultivated landscapes shared with humans a domesticated fire. Fire interacted with biotic technologies like wheat, sheep, and cattle as it did with axes and flints. The one, a catalyst, was a forcer of the environment; the other, a massive fulcrum by which to leverage fire practices into new fire regimes. More than an abstract model, fire was as much a tool of domestication as selective breeding. Most of the cultivated flora and fauna important to Europe emerged from lands subject to well-defined fire seasons—the monsoonal forests of eastern India and southeastern Asia, the mediterranean climates of Asia Minor. Filled with species adapted to fire disturbances, these were landscapes in which pyrophilic humans could thrive. Revealingly, the major centers of domestication are traditionally known as "hearths."[10]

The actual processes by which domestication proceeded are not known. Probably the earliest events occurred in southern and southeastern Asia and involved plants that could reproduce vegetatively, and animals that could be taken while young and literally brought into the household—taro, bananas, palms, bamboos, beadfruits, persimmons, citrus, spices; dogs, pigs, fowl, ducks, geese. In time, the idea as well as the species spread. Secondary hearths developed in China, Ethiopia, and the eastern Mediterranean. Further selection, in these novel environments, increased or reduced the agricultural ark's menagerie, and then radiated further, sometimes returning to the older hearths. Agriculture's passage from India to Europe followed the mountain-fringed southern rim of Eurasia.

The Mediterranean region added the date palm, the olive, the fig, and the grape to the register of cultigens reproduced primarily by cutting. More important, southwestern Asia became one of three hearths for seed cultigens and herd animals, for the cereals, milk, and meats so fundamental to the European diet.

Again the process of livestock domestication is speculative, perhaps originating from household pets or out of sacrificial needs, or through a combination of cultural preferences and environmental opportunities. Probably the major domesticates all began as milch animals and the practice of herding exclusively or on a massive scale represents a later evolution from a mixed economy of plants and animals. Certainly the combination of grasses and grazers is not accidental. Undoubtedly the originating environment was then, even more than it has become after millennia of abuse, a place richly mosaicked with fire regimes.[11]

(ii)

The work that fire did in such sites was much the same as it did in wild ones. It liberated nutrients such as calcium, phosphorus, potash, and proteins; it restructured the microclimate of sun and shade, heat and water; it drove off, for a time, soil microorganisms, predacious wildlife, and indigenous plants, enough that in the intervening ash bed humans could establish new species. It disturbed sites in particular ways, and plants would thrive that could seize such places either on their own or with human assistance.

There was plenty of precedent. Garden plots blossomed on burned sites much as bracken and fireweed did on burned windfall. Fire herding mimicked closely the practices of fire hunting; fire-assisted farming grew effortlessly out of the rootstock of fire foraging. European agriculture was rotational, its cycle turned by fire. Either it rotated the farm through the landscape or the landscape through the farm, the one shifting rapidly to newly fire-disturbed sites and the other specifying a controlled succession of plants and animals to occur on a fixed, regularly burned site. In both instances there was a time of fallow, in which the fuels could be regrown. The fallow itself, at various stages, also served grazing and foraging, and supplied household goods like thatch.

Each needed the other. Without unharvested trees, coppice, or grass, there was no fuel. Without sufficient fuel, fire could not liberate the fallow-captured nutrients, fumigate the soil, or purge the site of unwanted species. It could not do the two things fire ceremonies have always attributed to it and that farmers required of it—fertilize and purify. To reform one was to reform the other. Not until Enlightenment agronomy did reformers urge a systematic attack on the perceived problem of this linkage, but not until the exhumation of fossil hydrocarbons—fossil fuels and fossil fallow—were surrogates possible. Coal and petroleum powered industrial pyrotechnologies, and in derivative forms supplied agricultural nutrients, pesticides, and herbicides. In the process they also threatened the biodiversity of fallowed fields.

There is little agreement on what to call such agriculture. In practice, fire-fallow systems were as diverse as the natural fire-fuel systems that they mimicked.

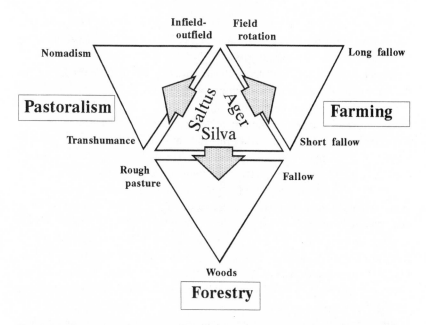

Europe's agricultural fire triangle. At its core are the three prime land uses: *ager* (arable fields), *silva* (woods), and *saltus* (pasture). Each practice, in turn, had distinctive patterns of fire and fallow, often overlapping. Abandoned fields, for example, could be used for rough grazing and then evolve into woods.

Every society had its own terms; and within each agricultural community there were typically dozens of names according to the special character of sites and techniques. Whether a locale contained organic soils or scrub, grass or woods, whether the woods were primary or secondary, pine or spruce, whether the combustibles were grown in situ or carried from surrounding sites, whether the fallow rested a long or short time—the variants were endless. There are good reasons to adopt the local language.

Yet the fire-fallow cycle begged for a common term, and anthropologists responded. Shifting cultivation, slash-and-burn agriculture, field-forest rotations have all served. But *swidden* has generally triumphed as the generic designation since the time it was introduced into the literature in 1951 by K. G. Izikowitz, a Swedish anthropologist studying French Indochina. Its origins are Norse, transferred to northern England during the Viking era. It referred, originally, to a burned clearing, specifically to burned heath. By the nineteenth century it was already archaic, even in Northumbrian dialects. By the twentieth century it was virtually forgotten. H. H. Bartlett scorned the choice, citing the many vernacular terms available in the cultures that still practiced it, and noting that the word was so obscure that it was not even in the *Oxford English Dictionary*. For that reason, perhaps, it lacked the denigratory connotations attached to alternative terms, and can serve ably as a generic expression. Certainly "swidden" is simpler than "fire-fallow system." But to call a practice "swidden" has roughly the same definitional power as calling a book "literature."[12]

Places immune to agriculture had either too little or too much fire potential. They were landscapes for which there was no adequate oscillating current of wet and dry periods, which meant insufficient or unavailable fuels; so there was no opportunity to jolt the site with fire. The gallery of such lands would include certain rainforests, deserts, and tundra. Alternatively there were landscapes for which anthropogenic fire provided almost universal access to the resident biota without the other manipulations—felling, plowing, sowing—that characterized European style agriculture. Australia, California, and the Brazilian *cerrado* are good examples. These places never developed formal agriculture until Europeans forcibly colonized them. Instead their indigenous peoples massaged the biota with a variety of fire techniques ("firestick farming," as one anthropologist has termed it) to extract their needs without the bother of introducing exotic flora and fauna.[13]

Such considerations reduce the practical distinctions between agriculture, horticulture, husbandry, herding, foraging, and hunting to the status of anthropological nominalism. At various times, one or several of these practices have coexisted; at other times, all have. Probably early Neolithic agriculturalists grew plots of cultigens on loess or later bottomlands and raised cattle, sheep, and pigs while they continued to hunt, fish, collect shellfish, gather nuts, berries, mushrooms, and honey, to ringbark (girdle) large trunks, pollard elm, alder, and hazel for fodder to feed cattle and goats, and to fossick among opportunistic burns. Probably agriculturalists tilled garden plots among broken forests and tended small flocks like extended household pets. Undoubtedly each practice had its trademark commitment to fire. The Neolithic economy was a kaleidoscope, twisted by the seasons and climate, its handle a torch. The encounter between early Europeans and Neolithic Europe, in brief, kindled a spectrum of fires, blurring one into the other like a kind of white light only broken into its individual bands by the force of conceptual prisms.[14]

Or almost. As agriculturalists refined their practices, they refined or specialized their fires as well. In particular, domestication demanded a fire as cultivated as its flora and fauna; and as domestication propagated throughout Europe, now flaring, now glowing like fiery moths on a wool blanket, it selected species of fire that differed from its progenitors as much as domestic sheep did from mouflons or oxen from wild aurochs. Cultivated fire could survive only in places created for it by humans; it was as dependent on human husbandry as milch cows, or einkorn that could no longer produce viable seed. It could not survive in the presence of predatory wildfire any more than fat-tailed sheep could with wolves, or wheat with thistles. If it was true that agriculture was marginal or downright impossible without fire, so it was also true that the fire regimes which the Neolithic revolution implanted across Europe would fail without constant tending, the combustion equivalent of sowing and weeding. Without human oversight, only feral fire would remain.

(iii)

Early in its history, agriculture evolved into more than the sum of its separate practices. After it boiled to a pithy core in Asia Minor, the Neolithic revolution approached Europe as a kind of miniature ark. It formed an ensemble, a stripped-down ecosystem complete with interdependent plants, animals, and microorganisms. Where early domesticators had planted a stalk or transplanted a species, the carriers of agriculture now shipped complete if simple biomes with their own cycling of nutrients and their own demands for site characteristics. The ensemble included grasses, forbs, legumes, trees, grazers, browsers, pollinating bees, and even a characteristic complex of weeds and vermin.

Among its most distinctive traits was the integration of farm and field, the fusion of cultigens with livestock. In some places and at some times plants dominated, while at others, animals did. But the norm—or where the norm was too remote, the ideal—was for the two to interact. Crops fed flocks, herds manured fields, the two bound by a closing circle of interdependence. When linked they made a functioning ecosystem that was also capable of moving, like a roving terrarium. No matter that the ark-bearing wagon often broke during its migrations, like a wooden wheel on a stony road. It advertised by its presence a pattern that Europe accepted as a Platonic ideal.

The synthesis occurred in the eastern Mediterranean between 10,000 and 8,000 years ago. Cereals and legumes, fruit and nut trees, browsers and grazers, vines, dogs, and fowl, all joined with the relic agriculture from southeastern Asia and consolidated in roughly the zone of ancestral wheat and barley. Then they moved outward where the environment permitted or could be made to accept it. By 8,000 B.P. it had spread throughout the Aegean; by 7,000 B.P. it filled the Fertile Crescent, excepting Egypt, and spilled into the Hungarian Plain. Over the next millennium it radiated by both land and sea, encrusting most of the Mediterranean littoral and tracking along the Danube and Rhine into central Europe. The needs of the newcomers led them to seek landscapes often different from those of Mesolithic peoples, interweaving the two economies into a new tapestry. By 5,000 B.P. Neolithic agriculture had seeped into most of the niches capable of supporting it. But then farmers and fire had helped define those niches: they made habitable what, of its own accord, was often not.

There were adjustments all around. Before a mediterranean-adapted biota

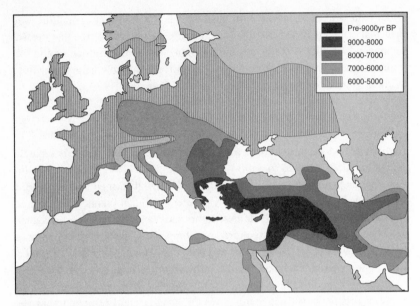

The Neolithic colonization of Europe. A mixed agricultural economy spreads west
and north across the continent. (Redrawn and modified from Roberts 1989 by the
University of Wisconsin Cartographic Lab)

could penetrate into temperate or boreal landscapes, it had to adapt to a regimen of summer instead of winter rains and to seasons of cold and hot rather
than dry and wet. That process of trial-and-error selection stalled the Neolithic
reformers on the Hungarian Plain for much of the seventh millennium B.P. When
they had arrived, their farm plots had hugged alluvial soils; when they departed,
the retooling completed, they seized fertile loess soils and relied on the more
regular rainfall regime of central Europe for the requisite moisture.

Before a complex of grasses and grazers could advance into mixed forest,
it needed the catalyst of disturbance. Something had to open the woodland
canopy, change soil pH from acidic to alkaline, wrench the existing flora and
fauna from dominance, fight off resident microbes, and displace the existing
humans. Pastoralism required sunny fields or forest steppes; gardening
demanded prepared plots suitable for cultigens but not for indigenous species.
The solution was a new regimen of fire in which the torch interacted with other
technologies. In the process, the newcomers fused with the old residents, often
with astonishing specificity, to fashion an environmental mosaic.

The initial points of contact were often small. But tiny villages or speckled
fields engaged the larger landscapes around them. Like their fires, the influence of pioneering agriculturalists could propagate. It was not necessary to fell

whole forests to change the dynamics of the forested environment. Swidden farmers worked small plots, leaving the woods to reclaim each cleared site over a fifty-year period, but from this base they also hunted, foraged, loosed herds of sheep, cattle, horses, and swine, and otherwise manipulated the surrounding landscape. Over a typical fifty-year cycle, even a small settlement could alter those forests extensively, and did. When the cycle returned, the newly felled and fired woods were different from the original ones. Continue this practice over centuries, and the forests of Europe might contain more or less the same species but operate in fundamentally different ways. While the amount of permanent clearing was small, the cumulative consequences of the new technology were pervasive and in some locales irreversible. As populations grew, so did the magnitude of their reclamation.[15]

Sedimentary records of preserved pollen hint at these effects. There is a record of initial contact, the fabled *landnam* by which Neolithic peoples first broke the landscape. Sediment cores testify to a dramatic decline in elm, a surge of coppicing hazel, a sprinkling of field weeds like ribwort plantain, stinging nettle, and sorrels, a persistence of grasses, a rise in light-hoarding species like beech, and of course charcoal, sometimes appearing in the pollen profile as a slashing spike or obscuring pall. On wetter sites, forest clearing probably stimulated peat formation, the biota no longer able to transpire away its excess subsurface waters. All of this derived from the need of agriculturalists to create an environment closer to those landscapes of Asia Minor from which their cultigens and domesticates had come. The actual techniques of reclamation adjusted to local circumstances.

The emigration of the Neolithic ark throughout the Mediterranean demanded the fewest internal adjustments, although it often induced the greatest external changes. Toughened though it might be, the Mediterranean landscape slowly degenerated under the remorseless assault of biotic tinkering. The passage of the ark into Europe's other environments came with less shock; both agriculturalist and landscape had to adjust, one to the other, like a parasite to its host. The outcome could be an extraordinary symbiosis of soils, plants, and practices, an ecological whole more complex than its unassisted parts. Especially along the margins, however, the agricultural synthesis fractured. Pastoralism predominated in the far north, the steppes, the upland moors, and from time to time around the Mediterranean. To an astonishing degree, however, a common template stamped Europe from Sweden to Spain, from Ireland to Russia.[16]

(iv)

This reflects in part a collective origin and commonly sought solutions to environmental challenges. But it also testifies to long centuries of persistent labor and to an agricultural model of great balance and adaptability. The complex could incorporate new members, as it did the horse. (Domestication of the horse most likely occurred around 4,000 years B.P., in the area of the Pontic steppes, probably sparing the species from extinction.) It soon became the symbol and enabling vehicle for the Indo-European exodus. The horse meant meat and milk, but also the chariot, the mounted warrior, the rituals of herding on wide-ranging grasslands. And the complex could also establish itself in an astonishing array of environments, from boreal forest to mediterranean scrub, from the borders of British moors to the fringe of Siberian muskeg. But well before the advent of historic records, the biotic technology for wholesale reclamation was complete.[17]

The ensemble did not again experience major additions and subtractions until Renaissance voyages imported the flora of other, long-segregated hearths, especially from the Americas. By then agriculture had so thoroughly reshaped Europe that the immigrant flora had to fit the minuscule niches it offered. The contrast between emigrant and immigrant species was striking. Voyaging naturalists like Joseph Hooker observed how frequently Eurasian species seized lands opened by contact, and how rarely imports to Europe did so. Starlings, cattle, rabbits, bluegrass, and blackberry—all infested lands exposed to colonization. But llamas, buffalo grass, and antelope failed to invade Europe with similar frenzy. The reasons are many, but prominent is the fact that European agriculture left few sites sufficiently untended for exotic weeds to invade, while the landscapes of the Americas and Australasia unraveled as fast as their indigenous societies.[18]

So powerful was the force of Europe's agricultural revolution that it not only reshaped the physical landscape of the continent—and later those of other continents—but impressed itself indelibly on the European mind. Agricultural reclamation, Europe's intellectuals believed, marked the chasm between the primitive and the progressive. So thorough was the European mode of agriculture that it denied, by default, that nonagricultural peoples had any power to remake nature. Their many manipulations were dismissed as inconsequential, and their land declared a *terra nullius,* available by legal and moral right to anyone who could use it. In practice, "use" meant "agriculture," and the taking of land was proclaimed an act of reclamation from its fallen state.

Where other agricultural systems existed, the European experience became the template for distinguishing the sustainable from the exploitative, the productive from the slovenly. Those who farmed according to European models with plow, fixed landownership, the integration of animal manure with crops, and so on were rational; those who used digging sticks and spruce harrows, who cycled through long-fallow forests or seized sites for one or two seasons, who massaged the indigenous biota rather than replace it, and above all who relied on fire—these were primitives.

While the actual criteria for judgment evolved as Europe's own reclamation intensified—the first continent to be subjected to its judgment was Europe itself—the agricultural ideal was stamped as completely on the mind as agricultural practices were on the land. Almost from the onset, intellectuals promoted reclamation as a paradigm for all relationships between humanity and nature. Its intensive agriculture became one of Europe's informing traits. Peoples and lands—and fires—that stood outside agriculture were beyond the pale of civilization. If fire had made it possible to reclaim and cultivate the garden, the garden defined the prospects and acceptable practices for fire.

But fire's agricultural revolution did not end with smoldering stubble and burned bushes. Other fire-catalyzed technologies such as metallurgy and ceramics intervened, outfitting agriculturalists with powerful tools by which to reorder landscapes and to process the goods harvested from them. These pyrotechnologies were as dependent on controlled fire as the ashy fields of the swidden farmer or the bracken patches of the forager. Not until the industrial revolution commenced the wholesale combustion of fossil fuels and the distillation of fossil fallow did open burning recede from its mandatory place in European agriculture.

When that time came, industrialization repositioned fire from the garden to the machine. It replaced the bonfire with the furnace, and the free-burning field fire with the combustion chamber. Increasingly fire seemed remote, mechanically partitioned from everyday experience, and the ecology behind agricultural burning as archaic as the fire science and botany of Theophrastus.

Pyrotechnia:
The Technology of Combustion

The dominion of fire did not end with the organic world: it extended also into the domain of rock, metal, lime, and clay, and it saturated the technics by which humans transformed whatever places they inhabited.

For some technologies fire was fundamental, with few if any alternatives, like the smelting of ore and the casting of cannon. For others, fire's effects were decorative, like the ashes rubbed into hides or the flame-induced coloration of amethyst and glass. The symbiosis that controlled fire fashioned between humans and the biota had its parallel in humanity's fire-fused relationship to the built environment. Besides, what fire gave to technology, technology returned with compound interest, each expanding the realm of the other. The culture hero who brought fire to the ancient Greeks, Prometheus, stated that fact with profound simplicity: "That is my record. You have it in a word: Prometheus founded all the arts of men."[19]

(i)

The range of fire-assisted technologies is staggering. In his survey of how human artifice counterfeits nature, Pliny the Elder pondered how

> fire is necessary for almost every operation. It takes the sands of the earth and melts them, now into glass, now into silver, or minium or one or other lead, or some substance useful to the painter or physician. By fire minerals are disintegrated and copper produced: in fire is iron burned and by fire is it subdued: by fire gold is purified: by fire stones are burned for the binding together of the walls of houses. . . . Fire is the immeasurable, uncontrollable element, concerning which it is hard to say whether it consumes more or produces more.

In fact almost no device or pursuit has lacked an element of combustion technology. And not a little of that technology has focused on fire itself.[20]

The process began early. Wherever humans needed heat, light, and power, they appealed to fire. It helped early hominids work with wood, stone, and probably bone, and even to acquire them. Controlled fire could char, harden, and sculpt wood whether as spearheads or dugouts. Applied to flint it allowed for special flaking, coloring, and tempering, giving lesser material the edge of obsidian. It could help shape horn and ivory. Certainly light and heat, and—where mosquitoes and flies were abundant—smoke, made possible worksites in otherwise impossible places.

But fire was also an enabling technology in acquiring raw materials. Selective burning felled trees, created deadwood for fuel, shaped willows and shrubs needed for baskets, and stimulated thatch. By stoking hot fires around or under cherty strata and then quenching them with water (or later vinegar or some other weak acid), miners could fracture refractory ore or undercut ore-bearing ledges. Fire quarrying persisted until the explosive combustion of gunpowder finally replaced it. And of course fire was ubiquitous in obtaining biotic goods through agriculture.

Few aspects of social life excluded it, from communications to sanitation. Well into the nineteenth century, parties of aborigines traveling outside their tribal lands habitually set signal fires to announce their presence, thus declaring themselves as hunters, not warriors bent on a surprise attack. Conversely, fire beacons warned of intruders or alerted the community to some other collective threat. From ashes came soap, and from fire-warmed water, baths. Infected clothes, dead bodies, and diseased environs were burned as a prophylaxis. Fire entertained; fir trees burned like Roman candles, torches illuminated plays, and later fireworks sparked the night sky. Around the communal fire, elders told stories, children learned tasks, groups danced in ceremonial rites and addressed their gods with sacrifice.

Out of the campfire evolved the stove, the furnace, and the kiln, and from cooking came the technologies of ceramics and metallurgy. Glass, glaze, enamel, bricks, clay linings for irrigation ditches and pipes, plaster and cement, pottery, and artifacts of tin, copper, bronze, gold, silver, and iron all enriched and reshaped human life, not only by society's direct absorption but indirectly by redefining what natural materials were valuable. Deposits of good clay became as valuable as caches of chert in Paleolithic times; copper lodes loomed as critical as prime soils.

As a paradigm of pyrotechnology, mining went beyond mere metaphor. Prospectors set fires on mountain slopes to expose likely outcrops (Lucretius even speculated that free-burning fires had melted ore and inspired metallurgy). Fire quarrying sank tunnels through soil, permafrost, and rock; candles and lanterns illuminated underground shafts for miners; the assayer's flame determined the character of prospective lodes; hot fires roasted raw ore and sustained its laborious smelting into metal; furnaces allowed casting into axes, knives, picks, coins, cannons, bells, jewelry. Without the concentrated power of fire, peoples had to rely on opportunistic foraging, on exposed veins of native copper, placered nuggets of gold, iron meteorites. With fire, however, they could literally force open the earth for raw material, forge new tools, and redefine their relationship to the landscape—to the biosphere as well as to the lithosphere because fire required fuel and the prodigious fires of great mines required equally immense mountains of fuelwood. It is estimated that the ancient mines at Laurion (Greece) consumed 0.6 million hectares of 20-year-old coppice, the Populonia mines (Etruria) burned 0.4 million hectares of forest, and the complex at Rio Tinto (Spain), engorging 42 tons of wood a day, consumed 3.2 million hectares over its life. Since such needs could not be met locally, fuel often traveled some distances, usually as charcoal. These restructured landscapes were, no less than those swiddened or fire-grazed, an outcome of anthropogenic burning.[21]

Smelting only hinted at the widening prospects for a chemical industry based on combustion. Fire distilled seawater into salt, wood into tar, resin into pitch and turpentine, grain and grape into alcohol; it transformed wood into ash and then into soap, and cooked calcitic rock into lime. Plaster and cement, in turn, encouraged new construction. The furnace-based transmutation of the base into the refined, even more than the hearth-based metamorphosis of the raw into the cooked, transformed thought as well as matter. From such observations, alchemy took its inspiration; and from the study of combustion, modern chemistry supplanted alchemy. The assayer's fire became a universal metaphor for testing, and ultimately a symbol of judgment and a test of character. *Philosophus per ignem* was chemistry's charge.

One pyrotechnology fed into another, all enlarging the scope of the humanized environment. Fire influenced warfare, urbanization, seaborne trade, natural philosophy, and religion; and through them it affected how humans interacted with the landscape. Much as pyrotechnology interbred with other technologies, including agriculture, so it displayed similar places of origin and parallel routes of emigration. Agrarian hearth had its close counterpart in industrial furnace. Departing armies, émigré colonists, traveling diplomats, all in ancient times carried the coals, if not the flames, of the tribal hearth with them.

(ii)

Those armies carried fire as weapon as well as symbol. The torch was sword, not merely banner. As long as cities were made of combustibles and citadels of wood, as long as armies clashed on fields and forests and bivouacked around campfires, as long as navies fought with wooden ships sealed with pine pitch, as long as combatants relied on a fire-fallowed agriculture for sustenance, fire was possible, and the torch-as-weapon likely. Armies hurled destroying flames against fort and besieger by means of arrows, fiery pots flung from catapults, even, if the Samson story is believed, with torches tied to the tales of foxes. Incendiaries were fundamental to arsenals. Armies needed fire control as much as artillery and battlements. Scorched earth became a policy of strategic retreat; fire and sword, the cry of conquerors and the plaint of the conquered; *incendit et vastavit*—they burned and laid waste—the melancholy entry of European chroniclers over the centuries. What fire had helped build, fire could help destroy. The pyrotechnologies that fashioned the sword assisted it in its deadly labors.

Incendiary weapons followed the logic of other pyrotechnologies. Free-burning fire, while used, was often undependable. It relied on suitable environmental conditions, and it was as likely to obscure a battlefield for the user as for the opponent. Most often it was applied as part of a scorched earth strategy, to cover a retreat, to flush out hostile forces from cover, or to destroy the agricultural fields that sustained an army. Instead, fire-as-incendiary became more specific. Besiegers attacked towns by hurling fire onto wooden or thatched roofs, seeking to burn or smoke out defenders as they would a bear from its den. Defenders responded with firefighting measures, tried to keep attackers out of range, and retaliated with incendiary weapons of their own—seeking to burn down wooden siege machines or enflame troops mustered at the walls. Greek fire, a liquid mixture of slow-burning combustibles, long remained the scourge of besieging armies and naval vessels. Eventually it was superseded by the explosive force of gunpowder, which gave new definition to the terms "firepower" and "fire control." Total war rekindled incendiaries for an industrial age. World War II saw the development of napalm, flamethrowers, aerial firebombs, thermite grenades, and aircraft and missiles by which to deliver the torch to city roofs. Not only the technologies but the targets evolved. Chemical torches were dropped from V-2s, Lancasters, and B-17s, and factories for tanks and ball bearings replaced field crops of cereals and pasture grasses. Not long afterward, the thermonuclear fireball replaced flame.[22]

The literature on fire and war is as old as literature. Homer's song of war, the *Iliad*, often reads as an extended fire metaphor. Soldiers' eyes "burn with fire," troops stoke their "fiery lust for battle," clashes rage "like a mass of whirling fire," field fights appear "as if the whole earth were devoured by wildfire." Poseidon calls a killing Hector a "firebrand"; Hephaestus forges Achilles' famed shield in fire, and Athena transforms him into a fiery pillar: "Charioteers were struck dumb when they saw that fire, relentless, terrible, burst from proud-hearted Achilles' head, blazing as fiery-eyed Athena fueled the flames." The epithet sticks: "blazing" Achilles. Homer, in fact, moves from epithet to extended simile:

On went Achilles: as a devouring conflagration rages through the valleys of a parched mountain height, and the thick forest blazes, while the wind rolls the flames to all sides in riotous confusion, so he stormed over the field like a fury, driving all before him, and killing until the earth was a a river of blood.

The epic ends with Achilles' funeral pyre, and the *Odyssey* opens with Troy's. So Vergil, in extended imitation, commences the *Aeneid* with the latter, repeats the extended fire simile in the clash between Aeneas and Turnus, and concludes with a rekindled vesta on the altars of Rome. As in Homer, the hearth replaces the forge.

Fire pervades ancient war as it does ancient landscapes. Other classics abound in fire weaponry. Incendiaries appear in Thucydides' *Peloponnesian War*, Xenophon's *Anabasis*, and Caesar's *Commentaries*, in which there were repeated burnings in forests as well as fortresses, sometimes by the Romans to flush the Gauls from their covering woods, sometimes by Vercingetorix to cover a retreat from the tenacious Caesar. (Caesar, like Achilles, also ended on a funeral pyre after his assassination.)[23]

Incendiaries, strategically applied, could change the field of fire for combatants. If armies used the woods for cover, then fire and ax could waste the fortress woods, as fire and sword could for walled cities. Caesar's attempt to reconfigure the battlefield with the torch was cognate to that of agriculturalists who burned to remake the wild more habitable. War could be reclamation by other means. Wholesale conversion became typical in guerrilla wars, or in conflicts where one side, committed to cavalry or drilled troops, needed open room to maneuver. Saracens slashed and burned in southern France; Turkish clearings in eastern Europe and the Balkans were so extensive that they may have led to permanent grasslands like the Alföld in Hungary and a pure pine forest in Bulgaria that, by the twentieth century, seemed virgin to German silviculturalists; the German *Wehrmacht* burned maquis in southern France and Greece to flush out insurgents. There were rules of war, even here, though they had meaning only if both parties acceded. Opposing Greek armies agreed not to destroy olive orchards, while Roman legions systematically sought out, felled, and burned groves sacred to Celtic druids.

Typically, then, war meant fire. It was abundant in Europe's interminable internecine wars, in Europe's expansionary campaigns beyond the continent, and in episodes of more local, civil unrest. During the Crusades, controlled fire became a prominent siege weapon. Guy of Lusignan was forced to surrender when Saladin surrounded with fire the hill on which he was entrenched. Subjugated Siberians called the Russian invaders the "fire people" for their weapons. The maritime empires of Portugal, Spain, Netherlands, and Britain were possible through the explosive fire of gunpowder. But more disturbing than martial fires set on the fringe of empire were those within. Arson became a weapon of insurrection, a chronic threat to the existing order. Rural burning—barns, ricks, fields—highlighted the 1830s riots in Britain and France, for example. The sheer breakdown in social order occasioned by war, unrest, or insurrection meant that fires, once regulated and kept in place, could now roam free. Even when not deliberate, fires trailed marching armies like other camp followers.

If war brought fire, it was not difficult to argue that fire, in its effects, was indistinguishable from war. For many European intellectuals, inhabiting cities, their experience of fire was the terror of urban conflagration, and for many cities this stemmed from the violence of armed conflict or rebellion. Moreover, episodic fire from warfare became a prominent if macabre fixture in Europe's kaleidoscope of fire regimes. Places like mixed deciduous forests that burned infrequently if ever under natural conditions, or only according to long-fallow swidden, kindled during the storm of battle, the slash and burn of an environmental warfare. The impact was far from trivial, not only in its direct effects but indirectly through changes in population, harvesting, and the general collapse of the social order that had impressed itself on the landscape. The fire ecology of central Europe, in particular, was closely related to warfare and social unrest, and that was a fact that its officials and naturalists were not likely or willing to overlook.

(iii)

To carry the torch, so often recognized as a symbolic act, was also a very practical one. The communal fire and the communal well were the two great public utilities. The common fire, in turn, was distributed to all the households of the larger group. Anyone who moved away from that fire took it with him as a firestick, coals, or a slow match. Even seaborne vessels held fire in their holds. When this was inconvenient or impossible, the traveler carried the means by which to rekindle new fire on demand. That fire kit included both apparatus and tinder.[24]

The means were many. The fire drill is probably the oldest and most universal implement. No doubt it originated from the hand rotation of a wood dowel, then acquired cords or mechanical bows to assist the process. Some drills operated vertically, some horizontally. The drill was known throughout Europe, and the horizontal drill was peculiar to it. A dry willow served as the dowel. Homer describes it in the *Odyssey,* Ezekiel refers to its use by the king of Babylon, and a reed serves as the cuneiform character for the Sumerian fire god, Gibil. Yorkshire's Settle cave contains fire-drill relics from Neolithic and Roman times. The techniques endured, particularly on the margins (such as northern Scandinavia) and for ceremonies (like the need fire).[25]

The fire saw, fire plow, fire thong, and fire piston reside primarily outside Europe, although again vestigial practices continued wherever folk culture thrived. The variety is astonishing. Swedes, for example, still kindled fire with drills, plows, and saws well into the nineteenth century. Similar findings are reported for the Balkans, Switzerland, and parts of Germany, their full extent limited, it appears, by the survival of traditional practices and the diligence of ethnographers to search them out. In effect, folk diversified their investment in fire appliances and thus ensured that they would always have fire from one source or another.[26]

The dominant device, however, was the strike-a-light. Dating from at least Neolithic times, it began with the percussion of pyrites and flint, later replaced by the—for Europe—universal reliance on steel and flint. This innovation postdates the metallurgical revolution in iron. But once developed, the method transcended all others for practical purposes, used alike for stove, musket, and tobacco pipe. Tinder and lighter joined buckled shoes and buckskin breeches as apparel. The apparatus became an important item of trade, disseminated eagerly to the Americas, to Inuit, Africans, Polynesians, whatever peoples Europe met on its voyages. The historical geography of steel-and-flint fire starters coincides remarkably with the global reach of European traders, missionaries, soldiers, and colonists.

Then the chemical revolution inspired better apparatus. The study of combustion, the discovery of oxygen, the use of sulfur to coat the pine tapers employed as miniature torches to light candles and stoves, the rediscovery of phosphorus which could ignite when exposed to air—all led, over a period of thirty years, to the invention of the modern match. There were many versions, but the one that triumphed, that provided the breeding stock for others, was the friction match, the vaunted "lucifer," invented by the English chemist John Walker in 1827.

The prototype was a wood splinter dipped in sulfur and then in a liquid of potassium chlorate, antimony sulfide, and gum water. It ignited when pulled through folded sandpaper. Walker met the rising demand for this immediately popular item by hiring the town's poor to split wood, and then dipping the splinters himself. He declined, however, to capitalize the process, set up a company, or even apply for a patent. He had, he claimed, wealth enough for his own wants. The lucifer he freely bestowed on his ever fire-starved fellow humans.

Development proceeded quickly, as much a part of industrialization as steel mills and railroads. The match complemented the new fire engines that powered the age of steam. By 1830 the first phosphorus matches were manufactured in Austria and Germany. But phosphorus was poisonous and prone to ignite accidently or even spontaneously. The Swedish manufacturer John Lundström solved the problems in 1852 by inventing the safety match, which could ignite only on contact with a specified surface of "red phosphorus."[27]

Despite monopolistic practices, the price plummeted and matches proliferated to the point of banality, the one artifact so cheap that people might freely ask a stranger for one. In olden times to mingle fires had been a solemn act, and the request to share another's fire a petition rich in symbolism and superstition. Now fire joined other industrially mass-produced objects, alienated from ancient associations, an act no longer dependent on intimate skill. The match replaced the torch much as the furnace superseded the open fire and as coal did fuelwood. But until other forms of power, notably electricity, challenged it, pyrotechnology continued to inform industry, field, and household, though increasingly it became invisible, vestigial, and archaic.

Like other fire devices, matches both ameliorated and worsened questions of fire safety. They made available to anyone a power to destroy whole cities, pastures, and forests; there was no control by cost, skill, or tradition on who had access to fire—children, idiots, criminals, soldiers, farmers, housewives, the rich and the poor could start fire with equal ease and profligacy; the old bonds of firetending and codes of fire behavior became irrelevant. Over and again, humanity had struggled to reconcile fire's powers with its dangers. Modernization only aggravated that problem by making ignition industrially abundant and concentrating fuels in cities.[28]

To be socially useful, fire had to be socialized. It had to obey the mutualistic logic of domestication. To survive, fire needed a shelter, and to prevent its extinction or escape, humans had to tend it. Fire could serve only if it was itself served. Neither fire nor firekeepers could afford to err. Each became bound to the other. Both required a *domus*. Both demanded a hearth.

HEARTH

*My hearth is piled with branches of pitch pine. Free burns my
faithful fire, and every hour my walls are black with smoke.*
                                                   —Vergil, *Eclogues* 7

Anthropogenic fire did not remain a wanderer among the wilds. It was too precious to trust to the opportunism of lightning, and too dangerous to abandon
to the vagaries of wind and scrub. If humans wanted fire at will, and wanted
to be shielded from wildfire, they would have to oversee flame themselves. The
result was a paradigm for domestication, the hearth its enduring emblem.

Along with its powers, fire imposed responsibilities. The needs of fire became
the necessities of humans. Fire was not a stone ax or a talisman, demanding
only that its possessor carry or store it. It was a process, as close to a living
being as any inanimate part of nature could be. Whoever desired fire would
have to feed it, breed it, train it, shelter it—to sustain it in an artificial environment in which the desired forms of fire could thrive. In domesticating fire,
however, humanity had to begin domesticating itself.

So fire was more than a natural phenomenon or a technology. If its ties to
the living world qualified it as metaorganic, its relations with humans rendered
it metacultural. With humanity it shared a common habitat, and with their mutual
domestication, fire entered into a social and cognitive world. The hearth
became one of the most intimate of social symbols; and the tended fire, a universal ceremony of species identity. Not accidentally did the centers of civilization become known as hearths.

The choices people made about how to use and interpret fire transcended
the biotic arrangement of combustibles and the diurnal rush of mountain winds.
They became, in a profound sense, moral questions for which the richness of
fire's symbolism was as significant as the moisture content of its fuels. The
cycle of fire went beyond the circuitry of carbon and phosphorus and entered
a mythic, ultimately moral universe that it has never since left.

DOMICILED FIRE:
HEARTH AND HOUSE

Anthropogenic fire demanded a habitation unique to its needs and duties. But humans could not exploit fire without being changed in the process. Fire's abode defined the focus of social life. (In Latin *focus* means "hearth.") Fire shaped the hearth, and the hearth the house. A family consisted of those who shared a fireside. The hearth became the archaeological tracer of human habitation, the one sure signature of human presence.

(i)

In the hearth, anthropogenic fire discovered a prime habitat. The hearth's design reflected the need to preserve, use, and control fire. Fuel had to enter, smoke escape, heat and light radiate, and fire remain. To maximize fire's benefits required reflector stones, chimneys, flues, and incombustible casings, and to minimize its hazards dictated the choice of building materials, the design of hearth and house, and even the arrangement of the dwellings themselves. If loosed, fire could propagate throughout the larger environment, not only the house but the aggregate of buildings that made up villages and metropolises. Domesticated fire could, if untended, become feral. Paradoxically, the hearth and chimney were often the only objects standing after a wildfire.

Domiciled fire had its ecology. The structure of cities reflected fire's influence as much as forests did: old, overgrown sections burned and rejuvenated buildings rose from the ashes. The buried past of ancient cities, from Troy to Nineveh, records a history of fire, layered like the charcoal varves of bogs. Many sites are known, and their chronicles dated, through the indestructible charcoal that they left behind. No less than with wildlands, urban history is a record of fire. Cities, too, had their fire regimes.

Some of the built landscapes burned often, a macabre parody of swidden agriculture in which forests were slashed in one site and burned in another. Those built of wildland materials burned like wildland fires—wooden dwellings flaming like windfall, daub-and-wattle huts torching like brush, thatch roofs flaring like the grasses they are. An archaeological experiment in Serbia found that in a typical peasant dwelling an uncontrolled cooking fire could enter the roof in three minutes, ignite it wholly in six, and lead to structural collapse in twenty. Vitruvius observed hopelessly that Rome's wood and thatch tenements were "made to catch fire, like torches." Gascony had a saying: "If covered with straw, don't let fire come near it." Tacitus observed in *Germania* that "every man leaves an open space round his house," and speculated that the reason was "as a precaution against the risk of fire."[1]

The same environmental conditions that promoted wildfire also favored urban fire. Similar fuels often burned in the mountains at the same time as in the streets. The largest fires required winds and drought, and wildfire in both settings propagated along the contours of the terrain, racing uphill and staggering down. But the built environment manufactured its own internal climate as well. Although the winter snows drove both humans and free-burning fire indoors, the relentless hearth desiccated the interior landscape like a kiln. What could not propagate freely outdoors because of the cold, the wet, or the dark could burn greedily within a house or along a cramped street. Accordingly, even in winter, fires often escaped, and burned with fatal abandon. In effect, instead of abolishing fire, the built environment added another season to it.

The regime of domiciled fire seemingly patterned itself after nature's prototypes. Fire burned most vigorously amid disturbed or old fuels, most uncontrollably in settlements recently hacked out of the woods or in overgrown, decadent slums—the city providing new slash or aging fallow. Romans feared the slums as they did the dark woods, as the scene for ambush and fire. Disturbed fuels bred fire. The great wave of agricultural reclamation that swept Europe and converted its woodlands to fields, an internal crusade, coincided with the Maunder maximum, a long span of warmer climate; together they inspired a legacy of fire. In medieval England, renters could lease a house until the first fire (*usque ad primam combustionem*). It is estimated that the average Russian village burned every twenty to thirty years, roughly the same frequency as the farmed forest on which these villages depended. But the large burned as well as the small. Fire razed urban complexes regularly, and sometimes massively, even discounting the savagery of war. Often fire followed pestilence, much as wildfire scoured beetle-killed or rust-blighted forests.[2]

Urban conflagration is a remorseless saga of Europe, as endemic to its combustible cities as rats and disease. Until cities no longer resembled reconstituted wildlands, fires rambled as readily as bears in the woods. The urban history of Moscow is a history of its conflagrations. Between 31 B.C. and A.D. 410, Rome suffered at least forty fires of sufficient magnitude to attract the attention of chroniclers, a fire frequency of roughly once every eleven years, approximately half that of the notorious *macchia* that clothed Italy's uncultivated wastelands. In pondering Rome's decline Edward Gibbon listed fire among the examples of the perishability of human art, noting especially that "in the days of distress and anarchy every wound is mortal, every fall irretrievable." The fires that Vergil urged for worn-out wheat fields, the shepherd fires that Silius Italicus saw ringing Rome like sentinels, had their lethal ecotype in the flames that swept through tenement *insulae* and that inspired frenzied reconstruction, new dwellings sprouting from the stony foundations like coppicing oak. Juvenal satirized Roman life as an "endless nightmare of fire and collapsing houses." The Christian vision of hell owed not a little of its metaphoric power to the experienced horrors of urban holocaust. By the Christian era the metaphors that animated fire's terrors were never drawn from wildlands and rarely from agriculture; they came almost exclusively from forge and town. Fire in stubble, heather, and gorse could not compete with the hell of a city aflame. Hell was indeed made by its inhabitants.[3]

(ii)

The conundrum of fire protection also echoed the eerie symmetry between city and country. For both, the need to protect fire was equaled by the need for protection from fire. There was no prospect, or desire, to abolish fire: every dwelling, every smith and tanner, every oven and stove, every lamp, every temple, every army bivouac, every sojourner through the evening streets required fire. Without fire the domicile was uninhabitable, the city unworkable.

The imperative was to exploit fire, not extinguish it. Just as the house was built around the hearth, so ancient villages and cities had a communal hearth, often a perpetual flame. Part of the rationale for permanent buildings was, after all, to nurture fire. French historian Fustel de Coulanges explained how it was "a sacred obligation for the master of the house to keep the fire up night and day. Woe to the house where it was extinguished." The last act at night was to bank the coals with ashes, the first act of morning to rekindle the embers. The enduring fire "ceased to glow upon the altar only when the entire family had perished; an extinguished hearth, an extinguished family, were synonymous expressions among the ancients." The same held for the communal fire. Those who failed to perpetuate it were punished, sometimes by death. For the sacred fire to expire was an omen of impending calamity.[4]

But domestic fires did escape. Even temple fires occasionally evaded their guards, and hostile fire appeared from time to time ignited by lightning, arson, and war. Urban life required aggressive fire protection. The best solution was prevention, which argued for better designed hearths and hearth surrogates. The driving force was often fuel. The scarcity of combustibles, particularly wood, compelled more efficient designs; eventually flame disappeared altogether into metal-encased stoves, to the delight of practical philosophers and the dismay of romantics. Substituting charcoal (and later fossil coal) for wood accelerated the process. Compared with flaming combustion, glowing combustion could release more heat with less volatility, but it brought its own demands for better ventilation. The control of draft led to designs for chimneys, flues, and bellows. Fluid combustibles like fuel oil and natural gas furthered the mechanization—and irrelevancy—of the fireplace. Electricity completed the chemical divorce by dispersing appliances for heat and light, and promoted a social segregation by installing electronic home entertainment centers where the flaming hearth had once stood.

Originally the house itself was the hearth—the fire situated securely in the center, the dwelling shaped to evacuate smoke through the roof. As structures elaborated, fire became more compartmentalized. The universal open hearth evolved into an array of specialized fire appliances, and the central fire disappeared into kitchen stoves and basement furnaces. Flues carried heat to rooms removed from the flames; candles, light; braziers and foot heaters, warmth. All this the architecture of dwellings reflected, for fire imposed limitations on how buildings could be shaped in order to capture the assets of fire while reducing its liabilities. No urban structure, moreover, was isolated. A fire in one building threatened all those around it. Not until the hearth ceased to command the center of the house—and conflagrations ceased to define the cycles of destruction and reconstruction of urban centers—could architecture consider dramatically new designs.

Urban life thus required fire codes. There are proscriptions, for example, in the Code of Hammurabi. By 450 B.C., Republican Rome decreed at what distance and to what height houses could be built, the regulations conceived primarily as a fire protection measure. There were rules too about maintaining buckets of water in tenements and prohibitions against open fires outside of specified hearths. After the outbreak of the Pyrrhic War in 281 B.C., wooden shingles were banned from roofs. Evidently builders and residents widely ignored all such prohibitions. Similar regulations applied to new towns created by rapid reclamation; the charter of A.D. 1200 for the village of Ipswich, England, for example, laid down rules for the approved arrangement of combustibles and the placement of tubs of water, along with duties for firewatching and firefighting. Legal sanctions threatened those responsible for accidental fire with restitution for damages, and those guilty of arson with criminal punishment. In an age before fire insurance companies, when a single fire could devastate whole city sectors and wipe out entire villages, there was little tolerance for carelessness, and none for arson, which was generally declared a capital offense.[5]

Still, fires inevitably broke out. Pioneering hamlets provided for firefighting— a bell as fire alarm, tools and water positioned as necessary, mandates for able-bodied men to assist when called. When fire did break out, villagers fought them as they would those in wildlands. They swatted and doused flames, cut firebreaks, pulled thatch from the line of fire, even set backfires when all else failed. Large cities like Rome sponsored firefighting crews, which had become as much a public service as aqueducts and roads. In Republican times, select senators supervised an official brigade (*familia publica*) of firefighting slaves. Its failings opened gaps for entrepreneurs to establish private brigades (*familia privata*).[6]

The most notorious entrepreneur may be Marcus Crassus (115–53 B.C.), a self-made man who, "if we may scandal him with a truth," according to Plutarch, secured his wealth "by fire and rapine, making his advantages of the public calamities." In particular, "observing how extremely subject the city was to fire," Crassus amassed 500 slaves who were builders and architects, then searched out buildings on fire, bought them and those of their nervous neighbors for a trifling, and used his men to halt the spreading fire, probably by tearing down adjacent structures. In this way, Plutarch marveled, "the greatest part of Rome, at one time or other, came into his hands." One suspects that arson accounted for not a few such fires. The unholy trinity of money, politics, and firefighting thus began early.[7]

Surely the most celebrated catastrophe was the conflagration of Rome in A.D. 64, a blaze that the contemporary historians Suetonius and Diodorus Cassius believed started under the orders of the emperor Nero, who wanted to clear land for palaces and parks. Tacitus reported at length on this "most terrible and destructive fire which Rome had ever experienced." Portentously the fire began on July 19, the anniversary of the sacking and burning of Rome by the Gauls. Begun amid shops selling "inflammable goods," fanned by wind, "encouraged" by "narrow winding streets and irregular blocks" and the absence of obstructions, the flames raged for days, until "enormous demolitions" cleared away combustibles. Even then it mysteriously rekindled. By the time it ended, the conflagration had incinerated, utterly or partly, ten of Rome's fourteen districts. With stark symbolism, it had even destroyed the Vestal shrine.[8]

Massive rebuilding followed, including an exorbitant palace for Nero. But unlike Rome's earlier burning by the Gauls, reconstruction was, Tacitus observed, not without plan: "Street-fronts were of regulated alignment, streets were broad, and houses built round courtyards. Their height was restricted, and their frontages protected by colonnades." Many of these reforms were intended to retard future fires. Edicts prescribed a fixed proportion of stone for buildings, ensured a greater availability of public water, and required that householders keep firefighting apparatus handy. There were sacrifices and prayers, persecutions of Christians, even an attempted rebellion by gladiators. But though all Italy was "ransacked for funds, and the provinces ruined" by the huge levies (and even temples looted), the reforms were soon forgotten. Rome endured other fires. For 1,600 years, however, its catastrophe stood as the paradigm of Europe's urban fire crisis.[9]

True or not, the rumor that Nero kindled or furthered the fire reveals a dark reality of urban life. For most cities, conflagrations were followed by new construction, which was, in fact, often prohibited in the absence of some widespread destruction. Not until urban fires ceased to rage over extended areas was it necessary to carry out urban renewal with dynamite and bulldozers. Until then, accident and arson often dictated urban rejuvenation, much as they did for the surrounding countryside.

One response was to upgrade public fire brigades. This Augustus did, motivated as much by politics as by public ardor. The *Vigiles* initially consisted of seven cohorts of 560 men each. As the name suggests, the primary chore was to watch for fires and attack them while they were still small. With buckets and

axes, there was little else possible. Among the duties of such brigades, however, was to enforce ordinances against open fire, both those legally kindled
and those nominally prohibited. But removing fire from hazardous workshops
and tenements was impossible. At least during the day if a fire escaped there
were people nearby to suppress it or sound an alarm. Authorities concentrated
on a nearly universal practice of covering open fires at night. Thus originated
the curfew (from the French *couvre-feu*).[10]

With or without special brigades, firefighting became a civic duty, and every
private fire a potential public threat. Many ordinances required that citizens spread
the alarm before attacking the source. Once the fire bell sounded, the public
mustered at the scene—guilds often dividing the labor among themselves, with
masons and carpenters tearing down roofs and walls, others covering adjacent
roofs with wet cloth, organizing chains of buckets to bring water, emptying threatened dwellings of their contents. If the fire spread, then crews fashioned firebreaks by demolishing nearby structures. The authorities sought to quell public
panic and looting, for a large fire threatened not only property but civil order.
Yet so long as cities were built of combustibles and crammed within walls, there
was little architectural control over the start and spread of urban fire.

(iii)

When such controls finally came, fires receded, and large fires became more
or less confined to outbreaks of war or riot. Real progress proceeded from
changes in building materials and urban design. Fire, as always, followed fuels.
(The *Aeneid* is full of references to firebrands hurled to the combustible roofs,
obviously a point of vulnerability.) In England, for example, urban fires more
or less paralleled the growth of urban sites. Wildfire burned sprawling suburbs
much as it would brush reclaiming a meadow. Overhung streets and densely
wooded suburbs burned as unquenchably as crown fires. So, too, the control
over urban fire mimicked the techniques used to control agrarian fires. That
pattern ceased only when masonry replaced timber; when cities, like farms,
substituted stone walls for woody hedgerows.

The transition coincided roughly with the London fire of 1666. The largest
city in Europe, London spawned the greatest fire. The city was still reeling from
more than a year of bubonic plague when on the morning of September 2, a
Sunday, fire broke out in a baker's house near Thames and Pudding Lane. The
streets were narrow, the overhanging houses were of aging timber, and everywhere were combustible materials; the dense houses themselves were stuffed
with pitch, tar, oil, wine, and wooden furniture. A long drought had drained
the city of moisture. An east wind fanned the flames into "an infinite great fire."[11]

The first response was tardy. This was, nominally, a day of rest. The affected
populace scurried to salvage their household possessions. Not until Charles II

issued a royal command did the authorities begin the necessary process of tearing down houses, many belonging to the wealthy, in advance of the flames. It
did little good. The wind rained down embers like a "shower of fire-drops,"
precipitating "flakes of fire" far in advance of the firefront. Streams of fire coa-
lesced into miniature firestorms. The diarist John Evelyn described the scene
at its climax:

> Oh the miserable and calamitous spectacle! such as happly the
> world had not seene the like since the foundation of it, nor be outdone
> till the universal conflagration of it. All the skie was of a fiery aspect,
> like the top of a burning oven, and the light seene above 40 miles round
> about for many nights. God grant mine eyes may never behold the like,
> who now saw above 10,000 houses all in one flame; the noise and crack-
> ing and thunder of the impetuous flames, the shrieking of women and
> children, the hurry of people, the fall of Towers, Houses and Churches,
> was like an hideous storme, and the aire all about so hot and inflam'd
> that at the last one was not able to approach it, so that they were forc'd
> to stand still and let the flames burn on, which they did for neere two
> miles in length and one in breadth. The clowds also of smoke were dis-
> mall and reach'd upon compution neer 56 miles in length.

Eventually the authorities resorted to gunpowder, while Samuel Pepys himself scoured the naval yards for "stout seamen" to use it. Gangs blew large firelines through thickets of dwellings. Then the wind dropped, firebrands ceased
to sail over roofs, and the flames quieted. The fire flared for days afterward,
the stones hot enough to heat leather shoes, some cellars still smoldering six
months later.

When it ended, the conflagration had consumed 373 acres within the city
walls, and another 63 outside it; only 75 acres within the city remained unburned.
In tallying the damages Pepys observed that the fire had burned as many parish
churches as "there were hours from the beginning to the end of the fire," and
that the number of churches spared equaled the number of unburned taverns.
"Here by the permission of Heaven," bore a commemorative inscription, "Hell
broke loose. . . . " After six years of reconstruction, however, a lecturer at Gre-
sham College could write architect Christopher Wren that "the Fire however
disastrous it might be to the then inhabitants, had prov'd infinitely beneficial
to their Posterity; conducing vastly to the Improvement and Increase, as well
of the Riches and Opulence, as of the Splendor of this City."

That in cameo had been the cycle of urban fire for several centuries. Disre-
garding the depravities of Nero, the great fire of London repeated, with
uncanny fidelity, the great fire of Rome. Evelyn's description is almost inter-

changeable with that of Tacitus. The catastrophe only magnified what occurred over and again in hamlets, towns, and cities. There were the same circumstances that bred fire like rats, the same mechanics of fire spread through crowded combustibles, an identical hysteria and hopelessness until the winds blew out or the fuel was exhausted. But this time, after the fire, a true change followed.

The great London conflagration sparked genuine, continuous reform. The old pattern broke down, in England first, but eventually throughout northern and central Europe. Edicts decreed standards for the layout and width of streets in new towns. The Enlightenment's scientific advances encouraged better firefighting technologies—pumps, hoses, fire appliances. More important, fire insurance companies proliferated, and by bringing fire codes into a capitalist economy they influenced the architecture of cities. In particular, brick and masonry replaced wood, and slate thatch. Mediterranean cities had earlier converted to stone and tile, partly as a measure of fire protection, more surely in response to the destruction of the surrounding woodlands, themselves forcibly metamorphosed into vineyards and fields, fired for pastoralism, or carted off for charcoal and fuelwood. Northern Europe had remained vulnerable to fire much longer.

As commerce forced cities to tear down their confining walls, streets widened, and as codes and capital rebuilt spacious squares on burned slums, the ability of fire to propagate from a single ignition over whole urban landscapes diminished. Between 1700 and 1900 the number and size of English cities expanded dramatically but the size and frequency of conflagrations shrank. The cities grew faster than they burned. The control of urban fire, it is argued, augmented the size of investment capital. The industrial revolution not only put fire into machines but removed it from heavily capitalized cities.[12]

Consider the case of thatch, the maligned tinder of urban conflagration. In France it was too abundant and too easily worked to dismiss, and sturdier roofs of slate or tile demanded construction that few peasants could afford. Not until the mid-nineteenth century when insurance companies became more aggressive and threshing machines replaced hand flails (the threshers broke the straw) did thatch recede from the rural economy. "Insurance rates had made thatch impractical for the prosperous," notes historian Eugen Weber, "machines made it almost impossible for the poor." Thatch—grown like grain, woven like baskets, or piled like haystacks—was a mainstay of a peasant economy. It disappeared when modernization submerged that economy. And so also vanished the fires it had sustained.[13]

Even so, the story is less one of fire exclusion than of fire's transformation. Thatch, after all, had been grown on sites burned to promote it, then harvested to burn in stoves or shocked into roofing, where it might burn in wildfire. But many of its replacement materials were themselves derived pyrotechnologies; they had already, as it were, passed through the flames. Tile, brick, lime for cement—all resulted from applied fire. Increasingly, combustion burned fossil fuels instead of contemporary ones, further breaking the shared ecology of town and country. Later, applied combustion in dynamos substituted electricity for the fire of oil lamps and pine tapers; gas stoves for the fireplace; oil furnaces for the central fire. Eventually, the cold flicker of television, not the warm flames of the hearth, became the focus of social life.

(iv)

Where it endured, fire survived as a vestige—the ceremony of the Yule log and birthday candle; the hearth a decorative feature like the wrought iron scrolling on a gate; the infrequently tended fire a kind of pet, like fish in an aquarium. Pondering the spectacle of caged fire, the American Nathaniel Hawthorne observed in 1843 that "in classical times, the exhortation to fight 'pro aris et focis'—for the altars and the hearths—was considered the strongest appeal that could be made to patriotism. And it seems an immortal utterance." (So it had remained, as cry or name, for patriotic and revolutionary clubs throughout the Romantic period.) "The holy Hearth! If any earthly and material thing—or rather, a divine idea, embodied in brick and mortar—might be supposed to possess the permanence of moral truth, it was this. All revered it." But now they revered steam, and the Second Nature they had made with fire became a Third Nature constructed with internal combustion.[14]

As urbanites' personal experience of fire waned, so did their tolerance of its consequences. They knew it only in its domiciled forms, as the servile hearth or the anarchic conflagration. As technology increasingly divorced them further from the former, they experienced only the latter. They saw fire as social horror. It threatened rather than informed the home. Fire's demands for fuel they considered exorbitant. Its smoke they condemned as a health hazard. If they could banish it, they would. The hearth became an optional feature of the house, an indulgence of the wealthy, the fireplace more expendable than a dishwasher or a stereo. As the power of the hearth to shape the house weakened, so also it lost its power over the social life within. No longer did the household gather around the central fire; no longer was the family that coherent group that shared a fireside. The dispersion of fire dispersed a social order as well.

What had begun as a dwelling in which to nurture fire now became a habitat inimical to it. And what was true to its singular experience, urban Europe projected onto nature, anthropomorphizing fire into terrorist and killer. Where their ancestors had hunted in the regrown thickets of burns and baited snares with the green pick of a freshly fired site, they now saw commuter rabbits disoriented by subway smoke and clerical deer fatally trapped in high-rise forests. Where aboriginal children had learned about fire by playing with it, urban Europeans learned as children never to touch the flame. The injunction against fire became one of the first and strongest of social prohibitions.

THE FIRE IN THE CAVE:
COMBUSTION AND COGNITION

For early hominids the known world was the world shaped and enlightened by fire. The world beyond the protective ring of anthropogenic fire, beyond the radiance of the hearth, was wild, unknown; what lay outside the transmuting power of fire was unknowable. Just as humans had used fire to shape their contrived worlds, the world of Second Nature and the world of domiciles, so it was perhaps inevitable that they should seek in fire an instrument for explicating those worlds.

Anthropogenic fire became a focus for understanding: it did for knowledge what it did for wildlands and dwellings. Fire was idea, symbol, subject, and tool. It could rework thought as it did metal or clay. If it required explanation, it could also explain. Fire was the ultimate dialectical tool, capable equally of deconstructing the text of the world into its constituent parts and of fusing them into a new synthesis. Within it gods were manifest, about it myths were told, by it philosophy was explored, and out of it a science evolved that would, in the end, destroy fire's magic, mystery, and metaphysic. "Fire," concluded Gaston Bachelard, "is thus a privileged phenomenon which can explain anything." It can even "contradict itself."[15]

(i)

Fire's power to destroy evil and promote good inspired stories, rites, and ceremonies, all of which had their source in the authority of nature—in the rich ash of swidden, in fire-flushed pastures, in flame-pruned thickets lush with berries. So the phoenix immolated itself every 500 years and rose, young and vigorous, from the ashes. So Demeter sought to bequeath immortality on Demophoön, the infant son of her host, by placing him next to the hearth on successive nights. Repeated fire was, paradoxically, a means of perpetual renewal. It was a simple matter to decide that a similar logic governed the cosmos, that the world might begin and end with fire or enjoy immortality by passing through fire-induced cycles of death and rebirth.

So much power demanded an explanation. The possession of fire was unique—this humans knew at their origins. More than anything else, fire defined them and segregated them from the rest of creation; myths that depict the origin of fire account equally for the origins of humans. Typically the proto humans are helpless. Typically some culture hero—an animal, a Titan, a cunning youth, a pitying god—steals fire from a potentate who hoards it as an expression, if not the source, of his own power. With fire, humans begin to act for themselves.[16]

Within Europe there were many variants on the theme. No myth embraced all peoples. There was disagreement, for example, even within Greece. The Argives insisted that their ancient King Phoroneus had discovered fire, and well into the Pax Romana they continued to honor his memory with a sacred fire at the great temple of Apollo Lycius. Even the celebrated story of Prometheus varied according to the license of poets and philosophers like Hesiod, Aeschylus, and Plato. Preserved in writing, adopted by the dominant civilizations, the myth of Prometheus eventually became Europe's own.

According to Hesiod's *Theogony,* Zeus the Cloud-Gatherer hid fire from mortal man. He had, after all, fought for supremacy with the aid of lightning, and through lightning, fire. Flames had swept the Cretan battleground between the Olympians and the Titans like a tidal wave. But the Titan Prometheus, who had sided with the Olympians, sympathized with the pathetic humans, pilfered some of Zeus' heavenly fire, and carried it to earth in a stalk of fennel—an herb often used as a slow match in ancient times, and possibly an echo of the reed that symbolized the Sumerian god of fire.

For this rash act Zeus punished both giver and receiver. To empowered man Zeus sent woman in the form of Pandora, whose mindless curiosity unleashed a host of evils. To Prometheus, rumored to know the identity of him prophesized to overthrow Zeus, Zeus added cruelty to fury by chaining him to a peak in the Caucasus Range. Each day without fail an eagle would appear before the hapless Prometheus and devour his liver; each night the organ would grow whole again; daily Zeus' rage smoldered and Prometheus' defiance swelled until after thirty or forty thousand years Hercules arrived to break the chains. It was this version that Aeschylus explored in his famous tragedy, *Prometheus Bound,* and it was this vision of the rebellious culture hero that attracted the Romantics.

Plato offered a more philosophical version. In the Socratic dialogue *Protagoras,* he described how the gods fashioned mortal creatures from compounds of earth and fire, two of the world's four elements. Creation took place underground at the direction of Hephaestus, god of the forge, and Athena, goddess of the arts. Once the creatures had been rudely fashioned, the gods assigned Prometheus and his brother Epimetheus the duty of refining and delivering them to the surface. As the etymology of their names suggests, Prometheus could think ahead; Epimetheus, only after. When the time came to equip the created beasts with their requisite powers and functions, Epimetheus convinced his brother that he could handle the task. Foolishly, Epimetheus distributed the valuable but limited skills to the animals as they appeared. By the time humans arrived, there was nothing left. Since the day fast approached when they must disgorge the finished creatures to the surface, there was no time to rectify the bungled creation.

But Prometheus was friendly to humanity, and he reasoned that if humans had fire and the mechanical skills allied to fire, they could survive. Zeus' warders closely guarded the Olympian fire, so Prometheus stole into the workshop of Hephaestus and removed fire from the forge. (Hephaestus himself and his fire had descended from the heavens after Zeus had hurled him into banishment. In this way the originating fire could trace its pedigree to lightning, not the forge.) Thus Prometheus could claim that he founded all the arts of men, and Plato could explain human dominance on the basis of pyrotechnology.

Regardless of particulars, the myths make clear that fire is power, it is not given freely, its presence joins humanity to nature, its possession distinguishes humans from the rest of base creation, and it unites the human with the divine.

(ii)

The ever-preserved fire must have indeed seemed godlike. In some societies, fire *was* a god; in others, a theophany, a manifestation of divine presence; in all, an inevitable part of sacrifice, ceremony, and theology. The older the religion, the closer and more vivid the presence of fire.

The Egyptian sun worship of Ra (or Horus) radiated fire imagery. The fire kindled daily on the altar reenacted the rising of the sun; the flame in the temple was his expression, and the fire on the altar, the triumphal Eye of Horus. "I am Horus, Prince of Eternity," read the Egyptian Book of the Dead, "a fire before your faces." New temples followed a consecration for which the torch was fundamental. Similarly, Ugaritic texts describe the dedication—purification—of Baal's temple with seven days of fire. Among Canaanite rituals to Baal and Moloch was apparently the sacrifice of burnt children, a practice condemned in Deuteronomy and Kings and by Jeremiah and reminiscent of the story of Abraham's near slaughter of Isaac. The terrifying messengers of Yamm before the council of El are depicted as a burning fire like a whetted sword, an image echoed in the Cherubim and flaming sword at the gate of Eden. Among the Sumerian-Akkadian pantheon was Gibil, a fire god associated with cane and reeds, where no doubt he most often manifested himself. Gilgamesh sent burnt offerings, full of "sweet savor," and the gods "gathered like flies over the sacrifice." Holy fire was theophany, a means of sacrifice, and a weapon of divine wrath.[17]

Early Indo-Europeans worshiped a god of the hearth. His progeny bred prolifically. He became Agni, the first god of the Hindu pantheon; Hestia and Vesta, the Greek and Roman goddesses of the hearth, respectively; Svarozhich, a Slavic avatar; Atar among the early Iranians; the hypostasis of Ahura Mazda, the Great

God of the Zoroastrians, among the first of the monotheisms. For the Zoroastrians the fire ritual was a core ceremony, the perpetual fire a central obsession, and the pure fire an uncompromising obligation. For it they erected and consecrated temples; through it they made sacrifices. Their priest, the Magus, gave rite and religion a final form; the Parsees preserved both against challengers, even carrying the sacred fire to India; and the Hebrews, during their Babylonian exile, incorporated many features into their own beliefs and practices. Such awkward adaptations may explain, for example, the story of Nadab and Abihu, whom Yahweh destroyed with devouring fire for bringing "strange fire"—that is, impure fire, probably in the Zoroastrian mode—before the altar.[18]

The Old Testament is in fact a cauldron of stories, rites, and beliefs simmering over a mix of religious fires. Probably the early Hebrews possessed a fire god in their history, as the Indo-Europeans did Atar. Apparently, like many peoples, they carried fire with them. Abraham, for example, *brought* fire—not made it—as he prepared for the Moloch-like sacrifice of Isaac. If so, that fire god vanished. In its place, the Hebrews honored fire as a manifestation of god, not as a god itself. Many of these expressions seem "strikingly archaic" to scholars, part of the Yahwist strata of the Pentateuch: Yahweh sealing the covenant with Abraham with a "smoking fire pot and a flaming torch," echoing rites (including Akkadian) in which objects and persons are purified by passage between theophanic flames; Yahweh descending on Sinai "in fire" and appearing to Moses "in the flame of fire in the midst of a bush," another covenant sealed with fire and another trope with analogues from Syria, Palestine, and Egypt; Yahweh leading his people through the wilderness with a pillar of fire; Yahweh repeatedly speaking to his people "from the midst of fire," a rekindling of the Sinai theophany. Prophetic reminders appear in Zechariah, Isaiah, and Ezekiel to whom Yahweh appeared as "the God of Fire." The Psalms repeat the imagery; "the voice of the Lord flashes forth flames of fire." In Daniel's vision Yahweh claims for "his throne a flame of fire," around which flows like a moat a river of fire. Fire is, in fact, as John Laughlin confirms, *the oldest symbol with which Yahweh is associated in the Old Testament.*"[19]

To these sources the Priestly tradition added other images and rites—the altar fire, the fire from heaven as a means of accepting or rejecting ritual sacrifice, the perpetual fire as a manifestation of God's immanence, the radiant fire as a symbol of God's glory, the devouring fire as an expression of God's power and anger; a plague, a weapon, a punishment, one of the most common motifs found in the Prophetic books. Fire—many fires of many origins to many purposes—blazes through the texts of the Old Testament.

Leviticus expounds the Priestly code for a perpetual fire, or holocaust since it must consume the sacrifice wholly: "The fire on the altar shall be kept burning on it, it shall not go out; the priest shall burn wood on it every morning, and he shall lay the burnt offering in order upon it, and shall burn on it the fat of the peace offerings." Such a practice had ample analogues among the Canaanites, the Greeks, and the Zoroastrians, whose ceremony parallels the Hebrew one closely. The Philistines, the Sea People, may in fact have descended from Greeks with a special worship of Hestia, the goddess of the hearth. It is worth remembering that even as they began their Babylon captivity, according to Maccabees (II 1:19), "the pious priests of that time took some fire from the altar and hid it in a pit" in the hopes that it might continue. Nehemiah later rekindled the fire, apparently extracting it with sunlight from "naphtha." The restored fire burned on the altar of the restored temple until Roman soldiers razed—by fire—the temple itself in A.D. 70.[20]

The success of the fire or the behavior of its smoke manifested the reaction of God to the "burnt offerings" presented by supplicants. The most spectacular exchange involved the infusion of direct fire from God himself. "Fire from heaven" consumed the troubled sacrifice of Manoah, decided the contested sacrifices of Elijah on Mount Carmel, accepted the offerings of David at Ornan, and filled the Solomonic temple during its dedication with the "glory of the Lord." The threat of punishment through divine fire—of Israel for its iniquities, and of Israel's enemies for their hostility—is so common that it became ritualistic, the literary cliché of the jeremiad.

The Bible's fire tropes have their history, however. The oldest images associate fire with lightning—the smoke, fire, and storm-spewed lightning that descend on Mount Sinai. Among the Prophets many relied on fire imagery derived from wildlands. Zechariah (11:1) speaks of the fire that "may devour your cedars." Jeremiah (21:14) has the Lord threaten, "I will kindle a fire in her forest, and it shall devour all that is round about her." Joel (1:19) lamented, "Unto thee, O Lord, I cry. For fire has devoured the pastures of the wilderness, and flame has burned all the trees of the field." Ezekiel (20:47) has the Lord God proclaim, "Behold, I will kindle a fire in you, and it shall devour every green tree in you and every dry tree; the blazing flame shall not be quenched, and all faces from south to north shall be scorched by it." Isaiah (10:17) declares that "the Light of Israel will become a fire, and his Holy One a flame; and it will burn and devour his thorns and briers in one day."

But most fire images derive from landscapes no longer wild. Wilderness fire was already a distant memory, a cultic cliché. More vivid metaphors, those with the power to speak to the prophet's society, came from agriculture and pyrotechnologies—the burning of stubble, old vines, and weedy thorns; the assayer's and refiner's fires; the fires of furnace and oven; the wasting fires of warfare, as Isaiah (66:15–16) graphically announces, "For behold, the Lord will come with fire, and with his chariots like a whirlwind, to render his anger with fury, and his rebuke with flames of fire. For by fire and by his sword will the Lord plead with all flesh." Even more abundant are allusions to altar fires and incense. (Even the pagan *Aeneid* constantly recounts sacred fires lit, saved, and extinguished, the accompaniment to any sacrifice or ceremony.) These are the tropes of urbanites, the fire metaphors of intellectuals removed from routine anthropogenic burning, of priests obsessed with symbolism, ritual, and formulaic idiom. As the universal fire was further parceled, packaged, and specialized, it lost its power as a metaphor of the universal.[21]

Christianity continued the metaphoric sublimation. It shed the final vestiges of the fire sacrifice, much as Buddhism did the fire ceremony of Hinduism. The altar fire shrank into the votive candle, and burnt offerings into the sweet fumes of incense. The routine wrath of Yahweh's fire visitations receded into the hallucinogenic apocrypha of a final conflagration. If the Last Judgment resembled the burning of tares, as Matthew likened it, this was a mild vision compared with the melting of mountains and the jealous fury that rained down "brimstone and fire" on Sodom and Gomorrah. The tongues of flame by which the Paraclete was manifested above the Apostles was a pale shadow of Baal's fiery messengers before which even the "gods do drop their heads, down upon their knees."[22]

(iii)

What happened in religion occurred also with natural philosophy. Fire as a phenomenon required explanation, and fire as a tool offered, in various ways, a means of explanation. Between theology and philosophy there was overlap; but it was obvious that fire existed apart from any divine agency, that the hearth and furnace were as central to the house and shop as the altar fire was to the temple, that an understanding of fire was mandatory for any improvement in the arts of field and forge. But from that exalted origin, fire endured a declension in philosophical status similar to that it experienced in theology.

Certainly fire was an obvious subject for contemplation. Wherever there were people, there was fire; whatever change people wrought in the world, they did so with fire. Anyone could see that fire was fundamental to the world and essential to any process of change. Was it not fire that transformed woodland into garden, clay into pottery, ore into swords? Whether, as Gaston Bachelard concluded, the hearth fire "was no doubt for man the first object of reverie," it was certainly an object of inquiry. Around campfires, before hearths, and beneath candles people talked, children learned, scholars read, poets sang. For most peoples fire was a manifestation—perhaps *the* manifestation—of god. For early Ionian philosophers like Heraclitus of Ephesus it embodied the essential principle of change: "all things are an exchange for fire, and fire for all things"; "this world . . . was ever, is now, and ever shall be an ever-living fire, with measures of it kindling, and measures going out." (Not for nothing was he known as Heraclitus the Dark). As Diogenes Laertius explained the later, Theophrastean doxography, the world itself "arises from fire, and is consumed by fire alternately through all eternity in certain cycles," culminating in a "final conflagration." Very likely Heraclitus, like Hebrew theologians, felt the influence of Zoroaster.[23]

Others opted for different informing principles—Thales for water, Anaximander for air. But fire claimed as central a role in thought as it did in the house; most ancient philosophies, Chinese as much as Greek, credited fire as an element. Anything emanating heat, light, or change (or for humans, passion) could be subsumed under the doctrine of a universal fire. The analogies to life were particularly powerful. That fire ate (feeding on *pabulum ignis*), grew, decayed, breathed, and died seemed to emulate the cycle of living beings. Plutarch believed that the ancients respected fire because it resembled animals and indeed because they imagined close analogies between fire and themselves. But any philosophy of natural change—the core of chemistry—had to explain fire and most often exploited fire as a model. "If all that changes slowly may be explained by life," Bachelard concluded, "all that changes quickly is explained by fire."[24]

Certainly the great schools all played with fire as an intellectual tool if not a cosmogenic obsession. Zeno centered the natural philosophy of Stoicism around the doctrine of an essential fire. A Greek successor, Diogenes Laertius, summed up Nature as "an artistically working fire," a phrase Cicero repeats in *De Natura Deorum* and a metaphor undoubtedly derived from the authority of pyrotechnologies. As fire animated the corporeal world, so the "fiery breath," the soul, animated the body. The cycles of fire informed even time, as history ended and renewed with periodic Great Fires.

The majority of philosophers followed the example of Empedocles, who orchestrated the competing principles of the Ionians into four elements (or "permanent roots")—earth, air, water, and fire. The Pythagoreans placed a "central fire" (different from the sun) in the middle, while around it the ten basic bodies including the earth revolved. Plato accepted the four elements, and elaborated the scheme in such dialogues as the *Protagoras, Phaedo,* and *Timaeus,* his creation story. His enduring contribution, however, was a critical passage in *The Republic* in which he describes the human condition. We are like slaves chained in a cave. All we see—all we can know—is what the flames of torches behind us throw into their treacherous light. We see only the shadows of objects that pass behind us, not the objects themselves. Compared with the pure sunlight outside the cave, firelight is a poor facsimile, offering an illusion of knowledge. The goal of the philosopher is to break those fetters and pass through the shadows to truth.[25]

But for most philosophic schools the world lit only by fire was the real world, and an explanation of fire was mandatory to understanding how that universe functioned. The torch, so to speak, passed to Aristotle, who accepted the Empedoclean four elements, identified them with the four primary qualities (hot, cold, dry, moist), organized them into the four sublunary spheres, and arranged them into dialectical couplings. As always fire was the odd element, the least tangible but also the most vital and the most protean. If it did not inform the material world, it was the model for chemical change—and would remain so into the nineteenth century.

There were critics, of course. The Atomists objected to the concept of elements, and persisted in their dissent from Leucippus through to Democritus, Epicurus, and the immense achievement of Lucretius. In *De Rerum Natura* he speculated on the origins of fire and through it the origins of metallurgy. The "penetrative fire" from a fierce conflagration could, he thought, have melted veins of metal ore. His descriptions of fire are naturalistic, however, caused by lightning, war, hunting, pastoralism; fire is a phenomenon of nature, not its spirit. "To say, as Heraclitus does, that everything is fire, and nothing can be numbered among things as a reality except fire, seems utterly crazy." Others wondered how it was that an "element" had to rely on air and food to survive.[26]

But the authority of Aristotle was immense. His student, Theophrastus, wrote a monograph on fire (*De Igne*), in which he affirmed that "of all the elemental substances fire has the most special powers" because only fire was self-generating. Few of the ancients ignored the Aristotelian canon; Pliny the Elder announced, with considerable exaggeration, that there were no dissenters from the Aristotelian doctrine of the four mutable elements. And all those who studied fire, Aristotle and Lucretius among them, were mesmerized by the common spectacle of the erupting flame. Fire was something that escaped during burning, or if not fire, then some equivalent inflammatory principle. If fire did not explain itself, then some other explanation was necessary; but until natural philosophy accounted for fire it was worthless, for it was through fire— *philosophus per ignem*—that philosophers, alchemists, smiths, and smelters worked their transmutations.[27]

By the late Renaissance the intellectual pillars of the old order were crumbling. John Donne pondered:

> *And new Philosophy calls all in doubt,*
> *The element of fire is quite put out.*

Paracelsus reduced the four elements to three (*tria prima*) and established one of them, "sulfur," as the principle of combustion. Others recombined elements, and found equivalents for "fire" in sulfur, oils, phlogiston, or caloric—something that could escape as flame, smoke, heat, and light. In his *Sceptical Chymist* (1661), Robert Boyle noted how the Aristotelians still relied on burning wood as a model. "The escaping fire in the flame, the smoke returning to its aerial source, the water boiling off from the sizzling end and the residual ashes," as Joshua Gregory summarizes, "seemed to embody the traditional four elements."

In 1720, Hermann Boerhaave reestablished the supremacy of fire by announcing that "if you make a mistake in your exposition of the Nature of Fire, your error will spread to all the branches of physics, and this is because, in all natural production, Fire . . . is always the chief agent." Pierre Macquer's *Dictionnaire de la Chymie* (1766) lamented the persistence of Aristotelian chemistry. In his *Philosophical Inquiry into the Cause of Animal Heat* (1778), Dr. Dugud Leslie resolved the "chymical analysis" of living matter into water, earth, air, and phlogiston—the latest fire surrogate.[28]

In fact, the Enlightenment was full of residual fires. Earth had its central fire, the solar system its solar fire, the heavens the celestial fire of the stars, comets, and quintessential aether. Electrical fire discharged as lightning. Inner fire provided the life force for plants and animals, the source of animal heat. And of course there was the ever-fascinating fire in the machine. Even Lavoisier's discovery of oxygen only replaced one fire principle, phlogiston, with another, the caloric. When Michael Faraday wanted to demonstrate the principles of natural philosophy in 1848, he chose, on ancient precedent, fire for his subject.[29]

But Faraday's *Chemical History of a Candle* also helped complete the intellectual transmutation of fire, its devolution from a universal cause to a chemical consequence, the mere motion of molecules, the quantum bonding of oxygen. The transition occurred, not incidentally, with fire's condemnation by agronomists and foresters, with its removal as a vital force in urban life, and therefore in the felt life of the intellectuals who resided there. Bachelard might boast that he "would rather fail to teach a good philosophy lesson than fail to light my morning fire," but most philosophers no longer lit fires or cared to understand them beyond their shared domiciles. The American Ben Franklin, for example, tamed "electrical fire" through his lightning rod, caged the wasteful hearth fire into a metal stove, and devoted his philosopher's mind to electricity rather than the elemental fire.[30]

That, in cameo, is what happened across Western civilization. Modern science reversed the ancient syllogisms and similes that had bound humans and nature. Ancient fire practices had mimicked nature; now technology provided the model for how nature worked, or ought to work. Industry invented new pyrotechnologies, and then suggested that heat engines were an analogue for animal heat. Natural philosophy found conceptual surrogates for fire. Chemistry subordinated fire to atomic reactions. Thermodynamics segregated fire from motion and heat. Electromagnetic theory divorced it from light. Fire had shrunk from Heraclitean universality to the laboratory demonstration of Faraday's candle.

Once the manifestation of god and the source of life—the most familiar of nature's Others, the most basic of tasks—fire had become alien, a destroyer of cities, a savager of soil, a befowler of air, an emblem (in science as in agriculture) of the hopelessly primitive. Whether or not they had broken humanity's chains, philosophy and modern science successfully extinguished the allegorical flame in the cave. Other devices illuminated the cavern; psychology replaced nature as muse, and machines, nature's models. Once an informing metaphor, philosophical fire had become a cliché, fit only for humanist scholars and the garish covers of romance novels.

But the world cave had housed more than humans, and fire had forms other than torch and hearth and purposes other than poetry and politics. Fire had come from nature, and unless humans utterly remade every particle of the Earth, nature's fire would persist—as it must necessarily persist in any theory of ecology; and as it had to persist for any philosophy or history that sought to explore the relationship of humans to the Earth. Fire was not arbitrary, its ecology not replicable, its meaning not expungeable. However uncertain its light, however compromised its flame, fire illuminated the world as it was. If the cave's fire was a poor facsimile of the Good, the True, and the Beautiful, so was the humanity that tended it.

NEED-FIRE, VESTAL FIRE: CEREMONY AND RITUAL

All over Europe, from very ancient times, people expressed their relationship to fire through rites and ceremonies. Of course, physically, fire was never far from ceremonial life. Whatever occurred at night or in dwellings required fire for light, and it was simple to fold the mandatory flame into the ceremony itself, to absorb the symbolism of fire into the cognitive ecology of the rite.

But there were other ceremonies—spectacular, tenacious, ubiquitous—for which fire was the center. From the Isle of Man to the Siberian taiga, from the Shetlands to Malta, from Morocco's Atlas Mountains to the windy steppes, a common core of fire festivals defined a shared culture of fire that persisted until the industrial revolution snuffed it out.

(i)

The originating rite was the need-fire—sometimes known in England as the "wild fire," in Germany as the "emergency fire" (*Notfeuer*), or among Slavs as the "living fire." The essential act was the recreation of a new fire and the use of this pure fire to fight off threats to the community. As fully as possible, humanity restarted its relationship to fire. And each community did so when some grave hardship threatened it.

The kindling of the need-fire thus came with strict prescriptions, although these varied from place to place. Sometimes the oldest resident of the village would set it, sometimes newlyweds, occasionally a naked couple, whatever seemed best to remember or recreate the initial capture of fire. The technology of fire-starting, too, had to be primitive—no flint-and-steel fire kits, only the friction of rubbed sticks, whether worked by hand or some kind of fire drill. Even the wood had its ritual ordinations; almost always the ceremony required oak, or in places that lacked oak, like the coniferous forests, poplar or pine. All fires in the surrounding community had to be extinguished. (Another version, sometimes found in Europe, often in India, was to accept a lightning-caused fire as a new fire, and to use this source to rekindle the hearth fires in the nearby villages.)[31]

What occurred next also assumed many local forms. But the ceremonial core was to have the new fire purify and fertilize the community and to prolong these benefits by using the need-fire to rekindle the hearth fires. From the need-fire the participants ignited a great bonfire. Into it they sometimes threw effigies of witches or burned animals like cattle or witch-identified creatures like cats. ("Bonfire" derives from *bone-fire*.) Through the bonfire's smoke and over its ebbing flames or coals, they passed their flocks—cattle stricken by murrain most commonly, but also pigs, geese, and horses in set order. Then they passed themselves. Next they carried the flame and smoke with torches through the countryside, their fields, orchards, and pastures. The ashes were sometimes scattered over the ground, and sometimes pressed over their faces. They carried the embers or tapers to their homes to reignite the hearth, and kept the extinguished brand in the house as a talisman against lightning, wildfire, and witchcraft.

A rich ceremony, this—reenacting the fundamental drama by which humanity distinguished itself from the rest of creation, playing on myths in which fire destroyed and renewed, appeasing the gods through burnt sacrifice, and exploiting the empirical evidence by which people used fire. The call for a need-fire was episodic, a response to calamity, most often recorded for outbreaks of cattle disease. When it failed, common opinion held that someone, probably a witch, had secretly hoarded some of the old (impure) fire. When the need-fire urged by Johannes Köhler of Neustadt failed, the populace decided the fault was his and later burned him as a witch.

(ii)

But as life became more settled, as agriculture and husbandry replaced a more migratory economy, and as pagan rites succumbed to a proselytizing Christianity, so the need-fire joined an agricultural almanac, kindled regularly according to seasonal rhythms, integrated into a sacred liturgy. The history of its fire festivals also recapitulates the fire history of Europe.

Curiously the festivals form pairs, each beginning and closing a cycle. Two—the fires of Beltane (May Day) and Halloween—derive from pastoralism and correspond to the seasons when the herds migrate between winter and summer pastures, when graziers are likely to fire the grasses and heath to stimulate new growth. Two others, those of Midwinter and Midsummer days, belong with a solar cycle, the times of maximum waning and waxing—a cycle of particular interest to agrarian peoples. The last two, the Lenten and Easter fire festivals, despite their Christian gloss, belong also with a pagan agricultural calendar and the use of fire to rouse field and paddock into new life. All trace their pedigree to the originating need-fire.

Of course the festivals varied according to season and purpose. The spring and summer fire festivals were generally more lively and widespread than those of fall and winter. Rough weather, for example, drove the Midwinter fire into houses, so that the hilltop blazes that lit the Midsummer sky were replaced by the glowing Yule log, and the symbolic burning of the landscape collapsed into the renewal of the hearth fire. Spring is the most critical time for farmer and herder, and the season when the power of fire for renewal, and prophylaxis, is greatest. Spring and summer, moreover, allow for the broadcasting of fire by torch procession, by flaming wheels rolled down hillsides, by fiery disks tossed into the air, and by the saturating of hilltops and crossroads with bonfires. In 1682, Sir Henry Piers wrote of the Midsummer fires in Ireland that "a stranger would go near to imagine the whole country was on fire."[32]

So in a symbolic sense it was. Part of the need-fire's purpose was to rekindle the hearth fire—to purify the sacred flame—but part was to impose a special fire on the landscape, to purify and renew the Earth. This was not primarily a symbolic act but an intensely practical one, without which the land was uninhabitable, and a potentially hazardous one, if the fires were set poorly. Clearly, regulation was necessary; no community could long tolerate promiscuous or random burning. Social control probably took the form of ritual that prescribed when and by whom the fires could be set. There is every reason to believe that the great fire ceremonies only codified into sanctified rite and a sacred almanac what people had once done openly, and what, in favored locales, they still did. Thus in Persia the Midwinter fire, a festival called *Sada* or *Saza,* not only kindled bonfires everywhere, but "kings and princes tied dry grass to the feet of birds and animals, set fire to the grass, and then let the birds and beasts fly or run blazing through the air or over the fields and mountains, so that the whole air and earth appeared to be on fire."[33]

Such practices could not continue in an increasingly sedentary, urban, and densely populated Europe. So as calendars became fixed, as new religions grafted themselves onto the fabulous ceremonies, as agrarian peoples moved from seasons defined by wet and dry to those best characterized by hot and cold, as fire practices proliferated in new landscapes, as bards sang in feast halls rather than over campfires, fire ceremonies became more and more emblematic. Once sublimated into symbol, fire entered a cognitive ecology in which it smoldered in the soil of the subconscious and convected into clouds of abstraction. It entered realms of imagery, mythology, and symbolism that had their metalogic, that shaped a landscape of the psyche. New associations became possible that were far removed from phosphorus released by burning pine, ticks and mites driven from surface litter, sheep and cattle fumigated by smoke, and ashes harrowed with spruce branches.

The ceremonial control of fire acquired new vigor with the spread of Christianity. Much as the Jews had fought with Canaanite fire cults and Zoroastrianism, so now Christians did, particularly with the fire rites of the pagan Indo-Europeans, and just as Judaism assimilated elements from their rivals, so too did Christians. Candle or lamp burned in tribute to the altar fire. The Church absorbed fire ceremonies into its sacred liturgy, baptizing the Midsummer and Midwinter fires into the feasts of Saint John the Baptist and Christmas, the fires of spring into the rite of Lent and Easter, the autumn fire into All Souls' Eve. Christmas log and Paschal candle replaced the pagan Yule log and the new fire. Missionaries condemned burnt sacrifices, further sublimating the practice with effigies and sometimes changing the putative victim's status from witch to Judas and even (after the Reformation) to Martin Luther.

But conversion required more than baptism, and the ceremonies persisted with stubborn defiance. In 734 a synod of prelates and nobles under Boniface included the need-fire in its Index of Superstitions and Heathenish Observances and forbade its practice. The ban was widely ignored, and in practice the Church continued to remake the ceremonies in its own image, so that, in time, priests even oversaw the rites and carried brands from the purified fire back to rekindle the altar fire. During the Crusades, as the Church intensified its temporal powers and sought to suppress spiritual rivals, the struggle against fire ceremonies renewed. The Church condemned practitioners as it did heretics and infidels; the written record of the fire festivals dates from this campaign. Equally, the Church reworked the imagery of fire—stoking hell with eternal flames, creating a fiery purgatory—and where suppression failed, tried co-option. How burning heretics at the stake was different from Druidical fire sacrifices was not obvious, but it had the sanction of the prevailing authorities. Thus auto-da-fé joined gruesome techniques of torture, often with fire, to create a vivid sense of hell among the public. "Probably the two kinds of agony were related," notes Johan Goudsblom, "and the fear of hell and purgatory was reinforced by the public executions with fire." The old practices acquired a new gloss, much as scholastics paraphrased the ancient texts of Aristotle and Galen.[34]

Still, the clerical campaign continued, at least officially. It intensified during the Reformation and Counter Reformation as competing religions sought to purge their own ranks of heretics or anything that might smack of a relic paganism. Gustavus Adolphus, for example, forbade the need-fire, but to little effect. Missionaries encountered fire rites among the lingering infidels of Europe's fringes, to say nothing of its overseas colonies, and could hardly damn the one while condoning the other. But the fires persisted; the prevalence of fire was too great to abolish by papal encyclical or clerical condemnation; and in the end the churches conceded, absorbing and adapting fire ceremonies as had early agriculturalists.

Nothing, it seems, could smother fire's presence in rural Europe. Lady Wilde provides a remarkably full account of the Midsummer's fire as it persisted in nineteenth-century Ireland.

In ancient times the sacred fire was lighted with great ceremony on Midsummer Eve; and on that night all the people of the adjacent country kept fixed watch on the western promontory of Howth, and the moment the first flash was seen from that spot the fact of ignition was announced with wild cries and cheers repeated from village to village, when all the local fires began to blaze, and Ireland was circled by a cordon of flame rising up from every hill. Then the dance and song began round every fire, and the wild hurrahs filled the air with the most frantic revelry. Many of these ancient customs are still continued, and the fires are still lighted on St. John's Eve on every hill in Ireland. When the fire has burned down to a red glow the young men strip to the waist and leap over or through the flames; this is done backwards and forwards several times, and he who braves the greatest blaze is considered the victor over the powers of evil, and is greeted with tremendous applause. When the fire burns still lower, the young girls leap the flame, and those who leap clean over three times back and forward will be certain of a speedy marriage and good luck in after-life, with many children. The married women then walk through the lines of the burning embers; and when the fire is nearly burnt and trampled down, the yearling cattle are driven through the hot ashes, and their back is singed with a lighten hazel twig. These rods are kept safely afterwards, being considered of immense power to drive the cattle to and from the watering places. As the fire diminishes the shouting grows fainter, and the song and dance commence; while professional story-tellers narrate tales of fairy-land, or of the good old times long ago, when the kings and princes of Ireland dwelt amongst their own people, and there was food to eat and wine to drink for all comers to the feast at the king's house. When the crowd at length separate, every one carries home a brand from the fire, and great virtue is attached to the lighted *brone* which is safely carried to the house without breaking or falling to the ground. Many contests also arise amongst the young men; for whoever enters his house first with the sacred fire brings the good luck of the year with him.[35]

(iii)

Nothing could dislodge such ceremonies—nothing except the suppression of the conditions on which they flourished. Remove the fuel, extinguish the fire. Secularize thought, and dismiss every ancient practice as wanton superstition. Urbanize the population, so that outdoor fires posed a hazard. Industrialize the landscape, substitute fossil fuels for biomass, make fire banal by mass-producing matches. The fire ceremonies faded, lingering longest among the more remote rural landscapes like Ireland, the Scottish Highlands, the Balkans, the Urals. Some persist today, mostly as versions of the Midsummer's fire— the Saint John's fire still prominent in Greece, the *Midsommersdagen* fire in Sweden, the Ivan Kupalo fire of rural Russia. But survivals have become a child's sport or a contrived commercialism. The last recorded need-fires in Britain correspond almost exactly with the invention of the lucifer match, the spread of the steam locomotive, and the creation of a chemistry no longer based on combustion. As fire lost its mystery, it lost its magic as well.

By the latter half of the nineteenth century, as ethnologists and folklorists began to collect data about the fire ceremonies, as they did about other antiquaries, they found themselves hard-pressed to explain the rites. Sir James Frazer outlined the two competing theories, the solar theory proposed by Wilhelm Mannhardt, and the purificatory theory advanced by Edward Westermarck. "On the one view," explains Frazer,

the fire, like sunshine in our latitude, is a genial creative power which fosters the growth of plants and the development of all that makes for health and happiness; on the other view, the fire is a fierce destructive power which blasts and consumes all the noxious elements, whether spiritual or material, that menace the life of men, of animals, and of plants. According to the one theory the fire is a stimulation, according to the other it is a disinfectant; on the one view its virtue is positive, according to the other it is negative.

Initially Frazer inclined to the former, then to the latter, which was, he admitted, the explanation most often given by the participants themselves. But he wanted a synthesis, if possible; and in pondering the question, "How did it come about that benefits so great and manifold were supposed to be attained by means so simple?" he dismisses any suggestion that "primitive man," such as Europe's peasantry, "acted first and invented his reasons to suit his action afterwards." No practical reason for the fires existed, and no theoretical argument could, in any event, derive from such empiricism. The fires were superstition. Their purpose, he concluded, was to burn witches.[36]

"The observance of such festivals flowed directly from their [the peasants'] overmastering fear of witchcraft and from their theory as to the best way of combating that dreadful evil." The two pastoral festivals, in particular, Beltane and Halloween, were evenings in which witches and other spirits disgorged upon the Earth and sought to work their black magic. The Eve of Beltane—Walpurgis Night—was literally the witching time, and to ring the countryside with hilltop bonfires and hurl flaming disks into the sky was a charm to ward them off as one would wild beasts. Wolves and witches were the two horrors of European herdsmen. In fact the two fears merged, since witches could assume many forms, preferably as wolves, vampires, and cats, all subject, along with witch effigies, to incineration by sacred fires. (The Midsummer's fire in Paris burned cats well into the eighteenth century; in 1648, Louis XIV lit the fire himself.) To destroy the witch was to protect the herds, so cattle and pigs and people passed over or between the flames to cleanse and protect.[37]

But the explanation proposed by the professional folklorists is hardly more credible, for they had lost the cause of the ceremonies as surely as the superstitious peasantry they chide. The first edition of Frazer's *Golden Bough*, with its dank compost of folklore, appeared in 1890, the same year that William James published his *Principles of Psychology;* and while the debate over the meaning of fire ceremonies raged among intellectuals, Sigmund Freud and Carl Jung scrutinized dream and myth for their revelations about the psychological membrane between belief and behavior. For these dialecticians, the mind guided the hand, not the hand the mind; they understood the fire festivals as originating in the murky womb of symbols, archetypes, and the primitive behavior of sympathetic magic. Neither the solar nor the purificatory theory, but a psychological theory best explains their attempts at interpretation. The fire ceremonies were, to their reading, a Freudian slip of European society, a recurring dream whose reality resided in a symbolic logic of subconscious associations. No one gave the slightest credence to the ecological behavior of fire.

But there, more probably, resided the origins of the beliefs that fire could purify and fertilize. The evidence lay all around. If phosphorus and calcium are more accessible after a fire than before; if sunlight strikes burned spring gardens more forcibly; if blackened soil warms faster and grasses sprout sooner; if the green pick of fresh-burned pasture has higher protein content than unburned sites and cattle and sheep grow sleek on it; if wheat and oats thrive in the ash of what was previously a dark woodland; if rye yields on new swidden are ten to fifteen times greater than elsewhere; if fire purges the preferred habitats of ticks and retards rust in grain; if weeds (at least temporarily) no longer throttle cultigens; if smoke stimulates the flowering of certain fruits; if

forbs and berries blossom more richly on burned sites; if orchids and geraniums flourish on recently fired plots but vanish in the absence of fire; if fires
keep wolves and bears away from flocks and homes, then by what criteria does
a folklorist or psychoanalyst dismiss the belief that fire destroys unwanted things
and promotes desired ones?

The superstition lies rather with an urban intelligentsia for whom fire was
no longer a necessary but only a decorative presence. The fire ceremonies persisted so long as fire remained a vital force in the life of rural Europe, for peasants could see for themselves the powers of fire to transform moor, forest, field,
and metal into the coin of nature's economy, and to make a hostile environment a habitable one. Once established, of course, the ceremonies reaped and
shed other meanings, guided by the syllogisms of the subconscious and the
symbolic. The burning of witches—the purgation of evil—most likely derived
by associating swidden with sacrifice. The abstracted bonfire became a burnt
offering. In many swidden societies today a religious rite precedes ignition.
Much as hill tribes in Thailand offer rice, so European herders sacrificed cattle.

The condemnation of fire ceremonies and rites as credulous folklore joined
other critiques of fire by Enlightenment agronomists and later foresters. The
traditional beliefs that free-burning fire could do good in woods and paddocks
they dismissed as no more than cultic lore, a residual superstition of a peasantry mired in millennia of ignorance. Yet those fire practices, like the fire ceremonies, stubbornly persisted, widening the chasm between an educated elite
and a populace that lived on the land. If intellectuals saw an unwarranted link
between bonfires and witches, between the fire ceremonies and the peasantry's
ideas about them, peasants could reply in kind. They could point to the vast
incongruity between what fire did in the landscape and the rationalized superstitions that urban elites held about it.

(iv)

The need-fire was temporary, an episodic response to crisis. The fire festivals
coded fire ritualistically into an agricultural calendar and a religious liturgy,
but while they were regularly rekindled, they were not permanent. The hearth
fire, by contrast, was. It burned as a perpetual fire, extinguished only at such
times as a new fire, purified by the above ceremonies, was ready to rekindle
it. The perpetual fire was the unpolluted source, maintained for itself as purely
as possible. The perpetual fire was the most solemn of fire rites, for it spoke
to the perpetuation of a people.

The utility of a continuous fire was obvious, and dates the practice to very
early times. But the shared, permanent fire became the focus, symbolically as
well as literally, for the human group. It defined the family, the tribe, the state,
the people, even humanity itself as the keeper of the flame for the biota. Among

Indo-Europeans the perpetual fire on the hearth was the center of family rites as the perpetual fire in the temple was for communal worship. Birth, death, marriage, servitude, adoption—all these binding rituals took place before the hearth, or with tokens from the hearth fire. Families sealed marriages and nations sealed treaties by mingling fires; newborn children were named before the hearth, new members (and even livestock) entered a family by circumambulating the hearth fire, exiles were banished from its presence, and in Rome the *interdictio ignis* forbade them even to possess fire in their own residence; a new owner took legal possession of a house by lighting its hearth fire. The authority of father and king derived from the hearth fire and communal fire. In fact, as Sir James Frazer points out, "the public hearth with its gods was a simple repetition of what was to be seen in every Roman house." Colonists, ambassadors, and armies carried the brands from the sacred fire with them when they departed. Alexander the Great carried the flame before him on his march. To borrow or lend fires to others was fraught with dangers. For the fire to go out was the greatest of catastrophes.[38]

Probably the best known were the related perpetual fires of Greece and Rome, the hearth of the Greek prytaneum dedicated to Hestia and the hearth devoted to the Roman Vesta. Similar practices appeared among the Celts of Gaul, Britain, and Ireland, the Lithuanians in the temple of Prauronia, and of course the Indo-European Persians and Hindus. But the practice spanned every continent and culture, from the Andaman Islands to the Iroquois, from the Aino of Japan to the ancient Israelites who carried their fire before them. What distinguished the European fires was their social context and accompanying rituals.

The administration of Europe's sacred fires told a political parable. From these communal hearths, originally tended in the house of the headman, came the brands for rekindling the home fires. Many words for ignition, like the English "kindle," also meant "beget"; thus the pedigree of the fire paralleled kinship lines, and its purity affirmed the legitimacy of family and especially of the royal line. The hearth was both the place of sacrifice and the place, in many myths such as those of Servius Tullius and even of Romulus and Remus, where kings were conceived. The wood fed to the fire the Romans called *materia*, likely related to *mater*, mother. The "sacrificial fireplace," Gregory Nagy argues, was "the generatrix of kingship and the authority of kingship," its symbolism "a matter of Indo-European heritage." The propagation of the fire thus manifested the prolongation of the reign; its extinction was the worst calamity that could occur, portending the dissolution of the state. The sacred fire was a scepter in flame. Although in time the places of king and fire separated (significantly the sacred hearth remained and the king moved to a palace), the authority invested in each remained.[39]

So did the rites that surrounded such fires. The fire could be used for some purposes and not others. It was sacrilege to mix the vestal fire with strange or impure fires and fatal to allow it to expire. The preferred fuel was oak, the tree most sacred to the sky god—Zeus, Jupiter, Thor, Perun—because it was, in temperate Europe, the tree most often struck by lightning. A study relating strikes to European tree species found that while oaks constituted 11 percent of the forest they absorbed 70 percent of lightning strikes. (By contrast, the laurel was rarely struck, which explains why laurel wreaths were awarded to heroes and emperors.) The vestal fire, like the Yule log, burned oak. The ruler—father, king, *pontifex maximus*—was the representative of the god and oversaw the fire.[40]

Perhaps the most curious aspect of the vestal fire was the cadre of vestal virgins who had the responsibility for tending it. This, too, had precedents not only in Indo-European lore but among such peoples as the Iroquois and Incas. The argument that Europe's ancient vestal fire also derives from the family hearth is probably correct. While the fire remained in principle under the direction of the paterfamilias, the practice of tending it devolved on his daughters as another chore of the household. So great were the household burdens, symbolized by tending the fire, that it is likely one daughter was obliged not to marry until after the death of her parents, thus remaining celibate.[41]

As the vestal fire segregated from the palace, so some leading families each contributed a daughter of age six to ten to tend the vestal fire. The vestal virgins numbered between four and six. Their service extended for a period of thirty years, after which the woman could return to society, her vows discharged. Celibacy was at first an assurance that the woman would remain in the household, later a symbol of the purity of the fire that she tended. Unfaithfulness through either illicit sex or the extinction of the fire was severely punished, even to the point of being buried alive. The vestal virgins thus remained under the *patria potestas* of the king or *pontifex maximus*—daughters, not concubines. The *ignis Vestae* was the family hearth fire writ large, purified, perpetual. From it each March 1 citizens renewed their domestic fires.

The shrine of Vesta was the oldest Roman temple, and the only one that did not have its four sides correspond to the four cardinal points. Instead it, alone, was round, and it alone had no inauguration but had always been. The shrine was an *aedes sacra,* not a *templum;* Rome's temples derived from it, and its perpetual hearth supplied the sacred fires to the other altars. If the vestal fire failed, it had to be rekindled from a need-fire. "The temple of Capitoline Jupiter, the shields of the Salii, and the perpetual fire of the house of Vesta: three signs, three chronological stages of the promise by which Rome lived," noted Georges Dumézil. "The fire was regarded as the most ancient." Even Nero, for all his public depravities, trembled when he entered Vesta's shrine and left in open fright.[42]

Something similar may be said for the larger civilization that emerged in Europe. Of all its many fires, the one Europe preferred, and the only one Europe's intelligentsia sanctioned, was the vestal fire. Europe sought the domesticated fire, the tended fire, the fire that merged the sacred with the social into a fixed order. This was an anthropomorphized fire: a fire that spoke to society, not to nature. The state had, in a sense, sought identification with this, the most ancient of Rome's sacred sites, not vice versa. But even more than politics, the vestal fire expressed the immanence of society. Its worship honored the tended fire, and the society that tended it.

The trend was progressive, like a road once taken that branches further with each league and never doubles back. In the end, Europe's censors and authorities wanted nothing to do with fires set by lightning, saw agricultural burning as degenerate and slovenly, condemned celebratory bonfires as heathen witch-burning, feared urban fire, knew free-burning flame best as a conflagrating weapon of war, and saw the popular torch as an instrument of social disorder, torture, property destruction, and hellish havoc. The one fire that survived was the vestal flame, perpetuated through generations of landscape and culture, pure only in its idealized conception, vestigial as it flickered over the Olympic games, before the dark stone of war memorials, and above white candles on the altar.

BOOK 2: EUROPE

Throughout Europe there was a common culture of fire that transcended the fire legacy bequeathed by nature. European fire was, first and last, anthropogenic fire, not the fire from heaven.

There was a characteristic European fire much as there developed, however complexly, a common civilization. Similar fire ceremonies lit hillsides from Killarney to Khabarovsk; similar styles of swidden slashed Scots pine and black-earth steppe; common institutions directed, however inaccurately, the shaping of landscapes, and collective ideas judged, however misguidedly, folk fire practices. There was a European fire ideal, as there had once been an Indo-European fire god.

But nature resisted. Whatever Europeans did, whatever they thought, by whatever rites they sought to placate natural forces, Europe's geographic hardware refused to run the submitted cultural software without glitches and occasionally crashes. The Platonic ideal corrupted on contact with stone, woods, rivers, droughts, and relentless rains. The Great Narrative fractured, like Chaucer's pilgrimage, into separate tales.

The encounter of fire with Europe, however, was no irresistible force meeting an immovable object. Both fire and European civilization were mutable, and the outcome of their encounter was less a mutual shattering than an environmental symbiosis. Europe could neither abolish nor wholly absorb fire, while fire would obey, and neither ignore nor incinerate, its tenders. In the end, the story of European fire had many texts, separately written on the distinctive scrolls of Europe's physical geography. The narrative itself was a dialectic, though one given a common cultural gloss by its learned commentators.

ETERNAL FLAME
Fire in Mediterranean Europe

*[Only] fire is naturally able to generate itself and to destroy
itself: the smaller fire generates the larger, and the larger
destroys the smaller.*

—Theophrastus, *De Igne*

PROLOGUE:
WEST OF EDEN

The Mediterranean is a place, a climate, a biota, and a paradigm. The shape of
the place and the contours of its climate have changed mightily over the eons,
but on the scale of human endeavor they appear as immutable facts of nature.
Biota and paradigm are more mobile and, more pertinently, they are inextricably intertwined with human history.

The place is a continental sea surrounded by mountains. More properly the
Mediterranean comprises that intricate littoral between shore and summit.
Where the mountains do not exist, as in Libya and Egypt, the Mediterranean
as a cultural landscape vanishes. Where the mountains are islands like Sicily
and Crete or narrow peninsulas like Greece and Italy, the Mediterranean dominates the whole; and where the land has more bulk, as with Spain, Turkey,
and the Atlas Mountains of northern Africa, the Mediterranean fades away
like fog toward the interior. The contours of the active fringe vary greatly: the
southern rim flows in relatively smooth curves, and the northern enfolds into
complex embayments and minor seas, as convoluted as a Mandelbrot set. While
the geographic spread of the region is large, its land mass is small, more an
archipelago like Indonesia than a landmass like the Eurasian plain. Its parts
communicate by sea.

The Mediterranean climate is defined by a imbalanced cycle of winter rains
followed by a long, droughty summer. This pattern too has its history. As the
sea drained and filled, the Sahara expanded and contracted. The encasing moun-

tains rose, eroded, and rebuilt, as the wild fluctuations of the Pleistocene spread ice sheets to the north, savannas to the south, and trapped the basin in a climatic warp between the temperate and the subtropical. But over the last 6,000 years or so, global climate and sea level have stabilized, and for the last 2,000 to 3,000 years the Mediterranean climate has been, by natural standards, relatively constant.

Brief wet winter, long dry summer—the climatic template stamps itself on every feature of the basin. The Mediterranean Sea itself has an excess of evaporation to fresh water influx and survives only through constant subsidies from the Atlantic. Soaked in this climatic brine the biota has responded by toughening leaves, driving down taproots, littering the soil with hard-cased seeds, and reacting quickly to revealed moisture or nutrients. Climatic stress became the model for accommodating browsing, cutting, and burning. A common suite of traits adapted to a common set of stresses. As humans quickened the tempo of disturbance, a scleromorphic biota displaced the others, and a pyrophytic biota, adapted to frequent grazing and fire, became the norm. The Provencal proverb captures it well:

Whoever cuts me doubles me
Whoever burns me fertilizes me.[1]

The Mediterranean became an utterly anthropogenic landscape. Its fire-sculpted biota is an artifact of human-wrought disturbances. Here complex pyrophytes met a complex pyrophylia; a fire-prone geography encountered a fire-wielding humanity; and the characteristic Mediterranean biota emerged out of this biotic forge softened by fire and hammered by ax and hoof. In effect, humans selected for those flora and fauna most responsive to fire, thus best suited to anthropogenic manipulation. What survived outright replacement by cultigens and domestic livestock endured because it could be integrated with those systems and because it could adjust to anthropogenic stresses, almost all of which involved fire as force or catalyst. The indigenous biota that persists is an artifact, as fully a relic as the ruins at Leptis Magna. For 10,000 years in its eastern lands and 4,000 years in the west, the natural history of the Mediterranean has been barely distinguishable from its social history.

The Mediterranean became the hearth of the European Neolithic. Symbolically, it was in the eastern Mediterranean that the Book of Genesis placed Eden. The eastern Mediterranean remained the historic corridor to Europe; through it came humans, the idea of agriculture, cultigens, livestock, and the accoutrements of civilization, from writing to mathematics. The intellectual contributions of the Mediterranean world equaled its technological. In the ancient Mediterranean, Europe found a paradigm of how humans and nature might interact, and in the story of Eden, an unhappy cameo of that promised history. The

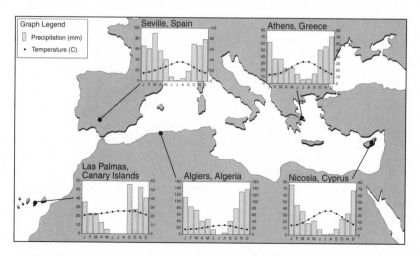

Mediterranean Europe: long, dry summers and short, wet winters, punctuated by frequent droughts and warm winds—an ideal climatic formula for fire, which made its extinction impossible. Even in 1990 some 95 percent of all European wildfires occurred in the Mediterranean. (University of Wisconsin Cartographic Lab)

Garden remained the ideal habitat; the Fall, the tragic (or ironic) chronicle of human failure to meet that ideal. It was a narrative often written with fire and preserved in ash.

If the flaming sword of the Cherubim barred reentry to Eden's east, a flaming torch assisted the passage west. The paradigms of fire ecology derived from the Mediterranean. So did the parables of fire practices, especially as fire joined ax and hoof into an unholy trinity of environmental disturbance. In the Mediterranean the perpetual hearth fire met an unceasing landscape fire, and it was difficult to decide to which flame, if not both, the phrase *flamma aeterna* best applied. Even by the end of the second millennium A.D. the Mediterranean continued, as it had since its Neolithic creation, to dominate the fire geography, and the fire philosophy, of Europe.

BEHOLD, BEFORE A GARDEN, BEHIND A WASTE

The flora is rich, its history dense. Here, where Africa, Europe, and Asia meet, where violent fluctuations in climate have pumped in and flushed out species like a bellows, where many cultigens have originated and others have gathered, where civilizations have long flourished and decayed, where land use has alternated between warfare and gardening, the biota has proliferated, toughened, endured, and degraded.[2]

Its diversity results as much because of those stresses as despite them. The

Mediterranean biota includes over 15,000 plant species, roughly three times that of temperate Europe; it features 100 types of trees compared to temperate Europe's 30. Even a small country like Tunisia hosts over a 1,000 different plant communities; the basin as a whole, on the order of several tens of thousands. The permutations are endless. And those figures do not include the intricate agricultural systems that command more than half the land surface. The flora is as hard as marble, as friable as limestone. Here, not surprisingly, the term "pyrophyte" (a fire-traited plant) originated. Its inventor observed that the Mediterranean biota was heavily pyrophytic, and in many regions, like his native Provence, almost wholly so.[3]

(i)

How this happened is apparent in outline, unclear in its details. From the time the modern climate stabilized, the Mediterranean's fire regimes obeyed the torch, not lightning. But the torch found plenty of raw, pliable material on which to work. The indigenous biota (if that term has any practical meaning) was preadapted to anthropogenic fire, or to related stresses that made an accommodation to fire simple. While few plants adapted to fire per se, they displayed suites of traits adapted to suites of related stresses; they adapted not to fire alone but to a landscape that made fire pervasive, that experienced drought, vigorous sunlight, browsing, impauperate soils, scarifying, windfall—a biota that could simmer readily over a chronic flame.

The botanical apexes of the Mediterranean fire triangle consist of woody evergreens, persistent aromatic shrubs, and geophytes, selectively larded with hardy grasses, some palatable, some not. The most vital trait they all share is the capacity to survive the Mediterranean summer. Some plants tolerate the desiccation by plunging roots deep into the water table. Some—the scleromorphs—evade it through tough leaves that slow or shut down transpiration during the periods of maximum stress or that partly shed excess leaves. Many plants store much of their biomass underground, and all adjust their propagation to avoid the drought and seize the quenching rains of winter. These adaptations merge with others—nutrient-poor soils, heavy browsing and grazing, frequent disturbances, and of course fire. Those species that could not accept the summer's annual forge and history's relentless blows disappeared. What Columella said of a stubborn shrub was true for most of the Mediterranean flora: "Obviously this hedge cannot be destroyed, unless you want to dig it up by the roots. There is no doubt that after fire damage it grows again better than before."[4]

Its many fire accommodations have made the Mediterranean biota as much a model for fire ecology as Greek statuary for Western art. No aspect of the regional flora lacks fire adaptations. Some features shield buds, boles, and seeds from fire. The cork oak thrives behind a thermal blanket of bark; ericaceous shrubs like many heath species store major organs underground, capable of resprouting after surface decapitation; annuals complete their growth cycle before the onset of summer dormancy. Fire prunes, but does not kill, such plants.

Other species, however, true pyrophytes, are stimulated by burning. They flower, release seeds, or germinate best following a fire, and in some cases only after a fire. Their numbers include trees, shrubs, forbs, and grasses, parts of virtually every biome. Mediterranean pines often have serotinous (late-developing) cones that release their seeds only when heat, especially induced by fire, melts their waxy seal. Many Mediterranean orchids flower following fires, evergreen shrubs resprout and renew themselves after a pruning burn, the seeds of *Cistus* germinate subsequent to violent heating. That fire was so abundant, and so routinely accompanied other disturbances, left the Mediterranean biota to marinate in pyrophytes.

More than affecting individual plants, fire helped arrange the composition of communities, and the overall fire regime profoundly influenced the stability of those biomes. They persist because a particular regimen of fire persists. So pervasive has fire been that almost no species thrives that cannot accept fire in some fashion; many characteristic species require fire to propagate; and the entire ensemble, the Mediterranean mosaic, is held together through the dynamic welds of recurrent fire. Burning affects the tempo as well as the direction of change. Soil and streams take geologic eons to change; woodlands require decades, if not centuries, to mature; but fire can occur in minutes. The issue is not whether fire affects the Mediterranean biota but how.

The ecological power of fire, moreover, is as great removed as applied. A biome accustomed to a regimen of frequent fire will suffer if those fires diminish as fully as a biome used to heavy rains will suffer from prolonged drought. If, in fact, it were possible to remove fire completely, many typical Mediterranean species would slide into insignificance, perhaps oblivion, and many common communities would metamorphose as dramatically as Kafka's Gregor Samsa. They would resemble those sacred groves from which fire, along with other disturbances, has been excluded and the genetic potential of the Mediterranean biota has blossomed into distinctive, often unique forms. The cedar groves of Lebanon resemble nothing else in the degraded landscapes of the Levant. The protected forests of Mount Athos differ from Thrace as much as modern Athens does from ancient Argos. The monastic groves on the Saint-Baume massif rise like an apparition from the maquis of Languedoc.

The explanation of the Mediterranean's typical landscape is the same as that for the groves: they are both anthropogenic creations. The anthropogenic landscapes of the Mediterranean favored pyrophytes as ancient sculptors favored marble. The actual composition and shapes of the Mediterranean mosaic were no more a product of lightning than the temple at Delphi was the outcome of natural erosion. Everywhere human artifice dominated, and because human technology, whether agricultural or industrial, relied on fire, the biomes that resulted favored species that could endure fire or that flourished best under a regimen of regular fire.

(ii)

Whatever its natural (or aboriginal) rates, the tempo of burning picked up with the Neolithic revolution. The requirements of converting landscapes, and the need to recycle those refashioned biomes, both demanded fire. But the new fire regimes would depend on how the Neolithic torch reconstituted the landscapes it encountered.

Many local biomes balanced like a steel ball on a glass hill, and the advent of agriculture gave it a critical nudge. More or less natural openings widened; clearing by ringbarking, basal fire, and browsing reduced the prevalence of closed-canopy forest, liberating understory shrubs, forbs, and grasses; broadcast burning prevented a reconquest. It is thought that the characteristic shrub lands of the region—call them the *maquis* for convenience—began their spread into dominance at this time, much as further north similar practices converted residual forest to heath and moor. What had existed previously in patches became widely prevalent. With the advent of classical agriculture, the landscape assumed the dimensions that would persist, with ebbs and flows, until the industrial revolution dissolved the aging grout that held the tiles of the Mediterranean mosaic together. The Mediterranean became a garden.[5]

The restructuring took three forms, each with its characteristic fire regimes. Some biomes were converted, some reshaped, and some irreversibly deformed. Sedentary agriculture accounted for the first, seasonal exploitation for the second, and extreme catastrophes—some fast, some slow, a few generic to the region, a few intensely tied to particular sites—for the third. The waves of reconstitution advanced from east to west like tidal bores, felt everywhere but with each site and embayment accommodating the passages differently. Thus locally there was both conversion and abandonment; cycles of erosion and rejuvenation passed like flocks migrating with the seasons; forests were felled and terraces cut into hills, only to be abandoned to maquis, reclaimed, recleared, eroded, rebuilt. But like the motion of a pendulum, each swing left the overall system a little less renewed. Each episode evaporated a little more from the biotic cistern. In some locales the cumulative effect, even after millennia, was minuscule. In others it was catastrophic.

Outright conversion to agriculture absorbed a large fraction of the Mediterranean landscape. Depending on local circumstances of environment and history, classical agriculture claimed as much as 40 to 60 percent of the land base. This grand mosaic built on tiles of three hues. There was *ager,* the cultivated field; *saltus,* the rough pasture or fallow; and *silva,* the woods. Each element has its distinctive niche. Arable farming occupied the lowlands; vineyards and orchards, the hillsides; and foraging, including pastoralism, roamed seasonally between lowlands and mountains. The pieces could transmute one to another. What was once silva might be cleared to ager, and what was once ager might, through calculation or chance, coarsen into saltus.[6]

All the parts of an ecosystem existed, each to its site—forbs and tubers in gardens, grasses in fields and pastures, vines in garden and vineyard, fruits and nuts in orchards, shrubs in semidomesticated maquis, and trees in planted and indigenous groves tended for resin, timber, and mast. Classic farming rested on a tripod of olives, vines, and cereals, particularly wheat; but these coexisted with a vigorous animal husbandry. Fauna included dogs, donkeys, horses, cattle, sheep, pigs, goats, and bees, that is, grazers, browsers, pollinators. New species of plants and animals funneled into the maelstrom, found niches or were discarded, and joined the colonizing arks as cultigens or weeds. Cotton, cat, fowl, apricot, lemon, melon, sesame, clover, cherry, peach, plum, fig, almond, chestnut, walnut, radish, flax, beetroot, rabbit, pheasants, camel, pigeon—all encountered the classical complex, and found niches or forced accommodations. Better tools and novel cultigens led to further conversions, of marsh as well as mountain. Greater populations led to more intensive packing, to the intercultivation of grain and orchard, to the pollarding of trees for animal fodder.[7]

Many landscapes became a vast garden, or a patchwork quilt of gardened sites stitched together by related cultivations. Directly or indirectly, almost nothing in the Mediterranean remained outside this matrix. What was not ager was saltus or silva. What was not farmed was grazed, tapped for resin, harvested for wood, foraged for mast, fed into flocks. Sometimes the parts were separated by either geography or season, stitched to a common fabric by long threads of migrating livestock. Sometimes they overlaid, so that farmers intercultivated cereals with olive groves, or grazed herds on stubble. No place was truly wild. And no place was spared fire.

Fire appeared with every patch, with any interstitial wildland in chrysalis from one state to another. For the agriculturalist, the torch was an implement of gardening like ax, plow, and rake. It broke new ground, recycled nutrients in fallow, disposed of waste, and fueled forge and hearth. Fire and ax readied sites for shifting cultivation, and then prepared them for sedentary farming. Fire assisted the harvest of olives and chestnuts by clearing the ground of debris. Farmers burned old and diseased branches, overgrown ditches and canals, agricultural residue, and especially stubble as part of an annual cycle of cleaning. Fire cleared away overgrown thickets, pruned vines, and disposed of briars, tares, and stubble. References to such practices abound in Old Testament, Talmudic, Hellenic, and Roman sources.

Wheat stubble, in particular, was unpalatable to sheep, which would seek out other cereals or even leafy weeds. If it was not burned, it rotted. Xenophon

(*Economics*) thought that "stubble may be burnt with advantage to the land." Vergil (*Georgics*) went further: "Often, too, it has been useful to fire barren fields, and burn the light stubble in crackling flames." Although he was uncertain what the burning did, he knew its happy consequences. Lucan told how "Mount Gargano and the fields of Vultur and the pastures of hot Matinus light up the countryside with a blaze of fire" when farmers burned the old fallow. Rustic calendars included stubble burning within their cycle of annual labors. Where stubble or fallow was inadequate, other debris like leaves and branches could add to the fuels. Cato recommended that farmers consider burning in their fields unused "faggots and brushwood." Columella thought such ashes "reasonably beneficial to the soil." Palladius urged that overgrown fields be segregated between the fertile and the infertile, that regular fallow guide the former and a longer five-year cycle of swidden the latter. "In this way you will enable the barren soil to compete on equal terms with the fertile."[8]

Side benefits included the temporary purging of pests. Kassianos Vassus thought field fires could retard caterpillars, fleas, even ants. Homer likened an Argive retreat to locusts fleeing before an "unwearied fire." Pliny argued that the "chief reason" for stubble fires was to "burn up the seeds of weeds." Out of such practices rose the great fire ceremonies in which torch processions paraded through orchards and fields, and from such experiences derived the metaphoric power of Prophetic allusions to the devouring fire.[9]

But field and garden were only part of the agricultural complex of classical civilization. The triumvirate granted silva and saltus equal standing to ager. Indigenous and planted woodlands furnished mast, timber, bark for tanning, charcoal and fuelwood, and naval stores of pitch, tar, and resin. Pine and oak, the forests most valued, were favored by proper burning. Trees tapped for resin were themselves protected from wildfire only by judiciously controlled underburning. The more important link, however, was pastoralism. Grazed field and rough pasture were inevitable complements to the hoed garden, and the herded flock was the faunal equivalent to the orchard and plowed field. Here, more than anywhere else, fire ranged freely.

(iii)

Ideally, flock and field were fused through the immutable nutrient cycles that linked consumption to production. Animals consumed biomass—fallow, waste—that otherwise went unused. They could feed on stubble or fodder crops, then consume lush mountain browse when the arable crops were growing. In return, they contributed manuring dung to cultivated fields—directly when "folded" into the field, and indirectly by storing the manure in barns or pens when the fields were dormant. Through those flocks, agriculture balanced output with input; through them saltus joined ager, and mountain pasture was linked with lowland field. But the rugged terrain of the mountainous Mediterranean required that the flocks move geographically as well as seasonally. Herds marched from winter pasture in the lowlands to summer pasture in the mountains.

Typically shepherds burned as they departed the mountains, in advance of the rains, and what escaped the autumnal flames they captured in the fires of spring. The tradition was already ancient, inherited from the vanguard of the Neolithic revolution whose fires and flocks had begun a revolution in land use that endured, in places, for 10,000 years. So Silius Italicus described the "multitude of fires that the shepherd sees from his seat on Mount Gargano [Apulia] when the grazing lands of Calabona are burned and blackened to improve the pasture." In the *Aeneid* Vergil referred to fires ignited by pastoralists

> . . . *when summer winds are risen*
> *In answer to his wish, at points apart*
> *The shepherd launches fires against the woods;*
> *And on a sudden, the mid spaces caught,*
> *Vulcan's grim line now spreads unbrokenly*
> *Across the stretching plain; he from high seat*
> *Victorious views the triumphs of the flames.*[10]

In practice, the cycle was often out of sync. The fields were too small or too unpalatable to permit folding the flock into stubble, or too precious to produce fodder to feed animals for their reciprocated dung. Instead, for half the year the migratory herds fertilized the hills instead of the farms. Pastoralism remained partly uncoupled, its dynamic weld easily ruptured, and its fires accounted for the vast proportion of quasi-natural burning, of those fires that combusted the ungardened landscape. Frequently, too, pastoral fire escaped; the Prophetic literature of the Old Testament has numerous allusions to pasture fires that burned badly or ran wild over orchard and field. The incendiary shepherd, promiscuous with fire, is a stock figure in the literature of the Mediterranean, routinely denounced by intellectuals, farmers, and outsiders. Thus in 1901, R. B. Richardson, after condemning the omnivorous goat, expressed his outrage at the equally lascivious fires, of which he once counted twenty-four in a sea journey from Piraeus to Nauplia and which for two consecutive evenings illuminated Athens by burning Pentelicus. The classical agronomists—Cato, Varro, Columella, Theophrastus—distrusted pastoralism, encouraging a smaller-scale husbandry in preference to herding. That husbandry and herding implied two often incompatible social orders was not lost on classical authorities.[11]

Whatever the social implications, the combination of fire and browsing shaped the indigenous biota into a spectacular shrub land of immense complexity. The generic maquis was a marvelously supple biome, dominated by pyrophytes, that soon acquired a litany of local names. A suite of traits converged to select for species that could thrive under a regimen of burning and often predatory browsing. Thus many plants had a high oil content that emitted vapors repugnant to casual browsers, giving the land its pungent aromas; but those same volatile oils made leaves highly combustible. (So bees, attracted also to the scents, became drawn into the cycle of burning, and thus honey and wax became major products for domestic use and trade.) The capacity to resprout from branch or root made for rapid recovery after defoliation by either tooth or flame.

The malleable maquis was the indigenous flora boiled by pastoral burning into a biotic sap, occasionally into a near-crystalline solid. The maquis was the Mediterranean biota in miniature, capable of being compressed or released as the pressures permitted. It composed most of the Roman saltus, provided the Mediterranean's ungardened pastures, and banked the region's nutrients like an imperial treasury. It was a mountainous outfield to the infield of lowland arable and terraced hillsides. It became the great arena of free-burning fire, one that filled the interstitial pores of Antiquity's mosaicked garden.

Ideally field fires were no more than hearth fires outdoors, like the Zoroastrian exemplar of a nurtured yet unhoused god. But inevitably the system proved porous. Flames leaked from field to forest, and by and through the maquis they could pass everywhere. Even free-burning wildfire could rage in remote sites, as it did in Homeric similes: "Through deep glens rageth fierce fire on some parched mountain side and the deep forest beneath, and the wind, driving it, whirleth everywhere the flame." The Pyrenees received their name from their frequent fires; one, reportedly in 200 B.C., fixed itself vividly in the imagination of the time. But already by Periclean times, Thucydides knew such heroic wildfires only as a literary trope, an allusion from "times past in the mountains." When Vergil likened the rush of Aeneas and Turnus to "fires lighted all about to burn / A parching wood and rustling brakes of bay," he spoke in epic simile. When Lucretius imagined a "fierce conflagration, roaring balefully" that has "devoured a forest down to the roots," he was speaking hypothetically; the melting of rock, not the dynamics of the fire commanded his interest.[12]

Still, the threat was real. It was "well known," as Theophrastus asserted, that fire would "seek a void toward which and in which it can move." Untended, abandoned, overgrown sites were just such landscape voids; they would draw fire like air sucking into a vacuum. The solution began with housekeeping on a massive scale. Burn debris as trash. Burn the land in patches. Burn the patches at different times. Prevent any one part of the agronomic order, particularly any practice that relied on fire, from assuming dominance. Keep society orderly, the land gardened, and the fire tended. As a final solution, eliminate fire altogether by promoting biotic or social surrogates for burning.[13]

Those first precepts the farmers of the Mediterranean have practiced since ancient times. The last, the classical agronomists repeatedly urged in their texts. The segregation between theory and practice, elite and peasant, thus began early. Agronomists wanted farmers to do with hand labor and manure what fire did with flame. They understood the integration in principle of flock and field, the concept of crop rotation, the necessity for manure—from dung to marl to pigeon guano—to maintain fertility. They sought endlessly to close the ecological cycle, to keep both people and land gardened. Almost all distrusted fire.

Fire was a difficult implement to control precisely, and the greater its free-burning range, the more problematic it became. Those who used it tended to resist the fixed order—the political economy—on which Mediterranean agronomy was predicated. Free-burning fire was the prerogative of free-ranging peoples, groups who wandered outside the fixed social order or who, by their mobility, threatened to destabilize that order and the landscape on which it depended. The ideal farm, or Roman *latifundium,* had no desire for the ecological serendipity of fire, and would, if confronted by agrarian rebellion, seek to suppress its unruly flames.

An equilibrium between field and flock was a paragon that neither geography nor history allowed. The agronomic paradigm demanded an integration of field crops and livestock through manure that the Mediterranean frustrated where it did not prohibit outright. Instead it proposed a more tenuous alliance between sedentary farming and a seasonal pastoralism. Antiquity's agronomic ideal also promoted a stability of land use, economics, government, and population that did not much persist beyond the Pax Romana, if it had ever really existed. Its immobile core was an agrarian order founded on sedentary farming.

Still, for a surprisingly long period this system prevailed. Political elites came and went, states fused and sundered, the Great Migrations, war, and plague emptied and refilled the villas and latifundia of the Roman imperium, agricultural laborers underwent metempsychosis as citizens, free peasants, resettled soldiers, *coloniae,* monks, slaves, serfs; but throughout the basic agrarian order endured. Not until geopolitics and an economic revolution finally broke the tremulous valences that, like a geographic van der Waals force, had bound field to flock did major reform occur.

(iv)

Fire there would be, but Mediterranean fire would exist in its anthropogenic form, and so would be subject to the same constraints as its human tenders. It would enter the same moral universe. It would experience identical social, political, and economic institutions, and undergo similar intellectual scrutiny. If mythology suggested that humans could not be understood apart from their possession of fire, so fire would not be seen apart from its human agents. The same judgments applied to each. The ancient Mediterranean, so formative for Europe's scholarship, would supply the narratives for Europe's environmental history, and through them, its fire history.

Its genesis was the story of Eden, symbolically located in the eastern Mediterranean. Eden was no wilderness: it was a garden. "The Lord God made to grow out of the ground all kinds of trees pleasant to the sight and good for food." Through the Garden ran rivers, from it sprang "the tree of life," out of its ground the Lord God fashioned "the beasts of the field and the birds of the air" and granted man dominion over them—the world began with a domesticated landscape. But Adam and Eve failed their test, and by eating the forbidden fruit knew they had failed. God cursed them, then "cursed the ground" because of them. "In toil shall you eat of it all the days of your life; thorns and thistles shall it bring forth to you, and you shall eat the plants of the field." From dust they had come and to dust they would return. The Lord God drove them out of the Garden, set the Cherubim to guard the gate, and instructed Adam "to till the ground from which he was taken."

In the greater Mediterranean, so long subject to agriculture, so long a source of European perception, Europe had an environmental paradigm, and in the story of Eden, an unhappy synecdoche of that region's promised history. With or without its Judeo-Christian theology, the story of the Garden served up not only a powerful creation myth but also a dominant set of metaphors for environmental history. The Garden remained the ideal habitat, the exemplar by which people should relate to the land; the Fall, the failure and collective condemnation of both land and people, or of land through people; the command to till and toil, an imperative to reclaim and, if only in a limited sense, redeem through cultivation and husbandry what had been lost.

The Fall, however, was not easily dismissed. The Mediterranean became a morality play of wise and abusive land use, and having tasted its fruit, Europe appeared condemned not only to endless toil but to the knowledge of failure. Over millennia the Edenic source became an environmental sink as thorns, thistles, and dust often did replace streams and orchards. Wild woodland fires joined those that had ravaged Carthage; untrammeled pastoral fires mimicked the barbaric hordes that picked over the carrion of the Roman Empire; swiddened hillsides and fired stubble barred reentry to the Garden as surely as the flaming swords of the Cherubim. The words of the prophet Joel (2:3) became the paradigm for a declensionist history: "Before them a fire devours, and after them a fire enkindles; like the garden of Eden is the land before them, and after them a desert waste; from them there is no escape." The fact that fire was everywhere—that almost every abusive practice involved fire in some fashion—made it easy to condemn fire itself as a common cause.

The Enlightenment secularized the story, as it did so much of scholarship. But the narrative and its moral matrix remained. Surveying the consequences of swidden in Finland and pastoral burning in South Africa, John Croumbie Brown quoted Fries of Lund to bring both landscapes under the ancient aegis of Garden and Fall:

> Before him lay original nature in her wild and sublime beauty. Behind him he leaves the desert, a deformed and ruined land. . . . and man himself flies terrified from the arena of his actions, leaving the impoverished earth to barbarous races or animals, so long as yet another spot in virgin beauty smiles before him.

So long as new Edens could be found, humans were doomed by their flawed ecological character to repeat the story over and again. So also the declensionist paradigm migrated westward with the course of empire and informed the tragic creation stories of Europe's colonies. "Thus did cultivation, driven out, leave the East, and the deserts perhaps previously robbed of their coverings; like the wild hordes of old over beautiful Greece, thus rolls this conquest with fearful rapidity from east to west through America."[14]

The agronomic ideal, which had persisted in northern Europe, enjoyed a revival as the Enlightenment witnessed an agricultural revolution which, while outfitted with new tools and fodder plants, reaffirmed the principles of classical agronomics, much as Neoclassicism did ancient aesthetics and literature. Surveying the Mediterranean, the Enlightenment pondered the melancholy meaning of its dramatic contrasts—the spectacle of a degraded society sunk into poverty and superstition amid the splendors of Antiquity, the specter of a land similarly debased into brush and gulley. The words of Plato's *Critias* hung hauntingly over the scene. "What now remains compared with what then existed is like the skeleton of a sick man, all the fat and soft earth having been wasted away, and only the bare framework of the land being left." Clearly the larger saga was one of loss, a mutual degradation that had consumed both land and people. What Edward Gibbon pondered amid the ruins of the Capitol, "while barefooted friars were singing vespers in the temple of Jupiter," others repeated amid the surrounding maquis, eroded hills, and abandoned terraces, while with equal promiscuity herds foraged and shepherds burned.[15]

It was not obvious, however, what had caused this debasement or how exactly the paradigm had declined. One school held that the devolution began with the ambivalent achievements of ancient civilization. Thus had George Perkins Marsh denounced as the *causa causarum* for the colossal wreckage of the Mediterranean the "brutal and exhausting despotism" of Rome, for "man cannot struggle at once against crushing oppression and the destructive forces of inorganic nature." A corrupt society had corrupted its land, and the decay in the one rebounded on the other. Thus were linked the internal rot of Roman society and soil erosion, the moral turpitude of Roman politics and wanton deforestation. Antiquity had raised its monuments at the cost of exorbitant environmental loans and a constantly debased ecological currency; and when those loans fell due with interest, the bloated edifice collapsed.[16]

Others disputed that political parable. They argued that, while ancient agronomy had failed locally, its principles were sound, and while agriculture had replaced the indigenous biomes, it had enhanced through artifice the productivity and beauty of a marginal land. In this conception it was the collapse, not the establishment, of ancient civilization that had initiated the long decline of regional ecology. The Fall was Rome's; its abandoned garden followed. Collapse resulted from the triumph of nomadism. It was the replacement of forest and field with pasture and steppe that had steadily ratcheted the region into a wasteland.

Itinerant pastoralism with its trampling hoofs, voracious mouths, and devouring fire was thus environmentally equivalent to the wandering tribes that preyed on the carrion of fallen Rome, to the wild bedouins enflamed with religious fanaticism who seized North Africa, the Levant, and Spain, to the banditry that infested Italy and the Balkans, to the wasting hordes of Mongol and Turk, felling woods with the same ruthless sadism by which they had leveled cities and raised pyramids of human heads. Mediterranean agriculture had resembled the dual administration of Roman armies by two consuls, who alternated their rule day by day. When that arrangement failed, an agronomic civil war broke out, in which a decoupled and despotic pastoralism triumphed, whether through the intimidation of the Greek goat herd, the untrammeled gullet of the Arab camel, or the organized terror of the Spanish Mesta. Under the crush of horde and herd, the maquis at first expanded and then itself degraded. Fire and hoof had vandalized the legacy of ancient agriculture as surely as fire and sword had its statecraft and temples.

Classic scenarios, these, still informing an understanding of why the Mediterranean landscape looks the way it does. Both implicated abusive fire. "Fire is the most powerful agent of life and death," Edward Gibbon observed. "The rapid mischief may be kindled and propagated by the industry or negligence of mankind; and every period of the Roman annals is marked by the repetition of similar calamities." He spoke of Rome, but he could as easily have referred to the Roman landscape. That was the hard judgment and inherited scholarship of the Enlightenment. But industrialization has so jolted the region that it has thrown into question not only the means of its environmental degradation but even the trajectory of that history. That many vegetation types relate to the maquis does not mean that they have devolved from it, or that the maquis is itself a debased habitat. Instead the biota displays incredible stability, rebounding like a cork under water when the pressures pass. Other interpretations suggest themselves.[17]

Degradation was a social, not an ecological, judgment. More sympathetically, it might be said that the Mediterranean suffers from fatigue. Several millennia of relentless human manipulation have worn down the biota and locally wasted away, along with its soils, its capacity for incidental recovery. The maligned maquis is a durable survivor of the indigenous flora, honorable in its pedigree, capable of regeneration if freed from abuse. The agronomic ideal, while still rich in symbolism, is a feeble relic of a lost age when the village had a greater claim than the modern metropolis, when the garden fed families, when pastoralism could command the power of the state. Old fire practices have vanished or gone feral, and inherited condemnations may have as little relevance as the agrarian epistles of Cicero or the grudging acquiescence of Columella.

ARCADIA AND ANARCHY:
MEDITERRANEAN PASTORALE

From the beginning, the Mediterranean had a fauna to match its flora. Early humans were hunters as much as foragers. Herders, with their walking larders, were the vanguard of the Neolithic revolution. Classical agriculture sought to integrate animal and plant, the one mobile and the other sedentary, into a common agrarian order. But practice and principle quarreled as often as shepherd and farmer. The Mediterranean landscape balanced on a razor's edge between arcadia and anarchy.

In principle, mountain pasture complemented lowland arable, together holding Mediterranean agriculture in suspension. If either landscape collapsed, the system came unhinged. Herds were freed of their social hobbles, ranging beyond designated pastures. Farms clawed up the slopes, forced to terrace to prevent excessive erosion. In practice, the alliance broke as often as it succeeded. Not only did herds roam seasonally and on lands outside the plowed field, they migrated across whole geographies. Mobile societies—invaders—traveled with their herds. Horse, camel, sheep, and goat became the vehicles no less than the symbols of conquest. Besides, the field needed the flock to close its ecological cycle, and economics often favored low-labor herding to labor-intensive husbandry, especially during times of depopulation. According to Cicero, when Cato was asked what is the most profitable thing in the management of one's estate, he answered "Good pasturage." What is the next best? "Fairly good pasturage." What is the third best? "Bad pasturage." What is the fourth best? "Tilling the soil."[18]

(i)

If Mediterranean geography made itinerant grazing mandatory, fire made it possible. The grazier burned not out of wantonness but of necessity. Fire retarded the final progression into full-blown forest, pruned and sweetened maquis, flushed new life into grasses and forbs, and in general kept ager and saltus in a state suitable for the herd. Even so, not every domesticated animal could participate. Horses, cattle, and mules, for example, required grass, which was not always abundant in the Mediterranean mountains and which restricted large herds to Asian steppes or the Spanish *meseta,* or to the well-watered northern mountains that bordered temperate Europe. That left swine, sheep, and goats.

Each had a characteristic niche, a preferred biome. Swine fed on the mast of oaks and beech; sheep and goats, on the browse of maquis. Thus herders had to tend landscapes as they did flocks. The Mediterranean became a vast kaleidoscope of pastures. The Spanish *dehesa* and Portuguese *montada,* stately with mature oak and grass, evolved to nurture cattle. Italian hills dappled with meadows and maquis fed sheep. Dry steppes held horses and camels. Oak and beech woodlands in the moister mountains hosted swine. (The expulsion of swine from the Levant and North Africa, an act reinforced by religious sanction, helped push those landscapes into other forms.) Everywhere the raucous scrub met the insatiable goat.

Flora and fauna tended to coevolve—and where the land degraded, they shared that mutual declension. Plants evolved in response to both fire and grazing, or rather in reply to those particular regimens of burning and browsing imposed by human will or allowed by accident. Pungent, thorny, quick-sprouting shrubs replaced trees; spiky bunchgrass succeeded swards; sheep took over land no longer fit for cattle or horses; and goats and camels replaced sheep. The prevalence of one species or other of livestock was partly environmental sense, partly cultural preference, and increasingly a historical compulsion imposed by the legacy of prior habits. The goat thrived because, in places, only the goat could survive. Macrobius has the goat chorus in his *Saturnalia* list lasciviously their omnivorous fare: "We dine on all manner of shrubs, browsing on tender shoots of pine, holly oak, and arbutus, and on spurge, legumes, and fragrant sage, and many leaved bindweed as well, wild olive and lentisk [mastic tree] and ash, fir, sea oak, ivy and heath, willow, thorn, mullein, and asphodel, rock rose, oak, thyme and savory." Most were stimulated by judicious burning.[19]

Threads of fire wove everywhere between the woof and warp of wild flora and domesticated fauna. It was not fire per se, or fire alone, but the immense synergism between burning and grazing that mattered most. The frequency, intensity, patch size, and seasonal timing of fire; the frequency, intensity, flock size, and seasonal timing of browsing—these determined whether the pasture evolved, devolved, or endured in its present form. Maquis that was burned every five years responded differently than maquis burned every ten; a site fired in the spring promoted different species than one fired in the fall; a large patch behaved differently than a small one. But likewise a site opened to cattle, a patch grazed immediately after burning, a pasture subjected to year-round browsing responded otherwise than one fed to goats, grazed after the winter rains, or left fallow for one or several seasons. The possible combinations were legion.

Fire prodded, fire cleared, fire converted; but fire alone did not abuse. The shepherd's torch only assisted other assaults, much as armies put cities to the torch only after the walls had fallen to siege engines and storming troops. Pastoral burning was as regulated (or riotous) as pastoralism. Fires swept wheat stubble annually, consumed rough pasture every two or three years, patch-burned maquis every five to eight, and cleaned out hand-pruned *dehesa* and woodlands as needed. Fire destroyed only when it was used destructively, when it armed combatants, abetted anarchy, inflamed vendettas, equipped exploiters; when the traditional order of society, and of socially ordered nature, broke down.

But abuses inevitably involved fire, and abused land was invariably burned. It was clear that fire and hoof could reshape biomes as forge and hammer could metal. Particularly for forests, it was obvious that recurring fire and incessant browsing retarded regeneration, that vandalism, greed, and ignorance could destroy a beautiful landscape. It was fire, however, that furnished the transcendent symbol, and bore the burden of barbarism. The character of pastoral fire was inextricable from the many expressions of Mediterranean pastoralism and the meanings attached to them.

(ii)

The best way to control pastoral burning was to control pastoralism. Husbandry sought to integrate herding into farming, transhumance to balance the two with seasonal migrations, and nomadism to challenge sedentary farming outright or to prey upon it. Each prescribed a different strategy of assimilation or containment.

Their varieties were many, however, as varied as the Greek village, the Berber tribe, the Roman latifundium, or the Spanish royal monopoly that in their own ways oversaw the herds. There were, moreover, profound regional differences between east and west, north and south, that reflected history rather than geography. Islamic pastoralism with origins in the steppes of central Asia, the deserts of Arabia, and the savannas of Africa differed in law and environmental impact from the pastoralism of Christendom, centered in the sown meadows and surveyed fields of a temperate Europe that had pushed itinerant herding to the outer margins of Norway, Scotland, and Wales. But everywhere in the Mediterranean some form of pastoralism thrived, and everywhere it hung like a sword of Damocles over the landscape.

Animal husbandry was possible where the herds were small, the natural meadows large, and the fields capable of growing fodder crops. Amid the littoral that harbored Mediterranean civilization, these conditions were rare. True husbandry was reserved for milch and draft animals, and for animals like horses and mules essential for military service. Minor herds of cattle grazed on large estates, sometimes ranging through woodlands rich in grass, but they shunned the prickly maquis. This remained the dominion of the great herds and flocks that migrated between lowland and mountain, summer pasture and winter, fallow ager and scrubby saltus.

Transhumance was the characteristic pastoralism of the Mediterranean. The rhythms began early, almost certainly predating sedentary farming. Communal rights widely supported herding; laws, like farming, had to accommodate that reality. The Roman *jus pascendi,* for example, provided wide access to feed by herds—in fact granted herds preference over other land uses. Under the Aquilian law of the Roman Republic landowners suffering damage from errant flocks could not confiscate or even drive off the offending creatures. Tradition sought, and law confirmed, instead to channel the movement into regular routes of passage—the *calles publicae* of Rome, the *tratturi* of Italy, the *carraires* and *drayes* of France, the *cañadas* of Spain. Thus transhumance, Fernand Braudel concluded, was "markedly institutionalized," protected "by safeguards, rules, and privileges," even when, like its shepherds ("always a race apart"), it stood somewhat outside the rest of society.[20]

Economics soon reinforced tradition. Stock raising was less labor intensive than farming, especially when slaves served as shepherds. Where land was abandoned, like much of central Italy following the second Punic War, herds, not farms, reclaimed it. After the Mediterranean became Rome's *mare nostrum* and grain was shipped freely around the basin, herds replaced cereals as a source of wealth. Whatever praises ancient authors sang to the farm and the virtues of the yeoman soldier ("the best citizens spring from the cultivators," asserted Cato), the farm was often little more than a brush dam against the ceaseless flow of pastoralism. Frequently, migrating flocks gorged on fields, fallow or otherwise, that lay along their routes. Herds moved into landscapes depopulated by pestilence, war, or economics.[21]

Whatever form it took, transhumance survived with the acquiescence, if not the collusion, of the state. If fire history is inextricably intertwined with pastoral history, so pastoralism is inseparable from politics. The consolidation of medieval states imposed a new order on all. Consider by way of comparison the dramatic contrasts between the three peninsulas—Iberia, Italy, and Greece—that like ancient Pillars of Hercules had supported classical civilizations. Greece exhibited a goat-centered pastoralism akin to anarchy, Spain an autocratic pastoralism of sheep and cattle, and Italy a garbled patchwork of the two superimposed over inextinguishable local traditions.

Always fragmented, after the final collapse of Byzantium, Greece disintegrated as a coherent political entity, submerged under the rule of the steppe-émigré Turks, with no larger order than that of tax collector and military governor. The pastoral triumphed over the arable. Ottoman land law helped subvert sedentary farming. So did the absence of anything like a cadastral survey; and so did continuous armed conflicts, social vendettas, depopulations, and a determination to clear the land of forests to lessen the prospects for ambush and to reduce the refuges available to rebels. Permission to harvest dry wood became an incentive to make fuelwood by burning, a practice that also expanded pasturage. "Perhaps nowhere," noted Bernhard Fernow, speaking for nineteenth-century foresters, "are forest fires more frequent, in spite of heavy penalties."[22]

Pastoralism—and especially pastoral burning—often resembled war, or at least political protest, carried on by other means. Throughout the peninsula, herders burned not only to promote pasture, but to destroy fields, intimidate farmers and villagers, escape the officers of the state, subvert edicts, destroy rivals, and in general keep society simmering over the flames of an ineradicable if feckless pastoralism. The rogue goat, or rather herds of free-ranging quasiferal goats, became the emblem of the Greek economy, and their swelling numbers the measure of a suicidal vendetta with its own land. The satyr that classical Greece had kept to the margin of society now seemed to rule it.

Iberia veered toward the other extreme, ruthlessly imposing a common pastoral economy that transcended both local and regional agriculture. The antecedents were ample; transhumance abounded locally, in the Pyrenees, the Cantabrians, the Trás-Os-Montes. But the hybridization of the merino sheep from African and Iberian stock, the growing traffic in wool vital to the European markets, and the acquisition of new lands through the centuries of the Reconquest, all fashioned a pastoralism that transcended local landscapes and moved across regions as well as between valley and *monte*. Armies took the field with attendant flocks; and the extension of Christian rule extended also the routes of migrating herds across the *meseta*. The victory over the Moors at Seville in 1252 suddenly opened up vast southern provinces to the pastoral economy. Herds could winter in Andalusia-Estremadura and summer in Castile-León. The routes of conquest became the *cañadas* of an imperial transhumance that branded the Spanish landscape as fully as absolutism and Inquisition stamped its politics.[23]

Early on, the process acquired direction. In 1273, Alfonso X of Castile issued to "all the shepherds of Castille" a royal charter of privilege, El Honrado Con-

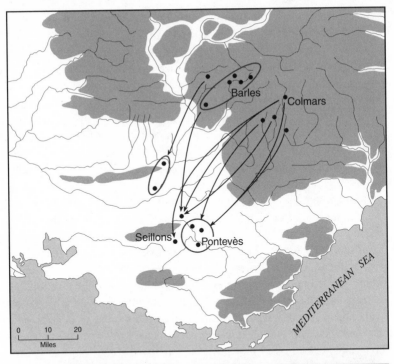

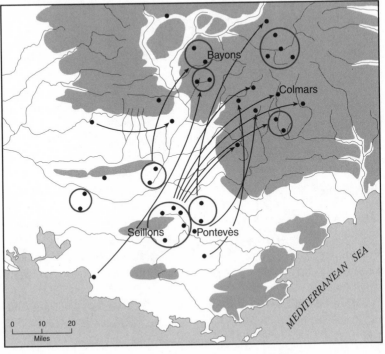

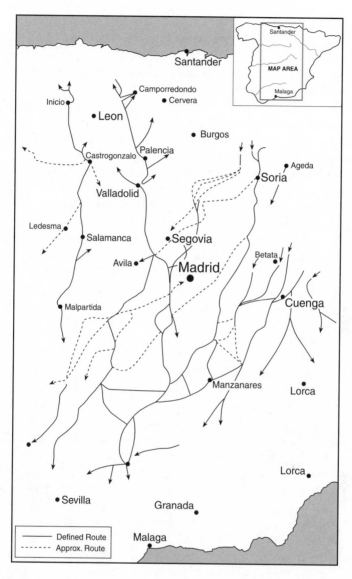

Transhumance. The variants were many, but two dominated: the mountain-and-valley pattern shown in (a) and (b) for southern France and the longer traverses (c) that evolved for the *meseta* in central Spain. In (a) the flocks move from the mountains to winter pastures in the lowlands, and in (b) back to the mountains for the summer. (Adapted, respectively, from Sclafert 1959 and Aitken 1945 by the University of Wisconsin Cartographic Lab)

cejo de la Mesta de Pastores, which sought to organize, protect, and extend to the furthest "extremities" the evolving system of seasonal migration. The herds supported the army; the army extended the dominions of the flock; the economics of the wool trade, regulated as a monopoly, poured into royal coffers and more than replaced the revenues lost from Moorish vassals who, defeated by the sword, no longer paid tribute. In 1476 the king became himself the Grand Master of the Mesta; with the merino sheep the Spanish monarchy formed its most powerful alliance. A decade following the final expulsion of the Moors, Ferdinand and Isabella recharted the Mesta (1501) and expanded its privileges. And for centuries after the Reconquest ended, ghost armies of sheep, cattle, and swine continued to march along the ancient *cañadas* in ritual memory.

The conversion of the Iberian landscape through transhumance was as profound as the conversion of Iberian society through the Reconquest. Grazing, particularly of sheep, was considered the apogee of land economics. What land could not support sheep was converted, forcibly if necessary; what compromised or encumbered the passage of sheep was trampled, with legal sanction if required. Pastoralism reigned, and the shepherd ruled with torch as much as staff. Burning not only helped shape the landscape, but helped to retain that imposed form, despite pressures by forest and *matorral* to regenerate. Still, deforestation was not the same as degradation; pastoralism was capable of creating stable, fertile landscapes such as the Spanish *dehesa* and Portuguese *montado;* and an agriculture adapted to livestock did not condemn Iberia to ecological despair. The problem was not pastoralism but the character of pastoralism as it evolved in Spain.

Absolutism can corrupt land use as it does politics, and Spanish pastoralism tended toward the absolute. The consolidation of political power under the monarchy of Ferdinand and Isabella, and the harsh uniformity of religion that the monarchy tried to impose on society through the Inquisition, the state applied to the landscape economically through the Mesta. What the Mesta did not rule directly, it shaped indirectly; its charter was to the landscape as the Escorial was to the state, the symbol of a central power, a determination to rule, not govern. Probably 80 percent of the forest area of Spain felt the impress. The reach of the Mesta deformed village economies by altering their own patterns of livestock rearing; its presence reveals the overall design of Iberian land use the way a lightning bolt can, in an instant, illuminate a dark countryside. The torch became the scepter of a pastoral tyranny. Spain evolved into the one country of western Europe dominated by a pastoral economy. Not until 1837 did a moribund monarchy, feeling the first tremors of industrialism, dissolve the medieval privileges of the Mesta.

If Greece lacked a geographic core, disintegrating into innumerable peninsulas and islands, Spain possessed one that loomed too large. Classical agriculture had developed around the Mediterranean littoral. To that coast clung the Roman imperium, grafting to its littoral rootstock such interior lands as Gaul, Iberia, and Illyricum. Power flowed from the sea inland. But the central plateau of Spain, the *meseta,* helped reverse this relationship. With the pastoralism forged during the Reconquest, the center dominated the periphery. The *cañada* replaced the Roman road as the route of imperial power, the woven strands of state rule. Over the intricate mosaic of Roman agriculture, Iberian pastoralism threw a vast wool blanket.

Italy experienced both extremes, but neither pervasively nor for long. Pastoral banditry on the Greek model triumphed locally on the peninsula where disorder prevailed and the regulation of pastoral fire collapsed along with other social institutions; and on islands like Sardinia and Sicily, continuing trends set into motion by Roman conquests transformed the interior into pastoral estates. Similarly, mini-Mestas sprang up where a state's land base was sufficiently large to support large-scale transhumance and its power sufficiently great to enforce a monopolistic charter. The purest expressions were kingdoms that fell under the control of the Spanish Habsburgs and experienced transplanted systems like the Mesta. Thus in Naples, for several centuries, Spanish-style pastoralism prevailed beginning in the fifteenth century.[24]

There was, however, no more a common Italian pastoralism than there was a unified Italy. An astonishing mosaic of pastures, changing political orders, and an evolving economy intimately related to maritime trade, all contributed to the variety of pastoral economies. One style thrived in the Alps, others along the Apennines, another yet, perhaps the most persistent, between Apulia and Abruzzi. Climate accounted for the peculiarities of the northern style; a preference for wheat, of the southern. Sheep and cattle, not goats, predominated, testimony to a more stable agrarian order and ligatures to the larger economy of Europe. Productive farmlands were the dikes that kept the flowing flocks within their *tratturi.* But new markets for wool or new rulers could send those flocks over the banks of their agrarian levees.

Southern Italy became a major center for large-scale transhumance, as herds moved like a seasonally alternating current between the Apennines and Tavoliere, between mountain and plain. Pastoralism here had a long pedigree. Roman agronomy had distrusted the dry limestone plains of Apulia, and preferred to graze sheep and horses on it. Still, wheat was a coveted cereal, and was grown where possible. When rural Rome suffered major depopulations, however, latifundia based more on pastoralism reclaimed the landscape. And then, no doubt looking with a covetous eye to Spain, the monarchy began to organize the annual migrations in order to siphon some of the flow into the royal coffers. The floodgates opened when Alfonso V of Aragon organized the Dogana system in 1447 or 1448. From an estimated 5.6 million sheep in 1400, the flocks swelled to 10 million by 1650.[25]

Like the Mesta, the Dogana oversaw the movement of flocks, and exercised, as George Kish notes, "absolute sway, not only over land that was part of the royal demesne, but over private lands as well." Its dominion extended, in its prime, over 15,500 square kilometers. Every movement of sheep, every landscape they might visit, every practice that affected pasture (and royal revenue) fell under its purview. The Dogana could control flocks by regulating the limited winter range, which dictated how large a flock could survive on the lowlands. Standard allotments gave every 100 sheep 24 hectares of saltus, 32 hectares of ager that had been cropped two years previously, or 48 hectares of recently harvested ager. This, of course, demanded strict control over cultivation. The migrations thus dictated the whole structure of land use.[26]

But increasing populations and, after the Napoleonic conquest, the abolition of the Dogana reerected the ancient dikes. The sheep population plummeted. It stood at 6.8 million in 1800, and 1.6 million a century later. While transhumance continued well past World War II, it became increasingly ritualistic. Its contemporary fires stand to those of the past as paschal candles do to Beltane bonfires. The ancient alliance of migratory fire and migratory flocks disappeared down an industrial drain.

(iii)

At least selectively. Where industrialization was feeble or only destabilized traditional societies, pastoralism persisted, and with it, fire. From the Maghreb to Anatolia, from the Levant to Iberia, from the Zagros Mountains to the Pyrenees, herding remains endemic to, as it helped found, the political economics of Mediterranean land use. Whether it was responsible for the degradation of the environment, as its detractors hold, or whether it reclaimed hillsides eroded by the hunger of increasing peasant populations for arable land, as its defenders argue, pastoralism has remained an ineradicable part of the agricultural ensemble. No place has lacked it, and in many places it has dominated.

To a remarkable degree pastoralism prescribed the historic dominion of anthropogenic fire. The geography of free-burning fire coincided with free-ranging pastoralism; browsing and burning amplified each other's power. Until recent decades, flame traced the winding routes of herders in spring and fall, while behind and before them clouds of smoke wreathed seasonal pastures. Fire fed on the flora with the same selectivity and voracity that the driven flocks did.

Infield and outfield were joined not by manure but by regulated routes of transit and by prescribed fires. The one was as constrained as the other. Only when Europe sailed beyond the pillars of Hercules and the Atlantic economy replaced the Mediterranean did that dominating alliance tremble, as maritime *tratturi* redefined the economics of wool and rerouted its traffic. But not until railroad tracks replaced *cañadas* and the transhumant tourist the shepherd did the balance of forces finally break and the land tumble irretrievably out of its ancient orbit.

Until then, too, the iconography of field and flock also informed competing claims to primacy in the evolving moral geography of the region. Thus the story of Garden and Fall had its complement in the story of Adam and Eve's two sons, Abel "a keeper of flocks" and Cain "a tiller of the soil." The Lord God "was pleased with Abel and his offerings; but for Cain and his offering he had no regard." In jealousy Cain slew Abel. But just as often over the millennia of Mediterranean history, Abel's descendants slew those of Cain. The civilizations of Antiquity—Hebrew, Greek, Roman, Arab—traced their origins to shepherds. The goat, the sheep, the camel, the bull, the horse, each emblemized the triumph of a new order. The rise and fall of ruling peoples recorded their passage in the relative status, economic and intellectual, accorded field and flock. The degree to which domestic plant and animal were integrated by the manured field, or paired through transhumance, or dissociated with some form of nomadism became an index of political and ecological order.

These considerations have profoundly influenced interpretations of Mediterranean environmental history. So has the fact that many critics have observed the scene from temperate Europe. The worrying flocks that agronomic critics witnessed browsing along the margins of the cultivated field, geopolitical critics saw around the cultured core of Europe—the cattle-herding Celts in the uplands of the British Isles, reindeer-rich Lapps in Scandinavia, well-horsed hordes on the steppes of Asia Minor, the far-ranging sheep, goats, and camels of Turk, Berber, and Arab. Many observers too were foresters, who saw any devolution from full-canopied woodland as an ecological recession, who imagined the high forest as the environmental analogue of high civilization and for whom the putative *Ur*-woodland was the standard against which all other change should be measured. To them maquis was only degraded forest, and pasture only a denuded woods.

Art and moral philosophy were more ambivalent. Neoclassicists and Romantics offered alternative images, seeing in the Vergilian pastoral an idyllic order undebauched by the artificial contrivances of Versailles or the Vatican, a middle ground between the city and the wild. Yet the dominant perception was one of condemnation. The dread of the nomad tugged more powerfully on European memory, accentuated by religious conflict. Not accidentally had the cloven-footed satan evolved out of the satyr; the demonization of the goat by foresters was only a further derivation. To critics, the Mediterranean pastoral was not a lyric but a tragedy, an ecological dementia that like some crazed Lear pulled everything around it down in mutual ruin.

Yet fire survived pastoralism. Wheat stubble continued to be burned, and as forestry began to reclaim old pasture—as silva replaced saltus—seasonal burning returned. By the 1980s incendiary fires throughout southern Italy had reached epidemic proportions, an estimated 49 to 65 percent of all known causes. Among the epicenters was Apulia. Even as the flocks ceased, the fires continued. Wildfire moved in to feast on the ancient fare of shrubs no longer consumed by the vanished sheep.[27]

In place of transhumant shepherds stood seasonal firefighters, hired by the state to combat incendiary fires on the hills. As shepherds had once used fire to intimidate farmers, so now locally recruited firefighters held the embryonic forests "as hostage," in the words of Vittorio Leone and Antonio Saracino, "to force the provision of short-term employment through the continuing fire menace." So long as they set fires, the state would hire them to fight the flames. Dismayed critics spoke of a perverse "fire industry" that had made itself fundamental to the economy of a chronically depressed region. Forest and city found themselves linked as tenuously as mountain and field had been before, joined by an eternal Mediterranean fire.[28]

GRAND TRAVERSE:
IMPERIAL FRANCE

The Mediterranean defined a political as well as a climatic geography. The mountains that framed its northern perimeter—the Pyrenees, the Alps, the Dinarics —traced the borders of states. The association was never exact, for Spain had Galicia and Asturias (*España Verde*), Italy the Po Valley and the Alps, the Balkan states a Mediterranean climate that clung to the coast and ventured little inland. But in all these instances the political core resided in the Mediterranean; the states and their cultures were Mediterranean; and attempts, like the Holy Roman Empire's, to weld them to temperate Europe were inherently unstable.

The grand exception was France. Along the south of France ruptures appeared in the engirdling ranges. No connecting mountains bound the Massif Central to the Alps or the Pyrenees; no geologic border segregated mediterranean from temperate Europe. The Rhone Valley, in particular, was a corridor between the two, assisting the penetration of the Roman imperium into Gaul and, later, promoting a rebound back in medieval times from a reconsolidated France. Here was a Mediterranean landscape not only under the jurisdiction of a temperate European power but absorbed into its national territory. France's center lay in Paris; its saga, like that of Muscovy, was one by which, as Jules Michelet penned in his *Journal*, "the least original part of the country took over all the rest." That included the exotic landscape of the Mediterranean. "The Île-de-France took over France," continued Michelet, "and France the world."[29]

The reality was light years short of such chauvinism. But the French reach to the Mediterranean was a profound event in European fire history. Alone among the nations of temperate Europe, France had to confront Mediterranean fire regimes. Thus it was France, not the Low Countries, that pioneered fire protection; France, not the German states, that summarized fire ecology across the globe; France, not Britain, that saw fire as something more than foreign exotica, like temple dancers or tigers. For France, mediterranean fire was part of its national estate. Even more remarkable, the imperial reach continued southward. It extended to Corsica in 1769; to Algeria and the Maghreb first in the 1830s and then, with renewed urgency, after 1870; to Morocco, beginning in 1912; to Mauretania, Mali, Chad, Senegal, Ghana, the Ivory Coast, the Congo. With cynical jealousy, France raced to Guiana, Madagascar, Indochina. When the scramble ended, imperial France claimed a swath of environments from the sodden fields of Flanders to the sweltering mangroves lining the Gulf of Guinea.

No other European nation absorbed so many fire regimes. No other sought, by quasi-Cartesian logic, to explain them or to rule them, or grafted fire history onto colonialism with such candor. Because so many of these acquired lands were administered as *départements* of national territory, not as colonies, their fire problems became France's. France confronted more fire directly than any of its rivals on the continent. And because France was a scientific as well as an imperial power, its experience diffused throughout Europe. The Code Colbert became an international standard for state-sponsored forestry and *dirigisme,* the political logic behind wildland fire control.

The French connection became a conduit. French fire practices were as widely disseminated as French art or the novels of Emile Zola, and the national forestry school at Nancy as much a pilgrimage site as the Louvre. Britain, for example, propagated many French practices through its own colonial forestry services, and America's founding foresters knew aspects of French fire history better than their own. With his story "In the Rukh," Rudyard Kipling describes how a British forester sought the *"reboisement* of all India" according to "the rules of Nancy," even though with time "he ceases to sing the naughty French songs he learned . . . and grows silent with the silent things of the underbrush." An early ranger with the U.S. Forest Service and lecturer at Yale University, Theodore Woolsey, Jr., asserted that "American foresters have very much to learn from the intensive methods of forest management and forest production on the Continent of Europe," and then outlined in detail, as the "best examples," the experience of imperial France.[30]

France's Grand Traverse was as much historical as geographical. It stretched from Paleolithic hunters to steam locomotives, from burned stubble to wildfires careening over Sainte-Victoire under the scream of the mistral. In southeastern France the fire history of the Mediterranean welded to the fire history of temperate Europe, so that not only the imperial fire encounters of France, but those of the continent, began when the Île-de-France sought to fuse Normandy with Provence, the Ardennes with the Cévennes, the conifer forests of the Jura with the maquis of the Esterel.

(i)

Separately considered, neither temperate nor mediterranean France had a fire history that was atypical. France's uniqueness lay with their fusion, and with the momentum of history that propelled French experience beyond the continent. If, by the twentieth century, the epicenter of French fire resided in the south, the origins of a national fire polity began in the north.

Temperate France had known fire, indispensable to agriculture, throughout its Holocene history. The agrarian order was an ensemble of infield and outfield, of ager with saltus. Around them, like planets orbiting binary suns, the agricultural year revolved. Arable, in particular, was long in the making and small in the overall spectrum of land usage. Varieties of swidden thrived alongside it—essartage in forests, écobuage on organic soils, an endless array of regular burning practices outside the arable, on lands as intensively foraged, grazed, and harvested as the population permitted. As late as 1908 forests along the Belgium border were slashed and burned; likewise in the Ardennes until World War I, and in the Midi well into the 1920s. Commonly, forests and fields were intercultivated, with cereals or pasture sown amid managed woodlands, and with strips of coppice ribbing fields like close-packed hedges—a source of branches to lay on the adjacent fields and burn as regularly as growth permitted. Broadcast fire was endemic in heath, especially prominent in Brittany and Gascony. Such sites were the temperate cognates of the mediterranean maquis, the product of burning and grazing in a wet rather than a dry climate. Ancient practices of farming and transhumance persisted in the Jura, the Hautes-Alpes, the Dauphiné Alps, the Midi, and the Pyrenees. Where foresters tapped pines for resin, wildfires were an occupational hazard and controlled underburning was an act of silvicultural hygiene. Not until well into the twentieth century did these fire practices finally break down. However mightily agronomists might ignore or condemn it, agricultural burning persisted at folk levels just as fire ceremonies did despite the fulminations of clerics.[31]

So, too, the fire history of mediterranean France does not differ radically from that of Italy and Spain. All experienced the same kinds of anthropogenic fires set for the same kinds of purposes; all received the Neolithic revolution probably by sea; similar entrepôts of colonizing Phoenicians, Carthaginians, and Greeks festooned their littoral; an identical agrarian order blossomed under Roman rule. Further inland, the archaeological evidence suggests that Neolithic pastoralism and horticulture early claimed the plateaus of Provence and the Massif Central such that climate and humans worked together to shape a distinctive biota. Neither departed completely.[32]

A characteristic ensemble took shape during medieval times and persisted until the nineteenth century. Pastoral burning and *écobuage* were characteristic of Languedoc and Roussillon, reaching a maximum between 1820 and 1830. In granitic Provence *essartage* was more pronounced. But the mountains experienced many forms of burning, both light and intense. Light burns served transhumant pastoralists by promoting grass and browse; accompanied hunters and smokers on their rounds; assisted the harvest of chestnuts, immense orchards of which were planted for fodder and flour, by clearing the understory; stimulated the kermes oak, which in turn promoted insects (genus *Kermes*) collected as a source of red dye for the wool industry; and shielded coniferous forests from wildfire.[33]

More severe burns testified to unrest, the fire only a flaming confirmation of a scrambled social order that was no longer able or willing to impose its image on the land. Uncontrolled fires broke out during the Revolution; the economic (and political) crisis that peaked in 1830 saw an outbreak of rural burning in Normandy. Potential incendiaries were many. They included political arsonists, discontented servants, peasants eager to seize new land, and soldiers. Among the burns were fires set to free land from legal bondage to the state, and fire as a weapon of guerrilla warfare. If, for example, an intense fire swept a forest of conifers, the land lost the shielding protection of forest laws because it was no longer "forested"; the local population could then log the dead trees and sow the ashy sites. Until title resided in a cadastral survey and not vegetative cover, officially proclaimed forests remained vulnerable to arson.[34]

Wars meanwhile were frequent enough and catastrophic enough to enter into the fire ecology of the region. Both the besieged and the besieger resorted to a scorched earth policy when it advanced their interests. The Gauls burned the woods to halt Caesar's advance, and Romans burned to compel Vercingetorix to retreat. In 970, invading Saracens (or the residents, or both, according to various accounts) burned back the forest to hinder ambushes. Marauding armies and brigands routinely set fire to field and forest. The sixteenth-century wars were especially memorable, with major incendiarism in 1524, 1536, and 1590; the 1536 episode followed from Charles V's determination to break local resistance by burning 300 square kilometers in the Esterel. Eugène de Savoie similarly covered his retreat in 1707 during the rebellion of the Camisards in the Cévennes. Even in World War II the French Resistance (known colloquially as the Maquis) and counterinsurgents fired the countryside, spurring major fire disasters in Var in 1943.[35]

But all this was more or less common throughout the Mediterranean. Unique to France was a national policy on forestry, legislated into the Code Colbert in 1669, that applied the powers of the state to certain land uses. That forest code, in theory, subjected all France to a single law. Just as new lands entered into the French polity as *départements,* so their biotas joined a collective environmental imperium, subject to common practices and expectations. Besides, France had the mistral.

France, in brief, had the Rhone Valley, a thoroughfare for the passage of Mediterranean civilization into the interior and a flume for the violent winds that blew through it in the spring and fall. Climate, people, and mistral—this was the formula that, according to French observers, had baptized Provence in particular as the *Region du feu.* Other Mediterranean provinces with a propensity for large fires had their own winds; but the power of France to abstract and propagate its experiences elevated the mistral and the fires it drove into a platonic type for them all.[36]

Paroxysms like the mistral threatened to whip every hunter's campfire, every field burn beneath groves of chestnuts, every *petit feu* of shepherd and forester into a wave of flame. What prevented this was that the indigenous population so exploited the land that there was little opportunity for a fire to spread. Blowing alone, no matter how fiercely, could not revive the flame of a taper that had burned to the bottom. Like the proverbial wolf the mistral might huff and puff furiously, but good housekeeping meant there was little extraneous tinder, and the land withstood its blows. Ager and saltus, orchard, field, garden, woodlot—all were tended, and when population pressures rose they were gleaned of every twig, pine litter, and dead branch. Peasants coppiced and pollarded even woodlots. Holm oaks were pruned to promote acorns, cork oaks were stripped regularly, and pines were tapped for resin. Shrubs, forbs, and grasses were used for browse and pasture, or foraged for berries, nuts, honey, and cooking and medicinal herbs. Little in the "waste" was in fact wasted.[37]

Population, however, rarely remained stable. When it swelled, land use intensified, conversion to arable expanded even on marginal land, and the harvest of the outfield could strip a land bare, trample it into powder, and instigate soil erosion. Every scrap of growth was used, every tree planted and pruned. Conversely, when population plummeted, the long-suffering indigenous biota reclaimed its old niches. Fourteenth-century plagues sent viticulture into a two-century retreat; sixteenth-century wars prompted an exodus from the mountains. As disease, conflict, social unrest, and changed economies, particularly the rush to industrialize, removed peasants, fields fell into abandonment, old fire barriers overgrew, and fuels went feral. Now, when the mistral found a flame, it could fan it into a conflagration.

Thus, paradoxically, begins a register of large fires, a chronology separate from that of plague or war. By the mid-nineteenth century the peasant economy was no longer self-sufficient, yet no systemic alternative replaced it. Elements of the traditional economy lingered, unpinned from former anchors, while herders laid claim to large extents of Mediterranean France subject to a revanchist maquis. The fire regime metamorphosed, but large fires existed outside the self-contained environments offered by traditional agriculture, as though they were the vents of a renewed volcanism. Abandoned fields no longer served as baffles, and deserted villages no longer sent out firefighters or watched warily over sanctioned burning. Fires were easy to start, difficult to control; and when the mistral rose, benign burns metastasized into a succession of disastrous wildfires that commanded the attention of all France.

The emergent mechanism for control was forestry. Over the centuries France had accumulated a melange of woodlands, some under royal dominion, others under ecclesiastic, communal, or private control. By the mid-seventeenth century cumulative attrition and indifference led to a situation in which the royal forests earned almost nothing, France found itself without adequate stocks of naval timbers, fuelwood was locally short, and overexploitation left woodlands degraded. Any hope of systematic management sank into a quagmire of folk practices, ancient rights of usage, and local exceptionalisms. The prospect alarmed Colbert, who established a commission that studied the question for eight years (1661–69), at which point Louis XIV promulgated its recommendations as the French Forest Ordinance of 1669, commonly known as the Code Colbert, which rationalized and redirected the administration of France's woods.

In goals as well as techniques forestry agreed with agronomy as it sought to maximize profit and serve the state. The law not only undertook the reformation of the royal forests, but instigated, with greater and lesser force, the penetration of eccelesiastical, communal, and even private forests as well. In this way the state had an influence over much of the land not in arable or towns. In fact, because agrarian life linked infield with outfield and self-sufficient communities could not live without both, the reforms could affect the whole ensemble of rural land use. In principle, forestry became an agent in the reconstitution of the French countryside. In practice, that did not occur until industrialization and steam engines began disassembling the economics of peasant life. Then forestry became virulent, and as it claimed more land and oversaw more communal landscapes, it met more and more fire that was no longer contained within the terraced slopes and tight-wrought fields of traditional society.

The French Revolution damaged state forestry and began a reduction, by sale, in the extent of the royal forests. Wildfires and arson were as rampant in the woods as torches in the streets. But reformation began with the establishment of a national forestry school at Nancy in 1824 and the forest law of 1827, which invested in the state Forest Department (Département des Eaux et Forêts) responsibility not only for state lands but also for those belonging to communes and public institutions, and even for some jointly held by public and private owners. The law mandated systematic management, under the direction of state foresters, for any such land capable of regular management. This affected primarily the lands held as village commons. The rural unrest of 1830 often targeted such lands for protest fires. The law of 1859 restricted the rights of even private landowners to deforest, a "striking anomaly" in French jurisprudence.[38]

In France, unlike Britain, enclosure meant a more intensive forestry. The reformers' purpose was primarily economic; they saw the communal woods as timber and resin, not as pannage, kitchen herbs, and leafy fodder. Among the strictest rules were those applied to grazing, and among the most unyielding prohibitions was that against the goat. In fact the law provided for the state to buy outright traditional rights, particularly those related to forest grazing; and as the peasant economy decayed, state foresters either acquired new lands or alienated old practices, the effects being identical. "The aim of the Department," summarized a British observer, "has always been to free the forests from such claims as far as possible." Still, in 1876, 82 percent of wood production was firewood, which meant that most forests remained as coppice.[39]

But as coal and later electricity replaced fuelwood, the conversion to sawtimber accelerated, and the transfer of usage from traditional forms to industrial forestry quickened its pace. The Forest Department also assumed responsibility for damaged lands, notably those in the dunes and heath of Gascony and the slumping summits of the French Alps. By 1877 the forestry service had completed regular working plans for two-thirds of the state forests and almost one-half of communal forests. Those schemes included measures for fire protection. At the forest of Montrieux, Major Frederic Bailey of the British Imperial Forest Service observed in 1877 that "the heads of the Department are anxious to raise a high forest of pines in places of the present crop, but the local officials are opposed to this project, as they are afraid of fires." They had reason to be.[40]

(ii)

As forestry spread, it reconstituted French fire. Regarding burning, the forest code was severe, prohibiting any fires within or adjacent to the protected forests. A law enacted in 1870 imposed even stricter limitations in Maures and Esterel. In 1876 the Forest Department suffered only 290 fires that burned a total of 950 hectares, almost all of that in mediterranean France. However large this loomed in the French imagination, it was vanishingly small by standards outside temperate Europe, and laughably tiny even by comparison with French agriculture. Big fire years followed wars, a further index of social disruption. But already forestry had demonized fire and the Mediterranean alliance between fire and herds, particularly goats. A ban on one was a ban on the other. Foresters often prohibited grazing of any kind on burned lands.[41]

Thus the problem of free-burning fire funneled southward into Languedoc, Var, and especially Provence, where big fires (by French measures) had struck in 1838, 1854, 1856, 1864, 1869, and 1877. Attention focused, in particular, on the forest of Esterel, "famous," as one visiting Briton noted, "as being the one forest in France to protect which from fire the most elaborate measures are taken." It was, according to E. E. Fernandez, conservator of forests for British India, "the model for the whole country." Even Americans were impressed, and one considered its infrastructure "much the best example of intensive Federal fire protection" in France. The details are worth exploring.[42]

In 1885 a group of British students and Major Frederic Bailey from the Forest School (along with "Mr. Takasima, a Japanese gentleman studying at the school") left Nancy for a tour of Provence and the Cévennes. They traveled by rail—already steam was supplanting mules for transport, as locomotives were replacing transhumant flocks and as steam-powered trade was redefining the cultural geography of forests. The landscapes they encountered, while undergoing rapid change, were fine-grained mosaics of public and private holdings, biotic patches as intensively cultivated as gardens. Even the sacred grove at Sainte-Baume, which stuck out amid the Provençal countryside like the Taj Mahal in the Gangetic plains (so "extraordinary," Bailey remarked, that "we could imagine ourselves suddenly transported back to Nancy"), there were "signs of ancient cultivation within the forest." The landscape bore the evidence of human handiwork everywhere. Gardens, woodlots, and terraced fields gleamed in the bright sun like refurbished monuments; even weeds resembled a kind of environmental graffiti. The only whiff of wildness they experienced came from a "night somewhat disturbed by the roaring of lions in a menagerie hard by."[43]

If less profuse outside Sainte-Baume's spring-fed grotto, other niches abounded. The group saw Scots and Aleppo pines, oaks, chestnuts, arbutus, grasses, heath, juniper, "green herbs," vines, cereals, olive orchards, oleander, broom, fields of "everlastings" exported "for making funeral wreaths," and arborescent heather whose grubbed-up roots were fashioned into "briar" wood pipes (from the French *bruyère,* or heather). Commercial trees were planted, grafted, and pruned. Officials preferred pine and, where it could grow, cork oak because of its value on the international market; locals wanted oak coppice for fuelwood and charcoal. Still, even as silviculture busily replaced horticulture, it nevertheless retained an agronomic ideal, and even though foresters might dispute which woods and techniques offered the best return on investment, they suffered no confusion over goals. There was no place for reckless burning.

The group halted at Esterel for a special lecture on fire protection. "Until we came to the Maures and Esterel," Bailey noted, "we had no idea that forest fires were such a serious question in any part of France, or that such complete arrangements existed for their suppression." But the economic forces that had propelled forestry into prominence had also, by unraveling traditional agriculture, created conditions that promoted wildfire. Temperate France could tolerate indifference; under the whine of the mistral, mediterranean France could not. Preliminary reforms began in 1869. After the great fires of 1870 a full-blown reconstruction occurred under the lash of new ordinances, including a special fire code for France's mediterranean *départements*. The resulting arrangements "might well serve as a model of how such things should be done in India."[44]

Fire protection resembled an army of occupation. People, after all, were the source of fires, either through carelessness or arson. Suppressing fire was not unlike suppressing popular unrest. The 1870 law (and 1883 amendment) prohibited anyone for burning within 183 meters of a forest boundary, or outside the designated season, and even then only with proper permits. Incendiary fires were punishable by imprisonment at forced labor for life, although, as one student observed, the penal code was "more terrifying on the statute books than in actual enforcement." Still, fires would occur. Elaborating on existing roads and paths, foresters laid out firebreaks from 15 to 40 meters wide. Some they cleared completely, even grubbing out roots, while in others they spared the commercially valuable cork oaks. The cut debris was burned either inside the lines or in piles outside. This elaborate labor broke up fuels, furnished lines for counterattacks and backfires, and provided rapid access to all points of the forest. Neighboring landowners had also to maintain firebreaks.[45]

But structuralism alone did not fight fires. During fire season, foresters maintained constant vigilance from hilltop lookouts and conducted ceaseless patrols. When a guard spotted a fire, he attacked it, and if he could not control it, he appealed for help. The telephone allowed for rapid communication. If the assembled forest guards could not control the fire, officials sounded the alarm to neighboring villages, who were compelled by law to assist. If this failed, officials turned to the army, who could dispatch "several companies of soldiers" within a few hours of a summons from the prefect. If direct attack failed, crews counterfired. A prolonged campaign required that officials requisition "wine and eatables" from local villages.[46]

The most curious practice, however—"believed to be peculiar to the Maures and the Esterel," Bailey thought—was the system of *petits feux,* or small fires. Foresters divided areas into vertical strips, and then burned a strip from the top down, beginning with those adjacent to the cleared firebreaks. Each year, in December, January, or February, a new strip was burned (the whole cycle requiring six or seven years), and sometimes more frequently "to prevent the undergrowth of shrubs from becoming so dense and tall, that the entry of an accidental fire would be attended with disastrous consequences." Typical patches were one or two acres in size. If the fires torched thickets of young pine, that was no loss because working plans sought to promote oak. (The biota was as sultry as the peasantry; the serotinous-coned pines seeded the burned sites with ferocious prodigality—"impossible," one observer thought, "to raise a finer crop of pines than that which follows the fire.") The *petit feu*, however, made the work of attacking conflagrations an "easy matter." Obviously the practice had evolved out of agricultural traditions, and inevitably intellectuals condemned it. The "lecture-hall at Nancy," Bailey repeated approvingly, railed against the practice as "'detestable from all points of view.'"[47]

In the end the Esterel exemplar was ambivalent. Everyone agreed that fire protection was outstanding, the finest in Europe. No other country, temperate or mediterranean, had anything like it within its national territory. But the land base after all was small. In 1897 the forest of Esterel comprised 6,744 hectares. Most forests in mediterranean France, state and communal, were smaller. Large fires could transcend political boundaries, so that a single conflagration might engulf a whole forest; this, however, the patchy landscape usually prohibited. The 1877 fire season that so staggered officials consisted of forty-eight fires and 6,420 hectares.

Moreover, while the resurgent maquis and afforestation grew, they did so along with the Forest Department. If industrial silviculture replaced traditional agriculture, then foresters had to replace peasants. If intensive cultivation failed to tend fuels, then fires flared uncontrollably. In this way large fires returned in 1918 and 1919 after the war years had restricted the labor the Forest Department could invest in its programs. After further bouts of fire and further decay of village life, major reorganizations followed in 1924. In particular, officials sought to replace the communal cooperation of villagers with formal "syndicates," private associations of landowners who could supplement fire protection under the supervision of the Forest Department. Still, the fires continued, any tear in the fabric of land use ripped wide by the mistral.[48]

So, while foreigners admired the French solution, they questioned its costs and doubted its universality. E. E. Fernandez observed sardonically that the French fire reformation began *after* that of British India, and at least in India, "we are so far ahead of the French or every European country, in the matter of protection against fire" that comparisons were silly. American francophiles like Theodore Woolsey, Jr., and William Greeley concurred. "Even costly protection has frequently failed and large areas have been burned," Woolsey admitted. The real secret—the essence of the French strategy—was that *"it is only by the clearance of brush and debris throughout the forest that crown fires are prevented."* Further, "unquestionably the fire prevention and fighting practice in the United States is on a greater scale and is farther advanced than in Europe." Apart from a demonstration that intensive cultivation can reduce the fuels that power wildfires, an extremely labor-intensive and expensive practice, France had far more to learn from Britain's colonial foresters and America's novices than they did from France.[49]

But of course the French solution was important to France. Sir David Hutchins, a proud graduate of Nancy, once declared that "all Foresters should be armed and soldiers of the State," sensible precautions against incendiary "marauders." For France, this injunction was literally true. Its foresters held commissions in the military; the students at Nancy received military instruction and drilling; in the event of war, the Forest Corps became an integral part of the army; and "in virtue of this service, a military uniform is prescribed for all grades." Of course fire protection put down social and economic insurrection at home; but France's real firefighting was done in its colonial wars. Languedoc and Provence were only bridgeheads to a wider conflict that spanned the Mediterranean Sea itself.[50]

(iii)

At one time in the geologic past, Corsica resided next to Côte d'Azur. It shared the same geology, and boasted the same flora and fauna. Then tectonic forces pivoted both it and Sardinia squarely into the western Mediterranean. By the Holocene, Corsica resembled a granitic castle surrounded by an immense moat. The island was wholly Mediterranean in character. It shared in the Neolithic colonizations that brought early agriculture to the region, evolved a typical Mediterranean economy, and became a port of call for every imperial venture into the western Mediterranean, from the Phoenicians and Etruscans to the Pisans and Genoese.[51]

Throughout, the Corsicans held to a fiercely rebellious temperament, originally communal, increasingly individualistic. Seneca's judgment stood as an epigraph for centuries: "Their first law is to revenge themselves, their second to live by plunder, their third to lie, and the fourth to deny the gods." Insurrection played out in the mountains as well as in politics. Wearied of yet another rebellion, Genoa sold the island to France in 1768. But what France stormed by purchase, it had to hold by force. It suppressed the latest insurrection, lost the island to Britain in 1794, and then regained it when Corsica's best-known native son, Napoleon Bonaparte, returned in 1796.

Here was a *département* that was segregated from continental France and that held an indigenous population more intractable than the peasants of Languedoc or the shepherds of Var. In principle Corsica became wholly integrated with France, and acquired French institutions along with the French language. In practice what didn't sink before it reached the docks at Ajaccio often burned up on the slopes of Mount Cinto. Corsica remained the one *département* that never recorded customary law. The old customs, often intensely communal, decayed without an institutional equivalent to replace them. Instead the Corsican came to exemplify a brutal individualism, aptly symbolized by the replacement of the long-dominant swine by the free-ranging goat as the basis of the island's pastoralism. So likewise with the island's fires. No longer tempered by tradition, burning flourished in vindictive and feckless forms. Corsica occupied the epicenter of western Mediterranean incendiarism, the notorious *zone rouge*.[52]

Metropolitan forestry was forced into compromise, as were other transplanted French institutions. Much of the incessant trespass and burning that exasperated foresters derived from traditional uses that persisted without traditional controls or that continued anachronistically—anarchically—amid a slowly industrializing economy. Lopping birch branches for goat feed, tapping pines for medicinal resin, stealing green wood for fuel, and burning to stimulate pasture were typical violations. So too was the destruction of signs, especially those proclaiming prohibitions. Equally symptomatic, Corsicans refused to convict offenders. Of 598 arrests made in 1911, an average year, 314 (52 percent) resulted in acquittal. Strict enforcement of forest law was impossible, and granted the inaccessibility of the higher mountains, intensive forestry was unnecessary. In particular, the valence between grazing and fire proved unshakable. An attempt in 1834 to regulate grazing in accordance with Nancy-style prescriptions led to armed opposition. Foresters backed down, though with inevitable face-saving gestures. Critics from the metropole, like Charles de Ribbé, denounced the "savage habits" of the Corsicans, but to little practical effect. The Corsicans ignored his words as fully as they did the foresters' posted prohibitions.[53]

Indigenous fires, in fact, forced forestry to change from the sanctioned regular (high forest) to more irregular (selection) methods. In 1900, Corsica's conservator of forests attributed the cause to "the fires, unfortunately so frequent in Corsica." Those remorseless fires, "disastrous and deadly," savaged the young and even-aged stands promoted by the high forest method. Only a less regimented silviculture, one that let the forest reseed from resistant resident trees, could survive. A friendly observer euphemistically remarked that forest administration was hampered "by an unruly population, by over-grazing, by fires, and, in past years, by lack of communication." Other accommodations to indigenes followed. Grazing trespass, an American observed in the 1920s, "is winked at in order to induce the local population not to set fires." This scheme, of course, only perpetuated the local regime.[54]

Every activity of Corsican rural life seemingly involved fire, and every fire defied the efforts of foresters to integrate Corsica into the national institutions of France. Fire protection was thus indispensable to reform, and its failure was an index of social pathologies. Compared with those of mediterranean France the methods in Corsica were, friendly critics concluded, "crude." Firelines, although of "unquestioned value," were too expensive and were maintained only with trespass labor. There were patrols, but no lookout towers, telephones, toolboxes, or program of public education. Foresters denounced the rural society with which they contended, compromised with its desires, and sought only to contain its worst outrages—the extraordinary conflagrations rather than the

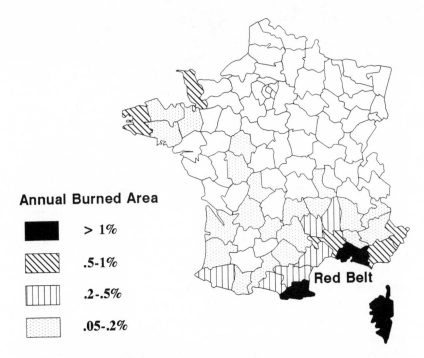

Imperial France. (Above) The geography of French fire: there is a patch of burning associated with the Brittany heaths, but otherwise the fires are concentrated in the south, most spectacularly on Corsica. (Facing page, top) The pattern of burned area in the Département du Var. Large fires tend to be associated with episodes of strong winds (mistral) and of social breakdown. (Facing page, bottom) The fire history of Algeria, 1890–1945. Despite some years of relative calm, the pattern is one of consistent outbreaks, not lessened by decades of colonial and civil wars after World War II. No quantitative summaries exist for the fires of 1853 and 1871, but they were recorded as "very important," and likely exceeded 150,000 ha each. (Data from *Revue Forestière Française* 1990, Seigue 1972, and Boudy 1948)

common burnings, the endless fires set from "incendiarism, burning brush, personal vengeance against guards after lawsuits, camp fires followed by high winds." The Marmano forest was typical: "the fires have run over the entire forest and the butts of almost all the large trees are charred by fires." The attempt to install a shelterwood system "proved a failure," officials conceded, "because of fires." The Vizzavona forest had its postlogging regeneration "wiped out by fire" in 1866. The forest reburned in 1896. Forestry could not control fire until it controlled Corsicans, and could not suppress one without the other. Forestry accommodated Corsican fire the way Sicily did the Mafia.[55]

This modus vivendi finally broke down completely when, along with the

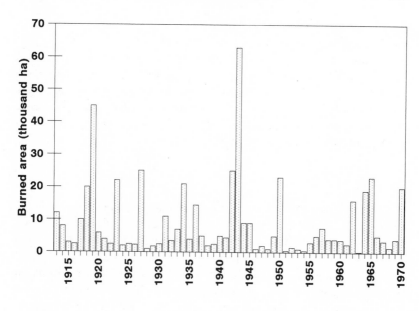

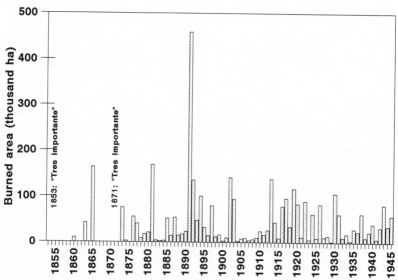

rest of the Mediterranean in the post–World War II era, Corsica's traditional economy could no longer withstand a wider market, resist urbanization, or repel tourism. However decayed, traditional practices had, like stone walls, helped contain the ubiquitous burning. Now those walls had fallen to rubble, the fires grew larger, and the efforts at containment shrank. Even within the context of the Mediterranean, the caldera of modern European wildfire, Corsica was infamous for the frequency and viciousness of its fires.

Wildfires attacked the new agents of reform as they had those of the past. In 1989, fires drove panicky tourists into boats. Two others died, trapped in a car; more than 10,000 hectares burned. Year by year the scenes repeated. Increasingly fires simply ate away at Corsica itself, like woodland maggots. Untrammeled burning looked less like Corsica's traditional sullenness than an act of self-immolation.[56]

(iv)

But at least Corsica was small, its failures hidden within elaborate administrative apparatus, and publicly French. The Maghreb was none of these. Tunisia, Morocco, and above all Algeria, however, boasted fire regimes that occupying France could not ignore and that instead it often enflamed. France could not dismiss its prolonged and fiery Algerian conflict as quaint, Corsican-like exceptionalism; inhabited Algeria was four-fifths the size of France. Collectively North Africa would test the militant commitment and methods of French foresters, whose success depended on fire control as fully as colonization did on military conquest.[57]

Between the Maghreb and southern France there were obvious continuities, almost an eerie symmetry, in climate and biota. Even the mistral had a twin in the desiccating sirocco that rushed northward out of the Sahara. From the Aurès Mountains, which come to a blunt point in Tunisia, the region flared out westward into two parallel chains of mountains spanned by a plateau. The terrain was high enough to capture sufficient moisture to support something like a Mediterranean economy. In ancient times the littoral had been a granary for the Roman Empire. Fire flourished under similar circumstances and to similar purposes as it did in the northern Mediterranean. Fire was endemic for swidden cultivation, fallow fields, and of course for pasture. Sheep, goats, and camels supplemented arable. The Maghreb was Provence or Corsica on the scale of Turkey.

But unlike mediterranean France, which pointed to temperate Europe, the Maghreb resembled an elevated island between the uncultivatable Mediterranean Sea and the sands of the Sahara. Its geography carried overland traffic primarily along an east-west axis, from one part of the Mediterranean or its neighboring deserts and steppes to another. Century by century invaders had passed through. Beginning with the Arabs in the seventh century, those invaders were uniformly Muslims and pastoralists.

Until the French. The French stumbled into Algeria in 1830 through a comic-opera diplomacy of insults, real or contrived, that led to punitive raids, and then through tragic escalation into a ferocious scorched earth campaign. Torch supplemented rifle. "We have burned everything, destroyed everything," exulted Louis-Adolphe Saint-Arnaud. When 500 Arabs, men, women, and children, sought refuge in a cave, the French kindled large fires at the mouth until all but ten died of asphyxiation. Later they repeated the tactic and killed 1,500. By 1837, France had conquered all of Algeria except Oran. After it finally fell in 1847, Algeria was divided into three *départements* and France undertook a putative assimilation. When he rose to protest this unwise adventurism, Baron Lacuée spoke prophetically in fire metaphors. "As long as you keep Algiers, you will be constantly at war with Africa; sometimes war will seem to end; but these people will not hate you any the less; it will be a half-extinguished fire that will smoulder under the ash and which, at the first opportunity, will burst into a vast conflagration."[58]

The legacy of France's conquest by fire was often more fire. Armed insurrection faded, but protest continued sub rosa. The battle shifted to the mountains and high plateau; foresters supplemented legionnaires. In the Tell, the mountainous littoral in which European colonization flourished, wildfires consumed 2,590 square kilometers of forest between 1861 and 1873, and "the damage done," a British forester proclaimed, was "enormous." That was only a down payment. By World War I it was estimated that over 1.2 million hectares of reserved forest had been burned over "one or more times during the past 40 years." And these statistics applied to official forests, not fields or uncultivated bush. Even so, the result was, as one sympathetic critic noted wryly, "not exactly a picture of well-preserved forest wealth!"[59]

There was more to come as French Algeria rushed to its fiery conclusion with almost Cartesian logic. While France pursued a program of aggressive colonization, indigenous fire practices became scrambled, and traditional fire control collapsed. With pacification, Europeans swept into Algeria and claimed or created farms, while foresters began demarking Algerian woodlands, particularly cork oak, for commercial exploitation; both acts pushed the resident Arab pastoralists aside. (Tellingly, officials prohibited agricultural colonization on reserved forests, allowing it only on former pastures.) Previously grazing had been a medley of village husbandry, transhumance, and outright nomadism in which whole tribes wandered in search of fodder. Previous conquests had exchanged arable for pasture, and kneaded new pastoralists into the existing dough.

The French conquest, however, reconverted quality pasture back into arable, and transformed that once-stable pastoral mosaic into a twisted kaleidoscope, constantly churning the pieces into temporary new patterns. In accord with both long tradition and economic necessity, the displaced graziers moved into the mountains. In protest they fired the reserved forests; to create new pastures, they burned across the mountains and especially the high plateau; to stimulate a further flush of forage from marginal land, they put whatever they could reach to the torch, and they burned as often as they could.

In the twentieth century the numbers swelled—of humans, of herds, of fires. Displaced peoples abraded against one another, and the friction created further fire. Open rebellion inspired still more fire. What the French seized with military firepower, Algerians began to reclaim with pastoral fire. Algeria threatened to become a permanently scorched earth.

Foresters arrived early on the scene. A graduate of Nancy, Victor Renou, toured French Algeria in the late 1830s and in 1842 published a comprehensive review of forestry's prospects; an embryonic Algerian Forest Service followed in 1843. Until then (and for some time afterward) the police and military dealt with fires. The forestry bureau remained under the Director of Finances. French officials tempered outrage with fiscal caution, for the forests existed to produce revenue. ("The budget is based upon the revenue rather than upon an ideal.") Not land but cork forests, and later Aleppo pines suitable for resin, were the objects of concern. No official was prepared to exceed the market value of those woodlands with massive investments in firefighting.

The consolidation of Algeria led to a reorganization and centralization of the Forest Service in 1849. The military regime meanwhile promulgated several edicts regarding burning. Then major fires broke out around La Calle (El Kala) and Philippeville (Skikda) in 1853, and shocked the authorities into further reform. Circulars sought to punish the culpable tribes and to deny them access to the burned land, either for wood or pasture. But other fires erupted in 1860, and major conflagrations in 1863 and 1865 despite the threat of military reprisals. More commissions, more reports, more resolve to act; foresters made the comparisons between Provence and North Africa explicit. Then, while the Franco-Prussian War distracted the French army in 1870–71, major incendiary fires swept the Tell and Algerian littoral as part of yet another insurrection that ran through 1871 and into 1872. As if seeking to make the linkage even more precise, wildfires afflicted both France and, with staggering damages, Algeria. The war and fires ended the Second Empire's experiments in Algerian forestry.[60]

The Forest Service reorganized in December 1873, following further study. After the debacle of the Franco-Prussian War, colonial officials were not inclined to tolerate any challenge to French arms, French rules, or French honor. In a sense, a reconstituted Algerian Forest Service would compensate for the march of German troops down the Champs-Élysées with patrols through the Great Kabylia, and for the surrender of Sedan with renewed defense of the Ouars cork forests. After all, Algeria was a *département* of France subject to the Interior Ministry, not, as were Tunisia and Morocco, colonies administered through the Foreign Ministry. Capping the reforms was the Forest Law of 1874.

At its reformist core was an elaborate fire code. The reforms invested the governor-general with special powers, but to preserve the power of the metropole an 1881 law stipulated that all the laws and rules that applied in France applied also in Algeria except where superseded by specific local legislation. Similarly, the Algerian Forest Service, initially autonomous, became incorporated into the French Forest Department. Practices followed precepts. French foresters countered Algerian fire with the Provence ensemble of fire protection, adjusting where necessary. In the case of Algeria, unlike Corsica, France was prepared to enact new codes and create special institutions; but in the Maghreb, unlike Corsica, it was not willing to adapt prescriptions to local circumstances. If France passed special fire codes cognizant of Algerian peculiarities, as the 1874 code was in principle, it was unwilling to compromise their enforcement. Intolerance did nothing to help tailor often ill-fitted regulations. As a result "trespass," especially in the form of grazing, became "the bane of the Algerian Forest Service"; and the incendiary burning of graziers and warriors established the prevailing fire regime.[61]

The methods of Provence, however, often worked poorly on the much vaster scale of the Maghreb and amid its more sullen population. Certainly firebreaks and roads alone were inadequate, and firefighting was often too late and too expensive. Instead the Algerian Forest Department sought to enlist, or where necessary forcibly conscript, the local population into prevention and suppression. Regardless, large fires continued; in 1881 a wave of incendiarism returned to Philippeville and Jemmapes and shattered any pretense that the reforms had ended the fire menace.[62]

There were further amendments to the code in 1885 and, following a forest commission established in 1900, substantial administrative reorganization and a revision and codification of forest law in 1903. As officials reviewed findings, two years of conflagrations—the largest fires since 1881—roared across the countryside. Clearly fire protection was as indispensable to the orderly administration of forests as police were to the administrative order of society. With considerable understatement, that ever-sympathetic American, Theodore Woolsey, Jr., admitted that "protection has not been altogether successful."[63]

The law addressed a spectrum of concerns. One thrust tried to prevent damaging fires, notably those set by pastoralists. The code prohibited burning of any kind on any forests, public or private, anywhere between July and November. Nor was burning allowed within four kilometers of any forest. Outside of this season, burning required official permission and requisite precautions to prevent escape. The complementary thrust was toward fire suppression. If a fire broke out, any persons, "European or Native," could be impressed into firefighting service. Incendiarism was punished not only by individual penalties but by additional sanctions against the entire tribe. If a forest burned, even rightholders could not graze livestock on the land for at least six years. And when fires "appear to have been lighted intentionally," forest officials could consider them "as resulting from acts of insurrection, and the lands of the offending tribe can be confiscated."[64]

But a new code that enforced the old outrages did not cool incendiary tempers. Criticism was so immediate that Governor Jonnart agreed to assemble a commission of inquiry in 1904. Addressing the commission, he urged a "permanent *entente cordiale*." Anyone with the slightest authority, he insisted, should be "zealous in the defense" of the Forest Department. Yet he chided the foresters for their too-rigorous attention to the "letter of the laws and regulations," and their indifference to the laws' "spirit" and the "higher interests of Algerian policy." Since forest administration was inseparable from fire protection, he urged the foresters to "never lose sight of the fact that the surest way to avoid fires is still to interest the natives in the existence of the forest, and to associate them in their conservation." Suppleness not rigor, flexibility not fanaticism—there had to be some place made for the indigenes and their fires. Further revisions in 1906 sought that toleration.[65]

It didn't happen. The French laid down their lines (literally) and held to them. Thus there was scant effort to accommodate local custom or adapt to local fire practices. Indigenous fire, like the indigenes, was to be swept off the land. So ferocious was the burning that even backfiring became suspect. "It is going too far," the Algerian Forest Commission declaimed, "when each native, each neighbor, each mayor or administrator, or each forest employee should assume the right of starting a new fire under the pretext of backfiring and of saving his hut, his property, his commune, or his beat."[66]

The real cancer, however, was the character of colonization. So long as European settlement continued to displace but not eliminate the indigenous peoples, fires would erupt at every point of friction. With nowhere to move, indigenes created space (and pasture) by burning. As France added Tunisia and then Morocco to its North African protectorate, these adjacent colonies, also part of the Maghreb, experienced nothing like the hopeless incendiarism endemic in Algeria. But they were French colonies, not French national territory. Colonies could tolerate some fire, while the metropole could not. In Tunisia, especially, French-styled fire protection enjoyed success.[67]

The commissions of the 1900–1904, the 1903 code, and its 1906 amendment concluded the "heroic age" of Algerian forestry and announced a more elaborate successor. For a while the fire scene stabilized. Then in 1913 conflagrations returned, biotic tremors like the earthquakes along the North African thrust zone. Excepting 1915, when wet weather dampened burning, the outbreak continued throughout the war years. The association of fire and war was hardly coincidental. The war encouraged heavy exploitation of the forests, reduced the capacity of the Forest Department to clear firebreaks, patrol, and dispose of slash, and diverted the military. Fires resulted, just as they did in metropolitan France.

Eventually the situation again stabilized until the Second World War reinvigorated the cycle. Vichy France suffered its worst fire seasons in centuries, the burned area even surpassing that of Algeria. In this case, however, it was the French who were the subject people, and the guerrilla war between the Resistance and the Nazis that stoked the flames. When the war ended, Paul Boudy's massive compendium of French forestry in North Africa concluded with words that eerily mimicked those that had begun the adventure. "Of all the dangers that menace the forests of North Africa," he intoned, none did such "irremedial damage" as fire, and unless the state addressed the real root of the problem, the scrambled land tenure surrounding forests, fire would continue its implacable destruction.[68]

Soon afterward the French imperium began to disintegrate. Relations in Algeria worsened, then culminated in a wretched civil war—another exercise in scorched earth—that carried incendiarism from the mountains to the city and even to the metropole. Incendiary bombs and napalm replaced fire drill and flint. Algerian guerrillas firebombed cafés and barracks; French military aircraft firebombed the backcountry and pine forests as putative rebel strongholds. When war finally ended in 1962, France had withdrawn from the Maghreb, French imperialism in Indochina and Madagascar had collapsed, French Africa had reconstituted itself into a shadow commonwealth of *la Francophonie,* and France was reconstructing its lost glories through the lurid megalomania of Charles de Gaulle. The battle lines withdrew to the metropole.[69]

By then, however, France no longer qualified as a global firepower. Even as fires etched the hills, exurbanites like Peter Mayle were reclaiming mediterranean France. This time, aircraft dropped water and retardant instead of napalm, but an old man could observe, "C'est comme la guerre, eh?" So, for France, it had always been.[70]

(v)

It was an accident of history—France's permanent acquisition of Mediterranean lands in the fifteenth century, and its centralizing tendencies (and pursuit of a self-proclaimed "mission to civilize")—that had distinguished France from the rest of temperate Europe. In hilly Provence, northern purposes fused with southern facts. Not only that, French forestry here succeeded in promoting solutions as a Cartesian QED of fire protection. With modifications—some admitted, some ignored—France propagated the ensemble southward, encountering more Mediterranean landscapes before leaping into such unlikely locales as the Ivory Coast, Madagascar, Réunion, and Indochina. Everywhere the French met fire. But similar encounters had characterized, and similar diffusions had seeped through, the much larger British empire, Russia's dominions in Siberia and the Far East, and even America's Trans-Mississippi West.

What made a difference was the power not only to propagate but to propagandize. Part of this was institutional, the national forestry school at Nancy, and part was the power of French forestry journals. But much derived from the character of French scholarship. The ambition of the metropole to centralize had a cultural counterpart in the desire of its intellectuals to consolidate and universalize according to first principles. They know everything, as critics have remarked of the graduates of the *grandes écoles;* and they know nothing else. That extended to fire.

In 1938, Georges Kuhnholtz-Lordat published a textbook, *La Terre Incendiée,* that was the first study, and for a long time the only one, that pretended to the status of a global survey of fire. Its audience was the students of agronomy at the Colonial Institute at Montpellier. Of course the book depended exclusively on French sources, its scope was that defined by the French imperium, and its science a pure strain of the European agronomic tradition. But if Kuhnholtz-Lordat, a botanist at the National Agricultural School, condemned fire, he also introduced the concept of a "pyrophyte," and if he measured every fire practice against French norms, he nonetheless introduced a comparative perspective that had no equivalent elsewhere. When the book was published, French fire science was as good as any in the world, and French fire protection as broadly experienced as anywhere. After the war, that changed.[71]

Fire science and fire technologies shifted, perhaps permanently, from the metropole to the periphery. Former European colonies in possession of large, and largely vacant, public wildlands became the focus of global attention. North America, in particular, dominated the arena of international fire. English, not French, became the lingua franca of fire science; American hotshot crews and air tankers, not peasant-grubbed firebreaks, established the technical standards for aggressive firefighting; Southern California, not Provence, became the type case for mediterranean fire ecology; aerial firefighting in Alaska, not patrols in Maures, served as the model for modernization, the ambition of developing countries as they sought a fire protection system that moved beyond traditional practices. Even within the Mediterranean proper, France had competitors, as Spain, Portugal, Italy, and Greece geared up to study fire's effects and sent CL-215 aircraft to attack fire's unwelcome resurgence. To America went students, from Canada came air tankers. Beyond the metropole, Esterel was a forgotten curiosity, a museum piece like a Louis XIV chair.

Yet France endured, France rebuilt, France returned. Almost uniquely among temperate Europe, fire ecology flourished. Outside of France fire scientists north of the Mediterranean could be counted on the fingers of one hand; in France, they held teaching posts and staffed institutes. As fires recycled back to the Mediterranean, French forestry modernized its firefighting forces, joined regional organs for fire management, and hosted symposia. Throughout, France tried to reclaim the renown it had enjoyed a century earlier.

Probably it could achieve that aspiration within the context of western Europe. Within the world, it could not. However chauvinistic, Kuhnholtz-Lordat could legitimately construct a cross section of fire ecology throughout the Francophile globe; his successors could not. Steady research on the Ivory Coast could not compensate for lost access in Asia, or disinterest in the Americas, Europe, and the rest of Africa. Where North Americans surveyed fire-seared mountains and conflagrations that burned half of Yellowstone National Park, French ecologists scrutinized fire-germinated seeds on sites the size of kitchen gardens. When Americans finally converted to the virtues of prescribed fire and became the international oracle for controlled burning as well as for high-tech fire control, the French searched through their national past and gratefully rediscovered a Gallic precedent in the *petit feu.*

Petit feu, indeed.

MEDITERRANEAN MINIATURE:
CYPRUS

The Mediterranean looked inward as well as out. If imperial France's leap across the western Mediterranean invites one summary of regional fire history, the Mediterranean islands dramatize another. Where centrifugal France bound the Mediterranean to temperate Europe and arid Africa, and then to the dispersed landscapes of a far-flung globe, the centripetal islands distilled, concentrating lessons like boiled resin. What happened to the region happened also to its islands and with greater intensity.

Those islands were both generic and unique. The character of Mediterranean land use did not penalize the islands for their smaller dimensions. The littoral-encrusting settlements of the Mediterranean were intricate ensembles, often on the scale of villages replicated one after another. Only in special circumstances such as the Spanish *meseta* or the micro-islands of the Aegean did the scale of land impose another order. Instead, the larger islands like Corsica, Sardinia, Sicily, Crete, and Cyprus captured all the elements of standard agriculture, from littoral to mountain. They were no more isolated from the larger civilization than many subregions for which the sea, not the land, provided transportation. Empires claimed them as they did such trunk-grafted hinterlands as Gaul. Many were only peninsulas one step further removed. They housed similar species, knew similar histories, experienced similar cycles of conquest. They were miniatures of Mediterranean history.

Yet they were different from the mainland, just as Turkey, Spain, Greece,

Italy, and the Maghreb were each distinct. What the islands experienced they intensified. There was no surrounding landscape to buffer major disturbances, no prospect for a seepage of species between one valley and another, no easy release from pressures pushing toward degradation, no ready diffusion of defiance. Islands were more easily convulsed; their recovery more onerous; their character more readily dominated by one feature or phenomenon, be it pastoralism, war, or population flux. Italy could absorb volcanoes like Vesuvius; an Aegean island like Thera could not, and in fact was obliterated by an eruption around 1638 B.C.

Islands became, repeatedly, centers of indifference to imperial wishes if not of outright hostility. If each island does not contain all the history of the Mediterranean, neither is any regional history complete without them. The littoral was the essence of the Mediterranean. Islands had at least that attribute, though some had nothing more. For that reason they are a kind of synecdoche of the Mediterranean environment, a cameo of its fire history.

(i)

Their isolation was relative. Some islands had once joined with the mainland, later to be wrenched apart by tectonic forces as happened with Corsica, Sardinia, and the Balearics, or were isolated by rising seas like Euboea, the Ionian islands, and many clusters in the Aegean. Some sprang from volcanoes, or were thrust up along plate boundaries. The recurring desiccation of the Mediterranean converted sea into land, although the fierce salt playas posed terrestrial barriers as formidable as the marine one that preceded and replaced them. Still, it was possible for the Mediterranean biota to populate the islands, however selectively. The littoral, not the lands behind it, was the interstitial tissue of its historical geography.

By Holocene times the islands overflowed with a relict flora and fauna, fractions of which had assumed exotic forms. Until the arrival of humans, none of the islands possessed major predators. The indigenous fauna evolved weirdly, with many small mainland species becoming huge and many large species downsizing dramatically. Hedgehogs, shrews, swans, and dormice swelled into giants, while deer, antelope, macaque, and hippos became dwarfs. Malta boasted three species of elephant, the largest seven feet high and the smallest only three. The flora likewise showed distortions. Crete held a relict population that dated back through five million years of isolation; Rhodes, possibly one million years; some Aegean islands, 20,000. Almost half of the Cretan flora (700 species) derives from that founding ensemble.[72]

Then humans stormed ashore. The chronology of colonization is not certain, for its record (even on the land) is a vast palimpsest in which each new text erased and overwrote the old. Undoubtedly there were contacts in Paleolithic times and possibly some seasonal if not permanent settlements during the Mesolith. Effective colonization, however, arrived only with the Neolithic complex, much of which dispersed throughout the basin by sea. The larger, near-coast islands felt the impact first, and the western Mediterranean earlier and more broadly than the eastern. Because the Mediterranean looked inward, its islands were not on the periphery, leading to dark unknown seas, but fell within the crenulated shadows of the great littoral, marking routes of travel like cairns, subdividing the larger basin into smaller units like so many witness trees, offering more valleys, bays, and mountain niches into which humans could insinuate their evolving flocks and seeds. No islands failed to succumb to the dominion of the humanized Mediterranean. By the Bronze Age few stood outside the Neolithic's evolving revolution in land use. A century or two before Homer, colonists had claimed them all.

Proportionately, colonization proceeded more rapidly in the western Mediterranean. Between the sixth and fourth millennia B.C. colonization seized more than half the islands' total landmass. The eastern Mediterranean did not achieve parity until the fourth and third millennia. One reason is simply the difference in constituent sizes. Six islands—biotic baronies, microcontinents almost—contribute virtually all (99 percent) of the western landmass. They were also relatively close to mainlands, or once had been. Their size reduced scale effects that were often critical to the flakes of land that speckled the Aegean, not all of which were able to sustain a viable agrarian population and instead depended on trade for sustenance. On the larger islands the whole panoply of Mediterranean agriculture could establish itself. Transhumance could evolve on Sardinia and Corsica on roughly the scale it did in Provence or the eastern Pyrenees.[73]

The shock wave hit many islands like the ancient tsunami that, by sinking the Cretan fleet, may have broken their cultural hegemony of Minoan civilization. Some of the relic biota survived, some adapted, some expired. Colonists leavened native flora with cultigens, native fauna with domesticates, and perturbed the remainder with new regimes of cutting, browsing, and burning. Endemism survived but at reduced rates—8 percent for Corsica and Sardinia, for example; 7 percent for the Balearics. The exotic megafauna—the pygmy hippo, the giant dormouse, the dwarf deer—vanished. In their place stood the tethered goat and milch cow, or roamed flocks of swine and sheep. Some went wild, to repopulate islands with mouflon devolved from sheep, for example. Roughly a third of Crete's flora descended directly from anthropogenic sources; but all of it responded to the patterns and whims of this congenital disrupter.[74]

The disturbances differed, too, both in character and timing. The islands had known major droughts, deluges, earthquakes, vulcanism, fire, and other convulsions, and had adapted to them. But humans introduced additional perturbations, just as they did novel flora and fauna. As maritime civilizations spread, they came into conflict with one another, and fought over island colonies. Carthage and Rome carried the Punic wars, for example, to Sicily and Sardinia as well as to Nubia and Tuscany. Desperate for arable land, Carthage made reforestation in its Sardinian colony a capital offense. Eager to make secure its title to acquired Sicily, Rome gave the island over to pastoralism. Populations rose, fell, poured in, or emigrated according to wars, plagues, treaties, and the economics of trade.

The islands experienced disturbance regimes that had their origins in the political economy of commerce; in religion, ambition, fear, and miscalculation; in unrest or disease in the mother polity, all of which stood far outside the ancient parameters of island ecology. The demand for sugar cane, the devastation wrought in vineyards by *Phylloxera,* competition for cotton, mines opened and closed, trade routes lost and reclaimed, taxes and debased currencies—all influenced the terraces that clawed up hillsides, the preference for sheep or goats, and the survival of forests. Massive emigration from Greek islands in the twentieth century reduced their overall population 30 to 50 percent, and in some instances to as low as 10 percent of what existed in 1910. The elastic bigger islands could absorb such disturbances, but the smaller ones were more brittle. From the excessive grazing that by the sixteenth century made myrtle so rare that tanners could no longer gather it to use in preparing goatskins, Sicily could recover. Suddenly stripped of its forests, Malta could not.[75]

Once established, island institutions became both more tenacious and more vulnerable. Many agrarian practices endured sufficiently to stamp a personality onto individual islands regardless of which mainland held sovereignty over it. All the large islands became extremist in some way, all resisted absorption by the mainland, all became notorious for their refractory residents intent on the continuance of traditional ways. France never fully assimilated Corsica, nor the Ottoman empire (or Greece) Crete, nor Italy Sicily. Whatever trend best characterized Mediterranean land use dominated the islands. All, in particular, became centers of pastoralism.

Sardinia was perhaps the most quiescent. But traditional practices persisted, if politically subdued. Customary rights survived both Roman land tenure and the feudalism of Aragon. In fact, most of classical agriculture continued well into modern times. In 1885, Robert Tennant observed that Sardinia still retained all the features and fire practices of ancient Rome. Farmers burned wheat straw, and pastoralists ignited the maquis. As much of the understory that "can be safely set fire to, without damage to the trees, they are burnt for the sake of improving the pasturage." Elsewhere, "no doubt," the Sardinian forests were "hardly and roughly used," with large tracts "wantonly fired by the shepherds for pasturage." There was "almost unlimited pasture" everywhere for the likewise "almost unlimited" herds of cattle, horses, pigs, sheep, and goats. Between its central mountains and enveloping lowlands, transhumance thrived, a miniature of Neapolitan Italy.[76]

But already economic modernization was groping into the hinterland and unraveling the threads of the agrarian tapestry that had draped the island. Malaria and unrest had kept farmers in villages and restricted the amount of land in arable; now, a larger market forced Sardinian wheat to compete with Ukraine and North America, and the precepts of a money economy gnawed like termites at the woody foundations of the agrarian equilibrium. Pastoralism expanded, reclaiming more and more of the landscape. In vain did the authorities attempt to dam the rising flood of fires. But threats meant little as emigration gathered pace. Sardinia steadily overtook the rest of Italy in the proportion of area burned and incendiary fires. Incredibly, the expansion did not cease at the island's edge. In a reversal of relationships, the island transferred its problems to the mainland. By the 1970s, Sardinia was exporting its shepherds to Italy, and with them an epidemic of pastoral fires.[77]

(ii)

No island quite captures the character of Mediterranean fire as acutely as Cyprus. Though, alone among the large islands, no mainland power now rules it, that has not removed Cyprus from the processes that have so influenced Mediterranean fire history. In fact its anomalous status has only institutionalized the unrest and endless warfare that have so shaped the region's natural history. Moreover, the story of Cyprus complements nicely the saga of the French-dominated Mediterranean—an arresting contrast between eastern Mediterranean and western, British imperialism and French, island miniature and grand traverse. Geopolitics has long argued for the island's strategic importance; so also do its fires.

Cyprus has a typical Mediterranean climate, landscape, biota, and history. Neolithic colonization began around 6000 B.C. and ended by 3000. Cypriot life thereafter centered in the village—metastable, adaptable, opportunistic. Farming, herding, and foraging all fed into the village economy; no single practice dominated for long. More critically, Cyprus also had goods valued for trade, and was strategically sited for the emerging maritime empires that hived off from Egypt, Greece, and the Levant. Its mineral wealth (copper, *cuprum*) gave the island its name. Its forests made it the Green Island of ancient lore. Its natural beauty confirmed it as the home of Aphrodite.

Cyprus was also prone to calamities, natural and social. It suffered earthquakes, floods, locusts, droughts—a moderate one every three years on average, a major episode every ten. Disease and famine struck with some regularity, the bubonic plague claiming 75 percent of the island's population in 1469. By the eighteenth century, malaria had made Cyprus notorious as a pestilential miasma. And of course there were wars. Whenever empires clashed in the region, they invaded strategic Cyprus. Conquerors from the west seized Cyprus as an offshore base, an island fortress from which to launch campaigns in the Levant; conquerors from the east subjugated it as a sentinel over the Near East littoral and a point of departure for maritime domination of the eastern Mediterranean. A century or two of peace might pass between major outbreaks, but the invaders always returned—Hittites, Egyptians, Greeks, Phoenicians, Assyrians, Persians, Macedonians, Romans, Byzantines, Arabs, Franks, Genoese, Venetians, Turks, and British—each killing, colonizing, ruling, extracting, taxing, kneading new ingredients into the Cypriot dough.

Within the spectrum of 10,000 years of remorseless conflict, earth tremors, famines, and ecological pillaging, a century of calm meant little. Cypriot society acquired the same properties of fatigue and resilience characteristic of its biota. Its fires were as endemic as its malaria, and as destructive as its episodic violence. Every practice, every shockwave, every point of contact threw sparks, and in the maquis and aromatic pine of its mediterranean mountains, those sparks kindled fires. Few sites escaped burning within the life cycle of their dominant flora. Even the remote Paphos forest deep in the Troodos Mountains burned at least once over a 200 year period. When people abandoned the land, lightning moved in. In the relatively quiescent decade of 1981–90, lightning accounted for almost 17 percent of all ignitions in state forests.[78]

The modern era commenced when the contest between Russian and British imperialism—Kipling's Great Game—focused again on the dry-rotting Ottoman empire, and when the Suez Canal, which opened in 1869, became Britain's primary conduit to India. Britain sought an Ottoman alliance, and it needed a military base from which to oversee the Suez. Dormant Cyprus, languishing under disease, agricultural decay, administrative corruption, and oppressive tax-farming, suddenly returned to geopolitical importance. In 1878, under a special treaty, Britain established a protectorate over Cyprus. Rapid reconnaissances quickly dispelled any illusions about the state of the landscape. Whatever the legal classifications of Ottoman land use, the largest category appeared to be *kapsalia,* burned land.

The Ottoman empire had attempted some reforms. It had instigated a new Land Registration Law in 1858, although it is unclear whether the provisions of that edict actually reached Cyprus. In 1870 it invited a French forester, Gérard de Montrichard, to report on the state of the empire's forests. He concluded that Cyprus, in particular, had suffered major, recent depradations, that over the previous twenty years the Cypriot forests had decreased in area by one-third and in productivity by probably one-half. Not the ax but the goat, he concluded, was the ultimate cause. The immediate agency of destruction, however, was broadcast burning. Most fires were set by herders.[79]

British observers not only seconded the dreadful status of the Cyprus forests but also confirmed that the havoc was comparatively contemporary. In 1869, Samuel Baker described vividly the wreckage of a forest hacked, burned, abandoned, and grazed, its broken and seared trunks standing like the pillars of a sacked city, as much a ruin of the Cypriot landscape as its melancholy monuments to antiquity. The sight, he ruminated, "would convey the impression that an enemy who conquered the country had determined to utterly destroy it, even to the primeval forest."[80]

The British administration promptly commissioned a forestry reconnaissance. The 1879 report by A. E. Wild, seconded from the Indian Forest Service, verified unequivocally that the devastation was both serious and recent. Agriculture had collapsed, pastoralism was expanding, and woodlands were receding before the blows of each. Forests were cleared for vineyards, for temporary cultivation, for pasturage, and for fuelwood, all of it executed with promiscuous fire. Woodcutters burned to kill standing forests and increase material available for fuelwood. Eager to augment the production of pitch, collectors slashed recklessly through the pinelands, and burned to stimulate the flow of resin. (Probably not 5 percent of the conifer forests had escaped such marring, Baker thought.) Vendettas abounded, vetted with torch as well as knife. Compromising if not abetting the situation was Ottoman land law which gave to the state all land but granted right of ownership to anyone who cultivated, at least once every three years, any waste or forest land over a ten-year period. The concept complemented perfectly the instincts of Mediterranean swidden. Few high forests could survive intact.[81]

Worse, everywhere pastoralists burned to promote grass and browse. Goats and sheep dominated land use, encroaching on arable and forest both. The national goat herd exceeded that of any island in the Mediterranean, probably double the size of the human population, almost 150 to the square mile; the number of sheep actually exceeded it; and together they obliterated any serious reforestation. Sir W. F. Thistleton-Dyer summed up the enduring British perception of Cyprus when he called it a "burnt-out cinder." The amount of damage, particularly firing, staggered the British, and the anarchic destruction filled them with the kind of contempt they felt toward the institutionalized corruption of Ottoman rule. Everywhere they looked, the Turk destroyed, while the British built.[82]

What Cyprus needed, Britain concluded, was a government of rational institutions and honest administration under the sovereignty of law. Almost immediately the British passed a Woods and Forest Ordinance in 1879 and revised it in 1881. The reformation of Cyprus depended on the rationalization of agriculture, which in turn was impossible without a rational forestry. The law's intent was to reforest the island, and by reestablishing its trees, stop this hemorrhage of soil and flooding, ameliorate the climate, and stabilize the society. A properly cultivated landscape could ensure an enlightened culture and a secure society. One strategy was to demarcate and protect the surviving forests, which they saw as an essential condition to the resuscitation of sedentary agriculture. (Despite the "not uncommon" fires, Baker asserted that "nothing could be easier than to defend" the mountain forests by an "efficient staff" drawn from Highland Scots or English gamekeepers.) Another was to prohibit exports of timber, charcoal, firewood, bark, and resin-derived products, which had the immediate effect of abolishing the migratory resin industry. There were plans too for afforestation, particularly around villages, as a source of ready fuelwood. And active protection, it was assumed, would follow readily. Administration of these laws passed to professional foresters. Within the context of British imperialism, only the Indian Forest Service predated its Cyprus cognate. Both, however, looked to France for administrative models.[83]

For such a forest reformation, there was no precedent in Cypriot history. An outraged Baker explained that "Be he Christian or Musselman, the Cypriot peasant is convinced that wood, like air or water, has no other master than the God who made it. It seems as natural for him to go where he will and cut wood as to drink at the brook hard by when he is thirsty." The result, as Paul-Gabriel Madon fumed, was "an aimless and inexcusable waste." But what one side saw as waste the other viewed as a resource, and what one praised as reasonable and sustainable, the other condemned as oppressive and ephemeral.[84]

They saw Cyprus with radically different perspectives. Britain's high commissioner came from an England that had not suffered invasion since William the Conqueror and had not fought a major war since it crushed Napoleon. It knew violence aplenty, but swept it to the periphery, to its colonies; otherwise, the Pax Britannica ruled. Britain was first among the industrializing nations, it harbored a domestically stable polity, and it boasted a globe-spanning imperium. Britons could afford to take the long view, to equate the long-growing high forest with a long-flourishing high civilization.

Cypriots could not. They knew everything could vanish with the next earthquake, drought, locust infestation, invasion, plague, or foreign ruler. They suspected that the British would pass away before long (which, considering the duration of Cyprus history, they did), and hesitated to commit their land to British designs that might prejudice their own extended existence. The Britons proposed improvement; the Cypriots sought survival. The essence of Cyprus life was the village, and the essence of the village economy was its ability to tap whichever of its latent land resources it needed to survive the latest crisis. The forest was less a woodland than a hedge against sudden change, now exploited, now left fallow, a ready source, when needed, for wood, pasture, arable, and fuel in whatever proportion the times required. In 1897, Patrick Geddes wrote: "Here we can see the geographical ruin in all its stages; here too the social ruin . . . the main survivals of the past, all the historic stages are in the living village." That of course was why the village was still there.[85]

The reconstitution of rural Cyprus—which was all of Cyprus—would pivot around the stabilizing power of forests. Forestry would root the Cypriot economy in something other than the village. The first appropriation was for £60, and "on what object this magnificent sum of money was spent," a forester sardonically wrote, "I have never met anyone who knew." Of course it was not enough money; there was never enough, because the British protectorate soon found itself in a firefight. The stabilization of agriculture did not eliminate free-ranging livestock. On the contrary, to the extent that sedentary agriculture expanded to accommodate a sharply rising population, reduction in fallow, and fields shielded from intimidating shepherds, it forced more flocks into the hills. But foresters were busy delineating those same mountains with the intention of growing high forest, which meant that they had to reduce herds and the fires without which herding was impossible. Attempts to "discipline" Cypriot pastoralism only led to incendiarism.[86]

Forest and flock seemed hopelessly incompatible. Britons mistrusted transhumance and nomadism, they vilified the fires set along seasonal migrations, and as northern Europeans they particularly detested the goat. Goats alone ate trees, even climbed trees, and their herders felled trees to feed them branches. Goats and fire became the twin terrors of Cypriot forestry, both relentlessly demonized by successive generations of foresters. Cypriots would not, however, get rid of the flocks, and the flocks had nowhere else to go. They swarmed over the mountain forests like incendiary locusts kindling fires wherever they alighted.

Thus Cyprus resembled Algeria—or almost any other patch of the Mediterranean. Unlike France, however, Britain had nothing in its national estate that resembled this in the slightest; the only analogue was Cape Colony, also a mediterranean-climate biota, and India, whose annual monsoon made fire even more prevalent than in Cyprus. Nor did Britain have foresters, a forestry school, a forest department, or a forest code; it hardly had anything that resembled a forest. British forestry did not involve extending national institutions outward so much as creating distinctive bureaucracies for the colonies, which then diffused from one outpost of the empire to another and portions of which (including forestry) eventually seeped back to Britain. Foresters joined hydraulic, mining, and civil engineers in the rationalizing of colonial economies and landscapes. But forestry was always something apart from Britain, something it acquired as it did St. Helena or the Elgin marbles, an extension of imperial reach like the Gate of India. British forestry was an artifact of empire and almost failed to survive the dissolution of that imperium.

Britain had occupied Cyprus for geopolitical reasons. When those purposes vanished, so, in theory, would the British high commissioner, the British Army, and the British-conceived Cyprus Forest Service. In the end, whenever it might come, the goal was self-governance. There was no colonization of Cyprus by supported immigration; no attempted assimilation into British national territory; no wholesale conversion of Cypriot society to English institutions or language. Like the French in Algeria, the British in Cyprus intended to civilize, but that did not mean transforming Cypriots into colonial clones or running Cyprus as one would a Northumbrian borough.

Yet forestry was different. It was transnational, like mining copper or building railroads or studying physics. British forestry, in particular, was imbued with French institutional ideals, and encumbered with a preference for *dirigisme* that was otherwise alien to British ambitions. Britain's first appeal for help went to the Indian Forest Service, which detailed A. E. Wild for his 1879 reconnaissance. With passage of the forest ordinance, however, Cyprus demanded a permanent presence and chose Paul-Gabriel Madon, a French forester previously stationed in Provence and Algeria. Madon immediately recognized the geographic similarities—the temporary, fire-flushed cultivations, the "excessive" fellings, the "barbarous methods," the waste, the "inexplicable modes" of resin tapping, and of course the displaced pastoralism. Madon commenced the ritual condemnation of the goat, that "eternal starveling" whose "cruel teeth" and "poisonous saliva" was destroying Cyprus as completely as Rome's legions had Carthage. In sum, he insisted that "the remaining forests of the island will not see the end of the century if radical measures are not adopted to put an end to this devastation."[87]

From his years in Algeria he knew what kind of radical measure was required. He epitomized, moreover, the French obsession with the primeval and the putatively natural. On Cyprus, as French colleagues would do on Mauritius and Madagascar and even America, he asserted the myth of an ancient Great Forest. Then he described its declension, and presented the classic dialectic between agricultural and pastoral life: "the former with its numerous resources, its brilliant future, the rise it gives to industry and commerce; the latter with its products more and more confined by its own abuses, its precarious future, and the mortal agony in which it plunges its people." The goat ate the Garden. And it was inseparable from the devouring fire.[88]

So Madon established fire as an index of environmental devastation and social insurrection. The great Paphos fires of 1881 (coincidental with those in Algeria) enraged him. "I, the chief of the service," he fumed, "had to work like a common labourer for eight days almost without rest and nourishment." He could get nothing from native laborers "without blows and threats." Even so 6,000 hectares burned. The indigenes' "contempt for the authorities," he concluded, "originates through the mistake made by the ignorant population of the island, in confusing mildness for weakness, and indulgence for fear." So sullen were the natives, so profound their indifference to any act save immediate gratification, that Madon could imagine a time when it would be "impossible, at least over half the island, for Government officers visiting the districts to obtain anything from the peasantry at all."[89]

Madon urged French solutions—strong codes, vigorous enforcement, punitive actions. Administration should proceed "without hesitation, interruption, and irregularity." High Commissioner Sir Robert Biddulph disagreed. Surely there was some point of compromise possible, some partial accession to tradition, some accommodation to grazing. Besides, Madon's schemes were costly. Britain rejected them, and Madon resigned. He took French *rayonnement* with him, and left a legacy of effective insight broken by ineffective application. "If care be not taken," he thundered, "the Mediterranean will soon count one island less and one rock more." Foresters might come and go but goats and fires went on forever.[90]

Gradually, however, there was progress. By 1896, the Forest Service had demarked, surveyed, and gazetted all the state forests. It negotiated with villagers and monasteries, one of which, Kikko, oversaw immense herds of goats. After Winston Churchill, then under-secretary of state for the colonies, toured Cyprus in 1907, appropriations increased, and after Sir David Hutchins, one of the empire's premier forestry authorities, inspected the island closely in 1909, the Forest Service renewed its convictions. Staff slowly increased, firebreaks and trails inched through the hinterlands, village afforestation projects sprang up, and legislation succeeded in partly controlling the herds and, more important, the herders.

Hutchins was willing to compromise on the goat question—to regulate rather than abolish. He noted, as had Baker, that fires were less devastating than their ubiquity suggested, and that through burning and grazing mature forests often had little understory to sustain conflagrations. Still, Hutchins had little doubt that the fires required attention. "The first point to establish," he insisted, "is the seriousness of forest fires in Cyprus." He castigated the "long neglect" that bordered on negligence. "For about 27 years," he noted, "that is to say, until within two or three years ago, more or less serious fires occurred every year in the Cyprus forests, *and no effectual measures could be taken to check them.*" That had to end; southern France and South Africa showed how to do it. The causes could be attacked, systematically and methodically—the revenge fires, the arson, the fires to get firewood, to practice swidden, to enhance grazing. The last was particularly critical, if politically inflammatory. But it was mandatory to break the unholy alliance between fire and goats. Nothing so symbolized Cypriot insolence and British exasperation as the persistence of semiferal goat herds, and of course the fires that traced their migrations. In 1908, villagers around the Kormakiti forest alone set ten fires to improve pasturage, and when according to forest law the lands were closed, raised a "political storm" along with a rash of retaliatory burning.[91]

Such stories—and the swelling herds—outraged professional foresters. Hutchins's vituperation was typical: "Unrestrained goat grazing and forestry cannot exist together in the same place any more than a cat and a mouse in the same room." Goats had invaded St. Helena and stripped it; temperate Europe had excluded goats and boasted a lush forest. There was a place for the goat, the poor-man's milch cow, as much a survivor as the Cypriot peasant. It was the one domesticated beast that could thrive under truly degraded conditions. (Recent studies suggest that short-term yields from goats run 15 to 30 percent, an extraordinary investment return.) But it was also identified inextricably with the depredating Turk, its numbers overwhelmed the battered Cypriot landscape, and its association with lawlessness and fire mocked systematic forestry and the British rule that identified a stable forest with social improvement. Follow this policy "resolutely," Hutchins insisted, and "the suppression of forest fires in Cyprus will become an easy matter."[92]

But nothing on Cyprus came easily. Gradually, however, there was progress, at least around lowland villages. Particularly effective was the Goat Law of 1913 which allowed villagers, by secret ballot, to exclude goats from communal lands. For the first time lowland villagers could move against goat herders without fear of retaliation and arson. By the time the British left, some 45 percent of villages had so voted. Other measures encouraged the substitution of sheep for goats, which burdened the island with a more or less constant population of migratory browsers but got the goats out of the trees; the extinction of herds by purchase; and the hiring of herders for forestry jobs, even fire control! But compromise, so fatal for forestry's ambitions, was exactly what Cyprus demanded and was unable to concoct.

(iii)

There was more at stake than the land alone. From the beginning of British administration the reigning Greek-speaking Cypriots had sought *enosis,* or political union, with Greece. Britain replied that it governed Cyprus under treaty with the Ottoman empire and had no authority to cede the island to anyone. When Turkey entered World War I as a German ally, however, Britain annexed Cyprus, offered it to Greece in 1915 (which Greece rejected), and finally created a British Crown Colony in 1925. While Greek Cypriots continued to press for union, the prospect alarmed Turkish Cypriots, now deprived of Turkey's protection. Thus the environmental conflict between goat and forester had its political counterpart in the quarrel between Greek and Turk Cypriot, neither willing to concede, each ready to respond with violence. Every ripple of unrest—

discontent among herders, ethnic suspicions within Cypriot society—ended in waves of incendiarism.

One celebrated episode occurred in 1912, two years before British annexation. A Greek forest guard, an autocrat known as the Lion of the Forests, attempted to enforce strictly the provisions of the forest law in the Kantara forests, notably regarding fuelwood and grazing. The local villagers were mostly Turkish, and they replied by systematically burning the forests from the Acanthu pass eastward to the Karpass peninsula, roughly 65 square kilometers. Not only was control hopeless and the forest damaged, but the land was again in a form the graziers most desired. The burned land remained treeless for fifty years. In the midst of this swirling, ethnically tiered civil war, the British presumption of rational institutions and preference for mature forest were doomed. An endlessly shifting cultivation, an endlessly opportunistic village economy, frustrated the ideal of an ordered landscape tended by a law-ordered society. Looking back on British stewardship, former conservator of forests Geoffrey Chapman listed accomplishments that seemed miraculous. "Only the problem of controlling forest fires remained"; and after the British departure, "still remains."[93]

If the Great War strengthened British sovereignty, it damaged Britain's claims to environmental legitimacy. Britain's war effort in the Near East demanded timber, so the peripheral Cyprus forests were cut, often with scant regard to silviculture, to satisfy it. Probably one-sixth of the forest was felled for the war effort, with "cataclysmic" consequences. Worse, grazing controls lapsed, herds returned, fires broke out, and attempts to restore the old order after the war only reinstated a kind of trench warfare between indigenous users and colonial overseers. What escaped wartime felling often burned; in 1919 the lusty Paphos forest, spared wartime ravages, suffered a series of major conflagrations. Sending Cypriots to Britain for forestry training, creating a Cyprus Forestry Association, reasserting the provisions of forestry laws, laying out roads and telephone lines, and hiring guards from local villages—none of these measures could compensate for a growing population and its demands, for an expanding and protected arable acreage, for herds that swarmed in ever greater numbers (by 1936 the number of shepherds had actually increased from 4,705 to 7,344), and for an intractable politics, of which the friction among indigenes at least equaled that between them and the imperial British.

Sparks kindled readily in the Cyprus tinderbox. An outbreak of arson in 1924 forced compromises, a relaxation in grazing control. Soon the state forests hosted a greater proportion of the national herd than ever before. Villagers refused to assist with firefighting. In 1927 the Cypriot Legislative Council rejected the forestry budget, prompting a constitutional crisis. In 1929, R. S. Troup, director of the Imperial Forestry Institute (then at Oxford), characterized the Cyprus

Forest Service as "overworked, overextended, and over-centralized." He could soon add "overwhelmed." In 1931 a global economic depression combined with record drought; the Forest Service withdrew from lowland to mountain forests; and illegal cutting, grazing, and firing washed over the abandoned lands like a spring tide.[94]

Increasingly fire dictated the pattern of forestry, not vice versa. The geography of burned sites determined the order of salvage logging, which often determined the overall schedule of harvesting; incendiarism decided the location and success of afforestation; grazier fires shaped the structure of forest and maquis; and wildfires informed the infrastructure and organization of the Forest Service. Incendiary burning etched the actual relations between forestry and society like a hot iron on leather. Where protection nominally continued, attempts to enforce legal strictures led to arson, which provoked retaliatory policing, which inspired further firing in an endless spiral. Every accomplishment proved ephemeral.

What was true for forestry was increasingly true for the Crown Colony overall. For Britain Cyprus became an imperial sink, costing more in outlays than it earned in revenue. The Cyprus quagmire threatened to do the same with institutions and ideas. After Britain proclaimed its protectorate over Egypt in 1882, the geopolitical value of Cyprus plummeted. Rational argument did not appear sufficient to reform Cypriot society, and armed enforcement was never considered. Change had to wait until the next global war.

During World War II, logging again accelerated, although this time with some silvicultural control. An important by-product was the renewed investment in forestry infrastructure, particularly road construction which not only opened lands formerly accessible solely by foot and donkey but plowed money into villages, reducing their incentive to joust with foresters over minor infractions and privileges. A Cyprus Volunteer Force, created when invasion seemed likely, evolved into a Forest Company that trained for firefighting. Equally, in 1943 Britain implemented a compulsory conversion from wood fuel to oil for industrial and domestic use. Almost overnight the pressures vanished for illicit firewood gathering, including incendiary firing to ready sites for harvest. This removed by far the greatest single depredation on forests adjacent to villages.

Not least, the war promised to recast colonial politics. In 1948, Britain introduced a new constitution. The Greek Cypriot community, however, rejected anything other than outright union with Greece. Britain soon displayed equal stubbornness, holding firmly to Cyprus even as it began to liberate colony after colony elsewhere. In 1947 it granted independence to an India eager for it (and foisted it off on a New Zealand reluctant to accept it); but it retained a Cyprus that it had once sought, with profound reluctance, only in order to protect its passage to India. With renewed resolve, Britain promulgated in 1950 a revised environmental constitution, as it were, in the form of the Forest Policy of Cyprus. Among its aspirations, the policy proposed to move forestry from protection into fuller production, endow a forestry college and a research establishment, and further technical infrastructure—from weather stations to the planting of poplars. But the policy still sought that chimera of British environmental rule, a balance between agriculture and forestry. The garden and the wood still defined the limits of British agronomic imagination; there was no formal place for pastoralism, which had two centuries before tramped over the Highlands, and there was only undying emnity for the free-ranging goat. So protest continued, its fires, as one Palestinian observed, "frequently malicious."[95]

Then folk unrest flared into outright insurrection. The demand for Greek union inspired a campaign of sabotage to force Britain to hand the island over to Greece or depart so the island could gravitate to Greece on its own. As a government agency, the Forest Service became a prime target. It was as vulnerable to political arson as it had been to economic arson. But if the British Army provoked attacks, it also helped to suppress them, if only out of self-defense. In June 1956, British troops were hotly pursuing George Grivas, military commander of EOKA, through the Paphos forest when smoke burst upon them, obviously a diversionary tactic. The ploy succeeded, however, as commanders ordered almost a thousand troops from a Scottish regiment to combat it; then the fire blew up through a rocky defile and killed twenty-two soldiers. Grivas and his cohorts escaped. Thereafter all British troops assigned to Cyprus underwent special training in firefighting. Captain A. G. Murdoch observed ruefully that "during its long history, the British Army has had to learn many important lessons the hard way."[96]

The issue went further than digging firelines. It was the whole culture of Cypriot burning that continued to baffle and outrage the British. They still felt the shock: they had come from an island legendary for its pyrophobia to one equally renowned for its pyrophilia. The persistent burning mocked their beliefs in ameliorative reform, as though the Cypriots saw no difference between British rectitude and Ottoman rapacity, between immediate exploitation and long-term cultivation. Harold Macmillan likened the political demands to a "baffling" children's puzzle "where the effort to get three or more balls into their right position is continually frustrated; two would fall into place but then the third would immediately escape." There was no rational political solution. Neither was there a balanced solution to chronic burning; what one group didn't burn, another would. Successful fire exclusion for a few years only added to the fuels (and intensity) of fires that inevitably followed. Insurrectory fires continued until a settlement in 1959 led to outright independence in 1960.[97]

But Britain was hardly the origin of the problem, and the withdrawal of British administration did not resolve abiding questions of pastoralism, of who had access to what forests for what purposes, of population pressures, and of the widening schism between Greek and Turkish Cypriots over *enosis*. Fires directed against British rule now found other targets. Without a common foe, Turk and Greek Cypriots rioted among themselves, culminating in civil war in 1963–64. Troops poured in from Greece; Turkey retaliated and established an extensive protectorate in the northern tier of the island. Predictably incendiarism raged through the mountains, the product of aerial attack and "forest sabotage groups." The losses in 1964 were exceeded by those of only four years since the advent of British administration. Another outbreak raged in 1966. "How much longer," wondered forest conservator Geoffrey Chapman, "will it be before the forest can be dissociated from political disturbances and before forest incendiarism ceases to be a stick to beat the Government." The answer was, not until there was no longer a government.[98]

Worse, the 1964 invasion displaced 180,000 Greek Cypriots. Unrest persisted, and in 1974 Turkey launched another invasion. The result was the largest outbreak of fire in modern Cyprus history. With two years of drought to help fuel its incendiary warfare (some kindled by the Turkish Air Force, some probably by rival factions among Greek Cypriots, some no doubt by opportunism and accident), 16 percent of all state forests and 30 percent of productive forests burned. Despite dramatic measures by the Forest Service, despite wholesale timber salvaging, and despite afforestation by bulldozed terraces across Troodos hillsides, violent fire had again subverted the promise of Cypriot forestry. Not even a truce brokered by the United Nations could abolish that fact. In the 1980s the three leading causes of fire were accident, lightning, and military exercises, and the largest proportion burned, by far, resulted from the operations of the U.N. peacekeeping forces.[99]

So the story ends, as it began, with fire. After a century of determined forestry, fire remained the one natural disturbance not controlled, and burned area—in 1980 almost 50 percent of the forest estate—the dominant presence in forest planning. The size of the coniferous forest was virtually identical to that at the time of the British accession. J. V. Thirgood concluded sadly that "the considerable forestry effort was, to a great extent, directed to husbanding a wasting resource." The Cyprus saga remained one of history by cataclysm.[100]

The source and character of fire had varied, of course. Its alliance with the goat had made each notorious. Remove the goat, however, and some other synergism would have evolved to take its place. Extirpate those maligned goats, and Cyprus's fuels, dry summers, and recurring droughts would remain, and with them fire. If controlling the goat would allow vast acres to reforest, that would only stash more combustibles for fire to seize. Eliminate fuelwood harvesting, and much of that wood will burn in situ instead of in hearths. The real compromise, controlled burning, seemed the one option that all parties ignored. But Cyprus was not a place for compromise.

EPILOGUE:
FIN-DE-SIÈCLE FIRE

For centuries the Mediterranean had defined a vast cultural watershed. Into it Europe flowed from the margins. Within its convoluted basin mixed all the elements of Western civilization—Greek with Iberian, Gaul with Phoenician. And from it Europe connected to civilizations in India, China, Mesoamerica, and Africa. Here originated Europe's premier agriculture, its commerce, its literature and art, its politics, its ideas of itself. Here Europe developed its ideals of landscape. "In fine," argued Cicero, surveying the Mediterranean landscape, "by means of our hands we essay to create as it were a second world within the world of nature." Here burned inextinguishably Europe's most expressive and vigorous flame. The Mediterranean was the original hearth of Western civilization.[101]

The Mediterranean's influence moved outward under the press of trade, missionizing, and conquest. There were climatic limits to the spread of its agriculture, and the transition from a regime of winter rain and summer drought was not easily overcome. Some flora and fauna, like the talismanic olive, failed to cross that climatic frontier. But many others, with adjustments, did. Goats could survive, although temperate Europe suppressed them in favor of cattle and sheep. Wheat flourished after modifications in planting techniques and breeding. No less vitally so did ideas of agronomy and proper land use. Classical texts spread with Roman legions and continued to diffuse, often through the Church, after Rome rotted apart. When Europe sailed beyond its enclosed seas, other mediterranean-climate lands became the sites for critical colonies; the transfer of mediterranean-borne cultigens and livestock became essential to the survival of nearly all colonies subject to mass immigration; and Mediterranean weeds scattered from the maquis to France, Britain, the Azores, Siberia, the Americas, and Australasia. What mariners had spread widely around the basin now disseminated throughout the littoral of the world ocean. Europe's global expansion began with the export of Mediterranean flora, fauna, and ideas.

But by the end of the nineteenth century those relative positions had reversed. Temperate Europe dominated and defined Western civilization, occupied the center of its moral geography, and prescribed the concepts of proper land use. Where Julius Caesar had once alluded casually to the migratory agriculture of the Gauls, and Tacitus had scorned the indifferent fields of *Germania,* now the triumphant descendants of Gaul and German scrutinized the impoverished progeny of Rome and declared them to be modern *sauvages,* sunk in a miasma of degradation, incapable of civilized husbandry. Where agronomists had once considered *silva* an appendage to farming, foresters now established the tree as the measure of environmental health and resurveyed the panorama of agriculture through the conceptual theodolites of silviculture. They saw the Mediterranean's fires, like its malarial swamps, as both a cause and symptom of its immense malaise.[102]

The Mediterranean remained, as it had always been, a disturbance-driven environment. Since the climate began to assume its modern shape, humans had controlled those disturbances, pruning, grazing, gathering, plowing, sowing, and burning. Their innumerable fires, in particular, had kept the agricultural cauldron simmering. But the disturbance was controlled only if the fire was tended. The vestal fire was not merely a social symbol but a paradigm of fire practices, and mediterranean Europe's fires were—as its critics contended—a useful index of its social order. Fire might be oppressive, anarchic, fragmented, gentle, abusive, restorative, vindictive, mild, or violent according not only to drought and wind but to the character and rate of change of its resident society.

The greatest outbreaks of fire conform closely with periods of rapid reform and social dislocation. The old order of fuels and flames breaks up, and fire expires, spills into old woodpiles, or is rekindled elsewhere. Displaced populations spread fire before them, as did symbolically the wandering Hebrews and the armies of Alexander the Great. Druze and Maronite in Lebanon, Kurd in the Zagros Mountains, Karijite and later Arab in the Atlas, Rif, and Kabylia Mountains, and indeed graziers everywhere driven from old pastures, no longer anchored in arable lands, spread fire in an effort to remake the landscape into forms more suitable to their needs. So did agriculturalists propelled by population pressures to convert waste into fields and pasture into terraced orchards. But no less dramatic was the sudden withdrawal of the human hand from a landscape. Together fresh fire and escaped fire inscribed the periods of Mediterranean history, flaming rubrics that announced new chapters and texts.[103]

The most violent fires occurred with that most violent of confrontations, war. The chronicle is relentless. No other fire practice so fills the preserved texts, and none was so capable of rewriting the biotic parchments of the landscape. Of course that record was biased by selective memory: incendiary warfare was not, day after day, the fire regime that sculpted the Mediterranean ecosystem. But rare events, if severe, can disproportionately influence an environment. A war-induced slashing and burning of biomes could shape a future landscape as fully as the sacking and burning of Rome or Syracuse could dominate urban history. And war in this pyrophytic milieu was inevitably fought with fire.

The Mediterranean biota had to accommodate warfare as it did earthquakes and droughts. Incendiary fighting was more than a Homeric simile or a Gibbonesque footnote. It belongs fully with other pyrotechnologies as an active shaper of the Mediterranean landscape; torches were flung into woods as well as wooden roofs, and Greek fire was poured over hillsides as much as onto besiegers. Not least, incendiary warfare has endured as an epitome of fire's ecological interpretation, such that all free-burning fire could be imagined as an assault on the land. The felling and burning of Mediterranean woodlands thus resembled the sacking and burning of its civilized citadels.[104]

By the nineteenth century, however, disturbance assumed a new character. Industrialization and the controlled combustion of fossil fuels began deranging what millennia of Mediterranean agriculture had for so long and so meticulously ordered. The weapons of conquest were chemical fertilizers, electricity, the internal combustion engine, and mass commerce overseas, not for spice, bullion, and slaves, but for wheat, cotton, steel, oil, machinery, and televisions. Under such blows, village life cracked; the countryside began to empty as urbanization replaced war, disease, and emigration as a demographic forcer; intensively managed garden plots became surplus and increasingly superfluous. Railroads replaced the *cañadas* of transhumance. Tourists substituted for agricultural laborers moving with the seasons. Forests rose on old vineyards and pastures. At different places, at different rates, the old order began to crumble, dissolving like a fresco exposed to corrosive steam.

This time the landscape would not rebuild out of the old materials, like Christian churches made from the stones of destroyed pagan temples. The agrarian mosaic had shattered, not merely shed its loose tiles. The prospect was that the industrial revolution would transcend everything since the Neolithic revolution and that, unlike the disturbances typical of its history, however violent, this disruption would not soon retire. This time, too, classical agronomy faced a competing authority as forestry engineers made a bold bid to be the arbiters of the evolving environment. With exquisite timing, foresters as emissaries of the new order collided with the relict practitioners of the old. Pastoralists and foresters, in particular, both moved into the exposed landscape left by the receding sea of traditional agriculture. Fire—to the one indispensable, to the other inexcusable—instantly defined the frontier between them.

In the postwar era, industrial reformation relentlessly pushed the Mediterranean into one of two extremes. In developing nations the populations rose dramatically, from 94 million in 1950 to 220 million in 1980. Their sheer numbers and poverty pushed agriculture, particularly pastoralism, to the limits. Between 1965 and 1976 forested lands receded at a rate of 1 to 2 percent per year; fuel requirements alone placed staggering burdens on woodlands. Where it was possible, many rural people emigrated or fled to cities, sometimes abandoning once arable land to industrial fallow. But in general, fuels burned in cookstoves, and free-burning fire, where it was possible, pushed the land toward a biotic meltdown.

For the developed nations, however, the permanent population remained stable, arable decreased by 9 percent and woodlands expanded by 13 percent often by aggressive afforestation. Tourism soared in exponential bounds, replacing resin tapping and grazing with hotels and gift shops; and if tourist development threatened the ecology of the littoral, it liberated the biota of the hinterland. Surplus fuels built up, firetending diminished, social unrest kindled new starts, and the threads of this unraveling tapestry became so many glowing fuses. Ironically, even more in the developed than the undeveloped nations, the Mediterranean reclaimed its lost standing as an epicenter of a new world order on fire.

All this, however, lay in the future, for the time after Europe had sailed beyond the Pillars of Hercules into the Atlantic and the Green Seas beyond, after vast discovered continents had replaced the Mediterranean's islands and parochial hinterlands, after science had overthrown the authority of the Ancients and steam the motive power of sail and oxen. Once the axis of Europe's *mappa mundi,* the Mediterranean became a tidepool in the vast ocean that was the global economy. Europe relocated to its temperate center, unmolested by Muslim invaders and unafflicted by the sharp oscillation of wet and dry seasons that endowed the Mediterranean with its dramatic climate and inexpungeable fires.

The torch passed from Europe's most fire-prone region to its least.

CONTROLLED COMBUSTION
Fire in Central Europe

Europe is so well gardened that it resembles a work of art, a
scientific theory, a neat metaphysical system. Man has recreated
Europe in his own image.

—Aldous Huxley, *Do What You Will*

PROLOGUE:
ASH AND EMBERS

The great reality of central Europe is that temperature, not precipitation, defines its seasons, and that while precipitation follows broad gradients—heavier along the coast, lighter toward the Eurasian interior—its annual distribution is relatively constant. Of course there are uncommon places and exceptional times. Some sites experience local rain shadows, some years know droughts, some epochs become moister or more arid, but there is no clearly articulated fire season, no regular dialectic of wet and dry that might synthesize into fire. There are few natural ignition sources, and few pyrophytes. Fires breaks out opportunistically whenever windfall and lightning create pockets of storm-driven swidden. The biota stabilizes around an immense deciduous forest that has left natural flame gnawing along its margins, like a savanna fire that expires when it strikes the damp border of rainforest.

So, too, Europe's fire history has flared and crackled around the temperate middle of the continent. Europe's central fire was the fire of its temperate core—socially controlled, conditioned by the garden, as servile as a milch cow. As temperate Europe became, in time, the principal repository of European civilization, so its fires became the standard for European experience. For all its ceaseless turmoil, central Europe survived intact or escaped the multiple invasions from the Asian steppes, the pagan northland, and the Muslim south that profoundly distorted the histories of the regions on its periphery. The center was, like its biota, stable, almost gyroscopic.

But of course its climate, biota, soils, and humans had all coevolved, woven into a fantastic tapestry of trees, rivers, livestock, humus, grasses, shrubs, and insects strung across the frame of this landscape loom. The enduring human contribution was agriculture. This too had metamorphosed over millennia, as much altered as altering. The garden, first crudely, then with greater rigor and intensity, modeled every aspect of life—how Europeans related to plants, to animals, to forests, moors, heaths, fens; how they defined society itself; how they interpreted their handiwork; how they understood fire.

The garden also defined Europe's moral geography. The coming of agriculture was the defining encounter; and *landnam,* the shock of first contact, was Europe's true creation story. Over and over Europe retold the saga, each time with more elaboration and fervor. But this folk epic was not unrecorded. Landnam's practitioners had scrawled their saga with charcoal and inscribed it on the parchment of bogs, lakes, and soils. They brought agricultural fire, then they guaranteed its survival.

Here in the center there was fire aplenty, and until very recent times combustion would persist with the stubbornness of smoldering peat. But fire was almost everywhere the instrument of humanity's contriving hand, an expression of human will, talent, blundering, avarice, desperation, and hope. Agriculture shaped fire as it did fire's supporting landscape—both of them planted, cultivated, bred, weeded, harvested, and above all controlled. Fire roamed woodlands as did domestic swine; it thrived on plots as did cabbages or wheat; it served agriculturalists as the furnace did potters or the forge blacksmiths. It faced little competition from lightning, and had scant opportunity for casual application or escape.

Along the periphery of central Europe, fire flamed and often raged, sometimes advancing like a wind-tossed surf, sometimes hurling far-ranging sparks. At the center, however, this profoundly agrarian landscape glowed like a smoldering hearth, full of ash and embers. In that ash humans sowed crops. With those embers they cleared land and cooked the harvest. This central fire warmed brightly when humans stirred or blew on its coals; it subsided when its human tenders banked it against hearthstones; it flared when they added suitable fuels.

LANDNAM: THE FIRE OF FIRST CONTACT

Even as the biota swarmed northward from its Pleistocene refugia, like bees from a broken hive, anthropogenic fire was present. But it served hunters, fishers, and foragers who exploited it as they would another flint-tipped lance or bone hook. The capacity of fire to propagate across landscapes depended on conditions beyond the control of Mesolithic culture: suitable fuels, suitably prepared; disturbances to keep the cauldron of combustibles astir; and the leveraging force of a fire season. A wet-dry cycle could pry open the biota as a freeze-thaw cycle could shatter rock. But the trend was otherwise. Temperate Europe became uniformly wet, its natural biota closed and shaded; and anthropogenic fire retreated into shelters or was carried like a spear. Free-burning fire became almost insignificant.

That changed with the Neolithic revolution. When agricultural fire colonized central Europe, it established patterns that lasted 6,000 years. The story is everywhere unique, full of local nuance. But consider Denmark as synechdoche. Twenty thousand years ago the Fennoscandinavian ice sheet had split Denmark in half, the east under ice, the west an open outwash plain and tundra. Postglacial adjustments in water and land left Denmark half of each, a peninsula and islands, not unlike Europe itself. Gradually the climate stabilized and precipitation spread more or less evenly across the year. A mixed deciduous forest established a natural equilibrium. When agriculture arrived, it struck with fire, ax, and hoof, and had consequences both typical and profound. Not least, Denmark's bogs preserved the record of this encounter and, once excavated, inspired the concept of landnam.

Landnam—literally, land-taking—is the Old Norse term for primary settlement and was used by Icelandic pioneers to describe colonization. The word was revived by Johannes Iversen and applied to the charcoal-laden stratigraphy of bogs and lakes, which everywhere throughout central and boreal Europe records the advent of ancient agriculture. If cattle, wheat, and ribwort were the signatures of the European Neolithic, controlled combustion notarized their documents for posterity.

(i)

The colonization of Denmark proceeded fitfully, its parts (by later standards) out of sync. The ice sheet left raw soil; the unburdened lands sprang upward; sea level rose; the Baltic filled with fresh water, then spilled catastrophically to the North Sea; the climate fluctuated like a blustering wind, now wet, now cold, now warm, now dry; and grasses, forbs, shrubs, and trees pushed north from Spanish and Balkan refugia at whatever rates they could manage. In the postglacial epoch all this had to coevolve—land and water with climate, climate with biota, biota with soils, humans along with elk, bear, and earthworms. The Mesolithic pattern that resulted is characteristic throughout temperate Europe. Carbon-14 determinations, as Iversen put it, "have confirmed that the maxima and minima in this curve occur simultaneously everywhere, from the Alps to Denmark and from Ireland to Poland."[1]

The sequence begins with Late-Glacial tundra, dry, dominated by a steppe flora, birch, and shrubs, stocked with megafauna like reindeer, bison, and horse. Between 8300 and 7000 B.C. Pre-Boreal forests of birch and pine define the

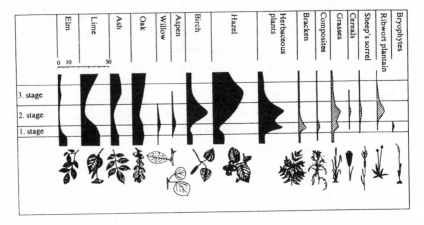

Landnam in Denmark: a generalized pattern based on preserved pollen, showing the three typical phases of *landnam*. (From Iversen 1973, by permission of the Denmark Geological Survey)

scene. Elk and auroch replace reindeer; hunters diversify accordingly, wield flint axes, and have dogs; the Baltic connects to the world ocean. Over the next millennia (the Boreal), hazel and pine dominate, but the future lay with the deciduous, shade-tolerant hazel. Hazel was a biotic scout for the wandering tribe of temperate shade trees that straggled north around the Pyrenees and across the Carpathians. Outpacing all the others, on suitable soils, the hazel found no serious competitors. Neither pine nor birch could reproduce well under shade, so where hazel established itself, it ruled, pushing the others, notably the pine, to the margins, to the poorer soils, to sites more routinely disturbed. Apparently it recruited an ally in humans, who feasted on its nuts and almost certainly helped propagate it wherever they wandered. "Endless nut groves" sustained, in Iversen's words, "the great blossoming of the Maglemose [Mesolithic] culture."[2]

But the Great Migration era of Europe's biota had only begun. Eventually the rest of the floral tribes arrived in an immense *omnium gatherum*. As elm, oak, ash, and linden moved in, they crowded the earlier genera to the sides. Meanwhile a rising sea segregated Denmark from Britain and Sweden, and then fractured it into a peninsula and archipelago, exchanging its sometimes continental climate for a more uniformly maritime one. The presence of ivy and mistletoe indicates that the summers had warmed, the growing season had lengthened, and lethal winter frosts had faded. Then, the migrations ceasing, the vital elements of climate, sea, and land converged into an approximation of a steady state. Earthworms mixed clay with humus into mull soil. The flora, lacking only beech, matured (6000–3000 B.C.) into the fabled primeval forest of Europe. At its immobile core, bestowing its name to the period, the Older Lime, stood *Tilia,* the European lime tree, the linden.

Self-referential, self-absorbed—linden was supremely indifferent to any presence save its own. Like other shade trees, its branches grew on one plane, but unlike the rest, each leaf adjusted to every other like a shimmering jigsaw puzzle that captured light and shunned shade. The canopy hoarded sunlight, spreading like a great unfolding umbrella. All beneath fell under its totalitarian shadow. When young its dark green leaves could survive in gloom; when mature, its light green canopy shone with sun-washed glare. Undisturbed, the linden could grow beneath oak, ash, pine, elm, or hazel, and then suppress them all. It did not flourish everywhere, but where it once intruded, it dominated, impervious to normal fungi and disease, resilient to injury, suckering from the roots if toppled. Beneath its funereal canopy no understory could thrive; the forest floor was open, spongy, decomposing with the slow rot of fungi; bare trunks stood like pillars in a dungeon; the land became a faunal desert, with only the wild boar to root among the litter. The linden forest grew over Denmark, burying the biota under its darkening dome. The end product of Europe's advancing biota was as empty as the land under the dead ice that wasted in the wake of the receding ice sheet. The linden's imponderable shade created a biotic black hole.

This ideal linden forest is an intellectual construct that probably stands to reality as the *Iliad* does to the sack of Troy. Nature was more turbulent, heterogenous, and vexatious. Mixed forests grew on pockets of wet land and poor soil, along the edges of shorelines and waterways that remained exposed to sunlight, and amid temporary openings. Oak and elm were tenacious competitors; hazel gave way grudgingly; but linden's natural rival, beech, still wandered uncertainly on the Eurasian plain. Yet the scenario is biologically plausible and more aptly describes the end of the temperate Mesolithic than alternatives. What the totalitarian linden seized, it held. Competitors died out beneath its suppressing shade. Rival species fled to the margins.

That includes humans, squeezed between rising seas and spreading shade forests. Mesolithic cultures joined pine and oak along streams and lakes and watched, with indifference or helplessness, as its hazel orchards succumbed, as edible forbs and tubers withered in the darkening shade, and as forest game fled. Worse, the opportunities for fire—their supreme technology—ebbed away. In the growing gloom, inexorable as nightfall, their fires were ineffective, and without fire Mesolithic peoples could not refashion a favorable habitat. Their torches alone could not resist this strangulation by shade; with the torch, they had a hammer but no wedge. Unless the ice returned, the seas rose, or the soil mutated, the linden forest could exist indefinitely, monolithic and immortal.

(ii)

But change came, arriving, as it had to, from outside the solipsistic shade. Around 3000 B.C. the climate cooled, perhaps by 2–3°C. The soil, particularly on sandy sites, deteriorated as rains relentlessly leached away its nutrient capital. The linden forest accepted these disturbances and repaired itself. Against the simultaneous blows of Neolithic humans, however, there could be no stability. The primeval forest, like Ozymandias sinking in the desert sands, at last succumbed.

With tool, tooth, and torch, agriculturalists began to rearrange the forest, selectively killing, pollarding, planting, stripping. They promoted shrubs, herbs, and forbs over trees, added new flora and fauna, served as a vector for disease and pest, and even altered the soil. They disassembled the linden forest as readily as they stripped away its bark and burned the residue. The implacable linden fell, like a great bole eaten out by fiery termites. The shade dome fractured, and in those widening fissures—that biotic enlightenment—species returned.

Landnam did not, at once, transform the deciduous forest into permanent arable. Instead it broke the monolith into smaller pieces. It promoted a greater diversity of plants and animals and allowed agriculturalists to insert their own cultigens and livestock into the cracks. The economy of a Neolithic culture (say, the Ertebølle) was mixed and opportunistic. It included cattle and swine, a few goats and sheep; it grew primitive cereals and pulses; and it foraged and hunted. For the former, it had to create habitats, and for the latter, to restore them. Cutting and burning—landnam—accomplished both tasks.

Landnamers carved small forest clearings with flint axes, then fired the residue. Probably the smaller trees were felled, the large ones ringbarked. This both created the fuelbed needed for burning and opened up the canopy to light. An experiment conducted in Denmark's Draved Forest in 1953 found that even inexperienced woodsmen wielding stone axes could treat a hectare of forest in fourteen days. Farmers left the felled wood to dry, then torched the patch. In the ash they sowed cereals or other crops. The resulting harvest exceeded anything possible in unprepared soil or on sites cleared but not burned. Yet the flush was ephemeral. Within a year, it was much diminished, and within two years, gone. So farmers cleared new plots year after year, each more an extended garden than an arable farm. In the aftermath of the burns, they grazed livestock, especially cattle.[3]

With the landnam plot as a haven, they and their herds could range widely in the surrounding countryside. Encountering these early Germanic tribes, Julius Caesar commented that they had "no private or marked-off land, and are not allowed to remain longer than a year in one place in order to till the soil. They do not use much grain, but live for the most part on milk and meat, and devote much time to hunting." As the forest regrew to fallow, it showed species and habitats far more usable to humans than tyrannical linden or beech. Projected over several thousand years, diffusing over large areas, landnam transformed the countryside. Out of its ashes, ultimately, grew Europe's mixed agriculture.[4]

Slashing and burning, however, was only part of a complex of practices. Landnamers also opened deep, empty forests by selective ringbarking. In the process, they promoted oak and hazel, the great mast orchards. They also spared ash and elm, whose leaves livestock ate greedily, and then pollarded these species regularly for the harvest. Leaf fodder became an important staple and winter fodder for penned stock, especially cattle, a critical source of milk and cheese. Other trees like linden and elm supplied bark for the same purpose, and large quantities were harvested as bast for fiber. Browsing, foraging, hunting, underburning—all further reworked a shade-tolerant high forest into a sun-flushed low forest, full of shrubs, grasses, forbs, and woody coppice. Into the cracks, too, moved field weeds like the ribwort plantain, white clover, and sheep's sorrel, all indicators of rough pasture, open pasture, and arable, respectively. Some weeds like rye, oats, barley, charlock, turnip, and wild radish later became cultigens in their own right. Amid this restored floral renaissance, animals returned and hunting revived.

Thus landnam inaugurated a sequence of biotic reforms. The pollen record stored in bogs suggests three phases. The first tells of liberation—a sudden efflorescence of herbaceous plants, of grasses, bracken, and Compositae along with some field cereals and weeds. Elm and linden recede. The second phase registers a time of fallow and recovery. The herbaceous cover remains, pioneering trees like willow and aspen increase, and above all birch sweeps over the site, another index that burning, not simply clearing, was the stamp of true landnam. Rough pastures replace temporary gardens. The third stage witnesses the return of shade trees, but primarily those that are more light-demanding and valuable to humans. Oak, ash, and hazel dominate, stocking woody pastures full of mast for swine and a source of leaf fodder. If undisturbed, the high forest can eventually return. In some places it did, and landnam had a second coming. In most places, a pattern of shifting cultivation or persistent foraging, grazing, and burning kept the land in some intermediate state, one ideally suited for an omnivore. Landnam was, as Iversen summarizes it, "a great collective clearance by burning, carried out simultaneously with the establishment of a settlement."[5]

Nor was settlement singular. Just as the parts of the primeval forest had arrived piecemeal, so did agriculture. New peoples immigrated, fought, displaced, or intermingled with resident tribes. They introduced tools made from bronze and iron, added cultigens like barley, millet, oats, and peas, nurtured the horse and the ox, and promoted vines like ivy and grape. By the Iron Age a more complex agriculture flourished complete with plows, regular fields, hay meadows, and hemp, all helping to anchor the restless opportunism of landnam.

Not until the Great Migrations ended, however, centuries after the breakup of Rome, did landnam become sedentary. Even so, it did not cease altogether, but persisted amid folk agriculture like spores in soil and in agronomic writing as durably as metaphysical debates about free will, ready to return whenever the cultural circumstances warranted; if no longer in Europe, then elsewhere. When Europeans spilled out of the continent into the Atlantic islands and across the Eurasian plains, and leaped to the Americas and Australia, they rekindled landnam and made it the mark of their possession.

By 500 B.C. climatic vicissitudes combined with anthropogenic pressures to close the Greater Linden period. The long postglacial warm phase ended. Wetter and cooler conditions, particularly colder summers, weaked the linden; except on prime sites, soils leached and compacted; the beech at last arrived, and as a valued source of mast replaced linden as a shade-dominant species and gave its name to the subsequent period. The deciduous forest fractured into a kaleidoscope of biomes. As with the Mediterranean, some of the changes stamped themselves indelibly on the landscape.

The indisputable logo of landnam was charcoal. Burning wrought changes that grazing and cutting alone could not impose. But every part of the ancient forest felt the effects of fire-assisted agriculture. It altered both the structure and the composition of the woods. Humans promoted mast producers like oak, beech, and hazel in place of linden. They pruned back the high forest into a more profuse and accessible scrub. What the primary Neolithic did to the primordial Mediterranean forest, the central European Neolithic did to its primeval temperate cognate. The differences lay in physical geography—the precipitation regime, which limited the power of free-ranging fire, and the absence of transhumance, which restricted the size and character of free-ranging herds. Mast supplanted maquis as pasture; the need for winter fodder replaced herding with husbandry; swine and cattle, not sheep and goats, prevailed. Temperate herders carried tree fodder to the flock, not the flock to the tree. But the results could be no less profound.

Perhaps the most spectacular effect was the sudden decline of the elm. Bog archives record a precipitous fall in elm pollen all over northern Europe at roughly the same time (3000 B.C.). Almost everywhere the plunge coincides with other indicators of landnam. Once discovered, the elm decline became one of the celebrated controversies of Europe's environmental history, a sliding index of the relative importance granted to nature and humans as authors of the Neolithic environment. One side argues that climatic cooling, soil deterioration, and disease explain the recession. Certainly the havoc caused by Dutch elm disease in North America (from 1929) and Central Asia (from 1939) offers a compelling analogue for the disease argument. The counterargument, however, notes the role of elm as leaf fodder and bast in the landnam economy and the rapid selection that ax and fire make against it. Besides, Dutch elm disease, too, had spread by means of human vectors. At a minimum, the combination of disease and novel Neolithic disturbances created a synergy that proved nearly fatal to elm.[6]

The forest—the whole ensemble of the temperate biota, not only its trees—felt the impact. Landnam also reconstituted shrubs, herbs, and soils, sometimes into new mosaics, sometimes into more singular biomes. On good (clayey) soils, fire and grazing spawned rough pasture and scrub forest. On poorly drained sites, it stimulated paludification, or a domination by organic humus. The wetter climate interacted with the removal of deep-rooted trees to raise the water table and drown out natural regeneration; the ancient trees that had functioned as biotic windmills, draining sites through transpiration, lay broken. In extreme cases, mires and upland bogs resulted that were capable of submerging the former forest under a blanket of *Sphagnum* peat; and just such bogs became increasingly prevalent. Elsewhere, mowing by iron scythe transformed alder swamps into hay meadows. Different regimens of burning, mowing, and grazing reworked shrub and grass into rough pasture, and then into grassy meadows. The spread of beech catalyzed the propagation of mor soils; infertile, acidic from the slow decomposition of leafy mold, hostile to other species.

More spectacular, similar practices could create heath. Here the shock of landnam followed by intensive grazing provoked a quick flush of moss and bracken and the disappearance of holly, alder, buckthorn, and rowan, while mature oak and beech persisted, spared in order to supply mast. On thick mor, grazing retarded regeneration; bracken and then grasses replaced woods; and through a continued regimen of burning and grazing, heath spread like an enormous fungus. Once established, heath supplied good fodder for sheep, turfy fuel for hearths, and humus for exhausted fields.

Gradually, however, the ancient nutrient reservoir drained away, eventually leaving barren sand or hardpan. Cutting, burning, and grazing persisted as the only means of exploitation possible, and so perpetuated the landscape. Almost without exception the expansive heaths of northern Europe, from Brittany to the Hebrides to Prussia, were anthropogenic. One wave of heath formation resulted from the Iron Age, another through land clearing in medieval times. Its heath, and other rough pastures of assorted "wastes," were to temperate Europe what the mountain maquis was to mediterranean Europe.

(iii)

Denmark's landnam is a microcosm for the Neolithic shock wave that hit central Europe. Of course there were innumerable variants and exceptions. There are sites in central Sweden and Switzerland, for example, that suggest the resident peoples adopted selected techniques of herding without slashing and burning. Surely immigrant and indigenous peoples coexisted in some places, and surely they exchanged fire and foraging practices just as they traded spear points and shells. But overall a similar scenario replayed throughout temperate Europe, from Ireland to Poland, from the Balkans to the Baltic. On marginal landscapes and during unsettled times, the initial impact of landnam might fade away, and a new landnam would have to restart the sequence. On prime sites, some form of settled farming might quickly mature into a sedentary swidden. For most of Europe, however, the paradigm holds well into the Iron Age, the Roman conquests, and the Great Migration era. In remote sites such as the Balkans and Cantabrians, elements of landnam continued into the nineteenth century.[7]

Landnam's fundamentals were not unique to temperate Europe. Wherever agriculture went, it claimed suzerainty by fire and ax. Similar landscape records track the coming of maize to North America, wheat to Han China, Bantu-borne millet to Africa, livestock to Vedic India, taro to Polynesia. Landnam horizons trace the movement of late-wandering Europeans into Karelia and the Crimea, the Sayan and Ussuri Mountains, Madeira and Greenland, Boston Harbor and Botany Bay. In all these cases the charcoal of anthropogenic fire commemorates First Contact. The absence of landnam in Neolithic Europe—that would be puzzling.

Still, those differences matter. Fire regimes are as characteristic of a culture as its architecture or literature. Fire, moreover, is the supreme interactive technology; its ecological effects vary with its mode of application and the practices that prompt or result from it. Unlike the Americas, Neolithic Europe possessed domesticated animals, and this made European landnam into a kind of wholesale browsing that had entirely different outcomes than mere slashing and burning for vegetables could ever produce. Unlike most other agricultural centers, temperate Europe lacked a definite fire season, so human command over fuels and torch brought far greater control over fire than was possible elsewhere.

For Europe landnam shattered what had been, at least in principle, a biotic empire, a vast deciduous forest. Grasslands, heaths, shrubby wastes, peat bogs, and of course fields and gardens now dappled the landscape, and where the forest persisted, it did so with a new composition. Roman Caesars might dismiss the Hercynian Forest as a dismal wilderness, but much of that putative gloom served its small-herding residents well. Almost every place knew some human use, and most places were shaped by human desires and technology. There were exceptions: clay soils resisted persistent agriculture until deep plows were invented; swamps and fens required drainage; permanent cultivation required manure, which meant that flocks had to feed on fallow or fodder crops. Still, Neolithic agriculture ranged from sandy Jutland to the snowy slopes of the Alps. The intensity of use depended largely on the density of human population. Chronically unsettled lands either inspired a renewed landnam or its derivative, a ceaselessly shifting cultivation.

The story of Bundsø from the Danish island Als is instructive. The preserved pollen record is more complete than for anywhere else in Denmark. Here landnam gave rise to rough pasture and sporadic fields, and when beech reestablished itself, a new round of felling and firing occurred. By the early Iron Age, Als was a typical medley of rough pasture, fields, and meadows. Then the rain of agricultural pollen stops. Its absence is as diagnostic as the deluge of ash that buried Pompeii.

On nearby Jutland, archaeologists have documented deserted fields and dwellings from the fourth century A.D.; similar evidence points to an abrupt collapse in Angeln. Some common cause afflicted a wide range of tribes and lands. The explanation may well be soil deterioration, which took different forms in sandy Jutland and in fertile Als and Angeln, but almost everywhere depleted the mull soil and left a degraded mor. As agriculture became increasingly difficult, the stressed tribes abruptly emigrated. The Venerable Bede describes how, at the beginning of the fifth century, the Saxons, Angles, and Jutes invaded England—precisely the Germanic tribes whose lands now lay deserted.

Once more, the old saga was retold. The land recovered, ready for another encounter with fire and ax. The émigré peoples brought their fire practices with them, as they did their legends and shields. The Jutland forest recovered, though with *Tilia* obliterated, beech now ranked supreme. The soils also recouped some of their losses. Then a new people, cultivating rye and hemp, arrived and rekindled landnam. Soon fields and pastures returned to their former dimensions.

But this time the Great Migration era was ending, and with it closed the migratory techniques by which Neolithic peoples had colonized temperate Europe. Where people stayed put, so would agriculture and so would the fire which fed on the fallow that agriculture cultivated for it and which transmuted the biotic dross of inedible shade forest into grain, vine, and fodder. There were still unexploited sites awaiting reclamation and conversion by missionizing ax and fire, but sedentary agriculture, not landnam, defined the coming era. The emigrating Saxons put England to the plow as well as to the sword. Increasingly the biota would cycle through a field, rather than the field through the forest.

RECLAMATION:
THE FIRE IN THE GARDEN

Landnam shattered the hegemony, real or latent, of the climax forest. After the Neolithic invasion, almost nothing remained completely beyond the pale of agriculture. In small plots the conversion was complete and control absolute. Elsewhere agriculturalists reshaped the indigenous materials, selecting certain trees, shrubs, and grasses over others. Servant species, in Alfred Crosby's striking phrase, projected the humanized presence widely. What remained was the useful, and what was useful was hoed and pruned into a garden. Abandoned or unused lands became "wastes," not "wilds."

But like all pioneering, landnam was a tragic act, destroying the conditions that made it possible. Eventually the Great Migrations—those of the biota, and those of humans—slowed; the shock of encounter passed, the biotic defibrillation ceased; and settlement succeeded wanderlust. Horticulture replaced swidden, and husbandry, herding. From time to time and place to place landnam might be revived, after vast depopulations from wars or plagues; but then its purpose was restorative. Increasingly the practices behind it, including anthropogenic fire, became sedentary. They contributed to an agricultural equilibrium that like the Sun, Moon, and Earth sought to balance ager, saltus, and silva, the complementary orbits of arable field, pasture, and woods. Fire turned the wheels of this agrarian orrery, and until fossil hydrocarbons replaced the fertilizing fallow and internal combustion engines its fodder-consuming draft animals, fire remained indispensable.

(i)

When the Great Migrations ended, Germanic peoples claimed the core of temperate Europe. Angles, Jutes, and Saxons invaded England, Franks absorbed Gaul, and other Germanic tribes occupied the lands between the Alps and the Baltic and shared a nebulous eastern border with north-migrating Slavs. The scene was set for an era, or rather a sequence of eras, of profound landscape transformation. Agriculture spread, intensified, and reordered itself. The jumbled fragments left by landnam fell into a new agrarian order. From centers in northern Gaul, the practices of a more sedentary agriculture radiated throughout temperate Europe. The Neolithic revolution evolved into an agricultural establishment. The Great Reclamation commenced.

The process consumed centuries. The reclamation of temperate Europe is the story of this secondary conversion, of its advances and retreats, of landscapes alternatively farmed and fallowed. Throughout, however, there was a tendency, driven by demographic pressures, to expand and intensify the most productive core, the arable fields and the cultivated pastures. Paradoxically the Ancients' agronomic ideal, so often frustrated in the Mediterranean, found its realization in temperate Europe.

Its fires trace the narrative of this history like vignettes adorning an illuminated manuscript. Agriculture remained a pyrotechnology. Each expansion applied clearing fires, each contraction allowed the feral fuels to replenish. Throughout, fire had become as much an artifact as the landscape that sustained it. Fuels went wild because humans ceased to tend them. Ignition followed the strike of metal on stone, and the abrasion of hand and wood. Controlled combustion traced the human presence as faithfully as the ruins of hilltop fortresses or a parish registry of births and weddings.

But controlled or wild, fire follows fuel. If central Europe wanted fire, it would have to furnish that fuel, and for an agricultural society, this meant humans would have to grow it. The fire economy of reclaimed Europe thus depended on its fallow. Whether of grass, peat, coppice, shrub, or woods, virtually every agricultural site except the most minutely manicured garden involved a period of fallow, little of which was random or accidental. Rather, fallow was part of a controlled succession in which fields and crops rotated in a prescribed order, at first with the species and at the rates typical of the indigenous biota, increasingly according to an artificially calculated regimen. When fuels reached the point that they could burn, fire returned. Fire, like crops, cycled through a sedentary field, and like its practitioners was progressively bound to the land, a serfdom of swidden.

On arable sites if stubble or accumulated fallow was insufficient for a good burn, other materials were brought to help feed the flames—turf, branches, broom, pine litter, old roots, composted manure, whatever was at hand. These were the combustion cognates to field fertilizers. So important was burning that temperate farmers even intercultivated their fields with fallow, much as mediterranean farmers did wheat with olive orchards. Gorse, furze, oak, or some other coppicing wood would be grown along the borders of permanent fields, or between narrow strips of arable. After a few years, peasants would cut them, lay the debris over the fields and burn the pile. Long poles with iron hooks allowed them to move the burning debris evenly over the site.

Burning was no less essential for lands outside the arable. Almost every use exploited fire. Saltus was sustained by systematic burning. Silva burned where herders needed a flush of grass, new browse, or a cleared path; where foragers wanted a fresh crop of berries or an easy harvesting of nuts; where hunters sought to shape the proportion of open *vert* to closed *covert* or draw deer to the succulent browse pushing through a fresh burn; and where social prohibitions broke down during times of unrest or disorder and once-contained fires, like the peasantry, rioted.

Fire and fallow were thus inextricable, the yin and yang of European agriculture. Without fallow there was no fire; without fire, fallow was mere waste, not fuel or fertilizer. The Reclamation had to cultivate fallow for fire just as it had to grow oats for horses. Without fire, farming was a four-cycle engine without a spark. The oft-maligned fallow was more than simple residue. It was grown to be burned according to an appropriate regimen. In the process it fluffed up the biodiversity of an agrarian landscape and furnished endless pharmaceuticals, herbs, flowers, and edible ephemerals that otherwise stood outside the castellated walls of European agronomy. The permutations of those arrangements were endless.

Its fallow—as much as its climate—helped make the fire regime of temperate Europe different from that of the Mediterranean. In temperate Europe, farm and flock could coexist more readily. Increasingly, the farm remained bound to its agrarian tenure, and crops rotated through it instead of the farm through the land. Agriculture settled into a system of infield and outfield, of intensively cultivated ager surrounded by extensive belts of saltus and silva that provided pasture, mast, fuelwood, forbs, and swidden plots. Over the winter, the animals could remain in their barns and consume fodder brought to them. Their accumulated manure could be worked into spring fields, thus promoting better crops and greater surpluses, and so close the loopholes in nature's economy.

In the Mediterranean, climate and geography—the often scanty fields available for ager, the inviting mountains of saltus and silva—wrenched the pastoral away from the arable. Instead of closing the circle, Mediterranean agriculture was forever trying to square it. What consumed whole landscapes in the Mediterranean could be done on the scale of a temperate European village. Agriculture ceased to wander, and moved between an infield of ager and an outfield of saltus and silva. Instead of farm and flock rotating through the landscape, the landscape, in effect, rotated through them. The broken cycle could be closed.

(ii)

The land was stubborn, the politics barbarous; progress was slow. Then around 1050 the Great Reclamation accelerated, announcing its heroic age. New technologies like horse collars and wheeled and moldboard plows; new crops like spelt, rye, oats, and buckwheat; newly valuable faunal domesticates like the rabbit and hybrid sheep: innovative adaptations that made three-field rotation possible; a renewed social discipline, with monasteries replacing slave-staffed latifundia; a restored sense of purpose, the medieval expansion or Christendom, an agricultural as much as military crusade—all fueled two or in some places three centuries of extraordinary land conversion.

The upshot was a medieval geographic synthesis analogous to its synthesis of scholarship, an environmental *summa*. Substituting sedentary farming for landnam did to European agriculture what Thomas Aquinas did for Christian theology by founding it on Aristotle instead of the Patristic canon. For the heroic age of reclamation, monasteries supplied the agrarian model, villagers the greatest labor, and east-migrating Germans the most dramatic saga.

The Benedictine monasteries laboring in the Dauphiné Alps and Île-de-France pioneered a model land use, complementing their proposed model society. They demonstrated the power of organized labor, religious conviction, and classical agronomy. Others, notably the Cistercians, revived the program in the twelfth century and sought out wildland and waste. Where the forest was dense, monks resorted to a religious landnam. The abbot would solemnly plant a cross, announce possession of the unreclaimed earth, and begin to chop. Thereafter, the work proceeded systematically and collectively. *Incisores* cut down or ring-barked trees, *extirpatores* removed the trunks, and *incensores* burned the residue. But unlike the Neolithic landnam, the scale was large, the conversion more or less permanent, and the preferred livestock sheep rather than cattle. Soon, lay brothers did much of the labor, and tenant farmers, not granges of brothers and monks, did the cultivation.[8]

Existing villages took up the cause. Population increased, and the climate warmed. Villagers extended fields and intensified their usage of waste and wood. Fields grew, primarily at the expense of woodlands, and conflicts erupted when ax met ax, and flock met field. Soon new villages proliferated about the countryside, not unlike the monasteries (and often around them). These clearings too involved fire, lending fire prefixes like *brent* and *brand* or suffixes like *-schwend* to the village names. Much of the surrounding woods served as fuel. Woodcutters and charcoal burners became as common a fixture of temperate Europe as shepherds were of the Mediterranean, and often as socially suspect.

What made colonization a crusade, however, was the eastward expansion of Germanic peoples across the Elbe-Saale border. A move southeast began in the tenth century, and a thrust to the northeast around 1100. The motives were many, both economic and religious. Along the Baltic certain military orders, first the Brethren of the Sword, and later the Teutonic Knights, reinforced the alliance of cross and commerce, much as Spain did at the same time. Along the southern frontier, German tribes moved down valley after valley, clearing, herding, and with major consequences, mining. Where they traveled they installed the new agrarian order, one apparently different from that typical of the Slavs. Like a slowly creeping fire, the Germanic front propagated unevenly, in long fingers or spots, moving rapidly as conditions permitted, extinguishing when circumstances became unfavorable.

There was intensification as well as expansion. Pressured by population, at times tremendous, the ager expanded, and as it did so it absorbed the outlying "wastes" into its own domain, subdividing the cultivated land into field and fallow. The movement between infield and outfield evolved into a system of field rotations. In the two-field rotation, field and fallow were of equal parts. In the three-field rotation that became the agronomic ideal, the fallow was reduced to a third. Agricultural burning obeyed the new order of fuels.

But the land remained nonetheless under a fire-fallow regimen. Agronomists further urged that the fallow be planted to fodder crops and abolished altogether. In principle, ager could so substitute for saltus and silva, or so dominate them, that pastoralism would become animal husbandry and woodland foraging a form of silviculture. Just as horticulture replaced foraging, so sown fodder would replace rough pasture. Close cultivation could extend everywhere. Fallow, and fire, could be weeded out of the garden altogether.

That was the theory, and as agriculture stabilized and population expanded, practice sought to reflect theory. In fact, conditions made it difficult. The three-field rotation was an agronomic ideal, as hypothetical as the composition of the Seraphim, and rarely were circumstances sufficiently stable long enough for it to attain a perfected state. Always there were interruptions and obstacles —breakdowns in the delicate social order that allowed this syncretic agriculture to work, obstinate wastelands that defied conversion to arable or sown pasture, climatic fluctuations that refused to conform to three-year cycles, and awkward imbalances between spring and fall crops.

It was also only too true that shifting cultivation prevailed along the margins of the emerging order, in Scotland, Britanny, Russia, Provence, and the Alps. And the borders between agrarian patches were often fluid, moving back and forth as need and opportunity availed. The conversion was more frequently a thinning rather than a full clearing of waste and woodlands, but the linkage held here as often as it broke in the Mediterranean, and the amount of land brought into composite cultivation steadily increased. Most spectacularly, the Great Reclamation transformed woodlands and later wetlands. Although the woods were too valuable a source of fuel, charcoal, pannage, leaf fodder, and timber to strip completely, they were remade and reintegrated with the arable into patterns that would shape the European landscape for more than a millennium.

Throughout, the fallow persisted. By most agricultural philosophers it was regretted and detested, infesting fields like weeds and forever lurking along the margins. Yet by practitioners it was welcomed as a great buffer against the viscissitudes of fortune, a natural reservoir of recaptured nutrients ready, when needed, to convert into crops and fodder, the fuel for mandatory fire. The three-field rotation on ager only miniaturized, not eliminated, the tripartite division of the landscape. Fallow persisted: and as long as fallow thrived, so did fire.

What fire did not convert outright, it cleaned. What humans and livestock (and vermin, birds, insects, and fungi) did not consume was sure to be burned in field or hearth or in wild accident. Field rotation was landnam domesticated; field fires, the pyric equivalent of the rotation of planted crops. Olivier de Serres, echoing Vergil, wrote that "many people handle the stubble still better by burning it on the land: the fire prepares the soil to admit the coulter and rids it of an infinity of weeds, insects and harmful seeds." So, too, was fire needed to soften rough pasture and sweeten foraged woods, to keep marsh and scrubland flush with palatable browse, to clean pollarded forests of residue, to prepare mast forests for harvest, to beat back intrusions of undesirable species, and to green up understories for loose-herded cattle and sheep. For the European gardener, the torch was broom, rake, shovel, and ax.[9]

By 1300 the long wave of the Great Reclamation broke. By the fourteenth century the land lay behind it like a great lagoon, the force of the wave's momentum spent. Exhaustion soon gave way to catastrophe. Terrible winters brought famines; the Black Death gutted Europe; prices fell, and the economy stagnated; lengthy wars of attrition broke out, from the Turks in the east to the Hundred Years' War between England and France in the west. The population pressures that had sustained agricultural colonization now imploded. Deserted fields and abandoned villages dotted the countryside, like candles blown out one by one in a great hall. The contriving hand was sick, dead, or fighting. The biota began its own reconquest. Rough pasture overran arable, scrub reclaimed saltus, shaggy forest grew over scrub. Its forests, peasants long proclaimed, "came back to France with the English."[10]

The nadir of the decline was the century between 1350 and 1450. Then came a renaissance, as much environmental as artistic. Much of the forsaken landscape was again reclaimed. Old fields were recleared and again experienced intensive farming. And like a rising lake, the eager waters of increased population fingered through old wastes and lapped up the slopes of the Alps. By the sixteenth century there were complaints, locally, about fuel famines, shortages in naval timbers, soil erosion, and flooding. With its fallows converted or consumed, the fields languished or degraded. By the seventeenth century alarms led in England to John Evelyn's *Sylva: A Discourse of Forest Trees* (1664) and in France to Colbert's Forest Ordinance (1669). The German states evaded the forecast crisis only by enduring the far worse wreckage of the Thirty Years' War (1618–48), then responded, in part, by inventing modern forestry. The English, however, turned to coal (in 1709, Abraham Darby smelted iron ore with coke), sought fresh supplies from its North American colonies and the Baltic trade, and applied the practical knowledge beloved by the Enlightenment to the problems of rationalizing agriculture. By the late eighteenth century Europe was again in the throes of revolution—political, economic, and agrarian.

(iii)

Landnam had wandered opportunistically through the land like a huge scrawl. The Great Reclamation had closed that line, but the resulting figure was far from the clean circle agronomists advocated. It was uneven, erratic, full of eccentric loops and digressions. A fire-driven agriculture followed the terrain of fallow, and fallow brought other putative evils, social as much as environmental. The only way to sharpen those contours was to reduce each increment of fallow, like infinitesimals approaching a limit. But fallow was not a mathematical abstraction, it was part of an ecological system.

The agronomic circle would close, only when humans could import energy

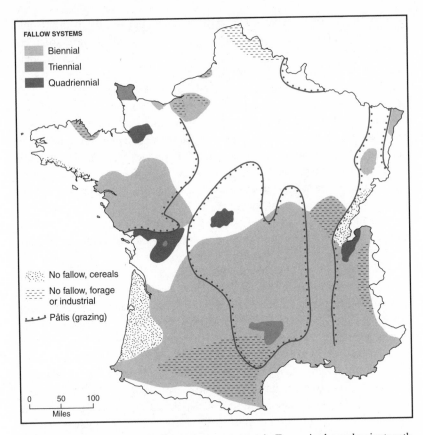

Fire-fallow agriculture. (Left) Crop rotation systems in France in the early nineteenth century. (Adapted from Braudel 1988 by the University of Wisconsin Cartographic Lab) (Right) "Burning the Fields in the Black Forest" by C. Rour, mid-nineteenth century. (Photo courtesy J. G. Goldammer)

and materials from outside the prevailing ecosphere. That process began with overseas colonies, which became an outfield to Europe's infield; but it achieved its apogee when fossil fallows replaced living, and fire was sublimated into machines. Coal and petroleum—extracted from sources far removed from existing ecosystems—poured into the agricultural economy like an infusion of plundered treasure. Applied to fields they brought fertilizers, pesticides, and herbicides; inside internal combustion engines, they rendered obsolete the fodder-demanding horse, donkey, and ox; embedded within a global economy of capital and trade, they shrank the agrarian circle to a vanishing point. Like commerce breaking down the walls of cities, this new agriculture, flush with imported biotic bullion, began literally redesigning the rural landscape with the

fanaticism of a modernist architect. Banning fallow abolished a good bit of bio-diversity and imposed its own ecological costs—an inflationary spiral of excess chemicals that piled up on land, seeped into waters, and clouded the air.

But, for a while, combusting fossil fallows allowed Europe to step outside the closing confines of its agrarian economy, and to achieve the platonic dream of ancient agronomists and modern philosophes: to banish fire from the gar-den. Since agriculture was the essence of landed Europe, and fire-fallow farm-ing the essence of agriculture, any such change would be revolutionary beyond the wildest imaginings of democrat, free-trader, or anarchist. Intensifying agriculture could reduce but not eliminate fallows. The true agricultural revolution had to wait for industry.

Until then the fallows remained, and with it the corruptible flames. Until then Europe's agronomists had to live with what François de Neufchâteau called "the disgrace of the fallows." It shamed agronomic revolutionaries much as autocrats did political theorists and monopolies did Enlightenment economists. The fallows' fires were the insurrections, superstitions, aristocratic privileges, mercantilist obstructionisms, and ineradicable poor of an irrational and arbitrary agriculture. The only way to close that circle, however, was to take a leap of ecological faith and transcend it. As Enlightenment Europe rebuilt the lost landscapes of the Great Reclamation, that ambition appeared impossibly idealistic. To many despairing philosophes it seemed that the fallows would always be with them.[11]

REVOLUTION:
THE ENLIGHTENMENT COMES TO AGRICULTURE

The Great Reclamation had its limits. Sometimes, as demanded by demographics, its wobbly circle swelled and sometimes contracted; but the reclamation could not alter those fundamental cycles without penalty. The apexes of the agrarian triangle—ager, saltus, and silva—remained in roughly constant proportion. In 1600, for example, France had 35 percent of its land in arable, 30 percent in pasture, and 33 percent in forest. They constituted the three estates of Europe's agricultural polity.

But the population began to build, and has not slackened to the present day; for over two centuries, agriculture has had to intensify and expand in order to satisfy those hungry mouths. As reclamation had replaced landnam, so an agricultural revolution reworked the reclamation. To the inherited mosaic, the revolution brought new shards, organized them into novel patterns, and carried the scheme to previously spared places, all with the intention of increasing the proportion of arable. Rebellion began to stir in the seventeenth century, then accelerated into full-blown revolution from the mid-eighteenth and into the nineteenth, breaking trail for the industrial revolution that followed. The conversion of old fields and the colonization of new ones continued. Between 1600 and 1890 the proportion of arable land in France exploded from 35 percent to 60 percent.[12]

Intensification required new crops and additional fertilizer. Cultigens such as maize, potatoes, and tomatoes arrived, all émigrés from American colonies, all soon integrated into field rotation, and all stimulants to higher productivity. Moreover, new fodder crops (again, the potato was a universal pablum, adapted equally to humans and hogs, and even distilled into liquor) reduced the need for rough pasture and woods pannage. Better, it encouraged the conversion of grazed and foraged lands into arable or at least artificial or sown pastures, and it meant that animals could be farmed as fully as plants.

So also the arrangement of the agricultural pieces changed. Much of this resulted from trial and error by peasants, a continuous jostling of parts to achieve a better fit. But agronomic philosophers—soon to be the fourth estate of agriculture—cast a skeptical, often scornful eye at the scene as well. An intellectual storm, founded on modern science, finally broke in the seventeenth century, aptly encapsulated by Isaac Newton's *Principia Mathematica* (1687) and John Locke's *Essay Concerning Human Understanding* (1690). The war between the Ancients and the Moderns heated up: the old was superstitious, the new enlightened; mathematics and experiment, not historical anecdote and literary essay, were the tools of understanding; modern natural philosophers like Newton, not ancient gossips like Pliny, explained how the natural world worked.

Inevitably the Enlightenment looked upon traditional agriculture as it did on inherited political structures or revealed religion. François Malouet might exult that "the works of nature, her spontaneous production and primitive creations have almost vanished under the strenuous efforts of the inhabitants of the old continent." But in 1787, on the eve of political revolution, the French agronomist F. H. Gilbert could denounce agriculture for having made no real progress since Roman times. Crop rotations and herding seemed the residue of mere tradition; the fallow was endlessly embarrassing. Clearly intervention was necessary. Surely enlightened reason could best—that is, most rationally— organize agriculture as it had physics, law, machinery, and would soon attempt in politics. If the Great Reclamation resembled an environmental *summa,* the agricultural revolution was a landscape *Encyclopédie.* A new generation of agronomists supplied not only lessons but standards. With few exceptions they condemned fallow, sought to convert waste with the same passion they might argue for inalienable natural rights, and labeled fire the prime criterion for discriminating the rational from the primitive.[13]

Meanwhile agrarian systems, new, old, and hybrid, pushed outward, not only to overseas colonies but over marsh and fen, alpine slopes and saltwater polder, to heath, upland moor, and scrub. This expansion of arable was a conversion of waste, not of wild. Much of that waste, like heath or peat, had resulted from the shock of landnam or had sunk, during centuries of reclamation, into a lethargy of inaccessible fallow. The intention was to expand the arable, either by direct conversion or indirectly through the production of more manure by enlarging pastures.

Its revival into arable, however, upset the reigning equilibriums that had governed the agricultural polity. Behind the aristocratic ager lay the increasing impoverishment of lower-grade saltus and silva. Expansion came through forced levies, ecological corvées, and environmental extortion paid ultimately with exhausted soils, mountain erosion, torrential floods, and biotic impauperment, until the landscape mimicked the gross disparities of the society that fashioned it. Threatened insurrection led to further oppression.

These conditions did not pass unnoticed. By the mid-eighteenth century, alarmed critics pondered the implications of the reclamation's *ancien régime.* By the end of that century, agronomic philosophes were aghast at its apparent decadence and stupidity, and saw the fired heaths of Brittany and the burned mountain slopes of Franche-Comté as agrarian cognates to the palace debauchery at Versailles, peasant superstitions, and mercantilist monopolies. Further revolution was inevitable: it only remained to determine means and ends. By the time the revolution had run its course, there were alternatives. Colonies, cities, and industry could sop up the surplus rural population; fossil hydrocarbons could substitute for fallow and firewood; and by the mid-nineteenth century the agricultural revolution had become secondary to the industrial.

Until then the revolution reorganized all three of agriculture's estates and restructured all three of the biota's strata, from its organic soils to its surface flora to its forests. Each part had evolved—and each was reclaimed—according to some variety of swidden. Demographics demanded increased productivity, and nature, for a while, supplied it, but only through the controlled combustion that drove agronomic theorists to distraction and set intellectuals' teeth on edge.

(i)

The conversion of soils was among the most spectacular of the revolution's practical reforms and among its most controversial. In effect, peasants applied the techniques of swidden to peat. While this allowed arable to expand into the domain of rough pasture, it also often incurred the same wrath and intellectual outrage as other expressions of slashing and burning. The controversy over paring and burning, as it was called in Britain (*écobuage* in France, *Rasenbrennen* and other terms in Germany), is a cameo of the Enlightenment's agricultural revolution, for it involved reclaiming land from a state degraded by Europe's ancestral agriculture.

Agriculture turned in on itself. The combination of a wetter, cooler climate and landnam had pushed many coastal landscapes, in particular, toward heath and hardpan and transformed exposed upland sites into bog or moor, too wet for cropping. Instead these lands stockpiled undecomposed debris, the ecological equivalent of stuffing hard currency into socks and mattresses. Such landscapes appeared to outsiders as vast wastelands. They served as rough pasture, and herders burned them according to various regimens. *Swidden,* after all, derived from an old Norse term for burning the Yorkshire ling or heath on a roughly ten-year cycle.

But now agriculture pursued the organic stratum beneath the surface mosses and heather. That stored organic matter was not so much infertile as inaccessible; its stockpiled nutrients were no worse than those locked up in trees, and they could sustain crops if properly liberated. The wealth of the biota, like the wealth of nations, was based on movement, on trade. But too much of Europe's was simple bullion, and too much was buried like the jewelry entombed with Iron Age kings. The problem was to get that specie back into the agricultural economy, and the techniques were the same for peat as for forest: cut and burn.

Where wood was scarce, peasants had long burned peat for fuel, and during droughts wildfires had routinely sent flames across moors and gnawed into pockets of peat like corroding acid. The innovation was to cut and burn the turf in situ for crops. In general, two strategies emerged. One imitated slash-and-burn forestry in which paring, drying, and burning occurred more or less on the site. The other mimicked charcoal, tar, or potash production, in which the cut turf was gathered into piles, often covered, sometimes placed into ovens, and slowly burned; peasants then carried the ashes back to the fields. In both forms a distinct crop rotation followed according to local prescriptions. The cycle varied from four to eight years and ended with a period of fallow in which the peat built up to the point that farmers could reinitiate the process. The analogy with swidden in forests was almost perfect.[14]

The practice achieved its greatest renown in Britain, which had upland bogs in abundance and was also the premier center for the new agronomy. Devonshire became such a point of dispersion that it lent its name to the operation, and paring and burning often propagated under the label "devonshiring" or "denshiring."

Naturally agronomists differed on its value. Advocates pointed to the successful conversion of otherwise sealed wastelands. This, together with improved stock breeding and the integration of fodder crops like potatoes and turnips into the rotation, encouraged the transformation of loose herding into animal husbandry, all of which were part of the agenda of Enlightenment agriculture. Critics, however, saw ruined humus and the perpetuation of swidden practices that should, by rights, be suppressed, not spread. They insisted that the long-term consequences were deadly, for denshiring was a profligate agriculture that would spend nature's biotic capital instead of living off its interest. A British forester, returned from India, compared the migratory paring and burning of the Low Countries with the practices of nomadic Tatars. Urban critics, especially, argued for *étrempage,* in which organic matter was added to a site, then plowed in, a green manure analogous to the compost of a garden; this was *écobuage* without fire. Their obsession was to build up, not diminish, the humus.

The normally pyrophobic British actually found proponents of paring and burning. In his compendium of West Country agriculture William Marshall (1796) concluded that "sodburning is essential to success." There was no other way to escalate productivity in otherwise marginal land. The indefatigable Reverend Arthur Young campaigned strenuously on behalf of the practice. In the Fens he observed that "it is scarcely possible, profitably, to bring boggy, mossy, peat soils, from a state of nature into cultivation, without the assistance of fire." In Sussex he declaimed that paring and burning was "one of the greatest improvements which land is susceptible of receiving." It gave the farmer that most valued of goods: a de facto dunghill, a mound of ashy manure, a ready cache of nutrients. The dosage, not the practice, determined its toxicity. Done poorly, paring and burning strip-mined the peat. Done well—not too deep, not too often, not on too sandy a soil—it liberated nutrients, reduced soil acidity, and improved soil hydrology.[15]

The British Isles remained the premier practitioner, but wherever the climate tended to be exceptionally sodden, there peat proliferated and arable agriculture struggled unless fire could break the remorseless accumulation of undecomposed biomass. The inspiration for cutting and burning organic soil was obvious, and had long folk precedents. What changed was its gradual assimilation into the agricultural revolution. A whole assemblage of secondary technologies—spades, plows, furnaces, turf cutters, field drainage—brought rigor to the process. Instead of a folk landnam of sod-burning, paring and burning evolved into a system, or rather applied the prevailing methods and ideas of the new agriculture to former wastes.

The Dutch adapted the practice in the early eighteenth century. From there it spread to Germany. The British example soon emboldened Scandinavians. The Reverend Young personally carried the cause to the continent, helping inspire the French, in particular, to expand the practice. By the mid-eighteenth century, écobuage had already assumed "classic" form in western France, much to the dismay and skepticism of agricultural philosophes including the Marquis de Turbilly (1761); hybrid versions sprang up in Midi and Provence. Still, the British exemplar, when it was explained fully, led to important revisions. By then variants had appeared wherever deep organic soils were prevalent. The practice penetrated into western Finland, Swiss cantons, Serbian hills, and Scottish highlands. It continued until forestry's saws replaced the breast plow and the industrial revolution sent it the way of the draft horse.[16]

(ii)

The great wastes were those given to rough pasture, the moors, heaths, marshes, and native prairies. They were traditionally fired as necessary; temperate pastoralists burned heath as their Mediterranean colleagues did maquis. An average cycle was ten years, which meant that roughly one-tenth of the total heath pasture burned in any one year. The benefits were self-evident, at least to those whose livelihood depended on healthy heath. Without regular firing the land became decadent, biodiversity shrank, and wildfires raged more intensely. In France the *landes* of Poitou, Brittany, Gascony, Auvergne, and Languedoc were all burned regularly well into the nineteenth century (and locally beyond then). On mountain pastures, too, transhumant pastoralists used fire to advance their spring march up the slopes amid rough grasses and browse and to cover their retreat in the fall. Here was a typical fire-fallow system, precisely what agricultural improvement sought to abolish.

The practice had ample problems, some real, some hypothetical. Spring burns were hazardous; too frequent firing, and intensive grazing too soon after a burn, degraded the heath; and nominally controlled fires often escaped to enter adjacent fields or woods. During droughts, normally innocuous fires could burn stubbornly. The historic record is full of pastoral fires set in upland moors that burned for weeks; Lower Saxony, for example, knew major outbreaks in 1645, 1664, 1719, 1776, 1780, 1780, and 1788. Brittany's experience during the 1976 drought shows the potential for wildfire where fuel and flame could meet. The best restraint was close management of the biota, good housekeeping that left few crumbs for a pestilent fire to feed upon. There were legal prohibitions against reckless burning everywhere (Denmark's Jutland Law dates to 1241); but decrees did not mean control. Where regulation was possible, pastoralists burned at night, under wet conditions, and with official permission. Since all this proved burdensome, illegal fires flourished.[17]

Worse, the burning did nothing to reform rough pasture into arable or its close cousin, sown pasture. Rotational burning sustained the status quo; revolution required improvement. The premise of artificial forage was that, with the right combination of plant and animal, manure and close grazing could substitute for fallow and controlled burning. The pasture could become as much a garden as the arable field. Rough pasture like heath, however, too often consisted of pyrophytes that stored much of their biomass below ground and compressed their growing season so that they were dormant (and combustible) over a prolonged spring and fall; this made fires both inevitable and innocuous. But high-yield forage that was also tolerant of trampling, like lucerne and white clover, lived differently: it stored more biomass above ground, accessible to grazers; and its season for growing began early and continued late, keeping to a minimum the need for supplementary fodder. Because such plants fixed nitrogen in the soil they brought an added bonus, but without adequate fire protection they were also easily harmed by burning in mixed fields.

Thus fires seemingly prolonged rough pasture, probably at the cost of cultivation, and they kept pastoralism alive, perhaps at the expense of animal husbandry. But full reclamation was difficult. The heath was stable as heath. To move it from that ecological inertia required the application of tremendous force, and the requisite biologic power could come only from social sources. To reform the heath would, in fact, have to reverse the legacy of landnam. Where Neolithic pioneers had struggled to render the landscape more fire-prone because they could then more readily influence it, their industrial progeny would have to make it less so because the new agriculture relied on other forms of combustion, and wanted flame in the hearth and furnace and nowhere else.

Perhaps the most spectacular reconversion was the second reclamation of Jutland. There is symbolic symmetry to the story, that Denmark, the exemplar of European landnam, should serve as the prime exhibit of its replacement. That it took an embryonic industrialization to install an aging agriculture was irrelevant, or rather was one of the endless ironies attendant to the story. The reclamation of the Jutland heath was metaphor as much as landscape, an emblem by which the rehabilitation of land could be coextensive with the restoration of society.

The heath was the result of fire-catalyzed clearing, and it had been renewed periodically by further burning to support extensive grazing. Soil charcoal records the major clearings—the classic landnam around 2000 to 2300 B.C., another at 400 B.C., and again about A.D. 400 at the onset of the Great Migrations, and yet again, a final surge that commenced around 1200. Where it wasn't deserted, western Jutland was an outfield to an east Jutland and Zealand infield.[18]

Still, the moors spread. The ecological conversion, once begun, was remarkably stable. The heath was as imperturbable as the shade forest it had succeeded. Soils and hydrology adjusted no less than flora, one to another, and made spontaneous reversion almost impossible. Without fire the biota sank into lassitude; with it alone, however, there could be no improvement. Fire recycled, but it could not add. The great wastes—empty, howling with the west wind, overrun (in Danish imagination) with wolves, populated by vagrants and outlaws—defied European conceptions of order. They were, the state perceived, a "lost province." So alien was the expanse that critics regarded it as a foreign colony, not unlike those being settled in North America or along the Volga. But experiments at deliberate colonization repeatedly failed.[19]

In 1751, Frederick V commissioned a survey of Alheden, and then recruited Captain Ludvig Kahlen, experienced in heath reclamation at Mecklenburg, who gathered a small band of German refugees from Westphalia. The center of the new estate was Kongenshus. Reclamation proceeded by cutting, burning, and plowing. The heath resisted; Danes refused to accept internal exile to such a forsaken place; and the Mecklenburgers, overwhelmed, fled one night. But German agronomic and cameralist influences were strong. Further recruiting renewed the colonization effort. By 1763, six small settlements clustered in Alheden. Enclosure of the commons helped. So did the potato. Together they sustained a resident population, although one that remained dependent on the heath (a stubbornly fire-fallow regime) for pasture, berries, fuel, and roofing. Fire was omnipresent, controlled burning mandatory, and wildfire a constant threat. Failure meant famine. A bad burn stimulated weeds, starved cultigens of nutrients, or burned pasture out of season. In 1763 an escaped fire threatened Groønhoøj and swept away all its heath. By 1805, heath claimed 40 percent of Jutland, and woods less than 2 percent.[20]

Ex nihilo nihil: more could not be produced from less. Inputs were needed from the outside, something to jolt Jutland out of its inertia. That happened with the loss of Schleswig-Holstein to Prussian arms in 1864. Overnight Denmark had surrendered a third of its agricultural lands. Worse, it suffered humiliation, because its own military had to pull back from the Dannevirke, which had defined its ancient border. A year later, Enrico M. Dalgas began a campaign of compensation. The reclamation of the Jutland heath, he argued, could counterbalance the lost landscapes and redeem the national honor. Rebuked by authorities, he took his cause to the public. In 1866 he, along with Drewsen Morville and Ferdinand Mourier-Petersen, formed the Danish Heath Society.[21]

Officials remained skeptical: they had been burned before in Jutland. An authority on the reclamation of the Belgian Campine, Lt. J. C. la Cour, argued that success required large markets, heavy fertilizing, and lots of capital. It required an economic investment sufficient to overcome the ecological deficits. But that, with the advent of railroads, was now possible. Vacant heath could be linked to urban centers, and fertilizer (first as marl, then artificial forms) could be imported in bulk. Cultivation and afforestation could reclaim Jutland's landscape, replacing waste with wealth. So, too, the public commitment could redeem Denmark. In 1872, Hans P. Holst wrote a motto for the Heath Society that became a national cry:

> *For every loss compensation can be found,*
> *What is lost without, that shall be won within.*[22]

The moral argument was probably decisive. As scientists focused on the heath, it became apparent that forests had once clothed Jutland, and that humans had cleared them and created the shameful wasteland. It should therefore be possible for humans to reverse that conversion. The moral charge that medieval cultivators had given reclamation on religious grounds, nationalists now promoted for secular reasons. The public rallied to Dalgas's patriotic appeal. He became the "hero of the heaths." The "heath cause" expanded by fire reclamation from moors to bogs. By 1950, heaths comprised only 8 percent of Jutland, and forests 9 percent.[23]

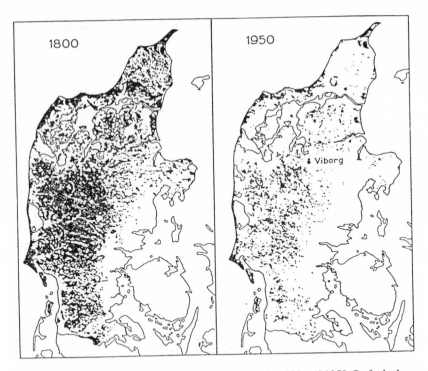

The conversion of Jutland. (Left) The extent of heath in 1800 and 1950. So far had the process gone that some Danes advocated heath protection as a matter of historic preservation. (From Thorpe 1957; by permission of the Institute of British Geographers) (Right) Changing land use around Frederiks. Agriculture claimed the greatest land, but forestry was also integral. (Data from Thorpe)

Despite the brazen nationalism of the Jutland cause (or perhaps because of it), similar coastal reclamations occurred throughout Europe. The techniques circulated with remarkable ease. Steensberg notes how, in the 1830s, bog burning around Copenhagen followed procedures described in England, but that the "local farmer had learned the method from a Dutch paper, which had been translated into German and printed in Lüneburg." Afforestation had become a pan-European craze, although in Jutland, as elsewhere, few of its claims to environmental amelioration were proved. Likewise the growth of international trade made conversion to intensive dairy farming feasible. And it was, in the largest sense, the development of fossil hydrocarbons that, like an infusion of ecological grace, made the conversion possible. But reclamation did not end with full immersion in fertilizer and steam.[24]

Perhaps inevitably there was a reaction. Deep burning without fertilizer ("dead

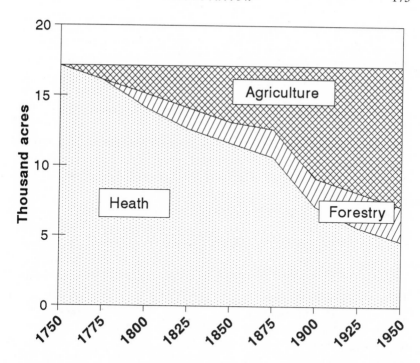

burning") drained nutrients. The great clouds of smoke necessary for reclamation burning drifted with the winds and immersed the urban metropole. In
Germany an Anti-Moorburning Society arose in 1881 to stop it. Another developed in Brussels. It was acceptable to link city and country with the smokestacks of locomotives, but less so with the stagnant palls of smoldering
moors.[25]

Even the intellectual (and patriotic) bonds weakened. The "Jutland movement" of artists, best known for Jeppe Jensen (Aakjaer), argued the case for
some heath preservation. Aakjaer noted that accessible heath was receding, and
thought the continued obsession with Jutland diverted attention from rural
reform on Denmark's better landscapes. He likened the rows of afforested
conifers to columns of Prussian soldiers, thus reversing the Heath Society's
patriotic call to arms. Save some heath, he pleaded. It was part of Denmark's
heritage, and only by preserving it could future generations appreciate the full
meaning of its reclamation. In a countermotto, he wrote:

> *Spare this remainder of seasoned ancient earth*
> *. . .*
> *Do not disparage the heath's "barren" gift;*
> *It is a poor country, which is nothing but garden.*

The new heath cause merged with the creation of the Danish Nature Conservation Society, and helped propel national park legislation in 1917. Appropriately, this initiative led to the establishment of a memorial park at Kongenshus.[26]

Appropriately, too, they could not abolish fire. If heath parks were not to be a garden, their fires could not be managed by cultivation. The waste would remain a permanent fallow. The parks would burn. They could not stand like the memorial statues of Dalgas and Aakjaer at Kongenshus. Without fire they would degenerate. Postindustrial Denmark found itself ironically returning protected landscapes to the age of landnam. The cracking of the primeval shade forest had created a profusion of niches into which species had insinuated themselves. By tearing down those structures, as decrepit as they perceived them to be, the Danes had removed the habitats altogether.

By the 1980s only fifty black grouse, a characteristic species of the heath, remained. The grouse could survive only if the heath endured, and the heath could flourish only if properly burned. Denmark was spending $10 million a year to practice what, for over a millennia, its leading authorities on land usage had condemned as unnecessary, baleful, and destructive. It found that reserves often needed fire, that burning was to nature preservation what scrubbing acid-rained statues in London and cleaning frescoes in Florence were to art preservation. The politics of combustion had been inverted. The smoldering moors had been replaced by smog-drenched factories and city streets, and now it was the misplaced combustion of the metropolis that threatened the heath.

(iii)

That left the third of the agrarian triumvirate, silva. Like heath, marsh, and moor, the woods were pasture; like peatlands, they were fuel; and like organic soils, they represented a storehouse of nutrient bullion. Unlike these classic "wastes," however, woods furnished other goods, notably timber, thus complicating its conversion to arable or meadow. Many places needed woody fuel or charcoal, and maritime powers found the absence of nautical oak and pine masts a military and commercial liability. So some high forest had to remain. But many woodlands could adapt to a more intensive agriculture, and the border between ager and silva rose and fell under the tidal pull of the new regime. The typical compromise was a species of swidden, a rotation between field and forest.

Most woods were communal, and most existed for fuel and forage, for firewood, charcoal, grasses, and mast. It was common in England, for example, to measure the size of a woods by the number of swine it could feed; there were 40-swine forests, 100-swine forests, and so on. Forest reserves existed, some for naval timber, more for royal hunting grounds. ("Forest" was a legal not biological term: the land might or might not be wooded, and if wooded it might or might not have many tall trees; probably not, since deer fed on browse and sought low covert, not high canopies.) The first clearing of woodlands sometimes resulted in their permanent conversion to field. Just as often it led to a new rhythm of fallowing.

The woods stood not aside from agriculture but in bonded servitude to it. Only later, with the triumph of forestry, did the belief arise that the barrier between forest and agriculture had to be absolute, that woods and field were implacable and exclusive rivals. Rather, infield needed outfield, ager needed silva—and woods needed arable land, for agriculture's demands were also the measure of society's protection. The woods were fallow and fuel as much as they were timber.

Of course the proportion of land devoted to each practice varied by place and time. Shifting cultivation was part of a shifting equilibrium. But traditional agronomy did not demand the extinction of woods: if the woods deteriorated, the fields also suffered. In mountain areas, resistant to deep plowing, farming was impossible without forest fallow. That "the forest enriches the soil" was a truism of later forestry. A graduate of Nancy elaborated how the forest is "the world's common soil-fertiliser, as firewood is the world's common fuel. Sometimes there is intermittent forestry and agriculture. Sometimes the forest litter is carted on to the fields. In Europe, the litter from the forest is removed as far as the forest will stand the process and put under the farm stock to form manure. This practice extends all through Europe."[27]

Fire cultivation of forests was characteristic of temperate Europe's perimeter —endemic throughout boreal Scandinavia, dominant in expansionist Russia, and common in Mediterranean mountains. Pockets persisted stubbornly in the Pyrenees, the Dinarics, the Carpathians, the Cantabrians, and the Massif Central. Within temperate Europe, the versions that most flourished were in sites similarly marginal to the ideals of garden farming, places like the Ardennes, the upper Rhine massif, the slopes of the Carpathians, and the splayed terrain of the greater Alps. Each region had its special features, its own descriptive terminology. Each displayed a range of variations according to the length of fallow, local climates, and larger agricultural systems in which the burning occurred. But they were clearly all of a type, like different-colored daisies in a common field. A quick sampling will demonstrate both their diversity and their commonality.[28]

In the Polish Carpathians, forest farming took three forms, depending on the length of fallow. Long fallow led to tall forests. These were cut in the autumn, dried over spring, burned in the summer, and planted to rye in the fall. It was possible to sow two, three, or even four crops, then burn the fallen trunks and standing stumps for another flush. By this time the old grazed sites returned to grass, eventually to woody thickets. If left alone the scrub restored itself ultimately into a tall forest. More commonly, the site became incorporated into a shorter rotation. Sometimes the clogged thickets were cut and burned, with cereals sown on the site or with the ashes gathered to carry to arable fields elsewhere. Often the forest, once broken to an agricultural harness, simply became a long-rotation field, slashing and burning the young (fifteen- to thirty-year-old) trees for three or four years of crops in regular sequence. In the southern Carpathians, forest fallow was combined with transhumance. Farmers needed the summer valleys cleared of herds, and the herds needed the extra fodder grown to tide them over winter.

All this was a calculated program: peasants sowed the required tree seeds with their cereals. The fallow was as much a deliberate part of the cultivation as wheat and turnips. Reportedly, the practice continued into the 1970s.[29]

In Austria's Steiermark (Styria) a related pattern evolved. Conversion of high forest commenced with logging for timber. Peasants then fired the slash. After cropping, the land served as pasture, then regrew to forest. Again, pine seeds were sown with the rye. In seventy years the cycle would begin anew. Where crops and pasture were more important than construction timber, the fallow shortened, to thirty to forty years. Trees were not only felled but their branches trimmed and spread evenly over the site. The resulting rye crop was, Axel Steensberg explains, "in great demand by farmers from elsewhere because it was practically free of seeds of other plants." For six to ten years after cropping, the site served as pasture. Then scrub overwhelmed the grasses.[30]

But high forest was not necessary. Younger woods were much easier to manipulate for fuel slash alone, so anxious peasants often shortened the fallow. (The rotation was typically twenty-five years in conifers; eighteen to twenty in birch, alder, and hazel; ten to twelve in pure alder.) Even the scrub was enough. On the poorest ground the practice was to divide the land into twelve or fifteen units, one of which was burned and sown every year, then grazed for four to six years. Large-scale swiddening continued until World War I, and in fact survived here and there into the 1960s.

In the Schwarzwald—Germany's famed Black Forest—fire farming was ancient. *Brandwirtschaft* took many forms, as always varying according to the length of the fallow and the purposes other than temporary arable to which the land was put. Probably less than 30 percent of the woodland was high forest (*Hochwald*), and that fifty to seventy years in age. Typically it was logged before burning. The remainder was low forest (*Niederwald*), the product of repeated cutting, grazing, and burning on a rotation of twelve to twenty years. But that is exactly what the peasants wanted: coppice for ready conversion to fuelwood or charcoal; woody slash for swidden farming; broom and thatch for housing and for byre bedding; oak bark for tanning (the bark should not be over seventeen years in age). Depending on what trees were most valued, oak or pine seeds were sown into the ash along with rye or potatoes. If this seeding failed, then hazel, birch, and hawthorn sprang up, although these too had their uses.[31]

Written references to *Brandwirtschaft* date back to the medieval period; observers saw it practiced well into the nineteenth century. Between the Ruhr and the Sieg, T. C. Banfield reported in 1846–48 how "a rotation of coppice or underwood, cut down every sixteen years, affords both bark for the numerous tanners and charcoal for the metallurgists; and both occupations alternate with the care of small farms belonging to these small manufacturers, as the rye is admitted into the forest rotation the year after the underwood is cut down." In 1871, V. Vogelmann noted that most of the population of the Schwarzwald survived through a mixed regime of swidden, known locally as *Reutberge* (hacked mountains), a practice that was "many centuries old." The forested mountains, he continued, are "stocked with coppice forests which are hacked after clearcut, fertilised by burning of litter (through a flaming fire) or by smouldering of grass, and utilised for growing rye, potatoes or oats."

An astonished Briton, familiar with swidden in Africa and India, saw *Reutberge* during a study tour of Germany, and called it by its Xhosa term, *kumri*, as a way of expressing his distaste: "All down the valley is poor, open, or devastated private forest with patches of Kumri, now burning about every quarter of a mile. The burning is done down hill with ten men on a width of about 30 yards. It is a perfectly calm, hot afternoon. The scene is like Kaffirland in spring. When the forest is done they burn heaped up soil and branches to get the ashes they want for the soil." He noted, equally fascinated and repelled by the spectacle, "This Kumri is recognized by law, and the burning of the forest not punished." The slash was carefully piled, the intervening grounds burned off, and large or escaped fires rare. The government even furnished conifer seedlings to help with replanting.[32]

The burning was regulated, as it had to be. Swiddeners fired fields in strips separated by firebreaks, not en masse; they smoothed out debris to ensure an even burn; they laid heavier logs along contours to prevent rolling brands from escaping and to retard soil erosion; they left some mature trees for seeding; they followed a rigorous if local prescription for crop sequencing; they restricted grazing, often denying access altogether for two years, then regulating access by sheep and goats in particular; and they notified neighbors, obtained permits, staffed firelines, and burned with free-burning flame or in piles as conditions warranted.

But fires could still escape, and did. Not everyone at every epoch took pains to restrict fire, especially during times of distress or war, and especially on commons. Often villages turned the worst common lands over to the landless poor, to farm as best they could. In times of stress the period of fallow shortened, going from perhaps twenty to thirty years to as little as twelve to fifteen. Forest fallow became coppice fallow. After centuries of continuous exploitation, the environment often suffered, although the constant rotation of plants catalyzed by swidden was better for the land than the monocultures of unburned forest that often succeeded them.

For centuries peasants had preferentially selected oak for its good properties as fuelwood, its tolerance of light, and the value of its bark for tanning. The growth properties of the bark influenced the length of the fallow period, while the extracted tannin linked cropping with the grazing that succeeded it. By sowing acorns in the ash with their cereals, *Brandwirtschaft* peasants closed the loop of their agricultural system. Their choices belonged with a larger equilibrium that cycled ager, saltus, and silva dynamically through the landscape, one after the other, making the Schwarzwald into a biotic kaleidoscope. The success of each part reinforced the others. But if one part failed, so did the others.

In 1850, variants of *Brandwirtschaft* claimed 60,000 to 70,000 hectares of the Schwarzwald. Decline, however, was already well advanced. Peasants were emigrating to cities or overseas colonies; cereal imports reduced the pressure for cropping on marginal land; industrial demands for softwood timber exceeded the agricultural values of hardwood mast, bark, and coppice; and trade with South America and later industrial chemistry ruined the market for oak tannin. By the late nineteenth century every part of the swidden ensemble was failing, as well as the social regulation that had prevented abuses. Foresters replaced farmers, silviculture took the place of agriculture, and fossil fuels supplanted the ancient fallows. By 1950 only 10,000 hectares of *Reutberge* survived. By 1970, *Brandwirtschaft* was gone.

The Ardennes, along the border between France and Belgium, knew similar practices (*sartage,* or *essartage*) and they too were ancient. Again, it is important to recognize that swidden formed a spectrum of practices, or better yet, a mixed-and-matched ensemble. Sometimes swiddeners used free-burning fire (*feu courant*), and sometimes fire was confined to piles or ovens (*feu couvert*), in which case the ash was carried and harrowed into the field. Bernard Palissy commented on one version in 1580. In this case *essartage* mingled with *écobuage* such that combustibles were collected and burned in small "furnaces," then distributed to the fields. One or two crops of rye followed, before the fallow was left for four to six years. In 1796 the *Encyclopédie Méthodique* gave a detailed account that follows closely contemporary descriptions from the Schwarzwald.[33]

A critical component was oak used for tanning. After eighteen to twenty years of fallow, residents felled the trees during the winter, stripped off the bark for tannic acid, and hauled away the largest chunks for fuelwood and charcoal. The remaining slash they spread across the field to dry and often added to it branches pollarded from the spared mature trees or other combustibles. In July or August they fired the slash, five to six hours being sufficient to burn over 40 hectares. Once the ash had cooled or been carried to and harrowed into the field, they sowed. Broom soon reclaimed the site, and what wasn't grazed was harvested after four or five years for byre bedding, where its nitrogen-fixing properties contributed handsomely to the stockpile of cattle manure. Meanwhile oak resprouted, and birch seized disturbed sites. After five years, young trees were beyond the reach of grazers.[34]

In the early 1880s, John Croumbie Brown, curious about this ancient art, witnessed its use, in both free-burning and covered forms, in the Ardennes.

> To prepare for the *Sartage,* the soil is stript bare—stript to the surface
> of herbage and turf; the wood having been barked while the spring sap
> was weak, and the wood having been carried off in the usual way, all
> chips, twigs, refuse, and *debris* are spread over the ground. The quan-
> tity thus spread is considerable. . . . On a calm day this is set on fire,
> and, the flames spreading, soon reduce the wood spread over the
> ground to ashes, precautions being taken against the spread of the con-
> flagration beyond the limits prescribed. . . . This mode of burning the
> small wood and *debris* is known as *Sartage a feu courant.*

Croumbie observed that the dates of the burning, while regular, varied from region to region. He also noted that it was customary to leave "around each felled and cleared portion of the forest a *cordon* of timber trees," which helped shelter the new growth. The other mode (*Sartage a feu couvert*) was used when "the ground is covered thickly with herbage, creeping plants, and turf."

> The soil is pared by means of a hoe, and of the vegetable product there
> are formed a number of little heaps to which fire is applied, and the
> ashes are scattered over the whole area of the ground which has been
> cleared, after which the procedure is the same as has been detailed.

From a forestry perspective, this mode was "not so advantageous as the other" because it yielded a less vigorous regrowth of wood. But each had its advantages, and the profusion of "brooms and other brushwoods [that] sprout up in great abundance, especially where the coppice has been subjected to *Sartage a feu courant,*" shielded young crops and trees during their first years, provided fuel and rough pasture, and were eventually overtaken by the woods. The preferred cycle of fallow was fifteen to twenty-five years.[35]

Like the Schwarzwald, the Ardennes surrendered its ancient practices grudgingly. Peasants preferred to adjust within the swidden cycle rather than abandon it altogether. But the same pressures that squeezed the Black Forest in an economic, ecological, and intellectual vice acted on the Ardennes forests as well. By 1896, French forestry officials allowed only 250 hectares of *essartage.* Still the practice, in both France and Belgium, continued, legally and illegally, until the Great War replaced its raked firelines with trenches, its axes and pollarding knives with barbed wire and bayonets, its smoke with mustard gas, and its flames with the firepower of mechanical ordnance. The industrialization that had promised to save the Ardennes from slow starvation by a peasant agriculture that had used fire like medicinal leeches instead destroyed it with the violence of controlled combustion at the hands of an uncontrolled society.

Mountains were no impediment, and if anything made the practice more necessary by reducing alternatives. Switzerland may have derived its name from the German for swidden.[36]

In Tyrol and the Swiss Alps, documentation for swidden dates back to 1190, when the towns of Bolsano and Keller prohibited swidden on their commons (the issue was not fire so much as trespass). Their fire regulations were more prescriptive, too, because the *Föhn* wind—dry, gusty, a European chinook—could whip incautious burns into wildfires. But while the regulation is more meticulous (and preserved), the practices are similar to those in Steiermark. Fire assisted the conversion to arable fields, swidden pastures, and seasonal transhumance. That, in fact, points to a vital distinction: the increased attention to herding. The mountains, after all, acquired their name from their prevalent pastoralism (*alp* originally meant "mountain pasture").[37]

The Alps were as much a pastoral economy as the Spanish *meseta,* but where the great plateau had flung herds across a subcontinent, here deep mountain valleys compressed them into ecological workings as intricate as a Swiss watch. What drove the system was the need for winter fodder so that herds could survive in barns. Transhumance could not take the flocks to winter pasture; it could only remove them from arable land on which grew the fodder and hay that would sustain them through the winter. Specifically, the herds, mostly dairy cattle, moved up the slopes in spring and down in autumn, and in most instances families or even villages moved with them.[38]

Between mountain pasture and valley arable stretched a succession of pastures, some rough, some sown. As the herds moved up the slopes, fields were cultivated for cereals, fodder, and especially hay. At intermediate levels, exploited in both the spring and fall, there were more pastures and with them often substantial residences. Only a handful of herders followed the animals as they pursued the ascending snow line. The dynamics of this pastoral system intensified as population pressures crowded the basins. Alpine society was as chocked with rules and prescriptions as glacial moraine with stone. By late medieval times peasants had established shielings above the timberline. By then, too (and not coincidentally), the timberline was moving downward, a harbinger of the environmental changes that overexploitation could induce.

It was in the creation of those vital pastures that fire mattered. Fire worked on the long-term rotation of fallow and pasture as sunlight did on the annual cycle of herbaceous growth and dormancy. Coppice or scrub replaced most high forest; repeated cutting, burning, and grazing of scrub led to grasslands. The conversion of woods to pasture was often intensive as peasants cleared stones, roots, and stumps from postburn sites, in effect cultivating a mountain grassland. Elsewhere (usually later, the eighteenth century) rules prescribed that stumps and mature seed trees should remain as a means of regeneration and soil stabilization. But such practices were common wherever temperate Europe engaged in forest swidden. Eventually—even in somnolent Switzerland, as drenched in peace as the rest of Europe was in war—rising populations intensified the conversions, and there were multiple breakdowns.

Along the alpine margins, particularly in France, there were fewer controls and no *cordon sanitaire* to shield, for example, the Dauphiné Alps from its own or outside excesses. Ancient habits—ineradicable practices such as *essartage,* and necessary practices like mountain grazing—swirled like eddies within a greater maelstrom of change. The rhythms of alpine transhumance now beat to the cycles of national (and international) economics, not the traditional husbandry of a mountain valley. Yet the panorama had to submit to a new environmentalism that was as much aesthetic as economic. When Sir Thomas Dick Lauder observed this "extirpation of Alpine forests" firsthand in 1832, he suggested that the "large patches are burned down by the inhabitants, as heath would be on a hillside in Scotland, merely to increase the herbage and the values of the pasturage of the places where the trees grow." That much was common condemnation. But Lauder went further:

> Uncouth black spots are thus frequently created in the middle of the dark green forests of the Swiss mountains, and the scenes of gloomy destruction which these exhibit when visited, with the huge trees standing half consumed, and stretching out their charred branches against the snowy peaks, and the clear blue sky, beggars description.

The Romantic critique was new.[39]

So was the response, first the environmental, then the political. In Switzerland small pressures acted on a mosaic of small landscapes; in France, especially, the stresses swelled to gargantuan proportions, and the land frequently buckled under the strain. In some locales, industrial interests and forestry sought to replace a stagnant agrarian regime. In others, the clearings, tramplings, and sheer weight of environmental pressures exceeded the land's elastic limit, leaving in its ashes a succession of avalanches, mass wasting, torrents, and soil erosion. The spectacle of mountain torrents, in particular, inspired reform. The trees that peasants had labored so hard to take out, the state was determined to put back.[40]

(iv)

The agricultural revolution could not, out of its own resources, break the vicious circle in which it increasingly found itself. Even as it moved outward, it was driven inward. There were no places left in which to expand, save overseas colonies; no methods available by which to further intensify utilization or shorten fallow; no ecological drafts upon which to draw to improve productivity without also diminishing the capital of soil, flora, and water.

What ultimately transcended the dilemma was industrialization, broadly conceived. Modern industry could, for a time at least, infuse a landscape with new energies and nutrients, even as it extracted old ones. It could redefine natural resources, thereby shifting the burdens elsewhere, and organize far-flung trade to reprogram the ecological hardware of nutrient cycling. It could extract fossil fallow to carry to famished fields and it could power plows without sowing oats or fodder. By so doing, an industrial economy could add another dimension to environmental geometries, rendering the closing circle into a globe-spanning sphere. Land—liberated from reclamation—was free for other purposes.

As often as not, the purpose was forestry. In 1848, in a dramatic reversal of Neolithic landnam, Switzerland prohibited forest grazing, which also had the effect of abolishing swidden. The woods responded with an impressive and spontaneous regrowth. In 1857, Switzerland made the reforestation of the Alps a national policy. The rest of central Europe was not far behind.[41]

REVOLUTION REDUX:
FORESTRY TAKES COMMAND

The woods had always been a part of agriculture. They meant fuel, and for many landscapes they meant long-term fallow and the biotic abundance that unruly fallow nurtured. Estates and villages grew woodlots for firewood and charcoal much as they cultivated gardens for kitchen spices and meadows for dairy cows. Woodlands meant pasture and forage, a source of mast, grass, mushrooms, berries, and medicinal herbs. Forests supplied construction timber, nurtured game, and yielded resin for distillation into naval stores. But as the agricultural revolution spread, the geography of forests shifted, like tectonic plates remaking the margins of continents, and the exploitation of the woodlands deepened.

The stresses on the silva mounted. Arable expanded into the woods; rising populations caused the period of woods fallow to shorten; and woodlands shrank in scope and deteriorated in quality. Felled trees were not the sole cause of degradation, and fired forests not the most vicious of abuses. But the burned woods typified them all. The felled and fired woods acquired for temperate Europe the weight of symbolic significance that the free-ranging goat had for mediterranean Europe.

What deforestation degraded, however, afforestation could, in principle, rehabilitate. Even as arable moved into the woods, the woods were moving into the wastelands. Initially, afforestation was another method of reclamation and supplemented agriculture by amplifying fuelwood and rough pasture. Trees could restock heaths, dunes, marshes, impoverished fields, and eroded hillsides, staunching a fatal hemorrhage of nutrients, damming loose waters, and gripping unstable soils. The woods could advance, just as arable could, both at the expense of rough-pastured wastes. Once established, the woods could restock village wood bins, guarantee a steady supply of charcoal to local smelters, ensure a flow of timber, and rebuild the organic soil. Woodlots were orchards for fuel instead of fruit; the agronomy of woodlands—silviculture—literally meant the extension of agriculture to trees. In this sense forests were farms.

But even as forest reclamation advanced, industrialization began redefining its purposes. Fossil fuels reduced the demand for firewood and charcoal; improved transportation allowed wood-scarce countries to trade for their timber needs; and the woods became more valuable as pulp and timber than as fuel, forage, and fallow. As an industrial order intensified, marginal agricultural lands became "surplus" and were even abandoned; and as the need for forest fallow receded, high woods replaced it. No longer integrated into a common agriculture, silva and ager became antagonists. Their economic separation led eventually to a segregation of ownership.

Increasingly, communal woodlands became industrial forests or state reserves. Some reserves existed for production, others for protection. The first met the demands of urbanization and industrialization for more timber, and later for pulp. The second promoted other environmental values, such as the stabilization of water supplies, the reclamation of wastelands, the enrichment of soils, aesthetic enhancement, and even a putative improvement of climate. Such extraeconomic values argued for public regulation, even ownership, and where necessary, for public coercion.

The emerging forests received their value from the economics of industry, and their meaning from an intelligentsia housed in urban centers. Forests and cities replaced farms and pastures as the most dynamic elements of the new landscape. For both, the tree became a vital environmental emblem, the standard of stewardship; and fire became a symbol of intolerable waste, of a peasant agriculture unwisely entangled with an industrial order. During that unstable transition fires broke out everywhere.

The Great Partition that removed the woods from the farm had also removed agriculture's methods of fire control. Forestry would have to invent a new regime. Agriculture had regulated fire by the close cropping of prospective fuels and by systematically burning and grazing the fallow. Forestry had to find surrogates, had to overcome the inevitable instabilities of an often fire-prone transition, and had to calm unruly biomass, a task no simpler than to quiet restless peasants removed from their traditional mark or commune. What had been a complex fallow now became a singular fuel. What had been woody fuel that burned benignly in the field or hearth too often became wildfire that smashed industrial plantations or reserved forests.

(i)

A legacy of Roman conquest, and later of Roman political scholarship, was the assertion that the superior power of the king translated into superior ownership of lands under his dominion. Rulers established *banforests*, "forest" designating a legal not biological status. Kings—the Norman monarchs of England were especially avid—thus established "forests" for hunting. It is estimated that as much as a fourth of medieval England was so "afforested," and as such subject to forest law rather than common law. That a Forest Charter to guarantee traditional rights of access complemented the Magna Carta is not surprising.[42]

But as the lure of the chase faded, and as monarchs scrounged for money to engage in their endless wars, the scale of royal forests shrank, and, where reinstigated, *banforests* often served ends other than hunting. Royal restrictions were established to guard oaks valuable as naval timbers, to ensure a steady supply of timber and charcoal to vital mines, and to stabilize diminishing fuelwood stocks. "Timber famines" loomed over villages like droughts and plagues, and local communities responded by enacting rules to lessen the overexploitation of oak bark, to prevent theft of timber or fuelwood, to prohibit grazing at certain times or by certain animals like goats, and to sustain such local industries as glassworks, potash, and the manufacture of wooden shoes. More than its timber losses alone, the woods suffered an agricultural assault from pasturing, the removal of litter, and "above all the fires." By 1750, forestry began its long chrysalis, aptly symbolized by the separation of the game warden from the forester.[43]

Germany, in all its complex principalities, led the way—the "fatherland of forestry," as Bernhard Fernow later called it. Economics was a primary goad. To officials the country seemed to be galloping toward a timber famine that would starve industry and agriculture both, threaten naval power, and throw domestic life into turmoil. Overcutting, exploitative harvesting of limbs and

litter, promiscuous grazing, and reckless burning were transforming productive woods into wastes. As agriculture expanded into marginal lands, peasants
trimmed trees of their branches, raked up forest litter for byre bedding, and
shortened fallow and coppice to suicidal brevity, while fires sprang up like oldfield weeds. The result was a nutrient deficit. Viewing the Nuremburg Reichs-
wald, a touring forester condemned the scene for showing "eloquently the state
to which an otherwise carefully managed forest may be reduced by the
removal, for centuries, of the litter." What the forest gave up it had to receive.
"This great natural law of the forest world," he lectured, "cannot long be broken with impunity." It mattered little whether the composting litter was lost to
barns or burns.[44]

Edicts against uncontrolled burning appeared alongside other proscriptions,
with as little effect. In 1778, foresters justified the expense of firebreaks
because "otherwise the still constantly recurring fires could not be checked";
because "not a single acre of forest could be found in the province that had not
been burnt in former or later times"; because "the people are still too much accustomed to the ruthless use of fires, so that no punishment can stop them." Despite
detailed regulations regarding smoking, burning debris, or agricultural swidden, fires broke out whenever excess fuel littered the landscape. In 1800, slash
sustained a fire that burned in the Württemberg woods for two weeks, despite
the efforts of a regiment called out to suppress it. (A thunderstorm finally did
the job.)[45]

But it is difficult to reconcile the reported abundance of free-burning fires
with a landscape simultaneously stripped to its stones, as critics charged. Where
utilization was most intensive, fire was rare—everything was burned in hearth
or furnace, or went into the gullet of the herds. Instead fires abounded in newly
colonized lands, on rough pasture, on soils too poor for cultivation; and the
protest over them was mutual. Peasants needed those fires to keep the land in
forms usable to their needs, exploiting fires to manage woodlands as shepherds
used dogs to help manage a flock. But foresters wanted high woods, not pasture, and rank humus, not dry heath. They perceived chronic fires as they did
theft, trespass, or bark beetles as an attack on timber and an affront to rational
management. When the eighteenth century began, foresters were weak; when
it ended, they increasingly dominated the agrarian polity, even assuming control over communal forests. As agents of the state, they, not peasants, determined land use; they, not farmers, decided to what purposes the revanchist woods
would be put; they, not herders, decided appropriate fire practices. Over the
course of the nineteenth century, forestry took command.

The reasons are transparent in retrospect. Clearly the agricultural revolution
could not continue as it had: its initial euphoria was yielding to an environmental reign of terror. Under its remorseless expansion to feed the appetite of

Europe's swelling populations, the size of the national estate in woodlands had shrunk disastrously, the exploited woods had degenerated in quality, and select but highly symbolic sites had given way to dunes, gulleys, landslides, and mountain torrents. The state could no longer afford to feed its woodlands into the maw of agriculture. The woods had other, higher economic uses; and forests promised bold means of restoring wastes that agriculture could not reclaim or had in fact created. Temperate Europe was littered with the agricultural equivalent of mining slag. Alarmed officials believed that it was necessary and desirable—through the coercion of the state if it came to that—to restrict traditional uses of woodlands and to redirect the state's reserved forests. Forestry was the means to do so.

It was a creation of the Enlightenment. It began as an exercise in codification, an encyclopedic gathering of empirical knowledge from hunt-masters and practitioners; but the theoretical framework came from university intellectuals seeking to reconcile field lore with first principles. What Linnaeus did with plants and Montesquieu did with legal codes, foresters like Wilhelm Gottfried von Moser and J. F. Stahl did in *Principles of Forest Economy* (1757) and a four-volume encyclopedia of forest, game, and fish practices, respectively. The agricultural revolution symbolized by Jethro Tull (new crop rotations, plows, enclosure, and intensive animal breeding) inspired a silvicultural reformation through rational harvest schedules, the replacement of axes by saws, the selective cultivation of oak and pine, the de facto enclosure of agrarian communes, and the reclamation of wastes.

Forestry was an Enlightenment enterprise in political economics, subject to the same logic, the same need to purge old superstitions and decadent court bureaucracies, and the same desire to replace folklore with experiment. It experienced the same awkward cultural shock as intellectuals and practitioners groped toward a common ground, as theorists sought to apply logic and mathematics to an inchoate mass of tradition, and as practical men sought some higher basis for judgment than appeals to personal authority and argument by vilification. Exuberantly, books tumbled out—dictionaries, encyclopedias, treatises on land law, silvicultural texts, mathematical analyses of forest growth and harvest schedules, and professional journals. Forestry schools appeared, first under the tutelage of published masters, then endowed by the state.

If the problems that forestry faced were pervasive and urgent, so were its responses. The agrarian economy needed reform: forestry could put antiquarian communes to more productive use. Modern states could ill afford unproductive wastelands, abandoned to coarse herding: forestry could reclaim them for timber. Here and there agriculture had degraded land into rock, marsh, torrents. Forestry could restore soil, drain malarial lowlands, and halt floods. Nearly everywhere, and with mounting force, marginal farmland or waste converted to forest. State-sponsored reclamation blossomed in Jutland's heath, Yugoslavia's notorious karst, the Sologne marshes outside Orleans, Russia's frontier steppes, the limey wastes of Champagne, malarial lowlands between Pisa and Naples, and transhumant corridors in the Pyrenees and Massif Central. The state's example could, in principle, inspire private owners as well. But most forest philosophers insisted that forests belonged to the state, or in a democracy, to the public; that they served higher purposes than economic exploitation alone; and that all woods, even those held privately, should conform to basic regulations in the name of the common good.

While forestry became a transcultural institution, national traditions were soon apparent. Germany pioneered silviculture and the prescriptions of forest economics. France excelled in grafting forestry's practices to the larger agenda of the state. That the premier forestry school resided in Nancy, along the border between France and Germany, only strengthened their fusion and the collective claim of Franco-German forestry to primacy. Germans primarily extended the precepts throughout Europe, to such unlikely modernizers as Spain, Italy, Greece, and Russia, as well as to Scandinavia, the Netherlands, and Britain. Imperial Britain, in turn, exported this fascinating hybrid to the rest of the world.

By the time the age of democratic revolutions broke out, German states like Prussia and Bavaria boasted new forest bureaucracies and "rational" forest policies. By the time the tremors of the French Revolution had died away, forestry had emerged as a confident agent of the modern state throughout central Europe. Forest policies were to land use what the new constitutions were to government. But forestry assumed more than political power: increasingly it claimed to speak for all environmental concerns. Conservation, it insisted, was its purview, if not its invention. Certainly, foresters became the arbiters of free-burning fire. And modernizers saw in fire control a technique of reform as useful as canals, reduced tariffs, and breech-loading rifles.

(ii)

A few spectacular episodes confirmed for critical observers both the economic logic and the environmental rationale of reformed forestry. In France the aftermath of the 1789 revolution and the onset of industrialization combined to wreck some landscapes, but a long traditional of state intervention suggested state-sponsored remedies. Forestry proposed an ecological cure.

The monarchy had long claimed, and interested itself in, its forest estate. But through greed, wars, neglect, and rights of popular access, the woodlands of France had shrunk. Regularly, kings issued new edicts, Règlement Général des Eaux et Forêts, and just as regularly these were ignored, perverted, or evaded. France, so the critics cried, would "perish through lack of woods." In 1543—

the year Copernicus published *De Revolutionibus*—Francis I extended to private forests the jurisdiction of the royal lords of the forest. But, as Cezanne reported in his study of French forestry, "the vices of the administration, religious discords, and civil and foreign war, rendered sterile these efforts." Henry IV tried to reaffirm control with another edict in 1597. The modern era, however, dates from the elaborate Forest Ordinance of 1669, better known eponymously for its principal architect, Jean-Baptiste Colbert, as the Code Colbert.[46]

A commissioned tour of French forests, published in 1661, documented the full spectrum of degradation. Rules were lacking or ignored; exceptions abounded, principles were reduced to a welter of customs and arbitrariness—exactly the sort of situation that infuriated Enlightenment philosophes and inspired them to rationalize and codify. Charles Colbert de Cressy wrote: "we are astounded by the number of fires which occur in the aforesaid woods, there being no forests in which there have not been many within a few years past." It "appears manifestly necessary," he continued, "that an endeavour should be made to find out some remedy which may prevent the occurrence of such disasters in the future." The primary causes, he noted, were "herds and people, who have no excuse for what they do."[47]

For eight years Colbert and twenty-one commissioners struggled to restore order (and ultimately recover revenue). During this period there was, in the royal forests, no logging, grazing, or fuelwood collection. Ultimately the lands had to be used. Louis XIV's wars alone demanded money. But the forests had to be exploited according to rational principles, and administered by principled officials. If, as John Croumbie Brown admits, the resulting Code Colbert was "more perfect in appearance than in reality," it was precisely the kind of rationalist ideal the Enlightenment sought. To it foresters referred as natural philosophers would to Newtonian physics. "No measure connected with the treatment of forest," Brown affirmed, "has yet excited so widespread and prolonged beneficial influence."[48]

Most of its provisions and administrative rigor were lost in the upheaval of revolution and were not reconstituted until 1827. Modern French forestry dates from that restoration. But when, during subsequent centuries, forestry argued the case for massive public investments, the Code Colbert conveyed political precedent and historical sanction. Those experiments, in turn, became exemplars for a new environmental order. Often they found wider expression in colonies than in the metropole, on far frontiers where indigenous protests could be dismissed or met with force.

The story of the Gascony dunes, and the reclaimed successor, the Landes, became one of the great morality tales of Enlightenment ecology. The moraine of Pleistocene seas, dunes lined the ocean perimeter of temperate Europe, from France to the Low Countries, Denmark, and the southern shores of the Baltic. Extensive coastal dunes had long defied systematic use, and where winds drove them inland they threatened more stable agriculture. By the eighteenth century, Prussia in particular was experimenting with reforestation by pine plantation along its Baltic shores. The protection, and later reclamation, of the dunes became a task of the agricultural revolution, and when it failed, of forestry.[49]

France soon claimed primacy by virtue of Gascony's notorious condition. Here the cancerous sands had plugged rivers, perverted soils, and buried or otherwise rendered worthless a once-settled landscape. Marsh and heath extended over more than a million hectares, a wedge driving dangerously across the French isthmus. Dunes (one version claimed that they originated after Vandals razed and burned the countryside in A.D. 407) spread like ecological gangrene, encroaching at rates of up to 30 to 100 feet a year. In 1786 the chief engineer of Bordeaux, Nicolas Brémontier, proposed a canal through the Landes and a program of dune stabilization. By 1793, experiments demonstrated suitable techniques, and in 1801 the revolutionary government created a Commission on Dunes to oversee the labor, the project later transferred to the Department of Bridges and Roads. Clearly France conceived the project as a massive public works program. Appropriations increased year by year, and in 1862, with approximately 80,000 hectares reforested, some lands, probably a fourth, reverted to local owners and communes while the rest became the responsibility of the Forest Department, which exploited the thriving pine woods for resin and timber. Not only had France stemmed the encroaching sands, it had recovered a handsome return on its investment.[50]

But if the encroaching dunes were stopped, the advancing woods were not. In 1737, experiments by an engineer with the Department of Bridges and Roads demonstrated that, with draining and planting, the vast wedge of sand, marsh, and heath that comprised the Landes could also grow maritime pine. From its beachhead on the coastal dunes, forestry marched inland. In 1857, a law committed the state to basic infrastructural improvements through drainage canals and roads while ordering the local villages to reforest their communal lands under the direction of state foresters; private owners soon joined the campaign. By 1892, state, commune, and private parties had afforested 700,000 hectares. Those labors had transformed a miasmal waste into productive woodlands, and as an American observer noted, they had remade a "shiftless class of 'poor whites' eking out a livelihood" into "one of the *most progressive* and perhaps *the most prosperous region in France*." When completed, Gascony boasted the largest forest in France, testimony to the reformative powers of state-directed forestry.[51]

Those resinous pines, however, were also fuel. The expanding afforestation broke down the natural barriers to fire spread—the stagnant ponds, the sand patches—and stacked layers of pine needles, branchwood, and understory heath like cordwood. The Landes had acquired a fire potential it had probably never known before. Almost immediately foresters escalated their fire-protection measures, particularly against the resident pastoralists who alone had roamed the wastes and who exploited fire to force the stubborn land to yield to their needs.

There was precedent in a 1741 law that forbade grazing for five years on burned forest land. But until there was a resident force of guards and a higher purpose, there was no prospect of enforcement. Both came with state-sponsored afforestation. In 1809 the prefect of Gironde decreed that "burning can under no circumstances extend over more than one-sixth the land owned by each commune," and then burning could proceed only after consultation with forest officers. So high was the hazard, however, that fire codes prohibited any burning within 100 meters of forest or heath, rigorously restricted charcoal burning, mandated spark arresters on sawmill stacks, and strictly denied contractors to smoke, light matches, or "carry fire of any kind whatsoever" through the protected forests. The special provisions mimicked those attached to Provence, and the Landes soon rivaled Maures and Esterel as a model of fire protection. In 1902, again on the pattern of Provence, foresters organized syndicates of local communes and landowners to assist.[52]

What they could not prevent, forest officers attacked aggressively. Firelines divided the land into Cartesian compartments. Primary firelines were 10 meters wide and 1,000 meters apart, with the interior landscape subdivided into blocks of 100 hectares surrounded by 10 meter blocks. The primary firelines, moreover, ran perpendicular to the prevailing winds, ideal for backfiring. Work areas contained tool caches; telephone lines connected sites with telegraph offices; and watchtowers scanned the green horizon for smoke. Foresters squelched fire as ruthlessly as a peasant revolt. Between 1883 and 1892, only 103 hectares burned per year in lands under Forest Department control, and only 4,703 hectares burned out of 600,019 hectares altogether.[53]

But those celebrated statistics were deceptive, too. Great fires—by French standards—swept the Landes in 1869–71, and in 1893 some 132 fires burned 35,589 hectares. Railroads and resin tappers superseded shepherds as a source of burning, malice often replaced carelessness, and the slashed pines, redolent with pitch, bristled like a forest of tapers. The pines did not suppress the old understory; at best, with studious cultivation, they rose above it. So, too, the afforested Landes did not at first eliminate the old order, but superimposed new practices and conditions. Only with relentless effort, conversion of the indigenous society, and fire suppression could the transplant resist the social antibodies that instinctively sought to reject it.

The real control over fire came through understory manipulation. "No measures are reasonably certain," Theodore Woolsey, Jr., concluded, "unless the underbrush is kept cleared." The forest was constantly swept clean. Whenever that strategy failed, as it did when the world wars stripped the forests of their labor force, then fires quickly returned. Large wildfires struck in 1918 and 1919,

French structuralism and fire suppression: firebreaks through maritime pine and sandy soils in the Landes. Note lightning scar on foreground tree. (Photo by Raphael Zon, courtesy U.S. Forest Service)

gorging on the luxurious growth that had gone feral during the war years. A similar round of fatal fires returned after World War II. By then the plummeting price of resin and a crisis of rural life made the economics of the monocultural pine problematic. The forest, however, remained, a vast living plug chinking the coastal armor of France.[54]

Equally diseased was the situation in the French Alps, which seemed to be consumed by a fever of peasant fires. By nature, mountains attracted heavy rains, released spring snowmelt, endured avalanches, spawned flash floods, and experienced the mass wasting of steep slopes. By the end of the eighteenth century, however, overuse had aggravated routine decay into full-blown degradation. For much of the Alps soil erosion, gullying, and flash floods marked the fracture-cracks of a landscape too long subject to the stress of human use, and now given to violent rupture instead of slow creep. What began with the extirpation of trees, the trampling of soils, and the burning of humus ended with massive earth slides and violent flooding.

Torrents—the catastrophic discharge of water and debris down narrow gorges—had become the norm, and *torrent* joined *dune* and *timber famine* as code words for environmental havoc. Unstable hillsides slid into and clogged valleys; from the exposed slopes the runoff of rain and soils accelerated; and the elevated streambeds hurled debris flows through gorges like express trains. Probably the best American analogue is the devastation wrought by hydraulic mining in the Sierra Nevada. Nature might repair the damages, but only over geologic time. Instead, one by one, the German states, Austria, Switzerland, and Italy adopted remedial measures, a mixture of engineered works to stabilize the land through dams and retaining walls and a national program of reforestation to restore the land to health. But dead works, critics noted, were less successful than living ones.

By the mid-nineteenth century it was estimated that France had two-thirds of the torrents of Europe. About 11 percent resided in the Pyrenees, 24 percent in the Massif Central, and the rest in the Alps. One extenuating circumstance was the mediterranean climate that brushed against the region; another, its mediterranean style transhumance, often with goats and sheep; and still another, roads and logging. The population pressures swelled, as local flocks competed with migratory flocks driven from Provence. The lower valleys soon buckled under the burden, and the flocks moved up the slopes. Small torrents became large.

But the initiating social torrent was apparently the French Revolution, which for a time revoked or neutered the restrictions that had dampened peasant exploitation. With little more arable possible to them, villages bursting with people surged up the slopes in a great pastoral sprawl. "It has, of course, been to the interest of the shepherds in charge to burn and destroy the forests in the higher regions as much as possible in order to gain more extensive grazing grounds," observed a British forester. The colonial parallels did not escape him: "the destruction of the forests thus proceeds in exactly the same manner as it does in some parts of the Himalayas at the present time."[55]

By the time the Second Republic restored order through the Forest Code of 1827, torrents were becoming common, and by midcentury, particularly after the great floods of 1840 and 1856, they were a national scandal. During the inundation of 1827, George Perkins Marsh calculated, "in a single day of flood, then, the Ardeche, a river too insignificant to be known except in the local topography of France, contributed to the Rhône once and a half, and for three consecutive days once and one third, as much as the average delivery of the Nile during the same periods, though the basin of the latter river contains 500,000 square miles of surface, or more than five hundred times as much as that of the former." And this was only one torrent, one time.[56]

The dam of resistance finally broke with the floods of 1856 that struck the Seine and Loire as well as the Rhône and Gironne. Tepid legislation from 1846 was reviewed, and the government promoted scientific inquiries into the causes of the catastrophe and possible solutions. The resulting law of 1860 redefined torrents from a local into a national problem, and committed the state to a solution. Emergency engineering would seek to stabilize the scene and establish a new hydrological regime, while forestry would attempt a longer-term restoration. The law charged the Forest Department to extinguish the torrents as it did fires. The means to this end was compulsory reforestation, partly through expropriation of private property by the state, and partly by the afforestation of communal lands under the supervision of state foresters.

But the official means served only to enrage local villagers, because restoring forests would suppress grazing and without grazing the villages could not survive. Seizing land and specifying suitable practices on communes, including tree planting, did nothing to endear foresters to local pastoralists. The villages, however, feared the torrents, and France, alarmed over the torrents' power to rip the guts out of its mountains and dismember whole *départements,* stiffened its resolve.

France was embarrassed. France was committed. France's *reboisement* of the Alps would restore France's *rayonnement* as a civilizing nation. A new law in 1882 removed the most egregious frictions, while reaffirming the state's commitment to afforestation, this time at greater public expense. By 1893 officials reckoned that, out of 1,462 torrents, they had controlled 163 completely and were "curing" another 654. By 1909 the state had purchased 106,735 hectares and afforested 78,607 of them. That meant, along with dams and retaining walls, the installation of a new fire regime as well.[57]

The rehabilitation of the Alps joined the reclamation of the Landes as the great exemplars of state forestry. Both were widely studied, loudly applauded, frequently imitated, and endlessly cited as testimony to the power of the new order. Both became templates against which critics measured land degradation and calculated the costs of restoration. The torrents of the Var were a lesson learned by the British and Americans as well. It was through the prism of France's 1827 torrents that American foresters saw the monster Mississippi floods of 1927, and it was from French experience that they argued for "living works"—massive reforestation—along with the dead works of levees and dams. The French solution merged structuralism, in the form of engineering, with the state, as a source of funds or coercion.[58]

That was also the classic French strategy for fire control. If forests were the means of environmental amelioration, then fire, the forests' implacable enemy, was an agent of degradation. The Landes and especially the Alps confirmed cutting, grazing, and burning as the unholy trinity of land abuse. Of the three, grazing and swidden were the *causae causarum,* but fire the essential catalyst. Although the initial cuts were small, they became septic, as it were, with fire, and as the infection spread, it rotted away ecological tissue. Fire sent up in smoke the nutrients that should have returned to the soil, ripped off standing vegetation that broke the momentum of descending raindrops that would otherwise scour the ground like pumice, and stripped away the protective humus that like a giant sponge could sop up the spillage of excess precipitation and prevent catastrophic runoff or landslips.

Control fire and you controlled clearing, trampling, browsing, and soil erosion. Control the fire regime and you controlled the hydrologic regime as well. A nation's rivers were at the mercy of its forests, its floods an inevitable aftermath of its fires. Professional forestry built its case with environmental similes almost Homeric in scope. British irrigation works in the Punjab and Uttar Pradesh would fail if torrents flooded the Himalayan foothills, and rivers would veer out of control if fires lit up the slopes. Stable agriculture demanded stable catchments. Likewise the compelling argument for the reservation of American forests was the protection of watershed. New American settlements in the arid West would crumble without stable watersheds to feed irrigable fields, and old landscapes in the humid East would suffer unreliable flows in their navigable rivers. But forest protection was meaningless without fire protection. Water was less a means of controlling fire than fire was for controlling water.

Even meteorology conspired to reinforce that sentiment. The *Föhn* winds that brought on the deluges were, except for their timing, the same winds that propelled the worst fires. Storming north from the Mediterranean they piled moisture on the mountains, spilling down slopes like rain off a slate roof, melting snowpack, and saturating unstable soils. But winds once drained of their moisture often swept over the mountains and plummeted downward, dry and warm—a Swiss Santa Ana. The classic wildfires of the Alps were driven by *Föhns.* A *Föhn* wind ruffled fuels like pages in an open book, blowing cooking fires into conflagrations. A *Föhn* wind brought bans on burning. If heavy rain followed a fierce fire, gulleys scratched across mountain meadows and torrents roared through deadly gorges. Wind and rain were unstoppable; but the landslips and torrents that followed, and the fire that precipitated them, were within the power of human institutions to contain. If forestry was to succeed, it would have to do just that.[59]

The French solution was widely studied, and usually envied. It promised that fire could be controlled much as flooding could, by suitable works and government power. When America's pioneer foresters looked for precedents, they turned to France. The "methods devised and practiced in France itself," Gifford Pinchot wrote, "probably cover a wider range of conditions and apply more closely to the needs and the problems of the American foresters than those of any other country of Europe." Even closer were the conditions in French colonies. The "management of cork oak and the construction of fire lines in Algeria," wrote Theodore Woolsey, Jr., "merits our admiration as surely as their success commands our attention."[60]

They dismissed German approaches as too rigidly bound to silviculture and close cultivation, something impossible under conditions of aggressive, sprawling settlement like those experienced in America. And more than technique, they coveted the commitment of the state, the monumental tradition of the Code Colbert. What the French strategy ignored, at least in principle and often in practice, however, was the indigenous population. Structures, living or dead; institutions, real or paper; state sponsorship, desired or detested—these were the means of control. Through and within them the local populace or its actions could be contained. It was a strategy best suited for the periphery, which is where it went. The metropole—*Mitteleuropa*—sought a more integral approach. But if its ability to control fire was greater, so much greater was the potential for cataclysm if it failed.

(iii)

These episodes all derived from the coastal or mountain margins of temperate Europe, and they were celebrated because, by reducing waste to field, they annexed those peripheral lands to the agricultural core. But Europe's great center was already farmed; the center's problem was one of evolution, of adapting new fire regimes to new forms of agriculture (or silviculture), of close-cultivating the fire in the garden.

No less than wheat and oak, fire was absorbed into the rhythms and geography of *Brandwirtschaft* in all its endless mutations. Free-burning fire thrived only in those niches that remained as hunting preserves or sacred groves or that still resisted agricultural reclamation. Wildfires, like crime, sought out the dark corners, the unkept slums, the empty lots; the heath, the bogs, the sandy woods. And they flourished, if briefly, during the period of transition, after the old order had gone to seed and before the new order could mature to harvest. Fuels mingled, fuels proliferated, fuels lay stacked, if temporarily, like stockpiled gunpowder.

Agriculture built fire control into its structure. It parsed the landscape into fragments, plowed their perimeters, planted noncombustible strips around fields ripe for firing, cut and burned according to regular prescriptions, and beat down fires that broke free. Fires escaped rarely, they found little room to roam if they did, and a hue and cry quickly brought down the power of the authorities on

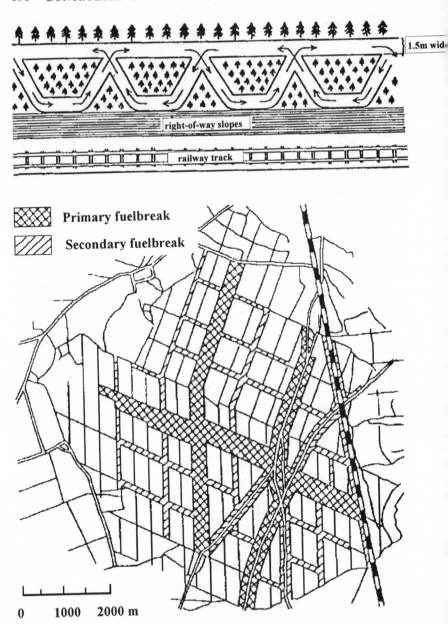

1.5m wide

right-of-way slopes

railway track

Primary fuelbreak

Secondary fuelbreak

0   1000   2000 m

Silva adapts to industry: (top) gardening around railroad tracks (*Schutzstreifen*), and (bottom) fuelbreak system in a pine plantation (*Waldbrandriegelsystem*). As silviculture was an adaptation of agriculture, so forestry accommodated industrialization. (Modified from Weck 1950 and Mißbach 1982) them. While wildfires loomed large in popular (and official) imagination, they were, like the landscapes they inhabited, a shrinking presence. They erupted mostly in times of distress, especially during periods of population upheaval.

Yet industrialization proposed just that, and on a more or less continual basis. The breakup of *Brandwirtschaft* left the fuels to fend for themselves while the tenders emigrated, traveled to the city, or worked at factories. Into that gap— and often widening it with hammer blows—came forestry.

Originally afforestation mimicked farming. Gaps that opened up were filled in with cultigens. Old wastelands now grew commercial forests. Fire bans were imposed around plantations, eventually exceeding a kilometer. As more and more patches of afforestation popped up like mushrooms, larger swaths of the interstitial landscape faced outright fire bans. This penumbral effect greatly expanded the fire regime of forestry, and the influence of foresters. Increasingly, foresters fenced off the countryside with firebreaks. The common landscape was, in effect, subjected to another enclosure movement, this time for trees instead of sheep.

The firebreaks followed agricultural precedents, and were themselves typically farmed. There were generous allowances for cleared areas—some grazed, some harvested for hay. Others were planted with a less combustible flora, a practice known as *Waldbrandriegel*. Potatoes were planted between pines, or along the routes of railroads (notorious for throwing sparks); birch or beech formed green dikes around lakes of conifers. The designs were sometimes intricate, as complex as miniature farms. The firebreaks themselves were abundant and expansive, sometimes as wide as 300 meters. In France critics protested that the obsession had gone too far, that committing one-sixth of a plantation to firebreaks, as some landowners did, was uneconomical. But the prudent knew that their absence rendered the young pines exceedingly vulnerable. Particularly in their early years, even-aged seedlings clothed the land like overgrown heather, and were often immersed in rough grasses or heath that could not be grazed down because livestock would trample and browse the conifers as well. A single fire could easily take it all.[61]

But inevitably fires appeared, and when weather and fuels favored them, they burned hot and sometimes long. With its vast sand plains, Prussia led the afforestation movement, and with its early grafting of forestry to the state bureaucracy, it fielded an aggressive program of fire control. Even so, fires increased along with the accelerating pace of official, private, and spontaneous afforestation. Between 1883 and 1927 half a million hectares were afforested, and large fires broke out in 1868, 1881, 1892, 1900, 1901, 1911, and 1928. Foresters rallied villagers to help control woods fires; when these forces failed, they called on the military. In extreme cases, where fire burned into peat or over unbroken terrain, campaigns could last for weeks. ("Large," however, is a relative concept. The 1892 *große Waldbrand* included conflagrations on the order of 17, 76, 32, 13, 46, and 56 hectares.) After the 1900 and 1901 seasons, the Prussian parliament staged a special debate over the spreading menace. Europe had long recognized that fire transmuted; what it now confronted was that industrial transmutation caused fire. Other reforms followed the 1928 and especially the 1934 fire seasons.[62]

These fires were different. Railroads, the absence of spark arresters on machinery, Sunday picnickers, careless smokers—none of these causes fit the profile of foragers, tramps, and pastoralists who had accounted for woods fires in the past. So, too, wildfire found new fuels. Like woodland creatures driven from their dens, fires roamed the landscapes in search of new habitats, and then took up residence. Likewise, traditional techniques could not always beat back the fires that broke out. The industrialization that had inspired the new regime had to develop methods to control it. In this way forestry policies replaced traditional fire practices, science addressed fire danger rating and fire behavior beyond the realm of folklore, and deliberate fire protection measures replaced the hue and cry of escaped wildfire. Lookout towers, patrols, water depots, and caches of fire tools, as well as prescriptions for land use around railroad tracks and fallow fields all furnished surrogates for folk fire control.

Already cosmopolitan, foresters looked to sources outside Europe for inspiration. Americans were particularly inventive, vigorously grafting the goals of European silviculture they had learned from Franco-German masters to a vast landscape capable of generating huge wildfires the size of German *Länder.* In America, agricultural analogies often surrendered to modernistic novelty, to recent technologies and radical ideas. Everywhere foresters moved against fire, *ein Feind des Waldes,* an enemy of the woods. As forestry assumed the ethos of engineering, foresters applied the same rigor to the theory and practice of forest fire control that chemical engineers did to the production of sulfuric acid or mechanical engineers did to the drivetrains of automobiles.

Yet forestry had its fire dissidents, just as agronomy did. In the beginning there were even attempts to adapt folk burning to forestry. Many observers noted how pine, in particular, often flourished after a fire. Agriculture had long disposed of fallow by fire—had grown the fallow in order to obtain the benefits of burning. There was no a priori reason why *Brandwirtschaft* could not grow rotations of timber and pulp trees as it had rye and turnips. After all, peasants had sown conifer seed and acorns into swiddened fields in order to ensure a new crop. Even in the woods, peasants had long contained the exuberance of the flammable understory by grazing, harvesting, and burning. But orthodox foresters saw agricultural burning as a threat, much as they saw agriculture as a competitor for scarce land.

A few argued for fire's utility, perhaps its indispensability. K. M. Müller protested that the pure pine forests of Bulgaria were a product of natural fire, suggesting that burning could thereby regenerate healthy pines elsewhere. Studying much the same landscape, Hesmer argued instead that anthropogenic burning (including wholesale clearing by the Turks) had done the work, but his conclusions were identical: fire had a firm place in Europe's "indigenous" ecology and a value as an instrument of forest management. Entomologists like A. Conrad argued that proper burning could contain outbreaks of insects; others that light surface fires could enhance regeneration and sanitize infected pines. Decrees dating back to the eighteenth century had encouraged burning as a means of purging fields of grasshoppers or other vermin. Dr. Thomas Meineke restated the case for heath burning. The agricultural precedents were legion. In brief, the German *kontrolliertes Feuer* could function as did French *petit feu*.[63]

Clearly, fire and forests need not be implacably hostile. But so they did become. Academic forestry, like academic agronomy, condemned fire, although practicing foresters, like farmers, frequently exploited it. Here forestry diverged from farming, because it fed, ultimately, into the metabolism of an industrializing society. Foresters wanted a barrier between forest and field, not a bridge. Especially during the transitional decades, rural burning posed threats much as rural economies posed competition. The drama lay in stopping fire, not accommodating it. Dissenters were overwhelmed by the drive to afforest, to improve productivity, and to counter social disaster. That so much land was so rich in young—which is to say, vulnerable—forests increased the sense of urgency.

Foresters and officials mobilized society to fight big fires as they would an invader. But such fires were "big" only in relative terms. A fire in excess of 100 hectares could qualify as a catastrophe. What had been small before became large as the overall context of burning shrank. Between 1883 and 1927, as it massively afforested, Prussia's annual losses to fire averaged only 79 hectares per 100,000 hectares of forest. Bavaria took more stringent measures and suffered even smaller outbreaks. Its penal code proscribed fire under any circumstances in hazardous woods, principally those with high grasses, föhn winds, or dry weather; demanded that all leaves and mosses be removed around any campfire; required that a woods fire be constantly watched; and banned grazing for several years after a burn. When a fire occurred, the villagers had to gather with tools to extinguish it. The populace took the instructions to heart. The 4,000 hectares Rothenbusch range suffered less than 42 square meters a year burned on average between 1870 and 1890, an amount that seemed quaint to touring British colonial foresters accustomed to horizon-sweeping veld and jungle fires.[64]

The gardened landscape remained, even if some plots grew birch and pine instead of wheat and potatoes. The *Waldbrandriegel* system successfully adapted the agricultural field structure to silviculture. The finely parceled, painstakingly manicured biota was itself the ideal check on large fires. That was the lesson forestry borrowed from farming. That was how Europe contained fire.

Even so, restrictions on agricultural burning tightened through the early years of the twentieth century. Forest burning became anathema, and through forestry's prohibitions, agricultural burning of all kinds. The internal combustion of fossil fuels and the distilling of fossil hydrocarbons replaced the open burning of biomass, the products of resin tapping, charcoaling, and potash manufacture. The only controlled combustion agronomists and foresters accepted was in the factories that produced artificial fertilizers, the coal-fired dynamos humming with electric power, and the oxen-replacing tractors. Steadily the constraints on burning acclerated and the techniques of fire control improved. Burning shrank to ritual, fire to symbol.

And then, with World War II, wildfire returned. The social landscape ended in shambles. The fire this time was a truly global conflagration. The hearth was perverted into a holocaust.

EPILOGUE:
HOLOCAUST

I wind the coil. Visions of future days
Tell me of Doom. On my abhorring gaze
There rise Valhalla's glorious halls ablaze.
The great Tree's riven limbs flame 'neath the walls.
'Mid smoke and lurid fire the Godhead falls.
Is this the dreadful Doom that is to be?
Is this the End of All?
> —Third Norn, in Richard Wagner,
> *The Ring of the Nibelung*

Like English denshiring, Dutch polders, and Swiss transhumance, German forestry was a graft on the great rootstock of European agriculture. It began by applying agronomic principles and rural values to the cultivation of trees. Silviculture was agriculture conducted by other means. The French expression for forest management, *jardinage,* establishes forestry's continuity with the garden. The triumvirate of ager, saltus, and silva had, by the twentieth century, evolved into field, forest, and city, each ideally in rough proportion. When the Bengali poet Rabindranath Tagore toured temperate Europe in 1878, he described the landscape as a "heroic love-adventure of the West, the active wooing of earth." It was, he noted, "the perfect union of man and nature."[65]

That was an ideal. It stood to landscapes as Max Weber's account of Prussian bureaucracy did to government. In citing Tagore, René Dubos had in mind the Île-de-France, a landscape produced by prolonged organic symbiosis between a physical environment and its human residents. The low hills and deep clays were no less productive for being farmed, and no less charming for reflecting human values about what made a land good and human aesthetics about what made it lovely. Even more than temperate France, unbalanced by its mediterranean south, the German states had achieved an almost perfect equilibrium between farm and forest. The act of cultivation itself was the essence of civilization. From it derived the concept of *culture.*

But the extension of this ecological exemplar was as badly compromised as the projection of Paris's power over the varied terranes of the French imperium. It was the outcome of a distinctive geography and history, not readily found along nontemperate Europe's margins, much less among Europe's colonies. The paradigm was itself a cultural construction, as little relevant to other landscapes as Latin verb conjugations were to Finnish or Senegalese. A fire-free agriculture was, for these others, a fantasy—or a nightmare—of reason. Attempting to abolish fire only pushed it to its extremities, the candle or the conflagration.

Everything in the garden had its place and time. Every plant, every animal, every person, every act—and every fire. There was no intrinsic reason to expunge fire. It had its role as much as spades, plows, and compost heaps. Symbolically, it extended the hearth over a domesticated landscape. Just as breeding was a way of preparing livestock for eating, so burning was a means of slow-cooking the cultivated biota. The combustion ideal was to bring the field to the hearth, or the hearth to the field; to feed turf and broom into the stove, or to carry the torch through garden and orchard. The eternal flames of antiquity survived as banked coals in the winter hearth; the fire god of Indo-European heritage shrank into the near invisibility of the Teutonic fire god whose worship is mentioned by Knut but who is never named, or the mischievous Loki of Nordic lore. Great fires flourished primarily in times of distress, when drought, plague, and war smashed the intricate gears and release springs of the agricultural cycle.[66]

For that reason alone wildfire was feared. But beyond that, intellectuals and officials ever distrusted it. Fire was dangerous, irrational, unpredictable, wasteful in its consumption, mischievous in its migratory habits, an inducement to sloth and violence. Fire was power. It was something to be controlled, something that had to be contained within the political order either by popular prohibition or state usurpation. Surely, better technology—more precisely controlled combustion or outright alternatives to combustion—could enhance yields still further and reduce losses, just as wheeled plows had replaced spruce harrows. That so much of the land was cultivated in order to be burned taunted agronomists as Euclid's fifth postulate did mathematicians. Surely, the fallow was not inevitable. Surely, alternative agricultures were possible if one assumed different axioms.

That is exactly what industrialization, or that part of industrialization committed to fossil hydrocarbons, did. The revolution left no aspect of the old order untouched. Artificial fertilizers, steam-powered trade, tractors, the pull of factories—all plowed under, each in its turn, the furrows and plots of the European garden. Intensive utilization slackened, rural laborers piled into cities, and subsistence farming gave way wholly to market cropping. Forests began replacing fallow, clean-stick forestry became more expensive and cumbersome, and fuels crept back like fungus spreading over a damp log.

Modern science reworked fire knowledge as mechanical combustion did the fire-tempered landscape. It was interesting, Axel Steensberg has written, "how in the late 18th and the 19th century genuine traditional techniques of fire-clearance became blurred by enlightened reformers' and agricultural organisations' reports of German and English literature." Fire lore became a tangle of tradition and novelty, confused in its techniques and purposes. Just as intellectuals objected to fire as an anachronistic agronomy, so urbanites protested its lingering nuisances, especially its smoke. By 1881 an Anti-Moorburning Society emerged to crusade against the rural fires in Holland and Hannover that annually immersed Germany in a "dense and sickly mist." The league, as well as others like it, was not merely an organization but an omen. The future of rural fire resided less with villages, flocks, and *Brandwirtschaft* than with cities, factories, and autobahns.[67]

None of this happened overnight, and the transition period, like all times of unrest, encouraged the uninvited fire. The land had not forgotten its fire-illumined past, nor had intellectuals forgiven it. The new fuels did not abolish the old; internal combustion did not eradicate all open burning; and the mechanical pyrotechnologies were means, not ends. During this confused transition, fuels often increased, not only in the uncultivated waste but through forests. Relic fire practices like *essartage* mingled with the embers blown from steam engines or thrown from iron brakeshoes, and new fire powers exceeded old fire restraints. In Europe's fire history there would be ample opportunity to indulge in modernism's addiction to irony. Controlled combustion would prove anything but controlled. Two world wars did not lead to fire's slow extinction but to its eruption.

World War II was a fire war in ways that Europe had never known and on a scale Europe had not experienced for centuries. Incendiary weapons poured out of industrial arsenals, and airpower allowed armies to hurl fire over the English Channel, not merely across moats. Both Allied advance and Nazi retreat formed fire fronts. For the Axis the burning of London and Coventry was an attempt to break a people's spirit. For the Allies, the deliberate burning of forests was a strategy to tie up manpower that might otherwise go to the front, and the firing of cities was both a military maneuver and an act of vengeance. As the Third Reich gathered for its *Götterdämmerung,* Reichsmarshal Hermann Göring ordered the great hunting preserves like those at Bialǿowieza, east of Warsaw, and Schorfheide, north of Berlin, put to the torch. Here—in cultural self-immolation—was the enduring vision that had haunted Europe for centuries, the specter of a fire that was consuming, purgative, uncontrolled. This time, however, unkept nature had not burned the cultivated landscape. A wild society had fired nature.[68]

Yet other images ultimately transcended those of Europe's classical fire heritage. Wildfire, malevolent fire, perverted fire, the dark fires that Europe had long dreaded in its nightmares, metamorphosed into new horrors. The enduring iconography of the war was, most often, cast in the imagery of combustion run amok, the conflagrations of London, the firestorms of Hamburg and Dresden, the ghastly ovens of Auschwitz and Dauchau, and from Japan the atomic immolation of Hiroshima and Nagasaki. The specter of uncontrolled fire, believed buried, had resurrected in more virulent technological forms. And this time the specter did not end with the armistice. The Cold War that followed brought the prospect that temperate Europe, beginning with Germany, could become ground zero for a nuclear holocaust that would announce World War III.

The belief that, for temperate Europe, fire was alien, unnecessary, and entirely controllable through proper cultivation, rational political institutions, and better technology proved spectacularly incorrect. The assumption that central Europe's very nature—its homogeneous, temperate climate—banished fire was false. On the contrary, that climate meant that fuels were abundant. By slashing trees, stripping peat, or smashing cities, it was simple to prepare them for burning as seasons and drought permitted. The assertion that its fires were a human artifact had surer grounding. The human hand had long ago erased or entombed anything like a natural fire regime. Undoubtedly such a regime could return; but whereas fire in mediterranean and boreal Europe was a constant negotiation between humans and nature, neither in a position to repeal the other, fire in temperate Europe was always a close gloss on human history.

Temperate Europe had predicated the control of fire on the control of society. When that social order broke, the new pyrotechnologies brought more fire, not less. The wildfires were not the precipitant of social disaster but one of its consequences. The twentieth century's thirty years' war showed that fact brilliantly; and fiery imagery that ended a hot war and inaugurated a cold one did nothing to dampen the belief that fire was both powerful and malicious. As Europe's rural population poured into urban centers, its folk knowledge of fire was lost in the torrent. Certainly for intellectuals, industrial Europe had even

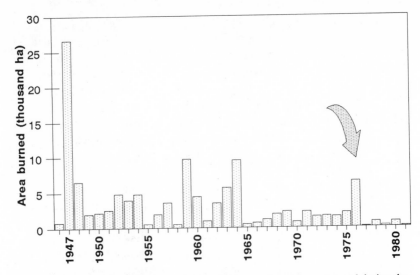

Götterdämmerung: fire follows war in East Germany. Forests were burned during the war, but the collapse of society led to major fires in 1947 (especially when the climate was favorable). Later outbreaks conform to a pattern of postwar harvesting, replanting, and reburning. Gradually the echoes fade. The arrow marks the *Waldbrandkatastrophe* of 1976, which, while comparatively large, is smaller than the other postwar outbreaks. (Modified from Weck 1950 and Mißbach 1982)

less use for fire than had agrarian Europe. Fire remained the stigmata of the primitive, the barbaric, and the dangerous.

But the postwar world that arose out of the ashes had its own fallows and wastes—parks and nature reserves among them. Where fallows flourished, fire would sooner or later follow.

Fallow was not expunged so much as metamorphosed, marbling forests and fields with fuel. If fallow had made fire possible, it had also disciplined it, integrating fire within an agricultural regime. An industrial regime would have to invent new forms of assimilation, new ways to apply and control combustion. The rural overpopulation that had once cleaned woodlands became a rural exodus that left forests littered if not overgrown. Hand labor was too expensive to justify close manipulation. The protest over smudgy moor fires surrendered to concerns over acid rain and the belching vapors of lignite power plants; nutrient loss from burned humus surrendered to the deposition of heavy metals and radionuclides; and the reclamation of wastes yielded to the creation of nature parks.

Postwar Europe, too, had its own rhythms of unrest. The belief that a green revolution and industrial technology could eliminate fire proved as illusory as

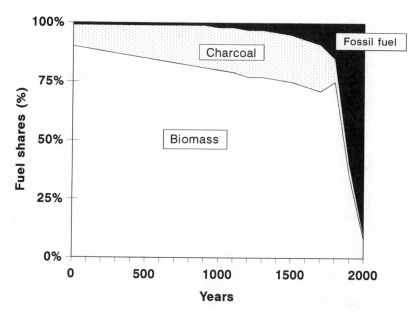

Industrial fire: fire follows fuel. The graph tracks the transition from biomass (or processed biomass, charcoal) to fossil fuels in the Old World. The distribution was uneven, with most of the early burning in Britain and a later center in Germany. Fire, however, is an ecological process, not simply a technology, and the removal of open burning can have unintented consequences. If the biomass is not consumed by traditional means, including controlled fire, it may burn catastrophically as wildfire. Data from Vaclav Smil, *Energy in World History* (Boulder, Co: Westview Press, 1994).

an earlier reliance on breast plows and marling. What persisted was the sense that temperate Europe was, above all, cultivated, and that fire, if essential, was not inevitable. What Europe wanted was pyrotechnology, not fire. But it got both, and soon discovered that it had too much of the former and not enough of the latter.

Quality, not quantity, threatened the biota this time—too much biomass, not enough biodiversity. The industrial transformation had done what it set out to do. It had restored humus, rebuilt forests, and protected nature reserves by restricting human practices within them. But without periodic removal, humus deepened and acidified. Without disturbances, protected forests returned to monocultures as exclusive as a Corbusier cityscape. Without fire-tending, landscapes like heath and the provincial highlands of the Harz Mountains degenerated. Central European forests suffered dieback not only from industrial pollution but because they were no longer slashed and burned but only logged and planted. If fire's damages were gone, so were its rejuvenating powers. The

Agricultural burning in organic soils, Friesland. The social discipline of fire as shown here, the central European tradition, is exactly what broke down during the war and its aftermath. The postwar reforms, however, went beyond the restoration of a social-ecological order and attempted to abolish fire altogether. Reproduced with permission of Freilichtmuseum, Kiekeberg.

problem had not been to abolish the human presence—or that of fire—but to redefine it.

Germany's is a controlled landscape. It has to be, given its population pressures. The German nature reserves constitute only 1.1 percent of the national landmass, with 200 of them less than 5 hectares in size; other restricted landscapes amount to 18 percent. None tolerate fire. Even outside these zones, agricultural burning is rigorously proscribed to specific seasons. The burning of hedges, in particular, has aroused strong condemnation over the centuries because it breaks down the careful borders of the political and propertied world, another illustration of fire as a manifestation of social disorder. That perception describes perfectly the difference between a landscape organized as a house instead of an ecosystem. Behind these fears lay the memory of the war's fire catastrophe.[69]

This has erected a "psychological barrier," in Henry Makowski's words, that makes controlled burning all but impossible. If fires from fields threaten reserves, then so too do fires in the reserves threaten the fields. Why farmers cannot burn fields (and hedges), but nature reserves can, exactly describes the dimensions of the conundrum. Nature reserves need to burn because there is no substitute for fire; farmers subliminate their fire into tractors. Paradoxically it is left to "uncontrolled fires" to demonstrate "how positive the effect of fire can be on the scenery and the maintenance of certain animal and plant species."[70]

That discovery should have shaken Europe's ecologists. Since the advent of its informing Neolithic, fire had been central to the life of temperate Europe, but the enduring assumption was that, like the rest of the garden, fire belonged wholly within the purview of the gardeners. It kindled at human discretion, spread because of human negligence, and raged through human malfeasance. It was no more natural than a stone hearth, and possessed no more autonomy than a steel and flint strike-a-light. That anthropogenic fire often failed was irrelevant; so did buildings, farming practices, and institutions. The solution to fire was better breeding, better education, a more encompassing set of social prescriptions.

Yet there it was, proclaiming the Otherness of Nature, defying the pyroeugenics of industrial technocracy, and declaring false the choice between hearth and holocaust. Perhaps temperate Europe's failures were not strictly political, but philosophical. Perhaps those breakdowns recurred precisely because a society had emerged that could no longer imagine beyond the self-referential landscapes it chose to call nature, that could see fire only as an artifact instead of a dialectic.

WILD HEARTH
Fire in Boreal Europe

The last and wildest stretch of earth
Where Europe's genius built a hearth.
                    —Zachris Topelius

But perhaps this was all possible because every farm had its
own comforter. One that came to rich and poor alike, that never
failed and never tired. . . . it was nothing but the fire, burning on
the hearth on a winter's night.
                    —Selma Lagerlöf, *The Löwensköld Ring*

PROLOGUE:
FIRE AND WATER

Its geography is a formidable collage of wet and dry. The last of Europe to emerge from Pleistocene ice and sea, the Nordic subcontinent became a stony matrix for innumerable rivers, lakes, mires, wetlands, spongy peat, and a littoral rising like a lithic raft as its burdens were lifted away. The air, too, mixed wet with dry. There were great changes in climate, the ice ages coming and going in sync with the mutable shorelines. Seasonality and droughts refined its gross dimensions, carving and abrading its contours like chisels and sandpaper. The lumpy landscape determined where fire could burn, and the often arhythmic climate declared when. What began with Pleistocene ice ended with Holocene fire.

For boreal Europe the Würm glaciation was not restricted to mountain cirques, periglacial tundra, meltwaters, and aeolian loess. The towering ice sheets had not only buried but depressed the land, and their recession not merely re-exposed old lands but set in motion their re-creation. An upspringing land, a rising sea, and restless meltwaters, probing for outlets, made and remade the region. Time and again the Baltic closed off, a vast freshwater lake. For

210

a while it flowed out across Sweden, from Stockholm to Göteborg. Coastlines migrated outward. Where the ice retreated, it left a deranged landscape, scoured, pocked, limned with eskers and moraines. These filled with waters, some flowing, some stagnant. The land shed those waters slowly, like a bear rising from a river. A cold, largely wet climate replaced the melting ice, but the water remained. Sweden became a land of lakes, mires, and rivers. The nineteenth-century Swedish-Finnish writer Zachris Topelius declared Finland "the Daughter of the Sea," whose emerging shores had added 1,000 square kilometers a century. Finland's national epic poem *Kalevala* claimed the dripping land as the creation of the Water Mother. And the folk epic *Tuli* likened the foaming Lake Alue to "spruces in the torment of the fire, / the flames' overwhelmingness."[1]

With inverted symmetry, boreal Europe mirrors mediterranean Europe. There is for both a core sea, and the same cluster of civilization around its littoral. Both orbit around a prolonged period of dormancy, winter for the north, summer for the south. Both frustrated the agricultural template of Europe's temperate core; neither could integrate grazing readily into the closed circuity of a three-field rotation; each required a seasonal outfield. Both defied the simple fire chronologies of central Europe. For one, fire was chronic, flaming, undeniable. For the other, fire smoldered, unleashed from time to time in volatile flareups. There are even similar attempts at national linkages between core and periphery. What France carried across the Mediterranean, striving toward the equator, Sweden attempted in a long traverse across the boreal zone, breaching the Arctic Circle.

Yet it seems an improbable place for fire. The long dormancy of winter, the brief efflorescence of summer growth and decay, the broken terrain of waters and waterlogged lands—all apparently argue for fire as ephemeral, limited, and anomalous. In fact, fire persisted like the famous *lördbrand,* the burn that smolders in organic soils beneath a winter snowpack, surviving from fall to spring. The Holocene biota that seeped and spilled across the emergent landscape brought the oldest of forests, the boreal conifers, into the youngest of subcontinents. That biota carried with it ancient adaptations to disturbance, including fire. That flora needed fire.

It required fire to counter the sodden climate, with its tendency to homogenize everything into mire and peat and acidic bog. Without fire the wetted land can become a vast sink of nutrients, like a stagnant pond that slowly silts in and chokes everything in its subsiding detritus. Accumulating raw humus can cover sites like an impermeable blanket. Allelopathic shrubs, shade-casting groves, and sphagnum mosses can spread like a fungal blight. Something needs to shake those nutrients free, to jolt the tepid spring into vigorous growth and stir the cauldron of biodiversity. Fire does just that.

To succeed, fire does not need to burn annually, although it can. In places, it keeps the biotic broth simmering, while elsewhere, from time to time, it brings the floral stew to a boil. It only matters that fire comes often enough to jar the otherwise slowed, boreal life cycle of the dominant trees and biomes. Accordingly fire appears opportunistically, when ignition captures fuel and drought, when continental conditions temporarily shove aside the prevailing maritime climate. Often it arrives explosively, crowding decades of biological work into a few short weeks. It appears in spurts, sometimes sweeping, sometimes creeping, shaping Fire Ages as lumpy as Ice Ages. Probably, under pre-Neolithic conditions, one percent of boreal Europe's wildlands burned each year. On average, major fire—crown fire—returned every century.[2]

There has been ample ignition. Humans prowled the ice flanks like the elk they hunted, so transmutative that there have been few places and few times when lightning has more or less defined the fire regime. But it has always been present, if not potent. At Sodankylä in Finland lightning accounts for 69 percent of the fires for which the cause is known. In the Ulvinsalo Strict Nature Reserve in northern Finland, fires have burned 50 percent of the area once in the lifetime of the oldest pines. Between 1712 and 1969, some 48 fires ignited, a frequency of 80 to 100 years. A similar history has characterized Muddus National Park in northern Sweden. In the twentieth century, fires broke out, presumably from lightning, in 1920, 1933, 1941, and 1947. Most were small, but the 1933 burn was part of a 200-fire complex and swept 20,000 hectares. As a place, Muddus is exceptional, resting imperturbably outside the thrust of dominant settlement, which is why it has survived more or less intact to become a park. As an index, it probably reflects the rhythms of an Arctic lightning fire regime. Farther south the pace of fire picks up.[3]

A survey of contemporary Swedish statistics hints at lightning's potential. Southern Sweden has more lightning fire than the north, the rain-shadowed east more than the maritime west, and the lowland forests more than the mountain *fjäll*. The gradient of lightning fires is, in fact, the gradient of Swedish fire from all causes. Lightning fire concentrates with close fidelity to the geography of some rare plants, notably several species of geraniums. Whether this reflects a historic pattern of natural ignition or simply a fire-prone landscape is unclear, so thoroughly have humans remade the scene. Today lightning fire flourishes only in nature reserves, as a scientific curiosity, like a rare orchid or a quarantined bacillus. But obviously lightning has lurked always in the background.[4]

Certainly fires, of whatever cause, have proved influential in site ecology. If fire alone has defined few sites, neither has it spared more than a few. Even-aged forests typically testify to past crown fires. The depths of mires and peat contain the record of past burns. Charcoal laces humus, settles into lakes, and

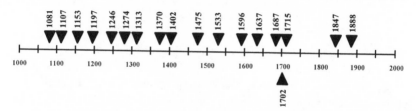

A fire-history chronology reconstructed from fire-scarred pine near Luleälven, Sweden. Each triangle and associated date indicates a fire. The major disturbance in this pattern occurs during the last two centuries with accelerated settlement. Logging cleared out most of the fire-recording old-growth, and, while it stimulated slash-powered wildfires (e.g., the 1888 burns), it mostly worked to reduce the background count of fires. Over a span of 900 years, fires returned, on average, every 47. (Data

decorates peat like marble. Even spruce swamp forests, long believed to be fire refugia, immune to burning, usually reveal on close inspection a fiery past. On the land's emergence, fire was there—drying, tempering, molding. Fire was a forge that helped make malleable the biota that nature and culture would shape into boreal Europe.[5]

The evidence of Europe's boreal fires is abundant. But perhaps most satisfying are those records that join fire with water. These take shape in the region's lakes that acquire annual layers of sediment, or varves. Stacked like the pages of an ancient chronicle, they are among the most reliable and, given the ubiquity of the region's lakes, the most common of its geographic archives. Varve muds define periods of erosion; varve pollen grains, the evolution of the surrounding flora; varve chemicals, epochs of acidification, mining, oxygen levels, and climate change. And varve charcoal records a fair sample of the region's fire load. That charcoal—carried through the air, flushed by streams—inscribes the region's fire regimes on the parchment silts like india ink.

But the varves are not alone. There are plentiful written documents, too. Three, in particular, are self-conscious cross sections through the region's natural history. They represent literary horizons as laced with fire references as the lake varves are with black carbon. If the varves bind water with fire, these books bind nature with culture. The *Historia* of Olaus Magnus, the travels of Carl von Linné, and Selma Lagerlöf's *Wonderful Adventures of Nils* trace the evolving fire history of boreal Europe as clearly as the fire scars on Scots pine and the macroscopic char embedded in lake sediments.

FIRE AND SWORD:
THE *Historia* OF OLAUS MAGNUS

They were tumultuous times. Christian II, king of Denmark, had at last tri-umphed over Swedish opposition and on November 4, 1520, assumed the Swedish throne in ceremonies at Stockholm. Three days later he had the cas-tle gates locked, announced trials, and brutally executed over fifty of his impris-oned guests, heaping the bodies on the square until, after three days, they were hauled outside and burned as heretics. The purge continued. But a counterin-surgency under Gustavus Vasa spread, and by 1523 he had driven the Danes from Sweden and installed himself as king. With exquisite timing the Swedish separatist movement merged with the Reformation. Gustavus Vasa embraced Lutheranism, seized church lands and wealth, and banished the leading Catholic prelates, among them the brothers Johannes and Olaus Magnus. They never returned.

Their personal counterreformation took the form of humanist writings. The elder Johannes wrote a history of the Goths and the kings of Sweden, the *His-toria de omnibus Gothorum Sveonumque regibus* (1554), a powerful political tract against the Vasa tyranny and Lutheran heresy. Olaus Magnus wrote an equally learned if disjunctive natural and human history of the Nordic peoples: *Historia de gentibus septentrionalibus* (1555). While it addressed the great con-tests of his day, it also enlarged their scope, so that the Nordic people struggle not only against heathen and heretic, tyrannical Danes and kingly usurpers, but against the forbidding if marvelous boreal landscape. The Swedish king-dom was a European frontier, a border that was ecological as well as political and ecclesiastical.

The north abounded with testimonies to nature's fecundity. But it was a harsh land that created a tough people, and the *Historia* offers much evidence of the capacity of the Nordic folk to struggle and endure. A jumbled thesaurus of prodigal wonders and practical works, the book became enormously pop-ular, was quickly translated into French, Italian, German, and English, and passed through twenty editions over the next century. It was, as John Granlund has recently remarked, "a superb cultural history—the first worthy of that name to appear in Europe." Between the revelations of Saint Birgitta and the trav-els of Linnaeus, Olaus Magnus's *Historia* was the great document of Swedish literature.[6]

It is also an extraordinary if eccentric encyclopedia of Nordic fire. Like other Nordic marvels, fire is presented as dangerous. The first book describes the hazards of lightning, including its capacity to kill and kindle. Later, Olaus relates the story of a lightning-caused fire that nearly destroyed Stockholm and sent 1,600 persons to their death as the ship on which they fled the conflagration sank. But fire is equally beneficial. Without it agriculture was impossible, and winter unbearable. To guide them through dark winter woods, folk would carry torches of oak bark, place tapers along pathways, and seek out special tree fungi (*eldticka*) that, when lit, would glow like candles. In this way, fire guaranteed safe passage. The wise traveler sought out such sites, places full of fire-carrying materials. And that is an example that chroniclers would do well to imitate.[7]

(i)

The *Historia* offers a reconnaissance of Nordic fires. There are the usual domestic fires for lighting, cooking, and warming. More vital to political economy is the pyrotechnology of mining and smelting, essential for both trade and weaponry. There are fires to assist fishing from small boats and ice floes, fires to drive off grasshoppers, fires to extract tar, fires for hunting, and fires for agriculture. There are ceremonial fires. The heathen Lithuanians worshiped fire along with forests and snakes; Christianized Lapps, by contrast, use fire to accompany rites of birth, death, and matrimony; ancient Goths practiced human sacrifice, reducing even kings (here Olaus sends a warning to Vasa) to burnt offerings; fire dances were common. But the chief benefit of the ceremony, Olaus hints, was as training for soldiers; and the principal display of fire practices in the *Historia*—far overwhelming all the others—resides in war. Half the *Historia* is devoted to the arts of war. The Nordic peoples possessed, it seemed, an inexhaustible arsenal of fire weaponry, equally deadly on land, sea, or ice.

Med eld och svärd, with fire and sword. So had the Danes invaded Sweden, Olaus observes, and so would the Swedes respond. Signal beacons along the shore warned of invading armies and called the populace to arms. Soldiers carried torches, rich in resin (they preferred spruce). Against citadels, armies shot flaming arrows, flung pots of liquid, catapulted heated iron and glowing slag, and hurled forest kindling. Miners sapped fortifications with tunnels, then built great fires that caused the walls to collapse. Peasants trapped errant enemy soldiers in houses, and then burned them alive. A scorched earth encumbered invaders. Cannon and other firearms added the explosive blast of gunpowder. The Norse hero Ragnar, it is said, devised a copper horse that breathed fire against his enemies. Burning fire shields sent smoke that confused hostile troops and masked maneuvers. The sea was no safer. Fire ships filled with tar and wood could burn bridges, scramble enemy fleets, and with the proper land breeze assist amphibious landings. Ship fires were, in fact, worse than land fires because there was no escape. The noise of burning ships, Olaus concluded, was more terrible than the rush of arrows. Nor did ice banish fire. The Nordics possessed fire sleds that, filled with combustibles and pulled by horses wild with fright, could plunge into enemy ranks, like war elephants sensing blood, thought Olaus.[8]

The *Historia* soon disabused those who believed that the north might be easy to conquer or was unsuitable to warfare. On the contrary, the prevalence of fire armaments dramatized the argument that civilization was present among the Nordics, even if it expressed itself through a profuse pyrotechnology of incendiary weapons. Those allusions—the charming woodcuts, the allegorical stories—connected the Nordic lands with European experience as fully as Olaus Magnus's citations from such ancient authorities as Julius Caesar, Seneca, Livy, and the inevitable Pliny. A frontier it might be, but it was as fortified as Hadrian's Wall, as much a border as the citadels that opposed the ravenous Turk. Revealingly, Olaus refers to the Lutheran reformation as itself a "world fire," so far unquenchable.[9]

In its obsession with fire weaponry, the *Historia* tacks close to the wind of historic records. More than any other practice, war dominates the chronicles of European fire, as it does Europe's written archives in general, and has since the *Iliad.* The expansion of one people typically came at the expense of another; conflict meant an exchange of fire; and flame traced the frontiers as surely as roads, villages, and trap lines. There was a strong tradition among the Nordics that one took possession of land by burning it. The surest means to conquer was to convert—if not the heathen, then the habitat; forcibly if necessary, by fire preferentially.

For this text, too, Olaus Magnus provides a gloss. He lavishes many pages on the violent, typically fiery, relationships with the Lapps in the north, the Russians to the east, and especially the Danes to the south. Often the conflicts focus on cities, and he depicts the paradoxes of urban fire, so essential when controlled in the hearth, so devastating when unleashed during war. But urban life, although favored by scribes, lords, and tradesmen, was a minor habitat compared with the immense countryside of wild and rural lands. For this also Olaus bears witness.[10]

The Nordic lands were an agricultural no less than an ecclesiastical and military borderland between temperate and boreal Europe. Friendly fire brought new land into cultivation, fertilized and purged old fields, and guarded against the encroaching forest, whose roots advanced like "poisonous snakes." But hostile fire, fire that through carelessness or enmity broke free from its assigned posts, was a marauding rebel and required a "war," as "against a deadly enemy," to suppress its depredating flames. Facing such outbreaks, whole districts could be called to arms.[11]

(ii)

Anthropogenic contact began early. Mesolithic tribes prowled along the receding ice sheets. They hunted elk, fished and foraged, and lived in skin longhouses outfitted with special heating apparatus (fireplaces located near doorways for draft, stone ducts to carry heat throughout the structure). In the climatic upheavals and migrations that followed, other peoples moved in, not unlike the spruce that, with later human settlement, massively invaded boreal Europe from east to west about 2,000 years ago. But the land was hard, and for the most part Neolithic pioneers established only beachheads, clinging like seals to the coast. Penetration inland came later, where it came at all.

Probably the subsequent settlement of Norrland mimics the nature of contact in the earliest eras. By the time Finns and Swedes probed inland, Lapps (Saami) were present.* Their origins are obscure. Who preceded them, or how elk-hunting Mesolithic clans evolved into or were supplanted by the tribes who bore the full brunt of contact with Neolithic peoples, is unknown. Probably, like the Finns, the Lapps had an ancient linkage with boreal peoples farther east, possibly beyond the Urals. For at least several centuries Lapps and Finns had shared a tenuous, contested frontier, steadily pushed northward. Some Lapp tribes specialized in hunting, some in fishing, but more than anything else the reindeer, domesticated for milk, meat, transport, and hunting decoy, distinguished their peculiar economy.[12]

The origins of domesticated reindeer too are murky. One theory argues that the practice diffused from a core region in southern Siberia; another holds that particular elements were widespread and selectively adapted; others point to the many contacts between reindeer herders and other pastoralists and the adaptation of the one's techniques to the other's dominant ungulate. Thus the reindeer replaced the dog and horse as a draft animal for sleds, the cow and goat as a source of milk, and sheep and cattle as providers of meat and hides. Tethered reindeer could be used to draw wild reindeer to hunting sites during rutting season. Harnessed reindeer could pull boatlike sleds effortlessly over vast frozen mires and wetlands. Above all, reindeer could survive on natural pasture through the endless winter. While other domesticates demanded fodder, typically cut from wet meadows, rough outfields, or even sown fields, reindeer could feed on lichens that hung from trees and carpeted the forest floor. Reindeer could thrive on the native forage of boreal Europe as the horse could on Eurasia's grassy steppes.

Probably reindeer pastoralism became established around A.D. 500. Almost certainly herds were small, not unlike the milch cows or draft oxen to which they were cognates. The stock complemented rather than replaced the mixed Lapp economy of hunting, fishing, foraging, and fur trapping. But as the system expanded and made possible a more intensive harvest, as it opened up inte-

---

* The people historically known as Lapps have recently adopted the name Saami (also, Samme, Sami). The term is not well known in English, so I have retained the old one.

riors otherwise blocked by winter, Lapps increasingly encountered the Finns and Swedes who probed inland from their coastal posts and who began to link them with the commercial markets of Europe.

The movement of furs and goods between inland forest and coastal village became more robust. And as herds began to increase, settlement moved upriver and spread from the littoral. This interaction triggered a full-blown pastoralism. A boreal transhumance developed as herds trudged between summer and winter ranges. Arable farming and pastoralism both expanded, guaranteeing that conflict would replace contact. In 1671 the Swedish monarchy proclaimed a formal boundary between the two groups, established designated points of contact, and sought to regulate their exchange, not least of all for purposes of taxation.

But the real border was environmental. However much trade worked to mutual advantage, the settlement patterns were incommensurable. Arable farming and pastoralism mingled as poorly in boreal as in mediterranean Europe. While everyone exploited whatever was available, the core of Finnish settlement was a swidden farm, of Swedish settlement a suite of rough cattle pastures, and of Lapp life the reindeer herd. These differences expressed themselves in characteristic fire practices, and they focused, with stunning precision, on lichens. Lapp pastoralism depended on abundant lichens for winter range, and as herds began to swell in the eighteenth and nineteenth centuries to unprecedented numbers, browsing pressure demanded more and more old-growth lichen prairies. But while, over the long run, lichens required fire for rejuvenation, the fire cycle was slow, almost the length of stand-replacing fires in pine. A mature site could require sixty to eighty years for full restoration. Adequate winter forage demanded accessible sites that were spared too-frequent fire, thus arguing for low populations and long treks.

Precise information on Lapp fire practices is, like so much about that elusive culture, not available. Certainly domestic fire was honored, and archaeologists now trace the movements of the prehistoric Lapps through their distinctive hearths. Fire assisted in hunting, particularly for bears; smudge fires brought relief to fly-crazed reindeer, and even served as bait to lure wild reindeer. Less clear are their free-burning fire practices. Friendly observers in the 1820s claimed that the Lapps exploited fire cautiously, that in fact they actively sought to exclude it from the lichen savannas that constituted their winter pastures, and that reckless or vicious burning by settlers drove them from ancestral lands as ruthlessly as armed troops.

But fire ecology was surely more complex. Success depended on keeping the size of the herds in sync with the size of the range, and that partly depended on fire regimes. Over their annual cycle of browsing, reindeer search out more recently burned sites, redolent with lush forbs and fireweeds, for spring foraging. By analogy to reindeer herders in Siberia, Lapps may have created spring pastures by deliberate burning. Like other ungulates, reindeer are attracted to recent burns; a large herd can, in fact, soon trample a small burned site into mud.

The problem was balance—the proportion of winter and summer pastures, of burned and unburned sites. In a broader frame it was the classic encounter between farmer, however committed to swidden, and pastoralist, however bound to his traditional lands. Both were pushing outward. Like swiddeners shortening their fallow, the exploding herds put ever greater pressure on mature or old lichen savannas, and this at a time when several economies, the Lapp only one among them, were expanding throughout Lappmark. There was less margin for maneuvering. There was less ecological slack with which to absorb fire of any sort, natural, careless, necessary, or vindictive. Ominously, their competitors needed a different fire regime. The Finns were swiddeners—among the greatest in Europe. Not only did they convert forest plots by slashing and burning, but their fires frequently escaped to scour away the lichen-rich understory of the surrounding woods. The Swedes also practiced swidden, but they were partial to burning for the improvement of grassy pasture, and since they required large and varied sites to ensure an ample harvest of winter forage, they spread their fires widely. Prospecting miners, treating the forest as though it were so much charcoal for smelting, were even more pernicious. The conflict between colonizers inevitably focused on fire.

The outcome appalled travelers and missionaries. In the 1820s, Petrus Laestadius condemned the settlers' "bad habit of burning forest near their farm in order to obtain good summer grazing pasture for their cattle." He regarded the practice as inherently evil, as well as a self-inflicted wound. Worse, the fires often propagated beyond control. "If the fires are not put out by rain, they can spread unchecked and lay leagues of land to waste. In the southern regions of Lapland this unfortunate practice has even spread so far that the Lapps cannot winter in their areas but are forced to move from the fells to among the farmers," thus intensifying the competition. Even in early twentieth century Finland, Jakob Fellman observed that forest fires were useful for the cattle rearing of the settlers: "The burned-over areas grow hay and grass which is much stronger and more conducive to milking than the sedge grass growing on the bogs. For this reason the settlers are often tempted to burn their forests." Worse still, settlers deliberately attacked the lichens, which drove off the reindeer, which dispelled the Lapps. The Lapps reciprocated, and turned to fire to drive off the interloping farmers and miners like so many wolves.[13]

Even Laestadius recognized that the settlers and forest Lapps harmed each other to some degree, that the reindeer damaged hay meadows and the settlers overfished lakes, and that such differences could not "be resolved in any final way: both parties must learn to live with them." But the calculated destruction of habitat was something else, worse because the Lapps had by now joined the panoply of "noble savages" and "children of nature" with whom European savants had populated the world's moral geography. Laestadius denounced the settlers' attempt "to destroy the Lapps means of livelihood in a more concrete and unnatural way," by setting fire to the forest. Where the clash was most severe, "immoral settlers," as Fellman called them, fired around fields and hay meadows and burned off the lichens. In this way, through a cordon sanitaire of fire, they protected haystacks and fields. Burning pushed the Lapps away from settlements—a practice more vigorously pursued in southern Lapland than in the north, where settlers too acquired some reindeer. Officials instinctively favored agriculture over pastoralism, but where legal means of removal or disengagement failed, arson might succeed.[14]

The pressures continued until industrial forestry in the late nineteenth century began restructuring Norrland more thoroughly than any process since the Fennoscandinavian glaciation. Timber, not agriculture or furs, became the basis of local economies. Foresters joined Lapps in protest against promiscuous fire, or indeed against burning of any sort. Fire melted away, like the residual ice sheet, and with that ecological burden lifted, the woods rebounded. Commercial species, notably pine and spruce, dominated forests, which became vast tree farms; mires were drained, clearing more land for forestry; tourism replaced seasonal fur trading; and reindeer herds continued to swell (by the 1980s they were herded by snowmobiles and helicopters), their demand for winter-forage lichens met in part by aggressive fire exclusion. Domestic reindeer dominated the understory of Lappmark forests as much as sheep and goats did Mediterranean landscapes. Herds even grazed on nature reserves such as Muddus National Park.

The ultimate consequences of the grazing regime were unknown, and unstudied. But the degradation wrought by its sustaining fire regime—one characterized by the expulsion of routine burning—became increasingly evident.

(iii)

The northern lands were exceptional, not only because of their indigenous peoples but because they frustrated classical agriculture. The farther north and the farther inland settlers went, the greater were the hazards and the more difficult their tasks. Pushing temperate agricultural systems into boreal climes was like rolling a snowball uphill. A full-blown Neolithic revolution first claimed the south and the littoral, and then selectively probed northward and into the interior. There it encountered a spreading but fragmented Neolithic in the form of reindeer pastoralism.[15]

Consider, as synecdoche, two paired histories, the first from Paimio along the coast of southwestern Finland and the second from the communes of Lammi and Sääksmäki farther inland. The first is representative for most of the Baltic littoral; the second, for the more distinctive interior colonization of Fennoscandinavia. Both stand in curious contrast to the fragment of temperate Europe lodged like a splinter in the south-reaching finger of Scandinavia.

Risen from the Pleistocene sea, Paimio dried and, readied by humans, it burned. What began as a spit of land evolved into an archipelago and then into a complex littoral of mixed landforms and offshore islands. At 8,000 B.P. it occupied 32 square kilometers, by 5,000 B.P. 155 square kilometers, and by 1,200 B.P., 233. Here was truly new land, and the great migrations of the Holocene colonized it for the first time.

The sequence was classically European. First came the pioneers, the pine and the quick-marching birch and alder whose "arrival and spread" was likely "due to fires." Then a chronically wet climate promoted a ponderous primeval forest that by Mesolithic times cast everything else under its shade until landnam broke open the tumulus landscape. By 2,600 years ago, assisted by the return of fire, the landscape experienced a far-reaching reconstruction: the forest restocked with birch and sturdy conifers, soils deteriorated, the biota fragmented into a complex mosaic of meadows, fields, heath, mires, and woods. Most spectacularly, spruce exploded through the region like a backdrafting fire through an open door. *Picea* and *Homo* spread in synchronization. By 1,200 B.P. conifers constituted 70 to 87 percent of the forest.[16]

What humans gave, they could take away, and more rapidly than paludifying soils, uplifting lands, and migrating trees. Population grew and agriculture intensified. The deciduous forest fell before ax and fire during the Roman Iron Age. The Viking era carried the search for pasture up river valleys and emergent wetlands. Settlements consolidated, swidden expanded, fallow shortened, and pasture-stimulation fires probed into peats, heath, and bogs. By A.D. 1000-1300 swidden settled into more sedentary forms, and grazing strengthened its grip through the harvesting of alluvial meadows, the conversion of conifer forest to rough pasture, and the use of seasonal shielings. The combined biotic shock created both spectacular meadows and degenerate heath. The forest thinned and shrank. The reclaimed landscapes spread like tendrils from a central European vine, attaching to the coarse latticework of the Baltic littoral.

This wholesale reformation involved far more than simple deforestation. Although cut and burned, the forest revived, often in different forms, each prompting another variant of swidden. For millennia the forest had returned, always serving the nuclear farm, always purged and revived by fire. By the nineteenth century, however, the forest not the field mesmerized observers, and it was anthropogenic fire more than any other practice that seemed to threaten those valorized woods.

The drama of Nordic fire moved inland, trekking to sites like Lammi. Perhaps because it is farther from the coast—through embedded within Finland's fabulous lake district—fires appear more frequently.[17]

The fire load rose and fell with climate and colonization. About 7,500 B.P. open pine and birch forests, rich in fireweed, flourished. Between 3,700 and 3,400 B.P. fires increased sharply, possibly of anthropogenic origin, a tentative landnam. By 1,700 B.P. spruce began its advance, and within 800 years or so accounted for 80 percent of the forested area. By the first century A.D. human expansion outpaced other boreal rhythms. Persistent agriculture found its way to lakeshores and riverbanks as farming began to nest instead of swarm. Still, agriculture meant fire—swidden farming, pastoral burning, fire-assisted foraging. But reclamation was at first tentative and episodic, its fire regime not dramatically different from what preceded it. From A.D. 470 to 900 swidden, or swidden in combination with natural ignition, shrank the fire return interval to 60 to 80 years. Then, from 900 to 1030, there was nothing. The site fell silent with abandonment.

Still, even frontier Finland felt the Great Reclamation and its ever-widening gyre. Between 1030 and 1616 swidden revived on a roughly 50 to 70 year cycle. The practice intensified, approximating European norms and transforming the fire-fallow cycle into something like field rotation. The cycle shortened to less than 30 years. By 1900 the fallow was so short and the forest so reduced that fires no longer deposited enough charcoal in Lake Lovojärvi to document their history. Swidden became impractical; not even peat and woody debris hauled from surrounding forests could carry fire adequately. The fallow shortened to 10 to 15 years, and yields plummeted by half. Once-heavy burns, purging raw humus and depositing rich strata of ash, yielded to light burns barely capable of propagation. Agriculture went from burning hefty logs to burning twigs and grass; from growing rye, turnips, and barley to raising cattle; from converting mixed, sometimes dense forests to massaging open fields, heath, and overgrazed plots of juniper. By the nineteenth century, the Lammi landscape was nearly treeless.

In 1915, after half a century during which foresters had contested with swiddeners, Olli Heikinheimo summed up the significance for Finland's woods:

> As a 25 year rotation time was used, sites have been burnt at least
> four times, ploughed at least twelve times and harrowed twelve times
> if there were three crop yields within each rotation time or altogether
> twelve crop yields. The area has been felled, burnt and used for fields
> for 20 years, for hay-making for 12 years and for pasture land for 68

years. Since slash-and-burn cultivation has been practiced continuously in many places for 500 to 1000 years, these figures must be multiplied by 5–10, in order to get an accurate picture of how extensive the use of that method was.

Even so, cultivated land was only part of the equation. To produce sufficient manure for arable fields, and to diversify a marginal economy, the ratio of meadows to fields had to be at least 2:1. Some of this came from abandoned swidden, the rest from wastelands immune to cultivation. These too were burned. Still, the system struggled. In the 1750s Peter Gadd argued that each decade consisted of two famine years, three scanty grain years, four fair grain years, and one productive grain year. With swidden, life was hard and uncertain, without it, impossible.[18]

In 1856, Finland created a national forest service, abolished legal swidden, and sought to restock its landscape with trees, which the international economy had made far more valuable than hemp, rye, and butter. This was a formidable task. Gone was maple; juniper and alder sprang up like pasture weeds; birch blanketed whole terrains like fireweed; only constant pruning held spruce in check; burning, deliberate and accidental, propagated widely. Mrs. Alec Tweedie, touring Finland in carts in 1911, saw fires everywhere. "One of the curses" of Finland, she concluded, and likened them to "locusts in Morocco." The country would soon suffer through two world wars, a civil war, a depression, the forced cession of 10 percent of its eastern border to the USSR, and punitive reparations.[19]

But trees triumphed. In the 1930s, assisted by the logic of a new economy, foresters removed not only swidden but pastoralism. Forest grazing ended in the Lammi region during the 1930s. In Paimio the amount of land in hay meadows plummeted from 1.4 million hectares in 1860 to 80,000 hectares by 1958. Draining, afforesting, fertilizing—all in the name of industrial forestry—restructured the landscape more thoroughly than at any time since the Holocene spruce invasion. Fires virtually vanished. The soot that sifted down to the varves of Lake Lovojärvi now came from fossil coal burned in power plants and factories, and gasoline exhausted from automobiles.

These two chronicles reveal the impress of a temperate template on a boreal environment, and the various accommodations—or, from a central European perspective, the distortions and agronomic perversions—that resulted. That Scandinavians could replicate that central paradigm was demonstrated by Denmark, and by that southernmost shard of Sweden long ruled by Denmark.

Fighting over the temperate provinces of Halland, Blekinge, and Skåne continued for another century after the *Historia* recorded the wars' gory tactics. In 1612 the Swedes stalled a Danish overland assault toward Stockholm with a scorched earth strategy. In 1658 the Treaty of Roskilde ceded the southern lands permanently to Sweden. Even so, only the narrow Øresund segregated Skåne from Sjaelland. Culturally and agriculturally the landscape belonged with Denmark, and its landscape history with central Europe.[20]

Landscape evolution followed a familiar scenario: landnam, reclamation, agricultural revolution, and that ineffable alliance of forestry with industry. In pre-landnam times, immense shade forests crowded Mesolithic society into lagoons and estuaries. The Neolithic arrived around 4,500 years B.P. introduced small-scale swidden, and loosed cattle and herds of mast-hungry swine. Within 400 to 500 years, landnam had fractured the monolithic forest into a mosaic, a coppicing woodland on a rotation of 40 to 50 years. Settlement dispersed, collectively browsing the forest into more favorable forms. Fires increased in abundance. By 2,300 to 2,200 B.P., agriculture had been restructured into more permanent fields, grasslands had expanded to enhance the production of manure, and fires had become not only frequent but routine. Biodiversity reached a probable maximum.

The next transition came as the Great Migration era succeeded the Great Reclamation. Between roughly A.D. 700 and 1200, agriculture consolidated and synchronized arable infield with pastoral outfield, and settled shifting cultivation into more or less permanent villages. Thereafter, with minor reversals, agriculture expanded and intensified. By the mid-seventeenth century, 93 percent of all farms were in villages. Between 1700 and 1800, with the three-field system dominant, arable lands assumed a greater proportion of the total landscape, increasing between 40 and 50 percent. Over the eighteenth century, however, population doubled and the weight of human numbers impressed itself on the land. The multifield system began to replace the three-field system and animal husbandry a looser herding, while marginal lands were colonized, productive lands enclosed, coppices decreased, peat exploited, rough pastures converted or degraded, and fallow shortened. Around 1875, population reached a maximum, then eased.

Gradually but relentlessly a capitalist agriculture intruded and an international market prevailed. Artificial fertilizers, draining, commercial cropping, arable ley farming, afforestation, and internal combustion engines substituted for fire-fallow cultivation. The logic of national agriculture policies proved more powerful than drought, the balance of trade more vital than the linkage of infield with outfield, the automobile more compelling than agglomerated villages. Landscapes begun with the Neolithic crumbled into ruin. Biodiversity at all scales, from species to landscape mosaics, diminished. Officials actively sought to exclude burning of any kind other than fossil fuels. Fire became as much a relic as rune stones.[21]

Those informing policies were derived from Sweden's southern provinces—from what they symbolized as much as what they produced. They bound Swe-

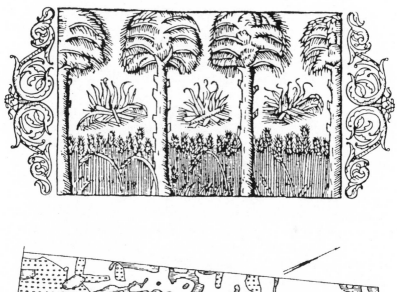

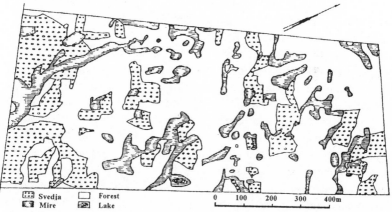

Svedjebruk: Swedish swidden. (Top) Recorded in Olaus Magnus, *Historia*. Note the trimmed branches on the trees. Where fuels were insufficient, peasants cut limbs from surrounding woods and carried the debris to the fields for burning. (Bottom) Dappled pattern of swidden plots (*svedja*), lakes, woods, and mires around Norums in 1900. (Adapted from Westin 1930)

den to the ideas, norms, institutions, and landscapes of central Europe; they had, in fact, been sought in order to establish a permanent link with central Europe. The acquisition of Skåne affected Swedish thinking as much as, in a later war, the loss of Finland did. It connected Norrland to central Europe as the Île-de-France did Provence. Skåne, not Stockholm, became the baseline for triangulating Swedish land use and moral geography. It is a curious inversion, as though Côte d'Azur supplanted Paris as a standard, or the Crimea, Muscovy. But the centripetal forces drawing Sweden to the center were greater than the centrifugal forces that pushed outward into the boreal wilds. Skåne became a cultural infield to the vast, swiddened outfield that was boreal Europe.

(iv)

Its peasants and pastoralists chronicled the region's fire history in the land, but its intellectuals, almost all of whom resided in cities, penned its written records. The urban landscape, not the rural, dictated fire consciousness. What high culture knew of fire is what intellectuals saw in houses, city blocks, and castles.

What they saw was fire-threatened towns and fire warfare. For cities the consequences of a fire set accidentally or one kindled by an enemy army were identical. In the *Historia,* Olaus Magnus locates urban firefighting after four chapters on warfare and before an explication of swidden. The city becomes another battleground with fire, and urbanites respond accordingly. A bell sounds the alarm. In the old days, Olaus notes approvingly, monks were first on the scene. Now, citizens assume the duty and organize with leather buckets, ladders, and hooks to rescue trapped persons, pull down thatch roofs, and guard against plundering. In such fires a person discovers the depths of his friendships. Good friends rush to help; others exploit the pandemonium to steal. If caught, thieves (and arsonists) were themselves thrown into the flames.[22]

With fire so common in urban settings—and in a cold climate, so essential— escapes were inevitable and wars sufficiently frequent to warrant speaking of urban fire regimes. The routine burning of cities, however, allowed for their rejuvenation. By the seventeenth century, fire protection became itself an element in urban design, not least as a military consideration. The fortified city had to cope with enemy fires as well as assault on its walls. The location of canals, the size of city blocks, and the movement of fire brigades were as vital as the placement of towers, the siting of armories, and the ability to mass troops. Legal codes sought to regulate the use of wood for construction. The introduction of piped water was as much for firefighting as for sanitation.[23]

Accordingly, streets were widened, structures built of stone, and geometric patterns laid down that provided ready access and compartmentalization. The 1650 expansion of Stockholm, for example, or the building of Göteborg reflected their fire history, and the fire consciousness of architects, as much as economics and defensibility. A razed site offered a chance to rebuild from scratch. The outcome was often streets as broad as plazas. John Murray's nineteenth-century guidebook alluded to the "air of desolation" that resulted from fire prevention planning, notably the wide streets. "But at least it is an improvement," William Mead has concluded, "on a situation in which everyone was likely to experience the destruction of his home by fire sometime in his life."[24]

Fire and sword. Olaus Magnus records (top) fire warfare and (bottom) urban firefighting. (From the *Historia*)

The same happened with Helsinki as it rose from the ashes of the 1809 fire, the war that cost Sweden its Finnish provinces. That disastrous conflict terminated Sweden's reign as a great power, removed it from Europe's military geography, and banished fire warfare from its landscape. But other former provinces were not so lucky. Long caught between the hammer and anvil of Swedish-Russian rivalry, Finland bore its wounds longer. The Nazi retreat from north Finland renewed scorched earth practices of a kind that seemed almost anachronistic amid an air war that sent V-2s to London and spawned firestorms in Dresden and Tokyo. From the Swedish side of the Torneå River, observers watched towns, cabins, and farms burn, their smoke columns tracing the tracks of the withdrawing Wehrmacht. That experience was, for Finland, all too common.

There are species—*Pteridium* (bracken) among them—that germinate after fire and then propagate by vegetative cloning. The growth of the clone can be regular, its size a chronometer of its life history. Not surprisingly, bracken fills fire-rich Finland, so prone to burning, so profuse in swidden and armed struggle. In principle, bracken can—should—flourish after firefights. So it did after World War II, in Finland as in Britain. And so it did after Finland's other great conflicts. The 1808–9 war doubled the frequency of bracken germination. Other spikes in the geography of bracken date to the war of 1788–90, the Little War (1741–43), the Great Northern War (1700–1721), the 1656–58 conflict with Russia, the Long War of 1570–95, even the 1489–97 Russian war. Still other clones coincide in place and time with invasions by Novgorodians in 1318, with Swedish settlements at Uusimaa in 1235 and Jämsä in 1100, with Karelian sites that date from 550–570 during the Great Migration era. Over the immense lifetime of the clones, fires have been so abundant that new fires have pruned back or wiped out the bracken that recorded the old burns.[25]

The sources of warring fire were many. During the 1808–9 conflict, mobile armies and refugees set campfires, Russian soldiers baked bread in special earth hearths, artillery shot incendiary ammunition (especially from ships), fleeing Swedes burned the forest on Sandö Island to mask their retreat, beacon fires proliferated and no doubt spread, wadding from firearms kindled ground fires, British naval forces cleared coastal forest areas, in part by burning, and Russian cavalry fought guerrillas by burning out sympathetic villages and enclaves. The ignition was varied, the opportunities for burning infinite.

Each scorched patch became a potential site for bracken spores to seize. As much as granite monuments and signed treaties, those patchy clones are, as Eino Oinonen has argued, "peculiar war monuments." They are ecological cognates to the woodcuts showing fire sleds and flung faggots with which Olaus Magnus documented the struggle to inhabit, and defend, boreal Europe.[26]

FIRE AND AX:
THE FINNISH COLONIZATION

Baltic civilization, like Mediterranean, was littoral. Where temperate climates prevailed, as in the southwest of Finland and in Sweden south of Stockholm, reclamation could move inland approximately on the central European model. In its historical geography Skåne is indistinguishable from Denmark, Halland from Jutland, Blekinge from the shores of Prussia. But the interior—the boreal backcountry—required other techniques, another dynamic of exploration and settlement. For the interior landscapes of the Mediterranean, Spain and

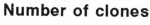

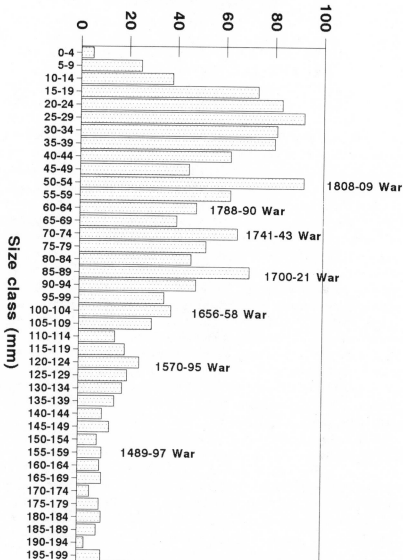

Fire and fern: bracken clones arranged by size class in Finland. Exceptional clusters of clones often coincide with major wars. (Redrawn from Oinonen 1967)

Turkey had discovered a solution in long-distance pastoralism. For the Eurasian plain, Russia had found an adequate propellant in the fur trade. For Fennoscandinavia, the answer was a virulent form of swidden that propagated through inland forests like cattle over Argentine pampas or sheep around Australian grasslands. The Finnish colonization informed boreal Europe as fully as the Reconquest did Iberia.

(i)

Its origins are obscure. The Finnish tribes who engaged in swidden were part of a diffuse linguistic group that stretched across the Urals and was distantly linked with the Magyars who settled Hungary. Increasingly, the expansion of Indo-European peoples had isolated and crowded them into the margins, left them to hunting, gathering, fishing, and most lucratively fur trading. Some time around the eleventh or twelfth century they met Novgorodian Slavs, who were then gathering steam for their great push eastward. Somehow the encounter transferred new cultigens, notably a hardy strain of rye; new agricultural practices, a species of swidden superbly adapted to the boreal forest; and new incentives that ignited the tribes into a northward push beyond the isthmus of Lake Ladoga, beyond the Baltic littoral, beyond the known realm of agricultural reclamation. Perhaps it was the demands of the fur trade that prompted a search for richer lands. Perhaps it was the relentless warring that made the Gulf of Finland a dark and bloody ground. Maybe an inspirational leader began it. Maybe the land hunger of dispossessed sons. Or curiosity. Or wanderlust. Or a bold accident. Whatever the subterranean causes, the tremor prompted a slow tsunami that broke through the berm of coastal settlement and flooded Karelia.

For a century or so swiddening Finns hovered around Lake Ladoga. Then they swarmed north like hiving bees. Within two centuries they had reached the Arctic Circle, pushed to the fringes of coastal settlements, and leaped the Gulf of Bothnia into the interior of central Sweden. Within another century they had banked around the northern Gulf, pushed the Lapps inland, and transported their pioneering ardor across the Atlantic to New Sweden on the shores of the Delaware River. The wave broke only with the royal 1671 proclamation that laid down the boundary with the Lapps, with changes in landownership laws (1684) that allowed sons to inherit a father's farm, with conflicts over standing timber involving mines and foresters, with enclosure, and with the simple exhaustion of virgin lands. Ultimately it subsided from the inherent tragedy of pioneering. Its success made its perpetuation impossible.

The indispensable core was swidden. From the start, however, slashing and burning melded with other elements of a highly versatile economy of loose cattle herding, fishing, long hunts, fur trapping, foraging for berries and mushrooms, and whatever else might serve a society of scattered homesteads far removed from routine trade routes, isolated from most affairs of state, speaking a non-Indo-European language, and cobbling together a viable economy out of a hardscrabble landscape still sloughing off the climatic grime of Pleistocene glaciations. But it was swidden that produced the phenomenal yields whose surplus made possible large families, that attracted pioneers to new lands, and that drove them from old ones. It was swidden that broke the boreal landscape to agriculture.

Swidden, however, was complex, and Finnish swidden, diabolically so. Classic Swedish swidden (*svedjebruk*) was an adaptation of central European techniques, a form of forest fallow agriculture, pastoral burning, and village life. It linked an arable infield (*inmark*) with an extensively exploited outfield (*utmark*), and agglomerated villages with a larger political state, whether medieval, manorial, or princely. Particularly in early settlement, the *utmark* could be vast and distant. Where alpinelike conditions prevailed (mountains and valleys like those in Norway), regular transhumance resulted on the Swiss model. Women drove the flocks of sheep, goats, and cattle to remote summer *saeters,* while men tilled the fields. Where the topographic contrasts were less sharp, the dispersion was more diffuse. Pastoral burning spread like spilled acid. But as in mediterranean Europe, the far-removed flocks made it impossible to gather more manure. The valences between field and flock were too weak.[27]

The classic Finnish swidden ("burnbeating," as Finnish scholars choose to translate it) had a different character. The swidden that punched into Savo-Karelia was a hybrid practice hived from the migrations of early Slavic farmers; it shunned clustered villages for family farmsteads flung over expanding hinterlands; and instead of revolving around an axis of manured arable, it orbited around a mélange of felled and fired forests, as uncentered as a bevy of asteroids. Swedish swidden belonged with a society that sought to stay put; Finnish swidden, with one that was too restless, too volatile, too full of momentum to do anything but move. The Swedes clung to the coast. The Finns drove inland.

Swidden assumed the character not only of its practitioners but of the landscapes that sustained it. Its versions were legion. They merged with fire cultivations of all sorts, the routine burning of raw land, rough pasture, and fallow, however constituted. Swidden practices diverged according to the age, composition, hydrology, soil chemistry, aspect, and elevation of that biomass, especially forests. Writing in 1899, Gösta Grotenfelt identified eight types by name; but variations were endless. Modern scholars typically cite two elementary versions that between them also describe the historical cycle of swiddening itself.[28]

One (*huuhta*) involved virgin, old (over seventy years), or coniferous forests. This was the true pioneering swidden, the landnam of boreal Europe. Prepa-

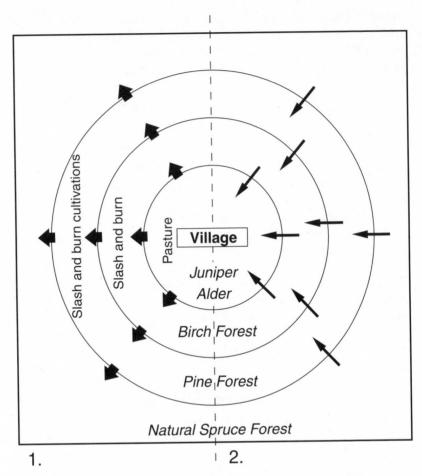

The swidden wave: the changes in flora as fire-fallow agriculture expands into spruce forest (left, 1) and then departs (right, 2). (Redrawn from Heikenheimo 1915 by the University of Wisconsin Cartographic Lab)

rations were far from simple. Scouts ranged widely and staked claims to promising sites with ax cuts. Probably they test-burned plots, probing the landscape with fire as a prospector might sample outcrops with a hammer. Daring "swidden kings" seized vast estates. Large trees were ringbarked, smaller ones notched, then felled all in one direction. The slash was left to dry for two years, then finally burned in July and immediately seeded with rye. Eventually a double burning evolved, with one fire conducted early in the season and a second two years later in midsummer. One cereal crop, occasionally two, resulted. The full swidden term thus required many years and many acres. "The *huuhta* cultivator," as Arvo Soininen notes, "had to prepare a new *huuhta* every year if he wanted to harvest a crop every year. Every summer he had one newly felled *huuhta,* a second cleared and possibly burnt once already in the spring, a third ready for firing and sowing, and a fourth growing a crop which the farmer could harvest at the appropriate time."[29]

But if the labor involved was great, so were the returns. The immense tangle of broken fuels stoked intense fires, opening the land to sunlight, purging pests, stripping away acidic humus, and blanketing the soil with ash. An outstanding burn could produce 100 bushels of grain per hectare, far beyond anything possible elsewhere in Europe. A strain of *svedjeråg* (swidden rye) that survived into twentieth century Värmland sprouted thirty shoots from a single grain on swiddened land. But the target crop was selective. Only rye thrived in *huuhta;* barley, the traditional Savo cereal, did not. That required swidden on other forest types and soils. With exquisite synchronization just such forests (usually dominated by birch) grew on lands recovering from *huuhta.* They were the raw material for the next swidden cycle.

This, the second variant (*kaski*), was the most popular and persistent practice. Deciduous forests were far easier to work with, could absorb grazing, regrew more quickly, and thus shortened the fallow cycle to fifteen to thirty years. In this case trees were felled in midsummer to ensure rapid drying, abandoned over the winter, then fired in early summer and sown with rye, oats, or where possible barley. If the burn was uneven, swiddeners—outfitted with special smocks and long, iron-hooked poles—rolled logs over the surface, and if the fuels were too light, brought additional wood from elsewhere to the site. A normal *kaski* field had a life of two or three years, sometimes up to seven. Depending on soils, swiddeners planted their crops in a regular sequence, ending with turnips, and after abandoning cultivation, with pasture. Observing the practice in 1792, Stephan Bennett labeled it "circulating svedjebruk," as distinguished from the pioneering version with which Savo Finns had converted their "wild deserts." For both purposes, he concluded, it was perfect.[30]

Ideal conditions were of course exceptional. Swiddeners adjusted to the opportunities presented to them, or those they could make. Johan Bureus in the 1590s reported that the Finns in Ångermanland cut their grain exceptionally high so that they would have enough stubble to fuel a second burn. Sometimes with a younger forest rich in humus it was necessary or possible, because of an early spring and sunny slopes, to complete the felling and burning in a single season, a practice known as *rieskamaa.* Sometimes it was helpful to convert, by ringbarking, a coniferous forest (usually pines with heath understories) into a deciduous one before burning could proceed. This technique, *pykälikkömaa,* required several years of advance preparation and could succeed only within a larger landscape in which swidden was already flourishing and within a culture long committed to it.[31]

But this was exactly the case with the Finnish colonizers. Each practice was linked with others across generations as well as geographies. The *huuhta* pioneers could not linger to enjoy *kaski* forty years later; they moved on, as they had to, as American pioneers outfitted with similar techniques did by breaching the Appalachians and sweeping, in a single generation, to the borders of the prairies. Later generations widened the cracks until the landscape broke open. Others filled in the gaps. Successors practiced *kaski;* and relying on vast tracts of land, they cycled through that restructured forest instead of lighting out for new territory. This the *huuhta* generation could not do. They could not stop, could grow no further crops until several decades of deciduous fallow had reclaimed a site. If the crop failed—if the fires burned poorly, if drought shriveled the growing grain—they hunted, fished, trapped, foraged, and moved on.

Finnish swidden was far from casual, slovenly, wasteful, thoughtless, extravagant, primitive—all epithets hurled at it by academic agronomists, foresters, missionaries, and other state officials appalled not merely by its rapid conversion of boreal wildlands but by its dynamism, its indifference to despotic states that required a fixed population amenable to tax collectors, military levies, mercantilism, established religion, and generally deferential to the constituted authorities. Instead, new swidden communities fissioned off. Their fires defied agronomic theory, and their smoke taunted the gardened society. Finnish swidden was an empirical system. That was its strength. It was also as corrosive of feudal agriculture as capitalism was of feudal cities.

(ii)

Finland could not contain it. At the time of the Vasa ascendancy, the kingdom of Sweden consisted of lands along coastal Finland and that part of the Swedish peninsula between the deciduous forest of the far south, then held by Denmark, and the northern coniferous forest, then inhabited almost wholly by Norrland's aborigines. Coastal Finland was strongly influenced, even settled, by Swedes. But Finns had crossed over, too, some during the medieval period, more with the enthusiastic encouragement of Gustavus Vasa (r. 1523–60). Most came from western Finland, settled in Uppland, or migrated to mining districts like Stora Kopparberget. They moved, that is, to centers of settlement or, if away from the coast, to sites of industrial concentration. Then, around 1570, a new wave of immigrants arrived, a slopover from the flood tide of swiddeners then cresting in eastern Finland.

Most came from Savo; most hurried to the coniferous interior. Before long *huuhta* pioneers had pushed west and north, searching out good swidden sites as they might mushrooms, hollowing out the boreal forest like wood borers in

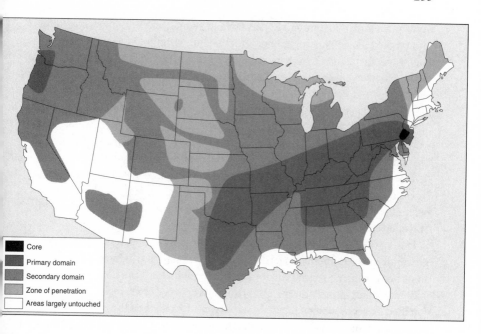

Core
Primary domain
Secondary domain
Zone of penetration
Areas largely untouched

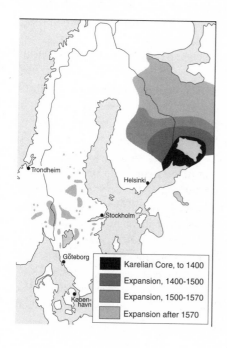

Karelian Core, to 1400
Expansion, 1400-1500
Expansion, 1500-1570
Expansion after 1570

The Finnish colonization: swidden explodes across Scandinavia, and then across the Atlantic to the Mid-American frontier. (Redrawn from Jordan and Kaups 1989 by the University of Wisconsin Cartographic Lab)

Scots pine, threading through Södermanland, Närke, and Värmland, crowding into (and over) the Norwegian border, punching north into Dalarna, Hälsingland, Medelpad, and Gävleborg until they met with Finnish swiddeners moving inland from other coastal enclaves. The prospects at first delighted officials, who deposited Finnish swiddeners into unsettled regions much as early mariners dropped off goats and sheep on uninhabited islands. In 1587, the duke of Södermanland (later King Charles IX) decreed that every settler should clear woods and plant rye. Excluding Ostrobothnia, whose emergent marshlands were unsuitable to *huuhta* (but not to other forms of fire cultivation), Finnish swiddeners soon encircled the Gulf of Bothnia and like pincers began to close on Norrland from both north and south. So prevalent was the practice that European savants like Henri Mallet and J. Hausmann argued that the etymology of "Sweden" derived from *svedje,* the swiddened plot.[32]

During the seventeenth century, Sweden claimed standing as one of Europe's great powers as it fought in Germany's Thirty Years' War, pummeled the Russians back from the coast, transformed the Baltic into a Nordic *mare nostrum,* and like other great powers established overseas colonies. In America it founded New Sweden on the Delaware River in 1638, then lost it to the Dutch seventeen years later. Not surprisingly the colonists included a substantial fraction of Finns, either from Finland or from *Finnskogar* Sweden. They carried in their heads, if not their hands, the coals from the Savo-Karelian hearth. Even after Dutch, and (from 1664) English control, Scandinavian immigration continued. Sweden absorbed its colonial losses; and geopoliticians and propagandists redirected their vision to Norrland. Norrland, they exulted, was Sweden's India. The new coastal towns were its trading factories, the swiddened interior its plantations.

Once started, however, the rapid reclamation of the boreal forest was difficult to stop. If swidden broke the land to agricultural harness, it kept only a light hand on the reins. Related fire cultivation practices followed its lead, or modeled themselves on its successes. Still, Sweden's ambitions were quelled, and after the Great Northern War (1700–1741) they receded in the ebb tide of defeat. During the 1808–9 war with Russia, it lost Finland altogether. Of necessity Sweden turned inward. Other economies, and other patterns of society, obsessed it. For paradigms it looked to the tended farmlands of Skåne, not the swiddened forest; to mining and ironworks, not long hunts and bunch rye; to stable communities that could be counted, taxed, controlled. It wanted manure, not ash, for fertilizer; craved timber for mine construction and smelting charcoal; and sought to preserve spruce for wood and pine for naval stores. In 1832, Bishop Agardt likened the swiddeners to Egypt's plague of grasshoppers. For so long left to his own ends, the swiddener found himself in stiff competition with others in his claim to the boreal forest.[33]

In 1647 a new Forestry Act, widely ignored, strove to rein in *svedjebruk*. Subsequent decrees, more or less effective, so began to squeeze swidden that, over time, even *kaski* lost its dynamism. Swiddening surrendered its forest fuels to its industrial competitors, and put down roots instead of burning them up. What the mines began, industrial logging concluded. Initially there was an almost seamless transfer of techniques as slash-and-burn forestry replaced slash-and-burn farming. But that too ended, and agrarian burning became as antiquarian a relic as boat burials.

(iii)

Swidden's recession was as uneven as its advance. It passed most quickly in Sweden, politically divorced from Finland, never quite comfortable with the immigrant Finns—so dispersed, so untrammeled by prevailing conventions, so often figures of alien superstition in lore and literature. The stronger Swedish state could impose gradual bans, industrial logging could compete more aggressively, and communal pressures could hammer down any individual nails that stood up. The practice survived longest in the old Finnish strongholds like Värmland and Dalarna. The last cultivated *svedjeråg* grew in 1918. The final swidden plot in Småland raised potatoes, for distillation into alcohol, in 1937. By then swidden practices were seen as an anachronism, if not a dangerous embarrassment.

So it appears in Vilhelm Moberg's tale of Kätill, a seventy-year-old farmer known as Svedjegubban (Old Man Swidden). As a young man, the landless youngest of brothers, he had fled to the stony *utmark* and there slashed and burned a life for himself. He had done better than most who were driven to the margins. In time his estate even exceeded that of his brothers, and it gave him satisfaction to watch the smoke from his plots waft tauntingly over the town.[34]

Now, as he prepares new plots for burning, he takes his two sons, both just out of adolescence, to assist with the burning, to educate them into the life he presumes they will inherit. But the fire escapes into some adjacent spruce, which erupts in flames and far-flung sparks. The cause is that Henrik, the elder son, indifferent to a life of swiddening, has left for the town. The old man and the young Edvin cannot by themselves contain the fire, which enters the field. They cut firebreaks, without effect; and they hurry to the birch grove to make a stand. Kätill pauses on a stump, then rushes impulsively from side to side. The flames surround him and the smoke blinds him. The fire seems oddly magical, or hexed. He trips over a root, throws his ax at the flames, senses the strangeness of it all, and dies in his swiddened pyre.

So, allegorically, did Sweden come to think of its self-destructive, swiddened past as it, like Henrik, hurried off to the new towns that gleamed on the industrial horizon.

The Finns surrendered swidden more reluctantly. The spread of sedentary farming, adapted, with the help of agricultural societies, from central European models; the economic and, later, political domination by foresters, who seethed as they watched sawtimber burn to stoke swidden plots; the diminution of recovering forests as the population built up and shortened the fallow cycle beyond the biota's elastic limits; the simple disappearance of the frontier; and competition with imported grains, field enclosure and new land laws, and the growth of a landless poor—all shrank the amount of land under swidden, the yields obtained from plots, and the relative contribution of Finnish swidden to the national economy. A tribe of bold pioneers ended up as a class of rural migrants, hired to slash and burn land they could no longer hope to own themselves. The national addiction to swidden, claimed intellectuals, condemned such people to poverty. Their reliance on fire branded them, in the eyes of agronomists and political economists, as primitives.

But in Finland, unlike Sweden, there were countercurrents. Against the rising sea of cosmopolitan modernity there was a riptide of ethnic celebration that sought a distinctively Finnish identity with which to contest the rigors of forced Russification. Attention focused on Savo-Karelia, on the curious practices that had claimed the Finnish interior and with it the Finnish soul. Here, not along the littoral, was the world of the *Kalevala*. Here, in such places and by such practices, resided the indelible character of Finland. The old swidden became an object of ethnographic curiosity, surviving in a world beyond agronomic condemnation. Here, it seemed, lay the secret of Finland's improbable survival.

The dreamscape of nationalist poets suffered a near-mortal test during World War II. Fighting the Soviets and expelling the Germans from the far north had savaged huge portions of the Finnish landscape, stripping it of effective settlements and disgorging tens of thousands of refugees. Equally devastating, the Soviet Union seized some 10 percent of the national estate along the eastern and southeastern borderlands, setting into motion more throngs of displaced Karelians. The colonization of Finland had to rekindle. The Land Resettlement Acts promoted more than 30,000 new farmsteads—the famous "cold farms"— that were carved by swidden out of standing forests. Existing farms, too, had to expand by the same folk techniques. The resettlement inspired, as William Mead has observed, "the most intensive episode of land clearance experienced in Finland's history." In a brutally practical way, postwar Finland emerged out of its pioneering past.[35]

The Finns did it, as they had done it so often before, with ax and fire.

FIRE AND FIELD:
THE TRAVELS OF LINNAEUS

His birthplace in Småland was a crossroads of Swedish geography. The village resided along an inlet of Lake Möckeln, a swath of flat arable surrounding the parish church. There were gardenlike meadows and rough pastures on wetlands and plains, and beyond that forests on the hills—beech to the south, pine to the north.

But his life was no less a crossroads of Swedish history. When Carl von Linné was born in 1707, Sweden was among Europe's great powers; the Enlightenment, grounded in the triumphs of mathematical mechanics, was beginning to retrofit the world according to Reason; agricultural reclamation had reached a state of stasis; and an expansive Europe had paused, content to endow plantations on tropical islands and erect trading factories in protected ports. When Linnaeus died in 1778, Sweden was imploding, natural history was challenging natural philosophy as the dominant oracle of scientific inspiration, and revolutions raged one after another—in land, with agriculture; in politics, with the onset of democratic revolts; and in economics, with the first throbbing pistons of industrialization. The rivalry between Britain and France had catalyzed a new global reconnaissance, and imperial contests sent Europe's soldiers, missionaries, traders, savants, and émigré folk across the Earth's continents.[36]

Those were the end points. The middle, where Linnaeus lived, was an age that prized the middle, that above all sought to consolidate, codify, and reorganize according to the dictates of reason. Alexander Pope's epitaph to Isaac Newton summarizes perfectly the Enlightenment's reigning spirit.

> *Nature, and Nature's Laws lay hid in Night.*
> *God said, Let Newton be, and All was Light.*

In the concise distillations of his *Essay on Man* (1733–34), Pope spoke for a generation that produced encyclopedias and dictionaries, that sought reason as a guide and order in "the mighty maze" of the world, that valued useful knowledge above metaphysical tropes, that preferred formal gardens to untended wilds and could even rewrite Shakespeare's delirious blank verse, as John Dryden did, into more disciplined heroic couplets. "Order," Pope wrote, "is Heav'n's first law." Moreover, the good man

> *But looks thro' Nature, up to Nature's God;*
> *Pursues that Chain which links th' immense design,*
> *Joins heav'n and earth, and mortal and divine . . .*

Such was Carl von Linné, the son of Nils Linnaeus, curate of Stenbrohult, and one of the Enlightenment's premier personalities, a Newton of natural history. It was said that God created but Linnaeus ordered. He gathered up the proliferating scraps of known nature and reforged the Great Chain of Being. In 1735, Linnaeus published the first edition of his *Systema Naturae*. In 1749 he wrote his apologia, *Oeconomia Naturae* (The Economy of Nature).

But his achievement, certainly his cherished public persona, rested on more than a scholar's desk and a taxonomer's zealotry. Linnaeus traveled. He traveled to central Europe, as a student from the boreal fringe had to do. In Holland he achieved notoriety by successfully growing a banana in a greenhouse. More significant, he traveled throughout Sweden, to Lapland in 1732, to Dalarna in 1734, to Gotland and Öland (1741), to Västergötland (1746), to Skåne (1749). These were commissioned travels, and Linnaeus sought the useful knowledge his instructions demanded—better clays for ceramics, prospective pharmaceutical herbs, the seaweed needed for burning soda, a better sedge for roofing —as well as his compulsive inquiry into the profusion of all nature that unfolded before him. "Oh, if only one could travel like this through all the Swedish provinces," he exclaimed to the governor at Umeå, "how much one could discover that would be of value to our country! How much one could learn from one province of how best to cultivate another." Written on his first journey, that became the model for them all. For Linnaeus there was always novelty with order, discovery with reason.[37]

The excursion, not the text, was his preferred form of botanical instruction, as the garden, not the library stacks, was his ideal herbarium. His local trips around Uppsala took to the field with a trailing entourage of students, friends, and picknickers that more resembled Chaucer's pilgrims on the road to Canterbury than formal academic proceedings. His wider travels, published as diaries, made Linnaeus a culture hero, a celebrant of Swedish identity as manifest in Swedish nature. "I have," Linnaeus wrote, "purposely described much that is common in Sweden because it is rare in other countries." Even today he is represented on two denominations of Swedish currency.[38]

But his influence ranged far beyond the collapsing Swedish empire. His natural history excursions served as a model for others, for what became a Grand Tour of Europe's natural marvels until, under the Promethean ambitions of Romanticism, they spilled out of their genteel genres and splashed across all the continents. Beside them—beside the South American explorations of Alexander von Humboldt, the voyage of Charles Darwin, the transcontinental trek of Lewis and Clark—Linnaeus's excursions seemed quaint. But those charming travels were, as the great botanist would have understood, the acorns from which sprang the mighty oaks of a second great age of discovery. They endure, a delightful varve from eighteenth-century Sweden and a curious cross section of boreal fire.

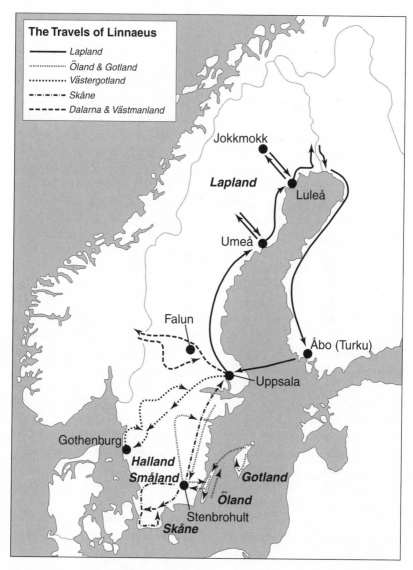

The travels of Linnaeus. (Sources from Blunt 1971, drawn by the University of Wisconsin Cartographic Lab)

(i)

In Lapland the young Linnaeus saw good fire cultivation and bad, useful on healthy Ångermanland soils, ruinous on thin Norrland sands. He saw landscapes burned to stone, and sites rejuvenated from burns with "Reindeer-moss" so abundant "as hardly to leave any room for the Ling." He saw farms carved by swidden. He visited Lapp huts filled with smoking fungus to drive off gnats and to inhale as a "specific," and experienced the chimneyless Finnish cabins clotted with smoke and incipient blindness. He passed through towns like Umeå and Turku not yet recovered from the flaming ravages of the last war. He noted hilltop beacons ready for kindling to warn of further attack. He wondered that Lapland residents did not burn more pine for tar and charcoal, why they did not burn to replenish marshy pastures, why they did not attempt, through burning, to free meadows "from their wart-like lumps." He saw evidence of fires, of endless causes, in abundance. They were as varied as Sweden's flowers.[39]

But this was only his inaugural journey, and that to the frontier. Some provinces specialized in other pyrotechnologies. Halland, Skåne, and Småland burned (and propagated) heath lands. Västergötland and Skåne practiced *kyttesbränning*, a form of swidden in peat. Småland was addicted to *svedjebruk* and heath burning. Tar and pitch were common among pine forests. Charcoal burning thrived around mines, burning to produce saltpeter and potash where wood was abundant, and lime burning wherever the right stone existed. With controlled fire, farmers supplemented manure to create additional fertilizer from peat, branches, even seaweed. *Brännodling*—fire cultivation—was everywhere, and almost everywhere necessary. From wildfire, villagers sought protection: escaped heath fires and swidden burns were all too common. So was the evidence of inappropriate fire in the unruly young forests, the spreading heath, the humus-glutted pine woods, and the barren hilltops like Gotland's Torborg.

Even dwellings bore the stamp of fire's threat. In Skåne, lightning had burned so many structures that churches seldom raised steeples, or else separated them from the main building. In Öland, houses had thatch roofs but interlayered with sod in such a way that fire was impossible. In Västergötland, the threat of wildfire led the town of Boras to prohibit milled wood for roofing, requiring the less flammable turf; and the city of Linköping, like many others, was laid out in a regular grid, with abundant streets and small blocks, for the purpose of frustrating wildfire. The history of Sweden's cities, Linnaeus believed, he could calculate by the age of their buildings, which in turn reflected the frequency and size of their fires.[40]

The interstitial tissue that held Swedish geography together was the field. It had done so for centuries. Agriculture dominated Sweden's economy, as it did

Sweden's landscape, as fully in Linnaeus's time as in Olaus Magnus's; and it was as much in need of Enlightenment as politics, celestial mechanics, and folk superstition. Agriculture was the practical charge of the Linnaean excursion. In summarizing his Öland and Gotland journeys, Linnaeus observed that "the habits of the farmers, their clothes, buildings, their farming methods, fields, meadows, forestry, tar boiling, charcoal burning and quarrying have been described, and I have now and then briefly indicated how methods could be improved." Even more, agriculture was the model for the balance of nature. Nature's economy was the farm's domestic housekeeping writ large.[41]

If the garden provided the standard for land use, agricultural burning was the norm for fire practices. Linnaeus's two most celebrated journeys—his first, to Lapland, and his last, to Skåne—graph almost exactly the gradient of Swedish fire. At one extreme was wildfire, which was by definition uncontrolled, dangerous, and damaging. At one point a lightning-kindled fire bore down on him and his guide with a "sudden noise" such as "I can only compare to what may be imagined among a large army attacked by an enemy." His flight from the flames made him feel "like an outlaw," for it placed him outside the ordered world of Nature's design. At the other extreme was Skåne's intensively cultivated arable on the central European model. Here fire was banned, at least in principle (though hardly in practice), and debate over fire's appropriate role plunged Linnaeus into a celebrated controversy.[42]

But most of Sweden was neither wholly wild nor wholly gardened, and for such lands fire cycled agriculture through stages of fallow or smelted down the refractory forest, like so much biotic ore, into tar, charcoal, potash, or other goods. In such contexts fire could be used well or ill. Linnaeus saw plenty of both. And he was of mixed—that is, of a practical—mind regarding fire's benefits and its liabilities. Some places needed more fire, others less. Northern Öland, for example, was a place without swidden, tar, or charcoal, and suffered as a result. By contrast, Västergötland and Skåne, because of population pressures, were so overrun with "pestilential" swiddeners that wood had become scarce and agricultural productivity had degraded. It was fire's context—its social environment—that determined whether it behaved like yeoman or outlaw. The standard for evaluation was utilitarian: the degree to which fire assisted or harmed the field.[43]

The boreal *utmark* offered more than rough pasture and long fallow. Settlers could cut and burn birch and spruce for potash and saltpeter, slash and burn pine into tar, stack and anerobically combust cordwood for charcoal. Each practice supplemented local economies, and each product was suitable for export; on some, particularly charcoal, depended local industries. Mining was impossible without the fuels with which to smelt crude ore. The early attempts by the Swedish state to regulate forest use concentrated, for this reason, around its mining districts. But if iron and copper were Sweden's two primary sources of export income, tar was not far behind.[44]

Tar—or its more refined distillate, pitch—had long formed a part of a diversified agrarian economy where pine forests thrived. It was, like grain distilled into alcohol, easily transported at higher rates of return than bulk lumber. Tar manufacture, by burning resin-impregnated wood under controlled conditions, was an ideal seasonal activity that most communities could synchronize with an agricultural calendar. It was little different in principle from gathering leaf fodder for winter feed or scything meadows. Where boat transport was possible, a tar industry could flourish well inland. These were precisely the conditions of Ostrobothnia and southern Karelia, and there tar became a basic cottage industry of boreal villages, an alternative to cottage textiles.[45]

Tar and shipping became mutually indispensable. After the breakup of the Hanseatic League in Germany, the center of the export industry shifted north to Sweden, especially its Finnish provinces. Naval needs and growing overseas trade escalated demand, and increased productivity quickly followed. In 1640, tar constituted half of Finland's exports. This fact was long disguised, however, because the Swedish state effectively imposed a tar cartel that required all exports to emanate from the monopoly market in Stockholm. "Stockholm tar" was, overwhelmingly, tar from Finland. Eastern Finland supplied many barrels, rafted down waterways to Viborg; but western Finland—Ostrobothnia—was the world's premier supplier. Tar burning continued, nonetheless, in Sweden, especially in well-wooded provinces like Småland. Linnaeus praised the practice as good for both "the farmer and the country," especially "in those places where the forest is more than sufficient and otherwise is used only for swidden," and urged it for the remote provinces of Norrland.[46]

He also rendered a detailed description of the technique, which differed from turpentining in that it used resin-saturated strips of wood rather than sap. The process began by paring away the bark from one side of the bole. The exposed area on the tree soon filled with protective resin. Each year flakes ("the size of a hand") could be chipped away, gathered into great bundles, and carried to a tar kiln. The "milking" of the scored pine could continue for ten years. The kiln was a kind of forest forge, built on a slope so that the distilled tar would run down a covered trough into a cauldron. The burning in the kiln was controlled—bellows rather than ambient airflow forced oxygen in, and a cover of sand and moss prevented the escape of tar-laden smoke. The burning might take up to two days. The secondary boiling of the pitch took perhaps another day. Again, combustion was tightly controlled, to prevent both flashover and boiling. The resulting tar went into barrels. About two barrels of tar would, in turn, distill into one barrel of pitch. Importers such as Britain and Holland usually oversaw secondary refinements to suit their particular needs. What Linnaeus described for Småland was typical, although contemporary accounts all

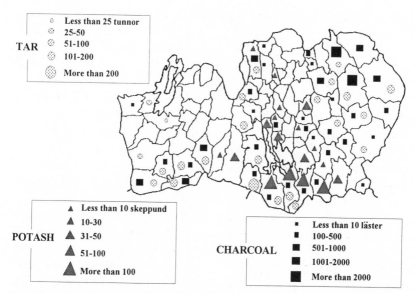

Småland: fire for chemical conversions. Here fire is used not for agriculture but for industrial purposes, transmuting forest into tar, potash, and charcoal. The units are archaic but translate roughly as follows: *tunnor* refers to "barrels" (125 liters each); *läster* is a bulk volume measure (1760–2000 liters); *skeppund* is a ship-based unit of weight (150–200 kg). (Adapted from Larsson 1989)

favored Ostrobothnian tar, which dominated the market not only in quality but in quantity.[47]

The cartel collapsed when, during the Great Northern War, Russia temporarily seized much of Finland in 1715. Sweden recovered both its Finnish provinces and the Stockholm monopoly until the next Russian war stripped it of both in 1809. Even as the Napoleonic Wars and overseas trade boosted demand for naval stores of all kinds, the nineteenth century saw the industry fade away. Russia redirected the trade and severed the eastern Finnish source. Iron ships replaced tar-caulked wooden ones. Steam power applied to saws created new mills; and applied to transport, created new markets. Tar burning faced increasing competition from other forest users. Above all, industrial logging asserted the primacy of pine for timber rather than tar. If loggers saw swidden as wanton, they viewed tar burning as vandalism. Enlightenment agronomists agreed. Burning a tree for its pitch was no different from burning soil for a quick jolt of phosphorus.

The primary use of the *utmark,* however, was for pasture. Lands too wet, rocky, sandy, or acidic for cultivation could be grazed or harvested for winter fodder, its grasses no less than its leaves. Writing from Finland in 1765, J. Krook noted how "the peasants are usually obliged the whole summer to collect grass and leafy twigs from bushes in the woods with the aid of sickles" to supplement whatever "straw and chaff" they could spare for their long-wintered cattle. The shieling (or in Norway, *saeter*) system of summer pasturing, a species of transhumance, further projected grazing's influence far beyond the dominion of cultivated fields. A largely subsistence practice, it also placed grazing beyond markets. In effect it was a social more than an economic institution. Like Alpine and unlike Mediterranean pastoralism, it involved families, typically women. Almost any site grazed would be burned in some way. Where insects were pesty, pastoralists left great fires constantly alight in fields, the smoke a sanctuary for humans and herds both.[48]

But most pasture was derived from swidden, the *primum mobile* of boreal agriculture. For several years, between the time cropping ceased and shrubs reclaimed the site, grasses and herbs flourished and grazing was good. Thus swidden's long cycle included pasture as well as field crops, and its already lengthy reach extended further, since every hectare of arable required at least two of pasture. Domestic livestock could not survive the winter without supplementary fodder, which meant that without the *utmark* there could be no arable. How the land responded depended not only on a site's climate and soil but on the kind of burning and grazing regime to which herders subjected it. As with swidden, the varieties were endless.

Lightly grazed and abandoned sites regrew into boreal forest, often spruce, ready for another round of swidden. Mast trees and birch woods were frequently tended into grassy parks, subsequently maintained as a grazed orchard. Lands grazed properly evolved into meadows; lands overgrazed degraded into gulleys and juniper. In this way grazing practices inscribed a biotic record as real as stone walls and tar pits. But its most spectacular expression was heath. Throughout southern Sweden, most staggeringly in Halland, great heathlands rolled to the horizon, first cousins to the *Calluna* heath then reaching its maximum across the sound in Jutland. Linnaeus wondered sourly if the spreading heath would take over all of Småland.[49]

The elements of heath—its floral particles—existed in the native forest. But their arrangement, and their dominance as a landscape, were an artifact of anthropogenic clearing, grazing, and burning. The Norse in Britain burned the ling every ten years or so. Southern Swedes burned their *ljung* every three years, then grazed with sheep or hardy long-haired cattle. The heath, too, they often swiddened; or where it formed peaty layers, they cut it up and carried it to fields to supplement fuels, or combined it with manures and burned it to make an enriched fertilizer. In effect, farmers mixed woody fuels with sparse manure much as, during famines, they scraped pine cambium into flour to make bark bread.

The heath was a creation of the field. It evolved from swidden, endured by burning and grazing, supplemented meadow, furnished fuel for home and garden, and like a tough exoskeleton helped give shape to the arable infield. It expanded with the Great Reclamation, reaching its apex in the early decades of the nineteenth century. But it was also accidental, stingy, often degraded, and frequently dangerous. Heath was not as productive as cultivated pasture or as versatile as forest. The fires that made it possible, that constantly reset its biotic clock, could also—and often did—run wild. The stringy heath was a fuse; the burning of *ljung* a match; and wildfire an all-too-common and unwanted detonation in the surrounding woods. Linnaeus related how, during his visit to Öland, he read in the parish records about a huge fire in 1624 that had raged in the heather until a "great effort" by the yeomen finally halted it.[50]

The same reasons that impelled Danes to convert Jutland's heath also rallied Swedes to reform the heathlands of Halland. But it was not easy to break the cycle. Until there were alternatives to the rough pasture of the heath, farmers could not cease grazing there, and as long as they loosed cattle and sheep to forage, they had to burn the *ljung* to ensure palatable fodder. Break that cycle and the forest would eventually return. Break that cycle and you also broke the pattern of traditional agriculture. That, of course, is exactly what Enlightenment reformers wanted.

The real reformation, however, came less with new ideas than with a new economy. Industrial forestry rolled back the heath from its edges like carpets of turf. In 1800, heath claimed some 30 percent of Halland; by 1950, only 3 percent; and by 1990 it survived only in symbolic enclaves. Coniferous forest overgrew the landscape like sphagnum moss burying an ancient woods. The once-majestic Halland heath at Mästocka shrank to the scale of a municipal playground, and only a fire set by schoolboys in 1933 probably spared it from being buried alive in a forest crypt. In 1955, officials, left with little choice but imbued with deep reluctance, began to burn the heath to save it.[51]

Cultivated fields were no more static than pastures. They, too, expanded as pushed by population and pulled by opportunity. In Linnaeus's day new fire practices were building on the old, adapting swidden as a means to rejuvenate old fields and to expand arable into novel environments. Some techniques added supplementary fuels from wetlands, some brought new fire in the form of rolling logs. Most spectacularly, *brännodling* (fire cultivation) carried farming into landscapes otherwise abandoned to marsh, peat, and moss. However much critics might split over the propriety of *svedjebruk*, they almost universally condemned its bastard offsprings. The purpose of farming, as Linnaeus reminded them, was to built up soil nutrients, not to vaporize them.[52]

The originating version appeared, not surprisingly, in Finland. Probably it began by adding peaty turf to woody fuels, often stacked, with the ash then

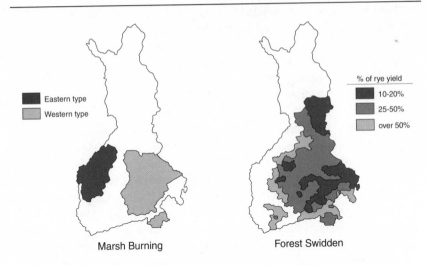

Finland: land of fire and fallow. Even in the 1830s fire remained fundamental to Finnish agriculture. Map on left shows concentrations of swidden in organic soils, while map on right documents the persistence of forest swidden. Both practices showed many local variants. Marsh burning, in particular, differed according to the recency of the land's emergence from water, resulting in distinctive "eastern" and "western" forms. (Redrawn from Soininen 1974 by the University of Wisconsin Cartographic Lab)

scattered over the field. The practice became known as *kyttlandsbruk* (from the Finnish *kyteä,* meaning to smolder or glow). Tavastland was the core region, but variants percolated outward into the surrounding Baltic lands and Russia. It was only a matter of time, however, before farmers carried the fire to the fuel instead of vice versa. With their torch they began cultivating landscapes rich in organic soils. At first these were relatively dry terrains; later, marshes.

The critical factor was an abundance of ready fuels. Drought could prepare these, and it was probably during a drought-nurtured burn (perhaps for pasture) that the possibilities for systematic fire-farming became apparent. But the same effects could result from draining, light plowing that exposed more moss to the air, and turf cutting and sometimes stacking. By controlling the water table, the depth of the ditching determined, in theory, the depth of the burning. Such preparations were the equivalent of *svedjebruk*'s ringbarking, felling, and firebreaks. Once properly dried, the site was burned and planted with root, fodder, or cereal crops before abandonment to peaty fallow or rough range. Instead of existing as natural pasture alone, the land thus passed periodically into field. Thus *kyttlandsbruk* was also often a prelude for meadows.

One fire led to another. After a fallow phase, the site could reburn, just as a swiddened forest could. But fresh pasture, too, needed further burning. And on really deep soils the first burn exposed peat, roots, and other buried debris that became available for continued firing. Such sites could burn again and again, supplemented by plucking out roots and combining them with other residuals left from the fire or simply stoked by the pool of peat left behind. Successive fires burned down through the column layer by layer, the fire stripping off the soil like the pointed shovels of peat miners.

The emerging lowlands of western Finland were ideal for the practice. By the early nineteenth century, Finnish farming, like a delicate balance, weighed eastern *svedjebruk* against western *kyttlandsbruk*. The technique crossed over the Gulf of Bothnia into Västerbotten. Probably Finnish emigrants carried it to central Sweden, cooking yet more landscapes into edible forms. Like other species of swidden, *brännodling* assumed many varieties, acquired many names, adapted to scores of environments, and attracted legions of critics. But even as Enlightenment agronomists pondered its ambiguous meanings, a potent rival—this time from England—wormed its way into Sweden's far-flung and vulnerable organic soils. By the mid-eighteenth century, paring and burning began to supplement swidden, displace *kyttlandsbruk*, add exotic tools to Swedish technology, and rekindle the controversies over the proper relationship between fire and farming.

Its most celebrated advocate, the Rev. Arthur Young, paraphrased folk sayings about fire as a good servant and bad master by declaiming that paring and burning, "properly managed," was "the most admirable of all improvements, and improperly, the most mischievous." Swedish critics summed up their reservations even more succinctly: *brännodling* made "rich parents but poor children." After a quick flush of crops, the land, it seemed, went to fallow, which meant, in their calculus, that it degenerated. Fire cultivation was the agricultural equivalent of strip-mining. Reporting on it during his travels, most notably in Västergötland, Linnaeus compared it to Finnish *kyttlandsbruk*, and denounced it as one of the "most harmful inventions" he had encountered. In his Skåne travels he thought peat a useful supplement to fuels, but condemned marsh swidden as "twenty times" worse than bad forest swidden. While both were unmitigated pests, he regarded turf-burning as far more destructive. Forests regenerated, marshes did not.[53]

Propagandists were alarmed, critics confused. Serious observers distinguished, as farmers did, between different practices and many kinds of organic soils—dry, wet, sandy, moldy, thin, thick. Some sites *brännodling* damaged; some it left unharmed, even renewed. In 1863, J. Arrhenius in his three-volume handbook of Swedish agriculture observed that "fire in the agriculturalist's hand is one of the most powerful and valuable means of land reclamation," but that it was also among the most ruinous. As with fire practices everywhere, the timing and techniques, not the fact of fire, brought good or evil.[54]

So, as with French *écobuage,* there were compromises. One was to cut and stack turf into piles or to carry it to kilns for burning, then return the ash to the site. This got the benefits of disturbance (paring) and ash (burning) but without the bother of running fire. Other critics wanted to use green fertilizer, to broadcast organic soil over arable fields as though it were so much compost. This also dispensed with burning. Whether on forest, marsh, or peat, warned Gösta Grotenfelt in his 1899 treatise, fire never led to "rational" agriculture. It was forever the stigma of primitivism, as irrational as burning a house to roast a pig. Organic fertilizer, not ash, was the only means of ultimate improvement. Between cultivating and burning, there could be no compromise.[55]

But farmers knew that fire did more than crudely fertilize. If it burned off some nutrients, it liberated others; if it vaporized nitrogen, it stimulated nitrogen producers and put nitrogen in forms more readily usable; if it killed trees and moss, it also wiped out inimical microorganisms and weeds, and passed through the biota like an electrical current, charging grains, grasses, and root crops like ions in a fluorescent lamp. If the effect was temporary, it was still an improvement over leaden peat and inert marsh. The antagonism between sedentary and shifting cultivation was a false premise. They were the grand polarities of boreal agriculture's alternating current.

And if there were plenty of critics of fire cultivation among the elite, there were also defenders. Here as elsewhere, they lost. In 1828 a decree banned swidden in organic soils on land owned by officials. Before long, industrialization's creation of artificial fertilizers and its revaluation of land use for forestry rendered the debate moot.[56]

(ii)

That put the burden on *svedjebruk.* It was the progenitor, the ancestral practice from which the others derived. Here, too, Linnaeus is an infallible guide.

All the contradictions about swidden's practice and theory appeared like mileposts during his travels. In Norrland he accepted it; in Västergötland he condemned it; in Gotland he lamented its absence; and in Småland he praised its usefulness. Traveling to Öland he noted the "excellent rye" that grew on old *svedjor* and watched the locals burn eagerly, "since the best time to burn is after a long drought when rain is expected." Traveling from Skåne he made similar observations about fire cultivation, noting that fire farmers "get an abundance of grain from otherwise quite worthless land." That passing comment plunged him into controversy and compelled him, then at the height of his fame, to recant.[57]

The incident is worth reviewing. Linnaeus had gone to Skåne reluctantly, at the request of Baron Hårleman, minister of agriculture, as relayed through the king. In 1749, Skåne was the fragment of Sweden that most resembled central Europe, and that could, for an Enlightened state, most serve as the model for agricultural reform. But traveling there from Uppsala took Linnaeus through Småland. He noted the one-field system commonly practiced; the value of the *utmark* for swiddening; and the rye, turnips, and pasture such sites yielded. *Svedjebruk* lands "which are everywhere seen among the forests here in Småland, and which are looked upon by some as profitable, by others as rather deleterious, we closely examined and the benefit and the injury done to the countryside were weighed against one another; one must not judge them according to the same rule in different districts."[58]

Then he mustered the arguments pro and con. Swidden consumed the "mould, which is the food of all growth," and hence impoverished the soil. But stony Småland was biotically "unpromising," and by slashing and burning the Smålander obtained from his "otherwise unprofitable forest and soil" good grain and pasture. Then came the heather, then the pine and spruce; then, another round of swidden. Deny *svedjebruk* to the inhabitants and they would "want for bread and be left with an empty stomach looking at a sterile waste, with expectations after a couple of hundred years for their own, or for others' descendants, who could however scarcely hope to reap any harvest from a thankless soil and stony Arabia infelix."[59]

The passage infuriated Hårleman. Not only had Linnaeus "not condemned" *svedjebruk*—"so pernicious for the country"—but he had "justified" and "sanctioned" the practice. Hårleman demanded that the offending passages be excised. To those for whom arable was a splinter from the True Cross, no good could come from expanding swidden in any of its heresies. Infield, not outfield, was the nucleus of farming; outfield, including swidden, had value only as a way station to a fully sedentary agriculture. Before the weight of such orthodoxy even Linnaeus, like the unrepentant Galileo, had to bow. In place of the offending passage he substituted an innocuous essay on manure and applauded the "common country custom" by which farmers carted wagonloads of heather, moss, needles, and other forest combustibles to mix with dung and burn into a sooty compost. Manure, not ash, was the lubricant of the agricultural revolution. In the temperate template, fire could not compete with bullshit.[60]

Thus European agronomists, like the Indonesian wet rice cultivators made famous by Clifford Geertz, turned inward—seeking a more intensive farming that would, in turn, become ever more extensive. Central Europe, like Java, became the involuted core, pushing swiddeners to the margins. But one might just as well have picked up the other end of the stick and argued that swidden was the norm, that sites of permanent arable were the anomalies—agrarian tumors, usually benign, sometimes malignant. Something like that might have happened had Skåne remained Danish. Instead it anchored Sweden, which twisted like a long ship moved about by the tides of climate and winds of reform but which never broke the chain.[61]

Against ideologues, Linnaeus could not prevail. But against the pragmatic logic of folk life neither could agronomic theories, laws, prohibitions, and decrees. Scattered throughout his text Linnaeus retained comments favorable to *svedjebruk,* and almost everywhere the folk ignored official pronouncements and did what they had to do to survive. In disputed matters they, like Linnaeus, deferred to Nature, "that true mother of all economy, who should be our best adviser in economy." They burned; and they continued to burn until an industrial revolution removed the whole matter from the realm of nature's economy altogether.[62]

It is clear, though, that Linnaeus felt no special ardor for fire. It was a tool with which to convert wildland into field. Agricultural burning served nature's economy as the hearth fire did a household's. Neither he nor Sweden's farmers would snuff out that vital flame until there was an adequate surrogate. The field, not the flame, was the standard of value. Fire had worth to the extent that it created, sustained, and renewed the garden. Otherwise it threatened an order too dearly won and a beauty too briefly known.

This, too, Linnaeus instinctively manifested. When on Öland he discovered a patch of *Linnaea borealis* ("my flower"), he knew "that the place has not been burnt within living memory." And when his Skåne travels took him, now at the end of his illustrious career, back to his childhood home at Stenbrohult, he described in detail the *svedjebruk* that had made that familiar Småland landscape and denounced the reckless burning that threatened to destroy fields and waste forest into heath. To his horror he discovered that a "violent wildfire" had struck even his home, had utterly destroyed his father's garden, once filled with the rarest plants in Sweden, and left him a "stranger" in the place of his youth. In those fears he spoke for all of Sweden.[63]

(iii)

In place of the Stenbrohult he remembered, Linnaeus wrote, a "new world" had come into being. The old world in which he had labored was one of exquisite balances. The economy of nature followed from the balance of nature. Nothing was wasted, nothing missing, nothing out of place. The hydrologic cycle was nature's informing metaphor, endlessly replicated throughout the kingdoms of rock, plant, and animal. Like Newton's planets, nature's biotic communities cycled through time in profound balance between the competing forces of growth and decay. Good husbandry imitated nature's example and sought to replace what it removed. It shoveled manure onto harvested arable, let forest fallow regrow, and never stripped the living humus from the land. Domestication was a process of rationalization that rectified nature's defects and redirected wild energies to human purpose, but that never defied nature's equilibrium. Even "circulating *svedjebruk*" was an imitation of natural rhythms, fire's cycle an avatar of water's. Nature was Design, Design manifested Reason, and Reason like Nature's Creator was immutable.[64]

The agriculture Linnaeus observed was, in significant ways, unchanged from the days of Olaus Magnus. There were more fields, more intensive manipulation, less random violence, and a better botany. But the process of reformation had only begun. *Storskifte*—Sweden's enclosure movement—took almost a century to complete, beginning in 1757 and accelerating after 1827. (The leader of the movement, Jacob Faggot, head of the Land Survey Office, was also a bitter opponent of *svedjebruk* and *brännodling,* which he saw as primitive and irrational, not unlike fragmented strip fields.) By the time it ended, chemical fertilizers were available; Sweden and Finland had experienced massive emigration; and industrialization, primarily forestry, was redefining the basis of land use. Linnaeus would have recognized the landscape of Olaus Magnus's *Historia;* he would have understood less well the landscapes that followed. Equilibrium gave way to evolution.[65]

Linnaeus had helped that happen. The Great Chain of Being he reforged became historicized; species became links over time, some disappearing, some newly created. So, too, the "new world" he saw at Stenbrohult would not merely recycle the old. Agriculture was soon in revolution; industry would quickly follow; and the Linnaean excursion donned seven league boots and strode over the Earth's continents and oceans. After he returned from Skåne, his own travels completed, eager students—his "apostles"—trekked to the ends of the Earth on his inspiration, helping to fuse science with imperial expansion into what William Goetzmann has called a Second Great Age of Discovery.[66]

They encompassed the world littoral. They toured Britain, Iceland, Spitsbergen, Brazil, Surinam, the Mediterranean, Arabia, and even Russia and Central Asia. They followed the trade routes to the Orient—trekking to West Africa, southern Africa, India, Ceylon, the East Indies, Indochina, China, and Japan. Peter Kalm went to North America. Daniel Carl Solander sailed on Captain James Cook's first voyage at the invitation and expense of Joseph Banks. Anders Sparman, having served his apprenticeship by travel to China, became the chief scientist of Cook's celebrated second voyage. Thus Linnaean students visited Australia, New Zealand, Tahiti and other Polynesian islands, South Georgia, and even glimpsed the ice islands that rafted from Antarctica. They were all of them difficult journeys. Much to Linnaeus's anguish, five of the apostles died; others were worn out; but all who published became famous, and one, Carl Peter Thunberg, having trekked across southern Africa and gathered plants from Shogun Japan, succeeded Linnaeus as professor of botany at Uppsala.

The closed world had broken. Growth, not circulation, characterized nature's economy, and progress, its larger design. Trade spanned the seven seas; Europe's great powers fought over plantations and hinterlands far removed from the civilizations of antiquity; European colonies, not merely trading factories, moved inland. Exploding inventories of nature too often shattered inherited intellectual schemas, Linnaeus's *systema naturae* among them. Nature's economy could no longer remain within the circulations of leaf, grass, and humus. Steadily, industrialization rewired its energy paths, reforged the links of its nutrient cycles, and set its trophic levels as much by the bullion of its specie as by the biodiversity of its species.

Europe's fire would not remain on the European hearth.

FIRE AND IRON:
THE ADVENTURES OF NILS

He was a boy "something like fourteen years old," and not good for much. His elderly parents had eked out a living on a hardscrabble south Skåne farm, but the father thought the son "dull and lazy," barely fit to tend geese, and his mother knew him to be "wild and bad, cruel to animals, and ill-tempered toward human beings."

Then one March morning while his parents trooped to church services, the boy captured and mistreated an elf who retaliated by shrinking the lad to his own diminutive size. Suddenly Nils—Tummetott, a Swedish Tom Thumb—began to experience the world from the perspective of the small, the oppressed, and the animals. "Little by little he began to understand what it meant to be no longer human." With his new enchantment came the gift of animal speech, and he listened while farm animals that he had tormented now debated whether to reciprocate. Then, when a flock of wild geese soared overhead and hurled taunts to farmyard flocks, the family's white goose, Morten Gander, impetuously flew to join them with the tiny boy clinging to his neck. So began the wonderful adventures of Nils Holgersson.

The saga commenced when Selma Lagerlöf was commissioned to write a book that would introduce elementary school children to Swedish geography. It was a great era for children's literature, an enthusiasm not limited to Sweden. So also had the use of animals as characters become popular. In the ten years before Lagerlöf wrote her two-volume *Adventures* (1906–7), Rudyard Kipling had published his *Jungle Books* and *Just So Stories* and Jack London had stormed American literature with his Yukon tales, best known for their wolf protagonists and the dog-wolf Buck in *The Call of the Wild*. But there the similarities end.[67]

If Nils and Morten Gander were part of a literary menagerie, they differed as much from Mowgli or Buck as the fields of Sweden did from the jungles of central India or the bleak wilds of Alaska. Flying about every province, Nils discovers not only geographic facts but the traits of Swedish life, and the essential character of what it means to be human. *The Wonderful Adventures of Nils* tracks a moral geography more than a physical one, and narrates a peculiarly Swedish romantic nationalism. In the end his experiences transform Nils. The boy grows up; the bratty Nils becomes, by choice, a decent human being, and is given back his human form. The story of his adventures acquired itself a kind of enchantment, and eventually was translated into forty languages.

The Sweden that Nils witnessed found itself, like him, suddenly transformed, equally unsure of its identity. Not for a century had the pugnacious Sweden of Olaus Magnus gone to war, and twice over the approaching century it would remain outside the conflicts that devastated twentieth-century Europe. The agricultural revolution launched in Linnaean times was accelerating into an industrial revolution. The old order reached a climax in the mid-nineteenth century: there was no more land to reclaim by existing technologies, no capacity to absorb still-growing rural populations.

The transition, however rapid, was difficult. Only in the 1850s does the expression "working class" (*arbetsklass*) enter the language; not until the late 1860s does famine cease to haunt boreal farmers; and it is even later before emigration is no longer considered an alternative to poverty and hunger ("Die or emigrate," warned Finland's Zachris Topelius). Not until the 1870s does wholesale logging of the Norrland forests make possible the capital accumulation to finance industrialization. Not until the turn of the century do fossil hydrocarbons restructure agriculture through trade and artificial fertilizers and rebuild Sweden's ancient iron works into a modern steel industry.

But change came, often with an abruptness that left society gasping. Steam transport, expanded trade, and liberalized tariffs began to dissolve the once self-sufficient local economies and then swept their pieces into urban eddies, themselves peripheral to the vortex of a global economy. Forests replaced fields, and steel the pyrotechnologies of wood smelting. Iron workers stood before blast furnaces outfitted with the white smocks that had once clothed *svedje-folk*. Steam replaced flame as the symbol of human power.[68]

In 1909, as Selma Lagerlöf was receiving the Nobel Prize for Literature, Swedish labor and capital clashed in a general strike that announced the parameters of an industrial social order as profoundly revolutionary as the enclosure movement had been for agriculture a century and a half earlier. Nils's search for an identity was also Sweden's. The refrain he and the wild geese chant over again, "Here am I, where are you?" is exactly the question to which industrializing Sweden had to reply.

(i)

For the Scandinavian landscape, logging was the engine of economic reform. Industrializing Britain demanded sawtimber, had almost none of its own, scoured the coastal forests of Norway, and then rolled into Sweden, advancing from south to north and coast to interior like an earthquake in slow motion. The first tremors were felt in the early nineteenth century; by the end of the century the shock wave had spent itself. When Erik Höjer observed that Swedes "have strangely enough great difficulty in imaging our country even at so recent a time as the beginning of the 19th century," the reason for that transformation was industrial forestry. Flying over Medelpad, Nils asked how people lived in country so inimical to farming. "Up here," he was told, "they have forests for fields."[69]

Forests were a commodity that northern Scandinavia had in abundance, unlike the rest of Europe. Freshly opened markets meshed with a newly accessible commodity. The catalyst was the combustion of fossil fuels. Steam engines powered mobile sawmills, transported bulk goods, substituted coal for fuelwood, and helped build up the wealth that Britain, in particular, translated into demand. Swedish timber exports boomed, first in the 1850s and again, farther north, in the 1870s. It was, in Eli Heckscher's words, "a gold-rush-like experience," unprecedented in Swedish history, "more truly American" in its frenzied character. Forest products became Sweden's premier export. In 1850, timber accounted for 15 percent of Sweden's total exports; by 1870, for 51 percent and had its export value more than triple. That proportion has continued to the present day.[70]

Logging was an industrial frontier. Timber and iron became complementary industries, as they had been in the past. Since at least the time of Gustavus Vasa, mines—principally iron, but also copper—had influenced forest policy in their surrounding landscapes. Smelting needed charcoal, and so conflicted with swidden to determine whether the woods would be burned for ore or crops. But now steel and timber fed into a common commodity market and gorged on common capital. Between them they catapulted Sweden into the industrial revolution.

The timber frontier restructured Swedish society as well. It attracted a large, migratory class of laborers cut loose from traditional society with whom logging companies had to negotiate and for whom it had to feed, transport, and build at least temporary towns. A surplus population that might otherwise have emigrated to the frontiers of North America now relocated to the frontiers of Norrland. The labor was largely unskilled, not bound to guild, craft, heritage, or place. The laborers were the woodland counterparts to textile and factory workers, and the mills their sweatshops. Unsurprisingly they spawned Sweden's first major labor conflict, a strike at Sundsvall in 1879.

But as new people moved in, industrial capital was moving older residents out. Wholesale logging was as extractive as open-pit mining: it needed vast reserves to throw into its mills, and to guarantee the supply it had to control the land. The state supported the task by transferring, as early as 1824, many state forests to private ownership, selling town forests, and partitioning communal forests. For southern Sweden this was enough. For Norrland, however, which constituted almost 60 percent of the national landmass, the original ownership rights had never been resolved. On lands sparsely settled by peasants, there had been less urgency to segregate clearly governmental from private lands. Much of the land between villages, in fact, was held in a kind of commons, a lease known as *avradsland.* The process of delineating public from private ownership on these amorphous holdings began in the eighteenth century in an attempt to accelerate agricultural settlement. As industrial markets replaced those of local agriculture, the state, committed to liberal economics, transferred the bulk of its public holdings to the local settlers, some of whom came to possess domains "as large as a small German principality." What had been commercially worthless in the early decades of the century became immensely valuable in its closing decades. Speculators quickly divested most of the land-rich, capital-poor peasantry from their princely estates.[71]

All this inspired a different society than had existed before, particularly in the north. But it created a vastly different landscape everywhere. The agriculture of Linnaean Sweden had exploited its forests for many goods, all supportive of farming and grazing, and had shaped those woodlands accordingly. Industrial logging wanted but one product, later two, and pursued those ambitions with a concentrated ruthlessness not seen since the advance of the last ice sheets. Domestic consumption boomed as mills created locally important markets. But wholesale logging for old-growth pine dominated the harvest. Between 1856 and 1896, sawtimber logging increased fourfold. By then a pulp industry had also matured that targeted spruce, and revisited the once-culled woodlands for another cut. Other forest products—tar, charcoal, fuelwood, swidden—found themselves in hopeless competition with commercial logging. Market forces succeeded where centuries of edicts and agronomic theories had failed. By the end of the nineteenth century the ancient forest lay in tatters.

Every attribute of the prelogged forest changed. Its composition shifted from a mixed woodlands to pine, then to spruce, then to a pine-spruce ensemble. Its age structure reformed from patchy old-growth trees to predominantly young reproduction. Nor did logging restrict its impacts to trees. Timber companies altered streams to ensure better floating for logs. Sawmills stimulated local communities, which projected farming over larger subregions. Everything else in the biota had to adjust accordingly. Soils became acidic. Marshes were drained. Moose and reindeer populations increased. Pastoral burning plummeted and wildfires proliferated.

Enthusiasts insisted, however, that the old forest had already been shredded by peasant agriculture, especially swidden. Of course, swidden had forcibly converted the old regime: that was its purpose. Yet its long cycles and small scales had, in many ways, only accelerated the tempo and expanded the dominion of the indigenous biota. It had shifted the composition of forests to softwoods, particularly birch, better suited for second-order *svedjebruk;* it had broken up large segments of the ecological mosaic and rearranged small ones; it made the forest undeniably different. But the sheer complexity of a properly swiddened landscape and the multiplicity of traditional exploitations, from charcoaling to tar burning, potash production, hunting, mushroom gathering, grazing, and selective logging, had argued for a biological diversity that would be impossible under a monoculture of commercial logging. Swedish loggers cleaned out old-growth pine as brusquely as Russian *promyshlenniki* had sable and American wildcatters had oil reserves, and were driven to seek out untapped sites by the same immutable logic.

Criticism of fire cultivation of all kinds reached a crescendo just as industrial logging exhausted the flush times made possible by easily worked old-growth forests. The denunciations called forth a long pedigree of antiswidden literature that dated back to the mid-eighteenth century. By the mid-nineteenth century competition for wood brought foresters into the fray. Foresters established commercial forests as the standard of land use, and timber as the measure of land's social worth. Neither valued fire. Fire burned forests, and it devalued wood to the status of a mere combustible, indistinguishable from peat or tussock. In the emerging land and fire disputes, foresters became the dominant dialecticians. From the pulpit of applied science they thundered against folk fire practices. Increasingly, they spoke with the authority of the state.

In fact, Sweden had a long legacy of (oft-ignored) forest legislation. Early reform had focused on landownership, the need to transfer control so that trees could enter the timber market. As the logging frontier slashed northward, the debate shifted to the competing needs of traditional agriculture and the emerging forest industry. A forestry institute (for teaching) was established in 1828, a national forestry corps in 1836, and a central forestry administration in 1859. Germany provided the appropriate models.[72]

In 1852, Ludwig Falkman reported to the Royal Forestry Institute on his two years of commissioned travels. It seemed to him that various elements of Swedish society were in "competition" to see "who could eradicate the forest first," and that if present rates of consumption did not diminish, the timber famine (*skogsbristen*) that already blighted certain regions would propagate across all of Sweden. While there were many causes, widespread burning, both deliberate and accidental, was the most inexcusable. Falkman identified the transfer of Finnish swidden as particularly notorious since it quickly spread "throughout the country" and "devastated forests" like a plague of bark beetles.[73]

Despite its annexation to Russia, Finland showed similar developments, partly because its intellectuals still published in Swedish, and partly because the spread of a global timber frontier and the diffusion of professional forestry kept them in loose synchronization. In 1851, Finland passed a new forest law that sought to restrain forest burning, and in 1857 legislation created a forestry service and banned swidden. Its imported foresters wasted little time with preliminaries. In 1858 Edmund von Berg, director of the Tharandt Forestry Institute in Germany, was commissioned to survey the state of Finland's forests. A year later he issued his report, whose conclusion was a ringing denunciation of Finnish settlement practices: "the destruction of forests, in which the Finns have become adept, is furthered by the careless and uncontrolled grazing of cattle, swidden practices and destructive forest fires. In other words, these three means are used for the same main aim, namely the destruction of the forests." Soon afterward a National Board of Forestry was established, and on the Tharandt example, the Evo School of Forestry in 1862, though the latter was not officially recognized until 1874. Its director, A. G. Blomqvist, later founded the Finnish Forestry Association (1877). Unsurprisingly, he committed his principal scholarship to a comprehensive survey of forest fires.[74]

Other critics followed, often in the form of official commissions. Three issued reports between 1874 and 1881: a Commission on Crown Forests, a Committee on the Conditions of Private Forests, and a Committee on Overcutting of Forests. The 1874 report reckoned that no less than 80 percent of existing forests were abused in some way. Regarding *svedjebruk,* it hedged. Certainly the practice harmed the sawtimber industry; certainly it led "mediately or immediately, to many fires, and consequently to much destruction of forest." But outright prohibition would throw the bulk of eastern Finland into poverty and deny the state needed taxes; better to regulate *svedjebruk* than to attempt to abolish it and thereby "place a part of the population of the country in the difficult position of either violating the law, or of suffering from the pangs of poverty"; and which of these options the majority would choose, the report added, there can be no doubt.[75]

Instead, further denunciations devolved onto professional scientists. The agronomic critique reached its apex in Gösta Grotenfelt's encyclopedic *Det primitive jordbrukets metoder i Finland under den historiska tiden* (1899), a detailed ethnography of Finnish traditional agriculture. The forestry critique culminated in Olli Heikenheimo's magisterial *Kaskeamisen vaikutus Suomen metsin* (1915). It is instructive that both targeted swidden, that both identified fire as the cause and stigmata of a primitive economy.[76]

Originally the task for Swedish reformers was to pour sufficient wood into the bottomless pit-mills of commercial forestry. But in a land still subject to famine, as Sweden was in the 1860s, the dimensions of the swath cut by the global timber frontier raised social issues as well. Not only mills but people had to be fed. Major commissions investigated the state of the forests in 1856 and 1871. Thereafter a steady drumbeat of reports and inquiries followed, many of them buried within the literature of a rapidly institutionalizing forestry establishment.[77]

All agreed that it was insane to incinerate commercial woodlands to sustain marginal agriculture. It was cheaper to import grain from Ukraine or North America than to grow it in Norrland or Finland. Already the oldest and most intensively swiddened regions of Savo-Karelia and Dalarna suffered from wood shortages. Given population pressures, swidden was no longer sustainable, and granted the market for sawtimber and pulp it was no longer affordable. Ultimately farmers had to become foresters; already foresters complemented agronomists as the censors of swidden. It was one thing for farmers and foresters to compete over whether a patch of timber should make rye or lumber; it was something else to have the woods burn up without apparent use to anyone. On that point agriculture and forestry could agree. More than ever fire had to go.

It became clear, however, that strip-mining forests could not continue, whatever the imperatives of international capitalism. Swidden worked because *kaski* succeeded *huuhta;* a regrown forest allowed for a truly circulating *svedjebruk.* That made pioneering swidden something more than plundering. Forestry could survive only if it could devise an equivalent system. It had to replace what it removed. Accordingly critics—critics of industrialization as well as critics upset by the self-destructive character of logging—agreed that silviculture, like agriculture before it, had to sow as well as reap. Their combined clamor, and extensive legislative reports issued in 1899 and 1901, resulted in the Forest Law of 1903, the first of a distinguished lineage and the inauguration of the modern Swedish landscape.

Unlike its predecessors, which had sought to regulate cutting for the sake of mines or naval stores, the 1903 legislation intended to regulate the whole timber industry. By mandating that owners reforest logged lands, it sought, in effect, to domesticate logging and industrialize farming. How this might occur was a social and political matter, not a strictly ecological one. The Swedish landscape would express the character of Sweden's evolving society. Nature's economy would follow, as it supported, society's. Sweden became a tree farm.

Traveling over Medelpad, Nils interpreted a stump-covered clearing as "dreadfully ugly and poverty-stricken." Then it was explained to him how every stage of the timber industry was analogous to the growing, harvesting, and milling he had known on his parents' Skåne farm. There was the field, here the woody sheaves, there the thresher and mill. That bleak forest—now that steam had replaced swidden—sustained the immense mills at Sundsvall. "What a great country we have!" Nils concluded. "Wherever I go there is always something for people to live upon."[78]

(ii)

Any change this profound of course affected regional fire regimes. But even as the field evolved into the factory, the flame did not retire to the furnace. Eliminating swidden and pastoral burning—smothering the rural economy—did not snuff out fire. While traditional ignition sources went into decline, new ones from combustion machinery took their place, and while forests were less often burned for ash and tar, they were also less meticulously tended and cleaned.

The ax did not clear fire from the land, it encouraged more of it. Logging broke down the ancient fuel structure, as it often broke down agrarian society. The control that rural Sweden had exerted over fire through its manipulation of fuels, often by means of deliberate firing, slipped away with land speculators and log flumes. Loggers extracted tree trunks but left the residue that swidden had carefully burned. It was still there to burn. And the more logging burst into uncut landscapes, the more debris it left behind. Wanton slashing promoted wanton burning.

If only temporarily, successful logging demanded fire control. It could not tolerate fire cultivation, especially swidden, which competed with it for trees; a controlled burn for the one was too often a wildfire for the other. Nor could it accept the profuse burning—from insect-inspired smudge fires to pastoral firings to the abandoned campfires of wayfarers—that crept, simmered, flared, and otherwise immersed the boreal forest in summer smoke. The complexly buffered rural landscape could absorb this kind of fire much more readily than could its successor. It had a fire elasticity that the more brittle industrial landscape lost. Foresters and foreign travelers routinely blasted the peasantry for its perceived carelessness, and its indifference to any free-burning wildfire except one that threatened home or field. Such a fire, however, the rural population could put to use. They could, as one Finnish critic put it, regard it "as a friend." In the biotic regeneration that flourished in its ash, they could hunt deer and moose, harvest firewood, gather cordwood for charcoal, and forage for berries and mushrooms. Obsessed with sawtimber, logging could only move on.[79]

But lightning and rural economies were not the only source of wildfire. Logging needed also to squelch its own accidental burning, which trailed it like cholera. The industry was as migratory and as eco-shattering as the pioneering Finns. It broke complex forest structures, rearranging fuels so that they rested, accessible, on the ground instead of in tree crowns; it homogenized what land and history had differentiated; it encouraged wooden milltowns, susceptible to urban fire. Even its attempts at fire control prevented the kind of burning that had helped insulate settlements against wildfire. Ultimately logging could control fire by reclaiming control over the landscape through the close cultivation of the forest, an obsessive silviculture, even to the point of removing snags, stumps, and windfall like so much roadside trash. Until then it had to protect itself from fire. Loggers became firefighters.

In the flush years, fire control depended on folk methods, except that logging camps replaced villages. For direct attack firefighters seized tree boughs for swatting, and cut and scraped firelines around the flaming perimeter. For a burn of any size, however, they had to seek out some preexisting firebreak such as a road, a river, or a swath of deciduous forest, and then set backfires. If the technology was crude, knowledge of fire behavior was often sophisticated, built on centuries of *svedjebruk* and *brännodling*. One technique was to tie tall grasses together and stand the bundles up between the firebreak and the approaching wildfire. When the fire's indrafts blew down the bundles, that was the signal to kindle the backfires.[80]

Probably what Nils witnessed in Ångermanland was typical. One morning he saw wisps of smoke rising from distant forest ridges. Surely, he thought, the smoke emanated from some farm. But soon the fire scaled up into a conflagration. "It would be best," he reasoned, "to be away from this." The smoke that he "drew in with every breath was a torture." He joined the animals in flight, lynx and adder and grouse, and these retreating refugees soon met people advancing to give battle. The small corps made their stand in a glen, along a brook, bordered by leafy trees. They widened that firebreak by felling conifers, wetted it by pouring water from the stream over heather and bog myrtle, dipped "great pine boughs" into the brook, and stood to face the flames. "There were not many men," Nils noted, "and it was strange to see them stand there, ready to fight, when all other living creatures were fleeing." But stream, leaf, and wetted bough held. When sparks started spot fires, the men brought water in buckets to extinguish them. When flames engulfed a tree, they felled it and suppressed the coals. When it crept through heather, they swatted the stealthy fire with boughs. Though the battleground was a shambles, "the forest fire was conquered." All that remained—"all there was left of the beautiful forest"— was "soft white smoke" from the ground and "black stumps."[81]

Folk methods were not good enough, however, when fire met heavy loads of slash dried by drought. Nor was it sufficient to appease officials drawn to timber's fire frontier like moths to a flame. The modern forestry era inaugurated a cavalcade of major wildfires. There were large fires in 1868, 1878, and 1888. An outbreak in 1876 burned approximately 1.2 percent of the state forests. The 1888 fires moved from felled forests to wooden towns. Nine years after it suffered industrial strikes, Sundsvall burned. So did Umeå, which rebuilt its oft-burned town center with fire-retarding birches. (It had burned regularly

before when Russian troops had invaded; now it burned from Sweden's industrial assault on nature.) So did Holmsund and Sandö and parishes in Jämtland,
Härjedalen, and Västmanland. While the fires struck Norrland hardest, smaller
echoes were heard outside Falun and Kalmar and elsewhere. The twentieth century's year of record came in 1901. Not far behind were the conflagrations of
1914, 1920, and, amid a drought of continental proportions, 1933.[82]

Those great fires hid as much as they exposed. The larger saga was one of
fires lost more than fires gained. The truest chronicle of Swedish fire was written best in its biota. The land, like a folk memory, chronicled the intricate
history of *svedjebruk, kyttlandsbruk, brännodling, saeter* burning, and wildfire—the patchy lichen savannas, the even-aged stands of conifers, the dappled deciduous woods, and the famed pine forest at Kulbäcksliden that dated
from regeneration that followed a conflagration in 1694. The advance of industrial forestry suppressed folk practices, just as it broke the land on which they
relied. The fires of the old regime faded away.

And the distinctive fires of the new regime became prominent in their stead.
With the institutionalization of forestry, large fires entered written literature
and became subjects for formal inquiry, even scientific investigation. The real
story was not a sudden eruption of wildfire. It was, rather, a dramatic reconstruction of fire regimes that saw spasmodic conflagrations increase and background burning diminish.

Swedish foresters recognized that their acquired fire problem was far less
severe than that of North America or Siberia. The horrific fires of 1876 consumed 26,920 hectares, not much above the 1 percent that seems to be the historic average of burned area for the boreal forest. The widely reported 1888
fires burned 11,650 hectares; the millennial 1901 fires, 10,475 hectares; the
1914 fires, which prompted a rash of official inquiries, 6,450 hectares; the 1920
fires, 3,830. These figures derive from state forests, but although critics
believed that two to three times as much burned on private lands, the overall
story is one of steady extinguishment. More and more land was protected, and
protected more intensively. Reviewing the 1933 fires, A. G. Högbom dismissed
as media exaggeration statements that "all of Norrland burned"; a truer figure
was one-thousandth of the landmass. Of two hundred fires, eight were responsible for 70 to 80 percent of the 20,000 hectares burned area.[83]

Fire causes too were changing. In an average year like 1925, locomotives
accounted for 20 percent of fires, "carelessness" another 20 percent, arson for
4 percent, and lightning for 26 percent. Of the remainder some were due to rifles,
housefires that spread into the woods, electrical lines, agricultural burning, and
"tobacco"; the shift from chewing tobacco to cigarettes (and matches), foresters
believed, led to many more fires. The big fire years resulted from unusual circumstances, not only drought but exceptional ignition; Högbom believed that

lightning accounted for possibly 70 percent of the 1933 fires. But of the traditional sources there was less and less. The overall fire load was in slow free-fall.

This trend accelerated after the 1903 Forest Law and its successors. Forestry could underpin the national wealth only if it put down roots, if it grew back for reharvest what it had stripped away. This meant that foresters had to design fire protection into young forests, not simply contain fires on old slashings. Sweden looked to Germany for inspiration in this, as in other matters. So did Finland, although some of that influence came indirectly through German-inspired reforms in Russian forestry. Regrowing forests would take time, however; probably several rotations would be needed to fully transform the woodlands, as it had taken several swidden cycles to convert the previous landscape. In the meanwhile there would be fires.

Foresters mustered to meet them. Lookout towers sprouted across the landscape like the fire beacons of earlier eras. Roads supplanted *saeter* trails, improving access equally for planting, harvesting, and fire control. Specialized handtools replaced pine boughs, and mechanical pumps replaced leather buckets. Scientific forestry organized symposia, sponsored research, and linked with professional colleagues in Europe and North America. Intellectuals and state officials discovered new reasons to distrust folk practices and detest fire. Not only was fire attacked, its traditional sources were searched out and destroyed. In Finland three decades of war, depression, and nation-building complicated the trend. In neutral Sweden hostile fires faded, like the nation's old soldiers, into history.[84]

(iii)

But fire, like the old rural landscape, did not vanish altogether. Between the fires of rural burning practices and the near-expulsion of all fires there was a fascinating transitional phase based on controlled burning for forestry. Just as swidden had mediated between wildland and arable, so *hyggesbränning* (slash burning), which derived from it, mediated between forestry's fear of wildfire and its passion for fire exclusion.

The statistics for Swedish fire are flawed because they capture only the damaging wildfires. The controlled burning that helped to slow fire's decline, that dampened the shock of fire's removal from the biota, does not appear in the ledgers of the logging economy. That omission says a great deal about forestry's official attitude toward fire.

Even as they advertised fire's threat to commercial logging, foresters recognized that almost all the fabulous pine they harvested for sawtimber had grown on burned sites. In remote areas these formative burns had originated as wildfires; elsewhere, as swidden or other fire cultivation. Norrland's timber frontier tracked precisely the centuries-old wake of crown fire and swidden. Without those fires the gluttonous sawtimber industry would have starved before it crossed into the boreal forest. So while fires, often worsened by logging's diabolical disturbances, menaced forestry's first harvest, it appeared to some observers that they might help stimulate a second. If sites once cut, save some seed trees, were properly burned, a new pine stand could flourish in its place. Forestry could adapt swidden to its own ends and grow pine instead of rye.[85]

So, even as forest commissions began investigating the great wildfires of the late nineteenth century, other institutions began a formal debate regarding *hyggesbränning*. Inevitably the discussion returned to *svedjebruk*, so fundamental to an agrarian society that exploited fire and itself so frequently a source of wildfire. Controlled burning entered the agendas of forest commissions charged with ensuring a steady flow of timber. In general, Finns were more sympathetic than Swedes, recognizing that without fire large sections of the country would plummet into poverty and admitting that without fire wet humus would not regenerate easily to pine.

The Finnish Forestry Association made regeneration burning the topic of its 1882 convention. That inaugurated a vigorous dialogue which, for both Sweden and Finland, ceased only in the 1960s. In many ways the controversy recycled the near-ritual discourse over swidden. There were those who claimed that the burning ruined humus, led to escaped fires, encouraged folk fire practices, and sanctioned a regime that modernization sought to eradicate. Practitioners were likened to a homeowner who burned the carpet to save the roof. Against those critics were foresters, largely field men, who began from the incontestable fact that pine reproduced best on burns, that controlled fire removed slash that might otherwise stoke wildfire, that without fire forestry was barely possible on the raw humus of the boreal environment. Jakob Fellman declared that only fire could reforest the cutover north. A. K. Cajander, founder of Finnish forestry, also supported controlled burning.

Both sides were right in principle, and right or wrong according to the particulars of place and time. Some sites were well suited for burning, some not. Some burns were well conducted, others not. It was not possible to segregate the two controversies. Foresters were reluctant to condemn *svedjebruk* for its use of fire yet praise *hyggesbränning* for what was essentially the same technique. The core issues were control over the land and the biotic privileging of trees, a quarrel expressed through competition to control the torch. A political declaration to that effect was probably too raw for popular digestion, however. It was easier to denounce folk farming because of its reliance on fire even if that argument restricted industrial forestry's access to fire as well.

Only a few researchers conceived fire as a unique process, not readily replicated by other technologies. This meant that if forestry was the goal, fire had value only to the extent that it promoted the same purpose. Other techniques could conceivably replace it. Since early foresters relied on natural regeneration, their burning was in effect a simulation of the quasi-natural processes that had spawned the forest; it was a swidden cognate. But a silviculture based on nursery-grown seedlings might argue otherwise. Eventually foresters prepared sites with tractors, planted trees as though they were turnips, and often promoted the fire-sensitive spruce sought by pulp mills rather than the fire-hardy pine. Until then, ironically, foresters often burned more area through *hyggesbränning* than they suppressed from wildfire.

But did it help or harm? Political economy had few doubts. Science, as always, was ambivalent. Local circumstances of site and burning seemed more important than generic principles. On dry soils with scanty humus a hot burn seemed to damage the site, propelling it toward heath. Elsewhere a good burn seemed to encourage pine regeneration. On sites ill-suited to natural reproduction there were few alternatives to fire, and the hotter the better.

The uncertainties were reflected in the persistence of field trials. G. Wrede undertook experiments at Parkano, Finland (1910); Edvard Wibeck demonstrated the value of burning for the afforestation of heath in southern Sweden (1912); Arvid Borg, head of the Finnish ranger school, attempted large-scale burning for conversion from stunted spruce to Scots pine (1911). Under Borg's leadership, but with the sanction of A. K. Cajander, head of the Finnish Forest Service, official approval for *hyggesbränning* on state forests came in 1919. Scattered foresters authorized its use in Sweden. (When Erik Lind began burning in 1923–24, it was said that "you must take this boy out of the woods or it will all go to hell.") But field success allowed the practice to scale up quickly. In 1928, O. Eneroth summarized the scientific findings for Sweden. By 1930 the practice moved beyond individual experimentation, became systematic, and reached an apogee. Then, just as quickly as it had climbed, it fell.[86]

The reasons were many, and they recycled once again the endless controversy over swidden. Poor techniques, faulty inspections (which reported poorer results than actually occurred), a desire for more spruce, a reliance on artificial seeding, vehement dissensions among professors, and the economic crisis of the Great Depression, all contributed. For Finland the Soviet invasion in 1939 temporarily ended controlled burning. But Sweden found a champion in J. E. Wretlind, keenly aware of fire's power to shape the character of the forest; and under his influence controlled burning percolated through Norrland's pine forests.

Wretlind reduced every component of the folk art to the prescriptions of a technical science. He described how to choose sites, how to leave seed trees, how to prepare firelines, how to ignite each parcel, and even how to deal with smoldering anthills. In 1948 he published *Nordsvensk hyggesbränning*, the summary of twenty-five years of practical experimentation at Malå. Controlled burning, he concluded, had "extraordinary meaning" for Norrland's forestry and was the best means to restore the land to "full productivity."[87]

Forestry boomed in the postwar era, yet the more Sweden cultivated its trees, the more it scorned its fires. During the conflict, Sweden's economy had been linked with Germany's, primarily exchanging iron for coal. Spared actual fighting, its gross national product had soared 20 percent. The rebuilding of Europe in the postwar era boosted Sweden's economy still higher. Forestry rode the crest, and *hyggesbränning* seemed an ideal mechanism—inexpensive and extensive—to regenerate the heavily cut forests. It became the topic of a special excursion for Norrland foresters in 1949. Sweden's success inspired Finland to rekindle its own prescribed fires. As it had during the 1920s, burned area rocketed up until the late 1950s when, once again, it collapsed. In 1958, Sweden burned 17,400 hectares of state forests; in 1988, only 131 hectares.[88]

The old critiques reappeared. Bad (too large, too intense) burns had produced bad results. There was less social tolerance for fire, and wildfires could, and did, escape. Public discussion persistently confused the effects of fire used for pastoralism, fire used in swidden or slash burning, and wildfire, despite their different character. The introduced fungus *Rhyzina undulata* attacked seedlings on burned sites, and the fear grew that burning might allow it to spread. (Apparently light burns assist spread, intense burns retard it.) Even more, the green revolution came to forestry, pushing reforestation into an intensified agronomic model, substituting artificial fertilizers for ash, planting with nursery stock rather than natural seeds liberated by heat, and readying sites with tractor-powered scarification and ditching instead of the cleansing sweep of flame. The organization of forest labor brought woodworkers into the Swedish holiday system. The month of July, once given to burning, now went to travel and summer homes. Social legislation was more powerful than natural laws.[89]

Hyggesbränning reeked of the archaic, and the postwar era was ready to consign it to libraries as no more relevant to Sweden's sleek modernism than Öland's windmills and Finnmark's spruce plows. When ecologists at Umeå prevailed on the state forestry service to preserve an area burned by wildfire at Åtmyrliden in Norrland, the site acquired the character of an open-air folk museum. Visitors could tour charred snags and fireweed thickets as they might examine Viking boat burials. Understanding fire ecology belonged with deciphering rune stones, a curiosity more antiquarian than practical. The expulsion of fire in boreal Europe was virtually complete. The welfare state had come to nature.

(iv)

Nils ends his adventures where he began them, by returning to the family farm at Vemmenhög. He is much changed. On his travels he has learned many virtues, not least of all courage, but most of all empathy for others. He soon desires more than anything else to be human again.

As word of his deeds on behalf of the geese spreads among the animals, it eventually reaches the elf who enchanted him. On the journey north Nils is told that he might regain his humanity if he takes the white goose, Morten, to Lapland and brings him safely back to Skåne; so Nils becomes the goose's protector. Returning south, however, he learns from the raven Bataki that the elf insists Nils will become "a normal human being again" only if he returns Morten Gander to Nils' mother, so that she "might lay him on the block and chop his head off." As the flock approaches Skåne, Nils, aching with homesickness, must decide whether to betray the white goose, and regain human form, or hold to a humanlike friendship with the goose and remain forever Tummetott.[90]

In his travels Nils goes everywhere, from Värmland to Gotland, from the harbor at Karlskrona to the summit of Kebnekaise in Lapland. But it is no accident that the moral geography of his adventures has its center in Skåne. It is the least boreal of all the Swedish provinces, a thorn of temperate Europe lodged in the side of the Scandinavian peninsula. Mother Akka, leader of the wild geese, flies Nils all over Skåne "just to let him see that his was a country which could compare favorably with any in the world." To the young geese making their first journey south she calls out, "Now look down! Look carefully! . . . Thus it is in foreign lands, from the Baltic coast all the way down to the high Alps."[91]

It could have been otherwise. Finland found its moral center in Karelia, and discovered in the storied fragments of the *Kalevala* a kind of creation myth of a pioneering folk. Nils' contemporary, the great dog Buck in *The Call of the Wild*, goes from civilization to wilderness, becoming an apotheosis of primitive virtue and frontier legends. It took a second book, *White Fang*, to try to bring him back. Nils' Indian cousin, the feral Mowgli, moves from the jungle to the man-village, but ends his career as a forest guard, protecting the wild, still conversing with his brothers the wolves. A Swedish saga might plausibly have brought Nils to Lapland and left him in wild innocence; or returned him halfway between boreal and temperate Europe; or brought him to Värmland, where fearless Finns had once begun the heroic task of breaking the boreal forest, where Lagerlöf had her family farm. Any such narrative would have left Nils on a frontier of boreal Europe. It would have defined Sweden as something unique, a fusion caused by the shock encounter of new and old, the temperate with the boreal.

But Sweden, so Lagerlöf implies, will define itself—all of itself—according to the standards of temperate Skåne. It will extend or rehabilitate Europe, not remake it. Even Norrland's forests will become farms. Nils does not create a new landscape but returns to the old homestead, healing an injured horse, returning the lost geese, rehabiliting himself, restoring family to hearth. His journeys were an adolescent adventure, an act of growing up, not of pioneering. Sadly, in becoming human Nils loses his ability to commune with the animals.

Morten Gander precipitates the choice. Like Nils he has matured, proven himself the equal of the wild geese, taken a wife, sired goslings. But he cannot refuse the chance to return. Eagerly he leads Dunfin and the goslings to his old goose pen. "Don't be afraid," he tells them, "there's no danger." They admire the "elegance and comfort" in which Morten had resided before he impulsively joined the wild geese. The trough, Morten explains, "was always filled with oats and water," unlike the hard scramble for food the wild geese experience. "Wait!" he cries. "There's some fodder in it now." He rushes to the trough, gobbles the oats, and then the door slams. They are trapped. Nils' mother takes Morten and Dunfin to the kitchen to cook them. If times were less severe, she says, she would let them live. Morten cries out—as he has over and again—for Nils. For an instant Nils hesitates. If he appears, he will be doomed to remain a Tummetott. But human virtues are more important than human form, and he rushes to save the white goose. As he crosses the threshold, he becomes his full size. "I'm a big boy," he exults to his parents. "I'm a human being again."[92]

So, too, Sweden faced a choice. Even as *The Wonderful Adventures of Nils* went to its schools, labor and capital were amalgamating in ways that would ultimately lead to a social democratic state, and when Europe plunged twice into war, Sweden remained neutral and unlike Norway and Finland suffered no invasion. In a sense Sweden, like Morten Gander, chose the security of the pen for the uncertainty of the migrating flock, a choice redeemed, as Morten was, by a commitment to human values. While Selma Lagerlöf looks back to an agrarian past, the values encoded in her book persisted throughout the century. They made Sweden a model of social security.

But if Sweden passed its moral crisis, it did not eliminate its environmental one. Before Nils' transformation, Mother Akka lectures him that "if you have learned anything at all from us, you no longer think that the humans should have the whole earth to themselves." Remember, she implores him, to leave "a few bare rocks, a few shallow lakes and swamps, a few desolate cliffs and remote forests to us poor animals, where we can be allowed to live in peace." Grant us, she asks, some refuge. Nils agrees but doubts that he should have much influence. On that count he was right. Skåne was more powerful than Lapland. The garden was mightier than the *vildmark*.[93]

EPILOGUE:
FINAL FLAME

By 1990 those tiny refuges of bare rocks and shallow lakes were all that remained to the wild animals. Something like 1.2 percent of Sweden belonged in nature reserves, little more than the scrap lumber left after commercial milling. Of twenty national parks, twelve were less than 25 square kilometers in size, and seven less than 25 square kilometers.

Instead Sweden had committed nature to the service of society. Industrial Sweden, the Sweden of the postwar boom and social democratic politics, restructured nature in its own image. Its values were stability, productivity, and security. Its environmental policy aimed at "securing every person's right to a good life environment, now and in the future, by limiting and preventing environmental disturbances and restoring damaged environments." Environmental protection meant protecting people from nature. It did not mean protecting nature from people.[94]

There was no place for fire. Fire epitomized the violence, the unpredictability, the disturbances that Sweden sought to stand apart from. With the aid of fossil fallow and fossil fuels, silviculturalists weeded fire out of the forest landscape. The 1990 forest volume published for the National Atlas declared that the "damage which is of the greatest significance" in Sweden is caused by "storm, fungi, moose, and insects"; only "previously" had fire been important. By the mid-1980s this, the most heavily statistical country on Earth, the creator of the modern census, no longer kept records on fires.[95]

Fire suppression accounted for part of the loss. The credit for most of the reduction, however, belongs to intensive silviculture. To promote full productivity and to guarantee social stability—timber for the mills, jobs for forest workers—forest laws became increasingly prescriptive. Even for private landowners the law eventually specified what kinds of trees might be planted, how they would be cultivated, and when they would be harvested. The 1903 statute led to many successes, with major reforms in 1923 and 1948 that made sustained yield a legal requirement. The law went beyond compulsory reforestation after harvest: it made harvest itself compulsory. Oversight committees discouraged unproductive lands, drained wetlands to develop plantations, set limits on the amount of deadwood allowed, and propelled industrial forestry to sites as remote as the timberline *fjäll* and offshore islands. Sweden, it seemed, had achieved the paired goals of agronomists and political theorists. Old fire-catalyzed practices became irrelevant. Fires became inconsequential.[96]

Only slowly have the costs of this fire famine become apparent. Industry spewed its own pollutants, prompted its own biochemical disturbances, and restructured the landscape in ways that suited its singular ambitions. Clearcutting proved worse than swidden, artificial fertilizers more potent than slash-burned soot, drained mires and scarified soils more damaging than stump plows and *kyttlandsbruk,* and dammed streams more destructive than forest grazing by *saeter.* While Sweden moved forcibly against industrial contamination that entered the country from outside (nuclear radiation, acid rain, ozone destruction), it addressed more reluctantly the internal environmental costs of its model society. The idea that nature somehow had rights was alien to a social philosophy predicated on *human* relations.

But ignoring nature had escalating costs. Biodiversity was one. Wildfire potential was another. But perhaps the most symbolic was that which once again joined fire with water.

Predictably (if paradoxically) the removal of fire-catalyzed landscapes in Sweden had affected even Norden's waterways. Many of Sweden's endless lakes rest on granitic rocks, and so, unlike lakes on calcareous strata, are poorly buffered against acids that rain or leach into them. Decomposing forest litter and mires offered steady sources of acid; spring melt often resulted in "acid surges"; and most of Sweden's lakes have probably lowered their pH over their lifetimes. But the ranks of the seriously acidified have increased dramatically throughout the twentieth century, accelerating in the postwar era. By the late 1970s an estimated 17,000 lakes larger than one hectare suffered some degree of acidification.[97]

There is little doubt that fossil-fuel combustion is a major cause. Industrial combustion for power plants, factories, and automobiles belched pollutants that rained down on sensitive lakes, overwhelmed their primitive capacity to neutralize, and purged the waters of some or all resident species. Sulfurous coals have provoked the most havoc. Land use practices, however, have supplemented this contribution significantly by increasing acidic sources and reducing alkaline sinks. Conifer forests are more prone than grassy fields to leach acids into waterways and so add to acidification. By contrast, burned landscapes become temporarily alkaline, sloughing those buffers into streams and ponds, and charcoal absorbs by-products that otherwise wash offsite. In brief, anthropogenic fire contributed to lake alkalization while fossil-fuel combustion accelerated lake acidification.

Anthropogenic fire had tempered waters as well as lands. In southwestern Sweden, lakes showed an interruption in their relentless acidification around 2,300 years ago, with the advent of landnam. By 2,000 years B.P. there was positive alkalization as the conversion to agriculture spilled, literally, into Sweden's waters. Undoubtedly the practice of burning around lakes to encourage reeds, the tradition of underburning forests and overburning mires, and the firing by chance or purpose of wetlands and bogs all increased alkalinity and counteracted the tendency toward acidification. But what agriculture gave, industry took away. Fossil-fuel combustion increased airborne sources of acidity, and fire-free forestry replaced alkaline-rich fields with acid-prone conifer woodlands. The process of reacidification thus began with the conversion to forests and the abolition of free-burning fire.

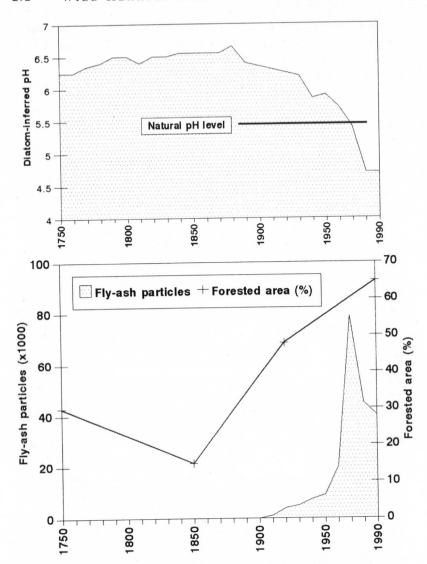

Industrial fire and fallow. Trends in lake acidification in southwestern Sweden (top) associated strongly with hydrocarbon combustion and somewhat more weakly with forest leaching (bottom). Both reforestation and the burning of fossil fallow are indexes of the industrial transformation of the landscape. At the same time, the reduction of biomass burning removed a buffering effect and allowed acidification to proceed. (Data from Renberg et al. 1993)

The acute acidification that has led to an environmental crisis, however, is the outcome of magnified industrial combustion of an order sufficient to overcharge even the older landscapes. Only an industrially equivalent process can counter it. So, in 1974, Sweden began to artificially lime lakes in an effort to reverse acidification, to increase pH to the point that indigenous flora and fauna could survive. In effect, Swedes did to their lakes what marl-carting Jutlanders had done to their heath. Some 6,000 lakes are now limed regularly with 200,000 tons of lime at an annual cost of 100 million Swedish kroner in an almost parodic adaptation of industrial agriculture. In some instances liming is done from boats or pontoons, as a farmer might spread artificial fertilizer. In other cases a special apparatus injects lime into streams like plasma from an IV bottle. For remote lakes, helicopters spray lime as they would pesticides.

Still, it is insufficient. The sources remain too great, the natural capacity to resist them too feeble. Having abolished swidden's obnoxious smoke columns, Sweden finds it must contend with sulfur-spewing smokestacks. Having eradicated prescribed fire, Sweden must now engage in prescribed liming to take its place.

The archival varves in those lakes now record a new combustion regime. Where once the soot of *svedjebruk,* pastoral burning, *kyttlandsbruk,* and wildfire had laced the annual laminations, now fly-ash, coarse carbonaceous soots, and sulfur compounds inscribe the region's geologic archives. Almost impervious to chemical degradation, spheroidal carbonaceous particles (SCP) have lodged in traditional carbon sinks, from soils to mires to lakes. They trace a host of processes for which this species of controlled combustion is a catalyst, the trace marker of an industrial landnam. SCPs transport metals, sulfur, and polyaromatic hydrocarbons; they accelerate the decay of calcareous stone, not least that used for buildings and monuments; and they probably interfere with natural weathering processes. They are found in even remote Norrland lakes.[98]

Their origin is complex. Most derive from local sources. But prevailing winds carry northeastward the immense combustion effluent that emanates from the urban and industrial centers of temperate Europe. Sweden could not declare neutrality from Europe's industrialization as it could from Europe's wars, and in fact had no desire to do so. As much as its trade relations, as much as Baron Hårelman's notions of proper agriculture or Selma Lagerlöf's decision to house Nils Holgersson on the Skåne coast, that stream of combusted carbon testifies to Sweden's linkage with Europe. With its great forests and relatively remote interior, Sweden might have fashioned a unique fire regime, a middle way between folklore and science, a fusion of the boreal with the temperate. Instead it exchanged the vestal fire for the industrial furnace.

The Swedes made that adjustment. Their land has not.

FLAMING FRONT
Fire in Eurasian Europe

. . . forested and wooden Rus' is even in a special, exceptional position in comparison with other countries: she is like an inextinguishable bonfire which, never going out completely, first weakens, then flames up with such monstrous force that any idea of fighting it vanishes: an entire sea of flames is spread by a whirlwind of fire from one end of our unfortunate land to the other, and destroys without a trace forests, planted fields, villages, settlements and towns.

—S. V. Maksimov (1896)[1]

PROLOGUE:
WOODEN RUS' IS LIKE A FIRE

Russia reversed Europe's geography, as it seemed to invert Europe's history. If Baron van Haxthausen's judgment is extreme ("Whoever would travel in Russia, earnestly study the condition of the country, and observe its national life with unprejudiced eyes, must first of all forget everything he has read in other countries upon the subject"), so are many of the circumstances of Russian fire. In Eurasia, Europe's vestal fire broke out of the temple.[2]

Western Europe thrust into the Atlantic like a fractured shoreline of seamounts, beaches, coves, estuaries, islands, and wave-scoured cliffs. Its smaller scale replicated its larger, as subcontinental peninsulas lunged into suboceanic seas. A west-trending Europe met an east-trending Gulf Stream, and each interpenetrated the other, until it was difficult to say whether the land was advancing onto the sea or the sea onto the land. But if Europe's internal seas flowed westward into the world ocean, its lands stretched eastward into the most massive of the world's continents. The Eurasian plain was as vast as South America, its flanking mountains arrayed like a stony windbreak around a campfire. From it, like kettles on hooks, hang the subcontinental peninsulas that decorate and define Eurasia.

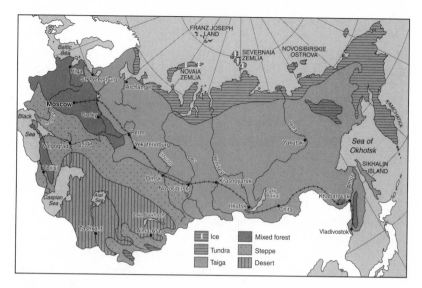

Major natural regions of the former USSR. Note the strong latitudinal trends, and the wedging out of the mixed European forest at the Urals. (University of Wisconsin Cartographic Lab)

The Eurasian plain offered no obvious natural barrier, no intrinsic geologic frame except the trans-Eurasian mountains to the south and the Arctic Ocean to the north. From central Europe to central Siberia the plain formed a lithic pond unruffled by tectonic winds. The Ural Mountains that have traditionally divided Europe from Asia were the scar tissue of ancient geologic suturing, long worn by erosion. They no more interrupted the flow of land, or of life, than rounded boulders in a river. In central Siberia the land rose in a shallow plateau, heavily dissected, but still remarkably uniform. Not until the plain met the great chain of trans-Eurasian mountains as they curved north to define the eastern perimeter of the continent did the great monolith truly end. Its climates likewise striped the plain in broad bands from east to west.

Climate, not geology, defines biotas. Maritime influences from the Atlantic push inland across central Europe and, beginning roughly at the classic Riga-Constantinople line, they abruptly narrow as the proportion of land to sea increases. The mixed forest of temperate Europe wedges to a point in the southern Urals. Above that belt stretches the boreal forest, the taiga; below it, a thick fringe of wooded steppe, and then steppe grasslands. Increasingly to the east a continental climate dominates. It squeezes even the taiga and steppe, the one grading into tundra, the other into desert. In the Far East, sustained by summer monsoons not blocked by the trans-Eurasian ranges, the forest splashes over its barriers and mingles with deciduous trees from the south. Thus a mixed

Asian forest thrives in the east in counterpoint to the mixed European forest in the west.[3]

The center was curiously dry. The Urals serve as a crude marker, a Eurasian analogue to North America's hundredth meridian. Beyond it, with few exceptions, precipitation falls below 20 inches a year. In Yakutia, precipitation ranges from 6 to 12 inches a year, roughly the same as the Sonora Desert. The dryness stalled glaciers: no ice sheets could penetrate into that dehydrated center. Instead groundwater froze into permafrost. In much of Siberia the seasonal thawing of that iced earth sustains the biota's coniferous core. The immensity of the landmass ensures that every place experiences drought at some time, and that every year it strikes somewhere.[4]

A seasonality that oscillates violently between winter dormancy and summer vibrancy; forests and grasslands that flourish amid a semiarid climate prone to droughts; a landscape of immense uniformity little broken by relief or cultivation—these are conditions that make fire naturally abundant, large fires potentially omnipresent, and wildfire free-ranging. Droughts ready this vast kindling for burning, and fires flare in an atonal dance. The mixed forest of European Russia knows fire more or less as central Europe does, with conditions toughening along a gradient to the east. The Far East experiences it in synchronization with the Asian monsoon that sustains another mixed forest. The rest—from the Carpathians to the Sikhote Alin 8,000 kilometers distant—supports fire everywhere, and big fires somewhere every year. In 1972 the Moscow oblast claimed the lion's share of Russia's fire load; in 1976 it was the Far East; in 1977, the Urals; in 1987 Transbaikalia; in 1992, Yakutia. Droughts occur every three to five years. Stand-replacing fires have occurred two or three times a century. Large fires materialize and vanish like an *ignis fatuus* in the taiga.[5]

Fuels, however invitingly arranged, still need a spark. Lightning forages, as ever, and in the drier interior it often gorges. But the dominant matrix and the fundamental rhythms are increasingly those of humans. Here the Eurasian plain invites a uniformity of people and purpose. The absence of a meaningful barrier encouraged propagation along climatic belts. Mounted steppe-dwellers moved over the grasslands much as Polynesians rode ocean winds and currents. Repeatedly, steppe tribes attempted to move north, across the biotic grain into forest, but with marginal success. What was needed was a people who could roam the taiga as pastoralists did the steppes.

That occurred when the Slavs, after centuries of churning in eastern Europe, massed around the Pripet marshes and then began to colonize outward in all directions. By 1580 they had breached the Urals. A century later, advance parties of Russian *promyshlenniki* and Cossacks reached the Pacific. From their forest ramparts they pressed southward, overriding steppe tribes, until they reached the trans-Eurasian ranges. The staggering uniformity of the Eurasian plain had, it seemed, yielded an equivalent uniformity of human settlement.

What transformed conquest into colonization was agriculture. If the Slavs were a forest people, they were also a farming people. The Russian settlers were different from Balts, Samoyeds, Mansi, Ostyaks, Evenki, and other forest foragers with whom they intermarried or displaced because they converted the landscape into something along the lines of European agriculture. What transfigured forest into farm was fire. As much as wildfire was a perpetual hazard, so was controlled fire a necessity. The tendency of Russian agriculture to expand rather than evolve and to oppress rather than intensify—to say nothing of the sheer immensity of the task—ensured that fire would not sublimate into mere symbol, smother in dung piles, vanish into pistons, or be snuffed out in the politics of social democracies.

"The illuminating torch, the broadcast fire, the purifying bonfire, and the fire of the hearth," Cathy Frierson has observed, "were the Russian peasant's assertion of his presence in the forest, his declaration of mastery over his cleared land, his definition of home, and an important symbol of his membership in a family of ancestors." Here fire returned to cultural consciousness—fire gods resuscitated, fire practices proliferated and persisted, fire ceremonies flourished, and fire appliances reclaimed their ancient centrality. Fire made the cold warm, the dark light, the damp dry, the oppressive hopeful, the forest's gloom bright, and the taiga's loneliness cheerful. For almost every wretchedness fire could compensate. "We put the kettle on the fire," wrote John Cochrane, traveling with a party of Yakuts and Cossacks, "and soon forgot the sufferings of the day." Against almost every landscape fire could transform. The candle and the torch became the emblems and tools of Europe's transfiguring march across Eurasia.[6]

Elsewhere fire had surrendered its standing—once supreme—in the pantheon of Indo-European gods. In mediterranean Europe it secularized into the vestal flame. In central Europe it expired among Celts, Franks, and Germans, lost to society as free-burning fire was to the sodden landscape. In boreal Europe it reappeared as Loki, somehow ineradicable, always mischievous. But among the Slavs the fire god survived as Svarozhich, son of Svarog, a deity that joined sun and hearth. Although he assumed many avatars, he probably descends from the Indo-European fire god. His identification of fire as a manifestation of a divine order has endured. Fire came from heaven; fire purified; its capture marked God's people; and with fire, good warred against evil. Novgorodians worshiped that fire god with an undying flame from burning oak. The tenth-century Arab traveler Ibn-Dustah declared that "all the Slavs are fire-worshipers." Only India, and to a lesser extent Iran, retained those ancient religious associations so completely or for so long. It may be no accident that the Slavs kept in contact with them far longer than did other Indo-European tribes.[7]

The Slavic hearth remained, as did its ancient Roman cognate, the focus of ancestor worship; the *izba* (peasant hut) was the "Slavs' first pagan temple"; the hearth fire was the "deity who protected the household and ensured the happiness of all the members of the family or kinship group." The hearth or stove claimed 20 to 25 percent of the *izba,* which grew around it. "A stove in the house," so a peasant saying from Viatka province went, "is the same as an altar in church." The *izba*'s interior was defined, as Cathy Frierson has noted, by two fires—the hearth at one corner, the sacramental candles below the icon in another.[8]

There were other fire-related figures, from the pre-Christian firebird beloved in Russian mythology to Ilya of Murom, the Christian hero of epic folklore. For the dominant figures there was a distinct pedigree. Herodotus recorded that the Slavs worshiped "Hestia in especial." Ilya was modeled on Elijah, the prophet, and Elijah was the successor of Perun, god of the thunderbolt. From Perun came both fire and ax, equally the apparatus of conquest and conversion, for lightning both shattered the tree and burned it. Here was the essence of swidden agriculture, transforming, purging, fertilizing. But here also was the essence of religious conversion. Holy fire transfigured the soul as profane fire did the land. To the pagan legacy of fire iconography Christianity added its own imagery; and Greek Orthodoxy, in particular, incorporated fire (often literally) into its liturgy. So Elijah (Saint Elias) succeeded Perun and dispersed celestial fire from his flaming chariot—hurling lightning at the devil, sprinkling cleansing fire like holy water, shielding the innocent from harm. At the entrance to every house a candle burned before an ancient icon.[9]

For the prophets of the eastern Church, fire was as central an image as it was for the Buddha at the caves of the Vindhya Hills. The fire sermon was standard fare. The mystic Dionysius proclaimed that "fire is in all things," a metaphor for the manifestation and presence of God. Angels were "living creatures of fire, men flashing with lightning, streams of flame." Justin Martyr asserted that "when Jesus went down into the water, a fire was kindled in the Jordan." So Origen asserted that Christ leaves baptism by water to his disciples, but reserves to himself "the power to baptize with the Holy Spirit and with fire." He who is near me, Origen has Christ further claim, "is near the fire." Gregory Thaumaturgus described his subsequent illumination by Origen "as if a spark fell into my soul, and caught fire, and blazed up." Orthodox missionaries to Rus' carried that imagery north, and there found ample symbolic tinder in Slavic myth and ceremony. The eremetic monk, the religious community, the missionary often became, as in Vedic India, the vanguard of colonization. So the holy fire propagated, spreading from the tongues of flame suspended by the Paraclete over the Apostles to the radiance of converted believers to the hellish conflagration of the Last Judgment.[10]

Fire was a universal intermediary between worlds, between heaven and earth, between sacred and profane, church and state, wilderness and farm, Slav and Tatar. It defined the borders between states of being, whether geographic or spiritual, and allowed for passage between them; for fire possessed, more than any other phenomenon, the power of transmutation. It could remake dark woods into food, and human clay into spirit; it could also destroy without remorse. Flame was the omnipotent metaphor for change. Wherever transformation occurred, on whatever scale, there was fire, and the more sudden the change the more violent the flames. The burning of forest began settlement; the burning of cities ended it. The holy fire that inspired a missionary could become the flaming stake that consumed martyr or heretic. Pyromantic visions foretelling the future appeared in fire, usually pillars of flame. Russians preferred Old Testament prophets of fire and the Christ who proclaimed, "I have come to send fire on the earth."[11]

Whether its flames came down or rose up, the tongue of flame symbolized the point of contact, the transforming act of conflict or conversion. To change was to burn; to countermand change was also to burn. The flames suspended between earthly fuel and heavenly glory—here was an icon of Russia. It thrived as a symbol of inspiration, protest, and revolt at large, from the Archpriest Avvakum in the seventeenth century to Michael Bakunin in the nineteenth, who prophesized that "tongues of flame" would descend again over Europe, this time in secular revolution.[12]

Perhaps the most spectacular, certainly most lurid, expression occurred during the Great Schism that sundered the Russian Orthodox Church in the seventeenth century. The attempt to introduce liturgical reforms began with the abolition of the rite by which, in imitation of Christ's injunction to "baptize with the Holy Ghost and with fire," candles were plunged into water. Traditionalists rose in protest, one tract (*On the Enlightening Fire*) declaring that reformers were trying to deny Russia "the tongue of fire that had descended upon the apostles." As the Patriarch Nikon, with the assistance of the Tsar Alexis, imposed further reforms, often with the burning stake, fundamentalist Old Believers also sought refuge in fire. Each side, that is, promoted reform or counterreform through their control over fire and its iconography.

The leader of the Old Believers, the Archpriest Avvakum, encouraged his followers by describing vividly fire's purgative power. "Burning your body, you commend your soul to God," he exhorted. "Run and jump into the flames." In the 1640s, ardent followers committed to the destroying flames whatever they could lay their hands on that was contaminated by foreign presence— musical instruments and realistic paintings no less than the foreign quarters outside Moscow. In 1667, Old Believers were officially condemned as heretics. Many declared themselves ready to suffer martyrdom by fire. Avvakum went to the stake in 1682 announcing to the crowd that fire would soon liberate his soul from the "dungeon of the body" and send it flying to heaven. An alarming number of followers voluntarily chose the same path. Between 1684 and 1690 some 20,000 Old Believers immolated themselves, whole families and congregations torching wooden churches to experience the cleansing flames.[13]

This was a civilization that needed fire, could not escape fire, could find no alternative to fire and demanded none. Fire routinely—sometimes gratefully, sometimes horribly—immersed their fields, their forests, their towns, their armies, their ceremonies, their literature, and, it would seem, their souls. It even capped their most distinctive architecture, the onion-dome steeple that adorned village church and metropolitan cathedral.

To the religious, those gilded domes shimmering above the forest epitomized the apostolic tongues of flame descending from heaven. To the more naturalistic, they manifested the all-too-tangible flames that rose from wooden Rus'. Regardless, the edifice was a nest of frozen flame. Whether conceived from the top down or the bottom up, fire symbolically crowned a building that, like its sustaining civilization, had risen out of the Eurasian forest.

THE CANDLE AND THE TORCH

Their origins are obscure. Possibly the Slavs had not strayed far from the Pontic steppes proposed as the Indo-European hearth; probably they are the agricultural tribes, the Wends, Antae to the west, Sklavini to the east, mentioned by Tacitus and Pliny as tributaries to the Scythians. Already they were farmers, already they understood the dynamics of the steppe-forest border. Certainly they exploited fire. Ancient chronicles most identified the steppe-dominant Scythians with two traits: they were mounted warriors, and they burned their grasslands, often retreating before a scorched earth. When Napoleon awoke to find Moscow aflame, he reportedly blurted out, "What a tremendous spectacle!—It is their own work! . . . These are Scythians indeed!"[14]

The gales of the Great Migration period, fanned by Hun and Turkish invasions, blew exactly through this corridor and scattered the Slavic tribes before them. Some moved into the Balkans, some skirted the Carpathians and seized most of eastern Europe, and others pushed north. They moved into forests and adapted their agriculture accordingly. The migration era sent its last tremors in the ninth century, as horse-mounted Magyars punched into the Hungarian Plain from the steppes and boat-coursing Norse probed Europe's seas and rivers. Slavic tribes continued to move north and east but had also moved back to the fringes of their old black-earth lands. By then the outline of a distinctive Slavic state, Kievan Russia, was apparent. Through its links with Byzantium its trade flourished and it became the pilot flame for the spread of Orthodox Christianity. But internal quarrels and incessant unrest along the steppe frontier broke the Kievan hegemony in 1054 and left a splatter of Russian principalities.

Then calamity. In 1237 the Mongols invaded, first slashing through the middle Volga region, later exploiting winter's frozen rivers to carry the horde into the previously impenetrable forest. With the onset of the spring thaw they returned to forest-steppe lands for further depredations. In 1240 they sacked Kiev. By the time the horde retired, save for punitive raids, to the congenial steppes, medieval Russia lay in ruins, permanently traumatized, stripped of towns, held as tributary subjects to predatory autocrats, severed from the Black Sea and Byzantium to the south, pressed away from the Baltic by Swedes and Germans, later by Lithuanians and Poles. Kievan Russia split into east and west along the lines of Mongol overlordship. For a while Novgorod, astride the northern fur trade, assumed the lost mantle of Kiev. But the future belonged with an obscure, immensely isolated principality along the Moskva River.

Muscovy grew like a crab adding shells, grew in a way not unlike imperial Rome, in a way not so different from the expansion of Île-de-France. From its core, the Kremlin ("fort"), the city added walls, one exoskeleton after another, then aggregated lands in a swirl like a chambered nautilus. In 1478 it subjugated Novgorod. Two years later it asserted independence from the Tatar Khanate. Disengagement was slow, expansion often halting. In 1571 a Crimean Tatar host dashed north and sacked and burned Moscow itself. Conquest was easiest to the north and east, where opposition was limited to forest tribes; it was hardest and least secure to the west, where Muscovy confronted a densely populated, modernizing Europe; to the south, against the steppe nomads, it was erratic but often spectacular. The Russian reconquest, like the Iberian, profoundly reshaped the national history. But where the latter encouraged a transhumant pastoralism, the former confirmed a migratory farming, the most spectacular display of swidden in recorded history. Each state, in response, imposed a peculiar absolutism.

Yet Moscow remained, at the core, the hearth of Russia. The great plaza at its center, later known as Red Square, the site of ritual processions that moved between Kremlin and cathedral, was popularly known as "the place of fire."[15]

(i)

When they scattered into the forests, the Slavic tribes carried a mixed farming economy with them. They were less committed than Germanic tribes to cattle, more prone to cereals and root crops. Their fields they supplemented with hunting, fishing, foraging, trapping, the gathering of herbs and medicinal plants, and in an age before refined sugar, the serious business of beekeeping. Still, they differed little from the agriculture of central Europe, and in fact had experienced it first. With uncanny fidelity the three apexes of Russian civilization—

Kiev, Novgorod, and Moscow—inscribe almost exactly the wedge of mixed forest that extends from temperate Europe eastward. Here the Russian land-nam resembled that practiced to the west.

But unlike the west, where clearing struck clearing and one agricultural people rammed against another, in ancient Rus' the prospects existed for expansion. Swidden bit like an ax into the great forest, scattering agricultural chips to all sides. Russian agriculture adapted to the forest steppe and then to the steppe proper, to the boreal forest and finally to the limitless taiga. Shifting cultivation prevailed over sedentary longer than in western Europe, and field rotations developed more by legal decree than economic logic. Only when serfs were bound to the land did two- and three-field rotations on the central European model become prominent. Even at the time of the October Revolution, they prevailed precisely in the mixed forest wedge.

The core practices were variants of swidden. They involved cutting, burning, planting, perhaps grazing, and fallowing. The longer the fallow the richer the crops. Woods were important because, until sod-busting plows became available, crops could not compete with deep-rooted steppe grasses unless the site was intensely burned. What Slavic tribes did carry away from the forest steppe were cereals—rye and barley especially—that were ideally suited for slashed and burned northern forests.

Somewhere around Novgorod, sometime around the eleventh century, while Kiev was yet in its prime, Novgorodians passed along this hybrid technology to their nonagricultural neighbors. The explosion of Savolax and Karelian tribes into Finland recapitulated on a small scale what the larger Russian tribes projected eastward. On the staggering immensity of the Eurasian plain there was ample room for expansion, and amid its numbing uniformity little need for further adaptations. A people on the move found a complex technology that not only aided but compelled their movement.

Still, their numbers were small, the process tedious and risky. It commenced with landnam, to which Russian pioneers gave many names. (Russian swidden was as generic and diverse as the Russian ax, sometimes specialized, more often locally adapted.) Advance parties led by specialists (*iskatel' novi,* seeker of new land) sought out and seized natural meadows and openings, higher sites spared early frost and late waterlogging, open to sunlight, typically flanked by a river. Preferred sites included alder or birch or a mixed forest, a likely sign of past fires and nitrogen-rich soils. Clearing proceeded by ringbarking and where necessary felling, taking pains to blanket the site with a uniform layer of fuels. Then the site dried, sometimes for months, sometimes for up to three years.[16]

The slash was fired in the spring on a warm, dry day with a breeze. The flames burned against the wind, where possible, thus spreading more slowly, consuming the fuels more thoroughly, allowing the burners to roll in additional material with long poles. If the first burn was incomplete, the residual fuels (and perhaps others) were refired, the notorious "black work." Another crop typically demanded another burn, searing off the black-humus sward and its weeds. A good burn required nothing more, only to sow the turnips, barley, flax, rye, wheat, oats, radish, or millet into the ash and harrow with brushwood or the crown of a dried spruce. One fantastic crop resulted; sometimes a second, lesser crop, was possible; rarely a third. The rhythm encoded itself in the name of months in the Old Slavic calendar: *sechen'*, the month of cutting; *berezozol'*, the month of burning.[17]

The Russian *zalezh'* (or *lvada*) thus corresponded to the Danish landnam and the Finnish *huuhta*. With it, natural cracks in the biota, the stress fractures of past disturbances including fires, became points of access by which to split and leverage the forest apart into large fragments and begin the arduous task of reconstruction. The forest was rebuilt into fields as its timbers were into forts and houses. The process was neither reckless nor random. Like Finnish colonizing, for which it had probably served as inspiration, the Russian *zalezh'* was a system that made possible other, less mobile systems. As it sailed east with the wind, swidden eddies swirled in its wake.

Agricultural burning flourished on the rich fallow that remained. Not for centuries—not in many places until recent decades—did farming transcend that forest fallow. In boreal or subboreal regions like much of ancient Rus', livestock were few, small, and difficult to maintain over the long winters; thus manure was limited (another argument for preferring the mixed forest wedge where leaf fodder could supplement hay). Domesticated bees, too, required the herbaceous- and shrub-rich landscapes of burned taiga. It is estimated that an apiary of 100 hives requires 5,000 hectares of such flora, a strong incentive to burn. So fire cultivation persisted. Its particular terminology and techniques derived from the characteristics of its sustaining landscape—whether forest or steppe, whether conifer or birch; on the cropping and landownership patterns within which it occurred; and on the length of its fallow. To know the fallow regime was to know the fire regime.[18]

Zalezh' applied to previously unbroken or long-abandoned lands. What came after it took many forms, of which two general variants persisted. In one, the farm cycled through the woods in classic swidden style. In the other, the fields remained permanent, and fallow rose and fell on them in prescribed sequence. Thus the first variation (*podseka*) resembled an infield-outfield agriculture or what in Finland had come to be called circulating *svedjebruk*. The second (*perelog*) was a version of field rotation. In nearly all regions these variations describe an evolution of stages, a movement, willed or imposed, toward more intensive cultivation.[19]

Fallowing was as intricate as other folk arts. In "unregulated" forms, a five to six year cropping cycle alternated with twenty to thirty years of fallow. In

Distribution

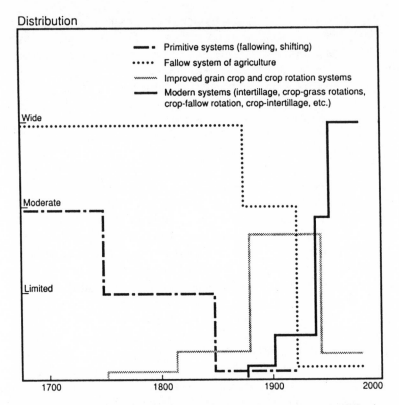

Russian fire-fallow farming. (Above) Historical developments among fallowing systems. Note their persistence until the advent of fossil fallow. (From Alayev et al. 1991, reprinted with the permission of Cambridge University Press) (Facing page) Geography of fallows, ca. 1900. Lower map shows that regions with long fallow remained prominent; top map shows the concentrations of shorter fallow. (Redrawn from Pallot and Shaw 1990)

more "regulated" forms, both cropping and fallow periods shortened, the latter often to as low as a nonsustainable three or four years. For several years after cropping ceased, the fallows would be grazed, another variant of the European outfield; in many landscapes, overgrown fields were the primary source of fodder. Where underbrush was the typical growth, it could be burned and its ashes spread over the field, a practice known as *kubysh*. Where grasslands were the norm, they too could be burned on either long or short rotation (*paly*). Where marshlands predominated, sod could be carried to the fields and burned, or burned in situ and the ashes brought to the waiting fields. By the eighteenth century, organic soils were pared and burned outright; Peter Pallas reported

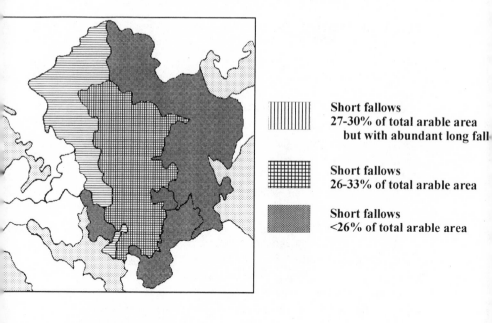

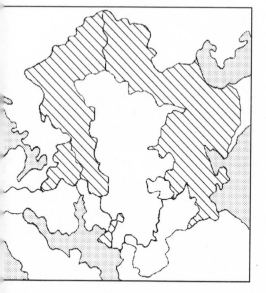

Short fallows
27-30% of total arable area
but with abundant long fall

Short fallows
26-33% of total arable area

Short fallows
<26% of total arable area

 Long fallows
>14% of total arable area

the practice from Yekaterinburg to Tyumen. In the boreal forest, there is little reason to believe that Russian swidden differed significantly from the Finnish.[20]

As in central Europe, demographic and economic pressures built up to shorten the time and abbreviate the extent of long-fallow fields. The short-fallow system followed the European precedents of the three-field rotation. It first stabilized shifting cultivation by assigning permanent status to pasture, meadow, and arable lands. A fixed land, however, required a fixed peasantry, and perhaps not coincidentally both the three-field system and serfdom become established in the sixteenth century.

They spread with the growth of Muscovy: they were, as in Europe, the agronomic paradigm. The system penetrated into the boreal forest with difficulty and into the steppes with various adaptations throughout the nineteenth century. While critics abounded—some hating any fallow, some believing that shortened fallow was a cause of degradation, and all of them dismayed by recurring famines—the system prevailed. By the turn of the century short fallow dominated agricultural landscapes in the mixed forest, the steppes, and much of the forest-steppe. But only in a few places did one system exclude the others; too often intensification meant degeneration; and almost everywhere outside the black-earth Ukraine, fallow flourished by design, necessity, or indifference. So, similarly, did that land burn from purpose, need, or accident.

By the beginning of the twentieth century the geography of Russian agriculture resembled a wedge pointing east, or rather a nested set of wedges, short fallows inside of long fallows resting inside of very long fallows. Short fallows typified the mixed forest and wooded steppe; long fallows, the periphery of boreal forest and steppe; *zalezh'*, the frontier. The closer they were to central Europe, the more Russian practices approximated European models. Short fallows belonged with organic fertilizers, intertillage crops like potatoes and maize, feed grasses, and pigs and cattle. Long fallow encouraged natural meadows or reburned fallow, preferred sheep to pigs, and left dung to be swept into rivers by spring floods. To the east the wedge narrowed; long and short fallows intermixed; and agriculture plowed along the contours of the forest-steppe. Beyond it *zalezh'* probed, tested, broke, softened, retreated, and otherwise assayed and readied the land for further settlement. Since fire follows fuels, Russia's fire regimes followed from its fallow regimes.[21]

Again, there were variants. The mixed forest enclave saw attempts to expand arable and pasture through swamp reclamation and more intensive cultivation, including sown grasses like clover and industrial crops like sugar beets. Commercial market gardens thrived outside Moscow and St. Petersburg, but often seemed as much a European import as the Academy of Sciences. Commercial cereal production, particularly in Ukraine, became possible with railroads and artificial fertilizers. And there were hybrids everywhere, the sign of an agriculture in transition.[22]

(ii)

The field was half the Russian hearth: the village was the other. For the most part Russians lived in and pioneered through collectivities—villages, monasteries, manors. Like their agriculture, their homes were constructed out of the forest, and like their adjacent forests and fields their built habitats were prone to fire. Houses, villages, and cities burned routinely. They burned, in fact, with almost the same regularity as their surrounding landscapes. Villages had their fire regimes. Wooden Rus' seemed to practice a kind of urban swidden.

There was no lack of ignition, or of kindling. All the sources of Russian fire were present, from lightning to torch. The Novgorod Chronicle records how lightning repeatedly struck the aspiring steeples of churches, and sent flames crashing through temple and town. What lightning missed, war and accident claimed.

The endless winters made perpetual fire in the home a matter of survival. Fire meant heat and light of course, but also warm tea, smoking tobacco, the flame before the icon, and the cleansing steam of the Russian sauna. A common practice was to relight the morning fire with the chimney closed (if there was a chimney) so that the cabin filled with suffocating smoke and heat, and only then to open the flue. "I conceived a hut that had been so well smoked every day," wrote Peter Dobell, an English counselor to the tsar's court, who struggled to explain this bizarre practice, "could not possibly afford a habitation for vermin."[23]

Until the advent of electricity there were open flames constantly in and around the house. The Abbé D'Auteroche noted the religious habit of burning unattended candles before icons: "Several fires happen from their carelessness in neglecting to change the lights before they are quite burnt out; by which the chapel, the saint, the cottage, and the whole village, are sometimes destroyed in a few hours. Such accidents are frequent, as this custom prevails all over Russia, even at the palace of the Empress." Even more hazardous were the fires required to dry harvested grain stored in barns. And around villages, farmers burned fallow fields and pastures every spring, swidden plots in midsummer, hunting grounds and berry patches as useful, and routes of travel annually; escapes were common. All this transpired within a built environment constructed out of wood, bark, thatch, turf, and chinking mosses.[24]

On the Eurasian plain, construction stone was difficult to locate and expensive to transport. But forests were everywhere, and the Scots pine, ramrod straight, its bole remarkably uniform from base to crown, was ideal for constructing cabins, stockades, cathedrals, and towns. It was easy to cut, simple to trim, and came in even-aged stands (the result of regeneration from past fires). Russians even paved their streets with planks and struggled to overcome spring bogs with corduroy roads of pine trunks. Lots between houses often bulged with firewood, lumber, and stacked logs. Like a kiln, incessant hearth fires drained house interiors of any moisture; drought did the same for the exterior. The outcome was as combustible as windfall, as volatile as thatch.

"It is estimated," George Wright explained in 1902, "that in Russia ten per cent of the houses are burnt every year." Until cities began to convert to stone and brick, there was probably less hyperbole to this figure than first seems likely. Admitting the value of a "dry and warm wood" as building material, Giles Fletcher in 1591 also observed their "greatest inconvenience," the "aptness for firing, which happeneth very oft and in fearful sort, by reason of the dryness and fatness of the fir, that being once fired, burneth like a torch, and is hardly quenched till all be burnt up." What Charles Scott observed traveling from the Baltic to the Crimea countless travelers echoed: "All Russian towns are frequently devastated by fire. In the course of our wanderings we scarcely ever entered a place free from signs of these sad visitations." Entering Kiachta a day or two after a fire, S. S. Hill noted that the fire had spread "with its accustomed rapidity whenever it breaks out in the Russian or Siberian towns," and that were it not for broad streets "scarce a village or two save the two capitals, where less inflammable materials are generally used for building, could survive twelve months." Partly rebuilt city blocks stood like burned taiga, desolate and melancholy.[25]

The only real solution required a change in construction materials, a revision in village design, a different, less fire-committed agriculture, and a less pyrotechnic domestic industry. That is, an environment other than forest, a society not crowded into wooden villages, a livelihood not dependent on swidden, grazing, hunting, foraging, fishing by firelight, and a source of power and heat not contingent on open combustion—in brief, a place other than Russia and a people other than Slavs. Instead village Russians—and this included almost all Russians—had to live with fire's hazards as the price of exploiting its powers. To survive they had to adapt.

"Loss of life and property from the effects of fire in Siberia," Hill noted, "are among the more frequent of the calamities which the people experience." A. S. Rappoport, soured by beggars endlessly pleading that their house had burned down, concluded that "perhaps in no other country so much cheating and swindling goes on, under the name of *fire,* as in Russia." Surely such routine calamities help account for the famous fatalism of the Russian peasantry toward fire. Until they "cease to view fire as a visitation from God which one must not go against," lamented M. K. Isaev in 1894, "until then fires will dispossess Orthodox Rus'." Isabel Hapgood related how lightning had kindled a fire on Saint Elias's Day, "so no earthly power could quench it but the milk from a jet-black cow, which no one chanced to have on hand." Instead an old woman grabbed her icon ("Virgin-of-the-Bush-that-burned-but-was-not-consumed"), faced the spreading flames, and uttered the proper prayer. "Immediately a strong wind arose and drove the flames off in a safe direction, and the village was saved."[26]

But peasant and villager were not prostrate. If they could not fight fire, they knew how to rebuild from it. Georg Brandes observed how well suited a liberated Russian peasantry was to colonize: "They can build new houses (*izbas*) for themselves in a few days anywhere." Brandes continued that "from a fear of fire, which in Russia, on account of the droughts and the construction of the houses, is more frequent than in other countries, the peasant never ornaments his *izba*. The new house contains everything which was contained in the old." It contained the enduring fire, too, which the peasant carried from old hearth to new, as he did to the landscape. Just as the new soil, wrung by cutting and burning, brought forth "as good a harvest as the old," so could the new house, or the new village. The log house was, in part, as much an adaptation to fire as was the forest from which it came. The village fire became a set piece of Russian literature, from Anton Chekhov's "Peasants" to Valentin Rasputin's *Siberia on Fire.*[27]

But even the larger cities burned. The story that Henry Lansdell told about the 1879 fire in Irkutsk was a scenario for virtually every wooden town—which is to say, virtually every Russian town—from the Gulf of Riga to the Sea of Okhotsk.

The fire savaged three-fourths of Irkutsk. It was July 7, and Lansdell's party "did not proceed far before we saw where fire had destroyed two blocks of buildings, the embers of which were still smoking." But he was neither worried nor surprised, since "it was only similar to what we had seen at Perm and Tagil." They checked into their hotel only to have another alarm sound, this one warning of a fire "not a dozen houses off." Wooden houses "of course" offered a spectacle, Lansdell thought, "much grander than that of flames coming through the windows of a brick structure, and the heat much more intense." In Irkutsk a fully involved structure threw enough radiant heat to ignite a building across the street. By now the city knew panic. "Men were running from all directions, not with the idle curiosity of a London crowd at a fire, but with the blanched faces and fear-stricken countenances of those who knew that the devastation might reach to them."[28]

Lansdell's party retired to the Angara River and crossed on a ferry. Meanwhile the fire spread. Later, his party returned, and met at the ferry a stream of refugees, "fleeing from the city, and carrying with them what was most valuable or most dear—an old woman tottering under a heavy load of valuable furs piled on her head; a poor half-blind nun, hugging an ikon, evidently the most precious of her possessions; a delicate young lady in tears, with her kitten in her arms; and boys tugging along that first requisite of a Russian home, the brazen *samovar.*" Terror lined every face. Residents struggled to salvage whatever they could. Crowds gathered, stores opened their shelves as the flames bore down and were stripped clean of exotic fruit tins, bonbons, and "huge family bottles of rye-brandy."

The fire "had everything in its favor." Attempts at control were ludicrous. The surest approach was to tear down buildings in the path of the flames, although wind-driven sparks could leap those barriers. Irkutsk mustered its fire brigade—"there were some English engines in the town," Landsdell noted approvingly—but the brigade had not drilled, there was no one in command, and although the Angara flowed around the city, there was no mechanism for delivering water from it to the engines except "in large barrels on wheels." (Less favorably sited, Kiachta was once saved from fire when "a train of camels laden with water" arrived in sufficient quantity to stay the flames.) The conviction swept the townspeople that nothing could be done. As evening approached, the line of fire strung a mile and a half long. "It seemed as if nothing could escape. Now one large building caught, and then another, the churches not excepted." Bells pealed out alarms, residents fled by the thousands, and toward midnight "the town presented a marvellous spectacle." Within twenty-four hours three-fourths of Irkutsk lay in ashes. The one exception was a small chapel in the city center, a "miraculous" occurrence and "so telegraphed to Petersburg." But the less credulous Reverend Lansdell observed that the sanctuary was made of brick, as were the structures adjacent to it, and he attributed to that fact— not divine intervention—its conspicuous survival.[29]

Nor were the metropoles spared. Between them Moscow and St. Petersburg held a third of the urban population of Russia, but fires struck as regularly as elsewhere. Drought, common wildland fuels, and endless sources of ignition brought town and country into synchronization.

Moscow's fire-return frequency eerily approximated that of its surrounding forest, with stand-replacing (district-devastating) fires roughly two or three times a century and lesser fires probably every ten to twenty years. Thus in the course of one century Moscow suffered major fires in 1571, 1611, 1626, and 1671. In 1688 every ruble in the Treasury went to rebuild Moscow after yet another burn. "In truth," Adolph Erman wrote in 1848, "conflagrations were common occurrences in the history of the city." The chronicles recorded at least seven "total destructions by fire, the most of them the work of victorious enemies." Thus it is understandable that "national historians" regard the conflagration during the French invasion, so monumental in the minds of Europeans, "not as the critical event of a remarkable campaign, but as an incidental affair of subordinate consequences." The city rebuilt, this time with a higher proportion of stone structures.[30]

Real protection required that the cities be other than what they were: constructed of other materials, built according to other designs, located in other climes. Unable to prevent fires officials sought to contain them. There were patrols organized through the police, and a system of towers, some in church steeples, to look for smoke. "Both in Petersburg and Moscow," Charles Scott reported, "we saw these solitary guardians, constantly on the alert, moving on their little spaces, with the restlessness and watchfulness of a wild beast in a cage."[31]

So precious was St. Petersburg to Peter the Great—"having cost the Czar such immense sums and his heart being so much set on the preservation of that place"—that he assigned to "all his Officers Military and Civil of all Degrees" special fire jobs and paid a special allowance. When the alarm sounded, drummers propagated the warning, officers rushed to their task, soldiers mustered, and "carpenters boys" hurried to the site clutching the axes and tools with which to carve out firebreaks. Often Peter led personally, and it was "a common thing" to see the Emperor of All-Russia "among the workmen with a hatchet in his hand, climbing to the top of the houses that are all in flames, with such danger to him that the spectators tremble at the sight of it."[32]

When the tsar was present, the fire was fought vigorously and intelligently. For all their frequency, fires rarely burned more than half a dozen structures. But "when the sovereign is absent," observed the Dane Just Juel, "things are very different. Then the people watch the fires with indifference and do nothing to help extinguish them. It is vain to lecture them or even offer them money; they merely wait for a chance to steal something." Others observed either lethargy or a useless bustle. Henry Morley chastised the police, pondering if their exclusive powers were perhaps "the reason that fires here never are put out, but are allowed to burn themselves out."[33]

If such breakdowns occurred in cities, so much less effective were village measures. Commands for villagers to keep barrels of water on rooftops and horses in readiness always seemed to find, "by some fatal coincidence, the barrels were always empty and the horses no where when needed." In all likelihood, the synchronization between wildland and village fires was probably very close in Siberia. Villagers fought fires in towns as they did in fields and forests. As with swidden, what fires destroyed they also renewed. The one compensation was that, in town as in country, regrowth followed fire.[34]

(iii)

Perhaps it was precisely this understanding that led to one of the most distinctive of Russian fire practices, the scorched earth. Chroniclers had identified it, particularly in the steppes, from the earliest times. Certainly Russians had no monopoly on military fire: victors burned and losers lamented. But it was a different matter to burn one's own land, to lay waste villages and fields in advance of an enemy. Yet this is precisely what Russia has done over the centuries. Russians shielded their Muscovy hearth with a protective ring of fire. They protected the Motherland as they did their villages, by a screen of prophylactic fire. If that failed, they resorted to the purgative fire.

Probably the practice evolved from centuries of warfare along the forest-steppe border. That biotic border was no more fixed than the region's cultural frontiers. Rather, it advanced and retreated according to climatic pressures, cultivation practices, and above all fire. The Eurasian steppes most likely belong with those other vast grasslands, from the African veld to the Brazilian *cerrado* to the North American tallgrass prairie, that were either created or sustained (or both) by anthropogenic burning. Without fire trees spontaneously reclaimed the landscape. But there was ample fire, and no need to wait for the arbitrary ignitions of lightning. Hunters, herders, warriors—all burned the land. The ancient chronicles spoke frequently of the steppes as "seas of flame."[35]

The steppes were indelibly linked with the mounted warrior. Probably in the Pontic steppes early Indo-Europeans first domesticated the horse. For herders of horses, cattle, and sheep the fired grasslands became an immense pasture. They also became a corridor for invasion across the underbelly of Eurasia, its grasses like a hemp rope lashing Europe to Asia. Across the steppes mounted armies could feed off the land; they needed only grass to maintain their momentum. Time and again the steppes became a grassy fuse that let nomadic hordes and migrating tribes detonate against sedentary Europe. Slavs regrouped in the dark forest, shielded by marshes, spring morass, ice-chocked streams, until the Mongol invasion temporarily shattered even these barriers. To that hostile frontier between forest and steppe both Russian and Tatar applied fire.

What mattered was timing. Invading hosts needed fresh grass, precisely what spring fires could furnish. But regrowth required several weeks, and its rate depended on soil moisture, weather, and various site conditions. In the absence of a systematic burn, the great hosts were forced to feed off older, less nutritious grasses and became vulnerable to wildfires that could race through the remaining dead stalks. But a fire too close to their arrival stripped the landscape of fodder in all directions. With nothing to feed their horses—baggage trains of hay were impossible—the army would have to leap over the burns or retreat. A fire that coincided with their arrival could, wind permitting, break their ranks as well. In this way whoever controlled the torch often controlled the battlefield.

Steadily, the Russian reconquest shut off corridors that allowed Tatar cavalry to move north. Soldier-colonists fenced the border with an abatis of felled trees and wooden stakes, a kind of forced afforestation. And they fired the grasses on notice of imminent invasion. After the 1571 Tatar incursion to Moscow, Prince Michael Vorotynski, on orders from the tsar, fired the steppes after the first frosts, with a strong dry wind blowing from the north, and Cossack villagers burned an immense area from the sources of the Vorona to the Dniester and Desna Rivers. As the frontier stabilized, however, it was not enough to have fires sweep in and out like flaming tides. Against the steppe's annual "sea of flame" the Russians built a breakwall. But when the time came for the Russians to advance onto the steppe, those same tactics could be turned against them. Time and again Russian incursions foundered on their inability to control the burning of the steppes.[36]

Perhaps the most infamous episode occurred in 1687. In May, Prince Vasily Golitsyn directed an army of 100,000 men south against the Crimean Tatars. The Tatars retired before them. Then, on June 13, smoke rose from the steppe and, driven by southerly winds, bore down on the Russian encampment north of Perekop. The flames wrecked havoc, and what was worse, denied to the Russians the fodder their horses required. (Rumors circulated that the Cossack hetman Samoilovich had ordered the fires after a quarrel with *streltsi* officers.) Regardless, the Russian host plunged south over an ever-blackened horizon. Eventually, it retreated, having lost 45,000 men and having never engaged the Tatars except through their proxy fires. When he mounted a new expedition in 1689, Golitsyn sent skirmishers well ahead to burn the steppes to the Russians' advantage.[37]

Eventually the strategy was applied to the forest and its converted fields, and even, when necessary, to its towns. Here the implacable isolation of Muscovy worked to its advantage. Invading armies had to trek overland for 800 to 1,600 poorly roaded kilometers to reach the Kremlin, far beyond the capabilities of ox-drawn baggage trains. In the winter the landscape was frozen, secluded from foraging; in the spring, it was a mire. Only in the summer did it offer food for horse and human, and this a determined defender could commit to fire.

Over and over the Russians have done precisely this. The agents of incendiarism were often Cossacks or Kalmyks, transported from the steppes. Against Charles XII, the army of Peter the Great fired swaths 190 kilometers wide. Against Napoleon's Grande Armée, Alexander I did the same. Against Nazi Germany, Stalin repeated the classic scorched earth practices, denying shelter and sustenance to the Wehrmacht. In his 1945 text *Forest Fire Control,* the doyen of Russian fire science, M. G. Nesterov, included a chapter on the use and extinction of "forest and field fires under war conditions." The chapter is unique in forestry literature.[38]

Certainly the most celebrated incident is the 1812 burning of Moscow. Even as Napoleon entered the city on the evening of September 14, rumors circulated about preparations for fires. Around midnight a "fire-balloon" alighted on the palace of Prince Trubetskoy. This, Count de Ségur, the quartermaster, concluded, "was a signal." At 2 A.M. a fire broke out in the exchange. Incendiarists wandered the streets with tarred lances, so "intoxicated with wine and the success of their crimes" that they burned openly, and "it was necessary to strike down their hands with sabres to oblige them to loose their hold." Drunken French, intent on looting, may have assisted the first fires, or contributed by negligence to their spread. Officers issued orders to shoot incendiaries on sight. Despite aggressive efforts, the fires still burned and by their light Napoleon finished dictating the terms of a proposed peace to Tsar Alexander. The fires were suppressed, and the offered treaty rejected.[39]

At midnight of the next day, more fires appeared. These had a strong north wind behind them that drove the flames directly at the Kremlin, where Napoleon and his army resided. A sudden wind shift to the west carried the flames away. But twice more new fires appeared, each cluster set so the inconstant wind might carry it to the walls and beyond. If their direction of spread was uncertain, their intensity was not. Wind and wood soon whipped minor fires into conflagrating whitecaps. Sparks rained down on the Kremlin. Sweepers stationed on the iron roofs were "not sufficient to keep them clear of the numerous flakes of fire" that drizzled down upon them. Napoleon watched as the conquest, "for which he had sacrificed every thing," vanished in a "mingled mass of smoke and flame."[40]

The fires raged for many days. Already the besieger had become the besieged, the conqueror saw the devouring flames consume his conquest. Eventually fire reached the Kremlin. What Napoleon had claimed by the sword, he lost to fire. "It was evident," de Ségur concluded, "that every thing was devoted to destruction, the ancient and sacred Kremlin itself not excepted." The Russian hearth had again become the place of fire. The purgative fires to which the Old Believers had committed themselves consumed a city. Napoleon fled the Kremlin, and then Moscow, and finally, disastrously, Russia.[41]

For years the wreckage remained. Visitors reckoned that the fires had devastated between two-thirds and four-fifths of the city, a ruin so thorough "as to render it difficult to recognize the lines of the various streets." Most of the surviving structures were stone or brick, many of them churches whose symbolic flames remained fixed on their onion-domed steeples. Moscow was, so European observers unanimously concluded, a "complete desert."[42]

But Russians, for all their suffering, saw the fire differently. The purgative fire was an old theme in Russian folklore and life. Fires kept wolves and bears at bay, drove off locusts, smoked away clouds of mosquitoes, thinned the habi-

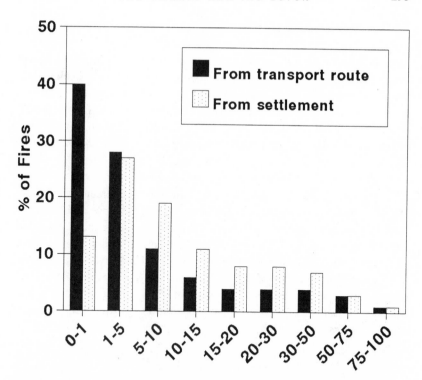

Lines of fire: the geography of corridor burning. Occupied zones were routinely fired in the spring, but kindling falls off rapidly away from settlements and thoroughfares. This pattern laid down a matrix of anthropogenic fire within which lightning had to operate. X-axis units in kilometers. (Data from Korovin 1996)

tats beloved by ticks, fumigated cattle against plagues, purified slashed forest into healthy field, and cleansed away an oppressive winter. They could, and repeatedly did, drive off invaders. Annually Russian peasants fired around their villages in the spring, reclaiming dormant land, stimulating fresh growth. Annually they rekindled fire ceremonies to purge evil spirits, personified in witch effigies, and to replace them with fertilizing powers. Russians preserved folk fire ceremonies like Ivan Kupalo (Saint John's Day fire) long after most western Europeans had sublimated them into pure symbol or relegated them to antiquarian curiosity. In wooden Rus' they survived.

In wooden Rus' they and the fire practices that they mimicked took on a more literal meaning. In ways that made the rest of Europe shudder and left intellectuals dumbfounded with disbelief, Russia, purged by fire, found itself renewed. The burned town, like the burned taiga, regrew.

LINES OF FIRE, FIELDS OF FIRE

From the Muscovy hearth Russian fire propagated outward. To the west it burned as against a wind, backing slowly, sometimes blowing out, stubborn but unable generally to cross Europe's firebreaks. To the south it met counterfires, and not until those preemptive burns were removed did the Russian flame spread, and then rapidly. But to the east, across the Eurasian plain, it ran with the prevailing winds, leaping over the Urals, ripping over steppes and taiga across Siberia, to Kamchatka, to Alaska, to Fort Ross, California.

Along divers lines of fire—rivers, tracks, and later railroads—Russia inscribed a new matrix of burning. Fire loads increased, fire frequencies quickened. New orders of burning mapped out novel fire geographies, and promoted a shift in species composition to favor the more aggressive pioneers of disturbed sites such as birch. The natives of Kamchatka, frightened by Russian weaponry, called the newcomers the "fire people." The Buryats believed that the Russian conquest was foretold in a shaman's vision in which a great fire destroyed the coniferous forest and replaced it with birch. So would the white Russians replace the dark Mongols. It was a prophesy written in the taiga's ecology no less than in folklore and imperial chronicles.[43]

(i)

The Russians did not advance into empty land. Pondering the Russian Empire from the nineteenth century, Baron von Haxthausen considered it an intermediary between two great throngs of nomads, one of the forest, the other of the steppe. And in fact the Russians thrived in the forest-steppe fringe, ideally suited to their mixed agricultural economy, and tracked it through Eurasia like a prospector tracing a vein of gold. In general, von Haxthausen's distinction holds. But the history of both "nomads" was as dynamic as their economy.[44]

Steppe peoples, in particular, could span vast distances. Conquering hordes snowballed by absorbing rather than exterminating conquered peoples. Time and again steppe pastoralists probed into the taiga, influencing the peoples with whom they came into contact, upsetting political geographies, prompting migrations that set off chain reactions, even transplanting themselves en masse, as the Yakuts did, into the cold core of Siberia. Long before the Russian reconquest they had reshaped the landscapes of Eurasia.[45]

The steppe tribes were the most similar in their domestic fire habits and the most formidable in their landscape burning. The grasslands were literally a field of fire: to start and stop fire was to control the cycle of growth and the movement of herds, including the itineraries of mounted hosts. Journeying from St. Petersburg to Peking in the early eighteenth century, John Bell recorded how a prince of the Kalmyks, the Kontaysha, defeated a numerically superior Chinese army sent to punish him. He waited until the Chinese were exhausted by long travel and heavy baggage trains, and then "sent out detachments of light horse to set fire to the grass, and lay waste the country," and otherwise harass the invaders. While the Chinese starved, the Tatars, "having always many spare horses to kill and eat," suffered little. "This method of carrying on war, by wasting the country," Bell observed, "is very ancient among the Tartars, and practised by all of them from the Danube eastward."[46]

But burning was a normal, and necessary, practice of steppe economy. Along the Russian-Chinese border Bell described how "this grass is often set on fire, by the Mongalls, in the spring, during high winds," for the purpose of procuring "early pasture for their cattle." The ashes sink into the melting snow, rendering "an excellent manure," so that the grass on such lands rises "as thick as a field of wheat." What they did not deliberately torch, an enemy or lightning would. Regardless of origin, the fiery spectacle was full of awful sublimity.

> At such times it burns, most furiously, running like wild-fire, and spreading its flames to the distance of perhaps ten or twenty miles, till its progress is interrupted by some river or barren hill. The impetuosity of these flames, their smoke and crackling noise, cannot easily be conceived by those who have not seen them.

Clearly such conflagrations were dangerous. For this reason "caravans, travellers with merchandise, but especially armies, never encamp upon this rank grass." Should someone find himself facing such fires, "the only method, by which he can save himself from their fury," Bell concluded, "is to kindle immediately the grass where he stands, and follow his own fire. For this purpose, every person is provided with flints, steel, and tinder." Twice Bell's expedition found itself threatened, surviving once by racing toward a rocky refuge, and the other time by reaching a hill, setting fire to the grass, and traveling "near a mile in a dismal cloud of smoke." Other members of the scattered party, "unprovided with flints," failed to start counterfires and "were put to hard shifts, having their hair and cloaths all singed." The best protection against hostile fire was controlled fire.[47]

Fire was no less central to domestic economy. It claimed the center of the yurt, which served to conserve and amplify fire's heat, light, and purifying force. Friar John of Plano Carpini who visited the Great Khan in the thirteenth century reported that the Mongols "believe, to put it shortly, that everything is purified by fire." Whoever appeared before the khan—"envoys or princes or any persons whatsoever"—were obliged "to pass between two fires, together with the gifts they are bringing, in order to be purified, lest perchance they have practised sorcery or brought poison or anything else injurious." When Grand

Duke Michael paid homage to Batu, he had to pass between the fires, not unlike the way Russian peasants, fearful of plague and witchcraft, ritually drove livestock between flame and smoke. The purifying fire extended to the bones of animals sacrificed to cure sickness, to the relatives of the recently deceased, to anyone near someone killed by lightning. Many eastern tribes adopted cremation to that same purpose. European travelers reported that the steppe tribes worshiped fire as they did the sun, moon, and water.[48]

Their fire practices they carried with them, no less than their yurts and herds of sheep, cattle, horses, and camels. Not only could fire renew pasture, it could extend it. In dry years spring burns did not halt at the forests' shaded snow line but propagated inward. Repeated burnings reached into the taiga like grasping fingers. Before the fires of spring, the dark woods melted away, leaving pools of new pasture. Corridors of travel widened; taiga thinned into forest steppes and forest savannas into prairies. As steppe tribes pushed outward, the land passed between their flames.

Probably much of the Ukrainian steppe was anthropogenic. The Hungarian Plain is almost certainly a creation of anthropogenic fire and grazing. Under the Turks, the Anatolian plains became more thoroughly grasslands and deforestation for military purposes became pervasive throughout the Balkans. Strips of grassland punched northward like knife thrusts across western and central Siberia. East of Baikal, Buryat fires fingered northward through wide valleys. Between the twelfth and fourteenth centuries the Yakuts broke out of Mongolia into the valleys of the Lena and brought their horses, cattle, and fires with them. In the Far East, mounted Manchus did the work. Even in the 1860s, Arthur Adams was struck by the "prodigious number of those charred and blackened trees that strew the ground in every direction," the outcome of "wandering shooting and fishing parties of Manchu tartars, who always fire the scrub and burn down the trees, to clear the land and make it yield good pasturage."[49]

No less incisive were the Tungus who transplanted steppe pastoralism to the taiga through the domestication of reindeer. From a Manchurian hearth the Tungus spread throughout Siberia and the Far East, repelled only by the stubborn Yakuts and the Chukchi on the forbidding tundras of the Anadyr Peninsula. Unlike the Lapps who exploited reindeer primarily as draft animals to pull sleds, Tungus tribes treated them like steppe livestock, devising pack frames like those on camels, mounting them like horses, milking them like mares and cows, and butchering them for meat or hides like sheep. And like those steppe herds they imitated, reindeer required burning.

The Tungus were, John Bell assured his readers, "Never at a loss for fire." If the preferred steel-and-flint tinderbox faltered, they kindled fire by rubbing wood. Nor were the Tungus or their alter ego, reindeer, ever far from fire, or its alter ego, smoke. To banish Siberia's infinite legions of mosquitoes, Tungus "light fires all around the place of their abode," Bell observed. They burned special moss in their hearths, carried smoking pots on their travels and even in their canoes, and fashioned special frames to house field fires for reindeer. The ethnographer Ellen Lindgren recorded that as much work "as possible is done in a dense smoke; and later, during our weeks in the taiga, we learned to eat and write up the day's notes standing directly over slow fires banked with grass." Their reindeer joined them, and so did the ethnographer's horse. In fact, a smudge fire attracted and held reindeer like a trap. (Even Cossacks refused to enter the taiga during early summer because of its mosquitoes.) When a clan moved its camp, men went ahead to cut poles for the new tipis and to "start fires." They used fire to spear fish at night. In the autumn they often burned grassy patches, hoping to attract game to those sites in the spring flush. Where they adopted some rudiments of agriculture, they practiced slash and burn, preparing the forest by ringbarking. Objects obtained from Russians or Chinese were always passed through the purgative smoke as though they were, like mosquitoes, so much vermin.[50]

But the reindeer was fundamental, and on the model of the Central Asian pastoralists who had inspired them, the Tungus burned to improve forage. The Evenki, a Tungus tribe, fired lowlands to promote especially a particular bog sedge (*Eriophorum Scheuchzeri hoppe*). Reindeer could survive a winter on lichens, but to thrive they needed a variety of fodder, especially in the spring. Accordingly the Tungus burned for their taiga herds as their ancestors had for steppe herds. In the 1990s the chronicle of that practice was still evident in the northern Khabarovsk region. Exploratory parties noted a high frequency of past fires that had shaped especially the lowland forests and even bared the upper mountains. Nor did the practice cease with the Russian conquest. Cossacks seized the torch and applied it to the same sites for their own purposes and their own preferred livestock.[51]

All of these incursions from the steppes adumbrated on other peoples, and still older peoples, dedicated exclusively to hunting, fishing, and foraging. There were Finno-Ugric tribes to the west, like the Mansi, Khanty, and Komi, the more Eurasian of the Finnish tribes that had merged with the expanding Slavs or spun off into Finland. Samoyed peoples dispersed throughout the trans-Urals; the Yukaghir and Chukchi roamed over vast Siberian landscapes. There were small tribes in Kamchatka, the Ainu in the Kurils, the Gilyaks on Sakhalin, and scores of clans and confederations crowding the borders of the steppes. It is estimated that Siberia may have hosted 120 languages.

But the expansion of Tungus, Yakuts, Buryats, and of course Cossacks and Russians broke those dominions, scattered their societies, and propelled the fragments into long treks. The strategy of Russian imperialism sought tribute, not land per se, and needed natives to harvest the furs with which to pay the mandatory *yasak*. Assimilation, forced or otherwise, was a common outcome. Inevitably, perhaps, diseases, war, and social and ecological disruption plunged native demographics into a recession from which the smallest clans never recovered. Scores of hearth fires went cold. In the process some aboriginal fire practices were transferred, and some were superseded. Many simply vanished.

Those practices are not known in any detail. Without agricultural fulcrums it was probably difficult to move much taiga. Many tribes probably foraged among the abundant burns kindled annually by lightning. They added their own fires as needed, burning in preferred hunting sites, stimulating berries and mushrooms, driving off noxious insects, clearing away windfall, warding off bears, wolves, and tigers. If the Cree of boreal Canada are analogous, then the aboriginal Siberians fired open grasslands and marshes; burned along thoroughfares of seasonal travel; and delicately fired along prospective trap lines. The fresh forbs and grasses that sprang up attracted small rodents, and on them fed the sable, fox, lynx, and wolverine prized for fur. Possibly large patches were burned to yield future firewood or to temporarily purge a scene of insects.[52]

Cossack exploratory parties encountered smoke almost everywhere, and fires of unknown origins frequently interrupted their progress. Forest, not riverine, tribes like the Udege and Evenki hunted browsers and forest rooters like deer, moose, squirrel, and boar: all fed on the grasses, shrubs, or mast of regularly burned woodlands or marshes. Many valley grasslands and oak-pine savannas encountered by first-contact Russians in the Far East, for example, were most likely the product of aboriginal fire. Contact itself was frequently an occasion for aggressive burning. The Evenki, it is reported, would burn forests to cover their retreat. As late as 1932, in retaliation for being dispossessed from ancestral lands, Evenki kindled savage fires around the new village of Komsomolsk. Sixty years later the land for 50 kilometers around remained treeless.[53]

The cumulative impact of all this aboriginal burning is uncertain. Probably it etched the taiga like bas reliefs chistled into cliffs, rather than quarrying it out for reconstruction, as agricultural burning did. Still, fire-wielding aborigines altered fire regimes, and when droughts multiplied fire's power to propagate, their small broadcast burns, their escaped campfires, smudge fires, and signal fires, and the cleansing fires they laid down around encampments could ramble through the taiga in earth-shattering roars. They knew only too intimately the terrible, implacable, necessary power of fire.

It is no surprise to learn that fire was sacred. The Ainu worshiped a fire goddess. The Yukaghir identified a spiritual Owner (or Man) of the Fire as the guardian of hearth and family. The Gilyaks nurtured the hearth fire as the symbol of the clan. When the group divided, they split the common fire, and protested any effort to loan that fire to someone outside the clan. The Koryaks maintained as sacred its fire-starting implements. Everywhere shamans stared into the flames for pyromantic inspiration. Universally fire and smoke purified, purging evil and sickness and readying the alien for acceptance into the hearth-defining clan. Altai tribes circulated the story of how fire would recycle the world:

> *Then the black earth bursts into flame . . .*
> *The earth now takes fire.*
> *In this way the end of the world will some day come about.*

All too soon, that legend became reality.[54]

(ii)

The taiga offered lines of fire, the steppes a field of fire. Taiga could burn routinely only where fine fuels like grasses flourished, and these were the sites most regularly fired and most eagerly sought after. Whether the forest proper, particularly its crowns, burned depended on complex formulas of fuel structure, growth, drought, and wind. But the grassy steppe could burn every year. It could even burn twice in one year, once in the spring and again in the fall. Only where the land was heavily grazed or converted to fields could fire slow or assume new, more domesticated forms. The Russian advance south was a colossal firebreak. Behind it, fire was subjected to the rhythms of the cultivated field, like a warhorse harnessed to the plow. Before it, free-burning fire roamed like mounted hosts of Cossacks and Tatars.[55]

For centuries the forest-steppe was a military as well as biotic frontier. In the sixteenth century, Muscovy constructed continuous lines of fortifications that blocked the main routes of Tatar incursion. The defenses were wooden, and the adjacent forest was preserved as a natural barrier. Settlers filled the protected lands. Then tsarist Russia pushed south, and founded new outposts along major routes and at strategic river fords. The fortifications attracted new settlers, leading to the need for further defense, which, beginning in 1637, evolved into the famous Belgorod line. Before it, a mobile shield, ranged Russian and Ukrainian Cossack regiments, the latter in exodus from Lithuania and Poland. In fact, the frontier (*Ukraine,* in Russian) gave its name to the whole region. To the east, the fortifications steadily extended Russian colonization along the steppe frontiers of central Asia, from the Simbirsk line to the Altai Mountains. Collectively they constituted Russia's Great Wall against steppe nomads.[56]

Behind that border, agriculture was classically Russian; but beyond it ranged a medley as great as a Cossack host. Whether the colonizing farms resided in forest, forest-steppe, or grasslands, swidden or long fallow-field systems prevailed. Fallowed sites in turn became centers for livestock grazing, and these were often extensive. Previously the pastoral economy had cultivated some arable, and field agriculture had encouraged animal husbandry; but along the frontier they often remained opposing systems, glaring across an agronomic Belgorod line, rather than mingling toward a new synthesis. Even in farmed areas, infield and outfield were poorly linked. The pattern was more mediterranean than temperate. South and east the conditions worsened. Droughts increased in frequency toward the Pontic steppes. Around the Caspian, westerly and northerly winds could swirl, dry, and thunder back toward the more humid steppes as the dreaded *sukhovei*. The Crimea's climate was mediterranean.[57]

Agriculture mimicked settlement. It was purer toward the mixed forest core, and more scrambled toward the periphery. The proportion of field to pasture decreased with the distance of newer settlements from older and as continentality imposed a hotter and drier climate. It increased as military pressure pacified the steppe tribes, absorbed the Cossacks, and permitted the transfer of manorial estates and state peasantry with all the apparatus of serfdom from the core to the perimeter. Intensification, like westernization, required an act of political will and the power of autocracy. Until then mobility remained high—the movement of fields, of swidden plots, of pastoralists, of peoples drawn or driven to the frontier.

"The boundless extent of virgin soil," as European travelers endlessly marveled, meant that the pioneer "need not worry about those rules of husbandry which we consider indispensable in Western Europe." Expansion was easier than evolution. In black-earth regions the peasantry was so indifferent to fertilization that they left manure to be swept away in spring floods. A disbelieving Briton, Robert Bremner, noted the sumptuous grasses, observed the feckless Ukrainians throwing their manure "into the rivers," and exclaimed how they then "must set fire to the fields in order to get rid of the surplus!" Having cropped one site, the "horde moves to some other district." He echoed A. Swinton, who in 1790 observed that the surplus fallow was "trodden under foot, or set on fire, by vagrant hordes, or by indolent husbandmen." The exhaustion of one field led to the creation of a new one, the filling of one region to the opening of another. The agronomic logic of swidden worked against the logic of autocracy like the paired blades of a scissors. Together they cut across the southern border.[58]

The steppes were a true fire frontier, in all its stages. Russian explorers frequently encountered wildfires. Peter Pallas found his scientific expedition "frustrated," for a "general conflagration of the steppe had devastated its surface and rendered it impossible for us to procure food for our horses." Later, fires sweeping the Kuma steppe forced his party to "escape at full gallop." Armies marched between fires and counterfires; from their fortified entrenchments, Russians sent flames racing southward, hoping to ward off assaults by steppe tribes during the critical early spring. Abbé D'Auteroche watched his Tatar and Cossack guides "set fire at certain distances to the fir-trees they met with on the road," illuminating the path and chronicling their trek with "a remarkable and curious" set of "fire-works." Pastoralists danced to the beat of steppe fires, set "sometimes by accident, and sometimes on purpose" and sometimes "on all the Points of the Compass," as John Perry wrote in 1716. Preferably kindled "as soon as the Snow is off the Ground," these immense conflagrations —thirty to sixty kilometers long—"may be seen at a great Distance when the Flames are reflected on the Clouds in a dark Night, and in a Cloud of Smoak in the Day." Farmers slashed and burned, and then fired fallow until it could be slashed properly again. They fertilized with ashes, not manure, and purged with flame, not plow. Surplus grass they burned rather than cut; straw left from field threshings they piled and fired when they had "some free time" and then tossed the ashes onto the fields. Even the new towns hugged the high ground on the east bank of rivers, not only to enhance fortification and avoid floods but to escape the fires that the prevailing westerlies would annually drive to the riverfront.[59]

The frontier glowed, a saga whose biotic manuscript was illuminated with vignettes of fire. "As darkness came on," observed M. P. Price, trekking into central Asia, "the grass fires, like little glowing lines on the hills beyond, denoted the presence of Russian colonies, where the peasants were burning the grass of the previous year. The glowing lines advanced, retreated, expanded, dwindled and grew again as the wind blew them hither and thither. They acted like beacon lights which led us on to the next Russian village."[60]

(iii)

The scale of Russian fire dwarfed its western European analogues. The steppes mocked pastoral cognates like Iberia's *meseta* or the Hungarian plain. The taiga relegated even boreal Europe to the status of miniatures. Here, across the largest contiguous forest on Earth, Russia did not expand trench by trench, like siege lines advancing on a Crimean encampment, but exploded in wild rushes. If Ukraine burned with the steady sweep of a grass fire, Siberia burned with the spotty torchings and violent eruptions of a conifer crown fire. European Russia was as large as the rest of Europe. At its maximum, the Soviet Union was as large as South America; its dimensions exceeded those of three continents. The saga of Russian fire moved east. In 1915, western Siberian fires spewed forth a smoke cloud the size of Europe.

The first Russian spark to reach Siberia's tinder was Yermak's expedition of Cossacks through the central Urals in 1581. The breakup of the Golden Horde had littered smaller khanates on both sides of the Urals, and one of these, Sibir',

Yermak invaded with a band of perhaps 1,600 men. Although he failed to depose the khan, Kuchum, he seized key sites east of the mountains, including Sibir' itself, and established forts at such places as Tobolsk and Tyumen. A midnight raid surprised him in 1585 and he drowned, in full armor, in the Irtysh River. Although Kuchum retook Sibir', the Russians returned and never looked back.

Yermak himself ended somewhere between mythology and pyromancy. Folklore held that his body was recovered and buried under a tree. "There," according to the Remozov Chronicle, "to this day the infidels see on the Saturdays of the commemoration of the dead a pillar of fire rising to the sky, and on ordinary Saturdays a great candle burning at his head. Thus God reveals his own." And thus the Russians revealed themselves to Siberia.[61]

The Russian sweep was not continuous but episodic, and although it built on experiences acquired during the expansion of Muscovy, the administrative apparatus was also overextended, patchy, and unevenly applied. Typically, tsarist Russia was obsessed with Europe and Ukraine but indifferent to Siberia apart from the annual tribute of sable and fox. Of the Russians who wandered east some came voluntarily in a search for furs, gold, or trade; in flight from religious persecution, serfdom, or legal warrants; or in expectation of good farm-

Holy fire. (a) St. Elijah, the Christian permutation of the Slavic fire god, in a cloud of flame. (By permission of Ikonen-Museum, Reckinghausen, Germany) (b) Yermak as burning bush, a pillar of fire before the infidels, as recorded in the short Kungur Siberian chronicle. (Reproduced from Armstrong 1975)

land. But many came by decree—administrators, state peasants, craftsmen, Orthodox churchmen, Cossacks, prisoners of war, political and religious exiles. For much of Siberia's history, Russia perversely held back those who wanted to go and sent those who did not. Major free immigration did not begin until after Emancipation in 1861. But the 550,000 peasants who then migrated to Siberia between 1860 and 1900 pale when compared to the more than two million Russians who emigrated to America between 1890 and 1910. No American frontier evoked woodcuts like "The Siberian Boundary Post," that featured chained convicts, armed soldiers, and wailing women at the Urals monument that officially separated Europe from Asia.[62]

Exploiting Siberia's fabled rivers, Russian *promyshlenniki* and Cossack conquistadors quickly overcame native resistance through a classic combination of firearms, iron will, disease, the use of indigenous guides and interpreters, and the exploitation of resident hostilities among the indigenes themselves that allowed even small numbers of Russians to divide and conquer. Russia had no European competitors; the Treaty of Nerchinsk (1689) early negotiated a border with China. Between 1586 and 1666, beginning with the stockaded town at Tyumen and concluding with Khabarovsk on the Amur River, imperial Russia constructed some fifty permanent settlements, all fortified, all supplemented by a bevy of satellite outposts, all surrounded by a penumbra of tribute-paying tribes. In less than a century Russia fixed the gross geography of Siberia's administrative apparatus—and scrawled an outline of Siberia's new fire regimes.

Travelers kindled fires wherever they halted, and routes of travel inscribed new lines of fire. No one traveled far without flint, steel, and tinder, or a native guide who could produce fire from friction. No one could survive long without innumerable campfires for cooking, light, warmth, protection, and comfort. A hot kettle boiled away the day's discomforts. A cordon of evening fires frightened off bears, tigers, wolves, boars, and gnats. No effort to obtain that fire was too extreme. Traveling up a frozen river, John Bell noted that his party had nowhere to warm themselves or cook "but in the thick overgrown woods." So they "made large fires" from the fallen trees, and "frequently set fire to the moss and dried fibres of these firs. In the space of a minute the fire mounts to the top of the tree, and has a very pretty effect. The kindling so many fires warmed all the air around." And "so by experience," Douglas Howard concluded, "every traveller learns that wherever there is fire, there, or thereabouts, is some kind of human being."[63]

Nothing was more common than fires strung along routes like beads on a cord, or less surprising than that many should escape. A recently constructed forest road had been made "partly by axe and partly by fire," observed Howard. But with a good wind servant soon became master, and "in all cases . . . there is on one or the other side, or on both sides of it, a blackened area of waste." Often the burned taiga made travel seem unearthly, and in moonlight, "inhuman," "weird," and fiendish. "Scarcely had we made our fire," Peter Dobell wrote, "when the grass all around us was in a blaze, obliging us to move to another spot; and the fire raged with such violence it was in vain to attempt extinguishing it. At length the woods,—the whole country around,—were on fire." At least, he concluded, the smoke helped drive off the "flying leeches" that were the scourge of Siberia. Cold, confronted with damp tinder, and presented with "a forest of fine trees, most of them in a fit state to burn," inspired John Cochrane's Yakut guide to "produce fire by friction" and apply it to the woods. The blaze quickly escaped. "From the danger of perishing by cold, I was now hurried into that of being consumed by fire."[64]

There was boredom to contend with as well. George Kennan related how, "after supper," his party "amused ourselves by building an immense bonfire of driftwood on the beach, and hurling blazing firebrands at the leaping salmon as they passed up river, and the frightened ducks." Peter Collins told how "in order to cheer our desolate bivouac we fired the old dried grass and bushes of the previous night still standing. It soon spread far and wide and lighted up the dark shore for several miles, making our camp more agreeable." Thomas Atkinson's party, wet and weary, camped on an island, and then "proposed to illuminate" it. They gathered kindling of branches and birch bark under a clump of picta-trees and selected smaller clumps on each side of the island. The wood burned slowly

> until some pine branches caught fire, when they blazed furiously, communicating the flames to the trees. In a few minutes there was a general conflagration; the fire ran up and along the branches like gunpowder, making a tremendous roar. There is so much terpentine in these trees that it caused the flames to rise to a great height. After our illumination we slept soundly until day dawned, and then resumed our voyage.

For such exercises newcomers had the example, and often the collusion, of the natives.[65]

Accordingly there were fires along rivers, roads, and railways, and of course around settlements. Even today the number and density of fires cluster close to developments and thoroughfares. At the right season or during the right year, such fires rambled into the interior and burned for weeks. "Then dusk came quickly down upon the river," wrote two travelers down the Shilka, "and the red eyes of scattered forest fires began to wink out from the hills above us." Maud Haviland watched a "forest fire which threw a lurid banner of smoke across the river," pondering whether the "atoms of ash in the atmosphere" accounted for the particularly gorgeous sunset that evening. Plying down the Amur, Anton Chekhov observed that along the right bank the "forest was on fire. The dense green mass belched scarlet flames; clouds of smoke merged into an elongated, black, stationary column which hung over the forest. The conflagration was enormous, but all around was quiet and tranquil; nobody cared that the forests were being destroyed." When he reached Sakhalin Island, large fires were raging that made the penal colony resemble a hell on earth. Wirt Gerrare related how a "heat haze thickened over the river; at times it devel-

oped into fog, or was increased in density by the smoke from immense, smouldering forest-fires. We passed through that fog in seven days, having scarcely
as many hours' clear sunshine. Ordinarily it was not clear enough to see distinctly from bank to bank, and on some occasions we had to lie-to when the
landmarks were invisible." Charles Wenyon spoke for legions of summer transients when he "found the river lit up for us by widespread forest-fires":

> How, in these unpopulated districts, such fires are kindled no one
> seems to know; perhaps by a flash of lightning, or a spark from a pass-
> ing steamer, or the smouldering brands of a camp-fire left by some
> careless hunter; but, however caused, when once started these confla-
> grations are beyond control. They burn for weeks, and spread over the
> forest-land for miles. One night we passed through a region where the
> whole mountain-side seemed to be in flames. We had seen other forest-
> fires before, but none on such a scale as this. It took our steamer nearly
> an hour to pass it. We heard the flames roar as they attacked new areas
> of stubble, and crackle among the prostrate trees; while the sky above,
> and the surrounding river, and the awe-struck faces of the people on our
> deck, reflected the red light.[66]

Roads and forest tracks had even greater need for fire. A burn stimulated
new forage for horses, removed the cover exploited by bear and bandit, and
helped open and dry out the immense quagmire of spring. Chekhov observed
the spectacle from his tarantass outside Tyumen: "On both sides of the road
and in the distance—serpentine fires: what is burning is last year's grass, which
they purposely set on fire." The aesthetic effects equaled the ecological:

> It is damp and slow in yielding to the flames, and so the fiery snakes
> creep unhurriedly, now breaking into segments, now vanishing, now
> flaring up again. The fires send up sparks, and above each flare there is
> a white cloud of smoke. When the flame suddenly enfolds tall grass, the
> spectacle is striking: a six-foot fiery column shoots up into the air,
> spouts a great roll of smoke, and promptly drops, as though sinking
> through the ground. The effect is even more beautiful when the snakes
> creep into a birch grove; it is all lit up at once, the white trunks are dis-
> tinctly visible, the shadows of the birches play against patches of light.
> There is something eerie about this illumination.

He was less charmed by the fire-scarred roads and railway in Sakhalin, littered
with the "charred stumps and trunks of larch trees, dried out by fire and wind,"
and ensconced in "swampy scorched earth."[67]
On his monumental 1912 expedition over Siberia's rivers and rails, Fridtjof

Nansen confirmed these impressions, and added others. "The coniferous forest has been destroyed by fire over and over again in the course of time along this river," he observed, citing abandoned campfires as a likely source. But "so it has gone on from time immemorial"; Russians only reclaimed ancient routes and augmented the regional fire load. "One cannot, therefore, expect to find primeval forest undisturbed anywhere along a river like this," Nansen concluded. Instead, expect young growth, deciduous trees, pioneering forbs and scrub. The same was true along roads, and especially along that steel wedge, the Trans-Siberian Railway, driven into the taiga by the sledge blows of industrial and imperial ambition. A realist, Nansen concluded that "one cannot expect to see much forest anywhere along the line." Not only had construction slashed and burned across the ecological grain, not only did construction and the trains themselves consume vast quantities of wood, but "because sparks from the engine often set fire to it; as the fuel is wood there is a continual stream of sparks, which easily catch the dry grass." The grass carried the flame to the forest. Slashings and clearings became tinder to carry fire to deep woods.[68]

But wandering did not confine itself to roads. Often paths served only as points of departure for hunters, prospectors, and refugees; and of course natives still circulated around their own traditional treks, although these now warped to capture or avoid the new corridors of traffic. The taiga simmered with seasonal fires, the worst ones often caused by prospectors. "The forests are destroyed by Russians who penetrate the *taiga* and burn them down," the anthropologist S. M. Shirov declared flatly. The destruction proceeded "partly due to accidental fires and partly to intentional practice of fire setting by the Russians settled in the gold-mining regions."[69]

Prospectors were by definition alien to a place and had scant concern about the particular consequences of their fires. Carelessness was endemic; in difficult terrain, clothed with vegetation or infested with insects, deliberate broadcast burns exposed rock and soil and drove off, if only temporarily, the plague of green flies, gnats, and mosquitoes; and in winter or where permafrost underlay the surface, fires made mining possible. Miners stacked and burned cordwood to melt the ground, and then scooped out the gold-flaked soil. Night and day the burning went on, and large fires in the surrounding landscape only readied the standing forest to serve, in turn, as fuelwood. A gold rush might or might not bring wealth to a particular miner, but it always brought fire to the land. Even today fire-scarred pine record when, in the late 1860s, gold fever poured fire over the banks of the Yenisei. In the 1950s diamonds in Yakutia brought the fire; in the 1970s, geophysical prospecting for oil.[70]

Ultimately, however, Russian colonization in Siberia was, like its colonization of the steppes, founded on agriculture. Siberian swidden was a clone of Russian methods. It replicated the latter's strengths, magnified its liabilities, and multiplied the possibilities for escape. V. B. Shostakovitch summarized the outcome: "In all these cases fire often gets beyond control, becoming immediately disastrous, the sparse Siberian population being absolutely powerless, and the fires, spreading out hundreds and thousands of miles, are stopped only by natural agencies. Such fires being repeated from year to year, most of the new Russian settlements within the taiga are surrounded with burned out forests. This sad picture is to be observed over millions of acres."[71]

Whatever dismay agronomists and foreign critics felt toward fire-based cultivation in Russia, its Siberian progeny fanned into outrage. In 1902 George Wright noted how "in the older portions of the empire," it was thought more advantageous to emigrate to new fields than to introduce "scientific and expensive modes" of intensive cultivation. That tendency swelled in Siberia, where the "superabundance of land" had made cultivation "even less thorough than in European Russia." Even Russian administrators, John Fraser reported, "bemoaned the way agriculture was pursued by peasants who have already settled. Their husbandry was wasteful. They would grow five or six crops on the same patch of land, never manure it, and when it was exhausted abandon it and move elsewhere." J. Stadling gave a somewhat more detailed, though equally dismissive, discussion of this system of "pillage and plunder" agriculture:

> The colonist now simply leaves his exhausted piece of land and commences to exhaust another piece. When all his land within the enclosure is thus worked out, he goes beyond its borders and finds out the most fertile spots, which he ploughs and reaps until they in their turn are exhausted. A Siberian colonist of the old type may thus have twenty different pieces of cultivated land scattered far and wide in the forest, some of them, perhaps, as much as a dozen miles away from his home.

In addition, he burned for pasture. The fallow was an easy target, but marshes, natural meadows, clearings of one sort or another, and even grass-understoried forests were candidates. Most settlers, too, supplemented their farms with fish, fur, wildlife, berries, and whatever else of use they could extract from the taiga. Gerrare thought they "were little better than the natives in depending upon the natural resources of the country." The "Siberian method of socialism," as European critics termed the tyranny of the commune, made for "a shockingly low level of slothful mediocrity."[72]

As always Nansen observed closely and while avoiding hyperbole was clearly awestruck by the magnitude of anthropogenic fire. Traveling east from Irkutsk "time after time," he observed, "we passed forest fires, the smoke of which extended for great distances." Here was the explanation for the puzzling absence of forest or old growth: "it is constantly being burnt." Residents fired the grasses in spring or fall (or occasionally both to mop up what earlier burns had missed).

"If this sets fire to the woods on the hillsides, nobody cares very much, and they may burn for weeks, without anyone being able or willing to stop the fire." In Manchuria he observed the same practice. "The natives have long been in the habit of burning off the long, dry grass, to provide better pasture for game; and perhaps the roving Chinese, who search for hartshorn, have done so too. In this way the forests also have been burnt." Advancing toward Vladivostok after dark, he "could see little of the country, except the fires here and there over the fields, where the grass was being burnt off."[73]

The consequences of all this burning were far from trivial. Like Shostakovitch—like virtually every other observer of the taiga and its grassy filigree—Fridtjof Nansen attributed to fire much of the character of Siberia. The Khingan Mountains' "primeval forest" of oak looked more like a "well-kept English deer park than an uninhabited country near the Amur." The explanation, Nansen concludes, was anthropogenic fire. Toward the end of his journey, he pondered how "it was strange, by the way, here, as everywhere in Siberia, how seldom one saw really big trees; the forest seemed often to consist of nothing but young trees; this is not because they are felled, but rather because they are wantonly burnt; and there is no end to these fires, one sees signs of them everywhere."[74]

But those fires were not wholly wanton, and they did more than attract wild game and fatten livestock. They protected the settlements from wildfire. Nansen captured this sense when he observed how flames had kindled a large haystack, which "as a rule" was shielded by one or two rings of protective burns. But here that practice had not succeeded. "The flames rose high and had a fantastic look in the black night; we were able to form an idea of the sight there must be at night, when the whole mountain is on fire and the forests burn for days and weeks." It is no accident that those environments most easily manipulated by anthropogenic fire were the ones most quickly colonized: they were the sites most readily transformed and most easily defended. Where humans had difficulty imposing their preferred fire regimes, the tension between them and the taiga was greatest.[75]

Since much of Siberia had just this status, conflagrations frequented the backcountry, and when wildfire struck around settlements, when it disturbed wholesale the existing hunting and trapping regimes, overthrew nut-bearing pine for birch, wrecked havoc on fields, and even threatened the wooden village itself, it epitomized the lonely terror of the taiga. Immense conflagrations hid the sun in smoke by day, and lit up the night with a lurid red glow like an emanation from hell. Against such horrors only God and rain—and a ring of protective burning—could offer salvation. When the Russian explorer Vladimir Arseniev and Dersu, his native guide, confronted a wildfire in the Ussuri Mountains, Dersu promptly sought an opening, and then ignited backfires. Later, when they found themselves trapped in windfall with a wildfire bearing down on them,

Dersu exclaimed, "Me little frightened. Grass no burn, but forest him burn." This time they could not fight back, they could only flee.[76]

In just such ways colonists had preemptively seized for their own purposes what lightning and accident would otherwise have seized for theirs. The biota then preserved that protective fire-ring long after the flames had died away.

Russia was indeed different. Once they crossed the border, European travelers noticed a different feel and character to the landscape, no less than to society. Gone was the obsessive fussiness, gone the oppressive ethos of gardening that characterized western Europe's land use. Russia had more room, greater woods, a starker contrast between the oppressed and the wild. However rigorous the European ideal, the vast lands and peoples of Rus' somehow resisted it. But this was even more true in Siberia. Settlements grew around rivers and railroads or scattered as widely as birch seed blown over snow on winter winds. The taiga was a green sea of trees, sprinkled by village atolls. Compared with temperate Europe, there was more open land, fewer sites spun into landscape lace or spaded into tidy kitchen gardens. Anthropogenic fire was an ax, not a chisel; wildfire, a conflagration not an escaped debris burn. Siberia boasted the largest fires on the planet.

And among the most necessary. Without fire humans could hardly survive, but with it, for all their differences, they could discover a mutual bond. Gazing into their protective fire Arseniev and Dersu, deep in the Ussuri Mountains, imagined "the silent witnesses of our talk and the mutual obligations we had undertaken." In their collective dependence on fire, moreover, Russian colonists and Siberian landscapes found a common cause. "When we awoke in the morning," Adolph Erman recalled, "we were covered an inch thick with snow, but became as lively as ever as soon as the fire was stirred afresh."[77]

So it was with all the taiga.

EMANCIPATION AND SUPPRESSION

The agricultural revolution came late to Russia. Like so many Western technologies and ideas, it arrived spasmodically and patchily, in fact only with the peculiar modernization made possible by fossil hydrocarbons. So long as new land and old fallow beckoned, it was easier to move on or to reuse traditional methods than to adopt modern ones; so long as autocracy bound serfs to manorial land, it was easier to command than to innovate. Productivity was poor, and Russia seemed as mired in tradition as wooden wheels in the rutted muck of its spring roads.

At the time of the Emancipation Statute (1861), almost all of Russia was rural. Tsarist Russia had fettered to the land forty million serfs, three-fourths of its total population, half of them "state" serfs assigned to crown lands or other official duties. Virtually all agriculture operated under village communes, which governed the partition of arable and the assignment of rights to commons of pasture and forest; Emancipation did little to alter that fact. Land modernization on western European models came haltingly. In 1914, 82 percent of the Russian population were still peasants. Genuine urban life flourished only in Moscow and St. Petersburg. European critics, Russian intelligentsia, and ardent agronomic reformers all bemoaned the slovenliness, lethargy, waste, and inexhaustible backwardness of Russian farming.

In an era when western Europe was preparing to plow under its last fire practices, Russia's peasants still kindled fires in woods and fields as instinctively as they nurtured glowing logs in the hearth and lit candles under icons. As the hearth defined the architecture of the *izba*, so Russia's fire practices shaped its farms and forests and the Russian peasant's understanding of the world. To modernists, however, fire farming, fire rituals, fire symbolism, and even the peasantry's fire fatalism all epitomized the implacable backwardness of rural Russia. They would have to go.[78]

From the time of their Slavic origins on the wooded steppe, the Russians were considered to be a forest people and a farming people. The reforms of the nineteenth century began to reorient farming away from swidden and subsistence and direct it toward field rotations, artificial fertilizers, and distant markets; they recalibrated forests for purposes other than as fuel for agricultural burning and as a rough garden for communal foraging, promoting their value as timber and pulp; and they reassessed the fires that had long joined field with woods. The new fire cycles would be set by internal combustion engines, not by open burning. The new field rotations would rely on the fossil fallows of coal and later petroleum rather than peat, brush, and trees.

From being an essential medium of exchange, a kind of ecological ether that had suffused field and forest, fire became a ghost in the garden, one that demanded exorcism. In accord with a Russian rhythm as ancient as the winter that followed summer, repression was followed by freedom. For Russian fire, emancipation meant—paradoxically—suppression.[79]

(i)

When academics in the late nineteenth century plotted Russia's agricultural geography, their maps inscribed a broad wedge pointing east, or rather a nested set of wedges. Short fallow systems nested within long fallow systems, which rested inside very long fallows enclosed by taiga, tundra, swamp, and steppe.

Some observers saw in this arrangement the structure of the Eurasian environment. The shape of agricultural regions reflected the narrowing of maritime influences, or conversely the greater impact of continental climates, both cold and hot, toward the center of Eurasia. Other scholars, like Alexander Chelint-sev, saw those different regions as stages of development. The collective arrow was a wedge of modernization driven eastward from Europe along the forest-steppe frontier. The arrowheads were the geographic expression of historical stages. In its passage, agriculture had broadened and evolved from the slashed-and-burned first contact at its Siberian point to three-field systems where the head was lashed to Europe's feathered shaft.[80]

In tsarist Russia both views were true and both false. Where conditions per-mitted, fallow had shortened and farming intensified. But for the most part Rus-sian agriculture had cloned and dispersed. Like a change in climate that in one place causes glaciers to advance while forcing others to retreat, changes in Rus-sia's climate of opinion, encoded in reforms like Emancipation, had diverse and often contradictory outcomes. They tended to accentuate as much as to replace existing structures. And wild incongruities often resulted when Enlight-enment encountered taiga. An Academy of Sciences boasting the likes of Leon-hard Euler rose in St. Petersburg in the eighteenth century amid the reclaimed swamps of the Neva delta. But when the Abbé D'Auteroche observed the tran-sit of Venus from Tobolsk, he was forced to burn the peat around the observa-tory to drive off the orbiting nebulae of insects.[81]

So the agricultural revolution came to Russia unevenly, as so many western models did, always suspect and precarious. But historical momentum supported reformation. Each change led to others, decree by decree, until the period from 1861 to 1874 became known as the Era of the Great Reforms. One agricul-tural strategy urged Russia to expand cultivation into wastes, another to inten-sify cultivation on its existing plots.

Russia's wastes were varied: marshes and cold swamps; organic soils of peat and roots; the taiga; the lonely landscapes of Siberia. In European Russia, recla-mation meant the drainage of wetlands. Amid organic soils, improvement involved paring and burning. Throughout woods and taiga it meant the con-version of more forests, replacing fur trapping, beekeeping, and the gathering of mushrooms and berries with pasture and arable. Most spectacularly it applied to the agricultural wedge prying open Siberia and the Far East.[82]

Its complement was a more intensive, scientific farming on Russia's exist-ing lands. But one feature of rural Russia could not change without affecting others, and four centuries could not be abolished in four years. Not only serfs but Russia's often autarkic economy needed Emancipation. Land reform, how-ever, was as incomplete as the adoption of European forms of field and crop rotations. After Emancipation some serfs received no land, and others received what they already possessed (2.5 hectares on average); but most of the trans-ferred lands went not to individuals but to village communes, which in turn redistributed them equally to all members. Additionally there were "redemption payments" due former landowners among the nobility for forty-nine years. All this added to financial burdens without contributing to agronomic improvement. The peasantry remained ignorant, poor, and collectivist. The boldest counterstroke, the Stolypin Land Reform enacted after the 1905 revolution, proposed to consolidate dispersed holdings and to replace communal lands with individual farms.

Such incomplete measures frequently encouraged the worst of both old and new. Instead of converting waste to arable, usable woods and accessible fields were too often degraded into waste. Forests were felled and pasture plowed for arable to feed more people; without extra forage, livestock numbers plummeted; without manure, arable degenerated; and without proper fallowing or supplementary fertilizer, fields were overworked and soil erosion became endemic. Loss of communal pasture and woods was matched by the decay of communal arable, which too often sank under indifference or the lethargy of large numbers. In an effort to give every household access to every kind of soil, communes partitioned hillsides in long strips from top to bottom. Since the only way to plow such strips was vertically, gulleys quickly gnawed through hills like steam shovels. By the 1890s the situation drew the attention of agronomists and by the end of the decade so scandalized the government that it dispatched formal commissions.[83]

The sad impoverishment of the forest-steppe region—the black earth of European Russia, the country's most richly endowed agricultural land—is instructive. Here, with Emancipation, the amount of land available to peasants actually shrank, often to a third of what they had known three centuries before. Estates retained a third of the lands, including much of the best; what remained, still under the control of the village commune, could not support growing families when subdivided with ever more exquisite equity. Probably 15 percent of the population were landless. Some immigrated to cities or Siberia; some worked for hire on the estates. The end result was too often more of the same: agriculture intensified without really modernizing. Population increased and productivity declined. Population swelled faster than new land could be brought into production, old lands could be improved, or excess people exported. The Stolypin reforms, in particular, had mixed results before falling victim to the apocalypse of war, famine, revolution, and tyranny.

What was needed were markets and alternatives to the closed ecology of fallow. Even as Russia gained ports in the Baltic and the Black Sea, it was the internal combustion engine and artificial fertilizer that broke open trade, made possible the intensification of agriculture, and promoted new worldviews. Tractors replaced horses, feeding on gasoline instead of oats, liberating more land for arable and more pasture for meat. Railways and steamships hauled Ukrainian grains to western markets, trading farm machinery for more hand labor. Artificial fertilizers (and later herbicides) could enrich fields without the bother of growing fallow to burn. Agriculture's real emancipation came from the liberation of long-shackled fossil hydrocarbons.

Until then Russia remained rural, its landscapes rife with waste, woods, marshes, and rough pasture, its agriculture dependent on fire and fallow. An increase in extensive farming encouraged more, not less, fire. Cultivation to the point of soil erosion swept fire away but at the cost of topsoil. Controlled burning remained a necessary implement, wildfire a threat, peasant fire practices an embarrassing emblem of Russian primitivism, and arson a vivid index of social unrest. "Like horse theft, household divisions, and *samosud* [mob law]," Cathy Frierson has observed, "fire was an established aspect of village culture which took on new significance for educated outsiders after the Emancipation who were quickly to perceive it as evidence of transformation and crisis in the countryside."[84]

Intellectuals grounded in European philosophy and values saw deliberate burning as a stigma of backwardness, as much an agricultural superstition as banks of candles were a liturgical one. They saw the peasantry's response to wildfires, especially those that so frequently savaged villages, as further evidence of social retardation. Typically, peasants believed that such fires were visitations, that against them protest was futile and perhaps wrong, and that one should submit to flame-fed devastations as a kind of judgment as one would to famine or plague. Urban, westernized elites asserted otherwise. There were alternatives to fire-fallow agriculture; there was no excuse for casual conflagrations along the frontier; and fires could be fought, like enemies, or prevented, like smallpox. How rapidly Russia expunged fire would reveal how successful it was at modernizing.

The metropolitan centers had something like formal fire brigades. The larger cities, even remote Irkutsk, had the semblance of an apparatus for firefighting, complete with imported engines. In the decade after Emancipation, rural lands acquired volunteer fire associations; and in 1893, members of the nobility and professions established, with royal patronage, the United Russian Fire Association to serve as an organizing center for those scattered associations. In the inaugural issue of its journal, *Pozharnoe delo,* M. K. Isaev declared that a full reformation demanded a change in the peasant's worldview, to the conviction that wildfire could be prevented and fought.[85]

The Association, however, was interested in more than the timeless scourge of village fires; this was not an act of post-Emancipation noblesse oblige. The Great Reforms wrenched traditional land uses, estates, forests, and peasants out of rural autarky and into a market economy that subjected rural fire to new scrutiny. Burning structures, incinerated woods, and fired pastures destroyed property, as that emerging economy defined it; they represented capital losses. Property owners sought to prevent those losses, fight the flames that threatened those values, or insure themselves against resulting damages. The border between old and new societies became, like so many other Russian boundaries, a fire frontier.

Thus wholesale reformations of the landscape and of village life demanded a change in fire practices. Enlightenment and rational improvement were impossible under migratory landnam, swiddened landscapes, routinely burned villages, and abject acquiescence to the heavenly flames of Saint Elias. If abolishing ancient fire practices destroyed peasant agriculture, then so much the better. The addiction to controlled fire, like the prostrate submission before wildfire, was both a cause and consequence of the peasantry's degraded condition and, worse, directly challenged the newly commercialized landscape. Nowhere was this more dramatically demonstrated than with industrial logging.

If Emancipation failed to free the plow, it did liberate the ax. Formerly communal lands were logged and sold, reducing to lumber what had once sustained a complex economy of farming, grazing, trapping, hunting, and foraging for foods and medicines. In retaliation, arsonists assaulted the stacked logs. Even more revealing was the situation that developed during the 1880s in Cherepovets district of Novgorod province. Wherever commercial loggers slashed, peasants burned. After all the hard work of felling was done; planting could follow. But logging companies did not see themselves as monastic orders; converting industrial forest to agricultural fallow was not what landowners desired, economists urged, or foresters prescribed. Such fires— the basis for millennia of Russian agriculture—were now arson. Willful or accidental, malicious or opportunistic, they stood by law outside the order of Emancipated Russia.[86]

The contest was not unique to Russia. Wherever traditional people heard steam's whistle or felt capitalism's steel, there similar firefights broke out. Identical conflicts were endemic throughout Europe's colonial empires. They occurred with Burmese swiddeners, India's mountain tribals, Sahel graziers, Australian Aborigines, Finnish *svedjefolk,* and American frontiersmen. Traditional societies needed free-burning fire; modernizing ones sublimated those flames into machines. In response, indigenes turned to the purgative flame, which destroyed the newly fashioned (and for them hostile) landscape and restored the conditions of the old one. The more that officials condemned fire, the more local protesters were likely to use it.

And without exception the architects of the new order did denounce traditional fire practices—British, French, and German colonial agronomists and foresters no less than westernized Russians and newly enlightened Americans. Progressives like Gifford Pinchot spoke of America's rural society in the same disparaging language used by Russian reformers. "I recall very well indeed," Pinchot wrote in 1910, how, in the early days of forest fires, they were considered simply and solely as acts of God, against which any opposition was hopeless and any attempt to control them not merely hopeless but childish. It was assumed that they came in the natural order of things, as inevitably as the seasons or the rising and setting of the sun. To-day we understand that forest fires are wholly within the control of men. . . . The first duty of the human race is to control the earth it lives upon.

No promoter for the United Russian Fire Association put it better.[87]

(ii)

But the extremes were greater in Russia. The contest between indigene and colonial power was here expressed between the castes of one society; and nowhere else, even North America, had forests on the scale of the Russian Empire. In 1900, forests still commanded 39 percent of European Russia; on a per capita basis, Russians had half as much forest as Swedes but seven times that of France or Germany. And then there was Siberia. No other European power held so much contiguous territory that it could think of dispatching criminals and other undesirables to "internal exile." Inevitably for a forest people settled on this much-forested land, Russia's fire wars were concentrated in its woods and taiga.

Russia had created itself from wood, and it had used ax and fire to do so. Pyrotechnologies dominated not only farming, grazing, hunting, and foraging, but primitive industries. Wood and charcoal were universal fuels: they sustained smelting, metallurgy, ceramics, glassworks, and distillation for tar, pitch, turpentine, and salt, to say nothing of domestic fires, saunas, smudge fires, and campfires. Even after the introduction of coal, fuelwood consumption in the early 1890s topped 73 million cubic meters a year. It is no accident that Russians had the hardest time colonizing those places where fire was most difficult to install or control. The pure steppes had too much free-ranging fire; the pure taiga, too much forest that either refused to burn or burned in conflagrations; and both required complex preparations. Their border, the wooded steppe, was ideal.[88]

But a fire that one group considered useful another might condemn as destructive. Broadcast burns set by early colonists to drive off bears also dispersed squirrels; what they kindled to attract deer in the spring might deprive cattle of winter fodder; woods that were burned for crops, trappers wanted for wildlife habitat and foresters wanted to sell for export. Times changed: the state might promote swidden fires at one time and denounce them as arson at another, and did just that. Meanwhile, wildfires, either simmering or boiling, were as common as gnats.

To control fire was to control land use. As the state assumed power over land, so it sought to dictate fire regimes so that the land would serve the purposes it most coveted. At various times, officials had sought fire protection to prevent undue damage to hunting, wild honey gathering, fuelwood, and the great forest wall along the Belgorod line. For each condition officials had promulgated a fire policy and then watched as flames, controlled or otherwise, catalyzed the transition.

Thus in the seventeenth century, fire prohibitions centered on the *yasak,* the notorious fur tax levied on non-Russians. While even sables, over the long term, relied on fire-cycled habitats, the short term *yasak* did not. Beginning in 1635, provincial governers began receiving charters admonishing them to exclude fire from sable-yielding taiga. (There was some cause for this sentiment. Vitus Bering's naturalist, Georg Steller, asserted that reckless Russian burning had displaced sable and fox from along the Lena River. Adolph Erman reported fears that fires along the Ob had likewise driven game away.) In 1683 the tsar prohibited, over all of Siberia, fires set in prime *yasak* forests and made fire-setting a capital offense. The imperial interest was in fur, not farms. There is no evidence that such ukases, however harsh, had the slightest effect.[89]

Perhaps the most intensive effort went into promoting metallurgy. The great mines of the Urals, in particular, were wholly dependent on wood for props and smelting. The amount of wood consumed was prodigious. Even in the nineteenth century the quantities staggered European observers like Adolph Erman and John Croumbie Brown. "Whole forests are set apart for this extravagant, and perhaps unnecessary, operation." Until coke became the dominant fuel for British industry, Russia reigned as the principal producer of European pig iron. Its fuels, not its ores, sustained Russia's supremacy; and it was essential to burn those fuels in furnaces, not in situ. Fire protection extended, in principle, to village and mine as well as woods. Even small towns like Achinsk assigned to each resident a special duty and responsibility for particular tools such as shovel or ax. Women organized bucket brigades; and leather workers had charge of the engine, since the leather hoses were the critical component. A "sign over each door" designated individual responsibilities.[90]

These were special zones, singled out like bee trees. More pervasive protection required that the forests themselves enjoy greater standing and that the state create permanent institutions to oversee them. Such was European style forestry, which began as one of Peter the Great's many western transplants and had its origins in his obsession to build a navy. In 1702 he decreed a ban on forest logging within 30 versts (about 32 kilometers) of rivers, later modified to 50 versts from major rivers and 20 from small ones. In 1723 he specified a fire code to prevent escaped fires and to mandate firefighting duties for everyone within 10 versts of a wildfire. Arson was punishable by death. To oversee the ukase he organized a bureau, headed by a German *Forstmeister* within the Admiralty Office.[91]

Like many of Peter's reforms, the concept of scientific forestry seemed alien to Russians. Peasants took what they regarded as reasonable precautions, because wildfire did them no good. But wind, drought, lightning, and the sheer backbreaking immensity of wooden Rus' frustrated any attempt to reduce forestry to gardening. This was a society that shaped ship timbers with axes, not saws. After Peter's death, Catherine I shrank the number of protected forests and abolished the forest administration.

The Empress Anna restored both. In 1732, following Peter's example, she imported German foresters to oversee forest policy. In 1735, endlessly annoyed by drought-fueled burns around St. Petersburg, she wrote to General Oushakov: "Andrei Ivanovich, it is so smoky here that one cannot even open a window, and that because the forest fire is raging as last year; it seems no one is attempting to put an end to this fire which has already been raging for a number of years. Order an investigation and see to it that men are dispatched to put out the blaze." She further commanded fire patrols, not only by the forestry corps but by communities. In Ingermanland she ordered, in 1738, that peasants not abandon swidden fires until the fire had expired, and even organized a cadre of "pickets" to spy on fire-careless travelers and mushroom pickers from "behind the trees."[92]

But the fires continued, indifferent to threats of decapitation or exile to Siberia. Burning, not cutting, accounted for the bulk of forest "destruction." More ukases followed. In 1744, Empress Elizabeth Petrona prohibited fires in Siberia that threatened sable harvests. In 1745 there was a general prohibition throughout the empire, one that assigned fire protection responsibility to local governers and *voivodes* and that commanded firefighters to place themselves under the direction of resident waldmeisters. Soon foresters were assuming control not only over wildfire fighting but over national fire policy. To protect wooden bridges and valued woodlands, the army organized patrols along the Moscow road. (Always suspect, transients were assumed to be a major cause of fire.) To set an example for the nation, Elizabeth further prohibited army regiments assigned to St. Petersburg from making temporary fires when they took their wives to gather berries and mushrooms. Wildfires broke out widely anyway. In 1752 they became so extensive in Ingermanland that the decree was reissued and army units sent to assist with suppression. Meanwhile, from Nerchinsk came the report that locals were using broadcast fire to drive bears and other beasts from sable-rich woods. There followed more decrees, more patrols, more threats. The severity of an edict's threatened punishment had little apparent bearing on its effectiveness. In 1772 the Admiralty codified and published its forest regulations.[93]

Catherine II then annulled most of the provisions and in 1788 liberalized forest use by landowners. The consequences, forester Feodor Arnold thundered, were such that even "strangers" were outraged at the havoc and waste. A decade later, while Europe suffered Napoleon's belligerence, a large fire swept Smolensk oblast and invaded Moscow and new orders streamed out to governers and voivodes to improve their vigilance against fire. On his travels Tsar Paul I saw evidence of casual and damaging fires everywhere, the insouciant result of letting agricultural burning creep and claw into the surrounding woods. Offended, he enjoined his governors to enact the prescribed precautions, established an autonomous Forest Department, and commanded the department to appoint village fire wardens drawn from "abstinent settlers of good behavior" to assist. In 1804, E. F. Ziablovski, a professor at the St. Petersburg naval academy, published the world's first textbook on forestry. In Russia, as throughout Europe, foresters had assumed administration over free-burning fire.[94]

As forestry's duties expanded, so did its institutional presence. Tsar Alexander I diffused forestry throughout whatever departments it touched upon. The purpose was not to abolish fire—that, if feasible, would exterminate agriculture—but to confine it. New laws required peasants to cooperate with the local *Forstmeister* before clearing new land. The process was applied first around Arkhangelsk, then more generally throughout European Russia, and—improbably—in Siberia. Meanwhile Russia moved to improve its technical standards. It endowed two new forestry schools, which officials consolidated into the St. Petersburg Forest Institute in 1813. The subsequent history of this institute—the focus for Russian training, research, and policy—is, in Bernhard Fernow's words, "practically the history of forestry in Russia."[95]

The inspiration and practical character of its forestry were heavily Germanic. German *Forstmeisters* staffed early departments, taught in colleges, and shaped the tenor of forest thinking. But Russia could never import enough of them, and to the extent that peasants had to interact with the foreign *Forstmeisters,* language was a barrier. So Germans trained Russians. Some Russians traveled to the German states, but most studied under German mentors brought to Russia. They spoke German, studied German texts, learned German practices; they became "the same as German forstmeisters but speaking Russian." Certainly the Forest Department's attitude toward fire was thoroughly Germanic.[96]

But like Darwin's finches in the Galápagos, the dispersion of Germanic forestry had brought about new species as it adapted to special niches in Spain, Turkey, India, the United States, and elsewhere. Not only cultural differences but the sheer scale of the Russian landscape compelled modifications. Translations from French and German did not overthrow folklore; forest institutes, the social drag of autocracy and serfdom; or *Forstmeisters,* even if they spoke Russian, the ancient patterns of land use and fire practices. The gap between peasant and forester never closed. In 1821 the post of Siberian *Forstmeister* was abolished on the grounds that Siberia's unlimited forests had no need of protection.

What forestry never lost, however, was its commitment to fire control. Thus 1832 witnessed both the founding of the Imperial Russian Society for the Advancement of Forestry complete with periodical, *Lesnoi Zhurnal,* and the promulgation of new regulations for forest protection through the creation of a forest guard. The guard drafted members from the ranks of retired military families and state peasants to serve for twenty-year tours. They complemented the network of village wardens, and bolstered the clout of the Forest Department. Both groups served, in principle, to contain agricultural burning, discourage careless firesetting by travelers, and combat wildfires.[97]

But bold initiatives in St Petersburg had a way of dissipating, like Napoleon's retreating Grande Armée, by the time they had traveled far across the Russian plain. Fires remained everywhere—necessary fires, nuisance fires, indifferent fires, holocaust fires. When Roderick Murchison completed his Russian expedition in 1842, Tsar Nicholas I asked the famous geologist what surprises he had discovered. Murchison replied that he was most impressed by the extent of "forest destruction" from logging and especially fire. He then implored the tsar, "in the name of the love of mankind," to take forceful measures to end it. Whatever the tsar and his ministries did or didn't do, and in whatever name they did or didn't do it, large fires continued; and explorers after Murchison, like those who preceded him, recorded the wreckage. "There are," Cl. Olanion observed,

> very often during the whole months here, in Siberia, unconquerable fires, kindled by some vagrant or runaway convict or sometimes by an ordinary peasant. Smoke from such enormous fires is spread over hundreds of versts. The taiga becomes evil and sad, no birds sing, beasts flee, gigantic trees—blackened almost to the top—are as ghosts, waving their long soot-covered hands until an ominous crack is heard and the trees crash down carrying their neighbors with them and these new dead bodies are buried among the other rotting trunks.[98]

What revolutionized forestry and fire was Emancipation. It freed forests from tradition as fully, and as unevenly, as it did serfs from the land. The new owners —peasants, nobility, the state—rushed both to apply proved methods to newly liberated lands and to haul the woodlands to market as rapidly as possible. Peasants cleared forests for more fields to feed expanding families. Estate landowners, deprived of previous incomes, sold off timber. So did the ever-ravenous state in its search for additional revenue. The industrialization of western Europe, especially Britain, created a massive export market. The quickening pace of Russian industrialization encouraged significant internal markets as well. Until coal reserves were developed, wood remained the principal fuel, and until stone and steel could replace it, wood dominated construction materials. Russia stripped off its European forests as through it were skinning a sable. Foreign critics like Fernow described the outcome as a "general slaughtering." What was struck by steel or rubbed with wood inevitably produced flame, and what was once slashed eventually burned.[99]

For European Russia, complaints compelled the tsar to initiate reforms that led to a succession of new forestry laws, beginning in 1867. Two years later the corps of forest inspectors replaced conscripted peasants with hired employees. Then the Valuyev Commission of 1872 documented wholesale deforestation in province after province. Ancient woodlands had vanished, river flows had dropped, and to the south soil erosion became endemic. That same year N. S. Shafranov published *Forest Protection,* the first text of its kind in Russian. The cumulative abuses inspired a forestry commission in 1875; its inquiry continued for years. Another text entitled *Forest Protection,* by N. V. Baranetski, appeared in 1880. Russia still looked west for guidance: its professors and forstmeisters still finished their education with a Grand Tour of central Europe, inspecting model German forests as aspiring painters might copy old masters hanging in the Louvre or architects draw the Parthenon and Coliseum. In 1887, Major Frederic Bailey reported on the visit of a Russian embassy to the French forestry school at Nancy.[100]

In the end, the commission's recommendations culminated in the comprehensive Forest Law of 1888. Its centerpiece was the "protective forest," a category of restrictive use applied principally to the north and south in an effort to stabilize waterways and soils. Such sites fell under plans prescribed by the Forest Department. Elsewhere the law established forest protection committees, locally constituted, to oversee forest conservation within the context of logging and farming. Most of the forested lands of Russia, however, belonged to the state. Of an estimated 200 million hectares (in 1901), the Crown controlled some 117 million. Gradually the provisions of the law extended to more remote provinces such as the Transcaucasia. Already, in 1884, western Siberia had its forest directorate restored.[101]

Still, exports thrived, forests frayed, and fires flared wherever woody debris littered the ground or droughts drained away peatland moisture. Investigations by the Forest Department in 1894 documented that the percentage of forest land on the Oka River's watershed had fallen from 15.8 to 3.6 and for the Don from 9.2 to 1.8. In Russia, as throughout Europe, logging had boomed with industry. Between 1861 and 1900, Russia's production of fossil fuels rose from 424,325 tons of coal and no oil to 17,809,125 tons of coal and 11,395,450 tons of oil, and its construction of railroad lines went from 2,200 kilometers to 53,200, including the mammoth Trans-Siberian Railway. By the end of the nineteenth century those coal-fired Russian railways transported four times the volume of timber they had carried in the 1870s. Between 1897 and 1908, exported logs increased from 1.6 million tons to 2.9, and sawn timber from 1.616 million tons to 2.72. Forest reduction coincided closely with population growth, as wooded land was, where possible, converted to fields. Between 1696 and 1914, European Russia lost 28 percent of its forests, some 67 million hectares. Even railways could not access Siberia's taiga to compensate. In 1895, the Far East was actually importing timber from the United States.[102]

Between Emancipation and Revolution the Russian forest underwent as profound a change as Russian society. In European Russia the forest decreased dramatically before stabilizing after the reforms of 1888. Along the once-wooded forest-steppes the state promoted afforestation, with mixed results. In Siberia some forest was lost to colonization, while more of the taiga recomposed itself to better adapt to the new fire regimes. Fires were everywhere, this time no longer contained within the rhythms of swidden and spring clearing.

Transitional eras are, for fires, the most volatile times. Russia's industrial transition—however primitive and however much over time it might quench the Russian hearth—initially increased the number and intensity of forest fires. It had stoked the hearth with slash and opened the social flue that had regulated the burning, and fires had quickened in response. Now Russia sought to dampen the pace, if not extinguish the fires altogether. The old Russian rhythm of release and repression reasserted itself. The one led to wildfire, the other to suppression.

(iii)

Everywhere officials recognized that it was easier to protect existing forests than to regrow those that were destroyed. Fire protection seemed an obvious solution, one that carried the sanction of European forestry. But against conflagrations the forester was as helpless as the much-maligned peasant. Only a dying wind could end a crown fire; only rain extinguish a long-smoldering burn in peat; only protective burning could shield settlements from taiga fires; and only backfires could, even in principle, check a running wildfire. Nor did institutional forestry end abuses. Fernow shrewdly characterized Russia's vaunted autocracy as really government by bureaucracy, and that tainted. Almost certainly he was correct when he concluded that "the general corruption of the bureaucracy is an almost insurmountable obstacle to improvement."[103]

Still, the fundamentals of fire control were known. They were integral to the German forestry transplanted to Russia in the nineteenth century, and as the doctrines of forest protection became systematized, those precepts trekked into taiga and woodlot. Their application, however, was patchy and often indifferent, especially prior to the 1888 forest law. Peasants and landowners frequently disagreed over fire practices and even over what constituted a wildfire. That peasants were shanghaied into firefighting gangs to work (unpaid) for landowners did little to inspire hard labor or careful attention to technique. As traditional methods broke down, foresters—and the state and landowners for whom they worked—sought to install a tougher regime. They had in their hands the blueprints for fire protection on the German model. Unfortunately, these proved considerably more difficult to copy than women's fashions, academic institutes, and battleships.

A good summary of Russian forestry's purpose and craft with regard to fire exists in S. T. Nat's 1902 exposition, *Forest Fires and Countermeasures Against Them.* The treatise begins with the ritual jeremiad against wildfire. "Fire and famine," Nat thundered, had become the norm. Between 1896 and 1899 the forest administration reported some 18,000 fires, of which two-thirds resulted from unknown causes. They weren't known because, too often, they weren't fought. Worse, the active conversion of woods to conifer plantations in defiance of their "natural succession" to less-flammable deciduous trees had "removed one of nature's more important means for resisting fire." Traditional Russian fatalism had, it seemed, combined with a landscape in upheaval to impress the Russian mind with "the idea that we must starve and burn." As agents of reform, it was left to foresters to show differently. In Russia as elsewhere fire control was the beginning of effective forestry.[104]

The task required scientific research, proper forest design, and aggressive fire control. The forces unleashed by Emancipation were rebuilding the forest no less than Russian society. The first impulse was often to strip-mine the woods. As long as avid logging and rapid changes in ownership littered the landscape with slash, and as long as the incentive to harvest exceeded the urge to protect, fires would thrive. But reforestation often brought little improvement. Instead of traditional fallow—birch and leafy hardwoods, nature's firebreaks—logged and burned landscapes were planted to commercial pine. The fire hazards continued without pause. "The more persistent and energetic our efforts" at reforestation, Nat observed, "the greater the risk of fire in these stands." Clearly firefighting was as much an occupational skill for foresters as timber cruising or raising nursery stock.

Ultimately, the premise of forestry was that good silviculture would contain fires as good farming did pests. Once incentives grew to shelter existing stocks and to nurture replacement trees, once forest law had strengthened the control of forstmeisters over general land use, the forest would acquire, in principle, as methodical a character as the farmed field. In place of plowed strips, foresters installed artificial firebreaks around and through blocks of forest—an artificial fuel mosaic—to substitute for the natural ones cut away and denied regrowth. So, too, the prudent landowner converted zones of high fire hazard into less hazardous conditions and sought to use roads, firebreaks, and stips of planted hardwoods to contain such fires as occurred. On German models, railroad right-of-ways could be planted to well-weeded gardens, burned clear of weeds, or stocked with incombustible hardwoods.

Failures were abundant, and fires profuse. The response was organized fire protection, whose essence was early detection and rapid attack, "force enough fast enough." Nat gave this universal maxim a Russian gloss by quoting Field Marshal Suvorov's formula for victory: "be quick, size up, and attack." A handful of firefighters could do in early moments what armies could not do days later. The "usual practice," Nat explained, was to designate "special horse-mounted fire guards," equip all forest guards with signal horns, and post sentries at villages "overlooking the forest." These were in addition to fire lookout towers, ideally plugged into a telegraph grid. The goal was to put "the entire forest under observation from 10 am to 6 or 7 pm."

But Emancipation had severed the social controls that had made it possible to herd peasants to the front lines. Former serfs were reluctant to suppress fires on land not their own, for a nobility they often resented, and for purposes with which they disagreed. Only close relations between landowner and peasant, Nat concluded, could achieve an acceptable level of fire protection. Instead, coercion replaced cooperation, as, sanctioned by forest laws, *Forstmeisters* and district police scoured villages for able-bodied men to serve as firefighters when the flames erupted. Even modest fires could command considerable manpower. Fire commanders needed firefighters on the lines, horsemen searching for spot fires, reserve forces to relieve exhausted firemen and for a final assault, and "large numbers of people" to mop up residual burning among ashy roots, charred trunks, and peat. Big fires or fires in organic soil could burn for days, even weeks. Many fires, however, occurred during planting and harvest when labor could hardly be diverted from the fields. Village elders stalled while they pondered who to send, or even convened an assembly to debate the order of dispatch. Occasionally they demanded an official document "in ink." Meanwhile, the fires grew.

The peasantry, however, often had little to gain from this fiery corvée. Nat had to appeal to landowners, as a "delicate matter," that they should ensure "at least that clean drinking water is provided for the workers." If hours or days of compulsory, soot-drenched labor resulted in, at best, a ladle of clean water, there was scant incentive to hurl oneself against the flames. Not infrequently peasant arsonists added to the load, firing the logged woods or the stacked timber that had formerly served as rough pasture and forage. Add to these circumstances famine, disease, economic distress, fractured communes, political terror, and handtools unchanged from the days of eleventh-century Novgorod, and the prospects for large fires swelled like a summer thunderhead. What officials condemned as philosophical fatalism had its empirical logic.

If foresters wanted to prove differently, then the task fell to them. The forester, Nat affirmed, "must always be ready to take personal charge of firefighting efforts." Suppression was neither easy nor elegant "when one unexpected thing after another happens, when all questions have to be answered, everything considered, everyone assigned, and plans developed to contain the fire, when one has to stay calm and strong in order to fight a raging fire without engangering the lives of many people, when any failure or mistake could result in irreversible losses." But precisely those conditions were the norm.

Techniques were primitive. Light fires could be attacked with shovels and pine boughs, trenches and swatting. Nat argued for the "beat and hold" technique, in which one struck the flames and then kept the flail on the flame for a few seconds. More vigorous fires required a flanking attack, pinching off the advancing head by parallel movements from behind. The most difficult technique to execute was the backfire, forestry's version of the scorched earth. Done properly the practice burned away the fuels from before a flaming front; done poorly, it added to the fire and demoralized crews.

The backfire required a firm firebreak and the clearing away of shrubby fuels that could carry the kindled fire into the canopy. Mostly, however, it depended on timing. A Forest Department circular from 1845 specified the terms under which such a fire could be set: only when "there is a perceptible draft of air toward the fire." Nat pleaded for a bolder, more flexible prescription. "Anyone who has stood face to face with a fire waiting for that moment and has had the wind whip the fire into a devouring wall that turns whole groups of trees into a solid hell of fire—that person will probably light the backfire sooner next time, and with good reason!"

In Emancipated Russia the conscience to protect lagged behind the lust to exploit. As conditions stabilized, however, a search for suitable models proceeded vigorously. The transnational character of professional forestry suggested that the principles of fire control were as universal as the physics of projectile motion, the periodic table, or the construction of high dams.

As North America engaged its enormous fires, Russians took notes. They recognized in Canada's boreal forest an analogue to their expansive taiga, and they scrutinized American suppression techniques for equivalents to the American agricultural machinery that had revolutionized Ukrainian farming. Perhaps technology could redeem what technology had condemned, and science drag a fire-fatalistic peasantry into modernity. But American and Canadian programs did not mature until after World War I, which is to say, after the Bolshevik Revolution, and their relevance for European Russia was unclear. They addressed empty lands, not those harboring a swidden-addicted peasantry and a logging-intoxicated nobility.

Until then, tsarist Russia had looked to Europe, especially Germany. Emblematic was the attention lavished on Dr. Kinitz, a forestry professor who had won a prize at the 1901 Paris world exhibition for his study of complex, gardened firebreaks by which to insulate railways. In 1912 the Russian journal *Lesnoi Zhurnal* reprinted the essay amid adulation and an appeal to emulation. The strategy embodied the European ideal: contain steam, as one would swidden, through cultivation. But close cropping had as little basis in Russian forestry as it did in Russian agriculture. West of the Urals Russia was farmed, not gardened. East of the Urals it was neither.[105]

WHEN THE SKY BURNED

Early on the morning of June 30, 1908, a great fireball, more brilliant than the sun, streaked across the Siberian sky. Its path crackled with a deafening roar. Shock waves scattered debris like chaff. Then at 7:17 A.M. it shattered the taiga along the Stony Tunguska River with a cataclysmic explosion, setting off seismographs as far away as Moscow, Jena, and Java. Immediately a flash of light seared the landscape in a great circle, a pillar of fire rose upward, and the taiga for a hundred miles round flared like a match head. The blast kindled a shock wave that struck the forest like an immense scythe; to all sides trees snapped off or blew down, leaving the taiga prostrate, bowing away from the source of the explosion.

The concussion blew apart Vanavara, a village 65 kilometers away; it blew away fences in Kirensk, 350 kilometers away; it rattled windows and lamps and overturned rafts in Kansk, 600 kilometers to the south; it forced the Trans-Siberian Express to halt while the tracks shook. The great whirlwind, having sucked up the broken and charred taiga into its vortex, now disgorged that burden with thunder and black rain. A Tungus herdsman, Vasily Okhchen, described how "the fire came by." He heard "an unbelievably loud and continuous thunder; the ground shook, burning trees fell, and all around there was smoke and haze. Soon the thunder stopped, the wind ceased, but the forest continued to burn." In Krasnoyarsk observers saw "a heavenly body of fiery appearance cut across the sky from south to north. . . . when the flying object touched the horizon a huge flame shot up that cut the sky in two."[106]

The Tungus attributed the event to a visitation from an angry Ogdy, the god of fire. Russian peasants no doubt saw in the spectacle the presence of Saint Elias riding across the sky in his thundering chariot, raining down tongues of flame, immanent in a pillar of fire. Prophets and augurers saw in it the portents of a political revolution begun in 1905, soon to end with the cataclysm of 1917. Expeditions from the Academy of Sciences sought to explain the phenomenon as a meteorite or comet, later as a miniature black hole, an antimatter collision, the atomic explosion of an alien spacecraft—none seems adequate. The original investigator, Leonid Kulik, overwhelmed by the immensity of the

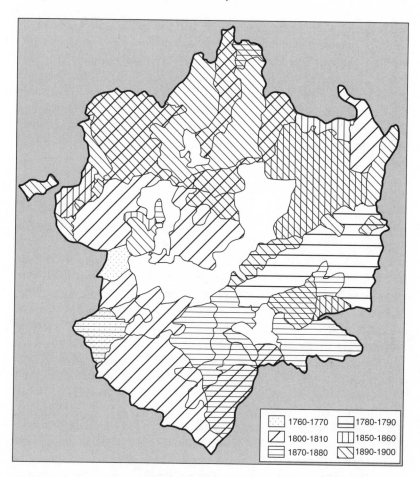

Big fires: the Tunguska event of 1908 superimposed on a forest whose age structure reflects the history of past large fires. Dates represent time of stand establishment (Redrawn from Bereshnoy and Drapkina 1964 by the University of Wisconsin Cartographic Lab)

destruction, sought an extraordinary cause because, even for Siberia, the consequences were awesome. Beyond the zone of devastation, he pondered, lay "the taiga, the endless, mighty taiga, for which terrestrial fires and winds hold no terrors, for they leave no greater scars than scratches on the hands and face of one of its people."[107]

Extraordinary, yes, because the episode was virtually instantaneous. But the Tunguska event was superimposed on a landscape mosaic, shaped by immense fires, whose individual imprints were as large as anything produced by the 1908 blast. In the 150 years preceding, all of the forest subjected to the explosion had burned in stand-replacing patches. What distinguished the Tunguska fire was its suddenness—the radiant flash that kindled whatever was exposed to its blast. Although shock waves shattered the forest, the fire itself was ephemeral, a surface scorching, like green wood doused in gasoline that burns brilliantly for a minute and then expires. The Tunguska event was a fascinating freak. The taiga absorbed it. Its core fire regimes obeyed the rhythms of drought and coniferous succession, its great fires burned deeply into peat and widely through canopies, and with eerie mimicry its fire complexes wrote an environmental subtext to the critical events of Russian history.[108]

(i)

The long Russian winter forced life to crowd itself into a few vibrant months. Spring came with violent abruptness as the biota hurried to grow, blossom, and reproduce. But decay was slower; almost nowhere did biological decomposition keep pace with biomass production. Peat, mires, and muskegs littered and in some regions dominated landscapes, hoarding nutrients into soggy biotic caches. Elsewhere the taiga grew, often slowly but with an incremental surplus of biomass stored to biomass lost. In dry permafrost regions it was often water that went underground and out of circulation. But the cumulative effect was like hoarding specie: it starved the biota. Nature's economy needed a freer circulation of nutrients, a recycling of species and habitats to match supply with demand. The only mechanism adequate to that task was fire.

For fire to function, however, there had to be ample fuel suitably available. The stockpile took time. For forests it was not only the load of biomass that mattered but its arrangement, the mixture of fine fuels by which to propagate the fire and of large fuels whose slower combustion liberated materials en masse. More often the limiting factor was their fuel moisture. Fires required dry fuel, and large fires—regional fire complexes—demanded drought. This was a precondition, not a cause. Drought no more kindled fire by spontaneous combustion than cold congealed itself into ice sheets.

What drought did was to homogenize the fuel array. Normally the components of a landscape had different moisture levels, such that pine needles differed from logs, standing trees from shrubs, forests from mires. Each was variously available for burning. Fire had to search out the dried fuels from the wet. Annually fire sputtered, probed, weaved through the taiga like a fox sniffing out food. With drought, however, everything was drained of moisture, everything became available for burning. While the speed and persistence of combustion varied with the density and structure of the fuelbed, all parts of the biota could burn. The fires of historic record thus document droughts; and thanks to the torch, droughts invariably led to great fires, not only in forests but in wooden villages. Drought and fire also meant famine, and famine brought pestilence and social unrest. Thus the Horsemen of the Apocalypse converged.

The Nikon Chronicle recorded for 1092 that "during that year there were no rains, the land was covered with fire, and many forests themselves and even the swamps were burning." In 1223 and 1298 the Suzdal' Chronicle alluded to great fires in forest and bog. In 1371 the Nikon Chronicle elaborated the imagery into nearly ritualistic form:

> That same summer there was a sign in the sun, there were dark spots
> like nails and a thick mist, so that one could not see seven feet ahead,
> and many human beings bumped into one another and suffered injuries;
> the birds were unable to fly in the air and fell to earth on the heads of
> humans, wild beasts wandered unseeingly along the countryside and
> cities, bears, wolves, foxes and the like mixed with men. The drought
> was so horrid and the heat so intense that beings became frightened and
> panicky; rivers, lakes, and marshes dried out, while the forest took fire,
> marshes too, and the earth burned; fear and panic enveloped the hearts
> of men.

In 1384 the terrors repeated themselves. "An intense darkness continued for many days and nights; the birds could not see where to fly and fell to the earth, and the people decided not to travel over the lakes and rivers." The Novgorod Chronicle recorded the great drought and fire of 1430. "The same autumn the water was exceeding low; the soil and forests burned, and very much smoke, some times people could not see each other, and fishes and birds died from that smoke; the fish stank of the smoke, for two years." The great drought of 1471 covered, it was said, most of the Russian plain and persisted for a whole year. Great fire complexes broke out in 1508, 1525, 1533, 1560, 1575, 1643, 1660, 1680, 1691, and 1696. A prolonged drought led to chronic burning between 1732 and 1737. The cycle repeated in 1780–81, and again in 1796–98. It continued through serfdom and Emancipation, through autocracy and industrialization; drought and fire gripped the land in 1833–34, 1840, 1848, 1859, 1865, 1876, 1881–83, and 1890–92. Despite better control over fire, the record increases with each century, most likely the product of increased settlement and better reporting.[109]

But all this related to European Russia alone. For Siberia and Central Asia only fires in well-traversed regions enter the chronicles. In 1908, for example, fires along the Trans-Siberian Railway between Tomsk and Krasnoyarsk were recorded, while the Tunguska event, in sparsely settled central Siberia, went almost unnoticed. The enduring chronicle was the one written in the landscape itself, in the depth of its peat, in the age-structure and composition of the taiga, in the flickering border between forest and steppe. For the most part the written records required some linkage with human society, which drought or travel, as well as flames, provided.

In Siberia fire rather than ax dominated, and in fulfillment of the Buryat prophecy, pine and especially birch had replaced fir and spruce over millions of taiga hectares. Exploring naturalists like I. G. Gmelin (1752), Peter Pallas (1776), and A. F. Middendorf (1867) recorded the shifts, and contemporary sedimentary pollen cores confirm it. The process accelerated with the advent of steam. Railways cracked open the taiga by encouraging settlement, threw fires to all sides, and melted the land down, like miners burrowing by bonfires into permafrost. Still, big fires disappeared into the taiga like bears, showing themselves from time to time to traveler or hunter. Almost every year featured a major fire complex somewhere. In 1909–10 great fires burned in Yeniseisk province. In autumn 1910, and again in spring 1911, a "wall of fire" stretched across the Far East. In 1912–14, central Siberia suffered "immense fires." Conflagrations were as common as black flies.

Eventually records become more systematic. Beginning in 1898, foresters extended their inspections across the Urals; by 1914, when more than half of European Russia had completed surveys, Siberian foresters had inspected 5 percent of Irkutsk province and 17 percent of Yeniseisk province. More methodically the state sponsored eight expeditions to Siberia between 1908 and 1912 to identify suitable sites for settlement. Academicians like G. A. Borovikov, R. I. Abolin, and M. F. Korotky weighed in with discussions of fire-forced biotic reformation in Yakutia and the Far East. All observed large fires, and where the forest regrew noted its changed composition. Collectively they corroborate Fridtjof Nansen's observations that the Siberian forest was young, that it overflowed with pioneering species, and that the concept of a "forest primeval" was increasingly difficult to maintain, if that fiction ever had any but literary meaning.[110]

"Forest fires," noted V. B. Shostakovitch of the Geophysical Observatory at Irkutsk, "are very common in Siberia. Nobody is surprised to observe them, much less alarmed." Normally, this was true. But even by Siberian standards the 1915 fires were millennial. So much of western and central Siberia burned that the fires could not be denied. For most of the twentieth century, the 1915 conflagration established the standard of reference east of the Urals.[111]

The obligatory drought began early and then intensified toward August. Around the drought's center, precipitation was 50 to 60 percent of normal, and at the core, 30 percent; and this within a semiarid forest. This time the inevitable fires did not expire in bogs or snuff out in wet duff. Fires that started in the spring burned throughout the summer. They burned everything in their path, and there was nothing short of the largest rivers to halt their spread. A detailed survey was of course impossible, but on the basis of 500 question-naires Shostakovitch composed a sketch of the conflagration. The domain of the fire was 1,813,000 square kilometers, "about one fifth of the area of all Europe." Of this, 8 percent, or 142,500 square kilometers, involved crown fires, an amount "equal of about one-third of western Europe (excluding Russia)." Peat burned as well as forest. (Interestingly, the southern Siberian taiga had experienced fires of a similar magnitude in 1871.)[112]

But what most drew attention to the burns was the smoke. "All of middle Siberia was enveloped by smoke, sometimes so thick that it was not possible to discern through it trees, houses, etc., at a distance of 14 feet." Altogether the smoke converged into a pall covering about 6,800,000 square kilometers, roughly "the whole of Europe." Navigation on Siberian rivers slowed, then halted; locally, the pall produced a terrifying darkness at noon; cereal crops that normally ripened early during dry spells required an additional ten to fif-teen days to grow, the direct result of diminished sunshine. Its fires set into motion an immense exodus of wildlife, moose, snakes, squirrels, birds, wolves, and bears. Normally phlegmatic journalists took note; newspapers obsessed with the collapsing Russian war effort found space for the great fires. The 1915 pall cast its shadow to European Russia even as the Great War darkened skies to the west.[113]

Salvation lay in sheer size. Over the course of two hundred years European Russia had by 1900 cleared 28 percent of its forest land; yet it still had 39 per-cent forested. Only a fraction of Siberia suffered permanent conversion; for the most part the forest had changed character but not metamorphosed into farms and factories. A 2,000 hectare fire in Bavaria could send shock waves through a community and burn itself into collective consciousness for a cen-tury. A 4,000 hectare fire in Provence was epochal. In Arkhangelsk it barely merited discussion. In Siberia it simply vanished.

There was cause for alarm in European Russia, now feeding its forests into the unquenchable maw of industrialization. Here forestry's emancipation demanded fire's suppression. In Siberia visitors, not residents, bemoaned the burning. Even so, not all of them agreed with the received revelations of forestry. Adolph Erman dismissed speculation that Siberia's "total and irremedial" fires would extinguish the indigenous peoples by destroying the taiga as the exter-mination of the buffalo had the plains tribes of North America. It is much more likely, he believed, that "in order to transform by extinction" the aboriginal peoples, "Christian brandy must be called in to the aid of the comparatively feeble conflagrations."[114]

And Anton Chekhov mused that if settlements the length of the Siberian high-way "conspired to destroy the *taiga* with the aid of fire and the axe, it would be another case of the titmouse who wanted to burn up the sea." He then told of a "learned traveler" who accidentally started a fire that cast into flame the landscape "as far as the eye could see." The savant believed he had caused a terrible calamity. Chekhov disagreed. "I venture to say that the learned man's labors probably made a larger dent on Nature than what he imagined to be a terrible calamity. On the spot ravaged by fire there probably grows an impassable thicket, where imperturbable bears ramble and hazel hens fly."[115]

So forestry's learned doctrines would do more harm than fires. In the taiga ordinary standards did not apply. Certainly Europe's experience with fire did not.

(ii)

Although Siberia drew foresters much as it attracted geologists to search for ore and civil engineers to build railroads, those professionals could hardly see the forest for the fires. There were three "primal forces" at work in the Siberian forest, Alexander Strogy lectured in 1911 to the National Congress of Forest Owners and Managers. They were natural renewal, ax, and fire. "Every acre of the modern Siberian forest is the result of the conflict between and the interaction of these forces." The first was slow, the ax quickening, and fires universal. Together they condemned the taiga to slow death. Even its immensity could not stay for long Siberia's melancholy execution.[116]

What was needed was a forest protection law, or barring that, effective fire control. Its fires, Strogy asserted, were "so horrible" that they overshadowed all other forms of destruction. Construction of the Trans-Siberian Railway had made wildfire "one of the most urgent and well-publicized problems in Siberia." The economic harm fires did was "colossal"; they overshadowed and trivialized even "rapacious management and destructive cutting"; they shamed Russian politics, embarrassed professional foresters, and morally blighted the countryside. As long as "the problem of forest fires remains unresolved," Siberian foresters could not be "true stewards, since they cannot ensure the integrity of the forest." Without fire protection all other reforms were meaningless. The fires were inexcusable. And within limits, within the domain of the most economically valuable stands, Strogy believed, they were controllable.

Reform had to begin with the "attitudes of the Siberian people," who viewed the forest differently than foresters did, who viewed foresters as another class of meddling officials from an unjust state, and who saw fire as an ally as much as an enemy. Abandoned campfires dotted the taiga as stars did the night sky. Hunters burned "to attract ruminant game" or "to encourage commercial game to move in a desired direction." Colonization cut and burned new woods, and the fires crept or flashed into the surrounding forest. Every spring burning around villages and along roads reclaimed the taiga for humans; and these fires necessarily probed into the adjacent wildlands. At the extremes of nature and industry, lightning and railroads kindled others. But Strogy was unshakable in his belief that the vast majority of fires were caused by humans. That meant that humans could suppress them, or that fire control began with control over human firebrands.

Early decrees banning fire in sable-rich forests Strogy dismissed as the expression of a "platonic desire." By the time foresters commenced serious investigations, Siberia was a shambles. The regulations of 1878 by which District Conferences of Peasant Supervisors were to prescribe periods for burning were "completely ignored." In 1899 the government took notice, and promulgated "Temporary Rules on Cautionary Measures Against Fires," which sought to regulate agricultural burning. The law required clearings around each burn plot and the presence of a Forest Department representative. This was impossible, and the edict ignored. "No peasant has ever informed the forest administration before burning a field," Strogy concluded. "Nor has anyone ever dug border trenches, nor turned the sod in a strip 'not less than two sazhens wide,' nor brought 'spades, brooms, buckets, and other suitable firefighting tools' to the site." Rather, the grasslands were fired at "about the same rate as before" and the forests were "in no way protected from these field burns." Lack of supervision—of peasants and primitive forest guards both—was "the crux of the problem."

The consequences of promiscuous fire spread like an ecological virus. The foresters assumed the mantle of Grand Inquisitor: the people had to be denied the freedom of fire for their own good. The peasants' ignorance, indifference, and sullen hostility only hurt themselves; escaped fires killed people, damaged bird life, harmed fishing, ruined forests, incinerated telegraph lines, slowed river travel, upset the water table, polluted everything with "a great evil." To seal his thesis Strogy even argued that "the probability of bear problems is directly proportional to the intensity of forest fires, which force the animals to search for food outside the forest." In 1900 the bears in Narym province, starved of food by summer conflagrations, spent the winter wandering instead of hibernating. Some migrated in groups like the biotic outcasts they had become, invaded settled areas, seized livestock, and were "so hungry they even attacked haystacks."

Countermeasures against fire were a prominent theme of provincial conferences by Siberian foresters in 1901. Their ambition was daunting. The state forests of Yeniseisk province alone totaled 7 million hectares, over which 180 mounted guards and 21 local guards offered "protection." Since direct attack on fires was impossible, foresters sought to restrict travel in the spring to main roads, require permits for fire-prone activities in state-owned forests, and conduct protective burns on state lands in the forest-steppe and "where possible, the taiga." The last was of course the most disconcerting. A Tomsk newspaper editorialized against the practice of "blacklining around forest parcels in order to protect them from fires. . . . This is of little help, and, who knows, might even increase the danger, since they don't have enough personnel to manage the fires properly or to guard against spot fires. Furthermore, these burns set a bad example for the peasants. We have heard them say things like: 'the forestry people do their own burning, and yet we're not allowed to.'"[117]

The practice confused foreigners, too. Traversing Siberia on the eve of revolution, Richardson Wright and Bassett Digby recited the ritualistic text about the "serious nuisance" presented by taiga fires, and quoted one official about a fire along the Angara River in which "the smoke rose, and, drifting, hung like a mighty pall over hundreds of square miles of central Siberia. For over a month the sun was nothing more than a red ball glowing dully through the yellow haze." This of course did nothing to help agricultural fields invariably hungry for sunshine. Further, the British visitors perceived an institutionalized rot so pervasive that even "forest fires afford ample opportunity for graft." Instead of laying down fireroads and firebreaks, guards submitted false reports, received funds for work half done, and left fires to ramble over whole mountains. Outrage reached a climax when the two travelers witnessed "respectable old men dismounting from their horses and firing the undergrowth for what to us at the time seemed the sheer fun of it." They interpreted the episode as further evidence of graft (guards were paid to fight fires); and perhaps it was. Equally likely they were witnessing protective burning. Clearly fire protection had become a bureaucratic conundrum of topological complexity. To a forestry elite the only way to undo this Gordian knot was to cut it with an unequivocal stroke of full suppression.[118]

The authorities tried. But the taiga was vast, villages scattered, and guards few. Peasants impressed into extended firefighting considered that duty another oppression, and were as likely as not to express their disapproval with more burning. Siberia itself rebelled. In 1909 Yeniseisk authorities moved against several large fires. They purchased supplies, brought in troops, loaded supply carts, and sent them into the trackless taiga "where there were no roads or paths of any kind." The local officials had taken forestry's injunction seriously, that wildfires did such harm that "all possible means must be employed" to fight them. The tsar's troops marched into the taiga like the British raj into Afghanistan. The expedition ended in futility. "The money was spent honestly," Strogy concluded, "and the fire was extinguished . . . by some timely rain."[119]

(iii)

Call Siberia an exaggeration, a perversion, a dark hope, an aberration. Conflagrations would persist there along with larch forests, cold swamps, pine savannas, and frozen mastodons. Fire control would take time, and it would, like ukases, mining concessions, and prison camps, center in Muscovy. In principle, European Russia could banish wildfire to the far taiga as it did Decembrists, thieves, and other disturbers of the social order. Siberia's fires were, in a sense, the price of European Russia's fire protection.

Yet there was reason for faith, if not hope. Technique and knowledge had steadily accumulated; reports, treatises, and texts like those of Nat and Strogy, and M. M. Orlov's *Principles of Forest Protection in Russia*, explained the fundamentals of fire control. Equally, O. I. Kusenava in the Far East, M. E. Tkachenko in the southwestern Russian plain, and various scientists attached to expeditions throughout the taiga—the Siberian immigration studies, for example—began reporting and analyzing the complex biological meaning of fire. The earliest studies emphasized the succession and transmutation of forest types under the shock of huge or routine fires, a record written widely across the landscape and branded into the memory of its oldest inhabitants.[120]

Two broad strategies emerged, well expressed by I. Yatsensko in 1914 and then by D. Kossovich in 1915. One sought to contain fires by land use, by adapting the European exemplar of silviculture. Reducing irregular forests to rational patterns could contain fire just as the organization of field and fallow did for agriculture and as urban design sought to do for cities. The other strategy recognized that firefighting, too, was essential. It wanted lookout towers, telephones, paths and firebreaks, ponds for emergency water supply, and ready pools of firefighters. Both could claim a certain logic and even viability in the more densely populated regions of European Russia, although only fire control had much meaning in Siberia. But measured against the Siberian holocaust of 1915, both were naive, and against the catastrophe of 1921, helpless.[121]

The implicit belief that fire could be banished to internal exile in Siberia was of course an illusion. As long as any part of Russia was unsettled, it could burn. Revolutionary ideologies had as little effect as tsarist ukases. In 1918 the Bolsheviks nationalized lands, in 1919 Lenin promulgated a special decree for forest protection, and in May 1920 the Executive Committee issued a special act to address "The Struggle with Forest Fires." The prescriptions called for the appointment of "knowledgeable people" to lead the fight and for sufficient forces to be available for call-up, principally forest workers and military units. To ensure adequate manpower, firefighting was to be included within general military training. Yet even as the revolutionary regime sought new firefighters, it gutted traditional controls, hamstrung voluntary brigades (which defied class conflicts), and incited arson. Real fire control depended on social control, and as long as the new regime relied on coercion rather than self-interest, it ensured ample room for fire.[122]

In 1921 there was little control and plenty of fire. The Great War, the Bolshevik Revolution, and the civil war had ripped the social fabric. Then drought throttled the Volga basin. From April through August no rain fell. Crops failed, the politics of War Communism failed, bureaucratic apparatus wracked by civil war and peasant revolts failed, and the year is best known for its horrific famine. But it was also a year of catastrophic fires. Desiccated crops, peat and mire, communal pasture and forest, wherever there was grass or wood, all became fuel. In Mari ASSR alone more than 200,000 hectares burned, a third of its forests. Villages burned, mills burned, cattle perished, and peasants, already burdened with famine, died in droves. The greatest damages, however, fell upon the Volga's pine forests, most of which were still rising from the ashes of the 1891 fire complex that followed wholesale clearcutting. The fires burned into November. Three years after the Bolsheviks had seized power and declared a revolutionary order, reactionary fires struck Russia's forests as famine did its fields.[123]

There is no record that anyone attempted to fight the 1915 Siberian conflagrations. If they did their actions were wholly local, probably restricted to protective backfires. The 1921 fires had, in principle, more opportunities for control. Access was better, the population denser, and the impress of forestry more vigorous. That fire suppression failed so massively in 1921 testifies not only to natural conditions but to the extraordinary social circumstances of the day. The fires grew large because of the strength of drought and wind, because much of the landscape resisted conversion to fields, because Russia's fallow-rich farmlands did not display the intensive gardening typical of western Europe, and because the scale of Russian forestry frustrated silvicultural conversions; but they also ran wild because a society shredded by war and famine and outfitted with shovels, axes, saws, pine boughs, and torches could not beat back the invading flames, and very likely augmented them. Inhabitants yielded to a scorched earth.

Between them those two fire complexes announce and for many decades dominate the fire history of twentieth-century Russia. The 1915 fire defined the characteristic conflagration for Siberia; the 1921 fires, for European Russia. Both occurred in times of intense drought. Both reburned areas not fully recovered (to maturity) from their last burn. Both occurred on a scale unimaginable in Europe. And both impressed themselves into history by association with human tragedies—for Russia, the cataclysm of war, revolution, and famine. For both the great fires were equally portent and fact.

The control of Russian fire, critics concluded, demanded more. It required a revolutionary ideology, not merely science; an implacable political commitment to effect a Great Transformation of Nature, not merely ways to finesse around fallow; and a fiery explosion more frightening and symbolic than the Tunguska event. It required Marxism, Bolsheviks, Stalin, and the atomic bomb. In the end, fire control would prove as wrenching, and often as futile, as forced collectivization. Until then the fissure between Western ideas and Russian reality remained. But the more Russia and its Soviet successor state tried to seal the cracks, the more flame spewed out of the chasm.

EPILOGUE:
FIRE IN THE MINDS OF MEN

Evil men in Kerzhents are burning
the green pine fortresses.
—Nicholas Kliuev, *Destruction: A Cycle of Poems*
(1934, written shortly before his arrest)

Between the fires of 1915 and 1921, crisis after crisis hammered Russia. Anything less than millennial fires simply merged with the general chaos of war, famine, and revolution. Fire imagery spiraled like firewhirls from the Russian mind. Lenin's *Spark* spread into open flame. In *Pillar of Fire,* Nicholas Gumilev declared that he was "ablaze with the flame which reaches up to heaven out of hell." Igor Stravinsky wrote the *Firebird* and *Fires of Spring;* Alexander Scriabin, his last symphony, *Prometheus: The Poem of Fire* (1909–10), of which a critic wrote, "His element is fire. . . . Fire, fire, fire; everywhere fire." There were real wildfires great and small to match those sparked by metaphor. Flames rushed through every gap in Russian society, like wind through a torn tent.[124]

But once kindled revolutionary ardor had to be suppressed along with the traditional fires that had sustained old Rus'. Imperial Russia reconstituted itself into the Soviet Union. The new Soviet society built on steel, coal, petroleum, tanks, concrete cities, and political terror. Forced collectivization and tractors would reform farming; fossil fuels would overcome, at last, the immense inertia of Russian fallow; ideology combined with science and steel to propose a Great Transformation of Nature and a New Soviet Man. During the revolution, fire protection launched no initiatives, fire science no inquiries. The 1920 edict was a useful precedent, though plenty already existed, no more successful. Even after the trauma of the 1921 conflagration, fire institutions advanced only fitfully. Not until Stalin consolidated his power did the Soviet Union erect a fire establishment. Of course it would be the largest in the world.

The old core remained in Leningrad with the Forest Academy. In 1928 the regional forest experiment stations founded a new center, also placed at Leningrad, and quickly reorganized a year later into the Central Scientific

Research Forestry Institute (CSRFI). For the next decade its studies fell largely within a triangle inscribed between Leningrad, Arkhangelsk, and Sverdlovsk. The principal instigator was M. E. Tkachenko, a leader of prerevolutionary forestry. Tkachenko held the forestry chair at the Forest Academy, knew three languages, and had lived for two years (1910–12) in the United States and Canada. He was instrumental in transferring North American research to Russia, particularly measurements of fire danger. In 1931 he oversaw the publication of a collection of papers on forest fire, the beginning of systematic fire science. In 1933 a "fire group" at CSRFI organized around P. P. Serebrennikov, a chemist turned forester, who helped direct it toward the questions of combustion chemistry as well as forestry. The Serebrennikov Group remained surprisingly international. America—which by now had the most aggressive fire research and fire suppression organization in the world—was a continuing and obvious source of data and experiences. But the group foraged avidly in the literature of Canada, Finland, Japan, and Germany. Their efforts culminated in two major programs.[125]

The most dramatic was aerial firefighting with chemical retardants. If it succeeded, the scheme promised to overcome the inertia imposed by Russia's vast distances. The idea also resonated nicely with Communist ideology. The chemical-laded airplane could do for forestry what the tractor and artificial fertilizer could do for farming; the contrast with pine-bough-wielding peasants was one the regime liked. Early trials in 1931 quickly resulted in two autonomous forest aviation programs. Experiments in dropping extinguishment bombs, the free-fall of dry chemicals, and other airborne means to attack fires followed. That the techniques failed did nothing to halt the persistence with which they were pursued.

Meanwhile Serebrennikov and V. V. Matreninsky published in 1937 the results of the group's collective investigations, *Forest Fires and How to Control Them,* a comprehensive survey that tapped a worldwide literature, the first Russian text on the topic. The group moved on many fronts—combustion chemistry, firefighting technologies, slash disposal, firebreaks, the design of fire lookout towers, fire-danger rating indices. But there, for a while, the story ended. What the purges didn't kill off, the Great Patriotic War did. Both Serebrennikov and Matreninsky died of starvation during the siege of Leningrad. Only two students, I. S. Melikhov and V. G. Nesterov, survived to rebuild Soviet fire science in the postwar era. The Soviet literature on fire remained virtually unknown to the West.

Still, droughts came, oblivious to the new socialist order, and fires broke through the cracks of the Great Transformation of Nature. It was easy to amass firefighting forces, easy to proclaim a doctrine of suppression. It was less easy to restructure nature or to board over the gaps between theory and fact. Fires could not be shot, purged, or exiled. The more society broke down, the more likely it was that fires would escape. Large fires struck European Russia in 1924 and 1927, and they came with special force during Stalin's purges in 1932 and the Great Terror from 1936 to 1939. The 1938 drought and fires ranged from the western border to the Urals. Collectivization, mechanization, and aerial fire-fighting could not suppress them.[126]

In the postwar era, the Soviet fire establishment became, in numbers, the largest on Earth. In output Soviet fire science rivaled that in the West. In the capacity to contain fires, Soviet suppression achieved, for a time, dramatic results. Even Yakutia, scene of the Soviet Union's largest fires, felt the impress. In the early 1970s approximately 700 fires a year burned an average of 150 hectares each. By the mid-1970s, 400 fires a year burned an average of 10 hectares. Almost certainly the official statistics are false, downgraded to meet mandated goals, but the trend is undoubtedly accurate. The real measure of what had changed, and what hadn't, came in 1972.[127]

The fires commemorated a half-century of Soviet rule. With bitter irony they struck the same regions seared by the 1921 conflagration. Drought again throt-tled most of European Russia, and although it was less prolonged than in 1921, no rain fell during July and August. In Mari ASSR, fires from April through June burned 87 hectares; from July 1 to August 25, 2,036 hectares; from August 26 to September 5, more than 180,000 hectares. Fires swept Gorky, Kostroma, Ryazan, Karelia, Komi, Arkhangelsk, Murmansk, and the Urals. They burned through the peat-laced suburbs of Moscow. Leningrad oblast alone experienced 2,363 fires, a record. Alarmed authorities flew in 1,100 elite firefighters from Siberia to help contain the flames. In ten days more land burned than in the previous ten years. Although fire experts attributed many of the fires to a freak dry-lightning storm, the official reports condemned careless—subversive—burning. In response the Brezhnev regime formally banned fire practices that had bound Russians to their land since their Neolithic ancesters had first farmed the forest steppe.[128]

It is hard to interpret the fires as other than political allegory, and even sci-entists did so. In 1921 the trans-Volga forests, if old and "overmature," were also majestic with dark history and folk meaning. They shrugged off light burns as a bear did fleas. They had survived big fires like those in 1815, 1823, 1848–51, and 1891, the last catalyzed by vigorous logging. But they could not survive the wild fury of the Bolsheviks. The woods burned to their roots. For decades the landscape was filled with the melancholy ruins of the old regime, the black wrecks of snags pointing accusingly, pleadingly, to the sky.[129]

The Bolshevik regime decreed that a new forest, created according to sci-entific principles, would replace it in a forestry equivalent to collectivization. It dispatched a special expedition of foresters, headed by Tkachenko, to rec-ommend reforms. The regime restocked woods, carved fifty meter wide firebreaks, replaced conifers with deciduous trees, erected lookout towers, and endowed a "mighty technic" to combat the antisocialist flames. Yet, although the 1972 drought was less intense, the capacity for firefighting immensely greater, and unrest replaced by the phlegmatic torpitude of the Brezhnev regime, the burned area for the two fire complexes was almost identical. The 1972 fires, in fact, virtually liquidated the forests replanted after 1921.[130]

Despite its vast forces of suppression, the Soviet state stood powerless before the elemental flames. There was no need this time for peasant arson to accelerate the burning, no reason to appeal to civil war, famine, forced collectivization, and the disintegration of village life to explain the damages; there was no lack of bureaucratic apparatus. The failure was structural, endemic, and absolute. The cause of collapse lay in the collectivist design of the planted pineries, the vast homogeneity of fuels, the corrupt chasm between conception and practice, the indifference of the resident populace to state prescriptions, the absence of traditional practices, including light fires. Projects boldly proclaimed had dribbled away, plantations had gone to weed and firebreaks had overgrown, scientific planning had ended in political cronyism and lethargy. Premature clearcutting and inadequate slash disposal had created sites of ready ignition. Instead of replacing one system with another, the Soviet regime had only destabilized the old and then relied on the iron fist of firefighting to hold its replacement in thrall. The fires of 1972 derived from the fires of 1921.

Mid-point in the Brezhnev era there was nothing left, not the old, not the new, only the ubiquitous symbols and fire-gutted rhetoric of the Communist state. Wooden Rus' was a memory, and its Soviet surrogate a burned-out wasteland. The official response was more suppression—more planes, more engines, more smokejumpers. But armed intervention could not suppress the fires as though they were placard-carrying dissidents on Red Square or an uprising in Hungary or Czechoslovakia. Fire responded to its own implacable dialectic, indifferent to purges, show trials, socialist appeals. If small fires were banned, large fires would replace them.

In 1972, however, other fires and technologies obsessed the Brezhnev regime. While around Moscow fires flashed through woods and smoldered in peat, the USSR and the United States negotiated an ABM Treaty. The threat of thermonuclear fire commanded international attention and symbolically announced the superpower status of the USSR. Among its provisions the Brezhnev regime successfully negotiated an exception for Muscovy. But the putative protection of an antiballistic missile network around the Kremlin was countered by the summer's surrounding fires, a symbol better grounded in Russian reality. Smoke covered the skies in a pall. Land collapsed over the subterranean cavities excavated by the implacable fires. Driving the ancient tongues of flame underground had not extinguished them. They burned on, and they would rise to the surface when conditions allowed.

SPOT FIRES
Fire in Atlantic Europe

A great flame follows a small spark.
—Dante, *Paradiso*

The European diamond shaped narratives of colonization as well as geographic lines of force. Moving north and south meant cutting across the grain of European geography. For agriculture, progress was slow, and adaptations frequent. At the mediterranean and boreal poles the valences that bonded mixed agriculture into a molecular whole broke. Swidden became the norm and pastoralism prevailed. But colonization east and west moved along climatic contours, even as the equilibrium between wet and dry—the proportions of land and sea—unbalanced in favor of one or the other. To the east, the land widened into the Eurasian plain, its water confined to rivers and bogs. To the west, the continent splintered into peninsulas and finally into islands. The one, eventually, brought under European influence the largest of the world's land empires; the other, the greatest of its maritime empires.

Of the two, the latter, the discovery and mastery of the world ocean, was the most profound. Paradoxically, it was the Earth's waters that carried European fire the farthest. Europe's world-spanning flames began as spot fires off its crenulated coasts.

The islands were, ecologically, a mixed lot. Some, like the British Isles and Greenland, were continental fragments separated from the mainland. Some were splinters of coastal mountains, isolated by rising seas or subsiding coasts. Others, including those deepest in the Atlantic, were volcanoes, a few active, many relic. The most spectacular was Iceland, balanced precariously—violently—atop the Mid-Atlantic Ridge. The offshore islands were easily found and quickly colonized. The impulse behind the discovery and settlement of the remote and scattered isles is considerably more complex. Expansion across the North Atlantic was much easier than in the south because there were far more (and larger) islands there, and those northern islands formed clusters rather than solitary points.

In Atlantic Europe the balance between oceanic and continental almost always favored the sea. Maritime influences bathe all the islands. The moderating sea makes the Grand Canary and Santa Maria Islands habitable, although they occupy, respectively, the same latitude as Plateau du Tademaït in the Algerian Sahara and Tonopah in North America's Great Basin. No less compelling is the northeast-trending Gulf Stream, shooting out from the Gulf of Mexico, shearing off into whirls of warm water and igniting storms before expiring in the North Atlantic. The Gulf Stream's warmth seeps over the region like fog. London, for example, rests on the same latitude as Irkutsk and Saskatoon, Saskatchewan. Oslo occupies the same latitude as Olekminsk in Yakutia and Fort Smith in Canada's Northwest Territories. Sea ice and bergs melt away before the Stream's surge. Along the flanks of Greenland, glacial ice shoots south and sea ice shuts down the coast, but between Norway and Iceland ice is sparse and broken. The Gulf Stream is the reason. Its modulating influence made coastal Norway and the Shetlands habitable in ways that Svalbard was not.

Atlantic Europe thus became more, not less, maritime, and its islands more, not less, accessible to seaborne traffic. If rivers accelerated the rapid reconnaissance of the Eurasian plain, islands assisted travel over the world ocean. For the most part the Atlantic plain, like the Eurasian, was settled by traverse as explorers and colonizers sailed along lines of latitude to the extent that wind and current allowed. Only later, after they understood the larger circulation of the trade winds, did they follow the fluid geography of the region, the recycling waters and winds. Until then boreal Europe settled the northern islands, and mediterranean Europe the southern. Near-shore Britain became a fascinating medley of central, boreal, and mediterranean cultural influences. To the extent that they resembled European lands, Atlantic islands were easily colonized. To the extent that they differed, particularly if they exhibited subtropical climates, they were prized.

The islands were far from a full miniaturization of Europe or Europe's subregions. Scale, accessibility, and the quirks of history rendered some—the largest and closest—into cameos of the continent and left others as little more than simpler and odder chips off the European block. Very small flakes could not exhibit much geologic or climatic complexity, and archipelagoes of earth-shards like the Shetlands or Faeroes were no greater than the sum of their parts. Larger isles, however, offered richer variety, especially if they spilled around a volcanic peak. Such islands were often more complex climatically than patches of similar size on the continent. So, too, were their highly filtered biotas.

Floral colonization was selective, and faunal colonization dramatically so. What plants thrived depended on what species could reach an island by the agency of sea, wind, and birds and which of those immigrant species could adapt to its conditions. The larger islands were complicated environments, rent with rain shadows, bursting with niches, and layered with life zones between shoreline and mountain summit. No species could seize them all. Still, there were great advantages for the pioneers: they had the land to themselves, and from their beachheads their progeny could adapt or evolve to claim dominions more diverse than any their predecessors had known. Their ancestral environs had defined their growth habits and ecological niches; now, like long-suppressed corks released from submersion, they popped up and rafted widely through the biota as competitor winds and nutrient waves allowed. The pedigree of individual species could be traced to mainland ancestries; the communities were boldly independent.

They were curiosities. Excepting Britain, the islands had many producers and few consumers. There were no indigenous grazing or browsing animals, no megafauna to push over trees, no foragers to root out tubers, and no herbivores to consume and promote grasses and forbs. With only storms and volcanic eruptions as primary disturbances, the biotas evolved into overgrown forests full of the trees and woody shrubs favored by the birds who migrated seasonally or permanently to the islands. Early European explorers reported hothouse landscapes overripe with woods and redolent with semidecomposed litter and humus.

Decade by decade Atlantic islands blithely stacked their green cordwood. Even where humans existed, even with anthropogenic fire, the accumulation often continued because people like the Guanches of the Canaries or Irish hermits on Iceland lacked a needed component to crack open a resistant biota. Or the isles possessed climates that were unruffled by the seasonal winds of wet and dry. Equally, islanders lacked access to distant markets and invasive species that could redirect the closed loop of island ecology into an epicycle in orbit around an economic sun of traded plants and animals.

The early fire histories of the islands are unclear. Natural archives like pollen-laden bogs and fire-scarred trees are rare, and written records few or absent altogether. Undoubtedly the colonizing biota brought fire adaptations with it from the mainland as part of its genetic heritage. Great storms, droughts, volcanic eruptions, and other disturbances must have, from time to time, created the requisite conditions for conflagration; and some ignition source, lava or lightning, surely kindled them. But without species added or removed, the ecosystem eventually restored itself to something like its old form. There was nothing to compound one disturbance with another, nothing to inhibit reconstruction on the old pattern. Nothing, that is, until Europeans arrived.

The newcomers were maritime colonizers of ancient expertise and had greater biotic firepower than petrels and seals. With the aid of islands, they had colonized the Mediterranean and the Baltic. With boats, they had rapidly disseminated the Neolithic revolution. Over millennia they had sought islands, fought one another for control of islands, traded and conquered from island outposts, and cultivated myths of islands in the Western Sea. To the Atlantic islands they carried their fire practices and even more, their agriculture, and with it a critical capacity to leverage fire. They quickly transformed islands corpulent with fuel into biotic forges in which to recast island ecology.

Even before they attempted systematic colonization, Europeans were depositing goats and sheep on uninhabited isles—these in addition to black rats and other escaped vermin. They introduced new flora and loosed pyrophytes, particularly those grasses and weeds long associated with their preferred livestock and whose seeds mixed with fodder or cereal grains. Island biotas became, at least in the short run, more fire prone; and on islands, unlike continents, the displaced species could not easily reclaim an old site or reestablish a prior ecosystem. There were fewer refugia, fewer opportunities to recolonize, and less resilience. Unique, specialized, disturbance-shy species died out; tough, generic, human-allied species thrived. For islands that had experienced fire infrequently or had known it without its fire-catalyzed confederates, the shock was intense. That the fuel load of many islands remained high—excessive by most standards—transformed shock, for some, into detonation. Colonization commenced with fire.

So the winds of European expansion scattered brands across the world ocean. European fire spread over Eurasia like a flaming front. But it crossed the Atlantic in a spray of spot fires as each island burst into flame and each flaming spire cast new sparks to the insistent wind.

IT WAS ALL A PLANTED GARDEN:
THE BRITISH ISLES

Europe's history is Britain's. More than this, the British Isles distill that history into one dramatic miniature. Although Britain became, over time, as insular as Russia was continental, the fire history of western Europe poured into it, and Britain in turn exported that experience more widely than any other nation. Its home fires burned on ships; and by the early decades of the twentieth century, the sun never set on Britain's imperial vesta.

It was all here. Just as Britain had rocks from every geologic era, so it had biotic outcrops of most European ecosystems and fossil relics of every fire practice. Britain was a synopsis of European fire history. The isles experienced the full brunt of Pleistocene climates—the recurrent glaciation; the eustatic tides of the Atlantic; the decline and fall, rise and recolonization by Europe's biota. It knew *Homo erectus,* then *Homo sapiens* in all his cultural avatars. Almost everywhere charcoal carpets the horizons of its organic soils, underscoring changes in biotic ensembles. Migrating Celts brought agriculture. Conquering Caesars bestowed the discipline of Roman roads and latifundia. Angles, Jutes, and Saxons, unsettled during the Great Migration era, relocated from worn-out fields of Jutland to new clearings in England. Viking raiders and Norse colonists put landscapes as well as villages to the torch, and confirmed the routine burning of ling and heath. Along with its peoples, plants, and animals, the fires from mediterranean, central, and boreal Europe funneled into Britain. It experienced landnam, not once but over and again. It knew fire-catalyzed transhumance along its upland, Celtic fringe. It saw a market-driven pastoralism arrogantly suppress a mixed agriculture in the Highlands. It led the agricultural revolution—the reclamation of organic soils by paring and burning, the exploitation of new fertilizers, the rotation of imported cereals and discovered tubers. It pioneered the revolution in wholesale fossil-fuel combustion. As much as any country could, Britain defined, not merely experienced, the European understanding of fire.

(i)

Fire is buried deep in the British landscape. Fusain derived from burnt ferns litters Lower Cretaceous deposits from the English Wealden. Probably the originating environment burned often. Pleistocene glaciations and seas, however, scrubbed off the residue of biotic history like barnacles from a ship's hull. Each onslaught of ice and water extinguished Britain's fires, and each return of land and sun rekindled them. When the contemporary climate turned sodden, fire history retreated into the refugia of genetic memory.[1]

As with continental Europe, the Pleistocene revolutions, while comprehensive, were variable. Some glaciations were more extensive than others; some spared sites that sheltered biotic refuges. A long-standing land bridge allowed species, including early humans, to advance and retreat. But the constant ebb and flow over rough terrain, the firing and quenching of the biota in the climatic forge, the cross-continental trekking to the Atlantic fringe by a cavalcade of species moving at different rates and by distinctive means, all filtered the biotic stream and steadily impoverished, relative to the continent, the species richness of Britain and even more of Ireland. During the Ipswichian interglacial, spotted hyenas, elephants, rhinos, hippos, woolly mammoths, and tarpans, the ancestral horse, had wandered these sunny isles. They all vanished of course, as they did from continental Europe. But after the last, Devensian glacial (ca. 18,000 to 15,000 years ago), so did rabbits, fallow deer, bison, spruce, and possibly hominids.

Paleolithic pioneers exploited the littoral, where they claimed caves and crowded the shores of major rivers and lakes. Their record is sparse, their impact on the landscape uncertain. How lightning fire fared is even more obscure. If suitable fuels were present, fires would follow; in 1970 a dry lightning storm kindled twenty-three fires in a single Scottish forest. But the collapse of the Pleistocene set in motion such immense changes that anthropogenic-induced disturbances were only more ripples on a stream already in flood. The surge of species that comprised the mixed deciduous forest of temperate Europe splashed over the geologic levees and inundated the newly exposed lands. Together they washed away in the cresting flood whatever fire regimes lightning had imposed.[2]

The distinctive reformation came when Mesolithic peoples and an ameliorating climate converged. As the isles became more temperate, they became more isolated. Even while the retreating ice exposed more land, the rising seas overran more of the North Sea plains that welded Ireland to Britain and Britain to the continent. Somewhere around 8,300 to 7,500 years ago the climate reached its modern equilibrium. Britain joined Atlantic Europe. Hereafter insular biogeography would prevail. Future colonization would have to cross a saltwater moat and besiege the Dover-cliffed castle. That required human troops. By now humans were, in fact, well established, and as the climate progressively warmed, they impressed themselves on the landscapes with slow persistence. Biotic imports came in their baggage trains, while the indigenous species were rooted out by hand and hoof. Through human agents, the landscape was homogenized with that of Europe. Over the centuries, Britain acquired one of the highest proportions of alien flora and one of the lowest of endemics of any island on the planet.

The landscape revolution that commenced in most of Europe with the Neolithic apparently began patchily in Britain with the Mesolithic. Upland landscapes across England, from Dartmoor, to the Southern Pennines, to Yorkshire, reveal vigorous fire and a floral shift, a kind of pre-landnam reformation.

As the Mesolithic matured, light-thirsty scrub like hazel replaced shade-domineering trees such as linden and elm; avid sprouters like oak, bracken, and heather replaced pine and ash; and species otherwise suppressed by great shade canopies into understory or pushed onto margins or openings erupted in profusion. Clearings encouraged fires, fires expanded clearings, and with help from grazers and browsers they thinned out the woods and widened the ecological stress fractures. The soil, too, began to reconstitute itself. Its deep-rooted trees had functioned like biotic pumps, draining the subsurface waters and venting them by transpiration to the air. With deforestation, the ground slowly flooded with excess water. The soil became podsolic, waterlogged, acidic, and burdened with undecomposable debris. Blanket bogs seized vulnerable locales.

On wet sites, lowland or upland both, deforestation led to peat; on drier sites, to heath and moor.

Disturbances such as these were magnified when coupled with climate changes. But the evidence for a climate-driven change simply does not exist. The British environment paused at a crossroads, and the path it took was the one its Mesolithic tribes chose—one from which Britain could never fully return. It has been estimated that, through such means, as much as five-eighths of England and Wales experienced soil acidification and disrupted nutrient cycles. In this immense reformation, fire was the likely catalyst, and burning the cardinal technology.[3]

Patch burning amid scrub and berries, underburning through pine savannas, broadcast burns to drive and draw game, escaped wildfires and high-intensity burns to clean out windfall after major storms—all set into motion changes that profoundly restructured the British biota. The evidence of fire is abundant. The shifts to sprouters, light-seeking species, and grasses and forbs are classic signs of fire-induced succession, particularly of a fire-browsing regime. In 1701, De la Bryme described excavated peat beneath which lay the ruins of an ancient forest. "It is very observable, and manifestly evident," he reported, "that many of these trees of all sorts have been burnt." Many also displayed marks of chopping or splitting with wedges. Modern stratigraphy has exhumed the same archives and has concluded that fire was extensive, recurrent, and potent at least in Mesolithic uplands, and of such regularity and magnitude and in such frequent association with Mesolithic tools that it is most likely anthropogenic. If the evidence is often circumstantial, it is, to quote Henry Thoreau, like the convincing circumstantiality of finding a trout in the milk.[4]

Yet doubts remain. Critics concede that *Neolithic* landnam could instigate such changes, but Europeans, especially Britons, find it difficult to imagine significant environmental reformation in the absence of agriculture. For centuries the British have viewed their isles as a tended garden, interpreting every transformation through the prism of mixed farming. They have cast into the category of waste and wildwood anything that existed before or apart from spades, plows, sheep, cattle, cereals, and ribwort plantain. It seems fantastic that Mesolithic tribes equipped with primitive stone technologies and without domesticated livestock could have induced such changes. But of course they could have done just that, if the environmental circumstances were favorable and if one is willing to see fire use as the norm and fire exclusion as the anomaly.

What Mesolithic peoples required above all else was a suitable seasonality, a cycling of wet and dry. They had tools sufficient to kindle, they had appropriate sites, and they had grazers and browsers in abundance—a Eurasian menagerie of deer, bison, aurochs, and field mice. And they had purpose. Why should Mesolithic Britons do less than Andaman Islanders, Kalahari bushmen,

Ghond tribesmen, Canadian Cree, California Miwoks, and endless other hunters and gatherers who successfully exploited fire to remake their habitats? Australian Aborigines engineered a biotic revolution in Australia with wooden spears, boomerangs, and firesticks at least 30,000 years before Mesolithic tribes wandered into Britain. Even the despised Fuegans, whom nineteenth-century Britons considered almost a freak of nature, a missing link, carried firesticks and remade their bleak steppes into a Tierra del Fuego.

Of course Mesolithic Britons used fire: to suggest otherwise is to excise them from the Great Chain of Being. What is not clear is whether their burning practices could propagate from hearth to landscape, and whether the torch passed merely over the surface or burned throughout the ecosystem. The most probable explanation is that they could, and that the biotic reformation we find recorded in bog pollen and charcoaled soil profiles is a fiery groundbreaking for what became the English garden.[5]

By the Neolithic there is no longer any doubt. Evidence clearly shows a recognizable agriculture around 5,000 years ago with all the classic symptoms of the landnam syndrome—elm decline, deforestation, soil changes, cultigens, weeds, livestock, and charcoal.

The biotic future of Britain belonged with its humans. They determined what grew and what perished, what lands degenerated and what would be reclaimed. Some slashings widened into permanent clearings; some regrew with forest or scrub useful for nuts and rough pasture, ready for further harvestings; and some sank into podsolization, spreading over the countryside as a scabby blanket of bogs and moors. Probably the climate was more continental, even as the rising seas isolated Britain from the continent proper. The subsequent return of a maritime climate (no place in Britain is more than 120 kilometers from the coast) only nurtured what early agriculturalists had planted. Often, accelerated clearing, grazing, and burning interacted with a revival of wet weather to lead to soil leaching and waterlogging.

The landnam phase in Britain lasted for centuries. It expanded Mesolithic precedents enormously, and it persisted through waves of new invaders—the Beaker people from the Rhine Basin, the Celts, the Romans, the Angles and Saxons, the Vikings, and the Normans. None of the newcomers imposed a dramatically different regime. Rather, if warriors, they seized political control over existing practices or, if settlers, accentuated trends that were already operating. They expanded the realm of agriculture, accelerated land clearing, introduced greater numbers of exotics in the form of crops, cereals, livestock, and faunal pests, and grimly continued to exterminate the wild competitors of those species. Cattle, sheep, pigs, dogs, and rabbits replaced aurochs, bears, wolves, and wild boars.

A critical moment came with the gradual promotion of sheep over cattle, because sheep could not be easily grazed in the woods. Domesticated sheep required pastures, which meant greater deforestation and the cultivation of special pasture grasses, and they could not coexist with deer, which further prevented their being grazed in forests. They demanded, too, the extirpation of predators, the substitution of the domesticated dog for the wild wolf, the establishment of transhumance and enclosure to carry them to seasonally suitable browse or to ensure sufficient paddocks. In brief, they required a wholesale overhaul of the British biota.

Through landnam, through migration and reclamation, through plague and abandonment, through restoration and agricultural revolution, the British garden grew. Probably its basic structure was complete by the time the Normans consolidated their hegemony. Thereafter it intensified, ever more complete in scope, ever fussier in details. Woods were confined to almost ceremonial groves, or were otherwise coppiced or pollarded. Underbrush was disciplined into hedges or driven into remote moors. Grasslands evolved into manured paddocks or manicured lawns. Herding became husbandry; specially bred flocks fed on specially cultivated grasses or field fodder crops. Everywhere the human hand shaped, pruned, felled, drained, plowed, planted, and replaced. "In a Word," Daniel Defoe said of the countryside, "it was all Nature, and yet look'd all Art."[6]

Even art, however, could be augmented by Reason. The Enlightenment rage for "improvement" drove landowners to rework old landscapes and reclaim new ones from waste. Reports poured out from Parliament, and local improvement societies urging systematic reform. The enclosure of the commons, the cultivation of moors and the draining of wetlands, the introduction of new fodder crops, fertilizers, crop rotations, and plows—while the old edifice remained, its decrepit guts were ripped out, its plumbing rebuilt, its power source reworked, and its interior refurbished with modern appliances. Even as the industrial revolution overtook its agricultural scout, the land remained a masterwork of human artifice. The garden surrounded the factory where it had previously enveloped the village. In the 1720s, Defoe reported approvingly the observations of two "Foreign Gentlemen" who remarked of Bushey Heath that "England was not like other Countrys, but it was all a planted Garden." Two and a half centuries later, it still was.[7]

(ii)

Britain became a veritable museum of Europe's landscapes, a thesaurus of its fire practices. The fires were there, though officials sought to keep them safely within the bound registers and behind their glass cases.

Throughout the Holocene, fires had almost everywhere dappled the scene, and charcoal sequestered in lakes and bogs preserves the archaeological record of those events as fully as stone axes and the cracked bones of deer and cattle. Spring fires burned prior to green-up; fall fires after curing; and summer fires, even in peat, during times of drought. There were fires for land clearing, fires for field cleaning, fires for pasturage, and fires for foraging and hunting. Even in historic times there are records of fires used to smoke out fowl in Scottish caves and of torches used while fishing illicitly for salmon. In keeping with the gardened scene of an island, fires were typically small, the agricultural equivalent to burning the leaves raked up beneath autumn trees. Burning became part of an English constitution of agriculture, never quite explicit but always there, always indispensable, and always part of the common law of land use.[8]

Mostly, British fire practices resembled those of Europe's temperate core. But there were differences. Woodlands vanished from Britain more quickly and thoroughly than in central Europe. The Domesday Book suggests that only 5 to 15 percent of the land remained wooded at the time of the Norman conquest; in Lincolnshire, only 3.4 percent. Except for the most remote, woodlands existed primarily for pannage, as semicultivated orchards for mast and fodder. Pasturage was, in fact, the dominant use for most of Britain's non-arable lands, a preference imprinted by the demographic implosion following the great plagues in which flocks refilled the vacated village fields. Along Britain's hilly fringe, transhumance carried livestock through Kent, Wales, Scotland, and Yorkshire.[9]

The torch was as much a complement of the flock as was the shepherd's staff, and flame as common a feature of the moor as the yellow and purple flowers of heather and ling. The charter of 1273, for example, granted to commoners around Ashdown Forest the right to burn scrub and broom to improve forage. In thirteenth-century Sherwood Forest, where heather and fern were considered "covert" for the king's deer, suspicious authorities inquired who "burnt them to get pasture for his animals." A statute of 1607 restricted muir (moor) burning in north England on the grounds that "there happeneth yerelie a great distruccion of the Broode of Wildfoule and Mooregame, and by the multitude of grosse Vapours and Clouds arrising from those great Fyers, the Aire is soe distempered and such unseasonable and unnaturall Stormes are ingendred . . . by the violence of those Fires driven with the Wynd, great Feildes of Corne growinge have been consumed." When in 1638 a John Harton was arraigned for burning in Exmoor Forest, he protested that the overgrown heather improperly entangled his sheep, thus limiting his right of passage. He argued further that the land had become rank with old heath that was fit browse for neither cattle nor deer. The land ought to be burnt to restore it, he insisted, a remedy "found by daily experience of burning commons not far from the forest." Well into the twentieth century, pastoralists in the Afran Valley of Wales "burned the mountain" in early spring to green up the grasses and forbs. Without burning, the principal fodder often became decadent and unpalatable, the underbrush overgrown and impenetrable. Without access to fire, commoners had no effective biological access to lands, whatever their legal rights of use. Accordingly herders burned *Calluna* heath on moors, gorse on hill pastures, and poorer grasses on downs. The moors and bogs stimulated by early landnam's fires became the principal scene for British burning over the millennia that followed.[10]

In one of the best-known examples, villagers regularly swiddened the ling swaying over Yorkshire moors. Later Yorkshiremen fired the patches according to an agricultural calendar that spanned seasons and years. Mostly they burned in the spring, and in theory they fired only the older, decadent *Calluna* heath on a roughly ten-year cycle. Pastoralists recognized that such practices introduced variety to the landscape and ensured vigorous growth. "Burning the ling" was also the preliminary stage in turf graving, the harvesting of turf and peat from drier moors.[11]

Not all fires were controlled. Some were accidental burns; some incendiary; and some the product of conflicting purposes. Even where allowed, moor burns often escaped, and in drought years they could range widely, by British standards, through field and woods. In 1762 it was said that "everything [was] burnt up, and the moors being on fire from Ewden to this [Broomhead] common and consumed several hundred acres. Cowel was for the most part on fire and almost all the moors in England and Wales." While moor fires were a general nuisance, they most enraged those landlords intent on establishing forest plantations whose young conifers were particularly vulnerable to fires that raced out of the heather. This, too, was an old conflict. Laws passed to prohibit malicious or careless burning were largely unenforceable. Queen Mary protested in 1566 that in the countries of Nairn and Moray the "divers of the inhabitants" were "making mureburne and raisis fyre . . . to the great hurt and destrouction of policie within our realms." In 1685, Parliament passed an act that prohibited muir burning after the end of March, thus regulating a tool rather than eliminating a nuisance. Other statutes followed. In 1693, three men accused of a heather fire that destroyed fir woods on the Craigmore of Abernethy had their ears nailed to the gallows on the moor of Belintomb.[12]

But burning was too entrenched to extirpate easily. Especially as the population increased, as the rage for sheep put more and more of the countryside into browse and grass, and as social conflicts scattered sparks far and wide, fires were common. Where not encased by arable lands, they could readily escape into waste or woods during dry years. The earl of Fifth almost despaired of eliminating fire in the waste, whose danger was "scarce to be conceived." A fire in Glen Urquhart in 1770 was halted only after gangs cut a firebreak some 500 yards wide. In his monumental *Manual of Forestry,* William Schlich confirmed that "forest fires are of frequent occurrence in the heathlands of Berkshire, Surrey, and Hampshire." In 1636, the lord chamberlain wrote the high sheriff of Staffordshire to explain that His Majesty knew of the "opinion entertained" that "the burning of Ferne [bracken] doth draw downe rain," and that since His Majesty planned to travel to that part of the realm, he "hath commanded me to write unto you, to cause all burning of Ferne to bee forborne, until his Majesty be passed the country." In the eighteenth century Gilbert White fumed over the persistence of folk burning in Selborne:

> Though (by statute 4 and 5 W. and Mary, c.23) "to burn on any waste, between Candlemas and Midsummer, any grig, ling, heath and furze, goss or fern, is punishable with whipping and confinement in the house of correction"; yet, in this forest, about March and April, according to the dryness of the season, such vast heath-fires are lighted up, that they often get to a masterless head, and, catching the hedges, have sometimes been communicated to the underwoods, woods, and coppices, where great damage has ensued. The plea for these burnings is, that, when the old coat of heath, etc., is consumed, young will sprout up, and afford much tender browse for cattle; but, where there is large furze, the fire, following the roots, consumes the very ground; so that for hundreds of acres nothing is to be seen but smother and desolation, the whole circuit round looking like the cinders of a volcano; and, the soil being quite exhausted, no traces of vegetation are to be found for years. These conflagrations, as they take place usually with a north-east or east wind, much annoy this village with their smoke, and often alarm the country; and, once in particular, I remember that a gentleman, who lives beyond Andover, coming to my house, when he got on the downs between that town and Winchester, at twenty-five miles distance, was surprised much with smoke and a hot smell of fire; and concluded that Alresford was in flames; but, when he came to that town, he then had apprehensions for the next village, and so on to the end of his journey.[13]

Free-burning fire had to compete, however, with controlled combustion. As Britain became ever more crowded, fire, like people and fields, had to keep its place. The originating fires became ceremonial vestas; the order of the garden determined the place of fire.

What had been, for example, among the most ubiquitous sources of prehistoric anthropogenic fire—hunting—became at best an accident. Although Shakespeare has King Lear proclaim that he would flush out his enemies by seizing a brand and then "drive them hence like foxes," fire hunting had long since vanished from Britain. Royal forests and chases, in particular, had become rigorously managed, with carefully prescribed rights of access and proportioning of browse and covert; foresters preferred to preserve that scene with cutting, grazing, harvesting, and other semicultivations rather than using fire. (It was commoners who demanded fire to give them ecological access for grazing and other traditional purposes.) The forest laws of 1662 proscribed muir burning within a quarter mile of young woods, and restricted burning to what would provide a year's fuel. The understory was more valuable as coppice for fuelwood than as habitat, as Gilbert White recognized: "Such forests and wastes, when their allurements to irregularities are removed, are of considerable service to neighborhoods that verge upon them, by furnishing them with peat and turf for their firing; with fuel for the burning of their lime; and with ashes for their grasses." Natural fuels were more likely to be combusted afar or in furnaces than burned in situ.[14]

Only on remote sites, inaccessible to arable agriculture, did broadcast burning persist, and then it was regulated as to season. John Evelyn reported in his *Sylva* (1664) that legislation prohibited moor and marsh burning between April and September because of the hazard of escaped fires, the obnoxious smoke, and the potential harm to nesting wildfowl. For their part, hunters, most of them transients, contributed wildfires from abandoned camps and smoldering wadding. By the nineteenth century, hunting had become a ritualized sport, and it was subjected to the same micromanagement as the rest of the British landscape. Dogs replaced fire as a means of flushing game.[15]

Something similar happened with Britain's other firebrands. Fire and sword swept Britain less frequently. The long period of ancient invasions had witnessed an outburst of burning—some in the fields and wastes, some in the villages (which, constructed of wattle and thatch, were really reconstituted woods and moors). Whether as an accident of record or a reflection of fact, the Vikings stand out as notable incendiaries, often firing upwind from a village and letting the flames drive the villagers from their cover, burning towns and fields, putting inhabited houses to the torch, and felling and firing the woods to prevent ambush and to deny sanctuary to enemies. It was an old Norse custom to establish title to land by burning it or, where more care was required, to carry a symbolic brand around the tract; in a sense this is what the raiders did, but with the frenzy of a berserker. In 1006 the *Anglo-Saxon Chronicle* recorded that "every shire in Wessex [was] sadly marked by burning and by plundering." The devastation increased during the long Norman war of conquest, and fire helped put many demenses into "waste." Border wars were fought with torch as well as pike. It was common practice for English marcher lords to fell and burn Scottish woods; it is said that John of Gaunt had his troops cut enormous quantities of trees which they gave "as fodder to the fire." The Scots reciprocated. After defeating the earl of Buchan, Robert the Bruce put the district to the torch; "marks of the fire," Archibald Geikie noted six centuries later, "are said to be visible on the trees in the neighbouring peatbogs." The civil war burned across much of England and Scotland. When a house inhabited by Jacobite rebels was torched in 1746, "some sparks catched hold of the young wood, and did irreparable mischief before it could be extinguished."[16]

Apart from war itself, fire was an expression of a chronic unsettledness that afflicted the less-developed regions of Britain, a violence that was only partly sublimated into rick burning and Beltane bonfires and never lost entirely. It was not enough to domesticate the landscape: the people had to be disciplined as well.

During Britain's second reclamation, fire was as critical a catalyst as for the first. Some burning targeted untouched or regrown forests—classic swidden cultivation. Thus, as the Reverend Arthur Young prescribed for Sussex, "if the forest be broken up for the first time, the furze, ling, broom, heath, with all other rubbish covering the surface, should be burnt as it stands, and then pared and burnt" preparatory to planting. Something analogous occurred where moss had advanced over formerly felled forests and smothered them in peat. An observer from Aberdeen and Banff noted that such sites feature "firm and fertile land, which, no doubt, is unfit for the plough unless it is burned, and then the crops luxuriate wonderfully with ashes. After a year or two new ashes must be made with new fires." Where surface fuels were too light to support deep burning, wood ashes (potash) were added and plowed into the soil.[17]

The reclamation of impoverished or organic soils—the farming of moor, heath, peat, and sod—propelled this enthusiasm further. That the practice was ancient in conception is likely: folk names abounded, and local adaptations flourished. Probably its origins trace to the culmination of the Great Reclamation in the thirteenth and fourteenth centuries. In Scotland alone it is possible to distinguish five classes of "ribbing and burning" on "Bruntlands." The timing, tools, depth of plowing, and length of burning varied according to climate, soil, and purpose, depending on whether farmers rotated through the peat in classic swidden style or attempted a permanent conversion to arable or to pasture, and then whether they cultivated for turnips, corn, heath, or clover.[18]

That the practice became pervasive is more certain. Soil swidden became an indispensable technology by which, in principle, waste could be converted to arable. Farmers collected peat as they would manure, then distributed their great mounds of ash where they were most needed. Their common cause was the recognition that peaty soils were both a nutrient reservoir and a combustible fuel, that fire was possible and combustion necessary for the transmutation. As early as 1662, Gordon of Straloch laid down both the prospects for the practice and the past from which they evolved:

> When, several centuries ago, all places were shaggy with woods to
> the great hindrance of tillage, as these forests were felled, or were rot-
> ting with age, moss grew over them, especially in wet and sunken
> places. The moss was at first light and spongy, but, increasing every

year by new additions, grew hard, and became firm and fertile land, which, no doubt, is unfit for the plough unless it is burned, and then the crops luxuriate wonderfully with the ashes. After a year or two new ashes must be had with new fires. Farmers, induced by this store of manure, eagerly desire these lands. The earth itself to a depth of eight, and sometimes twelve feet, is clothed with this layer; but when opened up it discloses huge trunks of trees parted from their roots or rotten with age, and in many instances destroyed by fire.

Britain's newly reclaimed fields rose literally out of the ashes of its old.[19]

As practitioners multiplied, so did critics. Academic agronomists never reconciled themselves to paring and burning, and in truth abuses were common and the margin for error often narrow. Burning too deep or too dry strip-mined the sod and replaced topsoil with stone. Any removal of organic materials, theorists reasoned, inherently impoverished the soil and upset its hydrology, while inevitable overcropping leached away the lifeblood of earth. Paring and burning too easily merged with muir burning, stubble burning, and other nefarious fire practices. Baron Courts routinely denounced the practice. So did many prominent agronomists, who could accept paring and burning as a vile but necessary means of conversion to sedentary agriculture but suspected it as a potential competitor. Critics who labored to expunge fire practices saw, to their dismay, the field of fire opening up. Farmers who exploited paring and burning were likened to profligate heirs who gambled away their capital instead of living off the interest. Soil swidden was the rural equivalent of speculative binges, the agricultural revolution's South Seas bubble.

But its promoters prevailed. In his compendium of West Country agriculture, William Marshall (1796) concluded that sodburning was essential to success. The practice spread northward to Scotland and acquired the sobriquet "denshiring" ("devonshiring"). In shallow heathland soils, denshiring converted waste to arable. In the Fens the Reverend Young observed that "it is scarcely possible, profitably, to bring boggy, mossy, peat soils, from a state of nature into cultivation, without the assistance of fire." In Sussex he declaimed that the practice of paring and burning was "one of the greatest improvements which land is susceptible of receiving." The farmer knows that, having slashed and fired the turf, he is "in possession of a dunghill." After four years of cropping, he dismisses the land to fallow, allowing the turf to rebuild until its next cycle of cultivation. England, in fact, field-tested the practice for all the continent.[20]

There remained, however, the need for more extensive pasture. The demand for wool to feed the textile industry through which Britain industrialized was insatiable. In England, as often as not, sheep crowded within the hedges of newly enclosured commons. The search for improved wool led to improved breeds of sheep, which required superior pasture, which argued for fodder like the nitrogen-fixing white clover, imported from the Low Countries. Slowly, as commercial husbandry replaced loose herding, grasses that thrived on close cropping and trampling replaced those stimulated by fire. In Scotland, however, the proliferating sheep followed behind a line of flame.

The Highlands and Islands persisted under the rule of clans and an agriculture not far removed from the Neolithic. Patch burning for subsistence plots, hunting, foraging, and cattle herding remained the norm. By the latter eighteenth century, however, the old economics had fractured under the blows of industrial demand. Highland chiefs initiated a century-long program of forced enclosure, the Clearances, that vacated whole landscapes. Into the vacuum rushed sheep, deer, and grouse as the great moors evolved into sheep runs and hunting plantations, better suited for a wider capital market. Into it too exploded fire, as if by a backdraft.[21]

The notorious Year of the Burnings that announced the Clearances had its environmental symbolism as well. The burned huts of evicted crofters had their counterpart in the transmutative fires that helped remake a Highland mosaic, long adapted to cattle, into a landscape fit for sheep. Muir burning itself was not new. What changed was its scale and purpose; what changed was the fire regime. The introduction of English sheep breeds like Cheviot and Blackface brought English style burning but without its social restraints. An observer to the Highlands in 1790 spoke of the "liberality, worthy of imitation" with which a lord "suffered the heath to be burnt." Others witnessed muir burning "practiced with advantage, by the sheep-farmers in the south country" and imitated them. In order to improve the range, it is reported that pastoralists, for example, kindled a great fire in Glen Strath-Farrer" that burned "twelve miles of pine, birch, and oak woods."[22]

The clearing of the Highland flora went hand in glove with the clearing of the Highland clans. Fires tracked the dormant heathlands behind the receding snows, and acquired new dimensions. Patch burning gave way to broadcast burning on a colossal scale, just as subsistence herding escalated into market pastoralism. As sheep multiplied across the landscape, more "wasteland" was burned and more woodlands felled and fired to support them. Under the synergy of fire and grazing, woods became heath, and heather became grass. Hordes of sheep trampled, plucked, and browsed a new pasture out of former woods and moor. When regulations governing muir burning were promulgated in 1685 and revised in 1772–73, they applied to Scotland, not England or Wales. Laws or not, some fires inevitably escaped to run wild. In 1790 the Reverend James Headrick wrote of "several instances" of widespread moor burning in the Highlands, and recalled especially "an extensive forest of native firs, which had been burnt by a fire kindled at the distance of many miles. The flame, urged by an impetuous wind, and acting upon the withered grass, and heath, in early spring, soon spread itself over many hills; until it caught this forest, where the blaze became tremendous."[23]

By the time steam engines added their metallic combustion to the national load, a Briton might well echo a couplet from Arthur Johnston's "Newcastle":

> *Why seek you fire in some exalted sphere?*
> *Earth's fruitful bosom will supply you here.*

There was fire aplenty, but except for the Highlands it was increasingly confined, sublimated, and restricted in place and season. On newly reclaimed lands, agriculture advanced under a cover of smoke, and during droughts fires could escape and rage through lands whose rough grazing left them rife with otherwise unconsumed biomass. On the increasing domains of arable lands, however, the agricultural revolution all but strangled fire out of the countryside. Instead peat was cut and burned as fuel; the woods were coppiced for fuelwood or converted to charcoal; understory was carefully manicured or harvested for fuel; grass and browse replaced domestic crops or were consumed by domesticated livestock. Excess growth was cut and burned in hearth or piles. Fire fertilized lands indirectly by preparing lime or readying heaps of rich ash to be plowed into spring furrows. Underwood, furze, and bracken were harvested for "hop-poles, hoops and cordwood" or rendered into charcoal. Villagers gathered small branches into faggots for hearth fires or to kindle the heartier fires that burned lime and brick. Coal replaced wood as a critical open fuel. So intensively was the land used that there was increasingly little opportunity for fire. Broadcast burns became debris fires, an implement of gardening like spades and rakes. As Robert Louis Stevenson put it in "Autumn Fires":

> *Sing a song of seasons!*
> *Something bright in all!*
> *Flowers in the summer,*
> *Fires in the fall!*[24]

So, too, were human firebrands restricted. The battle of Culloden in 1746 that opened the Highlands to clearance was the last land battle fought on the British mainland. Authorities eager to protect property strengthened the laws against arson and careless fire. Reckless burning destroyed hedgerows, the very measure of rural order and the rule of property. Worse, agrarian protesters burned haystacks and barns. The 1830 unrest led to rick burning on an alarming scale throughout southern England, as it had in France. In response, protesters were hanged or transported to Australia. Edward Wakefield pondered the outbreak and used the fires to advantage in promoting his colonization schemes to Australasia. But insurrection quickly died. When, in 1868, England next experienced coast-to-coast fires, drought had blanched the moors, and an ill-disciplined industrialization in the form of locomotives, not rural vagrants, cast the sparks. Britain's traditional home fires burned feebly, more symbol than fact.[25]

It had all gone too far. When William Brereton lamented in seventeenth-century Berwickshire that "here is a mighty want of fire in these moors," he referred to domestic fuels, but two centuries later there was an abundance of fire in furnaces and an absence of free-burning fires in the heather. Even among European nations Britain was exceptional for its pyrophobia, and even as its agricultural revolution matured, the industrial revolution overtook it, and the bright flames of the first subsided into the sullen coals of the second. Britain found in its coal beds the fossil fallow it needed to intensify agriculture, the fossil fuel it required to power factories and warm homes, and the flame-free combustion its intelligentsia longed for. Muir burning and straw burning became antiquarian relics like Scottish kilts and Yule logs, retained, or so critics believed, out of an endearing but irrational rural conservatism. In all this, too, Britain distilled the European ensemble. The black, coal-fired core, the flaming periphery, the fear of fire as disorder—again a cameo of the continent.

Certainly by the nineteenth century British fire history had largely moved to the empire's overseas dominions. Britain's own containment and occasional expulsion of fire perhaps made all the more intense the shock of rediscovering free-burning fire as an endemic and elemental phenomenon elsewhere. To travel to India, Africa, America, Canada, New Zealand, or Australia was to step back into British history to the early centuries of landnam and to engage environments where, unlike sodden Britain, nature could escalate bonfires into holocausts. So ill-equipped were the British that they lacked even foresters, and had to import German professionals to spearhead the administration of the conquered wildlands now nestled among their colonial commons.

(iii)

Fire receded and combustion advanced. That was the sanctioned scenario for improvement, and within limits that is what occurred. But fire had a logic if not a will of its own. It could not be arranged like quarried stone or painted over like a peeling post. Some places demanded fire, some attracted it, and some found it useful, even indispensable.

Britain's home fires never extinguished completely, and in odd ways some even rekindled. Fire lingered where the garden went to seed or where modern sticks twirled like a firedrill into ancient woodstocks. New ignition sources arose to supplement the old: railroads threw sparks liberally, recreationists replaced rural transients. Those who argued on behalf of fire generally advocated a traditional landscape. Those who wanted it removed were the voices of industry, spoken through forestry, and of urban populations, committed to nature conservation as they defined that term. Fire controversies—folk woods burning in England and Wales, muir burning in Scotland, and fire-excluding afforestation throughout Britain—were fundamentally social issues, secondarily environmental, and ultimately symbolic.

Fire traditions often died out slowly. Countryfolk continued to torch the year's rank growth with bonfires and broadcast burns. More insidiously they resorted to fire to protest the loss of traditional rights and landscapes. Often, commoners agitated for further burning on forest lands to retard the encroachment of scrub and woods on protected heaths and to make "pasturage more plentiful." Controversy over suitable fire regimes was a surrogate for controversy over land use, not only the purpose of land but the agency of its control. One group could legitimately view fire as essential to its interests; another, as detrimental. Not nature but society arbitrated the standard for judgment.[26]

Thus commoners with traditional rights of access to New Forest, for example, wanted more fire to keep heath healthy and to drive back woody vegetation that threatened to overrun pasturage, while Crown officials charged with promoting woods sought to prevent fires. By 1870, however, officials conceded and accepted controlled burning as a regular practice, though its dimensions were never as great as the commoners wished, and pines, in particular, gradually propagated like thistles over larger landscapes. Incendiary fires— a popular attempt to redress that imbalance—became increasingly frequent. In 1926, C. C. Dallas, a sportsman critic, lamented the legal and illegal fires that the "commoners" demanded "to improve the feed for their cattle and ponies" and the obsequious concessions of Crown officials who "fear that unless their [commoners'] wishes are complied with, there will be a risk of fires in the plantations." In fact, risk often became reality: "Not only is the Forest excessively burnt by the Crown servants but many incendiary fires take place which, during the dry weather of spring, can be seen burning day and night."[27]

So burning remained, but sub rosa. It was something peculiar to commoners, something that haunted the garden's slummy fringe, the countryside's East End, a topic not suitable for polite conversation. What could not be quarantined would be eliminated through land conversion.

Muir burning was not so readily disguised or dismissed. Its biotic logic remained in the genes of plants that reached toward the sun, grasped for sparse nutrients, and resprouted from severed stalks. Even a wholesale conversion of the moor to a sheeprun would change only fire's regime. Conservation of the heath meant, paradoxically, the conservation of fire. The controversy soon transcended local customs. As Parliament adjourned to the fall grouse hunt, its ministers could not avoid the moors' burning question.

When the Clearances remade the moors, red grouse proliferated alongside the sheep. By the middle of the nineteenth century, railways and sporting fashion had made recreational hunting as valuable as herding, and many landowners leased seasonal hunting rights and built lodges. What was good for sheep, so folklore held, was good for grouse. What lairds failed to recognize was the corollary, that if fire had promoted the heath for one, it had to remain for the other.

But as grouse replaced sheep, gamekeepers ceased to behave as shepherds. Sport hunting was more challenging if the heather grew tall. Gamekeepers sought to increase the covert, although "tall" also meant "old" and therefore decadent. The adage that "shepherds light the fire, the keepers put it out" became the narrative for a historical parable. Shepherds wanted one-tenth of the moor burned yearly; gamekeepers had bargained that figure down to one-hundredth, or even one-thousandth. "As early as 1857," one critic discovered, "there were reports of heather on certain moors 'man high'—by the sixties the whole effect of the shepherds' burning had passed away." What was good for sheep farming was, it seemed, no longer good for grouse hunting.[28]

Over appropriate fire practices—more fire for shepherds, less for gamekeepers—the two economies clashed. In 1871 and 1873 the controversy had festered openly enough to warrant a formal investigation by the Game Laws Commission. Even as the commission commenced its inquiry, and bag numbers were already falling, there occurred, with exquisite timing, an epidemic of strongyle, an intestinal worm, that devastated grouse populations. It was apparent to all that patch-burned moors were less affected than unburned moors. "The operation of burning is practically the only available means by which heather-growing can be successfully encouraged," observed Robert Wallace. A parliamentary committee subsequently concluded that "a well-burned moor can carry seven and a half times the stock of the moor burned on a hundred years' rotation, and nearly four times as much as that of the average moderately burned moor." To admit a role for fire, however, did not specify what fire's regime should be.[29]

So while landowners tried to restore fire, they had forgotten the originating conditions and mistook small burns as the antidote for not burning. The small burns failed. They were too complicated, too expensive, too subject to the whims of the seasons and workers, and much, much too little. The laws that regulated muir burning narrowed too greatly the times available for burning. The masses of unburned ling made reintroduction treacherous and often damaging. Fires escaped, soils baked, and heather recovered slowly or was replaced by bracken or grass. Sheep crowded onto freshly fired patches like looters at a burned building and pillaged the site. Like G. K. Chesterton's lament that Christianity had not been tried and found wanting, but tried and found difficult and therefore not really tried at all, timid patch burning had failed to do all it should have. Few understood how fire should function, and how a landscape badly corrupted by fire exclusion and wildfire could be restored. There were more epidemics, hybrid sheep became less hardy, and the fire environment degenerated into a landscape both less malleable and more volatile. Eventually Parliament commissioned an official inquiry, which issued its report in 1911.

The problem, put succinctly, was too little fire. The solution was to get more fire back into the land as soon as possible. Properly timed burns killed the strongyle larvae as it hid in moist, protected pockets; and these burns stimulated production of highly nutritious feed with which healthy grouse could resist infections. The parliamentary committee proposed a burning rotation of fifteen years as a working compromise; but it argued strenuously for much larger burns (up to a third of the estate) to reset the biological clocks, to free up the sclerotic arteries of the biota's nutrient cycles. "It is doubtful if too much burning can ever be done in any season," Lord Lovat observed, *"provided the areas of the fires are reduced in size as the patching and stripping of the moor progresses."* Large fires, even severe fires, were preferable to no fires. With regard to scale, "the answer can be given with no uncertain voice—patches are only a secondary consideration, the first essential is to see the proper proportion of the total acreage of the moor burned each year." The committee had even observed "one or two cases" of fires that burned through peat "to the bed rock" and had grown "excellent heather . . . on the mineral soil thus exposed."[30]

The committee urged big fires, a quick response, an enlargement of the season allowed for burning (earlier in the spring, later in the fall), and the use of autumnal fires particularly where old heather predominated. Such a program would promote heather over other plants, control the heather beetle as well as strongyle, benefit sheep as well as grouse, and, if the scale of burning was large enough, prevent sheep from overwhelming a fired site by overgrazing. The secret was to disperse the sheep by wide burning rather than concentrate them with small burns. "Burn Big" was the moral. Similarly the vigor of hybrid "hill sheep" depended on the vigor of their range, which depended in no small way on the vigor of a suitable fire regime.[31]

The fire-brokered alliance between hunting and herding that dated back to Neolithic times took on new life. Fire there had to be, but the form it took would vary. Scots wanted heather—a valuable winter fodder—and burned on a ten to fifteen year rotation ideally suited for it. But English and Welsh farmers preferred other flora, better suited to their breeds of sheep and styles of pastoralism, and burned accordingly. In Wales, mountain sheep were removed from the hills during the winter, so summer grass, not winter heather, was the critical pasturage. Hill farmers promoted grass by burning on a five to six year cycle. English hill farmers, too, turned to fire to help control dwarf furze and gorse and to stimulate grassy swards and rough pasture like purple moor grass. Gamekeepers sought a patchy mosaic of different aged heath and habitats.[32]

The urban folk of industrial Britain, by contrast, wanted fire abolished, like smallpox and cruelty to animals. Nature conservation groups worried that too frequent, too hot, or too extensive burning would reduce the diversity of habitats, eliminate desirable species, catalyze bracken, initiate soil erosion, and invade sacrosanct bird nesting areas. Exurbanites and recreationists distrusted rural fire and thought its smoke a pestilence. And foresters tolerated as little fire as possible, exploiting it defensively in order to create firebreaks around conifer plantations.

The emergence of forestry was something new under the overcast British sky. It did not intend to restore historic landscapes but to invent new ones. In spirit it belonged with other reclamations, a way of more closely cultivating nominal wastelands, leavened with modernism's obsession with novelty. But forestry's timing placed it within an industrial, not an agricultural, order, and its fire practices moved toward fire exclusion rather than fire use. The afforestation of Britain argued for less fire, not more.

Forestry was a novelty because Britain had long ago pruned its woodlands into coppice, leaf fodder, and pannage, and reduced its ancestral wildwood into the ceremonial arboriculture of estates. When it acquired vast forests with its empire, it had to hire foresters out of Germany. Those imperial foresters now returned to urge upon the Home Islands the same commitment to reforestation that Britain had cajoled and imposed on its overseas dominions. To their minds Britain deserved no less. "It is a remarkable fact that the nation which can boast of the most extensive forest department in one of her colonies," Bernhard Fernow observed in 1907, "has at home not yet been able to come to an intelligent conception even, not to speak of application, of proper forest policy or forest economy." John Croumbie Brown published sixteen volumes of forest reconnaissances from Cape Colony to the Urals, but almost nothing existed for the British Isles outside journals of arboriculture. William Schlich's *Manual of Forestry,* honed in British India, was the most comprehensive text in the world. Aspiring foresters from around the world were trained by Britain's imperial academy and carried those lessons back to their home countries. Eventually so did Britons.[33]

The scene was scandalous. Britain was by far the largest importer of wood in the world, yet marginal land rotted, seemingly useless, roughly grazed, pared and burned, fired to keep trees out of heath and moor grass, and unreclaimed by ameliorative afforestation. The scabrous fires damaged more than cosmetic appearances and deeply embarrassed reformers. Between 1820 and 1890, the Cooper's Hill region around Oxford—later (in 1905) the site of Britain's imperial forestry school—had suffered 150 hectares of burning that left it "only one-third stocked with regular forest." Patches and ribbons of unforested heather supplied the fuses until "regular fire lines" and patrols by vigilant students expunged them. Meanwhile, forestry's message merged seamlessly with reports like that from the Royal Commission on Coast Erosion (1909) that argued strenuously for afforestation as an ameliorative remedy for rural landscapes that were both overworked and underused.[34]

The Great War made that call more than a moral exhortation or an exercise in economic calculation. Britain, many believed, had suffered acutely from a near timber famine. Lloyd George thought the country had come closer to losing the war from lack of wood than from lack of food. Colonial sources were too distant, and in the case of India, too restive. Britain needed its own woodlots. Especially it craved the conifers its peoples had, since Mesolithic times, so assiduously stripped away. Afforestation could also reclaim wastelands otherwise abandoned to rough pasture and abused lands otherwise degraded into worthlessness. If they could not grow corn, the moors could grow forests. Trees promised ecological health, economic wealth, national security, and the transformation of fire-flushed moors into fire-free woods. In 1919 Britain created a Forestry Commission and charged it with afforesting the Isles.[35]

No one thought of fire. "Up to comparatively recent times," intoned A.D.C. LeSueur in 1925, "a humid atmosphere and a predominance of woodland composed of broad-leaved trees have together made the question of fire damage in English woodlands a matter of secondary importance." As I. G. Simmons has remarked in a different context, an English oak forest was "as likely to burst into flames after a lightning strike as a sackful of wet socks." Both should also have mentioned the relentless gardening of those residual woods. But fire proved a far graver threat than anyone had imagined. Britain's climate no more protected it from wildfire than its insular status, in an age of aircraft, saved it from warfare. Fire lay dormant, not dead. The era after the Great War carried the forest out of its hibernation in Highland glens and multiplied the opportunities for its kindling.[36]

There was the war itself, which so accelerated logging that "in every county," it was said, slash, grasses, brambles, and scrub grew into "dangerous fire traps." If such sites could avoid fire for a sufficient number of years, they would decompose into less volatile arrangements. But struck by drought, dry east winds, or careless ignition, they could explode. More threatening were the extensive softwood plantations promoted by the Forestry Commission. A fire at Glen Tanar near Aberdeen swept 830 hectares in a single rush; in June 1920 some 2,374 hectares burned in Scotland. The young conifers were as vulnerable as an old wheat field, little better than oily scrub mingled among the smoldering heather and grass. The industrial demand for wood plumped fuels; industrial transport by railway scattered sparks. Afforestation could succeed only if the new possibilities it created for wildfire were matched by equally aggressive countermeasures.[37]

Silviculture was plantation agriculture, and it first absorbed both farming's fire methods and its mores. Initial planting, particularly on moors, called for a preliminary burn "a year or so before the trees are planted." This practice, forestry's landnam, continued "irrespective of the nature of the site" even under the early direction of the Forestry Commission. Eventually plantations included firebreaks as part of their design, and burned around the perimeter to shield themselves from wildfires ranging like mad hounds across the moors. Ancient tools—fire beaters, brooms of birch—were stored at critical locations. Authorities laid down fire traces and fire belts—some breaks maintained by regular burning, others by planting to a more incombustible flora. Guards patrolled for fire at critically dry times. The Railway Fires Amendment Act of 1923 increased fines for carelessness. Articles about fire protection—long a staple of imperial forestry in India, Cape Colony, Sierra Leone, Australia, and Cyprus—now salted British forestry periodicals. The assumption had been that British fire would furnish the norm for the empire. But now, it seemed, Britain would learn from its imperial Outback.[38]

Still, droughts appeared and east winds blew, and as the twentieth century matured they found not manicured woodlots and leafy hardwoods but ready stacks of softwood kindling. The Forestry Commission devoted an entire issue of its *Journal* to the subject of the drought-driven 1933 fires. Having drained moors to plant pine, a Northumberland forester was shocked to discover that "fire in the spring months is an appalling risk in such a huge forest of conifers." In 1936, heavy rains prevented the burning of firebreaks, and then a hard frost followed and cured fuels early and dry winds drained them of moisture. Fires broke out—one started by an "Indian peddlar" who tossed out matches as he walked along rural roads—and propagated everywhere.[39]

Forest fires were prominent again because, for the first time in centuries, forests had become at least locally prominent again. They became a source, not merely a sink, for fire. As recreational usage by the public accelerated, with an inevitable increase in ignitions, one stunned forester proclaimed: "we have had almost completely to remodel our system of fire control." No British forester argued for routine burning within the woods; rather they argued against the wasteland fires that invaded tender tree plantations and the pressures for pastoral burning that insinuated a flaming virus into the forest itself. The *World Geography of Forest Resources* declared flatly that "the worst enemy of the forest is fire," and then cited as an illustration a 1948 blaze in Kielder that incinerated 290 hectares in two hours.[40]

As foresters patch-planted moors and marginal farmland, criticism arose not only from agriculturalists but from nature conservationists who worried that monocultural afforestations had become an ecological infection, blighting once-flowered moors and vital habitats for wildlife. But if they disagreed over the proportional value of pines, oaks, gorse, and dwarf furze, they found common cause in their fear and loathing of fire. Urban conservationists supplemented, and often supplanted, foresters as critics of burning. Moors became aesthetic landscapes and symbols, cherished as places visited, not places lived in.

When the Nature Conservancy convened a series of meetings in 1956 and 1957 to review the status of muir burning, the sessions revealed "a fundamental cleavage of opinion," as reported by D.N. McVean, "between the agricultural interests on the one hand and the foresters and conservationists on the other." Hill farmers argued for fire; they could hardly survive without it. Foresters distrusted it except as a catalyst for land conversion. Conservationists recognized that some fire was inevitable, but believed that "circumstantial evidence" was strong that burning, any burning, dissipated the humus that responsible agriculture had cultivated as the foundation of the English garden, and the precious vegetable mold leached away with exposed soils or vaporized into noxious smoke. By 1990 more Britons belonged to nature societies than were registered with political parties. They and the urban society in which they lived would decide the character of the countryside and the place of fire within it.[41]

(iv)

Postwar reforms were as dramatic for British land legislation and fire institutions as for British society. In 1946, the Hill Farming Act redefined the legal fire season and vested in Country Agricultural Executive Committees the responsibility for overseeing the code. In 1949, the Heather and Grass Burning Regulations expanded the reform to other landscapes; the New Forest Act restructured state-sponsored forestry and rural fire protection; and the Nature Conservancy received a Royal Charter of incorporation. As Britain changed so did its landscapes, and so inevitably did its fire regimes.[42]

Country Britain became an urban Britain, as its burgeoning population crowded into cities. A greater Britain became, in imperial terms, a lesser one as it shed its empire. The flow of fire expertise from the colonial periphery to the metropolitan core ceased. Urban elites established new norms for rural landscapes, rural aesthetics, and rural economics. For most urbanites, fire conjured up images of burning houses and stygian subway blazes, of television documentaries on rainforests savaged by slashing and burning, of the burning heather that called to arms Jacobite and Fenian rebels, of IRA firebombs, and of London during the Blitz. But there remained, within the genetic memory of Britain's indigenous biota, if not its population, the record of a more fire-conscious past. Heath and moors were only the most prominent expression of that heritage, because they were its most extensive relict.[43]

Even amid the dense stones of the City of London itself, the memory persisted. It took the firebombings of World War II, however, to liberate that buried past. Not since the Great Fire of 1666 had the 280 hectares of the City proper been so excavated, and not since the constructions that followed the Norman conquest had the City's land experienced such massive disturbance. Sites long covered were exposed to sun and rain, soils once stable were churned over like plowed sod, and resident species once immune to flame were fired like ceramics in a kiln. The City was, in effect, slashed and burned. And out of the ashes reappeared a flora long believed vanished. From pockets of brick dust and within the cracked walls of basements, standing like masonry pots, came an eruption of growth. Curiously, the most exuberant species returned Britain to its first record of fires, the burned ferns of the Wealden coals. Bracken staged an "amazing invasion" that, as K. W. Brad gushed, had "to be seen to be believed."[44]

If fire was an index of British land use, then bracken was a handy index of British fire. Both spanned geologic time; both persisted through all the declensions of the Quaternary; and both had found an ally and perhaps an alter ego in humanity. Probably, as L. Rymer notes, "bracken has achieved its present abundance and dominance through the activities of man," especially those acts branded by fire.[45]

Certainly bracken thrived as *Homo*'s ally and tracer, as a botanical vignette adorning the margins of Britain's parchment countryside. It joined other suppressed species liberated from the shade forest by Neolithic pioneers. Like so many others it favored the rough pastured landscape between closed woodland and arable field. Almost certainly it was promoted as a source of potash, fuel, thatch, bedding litter, compost, medicine, and food for humans and winter fodder for livestock. And like other allies turned parasites, it began to infest the overly humanized landscape, as ineradicable as it was ubiquitous. It has no known biological enemies. Only active harvesting, close gardening, and cattle herding (which trample down the stalks) contained it. The industrial breakdown of agriculture liberated bracken as the Neolithic had. Then it sprang up amid the burned and shattered ruins of London.[46]

Bracken was not alone, however. Other plants long thought to have been weeded out of the English garden struggled upward through the ash and rubble. The scene promised a reenactment of the biotic recolonization of Britain; the sterile City presented a tabula rasa not witnessed since the last glaciations. Bracken spread not by vegetative propagation but by seed, something almost unheard of in Britain's manicured countryside. But the experiment soon ended, "spoiled," in the words of Edward Lousley, "by the misguided efforts of well-meaning enthusiasts who have sown the seeds of garden plants broadcast in order to 'beautify' the ruins."[47]

The garden triumphed over the wild, and then the city reclaimed the sites with concrete, like a blanket bog. In that brief ontogeny, however, the Blitz recapitulated the phylogeny of British fire.

GREEN FIRE:
THE CELTIC ISLE

Beyond Britain lay Ireland. It was the outermost of the islands once connected with continental Europe—biotically among the most selective, climatically among the most maritime. Wholly open to the Atlantic, Ireland was both shielded from the continent by Britain and thrown into Britain's biotic shadow. Britain was source, filter, windbreak; whatever reached Ireland from Europe did so over a British dike; and of course not everything did. Everything that Ireland had, Britain had also; but not everything in Britain passed through to Ireland.

What did arrive was preserved. The role fire asserted in the hearth of an Irish cottage it also assumed in the Irish landscape. Estyn Evans wrote that he had "sat at fires which, it was claimed, had not been allowed to go out for over a century, or for as far back as family memory could go." At this "fireside seat," to which "the visitor was invited," tales of old times were told. Above all, the fire was "a shrine to which ancestral spirits return, a link with the living past." The last act of evening was to bury a live turf in the ashes, and the first act of morning was to revive it. That, in brief, was what Irish rural society did to its land as well.[48]

(i)

The biotic colonization of Ireland had to operate within a narrow geologic window. Perhaps as little as 1,500 years separated the retreat of the ice from the advance of the rising seas. Many plants faltered before they reached the Irish extremity. Of 260 flowering plants of general European provenance that settled in Britain, fewer than half crossed to Ireland. Of 889 floral species native to both, 15 Irish species were not known in Britain, but 409 British species were absent from Ireland. The process of naturalization showed the same gradient: some 51 British plants were naturalized in Ireland, and only 3 Irish ones in Britain. Not only the flora but the fauna of Ireland's woodlands were, relatively speaking, impoverished. Snakes, moles, weasels, fallow deer, elk—none arrived. While no Irish mammals were missing from Britain, at least 14 British mammals were absent from Ireland. Not only its isolation from the continent but its climate and topography account for the differences. More uniform than Britain, Ireland had fewer ecological niches.[49]

All this applied with equal force to its human history. The Mesolithic impact is unclear. Residual charcoal (the oldest: 8,150 years B.P.) appears to come from hearths, though high levels and an expansion of Scots pine and herbaceous species, both likely indicative of human activity, lace the archived peat. Neolithic landnam, however, branded the land with undeniable force. Around 3,500 years ago the first Neolithic surge broke over the British sea wall. Charcoal, cereals, pasture weeds, *Calluna* heath, elm decline, the initiation of blanket bogs, and a still wetter climate—all converge and collectively commemorate the conversion of Ireland's postglacial woodlands. The landscape that resulted would, within a range of tolerances, define Ireland for more than three millennia.[50]

The Irish landnam was most distinctive for its herds. Pastoralism, especially cattle, remained at its core. Eastern Ireland was somewhat drier and its soils better drained and could sustain sedentary arable; and cultivation repeatedly concentrated there, whether by Cistercian monasteries or English overlords. But central and western Ireland—the fringe of an island on the fringe of a continent—could not. Fire-assisted land clearing led to fire-mediated grazing. The Bronze Age Celts with their horse-drawn chariots and clan herds confirmed a pattern that elsewhere in Europe, like the Celts themselves, was plowed under. In Ireland they persisted. In Ireland bards fashioned a heroic literature around chariot chieftains like Cu Chulainn, while, improbably, cattle raids at Cooley and Regamna replaced the sack of Troy and the founding of Rome.

That the climate was mild enough to tolerate field grazing throughout the year also discouraged extensive infields. Typically the cattle fended for themselves, their numbers compensating for their low weight. In extreme cases, particularly in the wetter west, there was little fodder stored for winter, and little manure recycled to the fields. The herds remained in the open, the herders (indeed, the whole society) often with them, moving constantly between home field (*bally*) and summer shieling (*booley*), typically in mountains, bog, or other waste. Even the Irish chieftain was, as Maire and Conor Cruise O'Brien note,

> a semi-nomadic person, who spent long stretches of his life in the
> open air, on progress or campaign, hunting or, in earlier times, quite
> simply on the move with his herdsmen as his cattle changed pasture.
> Habitually he dined out of doors after the fashion of the Fenian legends.
> He continued to do so into Elizabethan times to the great scandal of
> English observers who also found his diet, of under-cooked meat, raw
> salads, milk products and little or no bread, an abomination.[51]

Under such blows the woods opened up or retreated outright, save those like hazel that also furnished mast. What replaced the shade-packed trees depended on the ensuing regimen of weather, fire, and grazing. Too-frequent fire and outright clearance pushed the system into blanket bog. Less frequent burning and forest fallowing encouraged heath. Either way, only the drying made possible by fire could counter the relentless wetting that rendered Ireland marginally habitable. The dampest and most overcast of Europe's lands became, ironically, a thesaurus of Europe's fire practices and a cultural hearth for its fire lore. The monks that preserved Europe's ancient learning had their complements in the folkways that saved its heritage of fire.

(ii)

Ireland was remote, but wholly insulated from European influence it was not. The Romans eyed it and dismissed it, declining to extend their invasion of Britain west. Instead Christianity, not Roman latifundia, introduced European agricultural techniques, and by A.D. 300 agricultural clearing slashed away many of the last vestiges of elm and ash. So a pattern emerged: Ireland was often invaded but not truly colonized. Its fire practices were attacked but never wholly suppressed.

For centuries, successive invaders spilled over the dike, but eventually the waters would recede and the land dry again. The Vikings raided the north and east coasts, erected towns, introduced their peculiar ling swiddening, and laid waste with fire, a pattern others were all too ready to emulate. (It is said that stone structures became common at this time because of the extent of Viking burning.) The Normans invaded Ireland after they mastered England, hybridizing land usage as the Norse had before them. Then Elizabethan England invaded, again claiming the more accessible and fertile eastern lands and beginning an assault on the residual woods that would sweep even hazel scrub into an Atlantic dustbin. Around Dublin, settlers introduced the three-field system; beyond the Pale, pastoralism prevailed amid small infields and a rough-pasture outfield periodically broken and burned. Edmund Spenser disparagingly likened the Irish herders to Scythians, for they lived "the most part of the yeare . . . pasturing upon the mountaine and waste wilde places . . . driving their cattle continually with them." But not until Cromwell was the conquest of all Ireland completed. And even before that final act, Bishop David Rothe remarked of the dispossessed that they "have no wealth but flocks and herds, they have no trade but agriculture or pasture," and for these reasons, it was "dangerous to drive them from their ancestral seats, to forbid them fire and water."[52]

Yet this was the ultimate ambition of the English invasion. The Britain that had long shielded Ireland from Europe now imposed a new (if eccentric) European order upon it. The Protestant Ascendancy commenced outright colonization that fundamentally restructured the countryside. Landownership passed from Irish chieftains and herders to English manorial lords. Wandering pastoralists, ever suspect, were to be replaced by a sedentary peasantry. The estates that Rome decided not to carry across the Irish Sea Britain did. That experience became, in turn, the model for Britain's overseas colonies in America. If it proved impossible to wring the water out of Ireland's bogs and to snuff out the fires from its ling, the British invasion did inscribe a grid within which agricultural reform could occur on a continental model. In reply, the "heather burning" became a rallying cry and symbol of Irish resistance.

Once a center of European learning, Ireland became an emblem of agrarian lassitude, an outfield to the English infield. Ancient agriculture piled on itself like blanket bog, and antiquarian fire practices smoldered like mounded peat. To folklorists Ireland was fecund; to Enlightenment agronomists and estate "improvers" it was as sterile as sand. As always, fire practices are a good index. The great fire ceremonies of Beltane, Midsummer's Day, and Halloween flourished, alongside a host of hearth-related superstitions. But the bonfires that blazed on every May Day hill stood for a score of fire-catalyzed purgatives and fertilizers: kelp was burned along the coast for ash; ling was fired decadally; the woods were kindled to prepare for cultivation and pasture; and where the woods' stumps were smothered under moss, peat was cut and burned in its place in peat-fired (or bracken- or straw-fired) kilns needed to dry corn and flax, the accumulated ashes of which were spaded into the fields or mixed with seed before sowing. In the seventeenth century, Gerard Boate observed that the contagion of heath burning involved both the Irish and the English, for after burning "the land bringeth reasonable good and sweet grass, fit for sheep to feed on; and with a little extra-ordinary labor and costs brought to bear corn."[53]

Such practices were universally condemned, if not by rational agronomists, then by Parliament. To improvers, pastoral fires belonged with the superstition that passed herds through smoke or brought the milch cow into the dwelling so that, seeing the cleansing fire, the cow might be cured of murrain. In 1743 the Irish Parliament prefaced an "Act to Prevent the Pernicious Practice of Burning Land" by declaring that good husbandry and agriculture were "greatly obstructed" by the habit, that dousing the landscape with flame did no more good than sprinkling it with holy water and passing a censer over it. Most agricultural theorists insisted that in fact it did positive harm.

But those landscape fires could no more be extinguished than the hearth fire or the candles that illuminated saints' statues in Catholic churches. "Faith in the use of fire," a meditative Evans wrote, "persisted longer than the woods." And beyond faith there was reason. Hely Dutton observed during his 1808 survey of Cork that "if a total abolition of this practice was to take place, as some people totally ignorant of rural economy seem to wish, a famine would be the result."[54]

Britain's second reclamation came to Ireland selectively. Enclosure was a by-product of land transfer, but it was too rarely effective, because the benefits often went to the estates of absentee English landlords. An agricultural divide increasingly segregated prosperous estates, given to horses and exotic trees, from impoverished small farms, which in their desperate search for fuel peeled upland peat to bare rock and hacked hedges into faggots. Still, the disincentives for reclamation were great, both for landlords and peasants. In its favor was a relentless rise in population that led Jonathan Swift to advance his "Modest Proposal"; that subsequently impressed the "Great Improver" himself, the Reverend Arthur Young, when he toured Ireland between 1776 and 1778; and that would, twenty years later, inspire Thomas Malthus to devise his famous formula by which productivity increases arithmetically but population geometrically. Critics believed that only the conversion of rough pasture to arable could head off starvation.[55]

The practical solution was paring and burning, readily adapted from Britain and ideally suited to the exotic potato. Pastoral "wastes" on hill and bog evolved into swiddened fields. The potato became as exclusive to the Irish diet as the cow had been before, but not as nutritious overall. The effect was no more an expression of Europe's mixed agricultural ideal than Ireland's ancient loose herding had been. Rural fire spread from the surface to the sod. In the early nineteenth century an estimated 90 percent of the potatoes grown in County Clare were raised on swiddened soils. Some 80 percent of all farms were less than 30 acres. Banning fire would ban the potato.[56]

Plague, not prohibitions, did that task. When blight struck the potato fields in the 1840s, even the smoke of the Beltane fires could not prevent catastrophe. The Great Famine resulted, and an Ireland that had chronicled its past through invasions from the outside now dated itself through its own outmigration. Its population crashed; probably one-fifth died, another one-sixth emigrated. The decline continued until 1930, leaving Ireland, in Frank Mitchell's words, as "one of the emptiest countries in Europe."[57]

The Great Famine seared Ireland's soul. Sir William Wilde observed in 1851 that "the closest ties of kinship were dissolved; the most ancient and long-cherished usages of the people were disregarded; the once proverbial gaiety and lightheartedness of the peasant people seemed to have vanished completely." But while the famine was a great divide in Irish folk history, it was not decisive in the history of the Irish countryside or of fire.[58]

True, there were new forces at work. There was the economic impress of a more liberal market, symbolized by Britain's repeal of the Corn Laws; there was the mechanical power of steam, epitomized by the locomotive; and there was the horror of the population crash and the revulsion it often instilled against archaic rural ways. There was little energy left, however, for wholesale agrarian rehabilitation. None of the new forces alone would restructure Ireland as powerfully as had the potato. Ireland had endured massive depopulations before—the Black Death, for example. After long decades it had always rebounded into a facsimile of its former self. It might well do so again.

But whether the old or the new, *something* would fill the vacated lands. European experience suggested that trees might be a better crop than potatoes. In 1883 a Dublin parliamentarian requested help from Denmark, which sent D. Howitz, an officer with its Forest Department. The reclamation of Jutland was of course an obvious analogue, though Howitz pointed beyond that to the example of the French Alps. "The question of re-afforesting these bare wastes," he insisted, "is a question of life or death to the Irish." No memorials, no "mere legislation," would "ever pacify that unhappy country" without the reclamation of those lost landscapes "by means of forest planting." As the world's largest importer of woods—its timber-trade imbalance "already an urgent question"—Britain, too, should take a keen interest in afforesting a degraded Ireland. It could become Britain's woodlot instead of its shieling. A quarter of Ireland, Howitz estimated, could grow commercial forests. That done, the country's "present meagre pastures and barren fields would become fertile meadows and smiling expanses of rich cultivation."[59]

Forestry was not the first plantation scheme for Ireland based more on faith than fact, though it fared better than many. Gradually, first on estates and then more generally, systematic reforestation proceeded, never quite as rapidly as enthusiasts recommended. The old pattern, like the outlines of Celtic fields still visible across the landscape, might prove ineradicable. Ireland's rage for reform diverted itself into the political fight for independence. Artificial fertilizers replaced kelp and sod as soil supplements, but this only confirmed Ireland's ancient status as an agricultural outfield to Europe.

Not until after World War II did industrialization become significant, and not until imported fossil hydrocarbons became widely available did Ireland have the surplus fuels and fallow it needed to electrify the countryside, diversify its diet, and replace the spade with the bulldozer and the donkey with the automobile. In 1973, Ireland joined the European Common Market, at last circumventing the British barrier. Its principal export, however, remained its people.

(iii)

This, too, was an old story.

Throughout Atlantic Europe, Ireland had supplied many of the skirmishers of the Neolithic, as it later furnished missionaries. Irish anchorites had a tradition of seeking solitude along coastal skerries or offshore isles. They sailed their currachs to ever more remote places, however, and had begun perturbing local sites as far away as the Faeroes and even Iceland. The first Faeroe was reached around A.D. 600–650. Legend holds that the annual migration of birds to this stony rookery inspired an Irish priest in the Shetlands to track their passage. Landnam followed. Quickly ferns gave way to grasses; weeds replaced junipers; burned peat substituted for wood as fuel. When the Vikings arrived around 800, they found landscapes already shaped by sheep. They named the archipelago Foøroyar, the Sheep Islands. Irish hermits reached Iceland, too, a far more harrowing voyage. Their numbers remained small, and their influence minor, however, when the Norse arrived to colonize in force. Probably some went farther west, as the legend of Saint Brendan suggests. If they did, they were too far from the Irish hearth to keep the cultural coals alive.[60]

Thereafter, by compulsion or choice, Ireland exported thralls to Norse settlements, soldiers to Europe and the British empire, convicts and diggers to Australia, and laborers and servants to North America. Early Scotch-Irish frontiersmen in colonial America lived much as their pastoral counterparts did in Ulster, Galloway, and the Scottish Highlands, and were condemned with equal vehemence for their feckless nomadism. "They go in gangs . . . ," wrote a seventeenth-century observer, "which move (like unto the ancient patriarchs of the modern Bedowins in Arabia) from forest to forest in a measure as the grass wears out or the planters approach them"; and along the way, they burned. The diaspora that accompanied the Great Famine, however, poured largely into cities. Those who had fled rural Ireland wanted no part in transplanting the old sod to new lands. Émigré Irish became urban.[61]

So, eventually, did those who remained. Firebombs in Londonderry replaced fired heath as an instrument of protest. Tractors took the place of dibble and spade, and nitrogenous fertilizers and manufactured biocides abolished the chemistry of flame. Burning peat became a stigma of poverty rather than a symbol of generational solidarity. The turf fires that had burned since before anyone could remember went cold.

NORTHERN MISTS, NORTHERN SMOKE: THE NORSE ISLANDS

They came with torch and ax.

Between A.D. 730 and 1030, Scandinavian raiders, traders, and colonists sprawled over Europe's northern littoral and many of its great rivers, from the Seine to the Volga. The Swedes faced east, viewing the Baltic as their *mare nostrum,* and penetrated into ancient Rus'. The Danes and Norse looked westward and ventured into the Atlantic. Danes crossed the North Sea to England; the western Norse more often skirted it, skipping like a stone across a pond from the Shetlands to the Orkneys, to the Hebrides, Scotland, and Ireland, then traversing west-racing lines of latitude to the Faeroes, Iceland, and Greenland, and ultimately to the New World. But if they traveled by water, they remade the lands they touched by fire.

All the tribes of this swarm had ample experience with islands. They inhabited shores and rivers, fished and hunted on skerries, and farmed the landscapes of the Danish archipelago. Norse villages that clustered like seal rookeries along the coast were de facto islands, their only means of travel by ship. To colonize the Shetlands or Faeroes was little different from entering a new fjord or settling offshore isles like the Lofoten. The etymology of "viking" is not clear, but one reasonable explanation is that it derives from *vik*, referring to a small, stream-fed coastal inlet. That was precisely the landscape best suited for their fabled dragon ships.

These dragons, like their mythical models, breathed fire. Raiders put to the torch villages and monasteries, and pushed Ireland into a defensive architecture of stone. Said the Orkney poet Arnor:

> The warrior laid waste
> now the Welsh, now the Irish,
> now feasted the Scots
> with fire and flame.[62]

They did the same to the land.

(i)

Landnam too traveled on the long ships. Settlers fired the land before unleashing herds of sheep, goats, and cattle to pillage the biota. With the Viking voyages the fire practices of northern Europe sailed across the Atlantic, a hybrid of raid and landnam.

From early times, boats carried elements of the Neolithic to western Norway. But unlike for Denmark, it is less clear that the new practices were the product of new peoples. It is just as likely that gardens and flocks were added to existing hunting, fishing, and gathering—the strongest components seeping by a kind of osmosis along the permeable membrane of Norway's rugged littoral. The contrast is sometimes sharp, but more often subtle. The Norse Neolithic was less a process of clearing and planting than of grafting. Populations were small and occupation episodic, horticulture tiny, herding extensive, and granted the maritime climate, the opportunities for fire limited. Even so, the change is real. The landscapes were increasingly artifacts of human settlement.[63]

On the offshore islands of northern Norway the earliest tremors of the Neolithic may date to 5,500 to 4,800 years ago, with sporadic evidence of goats, sheep, and barley. But steadier occupation dates later, particularly from the pre-Roman Iron Age. Woodlands—primarily birch—receded; the suppressed understory, now liberated, thickened into heaths and meadows; and a new vegetative mosaic emerged that included exotic weeds, grazed mires, blanket peat, trampled and heavily dunged grounds, agricultural fields, and fallow. Periods of intensive use ended with abandonment, and secondary reclamation on a rough cycle of 90 to 130 years. (It is believed that the western Norse derived from an earlier migration into Norway from Denmark and Sweden, and so brought swidden along with their broad axes and cattle.) Thus the most indisputable index of human influence was fire. The distance from a site to the colonized core, Karl-Dag Vorren notes, "may be indicated by the amount of charcoal." That is not a bad summary of fire-catalyzed settlement throughout the North Atlantic.[64]

More intensive settlement, especially more far-flung herding, blurred this simple geometry. For millennia the region's land use had centered on livestock, and the herds, on heath. The Norse herdsmen claimed the heath for open grazing and for the harvesting of heather as winter fodder. When the climate became wetter still, they turned the herds out on the heath for byre-free winter grazing. They used peat as fuel, manure, and byre bedding. What outfield woods remained, they seized for swidden. Marshlands they fired much as Swedes and Finns did with *kyttlandsbruk*. The vital heath had emerged as a distinct brome, literally out of the ashes of landnam, and it required periodic renewal by more fire.[65]

Even the slopes of glacial-scoured valleys could support livestock with regular burning. To free near-meadows for haying (for winter fodder) the *saeter* system carried herds to distant summer pastures, a Nordic transhumance system analogous to the one used in the Alps and the practice of shieling in upland Britain and the Hebrides. *Saeter* huts were intermediaries between summer and winter range, and so were visited twice a year, once traveling to the mountains and again when returning. Cattle predominated among the stock, a source of butter and cheese that could help sustain the herders over the winter. The practice projected the cultural landscape far inland and from the coast to the mountains.

But the press of population demanded more. From early times, offshore islands (an estimated 150,000 flank the coast) were exploited for rough pasture until the snows melted off the mountains. The amount of land was not large; only 4 percent of the Lofoten, for example, is cultivated, though rough pasture can claim a larger fraction. Where the flocks went, fire went also—quickening summer green-up, fighting back scrub and birch, promoting the tough heath that alone could feed flocks both winter and summer, and enriching spring pasture for animals thinned by the long winter. They were fires the Norse carried throughout the North Atlantic.[66]

On many of the closer islands, Vikings were not always the vanguard of the Neolithic, and came more as raiders than colonizers. The Shetlands experienced woodland clearing, grazing, burning, and heath and peat formation as early as 4,500 years ago. Thereafter the flora underwent local recovery and reclamation on an irregular basis but within the constraints of island biogeography. Elm, oak, alder, hazel, and birch gradually faded into extinction. The landscape evolved into rough pasture dominated by heath and blanket peat; meanwhile buried charcoal reached a maximum.

Over the last 3,000 years, that fundamental Shetlands geography has remained constant. It survived the probable arrival of the Picts (A.D. 500) and the known colonization of the Norse around A.D. 800. By then landnam was a historical fact, the old biotic order extinguished. The newcomers took over its deserted fields and brought them to life again by burning; the landscape is littered with fire-derived place names derived from *brenna* and *svi[d]a*. And Nordic fire practices, not Celtic, probably dominated. The same scenario replayed on the Faeroes, already ripe with Celtic sheep when the Vikings arrived in 800. But on Iceland, home to only a few Irish hermits, landnam was left to the Norse.[67]

The story began when King Harald the Fairhaired extended his hegemony throughout Norway. His unpopular rule prompted an exodus of Norse colonists throughout the North Atlantic. Harald, however, pursued them, and as he extended his claims to the Shetlands and the Orkneys and as Celtic pressure mounted on Norse enclaves in Scotland and Ireland, unhappy Vikings, often with Irish thralls but certainly with servant species of sheep, cattle, horses, cereals, and weeds, fled to the Faeroes and then to Iceland, the latter discovered by three Viking voyagers during the 860s. Iceland became the furthermost of Norway's isles, and its colonization, begun in 870 and recorded in the celebrated *Landnamabok,* followed a classic paradigm. Within sixty years Iceland was settled. Forty years later, overpopulated with people and beasts, it endured its first famine.[68]

Iceland was colder, climatically more marginal, and more subject to sea ice than western Norway or the islands of the North Sea. But otherwise it exhibited a cognate landscape of heath, moor, marsh, lichens, scattered groves of dwarf birch, willow, and ash, all packed into niches around the coast, a familiar ensemble. So was the history that resulted. Cattle dominated the early decades. Disaggregated homesteads amassed hay meadow infields, rough pastured outfields, and more distant grazings. Willows and birch furnished browse; and heath supplied fodder for summer and winter. But whatever the indigenous forms, Norse colonists soon reforged Iceland's landscapes with the torch.[69]

Not only did they burn heath, they introduced that most diagnostic of Scan-

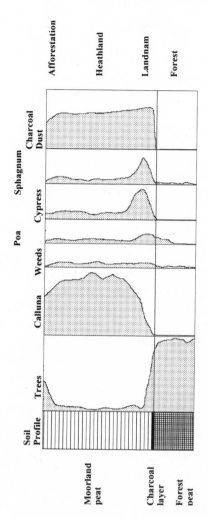

Norse *landnam*. This pollen diagram from western Norway records the conversion from forest to moor (and the more recent reclamation through afforestation). Norse colonists exported this practice—and left similar soil records—as they progressed westward across the Atlantic. (Redrawn from Kaland 1986)

dinavian fire practices: they swiddened. Where birch flourished, landnam meant fire cultivation. After barley (and oats), herbs and grasses sprouted in the ash. The Norse readily burned Iceland's existing heaths and moors, a familiar rite; and as a result of their felling, burning, and grazing they created still more heath and moor. Some of what they inherited they transformed into grasslands. Everywhere Icelandic landnam begins with a layer of charcoal. The names of thirty-one settlements contain references to those originating fires.[70]

So it was entirely appropriate, and in keeping with Norse antecedents, that conflicts over land claims should also appeal to fire. When later settlers protested the overly generous estates of the firstcomers, King Harald decreed that "no one should settle land more widely than he and his crew could carry fire round in one day."

> They must light a fire when the sun showed in the east. They must light
> further smoke-fires, so that each might be observed from the other, and
> those fires which were lighted when the sun showed in the east must
> burn till nightfall. Afterwards they must walk until the sun was in the
> west, and at that point light other fires.

With broadcast burns, the earliest pioneers had announced their claims. Now they verified those titles symbolically, with flames from the vestal hearth.[71]

For the Atlantic Norse, the journey to Iceland was the critical passage. From its western sea, less than the distance between Iceland and the Faeroes, it is possible to see Greenland, and from western Greenland to sight the outliers of the New World. Eric the Red spent his three outlawed years in Greenland, then returned to Iceland and came back with a colonizing party. In 985, fourteen ships packed with Norse Neolithic colonists reached southern Greenland. There they established Osterbygd (Eastern Settlement); later, they expanded to Vesterbygd (Western Settlement) up the Davis Strait, seasonally spared ice thanks to a tendril of warm water winding north from the braided Gulf Stream.

If the landscape was recognizable, so were the techniques of rendering it habitable. Shrub heaths dominated the coast; up the fjords there appeared groves of willow and birch, grasslands, fens, marshes, lakes, ferns, herbaceous cover on south-facing slopes, and tough heath in valleys routinely scoured by föhn winds off the ice sheet. Even so, the colonists were too far north for cereals, though with irrigation they could nurture some field crops. Instead they were thrown back on hunting, fishing, and livestock. Primarily this meant sheep and cattle, later a few pigs, goats, and horses. The legacy of landnam revived.[72]

The soils record the shock: the clearing of woods, the trampling and browsing, the stripping of sod for construction, the burning. The biota reconstituted itself with pioneering species drawn from its indigenous stock and with imported field weeds like *Rumex, Poa, Plantago,* and *Linum* (flax), all associated with cultivation, grazing, and disturbance, and all markers of Norse emigration as fully as broadswords and iron rings. The opportunities for biotic contamination were extensive. Ships carried local hay for fodder, filled their holds with soiled ballast, and exploited dunnage in the form of sawdust, wood chips, and twigs to secure their cargo. Weeds and insects traveled with the chaff. Half of the beetles on Iceland and Greenland are introduced species, probably from early Norse times. Species well adapted to the kind of disturbances practiced by the Norse sailed from one fjord to another across the Atlantic, a roster that includes the Norse themselves. With contact—Greenland's landnam—charcoal enters lakes and underlies peat.[73]

But as the centuries passed, the fires burned low. Between 400 and 500 colonists accompanied Red Eric to the Eastern Settlement. Like the pioneering Icelanders, they seized the prime lands at the head of the fjords, and with their flocks soon extended their reach. The settlement grew, additional immigrants came, another cluster fissured off at Vesterbygd, and others were attempted, if only seasonally, on the North American mainland. The Norse torch went to Markland (Labrador), L'Anse aux Meadows (Newfoundland), and the elusive Vinland, probably in New England. The archaeological record at L'Anse aux Meadows shows hearths, the forge of a smith, a pit kiln, and if the peat were peeled back would almost certainly reveal the char of burned moorlands. The ample charcoal, in fact, has made possible the carbon-14 dating of the site. Occupation, however, did not last long; these were the hearths of hunters and far-flung *saeters'* huts. On fjords and islands brushing the Arctic Circle a fire could brand a landscape for centuries. On a vast, milder continent like America the effect was soon buried beneath revanchist moors and thronging forests. The Norse colonization, in brief, quickly reached a maximum, and then, as had happened with Greenland, began to implode.[74]

On a marginal land not much was needed to tip the scales. Undoubtedly diseases from episodic contacts with Europe swept the settlements; conflicts worsened with migrating Inuits moving down the Davis Strait; the Little Ice Age meant climatic deterioration; no new ships flush with eager colonists arrived to replenish depleted stocks; and the traditional solution to island overpopulation—emigration—was not possible out of Greenland, which was effective neither as a source nor a sink. Vinland was inviting but hostile. Probably the environment suffered from overgrazing, from the sudden impact of unprecedented biotic stresses imposed on a land whose seasons turned with glacial slowness.

Whatever the plexus of causes, by the fourteenth century the Norse fire had expired, leaving the runes of char-inscribed stone in mute chronicle. Only the bardic ash remained to sing the deeds of forgotten heroes.

(ii)

Too often fire and ax had assaulted islands as they had villages along the Seine or fields beside the Humber. At their worst, Norse fire practices were a technology of raiding; at best, a craft of pioneering, of seizing and reworking the discovered biotic bullion. People and beasts had filled the best niches with stunning suddenness. Often Viking colonists melted down the biota as they did pillaged gold.

But birch and willow, the raw fuel of swidden, could not always resuscitate amid the bitter climate, close browsing, and leached soils; so swidden could not evolve into the circulating forms it had known in Sweden and Finland, and thus could not sustain itself. Those initial island woodlands were less a renewable resource than a biotic placer, plundered during flush times, the landscape left littered with the ecological equivalent of barrow pits and abandoned sluices. Over time, the dynamics that had made the land immediately habitable rendered it progressively less so. Island biogeography offered little escape from demographic pressures other than by emigration, famine, and disease.

The Norse isles knew them all. The furthest fires burned out; the nearer ones, from Iceland to Norway, banked their coals.

BLESSED ISLES, BURNED ISLES:
THE IBERIAN ISLANDS

The Norse brushed against, and often crossed, the outer limits of habitability. Between the Faeroes and Vinland only Greenland's Eastern Settlement approximated the climate of even northern Norway. But when the Portuguese and Spanish ventured into the Atlantic, they moved into balmier climes. They discovered islands rank with life and in the case of the Canaries—the Blessed, or Fortunate, Isles of ancient lore—rife with people. The archipelagoes of the eastern Atlantic formed a biogeographic region groaning with endemics, but like the Iberians who claimed them and the Genoese and Venetians who piloted many of the exploratory ships, they clearly derived from Mediterranean antecedents.

There was a synergy to settlement. One island led to another, as though they were detritus spilled from a Mediterranean stream into an Atlantic delta. Seize one island within an archipelago, and with luck and determination you had the others. Settle one archipelago and you had the advance base for colonizing a second or third. Eventually the clusters allowed Europeans to circumnavigate the world ocean. They led to cognate archipelagoes in Asia and America, the East and West Indies, from which voyagers could enter continents. The fires that burned on their towering peaks were the signal beacons of the caravanserai that lined Europe's maritime silk road.

They were also an ecological fact. The island biotas boasted a Mediterranean heritage of fire adaptations and for their lee sides, a trend toward sclerophylly. Undoubtedly lightning kindled fires from time to time. For the higher islands the prevailing winds distinguished between wet and dry sides, the broadly mediterranean climate (inspired by the cold Canaries current) defined wet and dry seasons, and drought from the subsiding Azores anticyclone imposed wet and dry periods. What the islands needed was routine ignition and the fulcrums and levers by which to ready fuels for kindling and to amplify fire's power to propagate, not only within an island but from one archipelago to another.[75]

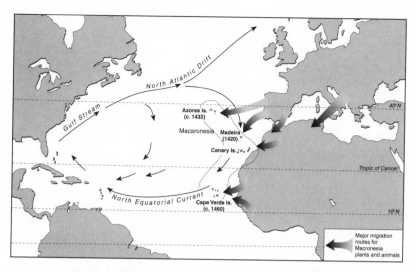

Iberian isles. Collectively called Macaronesia by biogeographers, the island groups derived their flora (and later fauna, and peoples) from West and North Africa and the Mediterranean, especially Iberia. Colonization followed ocean currents and winds, linking Atlantic Europe to the Antilles. (University of Wisconsin Cartographic Lab)

So their fire histories differ, from each according to its distinctive ecology, to each according to its niche in the political economy of European expansion. The Cape Verde Islands were too arid and too remote, and while ideally situated as a point of departure to the Americas, Portugal held them, not Spain, and so redirected the trajectory of travel south to Africa and India, not west to the Caribbean. Poor harbors, steep seacliffs, and a biota highly selected by arduous passage made the Azores formidable; and while westerly winds and currents made the archipelago a famous port of call for voyagers returning from the Americas or Africa, it was not an embarkation point for further discoveries. The Canary Islands had long been broken to the Neolithic harness, and had to be conquered rather than merely claimed. Madeira was a vast woods.

It was already an ancient and venerable practice to bring old fires to new worlds. The Canaries and Madeira furnished the basic paradigms, the one inhabited, the other not. In the Canaries, conquistadores took over the torch from the artful hand of the indigenous Guanches, and placed it under the boilers of sugar plantations. At Madeira colonists had to introduce anthropogenic fire for the first time, always an exaggerated exercise. In the Azores colonizers first sought help from faunal confederates, notably sheep, introduced by royal command in 1427. The sheep knew no competitors—no herbivores to challenge them for browse, no predators to contain their numbers. The avid herds worked like biotic sappers, readying the castellated isles for the formal assault authorized in 1439.

To each of the Iberian isles anthropogenic fire arrived in a different guise.
But to each it came.

(i)

The Canaries, a composite of continental and oceanic rocks, were an obvious
transition. The easternmost islands, Lanzarote and Fuerteventura, once enjoyed
land connections with the African mainland. (Fossils include ostrich eggs and
terrestrial turtles.) Deep but narrow straits surround the others like moats, fil-
tering the air- and seaborne pioneers from their sedentary neighbors. The largest
isles, Tenerife and Grand Canary, are often likened to microcontinents for the
complexity of their natural history. Of the 2,000 plant species known from the
archipelago, roughly 30 percent are endemic. The rest bear strong resemblances
to the Mediterranean biota, and like it are heavily salted with exotics.[76]

In their human history the Canaries also bridged land and sea. The process
of Mediterraneanizing the islands began with the Guanches, indigenes related
to the Berbers of North Africa. Probably the first wave of clans broke over the
eastern islands in the second millennium B.C., the last in the first centuries A.D.
The Canaries were, in effect, another of the Greater Mediterranean's many
islands, although thrust, anomalously, beyond the Pillars of Hercules. The
Guanches set about reclaiming the islands along customary Mediterranean principles. They brought cereals, pulses, dogs, pigs, goats, and sheep. Without consistent trade and further reinforcements, however, they lost or never received
metallurgy, horses, cattle, boats, and a written language.[77]

But they did possess fire, and with it they began the long task of cracking
apart the biota. The great pine forests that clothed the middle slopes of all but
the most arid islands were undoubtedly shaped by the Guanches' ambitious
burning and browsing as well as the seasonally arid, sometimes droughty climate. Like others of the genus, the Canary Island pine can send its taproot deep
in furious search of water. Uniquely, it can sprout epicormically from the trunk
after the loss of branches. Early inhabitants sought out resinous strips of pine
for torches. It is, in sum, a Mediterranean flora, well adjusted to disturbances
from drought, cutting, grazing, and firing. References to "thick trees" probably allude to savannas of thick-boled pine.[78]

Modern discovery commenced in 1336 with an expedition under Lanzarote
Malocello, followed by Catalan and Mallorcan (Majorcan) missionaries. Formal conquest of the Canaries lagged until 1402, when a Norman French force
sailing under the Castilian flag seized Lanzarote. A final reduction, however,
consumed nearly all the fifteenth century and required a cavalcade of military
expeditions and the aid of an epidemic disease, la peste. The last Guanches
capitulated on Tenerife in 1496. By then Columbus had returned from his sec-

ond, extended voyage to the New World, and Vasco da Gama was preparing to sail around Africa to India.

By then, too, Spanish settlers were completing the agricultural reclamation of the Canaries. Most of the Mediterranean domesticates found their way to the islands along with the rats, rabbits, pigs, insects, diseases, and other camp followers of European expansion. Irrigation, terraced hillsides, horses, sheep, figs, more cultigens including Old World vines and eventually New World grains and tubers like maize and potatoes, and conversion to export crops, notably sugar—all reformed the Canaries into something like Malta or the Mallorcas. In fact, an influx of Mallorcans actively assisted the process, along with Madeirans who by now had mastered the mechanics of island conversion.

That landscape of littoral and mountain, a biota toughened by climate and history, the controversies between peasant farmers and official elites, the elaborate ensemble of fire practices—as delicate as a fresco, as hard as basalt—all argue further that the Canaries belong with the fire chronicle of a Greater Mediterranean.

From early times the forests were exploited fully, and fears swelled that fire-catalyzed abuse would undermine their value. Tenerife was called the Burning Mountain for more than just its signal fires. As in Spain, livestock challenged the woodlands. The Canary Island pine was amply resilient to fire; in fact, it sprouted and seeded profusely after burning. But its capacity to endure abuse did have limits. The overharvesting of fuelwood, overgrazing of seedlings during the dry season, intensive browsing by exotic rabbits, clearing for greater pasturage, and resin tapping could push it into recession. As in Madeira and the Azores, sugar plantations exacted brutal levies from the woods to stoke their incessant furnaces.

But there were countervailing pressures for preservation. The peculiar climate of the taller islands made the pine belt into a fog drip forest that amplified the total precipitation as much as nine to ten times, so that the desire to fell the forests for fuel was met with the decision to perpetuate them for catchment, a biotic cistern from which to draft waters for irrigation. The differing water regimes between cleared and wooded sites were apparent to even casual eyes. (Unfortunately the total water budget remains little understood. It appears that the pines transpire more water out of the ground than they create from the clouds. The issue—as with fire—is one of proportion. Too few trees decrease the inflow; too many increase the outflow.)[79]

Protective measures included numerous restrictions, many directed against reckless burning. Common sources of fire such as night hunting during the dry season, pastoral burning, charcoal making, fuelwood cutting, and resin tapping were restricted or prohibited outright, and fires of any sort were proscribed under pain of "lashes, banishment, and even death." More and more, however, the isles resembled Iberia, itself almost insular behind the ramparts of the Pyrenees, except that pressures on the islands were more intense and the capacity for renewal and refuge less pronounced. Goats joined sheep, cattle, and even camels in the search for browse. With mounting force the Canaries mirrored the fate of other Mediterranean islands as graziers advanced behind a screen of smoke and as forests receded, leaving a few ceremonial groves to mark their passage.[80]

When the Sociedad Economica de Amigos del Pais organized in order to promote Englightened improvement, they targeted the dreadful state of the islands' forests. Their originating session, in 1777, cited in particular the plague of pastoral fires that sent flocks over clearings and stripped away the lush reproduction. In 1802 a wildfire gutted half of what remained of the famed Montaña Doramas woods in Grand Canary. Goats were demonized, here as throughout the Mediterranean. In 1836, official inspectors observed a "horrendous fire" that fed on a landscape "of mutilation," the outcome of poor regulation and abusive grazing.[81]

Still, there were many sources of fire, and until the rural population diminished or the agrarian economy metamorphosed, the burning would persist. On La Palma, peasants adapted the pine to coppice. Long-needled conifers salted the fields, their branches pruned every three or four years and burned in situ. The trees then sprouted new ones, and Canary swidden continued through another cycle. When critics protested the practice of raking up pine needles on a massive scale, peasants replied that they were only reducing the prospects for wildfire, which the authorities had proclaimed as an official goal.[82]

The islands' uniqueness was, after all, relative. The Canaries stood to Mediterranean islands as Iceland did to Norwegian fjords. In the ancient world, ships had apparently connected the Blessed Isles to Rome's *mare nostrum,* and they were known to geographers such as the elder Pliny. For western Europe they were closer than Cyprus, Byzantium, or the ports of the Black Sea. That link broke with the collapse of the Pax Romana. Now the isles became truly blessed because, unlike their Mediterranean cognates, the Canaries did not become cockpits for warring nations. If trade and migration ceased, so did marauding armies. The Canaries slumbered in an isolation both cultural and ecological, until Iberian mariners forcibly rejoined them to the Greater Mediterranean. Once done, however, the deed was not repeated. Conquest did not give way to reconquest in an endless regression. The Canaries became a port of call, not a point of conflict. The isles remained blessed, if burned.

(ii)

More spectacular was the colonization of Madeira. On Madeira, Portuguese *marinheiros* found an island sufficiently close to continents to have a rich biota and sufficiently distant to have selected species in often startling ways.

Madeira boasted a skewed ecology, a European flora without its complementary fauna other than birds and marine life and without the routine disturbances that seemed to rise and fall with the sun. The island was an immense woods, and for such it was named. With hand and hoof, however, it could be shaped into European analogues. Portuguese settlers soon flung open the windows of this Atlantic hothouse. They recreated Mediterranean agriculture de novo. Like humans everywhere, they began the process with fire.

In 1420 (or 1425, the date is uncertain) João Gonçalves, known as Zarco (the Blue-eyed), landed a colonizing party on the south shore of Madeira and promptly burned away the scrub to endow a settlement. He named the place Funchal, after *funcho,* the fennel, which abounded there. (Fennel was also the plant in which Prometheus hid the embers stolen from the Olympian hearth.) It is said that the Madeiran fire burned for seven years, that it soon escaped, and, as told to Alouise Cadamosto, one party "was forced, with all the men, women and children, to flee its fury and to take refuge in the sea, where they remained up to their necks in the water, and without food or drink for two days and two nights."[83]

It is a fantastic account. For those first-kindled fires to flare so furiously was a remarkable piece of timing. For fire to propagate over rugged terrain through dense forest (on the island there was said to be not "a foot of ground that was not entirely covered with great trees") is a rare event, and suggests that "big trees" did not mean closed forest, or that the settlers cleared as well as burned, or, rather unlikely, that woody Madeira was a quivering mound of kindling ready to explode at a spark. Probably the reality is that Zarco did set the first fires, that other settlements ignited others in tandem with aggressive forest clearing, and that the enormous mass of felled and homegrown woods fueled large, stubborn fires, most of which held to the drier and southern coasts and some of which threatened colonists (and burned wood houses in Santa Catarina and the church of Our Lady of Calhau, structures hardly credible for those first-fleeters fresh off their boats). Probably, as other chroniclers recorded, the initial wave of fires burned six months (the dry season), not seven years. By the time the explorer Cadamosto visited Madeira in 1455, the land reflected three decades of fire-catalyzed conversion. The great fire he described subsumes all those burns that had made the island, in his words, "more easily cultivated and also more rich and fertile." The Seven-Year fire is a mythic fire of creation.[84]

At first blush the deed, however brief or prolonged, seems incredible, arrogant, and stupid, the vandalism of ruthless ecological imperialists. In fact it is what humans moving into new country have always done. Pioneers broadcast burned to assert their claim to tenure. Travelers lit smoky signal fires to alert those whose lands they entered of their presence and peaceable intentions. Certainly the vanguards of the Neolithic were helpless without fire, and first sought areas that could burn. Pre-Neolithics had even greater need of free-burning fire, although they had less opportunity to leverage it as fully. Examples abound of first-contact fires. As Cadamosto noted for Madeira, it was "first of all neces-sary, when it was desired to people it, to set fire" to the land. It was amid just such Promethean ardor that Europe carried its vestal fire to lands previously outside the hominid hearth.[85]

A modern analogue occurred in 1972 when biologists from Australia's CSIRO visited the uninhabited Maria Island in the Gulf of Carpentaria. Abandoned for more than fifteen years, the island (40 square kilometers) had grown to a rank woods, strikingly different from the savanna of the mainland. With the party were four Aborigines whose tribe had jurisdiction over the island. While the scientists exulted in the lush "climax" forest, the Aborigines dismissed the scene as "dirty," a "rubbish country." Almost immediately on landing they set fires to clean it up. The scientists beat the flames out. Two days later the Abo-rigines succeeded in kindling a line of fires that swept the entire island in a wild surge. While the biologists lamented the loss of a unique biome, the Abo-rigines rejoiced that they had at last begun the process of rendering the place habitable, of reasserting their fire-mediated stewardship.[86]

That in a nutshell is what happened with all of Australia, the island conti-nent. And that is what happened on Madeira and on all the islands for which it is both emblem and paradigm.

The Madeiran archipelago consists of two islands, Madeira proper and Porto Santo, which is smaller, lower, and more arid. Both were soon heated over a Neolithic forge.

Madeira was the easier to convert. It had the broad features of a Mediter-ranean site—climate, winds, relief, littoral, ancestral biota—and the colonists lost little time in remaking the landscape according to classic Mediterranean patterns. Before long there were villages along the coast, terraces and canals across the hillsides, wooded copses hidden in remote ravines, and a panoply of roughly grazed landscapes overgrown with maquis, heath, grasslands, and bracken. The Noachian Portuguese brought a full complement of Mediterranean fauna, of which the domesticates included sheep, goats, pigs, poultry, cattle, dogs, and rabbits. A distinctive feature was the practice of housing dairy cattle in stalls, for which rough fodder had to be carried from the hills. The rabbits dumped on Porto Santo so proliferated that they drove off early colonists, who had to retreat to Madeira, rally, and mount a reconquest in midcentury; even so, the rabbits plagued the land like locusts. Madeira's export economy boomed with sugar cane.[87]

In such a landscape there were ample opportunities for fire. The Mediterranean climate argued for it; so did the archipelago's Mediterranean-derived biota; and so did the föhn winds that spilled down the flumes and valleys, and the Madeiran sirocco (the *este*) by which the Sahara from time to time blew away the northerly trade winds. Grottoes of presumed virgin woods, like the dense Caldeirão Verdo, disguised what was, in reality, a forest-heath, laced with latent maquis and scrub species. All this predated discovery. What Madeiran fire seemingly lacked was a spark. This, too, from time to time, it surely had.

But the old regime and its leisurely opportunities to restore itself over centuries ended with hominid colonization. The uniformity a rank forest had imposed was fractured by ax and animals. Equally, widespread clearing rendered more homogeneous the diversity of fire climates that had been created by the eroded terrains of a volcano thrust up from the floor of the Atlantic. There was more to burn, it burned more readily, and it was easier for a burn to propagate widely. The first shock of ignition freed fire, like Porto Santo's rabbits, to ramble.

After colonization there were more occasions for burning but less fuel to sustain it. Once that first flaming front had passed, the intensity of land use funneled the island's fuels into livestock, hearths, and kitchens; and rough pasture, if succulent only when burned, still worked to confine the overall fire regime. More and more the biota refined itself into a Mediterranean mosaic. So, indeed, fire found its place in the Madeiran garden, its strips of pastoral burning a kind of cognate to the island's irrigated terraces. Periodic immigration replaced the Mediterranean's usual wars as a means of bleeding off the surplus population. Madeira evolved into another Mediterranean miniature, the legendary fire of creation becoming little more than candles on the tablelands.[88]

The postwar economy began to rearrange the intricate Madeiran landscape as it did the rest of the Mediterranean mosaic. Goats lessened in value and decreased in numbers, cultivated pasture replaced bracken and heath, and forests swelled. In 1931 legislation empowered the Forestry Service to afforest with pines, acacias, eucalyptus, and vinhatico (*Persea indica*). As the contriving hand relaxed, the flora thrust out more buds and branches. Spared from voracious fuelwood gathering and browsing and replanted as a matter of official policy, woodlands reclaimed a larger proportion of the always limited land.[89]

Yet Madeira's fundamental conditions remained. What had made fire possible to Captain-Donatory João Gonçalves, and dangerous to his frightened followers, was available to his successors, provided that spark, fuel, and wind colluded in the proper proportions. That prospect was ever latent in the *este* and the scleromorphic scrub. From time to time it flashed into public consciousness, the biotic facsimile of a peasants' revolt. Not only in Madeira but throughout the Iberian isles, what had been won with fire and sword could be lost by it as well.

(iii)

With more than casual irony, fire crises have centered in the founding Canaries. Postwar reforms followed a Mediterranean scenario. Fossil fuels in the form of kerosene superseded fuelwood and charcoal, freeing woods from the consuming hearth. Mass tourism is supplanting an agrarian subsistence economy, downsizing flocks and committing resin tappers to economic purgatory. Souvenir shops are substituting a money economy for the bartered harvest of pine needles. Jumbo jets landing at Tenerife have become the caravels of a cosmopolitan economy of tourism. But instead of driving the indigenes into the hills, the moneyed invaders have sought to draw them out.

Nature's economy soon felt the flow of new money. With the close-pruning hand removed, trees (the Canary Island pine, especially) have spread like woody weeds. More spectacularly, an aggressive afforestation program, part of the *repoblación forestal* launched by the Franco regime, restored vast hillsides to woods, at the same time that an assertion of urbanite values has paradoxically stalled efforts to harvest this newest of the Canaries' plantation crops. The forest flourishes, redolent with litter, normally draped with fog drip, some 70,000 hectares throughout the archipelago, an artifact of aesthetics and affluence, an invention of the exurbanites who now reoccupied the islands. The uncut woods have become as much a symbol of contemporary progress as were the cleared woods of centuries before. The ancient fire-catalyzed abuses, this new society has asserted, would end.[90]

But fire had not arrived with Genoese captains, Spanish conquistadores, and Portuguese slavers, or for that matter with Guanche clans with their goats and wheat. Almost certainly it predated humans. For three thousand years, however, humans have influenced fire's regime, and for the last five hundred, have forced it, ever more rigorously, into certain molds. Colonists had shaped, not created, the archipelago's pyrologic regime as they had refashioned its hydrologic one. Their plantings and prunings, gardening and grazing had redistributed fire as their wells and canals had restructured the islands' water. The fires of the Blessed Isles had evolved with its flora, and would not end with afforestation. On the contrary, pine and eucalypt plantations added fuel. What happened in Côte d'Azur, Crete, and Corsica would happen also in the Canaries.

It happened most spectacularly, in fact, on the island of Gomera on September 11, 1984.[91]

A patrol of forest guards sighted the flames late in the evening of the 10th. Quickly the word spread, to the mayor, to the municipal police, and to the Civil Guard of nearby San Sebastián. The Spanish forestry service (ICONA) broadcast the alert throughout the island. Firefighting forces mobilized, and a stand was taken around the fields and village of La Laja. Still, the message propagated up through the chain of political command. It flashed to the government delegate, then to the governor, Francisco Javier Alfonso Carrillo, and to the government delegate for all the Canaries. Meanwhile, flames flapped in the wind and a terrain deeply incised by ravines frustrated firefighters as it had stymied conquistadores four centuries before. ICONA withdrew.

When its forces regrouped the next morning, they were joined by a convoy of politicians, having ferried to Gomera, and then driven to San Sebastián and there whisked to the field command post. For a time the fire paused, but then it advanced in a grand pincer movement that converged on the town of Ajila and the command post at Agando Rock. The ICONA commander ordered a withdrawal, a plea the officials ignored with "complete equanimity" until, minutes later, Agando Rock disappeared amid an "immense dark cloud of smoke." When it cleared and fire officials finally reclaimed the abandoned sites, they found twenty dead and fifteen injured, the governor among them.

Still, even as funeral services proceeded, the firefighting continued, shifting to mixed woodlands of pine and scrub within the Garajonay National Park, sites that had "suffered from outbreaks of fire over a period of many years." By the 15th, assisted by CL-215 air tankers dispatched from Spain, the fire was controlled. On September 19 it was extinguished by rains. An estimated 783 hectares had burned.

The industrial colonization of the Canaries would likely prove as exhausting as the old. Wildfire thrives on new fuels, flourishes on disturbance and rapid change, and waxes amid social controversy, all of which descended on the once blessed, now burned isles. As Spanish officials and island indigenes argued over what the islands should be, fire sought its own regime. Uncontrolled it could become the twentieth-century cognate of *la peste*. In August 1994 a wildfire raged through more than 1,500 hectares of protected forest habitat on La Palma. It was a harbinger of the future as surely as the Mallorcan missionaries and plagues of the fifteenth century.[92]

EPILOGUE:
THE WORLD ENCOMPASSED

The continual discovery of Atlantic islands encouraged further voyages. Each archipelago subdivided the Atlantic into smaller seas, and reorganized the world ocean into a patchwork of seas connected by straits and bridged by islands. For Europe's voyagers new continents were impediments, but new islands offered points of entry and egress. As scholars revised Ptolemy's *mappa mundi,* the islands of the world ocean shone like beacons, their importance so exaggerated that the Canaries loomed as big as Britain, and Mauritius as large as Ireland.

Rarely, and then with little success, did Europeans first land on continents. They seized offshore islands, or peninsulas defensible from good ports. The "world encompassed," as Francis Drake proclaimed after his circumnavigation, was a world linked by chains of islands. As island led to island within an archipelago, so each archipelago led to others until the world ocean itself became a European sea. Europeans organized West African trade from São Tomé and Dakar; they opened up India from Goa and Diu, and China from Macao and Hong Kong. And they launched the conquest of the New World from secure ports and reprovisioning points among the Antilles. The Greater Antilles were the first archipelago sacked and colonized by modern Europe that lay completely outside the pale of ancient Europe, the first outpost of a global imperium.

The sacred flames that ancient armies had carried before them around the Mediterranean, Europe's mariners now transported around the world ocean.

With uncanny symmetry, the small seas that encrusted Europe like atolled lagoons had a counterpart in the Gulf of Mexico and Caribbean Sea that, lying at the break point in the trade winds, carried Toledo steel into the heart of Mesoamerican civilizations. Christopher Columbus made landfall not on the mainland but in the Bahamas and did not sight America proper until his third voyage. Spain established the beachhead for its New World empire first at Hispaniola. From there it commanded the rest of the Antilles, and from Hispaniola and Cuba conquistadores launched their assault on *tierra firme*. These islands, like those in the Atlantic that had pointed the way, were especially susceptible to ecological reconstruction. What made them accessible and rapidly amenable to reform was that they had already been fired in a Neolithic kiln.

Hurricanes, droughts, volcanoes, and invasions—the Antilles were no stranger to disturbances and to often violently disturbed times. Anthropogenic fire helped stir the brew. In terms of cultural geography, Arawaks dominated the Greater Antilles; Caribs, the Lesser; while aboriginal peoples, preagricultural, crowded into the less usable mountains and peninsulas. But there was plenty of fire and the landscapes were, to various degrees, fire sustained.

Fire assisted the clearing of woodlands for the root crops like manioc that were the staples of the Arawak diet. While many fields appeared permanent, much of the residual forest was in fact fallow, filled with successional species of grass, cane, scrub, and trees. Maize was grown by "clearing the canebrakes and montes, which are then burned," Oviedo observed, "the ashes leaving the ground in better condition than if it had been manured." Mountain conifer forests were open, underlain by "short grass and many very tall pine trees spaced as olive trees are in the groves of Sevilla." Large savannas striped the lowlands, maintained by routine burning, both to drive and lure game. Martin Fernandez de Enciso and Pascual de Andagoya cite examples of fire hunting for deer, peccary, and *hutia:*

> The chiefs had hunting tracts (*cotos*) to which they went in summer [the dry season] to hunt deer. Fire was set on the windward side and since the plants (*yerba*) grew tall the fire was great. Indians were placed in file at a position where the fire would come to a stop. The deer, massed in their flight and blinded by the smoke, were thus driven by fire to the place where Indians were waiting with their dart throwers and stone points so that few creatures escaped.

Fire in canoes assisted with night fishing. Probably fires helped in myriad crafts and tasks, from growing thatch to harvesting fruits and flowers, as they have done in similar environments the world over. Houses were scattered; not clustered, possibly as a measure of reducing fire hazard; some were constructed on marshes or open water "in order," Oviedo thought, "to be secure from animals, wild beasts, and their enemies, and to be safer, and without any danger from fire." Probably fire was loosed by prospecting parties to clear dry-season vegetation from rocky outcrops and lodes, much as indigenes did in Mesoamerica or, for that matter, Europeans had done. Probably the Greater Antilles experienced a similar fire history to that recorded in the charcoal of ocean sediments off the Nicaraguan coast. There the highest flux occurred in the fifty years prior to the Spanish conquest.[93]

Direct evidence is scanty. But the commonality in land usage throughout the aboriginal and agricultural Antilles, the similarities in the biotic history of Jamaica, Cuba, and Martinique, the suddenness with which a single generation of marauding Spaniards infested island after island, like Vikings descending on Irish monasteries, all suggest that what occurred on Hispaniola was paradigmatic for the whole Caribbean. Gather those separate chronicles together and there are enough points to suggest that if the dots were connected they would reveal a gardened biota, one densely populated with agriculturalists and hunters, for which fire appeared liberally in field, savanna, and fallow. It was, accordingly, a landscape highly susceptible to sudden changes in the amount and pattern of fires applied and withheld. The invading Spaniards upset both. In less than three decades Hispaniola was a shambles.

The indigenous population died off in biblical proportions. Through slaving, disease, war, murder, and social chaos their numbers plummeted. Within forty years the Spanish had virtually depopulated the island and abandoned it to weeds, wild animals, and feral conquistadores. *Cunoco* fields shrank or went untended; cattle and pigs invaded savannas, cropped grasses, and displaced native grazers; wild dogs roamed hills and ran down indigenes and local wildlife; woodlands reclaimed clearings and fire-starved prairies; weeds, rats, horses, and cereals replaced old fields and infested disturbed sites, while roaming soldiers and gold-seekers made social disturbance as common as thunderstorms. The inelasticity of island biogeography meant that the cruel blows often shattered the land rather than deforming it. There was little rebound, no reconstruction of old materials according to new designs.

Collapse sent the adventurers to other islands, and when those crashed, to the mainland. Like California dispatching its forty-niners throughout the Old West, Hispaniola disgorged its flotsam of vagabonds and conquistadores throughout the new world. What Bartolemé de Las Casas believed was "perhaps the most densely populated place in the world," as though "God had crowded into these lands the great majority of mankind" (in fact, all the Antilles, he thought, were "veritable gardens and beehives"), became a "land laid waste and turned into a desert." The Spaniards had wasted with fire and sword; Pedro de Alvarado "set ablaze, as if with fire from Heaven, the entire coastal land" of Guatemala. The "inferno of the Indies," as Las Casas called it, was a human holocaust: the fires were applied not only to fields but to villages, to thatched houses crowded with indigenes, to the torment of captured caciques, tortured with flame and burned at the stake. Pestilence followed fire and war until, in the end, "the land stretches empty, burnt, destroyed." There was no one left to cultivate it. It became a green desert. Europe found that its classic critique of the nomad now applied to itself.[94]

So great was the wreckage that when Lopez de Valasco assembled his geography of Spanish America in 1569, there were only a thousand Spaniards left in Hispaniola, half of them in the town of Santo Domingo. The Arawaks were gone; black African slaves constituted the bulk of the resident population. Added to the diseases native to the Antilles were those of Europe and West Africa. The "old Spanish Main," in Carl Sauer's words, "had become a shabby fringe" to the wealthy vice royalties in Mexico and Peru, the bulk of the *islas* "repossessed by wild growth of tropical vegetation." When northern European powers began their contest for the Caribbean, they had to reclear, replant, and repopulate.[95]

Unlike the Canaries or even Iceland, the Antilles had never belonged within a European orbit. The Norse islands were replicas of Norwegian landforms and the North Atlantic biota; the Iberian islands, of the Mediterranean. Stubborn Grand Canary resembled recalcitrant Corsica, and Tenerife the Aetna-looming landscape of Sicily. Their biotas had once shared evolutionary ancestors, and still knew a similar climate. In the Canaries Spain reconnected what had, a millennium before, once belonged to the Greater Mediterranean. The Canaries completed the Reconquista.

The Antilles, however, were new to Europe, an *otro mundo,* as even Columbus reluctantly recognized. Like captured asteroids in unstable orbit, the island arc circled Europe's commanding mass for a while, then escaped. Its fire history was transitional, the torches and bivouacs of an invading army. The native fires went out; the émigré fires passed on to the mainland. Only two centuries later did European regimes reclaim the islands and convert them to productive plantations. Increasingly the Antilles moved beyond Europe's grasp, if not beyond its reach.

The world encountered was fast becoming a world encompassed. The European torch passed beyond the Pillars of Hercules, the geographies of Strabo and Ptolemy, and the natural histories of Pliny and Theophrastus. Everywhere the voyagers encountered strange fires. And like Nadab and Abihu, pre-Columbian peoples in the Americas and Australasia met a devouring fire in reply. Through its mariners, from fire-beaconed island to island, Europe's unleashed vestal fire filled the Earth.

BOOK 3: EARTH

. . . Then having gained
At length the land it passed our hope to reach,
We sacrifice to Jove, and for our gifts
Light up the altar-fires.
                    —Vergil, *Aeneid,* Book III

ISLANDS

As Delos and Ithaca and Sardinia had helped Europeans colonize the Mediterranean, as Gotland and Åland and innumerable skerries had the Baltic, and as the Faeroes and Shetlands had the North Sea, so the Atlantic isles readied Europe's voyagers for the islands of the world ocean, and through them, the continents of the Old World and the New and those lands, like Australia and Antarctica, strange beyond newness. For seafarers, islands were portal, sanctuary, and fortress; the stitches that sewed the world's multitudinous seas into a common quilt; storm lanterns lighting the sea of darkness. Islands concentrated, islands exaggerated, islands propagated.

With the aid of provisioning islands such as Cape Verde and Hawaii, a seaborne Europe voyaged throughout the Earth. Through offshore islands like Fernando Po, as impregnable as moated castles, a militant Europe commanded the littoral of the world sea. Even its expeditions to Antarctica preferentially departed from offshore bases like the volcanic Ross Island rather than unstable if continental ice shelves. On tropical islands like Jamaica and Java, a newly capitalist Europe conducted its critical experiments in the political economy of imperialism. Out of the extinctions of dodos and tortoises, the despoliation of St. Helena's forests into torrents, the desiccation of the mountain springs of Mauritius into arid gulleys, the destruction of Hispaniola's landscape no less than its people, Europe wrote the prescriptions for an environmental ethos.

Inevitably those encounters kindled and extinguished fires. The strike of European steel on indigenous flint scattered sparks across the globe until the spinning Earth itself resembled a great whetstone flinging embers, wherever it met the bite of ax or sword. The winds of European expansion blew those embers everywhere. Out of exploration and empire came new fires, strange fires, and sacred fires. Voyaging Europeans brought anthropogenic fire to places that had not known it. They carried European fire to places not naturally receptive to it or already purged with anthropogenic flame. And they nurtured symbolic fires around which Europe's savants told environmental parables and rekindled vestas that guarded the encountered Edens.

NEW FIRE:
THE COMING OF ANTHROPOGENIC FIRE

In the fifteenth century the world ocean still bristled with uninhabited islands. By 1859 even the most remote Pacific isle, the atoll at Midway, had been found. By the end of the century miners were excavating coal on Svalbard, anthropologists were searching for Inuit amid the Canadian archipelago, and whalers, prowling the ice-crusted Southern Ocean, had established a base on South Georgia. To all they brought fire.

Not every isle could nurture it. For the polar islands, fire came only through human agency. It was sustained with imported fuels and thrived only because habitation was impossible without it. For temperate and especially tropical islands, however, fire stayed. It was as quickly naturalized as the dogs, rats, goats, citrus, and cane Europeans brought on purpose or by accident and that catalyzed a new ecology. Fires preserved in the holds of ships sailed from Europe to Guam, Norfolk, Ascension, Juan Fernández, Réunion, the Galápagos, Tristan da Cunha, Kerguelen, and scores of other deep-water isles and set them to boil like so many biotic pots.

(i)

The uninhabited isles were, their first explorers exulted, "new worlds," prelapsarian miniatures of the Creation. But they were far from complete worlds.

They had evolved with what wind, wave, and far-vagrant birds had brought to them. High islands, large islands, archipelagoes of islands, and tropical islands offered more niches than did low, small, isolated, or subpolar islands, and thus boasted greater biodiversity. But compared with continents, their biotic constitution was limited and eccentric. There were among them islands empty of grasses, landscapes without conifers, and biotas lacking grazers, browsers, or carnivores. There were islands without snakes, and some without mammals. Evolution's invisible hand had prodded and sculpted the available materials into new growth habits or fashioned new species outright. On remote islands explorers found a menagerie of flightless birds that in their various avatars hunted like wolves, browsed like cattle, or grazed and rooted like rabbits and swine. What on nearby mainlands were suppressed shrubs blossomed into majestic trees. On the Galápagos archipelago the fast-colonizing finch eventually assumed also the roles of starling, grosbeak, and parrot, while immense tortoises browsed where elephants or wood bison might have done in Africa or North America.

If isolation made these islands special, it also made them precarious. Even complex biotas could be immensely vulnerable to immigration and to successive, unusual disturbances. When new species had arrived in the past, they had done so tentatively and singly, and if they naturalized, they cultivated niches over long centuries or millennia. Now the storms of a blustering Europe hurled roving arks and biotic flotsam to their littorals in a surge. Dozens of species struck the shores, often in concert, so that voracious goats and trampling cattle, for example, created opportunities for brome and ribwort. Typically, few uninhabited islands had experienced routine fire, or fire over all its surfaces. Contact thus meant a quantum leap in fire loads and a transmutation of fire regimes. Like its need-fire ceremonies, Europe's fresh-kindled fires reenacted an old saga, the creation story of a fire creature.

The consequences of first contact were often dramatic. Islands empty of browsers and grazers soon swarmed with cows, goats, sheep, rabbits, and sometimes horses and asses and even camels and reindeer. Often in advance of settlement explorers deposited goats and sheep to commence the labors of reclamation. The few goats deposited on St. Helena in 1513 bred so successfully that in 1588, according to Captain Cavendish, they were thousands and formed flocks a mile long. Cattle released on Nouvelle Amsterdam in 1871 soon reached epidemic proportions and stripped the native flora away, leaving erosional scoring and swards of Eurasian weeds accustomed to trampling and cropping. Rabbits released on Crozet, Kerguelen, and Macquarie Islands soon gutted those landscapes of tussock and heath and replaced them with gulleys. The Falkland Islands tussock was so majestic that a seventeenth-century visitor mistook it for a forest canopy. It soon disappeared before the teeth and hooves of proliferating sheep.[1]

So the process went. Islands without mammals got dogs, rats, cats, mice, donkeys, mongooses, and pigs. Islands thinly stocked with invertebrates received insects and microfauna, from flies and mosquitoes to beetles, aphids, earthworms, millipedes, termites, centipedes, weevils, ants, and other stowaways that entered soils, and helped refine the resident biota. Ships deposited bales of cereals and a ballast of weeds. Sugar cane supplanted ebony. Maize displaced laurel. Acacias, citrus, oaks, pines, and later eucalypts shouldered aside native palms and hardwoods. Unique species receded, generic species, toughened by successive acclimatizations, thrived. Soils altered, soils eroded.

Paradoxically, while endemism suffered, biodiversity boomed. "He who admits the doctrine of the creation of each separate species," Charles Darwin wryly observed, "will have to admit that a sufficient number of the best adapted plants and animals were not created for oceanic islands; for man has unintentionally stocked them far more fully and perfectly than did nature." Species counts bear him out. Tristan da Cunha hosts 70 indigenous flora and 97 alien. The Seychelles feature 233 indigenes and 247 aliens. In the Mascarenes of the south Indian Ocean, Rodriguez has 145 native plants and 108 introduced, and the Comoros have 416 indigenes and 519 aliens. In precontact conditions, Ascension Island had fewer than half a dozen plant species; today, it has scores.[2]

Above all, the islands got people. They got axes, hoes, plows, trade, institutions, desires, beliefs; they acquired a regimen of chronic, sometimes violent disturbances; they got whatever plants and animals and land use practices people carried with them; and they got fire.

Fire leveraged those other technologies, exactly as those practices amplified fire's own powers. Just as migratory birds had carried the seeds of those plants most useful to them, and thus remade their island landfalls into a more favorable habitat, so did humans. Cutting, browsing, and grazing, in particular, fractured compact biotas and pried open niches for fire. Cultivated sites became points of infection. Domesticates went feral; and fires escaped from fields into adjacent forests and scrub. In this way islands with no meaningful fire regime previously often became cauldrons simmering over an anthropogenic flame, while islands that had indigenous fire saw it as fully transfigured as the landscapes on which ferns and finches had once thrived but which now grew maize and wild dogs. If humans exploited fire to recast island biotas, so the shock wave of settlement, like windfall before lightning, created ideal conditions for burning.

But if fire magnified the effects of colonization, so did the dynamics of island biology. On islands, the small could become large, and the common, unique. Origin and extinction had the same meanings for fire as they did for species. High islands featured wet and dry sides on their windward and lee flanks, respectively. Tropical islands experienced wet and dry seasons. Islands in the Indian Ocean swayed in the wet-dry rhythms of the monsoon. Islands in the Pacific pulsed to the atonal cadence of the El Niño-Southern Oscillation; an abnormally warm, wet year could fluff an archipelago like the Galápagos with fuels and then blast it with drought, while archipelagoes in the southwestern Pacific, normally wet, could shed their moisture like air escaping through a punctured tire. Humans accelerated the tempo of disturbance, introduced more pyrophytic species, and ensured that ignition was always possible, and in fact always present.

The shock of European encounter led to a chain of disturbances that far transcended the winds, waves, and migratory flocks that had routinely visited the archipelagoes. Flora and fauna, once introduced, would not easily leave. Trade routes superimposed new nutrient cycles on indigenous ecosystems. Islands experienced not only the pulse of storm and surf but the stimulant of ambition and desire; nature's subsistence economies became integrated into a global market of escalating supply and demand. They became articles of contention and trade in imperial rivalries among European contestants to control that flow of goods and monies. Geopolitical cycles supplemented those of geochemistry. Disturbance would not end: there could be no local equilibrium. In all this fire was cause, consequence, and catalyst.

Fire sprang from first contact as though from a lightning-struck tree, and flame brought instantly to the minds of critical observers the parable of Madeira with its colonization by an isle-engulfing conflagration. But the Madeiran model had limitations because it applied to an archipelago that, in climate and biotic heritage, belonged within the penumbra of Mediterranean Europe. Madeira could be smelted in the same forge that had shaped Crete or Corsica. Serious scholars knew its informing fire was not one but many. Practioners knew that with time they could hammer and quench its flame-softened biota into approximations of gardened Europe.

Tropical isles stood outside the realm of European experience. Their biotas beat to different rhythms, not only because they were islands peculiarly stocked with species but because that biota derived from sources in Asia, Africa, or the Americas and thrived in a tropical, not temperate, climate. For their fire regimes, either existing or potential, there was no ready European analogue, and for the fiery consumption of those landscapes often there seemed no justification, as horrified naturalists watched lush woodlands reduced to ash and *philosophes* pondered paradisiacal landscapes consigned to a human hell. Nothing was more instinctive than for settlers to exploit fire, and nothing so rankled educated critics. It was not simply that valuable woods were felled and exotic flowers despoiled, but that they were *burned.* From the flames of perdition there was no redemption. For fire's critics, allegory took the place of analysis.

The debate rekindled in the eighteenth century as Europe renewed its long-paused expansion. A wave of circumnavigations quickly discovered the remaining islands of the world ocean and occupied or reoccupied the others. The sails of those world-spanning ships were filled by the rivalry between France and Britain, their holds stocked by the culture of the Enlightenment. In particular, the reconnaissance compounded the excursions of Linnaeus with the traveling connoisseurs of the Grand Tour, and then held both, like a suspended oil drop, between the charged plates of modern sciences. By the end of the century it projected a cultural sensibility, in part a reaction to the inflated presumptions of Reason, known as Romanticism. It also commemorates, as Richard Grove has elucidated, a new epoch of environmental understanding in which once-uninhabited islands became not merely experiments but exemplars.[3]

Eden met Enlightenment. The Age of Reason rewrote the Book of Genesis into a secular language—the vernaculars of Newtonian mechanics and Linnaean natural history—and it located the Garden on tropical isles. Adventuring Crusoes of moral philosophy, their old narrative vessels smashed on the reefs of an uncharted *mappa mundi,* found themselves cast to the shores of desert isles. Probably the two most critical—the symbolic twins—were St. Helena and Mauritius. That new text was often read by the light of landscape fires.

(ii)

Sighted by the Portuguese in 1502, St. Helena soon became a way station on the passage to India both literally and conceptually. Voyagers paused here on their trek, and found in this isolated isle a reference point, an experiment, a metaphor, and a tragedy. It became the dark twin, the secular restatement of the Fall.

The preliminaries began early as the Portuguese deposited goats, then commenced formal colonization when Fernando Lopez, seeking sanctuary from India, settled in 1533. He brought the fruits and beasts of two gardens, Europe and India, and soon transplanted cereals, gourds, pomegranates, palm trees, orange trees, ducks, hens, sheep, and goats, "all of which increased largely, and all became wild in the woods." Even as travelers praised the Edenic quality of the isle and its provisions—as well they might after arduous months at sea—the enveloping forests were receding. The cut woods, rife with goats, failed to regenerate. Meanwhile both the Dutch and English East India Companies quarreled over St. Helena, the English first arriving in 1659, the Dutch eventually decamping to the Cape of Good Hope.[4]

The British attempted to impose a tropical plantation model, hoping to extract profit as well as provisions. Sugar, rice, cattle, and swine soon added to the congestion. By now goats and rats had reached epidemic numbers, wood had become scarce (not helped by the practice of constantly distilling arrack—the principal liquor—over endless fires), reliable springs had shriveled, and soil had begun to slough off the rocky slopes and run through newly entrenched gulleys. By 1709, governors were warning the Court of Directors that "once this wood [the indigenous forest] is gone the island will soon be ruined." A major drought in 1712–13 brought the island economy to its knees, not assuaged by the increased consumption of arrack. Social disorder mimicked ecological disarray. ("The people," Governor Roberts reported, "are grown sottish.") What rainfall there was rushed away in sheets or torrents. The belief grew that colonization had altered the climate. Deforestation, it was argued, had led to desiccation.[5]

If the loss of its woods had condemned the island, their restoration might rehabilitate it. The first attempts at reforestation began by planting Mediterranean pine in 1715. The St. Helena Forest Act followed in 1731, seeking protection for remaining woods, urging afforestation (with furze if nothing else) for both fuel and water, while attempting to control feral populations of goats. The goat, once admired as a foodstock, had now become demonized, a cloven-hoofed satan that had perverted another Eden. In 1794 a comprehensive forest law was promulgated, modeled on the 1791 legislation developed for St. Vincent in the Caribbean. By then, however, the damage was too extensive for more than palliatives. Restoration of the indigenous landscape was impossible.

The symbolism was sharpened because St. Helena had restated the immemorial contest between fire and water. It was during his stay on the island in 1676 to observe the transit of Venus that Edmund Halley elaborated the modern conception of the hydrologic cycle, and it was the St. Helena example, among others, that demonstrated the consequences of melting down the links of that chain. If it was a commonplace that water could extinguish fire, it became equally axiomatic that fire could eliminate water. On tropic mountains no less than on the slopes of the Dauphiné Alps an excess of burning led to both flooding and a groundwater deficit.

What growth built up, consumption removed. Combustion not only destroyed the rain-attracting forests and the water-retaining humus but liberated in vast amounts precisely those vapors that polluted the air. "The effluvia of vegetables," lectured Edward Long in 1774, are imbued "with the power of reviving common air, that has been vitiated, or fouled, by fire or respiration." Burn, and you add to the contaminants and remove the scrubbers. In fact, St. Helena lacked the record of an isle-consuming fire so common to the mythology (if not the ecology) of first-contact islands. The burning of the island had proceeded secondhand, through fuelwood for arrack and browse for goats. Regardless, the outcome was identical.[6]

By demonstrating the consequences of denudation, by whatever means, St. Helena became one of the great cautionary tales of Enlightenment environmentalism, whose melancholy history was endlessly recited by the major naturalists of the age—from Joseph Banks to Joseph Hooker, from Charles Darwin to Alfred Wallace, all of whom stopped at St. Helena during their long voyages and incorporated its lessons into their larger texts. The connection grew beyond a passage to India. As exploration and empire probed further, Europe discovered other islands, similarly degraded; as Europe watched its own alpine soils apparently degrade and mountain torrents spread like a carcinoma, it reread the parables learned on remote isles; and as scientific theories linked woods, water, and soil, European savants had a formula by which to explain the chain of causation that could reduce a once-luxuriant natural economy to paupery. If the "devastation" also involved fire, the world was so much the worse for the wreckage. Contemporary alarm over global climate change through promiscuous burning is its linear descendant.

(iii)

St. Helena's geographic (and literary) double was Mauritius, situated on the Indian Ocean side of Africa. What St. Helena was to imperial Britain, Mauritius was to imperial France. But where British merchants bemoaned the lost capital of a degraded port of call, French philosophes bewailed a lost Eden.

The usual suspects discovered, claimed, variously occupied, plundered, and colonized the island in the usual sequence—Portuguese, Spanish, Dutch, French, and British. The Portuguese shunned formal settlement but left their signatory residue of goats and pigs, along with some commandeered deer and monkeys. The Dutch introduced beans, peas, fruit trees, Javanese deer, Chinese pigs, sugar cane, tobacco, sweet potatoes, more goats, and feral dogs, cats, and rats, and along the way oversaw the extermination of the Mauritian land tortoise and the dodo by hunting and introduced rats, and the virtual extinction of the lowland palms by fire. But what most obsessed them was the island's stock of ebony, which they proceeded to log off in prodigious quantities before temporarily abandoning the island in 1657.

Instead, it was the French who crafted the island's enduring, ambivalent landscape and who defined its symbolic significance—a French intelligentsia caught between the vision of Edenic nature and Cartesian landscaping, between the fresh innocence of untrammeled nature and the contaminating artifice of civilization, between visions of Tahiti and Versailles.[7]

The French reign lasted through most of the eighteenth century and was noteworthy less because it inaugurated systematic colonization than because, once the French East India Company sold the isle to the Crown, it inspired Governor Pierre Poivre (1767–72) to envision Mauritius as something more than a village commune condemned to ignorance and doomed to overexploitation. Through Poivre and his collaborators, Philibert Commerson and Bernardin de Saint-Pierre, Mauritius proposed an alternative future to the endless degradation that characterized St. Helena. Collectively they envisioned Mauritius as a Utopia that, like Thomas More's, rested securely on a remote island but unlike More's derived its moral authority from the uncorrupted world of Nature with which it coexisted. Saint-Pierre captured the sentiments exactly when he wrote that he had "not had the felicity, like the primitive navigators, who discovered uninhabited islands, to contemplate the face of the ground as it came from the hand of the Creator." But he could study and protect those sacred groves that remained. If Eden could not be recreated, it could be preserved.[8]

For Mauritius, in truth, did more than epitomize the ideologies of Physiocrats and Rousseauist romantics: no less than St. Helena (or Tobago or St. Vincent in the Caribbean), it vividly demonstrated the climatic consequences of defor- estation, and like them it argued for—and institutionally pioneered—the use of state-sponsored intervention to arrest and, if possible, reverse that degener- ation. Such action was necessary both to preserve the natural order (which was intrinsically superior to any artifice of humanity) and to redeem those lands that had already succumbed to the vices of civilization. In 1769, a century after the Code Colbert, Poivre instigated a Forest Ordinance for Mauritius that estab- lished mechanisms for reserving mountain forests and replanting cleared woodlands; it also prohibited fires. The gesture was quixotic and soon over- turned or ignored, though never completely and not without ramifications. Mau- ritius, like St. Helena, was often visited by savants traveling to the East. They collected the seeds of Poivre's potent scheme and found hospitable lands in which to plant them. In time the idea also took root in Mauritius.

The philosophes had no place for fire. It was hard to see how reducing indige- nous forest to a burnt offering was pleasing either to Nature or to Nature's God. The Dutch had destroyed the coastal palm biome by cutting and burning (includ- ing its exploitation as fuel for the production of spiritous arrack). In 1756, Poivre's predecessor, Governor René de Magon, denounced grass burning as an accomplice to deforestation and desiccation. The annual fires "dry up trees every year and kill them," he fulminated. A year later he complained that "each inhabitant who clears up a well-wooded piece of land sets fire to it," making forest regeneration impossible. In 1763, Poivre condemned, as "the greatest fault which has been committed in the island, and which has proved most prej- udicial to cultivation," the practice "of clearing the woods from off the ground by fire." Instead of selective felling, settlers indiscriminately fired; instead of gardening—weeding, planting, manuring—they burned; and instead of hus- banding their flocks, they burned the rough pasture. The stubble and grasses they "left lying," to be "kindled here by a thousand accidents," and the result- ing fires consumed not only the straw but "frequently part of the neighbour- ing forests." This left herds to "wander about and languish" in the woods, thus encouraging herders to stray still further afield. When Bernardin de Saint-Pierre arrived in 1768, he lamented that the mountains around Port Louis are "cov- ered during six months of the year with burnt grass, which renders the land- scape as black as a charcoal yard." Once cracked, Mauritius's forest canopy could not resist the frequent cyclones that slammed the island, widening the woody rifts and strewing more fuels.[9]

Social order and environmental order—the two were inextricable, and both suffered from promiscuous fire whose changes threatened even the climate. "Reckless and ignorant men," Poivre lectured, "thinking of nothing but them- selves, have ravaged the island, destroying the trees by fire to make a fortune at the expense of the colony, leaving nothing for their successors but arid lands

abandoned by rain and exposed without relief to storms and the burning sun."
Plains—"made so through fire"—had suffered from "surprising aridity." Worse,
as later governors testified, the inhabitants were not much interested in farming; they wanted only to make their fortune "by any means they think permissible" and then return to France. The island's debasement resulted not from
ignorance or irony but greed. Human vice corrupted natural innocence. Laws,
Bernardin de Saint-Pierre concluded sadly, "cannot overrule the emotions."[10]

But emotions could give rise to new laws. That settlers required fire to transform an exotic landscape into a useful habitat only furthered the thesis that
humans invariably pollute what they touch. On Mauritius, settlers had burned
away the leaves that should have covered their shame. Redemption demanded
humanity's humbled withdrawal, and the penitent replanting of "those lands
formerly devastated by fire." Fire control was mandatory; fire exclusion, ideal.
And the legal regime that proclaimed that goal, while oft ignored in practice,
endured as a literary and philosophical and eventually political vision.[11]

Poivre's was a powerful paradigm. However compromised, the mountain
and river reserves did spare much of the island's forests from felling. When
Britain seized Mauritius in 1810, it inherited both the fact and the ideology of
those reserves. By then its own dark exemplars in St. Helena and the Caribbean
reinforced the sentiment that mountain forests were environmental shields, like
a later generation's views of stratospheric ozone.

When Major F. A. Mackenzie Fraser published a map of Mauritius in 1835,
nearly two-thirds of the landscape remained "under primeval forest." That was
soon to change as emancipated slaves moved into the forests and quickened
trade led to wholesale logging. The woods could more easily survive tropical
cyclones than the gusts of liberal economics. By 1872, deputy conservator of
forests Thompson reported that the "great mass of the aboriginal forest" had
disappeared, reduced to 29,000 hectares, and by 1881 diminished further to
14,600 hectares. The formal reserves has shrunk; other categories of forest lay
in various states of "ruin"; breaking open the primeval canopy exposed the Mauritian forests to storm and cyclone; and where forests regenerated they did so
by restocking with exotic species.[12]

Yet there were powerful counterforces. The apparatus of mountain reserves
and forest guards remained, if moribund, ready to revive with the proper stimulant. That came in the linkage of disease and desiccation with deforestation.
Malaria had become rampant with immigration from India, watersheds appeared
unstable, drought and storm more frequent, and the climate increasingly more
unwholesome. Forests—preserved, replanted, "sanitary"—were a public health
measure. New proclamations replaced old, culminating in the the Forest Law
of 1875. If it could not restore paradiasical visions, the ordinance could at least
protect some semblance of the ancient nature that had inspired them. And while

fires persisted, they remained where they had always been. Fire and forest each kept to its place.[13]

In 1903 the conservator of forests Frank Gleadow analyzed the situation. It was clear that fires were as eclectic and hybridized as the Mauritian populace. Sites long settled, areas recently disturbed, places subject to seasonal dry winds or secular drought, here fires clustered. There were two fires reported in 1895, sixty-eight in 1900. In ten years Port Louis recorded fifty-seven fires, and Moka none. Fires flared, in Gleadow's words, in "the dry hot forests round the coast, principally on the west." As clearance for crops or logging spread, however, so did the zone of burning. Fractured forests subsequently plucked by winds became vulnerable as well. Still, the fires did little damage except to potential plantations. Much of the burning swept grasslands. Many of the "forests" regularly burned were really coppices that resprouted greedily after fire-pruning. Among the side benefits was the "severe check" fire gave prickly pear, a weedy cactus mistakenly introduced to the island, which grew "so thick as to close the forest to anything larger than pigs and goats."[14]

The sources of fire were typical for still-colonizing lands, although they had an Indian flavor that reflected the origins of the most recent immigrants, brought by British planters to work sugar cane. Most fires originated from graziers or "grass cutters." Many spread from nearby "cultivators carelessly burning to clear their land." Travelers accounted for some. Not a few started from "native boys or soldiers" who "sometimes throw in a match for the pleasure of seeing a blaze." Countermeasures took the form of beating flames out with boughs, igniting backfires, or simply letting the blaze run its course through "impenetrably thorny" sites to the nearest firebreak, of which, in official opinion, there were never enough.[15]

In the years prior to independence little changed. Fires swept Crown forest lands annually around Port Louis. Deliberately set, the burns were defiantly accepted by the local population as "no more than unsightly bare and blackened hill sides which have become such familiar 'land marks' that they call for no comment." The annual fire-monsoon, however, prevented any serious afforestation. Contemplating eucalypt plantations on Signal Mountain, "badly scorched again," officials concluded that until these fires could be "fully controlled or wholly prevented" reforestation had "no future whatsoever." Instead, imported pests (including exotic fire) would degrade the flora, a relentless sun would bake the denuded landscape, and rains would scour away the soils. Foresters little doubted that "the reclothing of the slopes would add to the amenities of the capital city," but for any amelioration of the Mauritian climate, whether natural or social, "there must be complete protection from fire." In 1957 a phenomenal drought saw fires break out in Nouvelle Découverte, Monneron and Desenne, Grand Bassin Range, and the Midlands Range that affected plantations of pine, araucaria, and eucalypt, exotics all. Meanwhile the usual spate of April-to-June fires swept the Port Louis region. Two centuries after Governor René de Magon denounced its fires, Mauritius still burned, in much the same way, for much the same reasons, amid much the same official displeasure.[16]

Mauritian fire thus retold the story of Mauritian colonization. Humanity made its claims to the island through Europe, and Europe, like all peoples, had imposed title with the torch. The resulting cultural landscape looked a little like Europe, a little like India and Africa (the sources of its laborers), and a lot like other tropical islands, once uninhabited, now awkwardly remade in that most elementary of environmental dramas, sudden fall and a long, painful redemption. The special contribution of Mauritius was the paradigm of its reserves. The contrast with St. Helena and other provisioning points on the passage to India was obvious. The Dutch at the Cape had made a desert into a garden, the French at Mauritius had, with difficulty, preserved elements of the native garden, while at St. Helena the British East India Company, in the words of an outraged Joseph Banks, had transformed a natural garden into a "desert." By the time Britain held both islands, Mauritius was ripe for further development and St. Helena fit only for the exile of deposed emperors.[17]

It was the classic European dichotomy—the garden, natural or cultivated; the desert, innate or contrived. The narratives that linked garden and desert stepped from truism to truism with the inflexible rigor of a Latin verb conjugation. The social order and the order of nature were interdependent, the hybridization of *hortus* and *cultus*. Because fire was so intrinsic to both, it also had to submit to their common regime. That, too, was the classic European prescription.

But if the European encounter shocked uninhabited islands, the islands also electrified Europe. The contrast between the wild and the cultivated forced Europe's savants to reexamine their premises about the order of the world. The unpeopled island, especially one that was tropically lush, stood outside the ancient discourse that had discriminated between the savage, the barbaric, and the civilized. Such islands were the creation of no society. They had not fallen, as populated lands obviously had, and would only share in the Fall to the extent that humans colonized them. They challenged natural history with unknown facts, unsettled moral philosophy with curious cultures, and confronted imperialism with a Nature for which calls to conversion or pronouncements of a just war rang as hollow as a metal ax on ebony. These conundrums were not, however, equally apparent to those settlers who actually contested the refractory forests and soils with ax and spade.

So even as Europe rekindled its ancestral vestas, it also renewed the ancient debate between elites and folk over the proper regimen for fire, between those for whom fire was symbol and those for whom it was tool, between the vision of an Eden guarded around by prohibitive flame and a fallen Earth for which penitential fire was an essential means of reclamation. On the ground, the debate was never seriously in doubt. The colonizers turned, instinctively, to fire. They did so as the agents of humanity, the evolutionary keeper of the Earth's flame.

STRANGE FIRE:
THE COMING OF EUROPEAN FIRE

By the time of European contact, most of the inhabitable islands of the Earth were already claimed. Clusters of maritime cultures trafficked around the Caribbean and the monsoon tides of the Indian Ocean, and even along the spiny Aleutians. Civilizations flourished throughout the great triangle of the East Indies that has one apex at the Philippines and the other two at Sumatra and New Guinea. Convoys of outrigged canoes sailed colonizers across the Pacific from the Marianas to Easter Island, from Hawaii to New Zealand. Only the Atlantic and Subantarctic islands were, in any systematic way, uninhabited, and these were, not incidentally, the medium for Europe's expansion.

All the indigenes had fire. The Andaman Islanders had little else; Polynesians also hauled pigs, fowl, taro, yams, coconuts, stone adzes, dogs, probably rats, and certainly swidden, with which to leverage the land across fire's fulcrum. In some landscapes the process of transformation had barely begun, or would progress poorly without the interaction of imported grazers and pyrophytic weeds. For others, Europeans were only the latest in a succession of fire encounters, their presence (and their imposed fire regimes) no more enduring than a lava flow down Mauna Loa. Fire ecology was more complex when applied to larger islands, some of which like Madagascar and New Guinea could be considered microcontinents and most of which experienced fire in ways that would make its extirpation difficult or ecologically ruinous. Fire regimes were more problematic where indigenes had already baked the landscape in a hominid hearth.

Fire was there, and it remained for Europeans to define new relationships. In Madagascar they redirected it, in Hispaniola they suppressed it, in New Zealand they co-opted it, in Indonesia they intensified it, and in Tasmania they exterminated and replaced it. At Easter Island they reclaimed an isle already colonized, degraded, and abandoned. At Jamaica they deconstructed a settled landscape and then repopulated it with new plants, animals, and peoples. Everywhere, smoke by day and flame by night was, in the words of Captain James Cook, "a Certain sign that the Country is inhabited." Natives set fires that confirmed their presence. Castaways lit signal fires to aid their escape. Fire and people—to find one was to find the other.[18]

The contrast between inhabited and uninhabited isles had its complement

in the contrast between those whose populations exploded after contact and
those whose demography crashed, and especially between the two Indies, East
and West, the one Europe sought and the one it colonized. Beyond the hard
lessons they posed to biogeography were the tougher parables the isles proposed to moral geography.

(i)

The West Indies rimmed the Caribbean like a reef, and on it the European ark
that sailed to the Americas first smashed. The Great Encounter had plenty of
analogues, but because it commemorated contact with a New World, not a recon-
nection with the passage to India, it propounded a creation story for the civilization that followed. The Myth of the Encounter pitted an innocent America
against a decadent Europe. In fact, much of the New World had known anthropogenic change longer than much of the Old.

The ark's passengers found a habitat already aswarm. The Lesser Antilles
cascade out from South America like boulders disgorged from a stream in flood.
And that is in fact how the archipelago received much of its flora, as seeds
washed up on the beaches from the surging Orinoco and Guyana Rivers, and
even the Amazon. It appears that successive colonizers followed their track,
the Tainos spilling out the Orinoco River to Trinidad, the Arawaks from Guyana,
and then paddling up through the Windward Islands, and from there to the
Greater Antilles, pointing like a bony finger into the Gulf of Mexico. Each new
wave of invaders squeezed the residents of older invasions tighter, until the
aboriginal peoples were thrown off the lithic raft altogether or crowded into
remote or inhospitable niches, like the Ciguayos of Hispaniola and the Gua-
najatabeys of Cuba. Their Taino-speaking successors possessed agriculture, and
to varying degrees carried practices like swidden and savanna-burning inland.
Some islands were densely crowded, and others—along contested frontiers—
hardly at all.[19]

War, slaving, and disease decimated the indigenes of the Greater Antilles,
and with them the landscape they had sculpted and the fires they tended. But
as Alfred Crosby has emphasized, the Europeans had ecological allies. Cattle,
horses, swine, goats, dogs, many of which went feral, and a bewildering cornucopia of European and African cultigens, heavily laced with weeds, soon
dismantled the biota. Within a few decades, the natives of Hispaniola, Cuba,
Puerto Rico, and Jamaica were largely gone, and their cultural landscapes
degraded or overgrown. The effects propagated throughout the arc, though from
raiding and disease rather than by colonization. Within another century the Spanish were, for practical purposes, gone as well. Northern European settlement
commenced in 1624 when English and French colonists arrived on St. Kitts

The West Indies (University of Wisconsin Cartographic Lab)

amid the Lesser Antilles and replaced the strategy of the Spanish *repartimiento* and *encomiendo* with the plantation and the estate.[20]

Here was disturbance on a grand scale. But the islands had always known hurricanes, fluctuating sea levels, and for some, volcanic eruptions, not to mention repeated colonizations that had culled, planted, rearranged, and burned. The newcomers probed a landscape whose cultural origins traced back as far as 5,000 years B.P. By the time of European contact, much of the forest land was part of a fire-fallow agricultural complex, dry scrublands and coastal meadows were probably continuing to expand, and fires dappled the landscape, pushing beyond fields during droughts and most likely flaring after hurricanes slashed exposed woodlands. (Following Hurricane Gilbert, which slashed through the Yucatán in September 1988, traditional burns during the dry season of 1989 seized on a fuel-fluffed peninsula and gobbled the debris up in an orgy of wildfires that consumed 100,000 hectares. Undoubtedly similar events occurred in the prehistoric Antilles.) Spain plundered and extorted, and secondarily attempted to transplant European agriculture with native labor, and when that failed, with African slaves. The Antilles were left as broken shards. But islands that had known rising seas, landscape-cleansing eruptions of ash and incendiary gas, and repeated invasions from seaborne weeds, Taino colonizers, and Carib raiders had the capacity to regrow, if not restore. The question was how and to what end.

The first fleets that sailed from England, France, and Holland in the seventeenth century were ill-equipped to attempt wholesale colonization, and instead

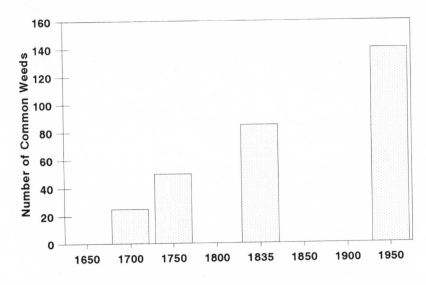

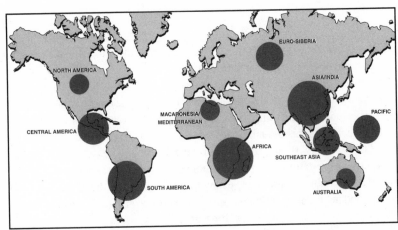

Biotic recolonizations. (Top) Rate of arrival of weeds in Barbados. (Data from Watts 1985) (Bottom) Source areas for the exotic plants of Martinique, many of them a reflection of the French imperium. (Adapted from Kimber 1988; University of Wisconsin Cartographic Lab)

adapted native practices. They recleared and reburned what declining indigenous populations had abandoned. The newcomers filled the ecological vacuum with cosmopolitan exotics, from bananas to camels, beans to donkeys. Coconuts clothed littorals; citrus penetrated fallow to become a major weed; lantana, liberated from pre-Columbian suppression, ran riot. The biota was as syncretic as it was synthetic; spillage from European trade routes replaced the flotsam of flooding South American rivers.[21]

The subsequent fire histories of the islands depended on the presence of livestock, on contacts with metropolitan Europe, on the development of commodity plantations, and on whether or not the indigenes remained. On some islands the Caribs were expelled or assimilated; on others, they survived. From the mid-seventeenth century to the mid-eighteenth, however, a more powerful force appeared, an informing principle. Estates boomed as the political economy of cacao, coffee, and especially sugar reconstructed island geography wholesale. The islands became sufficiently valuable that Europe's great powers fought wars and conducted diplomacy over them for 150 years, their commercial value far greater than North American outposts.

If the Lesser Antilles avoided a biotic meltdown, the colonizing fires made them malleable enough to be reshaped into the preferred patterns of a mercantilist ecology. Plantations replaced plunder. Forests were fired to fashion permanent fields, and these fields were regularly fired to renew cropping. Cane fields were burned to remove residue, rats, and poisonous snakes, to prepare the cane for harvest, and to protest oppression or poverty. Fuelwood was combusted into charcoal, or burned relentlessly to distill the cane into syrup; and when wood became too scarce, bagasse, the waste from harvested cane, did the job. Savannas, scrub, and meadows were fired to provide better pasturage. Charcoalers burned out pockets of woods like moths chewing a sweater. Escaped fires scratched into old fallow or forest. On the windward side, field burning presented few problems except in times of drought. On the dry coasts the fires often propagated. Watching the spectacle in Barbados, Sir Henry Colt fumed that "all the earth is black with cinders." On Martinique, G. T. F. Raynal thought the fires a good purgative and their ash a sound fertilizer. Steadily, fires moved up the slopes with settlement, and seasonally smoke filled the sky.[22]

To Enlightenment environmentalists the Antilles were of a piece with St. Helena and Mauritius, the causes of their degradation identical and the potential solutions quite similar. If reserving critical landscapes from human habitation seemed harsh, the practice was on a par with other rationalizing reforms of Enlightened despotism, all considered necessary for the public good to triumph over the practices of a superstitious folk. That humans inhabited these landscapes did not invalidate the syllogism: the savages could be ennobled and their ecological impacts trivialized as little different from those of deer or monkeys. Besides, they were few and becoming fewer. Where this was so, or where the islands were forcibly depopulated by chronic wars, the landscapes became truly deserted, a second-order new world. The essence of forest reserves after all was to remove people: only then could a truly natural order thrive. But the problem of preserving lands in advance of colonizing was very different from that of preserving lands that were already occupied. The Lesser Antilles soon showed those distinctions.

At the end of the Seven Years' War, France ceded Dominica, Grenada, St. Vincent, and Tobago to Britain, which already possessed other shards of the archipelago. Within a year, learning from its mounting experiences with island biology—not least from Barbados, which was in the throes of an ecological crisis as intense as St. Helena had known—Britain introduced a strategy of forest reserves, not unlike those on Mauritius. Grenada received a forest ordinance in 1764, and Barbados in 1765; these served, in turn, as templates for the other islands.[23]

The problem with applying the Mauritian model was that the Antilles were already inhabited, and an Antillean Eden could be created only by the expulsion of its residents, either through force or accident. Some islands indeed had been emptied during contact, although others would remain inhabited or be restocked with colonists, creoles, liberated slaves, and surviving indigenes, all of whom had very different designs on mountain forests and different perceptions about the place of fire in them. Often the outcome was to create a surrogate indigenous population. Even so, the debate was less between indigene and alien than between an elite who saw reserves as a means of limiting environmental degradation and folk populations who saw those reserves as threatening a way of life. In this respect, Europe transplanted its environmental debates along with its plantations, frigates, and weeds.

All this was apparent in the Lesser Antilles. On Tobago, British strategy called for extensive reserves because the British had managed to alienate the resident Caribs, who subsequently disappeared. On the other islands, notably St. Vincent, a thriving population of Caribs and escaped slaves successfully resisted. Infuriating the ecological reformers of the Age of Reason, these inhabitants managed to turn the uncleared woods of the proclaimed reserve to military advantage. Instead of sheltering colonial estates, the mountain forests ("reserved and appropriated for the purpose of attracting the clouds and rain") harbored hostile insurgents. By stalling boundary surveys, and aided by French occupation between 1779 and 1783, the rebels retarded resettlement. In 1791 they forced the British into compromised legislation, the King's Hill Forest Act, which reserved wooded land but on a small scale. Eventually a failed uprising in 1795 ended in the Caribs' deportation, but the redefinition of mountain reserves persisted, and the St. Vincent legislation became the basis for reform in St. Helena, now populated, and those lands for which indigenes would prove as immovable as the hills.[24]

Unfortunately the hills of the Antilles seemed themselves to be moving. However powerful the symbolism of the King's Hill reserve, erosion put more land into scrub than forest ordinances enclosed. Land clearing reached a maximum during the Napoleonic Wars before the two economies, nature's and mercantilism's, once more threw marginal land into pasture or fallow. Another episode of colonization followed the abolition of slavery, as freedmen took to the mountains in search of land. As quickly as one indigenous group faded away, another appeared. As soon as one economy expired, another reclaimed the woods.[25]

By the mid-nineteenth century, however, the West Indies ceased to be a story of contact. New fires had naturalized, and strange fires had reconciled or been expelled. Environmental crises were recycled, not recreated. Fire burned where humans prescribed, where they felled woods or cane to fuel it, where they imported grasses from Africa to fashion fire-flushed savannas capable of feeding their alien cattle, and where they cooked meals or roasted wood into charcoal. In Europe's global economy, the West Indies had gone from estate to kitchen garden. Among environmental paradigms, the West Indies' forest reserve shrank from the status of allegory to anecdote. Environmentalism, like the flag, followed trade to the continents, especially India, where scientists confronted ecological change on the scale of subcontinents instead of island miniatures. There the critical debates raged, where the lands were larger, the indigenous populations bigger, and fire more powerful and rampant.

(ii)

These were also the conditions of the other Indies, the one that Europe's explorers had so strenuously sought. The East Indies lay astride the Asian monsoon, with its planetary rhythm of water and fire. The isles already had livestock and wild megafauna and an indigenous flora of teak and spice that Europeans lusted after, not a following landscape like the abandoned Antilles. Their stories differed accordingly. In the West Indies Europe dominated, disassembled, and rebuilt; in the East, it was repulsed.

The East Indies were larger, more complex, more stubbornly populated, and endowed with an environmental mandate for fire. The complexity of the southeast Asian peninsulas and archipelago is staggering—the geographic stew of high islands and mingled seas, the chronicle of dramatic disturbances, the astonishing biodiversity. The rising and falling of the Pleistocene seas opened islands west of the Wallace Line to foot traffic from Asia, so that the archipelago hosted monkeys, tigers, elephants, and even *Homo erectus*. Active volcanoes rewrite the ecological palimpsest regularly; in 1883 the island of Krakatoa vanished in an eruption that soaked the stratosphere in dust for over two years. Cyclones smash the forests, tidal waves the shores. With its deeply sculpted, isolated val-

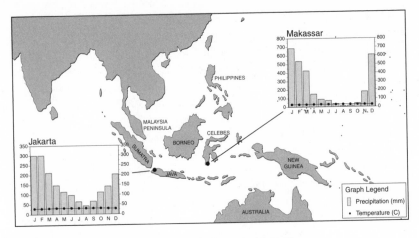

The East Indies (University of Wisconsin Cartographic Lab)

leys, New Guinea, it is estimated, holds one-fifth of the world's languages. It comes as no surprise that the codiscoverer of evolution by natural selection, Alfred Wallace, should have conceived of that idea after his extensive travels in the Greater Indies.

The similarities in fire practices and fire-tempered geography are no less strik-ing. Throughout, there is a broadly common, disturbance-adapted biota, a fire-wielding species, and most tellingly, the commanding rhythm of the Asian monsoon. The Equator split the East Indies in half geographically, but the mon-soon split its climate, and the dry half burned. Yearly the lands pass through a wet and a dry phase, an alternating current that charges its biogeography with rain and fire. Each polarity has had its distinctive agricultural practice. The first exploited the dry season, the second the wet. The first was infinitely malleable; the second, capable of indefinite intensification. Together *ladang,* or Indone-sian swidden, and *sawah,* wet rice cultivation, transcended nuances of island geography and cultural preferences. Together they define the twin cores—the hearth and the well—of the region's historical geography.[26]

They also defined one of the great hearths of anthropogenic fire. Through-out the region, there exists an astonishing commonality of tools, terms, and purposes. More remarkable, the insular triangle that inscribes the East Indies reflects an inverted, continental counterpart, with its apexes in Bengal, Hunan, and Malaysia. The Malay Peninsula joins these two fire triangles, as indeed Malayan words, technologies, and cultigens bridge them. The Malay word for fire, *api,* reappears as the Polynesian *afi;* the term for house or clearing, *uma,* is the *jhum* of eastern India swiddeners. Almost everywhere, at the time of con-tact, fire and fallow, especially shifting cultivation, was the basis for agricul-

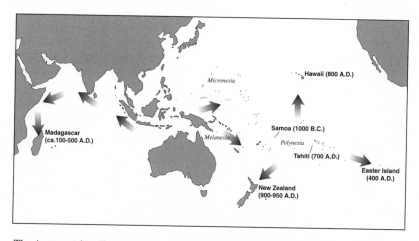

The Austronesian diaspora, east and west. (University of Wisconsin Cartographic Lab)

ture. Some places—lowland rainforests in Borneo, for example—were too perennially wet, and some well-watered sites exploited wet-field cultivation. Still, the informing fact was a fire-fallow regime.[27]

Nor did the fires stop at the swidden plots' edge. Even the magnificent forests of spices, teak, tropical hardwoods, fruits, and in the Philippines, pine, were probably a cultural landscape, a curried fallow of tropical forest. When Hugh Cleghorn celebrated the biotic profusion of the Western Ghats, he titled his book *Forests and Gardens of South India,* and understood swidden as the link between forest and garden, as indeed it was throughout the Indies. Many monsoonal forests were routinely, even annually, underburned—teak, sal, and pine, primarily. In places where fallow was fired soon after abandonment and tropical grasses were present, they converted to tough grasslands like bamboo or, where *Imperata* was present, the notorious *alang-alang,* dappling the landscape and often crowning the summits of New Guinea hills. Only very slowly, and then in the absence of fire, did forests reclaim these fire-hoarding grasses. On Borneo, coal seams have burned for at least 13,000 years, and have rekindled fire in the surrounding forests whenever recurring drought allowed.[28]

Nor, again, did the informing fires remain on the ancient proto-Malaysian hearth. They joined a great diaspora of fire that sailed throughout the Indonesian archipelago and then beyond, from Easter Island to Madagascar. Only Australia was spared, although the introduction of a microlithic toolkit and the dingo probably resulted from contact with the far-voyaging folk who carried fire throughout the Indian and Pacific Oceans.

Unlike the Antilles, the Indonesian archipelago was not emptied. Europe sought to take over a flourishing biota, not rebuild a shattered one. Whatever fires Europe might loose met a swarm of counterfires; whatever flames they suppressed were rekindled. The answer to fire, it concluded, was water.

The Europe that sought out the Indies thought it understood the relationship between water and fire. The syllogism stated that the two were antagonists, and that the more you had of one the less you had of the other. If you controlled one, you controlled the other. If you burned the tropical forest, you set into motion a declension of environmental degradations. By contrast, if you watered, or if you promoted forests and watersheds that attracted and held water, you enriched the land. If, on uninhabited isles, the misuse of fire by European settlers had led to a loss of waters, in the East Indies authorities sought to reverse the flow and use water to replace fire.

In its encounters with the Greater Indies, Europe was baffled, pragmatic, dismayed, and dogmatic. The earliest European powers wanted trade, not colonies. Trading companies, not governments, created factories and plantations. Only when regional politics compelled them did companies advance from the coast to the interior, and this expansion forced governments to plant the flag beside their trading posts. Europe didn't trust roving villages, didn't believe shifting cultivation was sustainable, didn't ascribe the value to "minor forest products" that foraging natives did, and didn't like fire. As long as trade alone mattered, how the natives obtained the vital goods was their own business. So long as the spices, coffee, rice, and timber poured into ships' holds, it mattered little to overseers if the indigenes cut, planted, and burned.

But as more direct colonial rule spread, pressures grew for more agricultural lands, more commodity production, and more industrial use of forests—such as harvesting teak for railways instead of houses and ships. In contrast to the West Indies, the indigenous population swelled. As stresses built, cleavage planes ruptured across the landscape. Fixed-field, water-based farming replaced shifting cultivation, a transformation that Europeans overall applauded. Increasingly authorities began to treat the land as they would in Europe. Savants, in particular, rarely recognized the kinship between shifting cultivation in the Indies that left valuable trees (fruit producers or large-boled trees suitable for dugouts) in garden plots and the European tradition of sowing pine or oak among the barley. They saw burning *alang-alang* as no better than firing heathy wastelands, and vowed to bring rational improvement. They interpreted underburning in teak as the combustion equivalent of scalping the soil, or sheet erosion. If untreated, the East Indies would follow the models for tropical degradation prominent in the West Indies, St. Helena, and Mauritius.

The confusion extended—still extends—even to the names for common fire practices. The indefatigable H. H. Bartlett marveled with barely suppressed sarcasm how "swidden" had become a "general term for shifting agriculture," shoving aside perfectly usable indigenous expressions like *ladang, kaingin,* and *jhum*. Swidden—"revived from obscure dialectical English"—could not even be found in the *Oxford English Dictionary* in 1957. It was, Bartlett concluded, "a quite unnecessary term, except perhaps in discussion of obsolete phases of north European agriculture." Nonetheless, a word transported to Northumbria by Norse invaders to describe burning the ling now subsumed the spectrum of East Indian fire-fallow systems that were as varied as the region's orchids and beetles. In 1954, Harold Conklin applied the term to the Philippines, and by 1963 Clifford Geertz enshrined it permanently into the anthropological literature with his study of Indonesian agriculture.[29]

There was more to this fire-catalyzed landscape than swidden plots. While their origins are obscure, Indonesian teak forests and Philippine pine appear to be largely anthropogenic. Probably teak could have migrated through the islands along with so many other continental species. Varied evidence suggests nonetheless that teak was introduced in the tenth century, likely as part of the colonizing surge that brought so much Indic civilization to the archipelago. Certainly it was vital to shipbuilding, an enterprise well developed by Javanese and Chinese traders considerably in advance of European contact. Like other valuable species, teak was planted as well as harvested. The Dutch divided the Javanese forests into two categories: teak, which they managed, and jungle, "from the destruction of which nobody suffers." Both burned, the jungle after swiddening, the teak almost annually.[30]

The colonizing Dutch, interested in trade, at first tolerated the scene. A report in 1776 explained that such fires were customary and of great antiquity and listed as the Javanese (or Kalang) motivations that fire denied cover to wild predators (particularly tigers), fought down weeds, stripped away debris (whether natural or from felling), fertilized, rejuvenated tropical grasses in a form suitable for grazing, stimulated teak regeneration, and in general kept the land open, appealing, and habitable. While the spectacle appalled trained foresters and agronomists, the forest overseers (*boschgangers*), who were drafted from the ranks of soldiers and traders, cared only that the result produced abundant teak. For a while *boschgangers* were actually instructed to kindle "small fires" to clean up felling refuse, or to underburn lightly where teak saplings could not be harmed. They were even to burn teak seed before planting, on the realization that heating accelerated sprouting.[31]

Increasingly a colonial order replaced, or at least redirected, the indigenous. The Dutch Republic assumed control over the Dutch East Indies Company's holdings in 1800 and instigated a typical slate of colonial reforms that eventually included centralizing forest administration, hiring professional foresters, and reserving forests on "waste" lands as Crown property (beginning in 1836). A succession of forestry boards or forest departments assisted the transition. Forestry was thus congruous with other reforms of the cultivation system. All this did not end logging, which in fact accelerated, but it did transfer both ax and torch from indigenes to colonial officials. As state-sponsored conservation replaced commercial exploitation, fire-farming cultivation was rooted out. The 1829 forest regulations for Java still sanctioned controlled fire; by 1857 they forbade it. Two years later, Professor de Vriese forecast that continued deforestation on the mountains would, as on other tropical isles, lead to desiccation and soil erosion. In 1865, Dutch East India passed its first forest law.[32]

With remarkable fidelity, developments in Dutch Indonesia paralleled those in British India. Both felt the shock of industrial forestry and the demand for teak, in particular; and thoughtful observers in both countries were appalled by the waste of early contract logging. In 1857 the Dutch government dispatched four supervisors to oversee operations; a year later it appointed the German forester von Rössler, long active in the Indies, as inspector-general. As in British India, the forests were divided into three classes. The primary teak woods were placed under the direction of professional foresters; others were turned over to public administrators; and all the wild (that is, noncommercial) forests fell outside strict control. Native practices continued to prevail on all but the first category. By 1874, most such woods were, to official eyes, "ruined," and were eventually brought under government supervision. By 1884, forest reserves had expanded into the long-fallowed forests of village swidden. Even so, private contractors continued to do the cutting, over the strenuous protests of foresters, who argued that only the state could ensure proper regulation. Reluctantly, the state was forced to agree.[33]

The colonial government both intensified and expanded its control over the East Indies forests. Between 1903 and 1921 the state replaced almost three-fourths of private operations with its own. And it began to probe beyond Java, which held only 2 percent of the total forest estate but claimed 92 percent of the state's forestry budget. A supervisor traveled to southern Sumatra in 1900. A forest inspector toured other islands between 1903 and 1905, more to prospect for timber and possible reserves than to regulate. In 1908 the forestry service created the post of permanent inspector for forests outside Java. Staff built up steadily. German forestry remained both a source and an inspiration, and students continued to do their "practical work" in Germany even after formal schooling had transferred to the Agricultural College at Wageningen.[34]

Where professional foresters went, fire control followed. The condemnation of indigenous fire was, as a matter of official policy, universal. When C. O. R. Spalteholz listed "theft, grazing, and forest fires" as the prime threats to teak, he spoke with forestry's imprimatur. In practice, there were complications. The wet season continued to grow fuels profusely, and the dry one to ready them for burning. During really severe droughts, even the nominally evergreen forests as well as the deciduous ones shed their leaves and created an understory piled with fuel and exposed to the searing sun; untreated logging slash added to the stockpile; and fires abounded. Teak, however, seemed impervious. A British observer noted that every year "large areas were burnt over by leaf fires in the dry season," yet they did so "without damaging the teak itself" (the loss of humus, however, concerned him). Worse, there was no end to ignitions. Much of what passed for theft was *ladang*. Forest grazing could not be banned because the Javanese had never fed their cattle in any other way. Both practices depended on free-burning fire. Inevitably fires would escape, and land committed to one fire regime would be subjected to another.[35]

There was also the inextinguishable protest of folk arson. The more the Dutch objected to fire, the more often the natives were inclined to use it. Attempts at wholesale suppression failed. In 1902, alarmed by drought, Kalimantan officials attempted as a conservation measure to reduce swidden and grassland burning particularly by Banjarese and Dayaks, only to have the experiment quickly collapse. There was too much land adapted to fire and too many fire-dependent cultivators. The more Dutch forestry expanded outward, the greater its fire frontier, and the more abundant its firefights. It could not hope to contain them all.[36]

In 1929, Coert duBois, principal architect of America's strategy of systematic fire protection, now American consul to Java, compared the scene with what he had known in California. The easterly monsoon blowing from central Australia created the climatic opportunity for fire, and the leaf-shedding teak the fuel. By September the mixture was combustible. If the rains stalled until December, conditions invited "disastrous fires." Java could expect 5,000 fires a year. But only those that threatened commercial teak forests concerned revenue-conscious governors.[37]

For their protection, well before the advent of the fire season, Dutch foresters prepared plans and arranged the distribution of woods laborers "with reference to their use as fire fighters." Each crew had special training. When these proved inadequate, local villagers were called to their aid. Roads, trails, and tramways provided access; these were cleaned of debris annually into firebreaks, along with other clearings "on the windward side" of protected sites. Detection relied on patrols and fixed lookouts. Communication depended on special codes rapped out on hollow log drums suspended from every lookout platform and in the "alun-alun or gathering place of every native village." The level of protection represented "a considerably higher degree of intensiveness" than known on American national forests. But for that the Dutch could thank their reluctance to pursue fire into the normally incombustible rainforest and the presence, paradoxically, of native villages. It was no accident that teak grew preferentially on those sites subject to dry winds and regular fire.[38]

Real reform would require more than log drums and firebreaks. Fire-suppressing foresters had to replace fire-setting folk, which is what forest reserves and wage-earning rather than village-based labor tried to do; and a fire-retarding flora had to substitute for a fire-promoting one, which was, as always, the holy grail of silviculture. Alone, firefighting too much resembled a police action, sure to fail against determined ecological insurrection.

As forestry professor D. Burger lectured in Jakarta, half measures only worsened the circumstances. Preventing some fires allowed more fuels to pile up, which made fire more damaging. There had to be regular fires or no fires. In "such conditions," Professor Burger argued, "the dry material should be carried away and if necessary trees are to be planted." Just where that woody compost should be taken, he didn't say. But the pacifying trees should be intolerant evergreens that burned poorly and opened an umbrella of smothering shade over the sites beneath them. In conditions like those of the Indies, the solution was to garden the forest, and to weed fire out of the mulch.[39]

Instead, water policy progressively determined fire policy. More and more, a spreading pool of irrigation drove fire to the margins. The apparatus of intensive colonization would, as theory forecast, replace a fire-fallow with a water-commodity agriculture.

The compulsory cultivation system, inaugurated with liberal fanfare around 1850, had boosted export commodities like coffee and sugar at the expense of traditional *ladang* and mountain fallow. Coffee could replace swidden; sugar, wet-rice *sawah*. But as sugar came to dominate exports and rice domestic consumption, the system demanded a stable water cycle and, increasingly, irrigation. Observers detected an alarming volatility of drought and floods, the desiccation that appeared to follow tropical deforestation as predictably as vultures did carrion. For watershed protection, both foresters and hydrologists promoted mountain reserves and reforestation. And reforestation was predicated on—was impossible without—fire protection.

By the time the cultivation system was repealed in 1916, much land was already abandoned, converted to *alang-alang,* or overgrown with exotic shrubs such as lantana. Behind every such deterioration officials saw fire—fires that annually rejuvenated the *alang-alang,* propagated exotic pyrophytes, pushed back the forest frontier, and scoured humus off unstable soils. The prescription for protection was as familiar as its analysis. Restrict graziers, swiddeners, charcoalers, and burners of any kind; if possible, close the forest to traditional use. Then reforest the lands with fire-dampening flora. The future lay with water, which alone could support the commodity crops and *sawah* on which the metastasizing population depended.[40]

And so it went. Water shaped Inner Indonesia; fire, retreating beyond water's flow, the islands of Outer Indonesia. *Sawah* became a black hole, deforming the population of the Indonesian archipelago. In 1942 the Japanese arrived, and in 1949 the Dutch left, but the patterns of fire and water remained and intensified, as enduring as the monsoon. Or they did until the transmigration programs and industrial logging of the 1980s exploded swidden and slash fires into the outer islands, particularly Borneo, like a supernova. In 1983–84, logging, *ladang,* and drought turned 4.5 million hectares of East Kalimantan rainforest into a smoking hole. The cycle repeated in 1987, and again in 1994.[41]

So vast were the smoke palls that they obscured the skies more thoroughly than Krakatoa, and so dense that Singapore repeatedly had to shut down its airport. The spectacle was visible from space, its smoke by day and fire by night recorded with remote-sensing satellites and ogling space shuttles, testimony to near-Earth voyagers that humans were present. Industrial swidden—geopolitical swidden—burned forests as though they were rice straw, and lit up the archipelago in a ring of almost volcanic fire. Even the wet fields of *sawah* could not extinguish them.

(iii)

The explosion of Indies fire had, in fact, ample antecedents. For millennia the region had been a fire source rather than a fire sink. Probably only Europe rivaled the region as a spawning ground of maritime colonizers; and over the course of several years, a great diaspora had cast sparks out of a proto-Malayan hearth. A branch of Malayo-Polynesian speakers, departing Borneo, skirted the fringe of the Indian Ocean and landed in Madagascar in several pulses beginning around A.D. 500. Waves of related colonizers carried the firestick throughout the spangled Pacific, lighting new archipelagoes like candelabra. The first groups probably entered Polynesia proper around 1300 B.C. For nearly a thousand years they nestled in Samoa and Tonga, then burst out in an ocean-spanning triangle. They reached Easter Island by A.D. 500, Hawaii by 600, and New Zealand around 950.[42]

If clouds announced islands, smoke and flame proclaimed settlement. In his cruises through the Pacific, Captain James Cook observed: "We saw either smoke by day, or fires by night, wherever we came." In the New Hebrides the "country was illuminated with fires, from the sea-shore to the summits of the mountains." At New Caledonia, after descending the central mountains, "the first thing I observed they [the natives] did, was to set fire to the grass, etc., which had over-run the surface." Swidden was universal, "observed by all the nations in this sea." Joseph Banks concurred, "frequently" observing "large fires . . . in the islands and New Zealand made by the Natives in order to clear the ground for cultivation." By the time Europeans arrived and began to cultivate the myth of Tahiti, colonizing swarms had already tilled the biota and fired the landscape in a hominid kiln.[43]

In this panorama two islands, or microcontinents, again stand as doubles. Together they flank the two extremes of the Greater Indies diaspora. A relatively homogeneous people colonized New Zealand for as much as 800 years prior to European contact. By contrast, the colonizers of Madagascar were, by the time of European arrival, culturally syncretic from contact with other peoples, and Madagascar was the end of a long hegira. Both islands—one largely temperate, the other tropical—were rich with endemics and strikingly peculiar in their composite biota. Under the blows of settlement both fractured along biotic stress planes. And both, by the time of European contact, were as well fired as a ceramic bowl.

There is a Maori tradition that when the first settlers saw Aotearoa, it was heavily forested, the canopy broken only at a few sterile sites. Then "Kupe and other early immigrants arrived" and "lit fires at all places whereat they landed, and so much forest was destroyed, also the moa perished in those fires." Aotearoa, in brief, became a Maori Madeira.[44]

What happened was no different in type from what occurred throughout Polynesia, though the outcome was particularly dramatic because New Zealand was larger, more temperate in climate, its eccentric ark full of endemics. Except for an Australian bat, no mammals inhabited the islands. Every vertebrate niche was filled with birds, including a genus of flightless birds known collectively as moas, from eleven to twenty-eight species. New Zealand forests, highly sensitive to fire, were rich with *Podocarpus, Nothofagus,* and *Agathis,* a taxa as exotic to Tahiti as to Britain. Under the impact of colonization, the moas became extinct, and the indigenous forest retreated to half its precontact size.[45]

There had been fires before humans, some extensive, all absorbed into a frequently disturbed landscape. Especially on the thermally active North Island, earthquakes, eruptions, and landslides kneaded the biota like bread dough. But fire often put them to bake. New Zealand's mountain spine created a rain shadow to the east, a suitable geography of wet and dry; from time to time there were droughts, forest die-offs, and storm-wracked slash; *Föhn* winds regularly swept the Canterbury Plains and Hawke's Bay region like an avalanche; and lightning kindled fires. Under wholly natural conditions, large fires had swept both North and South Islands between 2,500 and 1,500 years ago. Within 500 years after that spontaneous Ragnarok, a unique fire species arrived to seize the fire-sculpted land.[46]

Still, the span of time to recover was great, and the old order eventually reestablished itself. Precontact New Zealand, though rich in pioneering species, possessed no true pyrophytes; the biota restored itself by being left alone. But once begun and perpetuated, once rekindled again and again by a determined pyrophile, fire could become self-sustaining, slowly buckling the surrounding woods like a fault whose cumulative stresses exceed its elastic limits. Even Europeans found the native woods unusually fire sensitive; burned sites were quickly overwhelmed with pioneering species like bracken and tutu (*Coriaria ruscifolia*). What had preserved the forests—a long fallowing between catastrophic disturbance—vanished when far-sailing humans arrived for whom the forests offered neither shelter nor sustenance. "The forests of New Zealand," concluded M. S. McGlone, "lacking resistance to fire, slow-growing and without substantial food resources, were doomed from the moment of first human settlement."[47]

Its first fleets arrived probably around A.D. 950. Legend holds that others came in their wake during the centuries that followed; some speak of a later, Great Migration in the fourteenth century. Regardless, Aotearoa became the largest island by far in Polynesia. And like those others, it soon learned of anthropogenic fire. The new colonists burned for all the reasons their ancestors had. They burned to establish horticultural plots, to ease travel and keep open thoroughfares, to hunt and sustain habitat, and—not insignificant for a people so congenitally aggressive—for war and defense. Dense woods invited ambush; forests that crowded settlements encouraged attacks, or fire-assisted assaults.[48]

But they also burned to render an alien land more habitable. South Island, in particular, resisted traditional Polynesian agriculture. Fire hunting for moas replaced swidden for kumara (*Ipomoea batatas*), a tuber. The Maoris could not melt down and recast Aotearoa into Samoa (or mythical Hawaiki), but they could heat and bend it into more usable forms. Of critical importance was bracken, which thrived and whose root seems to have replaced taro and yam as a carbohydrate food source. Hot fires stimulated bracken, repeated fires rejuvenated it, and fast-burning bracken often carried fire into surrounding woods, especially during times of drought or föhn wind. By the 1830s, Charles Darwin observed that "the whole country abounds with fern," that its sheer pervasiveness gave the "whole scene, in spite of its green colour, . . . a rather desolate aspect." Moreover, it was not necessary to clear off a site to prepare it for fire, only to open its surface to light, slash its understory, and kill its large trees by ringbarking or kindling basal fires. In this way a productive, fire-dependent biome quickly replaced a less usable, fire-sensitive one.[49]

There were other causes, and other effects. Undoubtedly campfires and miscellaneous burnings got away. Kauri, often rich in resin, held fire in their roots for long periods, another source of errant burns. Colonizers would test landscapes with fire as they might assay rock. The islands were new to the Maoris; only in time would they learn what fires best suited what places. If their hunting killed off the moas, their fire practices destroyed the forests on which the moas depended to recover. Besides, accidents happened, fires escaped. And, Janet Davidson reminds us, there is the "sheer delight of a big burn-off, with or without reason." European pioneers to New Zealand "felt it," and European explorers throughout Polynesia catalogued a constellation of fire practices as dazzling as they often were baffling. Nothing so declared the human presence as a fire.[50]

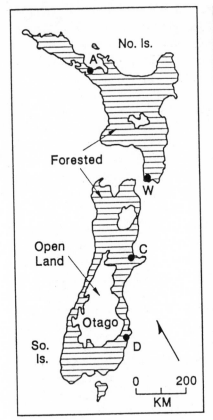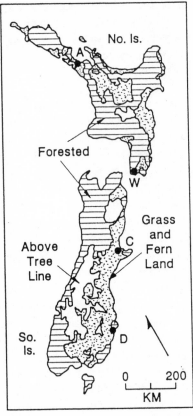

The Maori colonization of Aotearoa. The general vegetative cover of New Zealand at the time of Maori contact (left) and prior to major European settlement, ca. 1840 (right). (From Dickinson 1995, reproduced by permission of the Geological Society of America)

By the time of European contact, the Maoris' fires had branded the land-scape with distinctive patterns. The main burst of clearing and burning had occurred between A.D. 1000 and 1200. The lowland podocarp forests of South Island were burned between about 1200 and 1400, and the interior beech forests between 1300 and 1500. Now, tussock and bracken dominated the eastern flanks and lowlands, and other changes rumbled like caissons behind: dune forma-tion, soil erosion, faunal extinctions, the release of exotic mammals like dogs and rats. Hunting and habitat conversion drove the moa, all dozen or score of species, over an evolutionary cliff. The Maori clans had attacked the land as ferociously as they attacked each other.

If its biotic alienness prevented Aotearoa from becoming another Samoa, its size probably spared it from becoming another Easter Island, a suicidal seduction of deforestation, wars, and sumptuary temples. On Aotearoa, human populations ratcheted upward. By the time the HMS *Endeavour* rediscovered New Zealand, its coasts swarmed with Maori.[51]

If this extraordinary reconstruction of the landscape abolished many niches, it also created others. The horticultural clearings and fallowed woods were open to an agriculture whose crops could thrive in the New Zealand climate, and the expansive grasslands begged for grazers. Colonizing Europeans had both. In the seafaring British the far-ranging Polynesians met a nautical and military equal. Their biotic ordnance, however, gave the British far more firepower.

The Maoris had done the bulk pioneering, and continued to do so after European contact. Just as guns propelled intertribal warfare to new intensities, so European markets and introduced tubers like the hardy potato accelerated land conversion. Maori warriors set out on long voyages and cleaned out ethnic rivals in what would become prime sites for European settlement. Clans disappeared like species of moa. (In one notorious episode, Ngati Tama and Ngati Mutunga contracted with a British ship to visit Chatham Island, where they slaughtered everyone and carried the heads back for sale and other body parts for the pot. The incident forced Britain to reconsider its laissez-faire policy toward New Zealand.) Potato gardens replaced kumara, and expanded into former woods. Even as European settlers spread, they often contracted with Maoris for land clearing.

If the Maoris labored to remake the islands in the image of mythic Hawaiki, the English sought to replicate a gardened (no less mythic) England. In 1835, Darwin reported patches of English farms sewn on the landscape like appliqués:

> On the adjoining slope, fine crops of barley and wheat were standing in full ear; and in another part, fields of potatoes and clover. But I cannot attempt to describe all I saw; there were large gardens, with every fruit and vegetable which England produces; and many belonging to a warmer clime. I may instance asparagus, kidney beans, cucumbers, rhubarb, apples, pears, figs, peaches, apricots, grapes, olives, gooseberries, currants, hops, gorse for fences, and English oaks; also many kinds of flowers. Around the farm-yard there were stables, a thrashing-barn with its winnowing machine, a blacksmith's forge, and on the ground ploughshares and other tools; in the middle was that happy mixture of pigs and poultry, lying comfortably together, as in every English farm-yard. At the distance . . . there was a large and substantial water-mill.[52]

The process quickened after the Treaty of Waitangi in 1840. War and disease eventually displaced the Maori, sheep invaded the tussocks, loggers removed many of the remaining forests, European cereals and root crops sprouted from old and new fields, and New Zealand was soon as overrun with English expatriates, from swans to hedgehogs. From other lands came llamas, Himalayan thars (wild goats), eucalypts, Monterey pine, Australian possums. As the landscape struggled to acquire British forms, it displayed an often unBritish preference for fire. The "first impression of New Zealand," Joan Druett noted, "was often of flames leaping up into the sky."[53]

The English colonists went at their task with as much zeal as the Maoris, and considerably more ecological leverage. To pioneers, fire was a philosopher's stone, transmuting New Zealand's weird dross into familiar gold. Edwin Fairburn wrote how the "steep hillsides are cleared of timber which is burnt to the ground. Then grass is sown in the ashes." The task continued well into the twentieth century. "Fire played an indispensable part in the development of bush and scrub land," Briscoe Moore, a bush farmer, observed simply, "and one had to use it." Success or failure hinged on the burn, and on the morning following it, the "settler will be elated or depressed accordingly." Farmers routinely spring-burned planted fields, native bush, weeds, and flax stubble. Firewood gatherers, a British forester proclaimed, toss lighted matches "to the mass of tops and spray not deemed of sufficient value to defray the cost of removal: the mountain-slope is quickly lighted up with a bright blaze." Logging slash fed outbreaks of dry-season wildfires. Confronted with tough country, pioneers resorted to "the simple device of burning their way into and through" it.[54]

Still, pastoralism, not potatoes, was the instrument of wholesale reformation. Exploring pastoralists like J. B. A. Acland noted in 1855 that "the only way in which a sheep-walk, or 'run' is cultivated, and the pasturage improved, is by putting a lucifer-match under a tuft of grass and setting the whole country ablaze." Tussock burned like cane, and flowered in the aftermath. Samuel Butler recorded how, after an exploring trip to the mountains, "we burnt the flats as we rode down, and made a smoke which was noticed between fifty and sixty miles off. I have seen no grander sight than the fire upon a country which has never before been burnt." Surveyors around Mount Peel did the same; John Acland estimated their burns extended 20,235 hectares and were visible 97 kilometers away. "By 7 P.M.," he recorded, "our fires had extended for miles. . . . [By their light] I could read and write my diary as I did." Sheep and other imported fauna soon interacted synergistically with fire to remake vast landscapes with a thoroughness unavailable to the Maoris.[55]

Exhilarating, the burning went beyond necessity. Even Lady Barker in the 1850s succumbed to the "exceeding joy of 'burning'" and competed with rivals to set the most spectacular fire. She lamented having missed the great fires that had undoubtedly accompanied first contact. Others, glad for fire's assistance, were less pleased that the more the bush was cleared, the more it burned with wildfires. Large fires broke out along Banks Peninsula in 1853, in south Canterbury in 1859 and again in 1863, and, spectacularly, in Waimate in 1878. Still, pastoral burning was less deadly than woods burning, and of tussock burning, Lady Barker wrote, the residents "never were allowed to have half enough of it."[56]

It is not easy to smash a biota. In retrospect, it happened to New Zealand in little more than a geologic heartbeat. To those on the scene, however, it occurred only with monumental labor, and then amid grave uncertainties about the outcome. The old scenarios for postfire recovery literally went up in smoke. "Previous to the 'eighties," observed Herbert Guthrie-Smith, "the effects of burning out the indigenous vegetation of the run had been almost imperceptible; ground temporarily cleared had immediately lapsed into its former condition." But now local weeds like manuka (*Leptospermum scoparium*) competed with alien weeds, and the structure of the burned site—trees plucked out by their roots, peat burned away, ground trampled by alien hoofs—deleted the traditional narratives by which the land had retold its story. Conversion opened a Pandora's box of plagues. Pieces proliferated, patterns proved elusive. Even fireweeds were unpredictable in their exuberance. Successive fires yielded new, rarely repeating growth.[57]

It was not obvious how the conversion would end, with how much tragedy or irony. B. E. Baughan captured this unease in her gritty poem, "A Bush Section":

> *For along the paddock, and down the gully,*
> *Over the multitudinous ridges,*
> *Through valley and spur,*
> *Fire has been!*
> *Ay, the Fire went through and the Bush has departed,*
> *The green Bush departed, green Clearing is not yet come.*
> *'Tis a silent, skeleton world;*
> *Dead, and not yet re-born,*
> *Made, unmade, and scarcely as yet in the making;*
> *Ruin'd, forlorn, and blank.*[58]

The disintegration—the ecological equivalent to the ceaseless Maori wars—could not continue. In 1874 a preliminary Forest Conservation Act was passed, surprisingly with the approval of Prime Minister Julius Vogel. Officials subsequently arranged for a forester, Captain Inches Campbell-Walker, to be deputed from India. His inspection tour added to the growing conviction—and clamor—of imperial intellectuals who believed that forests stabilized climate and that fires destabilized it. Regardless, the act proved premature. Campbell-Walker's report was buried, leaving Vogel himself to protest: "The experience of the world is against it. State forests are the most cherished institutions of the countries that possess them." Meanwhile, bushfires raged, also set into motion by Vogel's program to accelerate settlement. A new Great Migration was remaking New Zealand as profoundly as the old. Railroads cracked open sealed woods, and fires scurried through the fissures. In reply, a miscellany of firefighting corps, mostly centered in towns, organized in 1878 into the United Fire Brigades' Association of New Zealand. And in September 1885, in a decision echoed throughout much of the British Empire, from Tasmania to Ontario, New Zealand legislated into existence a reservation system of state forests and hired forest rangers to oversee them. One of their charges was to protect the land from fire. Without control over land, however, control over fire proved impossible. "With little exaggeration it could be said that, for the next several decades, a pall of smoke hung over the North Island."[59]

Horrifically, within months, a 100-year drought plunged New Zealand into a maelstrom of fire, its vortices swirling through newly hacked bush settlements around Mount Taranaki and Hawke's Bay. The great fires fed largely on slash accumulated during the 1870s and early 1880s after a truce had calmed the Maori guerrilla wars and the Vogel reforms, particularly regarding railways, had wrenched open the interior. The extreme weather encouraged rather than dampened burning off, and once set in motion protective burning was often the only, desperate response. The fires multiplied to epidemic numbers and heroic size; they affected all parts of the disassembled New Zealand landscape, claiming towns as well as bush paddocks. So, too, their attempted control makes a fascinating complement to the evolving landscape: there were railroads and fire engines amid ax-felled bush and ox-cart roads. The compound was volatile, the landscape still immersed in the alchemy of fire transmutation.[60]

The conflagrations mocked the presumption of Wakefieldian settlement, an antipodean England, the planned promise of security and prosperity that had attracted colonists. But if fire alarmed boosters, it horrified naturalists. Even exotic flora, prone to weediness, invited fire. Gorse and broom mingled with manuka and bracken, as environmentally volatile as the political mixing of Briton and Maori. Worse, it appeared that New Zealanders had consigned a unique bush to the flames and had grown in its ash a cosmopolitan flora of weeds, blackberries, and English thrush. The fires' residue facilitated the "luxuriant growth of goundsel, thistles, piripiri, and other weeds, diversified only by scattered bushes of bush-lawyer, and similar unwelcome growths," lamented a British forester. "The transformation is now complete, the grace and beauty of nature are replaced by rugged untidiness." Another island garden was becoming desert. Social disorder would inevitably follow environmental anarchy.[61]

Gradually economic logic imposed an ecological order. What eventually sculpted the puttied landscape was the contriving, not very invisible, hand of a global market. After refrigerator ships linked New Zealand dairy and meat products with Britain, New Zealand evolved into Britain's offshore market garden.

Indigenous Aotearoa, reduced but not removed, stabilized as aliens and natives came into rough equilibrium, and biodiversity, paradoxically, increased. New Zealand was large enough and the Maoris stubborn enough not to crumble completely. (Maori farmers adopted potatoes and maize, and sheep stations hired Maori shearers.) Small dairy farms succeeded pastoral sheep-walks, and sown pasture, the expanses of burned tussock. So also wholesale conversion burning gave way to more selective firing; legislation regulated the place and timing of burning; and debris burns replaced great clearing fires. Herbert Guthrie-Smith documented the transition from Tutira, his sheep-run microcosm of New Zealand. The land had absorbed the first fires, as it did earthquakes, with a shudder, before returning to the status quo. The truly transforming fires came later, once outfitted with exotics like vandals with crowbars and hammers, and deconstructed the native bush in ways both damaging and unpredictable. (When redemption came, however, it was the transmuting fire, as much as the trampling sheep and reliable credit, that achieved that end.)

Yet the green field not the blackened paddock remained the ideal. Agronomists routinely condemned pastoral burning as the cause of grassland deterioration, soil erosion, weed encroachment, and watershed decay. Foresters saw fire feeding on slash as sanitary engineers might watch rats feeding on garbage; fire had no obvious place in indigenous forests and certainly none in commercial plantations of exotic pine. Conservationists saw bare soil and gulleying in mountain paddocks, the scene of fire-catalyzed sheepgrazing. The solution was obvious. As the Department of Forestry put it in 1919, "Fire-protection is simply a matter of staff and the adoption of correct methods."[62]

That became possible with the Forest Act of 1919, as reconstituted in 1921–22. That year 20,000 hectares of Crown forest land burned. The first director of the Forest Service, L. MacIntosh Ellis, wasted no time in identifying fire as the "archangel of devastation," the "greatest enemy to successful forest-management in New Zealand. Until and unless this arch-enemy can be controlled no forest plans are worth the paper they are written on." Fire protection was "the first step to forest-perpetuation," and the first requirement of New Zealand's ambitious afforestation schemes. Granted that its "primitive" trees were more susceptible to fire than exotics, fire control had to become "much more complete than in countries of the Northern Hemisphere."[63]

With forestry's fanaticism, the new economy's firm hand, and the Forest Service as an institutional matrix, New Zealand quickly tamed fire. Settlement and more intensive husbandry controlled fuels; a system of burning permits helped control burning; and the creation of rural fire districts controlled wildfires. Fire became naturalized, sometimes benignly like honey bees and white clover, sometimes more malevolently like ferrets and possums. Rural burning persisted—farming was impossible without it—but like the farmers themselves it became integrated with a stable, agricultural mosaic that comprised rural New Zealand.

But it only worked with those parts of New Zealand that belonged to the new order. A part that didn't exploded in the summer of 1946. On state forest lands 62 fires burned 6,800 hectares, while outside state lands 311 fires (200 kindled by railroads) burned 240,000 hectares, the greatest part through "scrub, fern, and tussock."[64] A new Forest and Rural Fires Act (1947) moved to plug the institutional hole. Urban fires in Rongotai and Christchurch prompted a royal commission in 1947, whose recommendation for a national fire service became law in 1949. Meanwhile there was the example and determination of Britain. In 1947 Britain nationalized its fire services and gently nudged the Kiwis, reluctant to sever links, out of the imperial nest; New Zealand became independent. Economic ties, however, strengthened. Demand for New Zealand's rural products boomed. As more land was brought into the economic regime, so it was also absorbed into an institutional fabric of fire protection.

Progressively, fire became enveloped into the cocoon of a welfare state. Even rural firing, outside high country paddocks, was reduced to the equivalent of burning raked leaves on a lawn. Wildfires became rare. Reforms extended even to mountain tussock. Catchment boards restricted agricultural burning through permits, and after the Land Act of 1948, on Crown lands as well. To the public mind, fire and erosion became synonyms. Although a 1949 royal commission concluded that agricultural burning was necessary if dangerous, the prevailing sentiments condemned the practice as environmentally destructive. To quibble over appropriate fire regimes or postfire practices was pointless: the best way to limit the damages wrought by fire was to abolish fire altogether.[65]

And the best means of fire prevention was to convert the land to fire-immune forms. Technology colluded with markets to cultivate even remote paddocks. It became possible, through aircraft, to sow pastures, introduce legumes, and top-dress with superphosphate fertilizers. It was possible to replace tussock, and to abolish the fires that tussock had required. Ironically, catchment boards preferred to destroy a biome rather than preserve it with fire. However compromised had been New Zealand's attempt to transplant England's biota, it had adopted unreservedly England's pyrophobia.[66]

Like so many of its landslipped hillsides, however, the reconstructed New Zealand order began to disintegrate. It lost the discipline imposed by a larger economy when Britain joined the Common Market, when global competition began to glut the commodities market for agriculture, and when the cost of imported oil skyrocketed. No longer could pastoralism support New Zealand; nor, increasingly, could New Zealand support 90 million sheep and cattle.

Reluctantly—stunningly, under the direction of a newly elected Labour government in 1984—New Zealand began to devolve its welfare state, and its landscape followed suit. The much publicized renegotiation of the Treaty of Waitangi begged for an environmental cognate. Old farms were converted to planted forests; and retired pastures to woods, nature reserves, or flammable scrub. In 1987 the two trends converged when the state disestablished its Forest Service. Protection forests reverted to a Department of Conservation; production forests, including its world-class afforestation projects, were privatized. No longer Britain's offshore market garden, New Zealand was instead becoming Asia's offshore tree farm.[67]

So the land was changing again. In each of its great transmutations, some species, like radioactive tracers, had illuminated not only the dominant landscapes but the presence of fire. For the Gondwana Ur-woods, it was the towering kauri, as sensitive to fire as the banana to frost. For the Maori occupation it was bracken and tussock, defining the domain of colonization as surely as lava and ash did the volcanic fields of Ruapehu. And perhaps more than anything else, gorse has defined the age of British settlement.

Imported from Britain as a hedge, gorse was intended to delimit wildlands into fields and paddocks. As it kept the landscape in order, so also sheep, goats, farmers, and fires held it in check, as they had for millennia in Europe. There, symbolized in the gorse hedgerow, was the transplanted British landscape. Today gorse is more likely to range over whole hillsides and metastasize into tumorous patches on lands abandoned by the old pastoralism yet not converted fully to forestry or suburbs. The fire protection system that the Forest Service had overseen disintegrated.

Gorse burns explosively, and like a pyrophyte, to burn it is to stimulate it. Fired gorse can liberate 40 million seeds in a hectare, seeds that can remain viable in the soil for up to a century. Fire and gorse became linked: propagate one and you propagate the other. Previously, gorse had been contained by its tended rows, gardened as much as maize or cabbages. Place it under shade trees for a century and it will wither away. But that kind of stability is gone, and there may be little to halt the flames, save the normally benign climate and mechanical counterforce. To keep prospective fire from suburbs, firebreaks line the mountains around Hutt Valley, and to limit its threat to Monterey pine plantations gorse is suppressed with herbicides, bulldozers, and when it catches fire, with engines, pumps, and helicopter buckets.

Isolation—geographic or economic—did not mean stability. The fires that a rural New Zealand had to accept, because it had no option, an industrial New Zealand is no longer willing to tolerate. If it chooses to preserve its past, it will

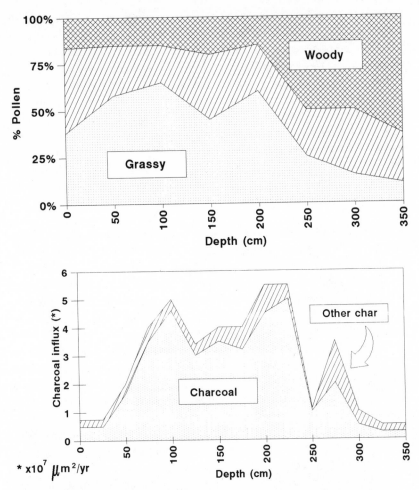

The Malagasy colonization of Madagascar. The timelines read right (past) to left (present). With first contact, fires proliferate—events recorded by a rapid increase in charcoal (top). Simultaneously, preserved pollen indicates a larger shift in floral composition from forests to grasslands (bottom). (Data from Burney 1986)

have to retain fire. But such was New Zealand's pyrophobia that it might well decide that tussock, manuka, and bracken were not worth the cost, if the price was fire. It was slower to learn that fire-free landscapes also had their price.

(iv)

If the Maori had set their biotic pot to simmer, the Malagasy had apparently let theirs boil over. New Zealand represented a landscape that, to European eyes, had been incompletely converted, and pioneers soon added English fuel to the flames to complete the transformation. But Red Madagascar exhibited a landscape that had evidently exceeded the elastic limits of its indigenous ecology. French naturalists and colonial officials recoiled in horror from the excess. The imperial task was to suppress, not settle.

Once attached to Africa, Madagascar had broken away with India, then lagged as India plowed north into Asia and left the Seychelles in its furrowed wake. It was a miniature Africa, a plateau flanked by coastal lowlands, its climate subject to ample rains between a prolonged (seven-month) dry season. Sediment cores from lakes in the island's center suggest a long history of fire. A 36,000-year profile from Lake Tritrivakely traces a steady rain of charcoal, ebbing and flowing with climatic pulses, that slackened only around 4,000 years ago. Pollen residue recommends a biota that, while rich in endemics, was structurally similar to the *miombo* woodland that prevailed on the mainland. The record sketches a loosely woven fabric of grasslands and savanna woodlands, knotted here and there into dense forests. A significant fraction of the charcoal derives from grasses. For the next 2,000 years charcoal influx remained low, while the proportion of pollen from woody species rose. The island housed a relict bestiary of lemurs, pygmy hippos, an endemic aardvark, a carnivorous viverrid, and the usual Gondwana aviary of flightless birds, including an elephant bird that stood three meters tall. But the island was uninhabited by humans.[68]

The Austronesian diaspora filled that void some time between the first and sixth centuries. Sooner or later wind and currents would carry determined mariners to the shore; pumice from Krakatoa, for example, washed up on Madagascan beaches two years after the explosion. But settlement, not trade, had to provide the motive, and it was far from obvious that voyagers whose closest linguistic affiliations are with Malayan speakers in Borneo and Moluccas would survive as a colonizing force from their extended transit around the Indian Ocean, all of which was populated, all of whose coasts were heavy with traffic. Certainly Madagascar was known; yet without inhabitants, which is to say without trade, there was little reason to travel there. There was scant incentive to colonize.

Probably the voyagers stayed for many years along the east African coast, and out of their wandering in that Swahili Sinai they acquired tools, knowledge, African slaves, and above all zebu cattle. By the time they renewed their migration, they were a complex, creolized society. The Proto-Malagasy exodus likely made landfall in Madagascar around A.D. 100. A major colonizing push commenced around 500, possibly the result of secondary migrations. Like travelers announcing their entry into new country with a signal fire, the Proto-Malagasy kindled blazes. Legend holds that landfall began the *afotroa,* a "great conflagration" that remade the island. Lake sediments testify to a reality behind that memory: charcoal spikes abruptly reach levels not known for at least four millennia.[69]

Reconstruction came quickly. By the ninth or tenth century Madagascar was effectively settled by cattle pastoralists and swidden (*tavy*) farmers. By the advent of European contact the Malagasy had fragmented into at least eighteen rival ethnic groups. The new megafauna, however, had no sympathy with the old. In short order a wave of extinctions swept over the island comparable to those experienced in New Zealand, Australia, and North America. Swept out with the evolutionary tide were seven genera of lemur, the pygmy hippo, aardvark, viverrid, giant land tortoise, and the ratites—the Madagascan dodos and moas. By A.D. 900 the megafaunal holocaust ended.[70]

The fires did not. Fire was part of the natural heritage of Madagascar in ways it evidently was not in New Zealand or Java, and mosaicked grasslands receptive to fire flourished even to the time of contact. These patches became points of entry by which anthropogenic fire, *tavy* swiddeners, and pastoralists could pry open unfavorable biomes. Grazing, cutting, and burning soon culled the savannas of trees, drove dense woods into ravines or remote hillsides, and remade the Madagascan plateau into a cognate of the high African veld. The proportion of grass to woody charcoal increased. By the time French naturalists began their reconnaissances the central plateau was 70 to 80 percent prairie, an eerie, unsettling emptiness. Annual fires kept it that way.

France and Britain had long but lightly sparred over Madagascar, an island that never commanded the geopolitical significance its location along Europe's passage to the east suggested it should have. Uninhabited islands were better suited for provisioning than places like Madagascar, then subject to the Merina dynasty, a monarchy-ruled caste society not unlike India's. European influence was propagated mostly by missionaries, especially British. The French—the most shameless of Europe's imperialists—commenced conquest in 1883 on the basis of a dubious 1840 concession to western ports from the Sakalava tribe. Hostilities ended with a treaty signed in December 1885 in which France announced a protectorate over the whole island, a status confirmed by the Berlin Conference, this after the Suez Canal had redirected Indian trade and made Cyprus more vital than Madagascar.[71]

Soon a combination of French ambition and presumed grievances against French honor culminated in outright invasion. The war lasted six months before a detached column seized Antananarivo, the Merina capital. Of the 14,773 troops who landed, 14 died of fighting and 9,337 of disease. There followed a period of episodic chaos until Governor-General Joseph-Simon Gallieni finally suppressed unrest and for good measure abolished slavery, caste, and the monarchy. By then French scientists, military engineers, and officials of occupation sprawled over an island larger than metropolitan France to determine what their outburst had gained them.

Red Madagascar, it was soon titled—red for the laterite soils baking under the tropical sun, red for the blood shed in conquest, red for the flames that enveloped it like the sea. Earlier travelers were mostly Christian missionaries among the animists and Moslems of the island. The European, Samuel Copland exclaimed in 1822, "is lost in astonishment in traversing the vast plains and forests." William Ellis explained that the Malagasy burn their luxuriant grasslands at the end of the dry season, at which time "the fires may be seen at an immense distance illuminating the horizon in a most splendid manner, for many miles in extent." They practiced *sawah* in select lowlands but swidden throughout the mountains, save some sacred groves. Their endless cattle—three zebu to every human—were their primary livelihood; and only fire could flush the stubborn tropical grasses into palatability. Moreover, itinerant Europeans were not above contributing to the island's fire load. In 1876, Charles Frederick Moss described how, on a clear night, his party watched the great grassfires "among the wild hills and moorlands." They counted twenty in various directions, and saw streams of flame, "distinctly visible," on the slopes of Mount Ankaratra 80 kilometers distant. Later, when luggage bearers fell behind, Moss ignited grass fires to serve as beacons. While those "glorious blazes" helped guide the Malagasy, the routine burning of the central plateau only confounded the Europeans, who "groped [their] way" to their destination. For the visitors the resident fires blinded rather than illuminated.[72]

Instead the French conducted their own reconnaissance by fire. Their level of initial ignorance was appalling. (They had predicated their conquest on rapid marches with the *wagon Lefebvre* only to discover, on landing, that Madagascar had almost no horses, no oxen trained to the harness, no wheeled vehicles, and in fact no roads. Instead of a flying column racing to the imperial capital over highways, the army labored like ants to build one.) From 1895 to 1900 French officials and savants scrutinized this peculiar land, so rich in endemics, so odd in its customs. Louis Catat concluded that fire and ax had deforested the plateau, that the indolent Sakalava made no pastoral improvements but only burned the prairie, a "barbarous" practice. A. Charon thought that burning was so universal, so instinctive, that only exceptional sites escaped; that such fires had converted forest to prairie; and that the custom was "harmful," "savage," a "hereditary mania." A. Durand asserted that, because of *tavy* and its successor fires, only small fragments of a primeval Great Forest remained along the eastern mountains, hiding in protected pockets like frightened lemurs.

In the far north, long marches through once-wooded terrain by Lieutenant S.-V. Duruy revealed nothing but "charred trunks," and north of Benavony he witnessed what he perceived as a disastrous conflagration but what the Malagasy regarded with "complete indifference." The remainder of the coun-

try, as H. H. Bartlett has summarized the literature, "was absolutely devastated by the habit of all the Malagasy, even in passing, to set fire to the herbage,
under the pretext of improving the pasturage, even if there were no herds."
Those fire practices reflected, as they had helped cause, the apparently
debauched state of the Malagasy. The outcome seemed not only a degraded
landscape but a society of callous nomads, wandering herders, and shifting
cultivators, inimical to stable civilization. Madagascar, it seemed, was an island
Maghreb.[73]

Here was a familiar environmental allegory: the melancholy destruction—
desecration is not too strong a word—of an ancient woods by a barbaric
nomadism. Worse, those debauched morals could infect the civilized as well
as the heathen.

Above 1,000 meters, Mount Tsaratanana, for example, had not suffered the
perversions of Malagasy fire, spared by damp ravines and a reluctance of agriculturalists to approach it. When two French captains tried to ascend it in 1899,
they were beaten back by the weather; then their "porters," it was stated, then
started a fire that swept to the summit and incinerated everything in its path.
Subsequently a Professor Lemoine, a geologist, ascended the mountain three
times early in the century, always in the dry season and always, apparently,
accompanied by fire. That *feu d'artifice* created, to Lemoine's eye, a magnificent spectacle and left his northeastern approach denuded. Perhaps a geologist preferred to see the rocks, but botanists emphatically chose trees. When
Perrier de la Bathie engineered his own ascent in 1912, he found to his dismay
that the ancestral forest had been reduced to charred stalks. He retired for two
months to the still-verdant west flank, and after long delays occasioned by the
world war, mounted an expedition in 1924 to explore the mountain thoroughly.
By then other climbers and other "porters" had completed the task of firing the
woods. Enraged and bitter, he reconstructed his lost paradise from the vestigial shards that had miraculously escaped the flames.[74]

The saga of Mount Tsaratanana became, in Perrier de la Bathie's mind, a
metaphor for all of Madagascar. Once, in a prelapsarian age before the arrival
of humans, a majestic forest of rare endemics and precious hardwoods had
cloaked the island. Then, with fire, the Malagasy had wantonly stripped it away,
pillaging and vandalizing that botanical monument. Meanwhile, Henri Humbert, a professor of botany in Algeria, joined a scientific mission to the island
in 1924, added his own observations to those of Perrier de la Bathie, and reached
a complementary conclusion. The fire practices of the Malagasy had replaced
a complex tropical flora with a degraded savanna; the domineering prairie that
now covered upland Madagascar was wholly anthropogenic. In 1927 both men
published their conclusions as memoirs of the L'Académie Malgache. Together
they so established the myth of the Great Forest that it became a genre of the

scientific literature. Mythological Madagascar, however, had more in common with Pierre Poivre's Mauritius than with the contemporary Africa that it most approximated or Java whose history it resembled.[75]

France's mission to civilize thus extended to the preservation of rainforests and lemurs as well as the protection of persecuted Christians, the redemption of national honor, and the *présence Française*. The prescription required that imperial France should commit residual forests to national parks or nature preserves; should afforest red-soil grasslands, with exotic acacias and eucalypts if necessary; should wean herders away from rangy zebu and toward selectively bred cattle, and farmers from *tavy* in favor of sedentary cropping; and should, at a minimum, build roads—lots and lots of roads. Shortly after Perrier de la Bathie and Humbert published their classic accounts of a fire-declined biota, colonial officials agreed to set aside nature reserves and national parks. By the time of independence these embraced fourteen major sites and more than 700,000 hectares, initially committed to the patronage of the French Natural History Museum.[76]

The Great Island was a spectacular island ark. It was obvious that unique species had vanished, and that more were doomed without state intervention. It was also apparent to even casual observers that forests could regrow over the plateau were they not beaten back by ax, fire, and hoof, and that annual fires abraded the forest like a storm-wracked sea eroding away seacliffs. In this way the vision of the lost Great Forest gained validity and the prospect of its restoration, plausibility. Restrictions on *tavy* and firebreaks against pastoral burning served like jetties and seawalls to break the force of the firestorms. The Service des Eaux et Forêts, modeled on that of metropolitan France and guided by a Code Forestier (1930), imposed a strict regime over reserved forests and parks, and announced severe penalties for misused fire. Not incidentally, control of fire also meant control over the Malagasy. (Critics hinted darkly that, without rigorous policing, the reserves were becoming sanctuaries for cattle thieves and "tax evaders.") In such a landscape, to control the torch was to control the character of human life.[77]

But of course control was never more than marginal, however imposing the colonial edifice. Even with the threat of prosecutions, the central grasslands burned at least once every three years. Land burned whenever it was possible or necessary. Effective fire reform required a level of knowledge that the French did not possess and a degree of social control that remote France could not impose. Indigenous Madagascar did not, apparently, include its indigenes. The prevailing sentiment was that voiced by a British traveler, Walter Marcuse. "The Malagasies regularly burn the forest," he explained, while "the French colonists have made a great point of the need for legislation to prevent the Malagasies from burning the forest."[78]

Gradually, naturalists began to discriminate among different fires and their consequences. Some quietly wondered how Madagascar had come to display so many fire-adapted species if it had been immune to fire in prehistoric times. A skeptical H. H. Bartlett accepted that "man's destructiveness in Madagascar has been inconceivably bad," but argued against "making it out to have been worse than the evidence indicates." If the past was lost in smoke, however, the present was only too well illuminated by flames, and promised to replicate the experience of Perrier de la Bathie on the slopes of Mount Tsaratanana. Endemic Madagascar would soon vanish in the fires of an ignorant peasantry. Red Madagascar joined goat-plagued Cyprus as an international emblem of environmental abuse. Conservationists demanded an "absolute prohibition of burning" around any preserve. "When the house is on fire," alarmed critics explained, "one should not send the town clerk to help, but the fire brigade with all its fire-fighting equipment."[79]

Still, Madagascar remained what it had always been, a biotic backwater, an afterthought of colonization. French rule, however brutal, was short-lived, and French fire control, however misinformed and well-intentioned, was both ephemeral and ineffective outside the most strict reserves. The Great Forest had more to say about France than about Madagascar. The island remained a "museum of living fossils," a biotic Parthenon whose value to natives lay in the usefulness of its recycled stone and to Europeans in the power of its idea. That Red Madagascar persists as one of the enduring emblems of a degraded planet speaks more fully about contemporary Europe than about either that putative island Eden or the aboriginal Earth.[80]

SACRED FIRE:
THE COMING OF CONSERVATION

From the beginning, islands were also ideas. Mythic isles like Brasil, the "Island of the Blest," helped inspire mariners to venture across the Atlantic; and imagined islands housed utopias like those of Thomas More and Francis Bacon. Discovered isles often acquired philosophical stature. If they were uninhabited, they were "new worlds," fresh from the creation; if populated like Tahiti, they were miniature paradises secure in their remoteness from the corruption of artificial civilization. Either way tropical islands, in particular, were symbolic clones of the original Garden of Eden, and like that prototype they recited over and again, like a traveling bard, the paired, heroic narratives of Fall and Redemption.

By the Enlightenment that religious metaphor was fast becoming secularized. Natural innocence seemed more original than sin, and progress more plausible than mere redemption. Islands left the landscape of literary allegory and entered the geography of science; scholars perceived them as semicontrolled experiments in natural history. On islands, processes happened quickly and openly that on continents might take centuries or be disguised amid the sheer complexity of a nature riotous in its exuberance or amid the opaqueness of a landscape dominated by humans. *Philosophes* keen to reconstruct the City of God out of secular stones also retold the story of the Garden in more naturalistic verse. Islands were miniature Ararats on which Nature's prolific arks had come to rest. The creation of lush profusion from an aboriginal few became a model for evolution, the progress of Nature's Design. So also did secular serpents encourage collapse by inviting the earliest colonists to consume the tree of life. The environmental wreckage of islands like St. Helena became microcosmic warnings of macrocosmic doom. As examples mounted, the decline seemed to proceed with almost thermodynamic inevitability.

But it was no longer necessary to accept the world as revealed. On the model of the laboratory, it was possible to invent. If islands could be destroyed, they could also be created. It was conceivable to set aside lands as nature preserves, to design biotic islands that could be shielded from the pollution of human behavior. Ideally such sites could be carved out of places yet untrammeled by colonizing humans, especially the emissaries of a market capitalism that seemed to empty wild landscapes like termites hollowing out a eucalypt. There were ample precedents. Sacred groves, hunting reserves, royal forests, botanical gardens, zoos, mountain catchment reserves, all offered ancient models. Every society, Europe not least of all, had places that it considered sacred, places to which it regulated access or from which it abolished certain practices.

By the nineteenth century, however, as whole continents were changing at rates previously reserved for isolated islands, a countermovement emerged to endow preserves for scientific, aesthetic, historical, nationalistic, and even economic purposes. An industrial landscape, too, needed its sacred groves, an urban society its wilderness, a scientific intelligentsia its environmental utopias.

(i)

The crisis seemed greatest along the colonial periphery, where the shock of encounter was most apparent. In fact, it can be argued that Europe itself was the first land to be subjected to European imperialism, to the corrosive impact of modern science on religion and folklore, to the massive changes in land use stimulated by global markets, errant capitalism, and industrialism. But consequences were more visible to European eyes when acted out elsewhere, and wholesale reform was certainly more amenable to political action beyond the mobs and conspiracies of the capital. Accordingly continental Europe created reserves hesitatingly and on a small scale, while imperial Europe imposed, or made possible, their creation on a vast scale in colonies and former colonies. The greater the contrast, the greater the cultural power of the sacred grove.

Enthusiasm for reserves thus varied in seemingly inverse relation to distance. It took a German, Alexander von Humboldt, to explain the meaning of deforestation in Venezuela; a Scot, Hugh Cleghorn, to elucidate the denudation crisis in India; a Frenchman, Bernardin de Saint-Pierre, to delineate the destruction of Mauritius; and, revealingly, an American, George Perkins Marsh, to trace the outlines of environmental abuse in Europe. So mountain reserves were easier to promulgate on Tobago and St. Vincent than in England's Lake District, forest reserves were far vaster in central India than in the Schwarzwald, and national parks dotted the Rocky Mountains of North America rather than the Ardennes or the Apennines. Great Britain summarizes the circumstances perfectly—insular Britain, the archetype of an island biotically impoverished by colonization (reduced to less than one percent endemism); industrial Britain, the prototypical landscape remade by market capitalism and steam; imperial Britain, the vigorous promulgator of forest reserves and advocate of nature protection in Africa, Asia, Australia, and North America; and insouciant Britain, adopting a national park act for the Home Islands only in 1949.

The ideological reasons were far from trivial. However lovely the English countryside (to the English), it was impossible to imagine that scene as other than a cultural creation. The landscape was a cultivated garden, as ordered as English society, compared to which fens and moors seemed wild. England was a model for a reclaimed landscape, not a prelapsarian one. For nature still fresh from the Creation or raw with primitive vitality, it was necessary to move beyond hedgerows and plowed fields. The cultivated was, by definition, the civilized. Wild nature prowled along its periphery. Reclaimed nature was admirable to the extent it reflected the faith and good works of its sustaining society; sacred nature inspired and instructed in proportion as it was removed from that society.

The political reasons for the disparity were no less compelling. Wild nature might be wasteful and extravagant, its rivers and cataracts might exhibit an unconscionable squandering of energy, and its relentless overpopulation and mass extinctions might restate a parody of Malthusian ruthlessness; but only humans caused outright destruction. Europe's colonization of uninhabited islands proved conclusively that humanity could shatter Design and break the links of the Great Chain of Being. The greater the contact with humanity the greater the potential for degradation. Intellectual narratives of encounter (as distinct from folk stories) are almost universally declensionist, tragedies propelled by fundamental human flaws, the original sins of ignorance and greed. The story of island collapse was restaged in place after place with the predictability of a medieval morality play. Its science described an ecology of atavism.

The shock of the dislocations, social and environmental, frequently inspired a reaction among thoughtful observers. Call it, as a later generation did, conservation—a varied, often inchoate counterrevolution that sought, among other things, to preserve the indigenous, to protect resources from the worst excesses of exploitation, and to rehabilitate lands already damaged. Proponents wanted to tame nature's wantonness, to discipline society's waste, and to preserve some elements of natural splendor and Design. For the more outraged critics, that was insufficient. If conservation sought to regulate human contact, its rival environmental philosophy, preservation, wanted to eliminate that contamination altogether. Only expulsion could preserve the Garden. Both, however, began with the control of people.

"I got into a conversation" with a Canadian colleague, explained Sir William Schlich, retired from the Indian Forestry Service. This "high official of the Dominion" protested the establishment of forest reserves "because our people will go and settle in the middle of them, and are we to cut them out again afterwards?" That, replied Schlich, begged the question. "The thing is to select areas and to declare them a reserve forest and not allow the people to go inside. Unless that is done the reservation has no meaning." And what was true for forests was trebly true for parks. A landscape with indigenes could not be protected. A sacred grove inhabited by humans was a contradiction, or a travesty.[81]

Such a strategy, however, was unlikely in a Europe long crowded with people, and it seemed unnecessary in a Europe that had long ago cultivated out any vestige of the wild. But on both counts it was possible in landscapes lightly populated by aborigines or nomadic pastoralists, or in lands firmly under the political domination of colonial powers. Here were vacant lands or lands that could be emptied of people. Here it was possible to establish biotic islands in the form of parks, hunting preserves, catchment areas, and scientific study areas that could preserve, or where necessary create, the uninhabited islands that had decorated the geography of European utopianism. Without humans there could be no Fall. Without human artifice Nature could be studied in its platonic purity, its revealed texts uncluttered with the glosses of human commentary. That ideal landscape was the metric by which human-wrought deviations could be measured. Here the sun, not the shadow-casting fire, could illuminate.

The Garden had its counterpart in the Hearth, the sacred grove had its vestal fire. Fire there would be. But what kind, and to what end?

In Europe's philosophy of fire, two conceptions prevailed. One, accepted by the folk, was the Franciscan fire, a flame that was a part of nature yet shared by humans. In his *Song of the Creatures,* Saint Francis of Assisi praised God "for our brother fire, through whom thou givest us light in the darkness: and he is bright and pleasant and very mighty and strong." Its dark double was the Nietzschean fire, favored by intellectuals and officials, a fire emblematic of humans and their diabolical transmutations. "Surely flame is what I am," Friedrich Nietzsche proclaimed in *Ecce Homo,* consuming, "never sated," leaving "behind me ashes."

But which of these fires belonged in the Garden? Was fire a force of nature, as vital as sun and soil, sampled but never controlled by humanity? Or was it a contrivance of hand and mind, sometimes obstreperous when not properly tended but meaningless outside the domus of dwelling and the tended landscape? Was the vestal fire an abstraction of nature or a projection of humanity? If fire were not solely under humanity's control, it might threaten the existence of the grove, yet if it were under human governance, it might not suit the grove's sacred character. Was fire an evil or a good; a necessity, a tool, a presence, or a decoration?

As Europe ranged though the world, it sought to bring order to broken landscapes and to protect some fragments of the lands it encountered, and this required that Europe choose for those biotic isles what kind of fire, if any, they would have. Over time, three possibilities were proposed. One, the Franciscan fire, argued that fire belonged but only under strict human control. Another, the Nietzschean fire, argued that fire of any source had no place because it could not be segregated from its human tenders and in mimicry of them it ended in self-immolation. Fire's role, like that of the flaming swords of the Cherubim outside Eden, was to shield but not to enter.

The third possibility, promoted eventually in America, held that fire belonged but only in a purely natural form, a flame untouched by people. To Europeans, a fire without humans was meaningless, like a landscape without artifice, or worse, an aberration like a monstrous birth. To Americans a natural reserve with a tended fire was a contradiction, if not a sacrilege. That both visions found their most vigorous expression outside Europe proper betrays their origins in the utopian, the Edenic, the Romantic, and the imperial.

(ii)

It is no accident that America created the first modern nature reserves, for it possessed landscapes that seemed not only sublime and monumental to European sensibilities but that were in the semi-arid West and relatively vacant of people. They conveyed the sense, otherwise found only on desert isles, that they had escaped the Fall.

Through diseases, wars, contracts, treaties, and forced relocations, colonizing Europeans had largely swept America's indigenes from the land or sequestered them onto special reservations. In the eastern United States agriculturalists quickly seized the vacated sites. In much of the remote, arid West, however, agricultural settlement stalled. Miners, loggers, and open-range graziers passed through like a squall, leaving overturned and trampled landscapes to be blown away like so much biotic dust. Permanent settlement, by and large, did not follow. For several decades the American West experienced a condition known little to the world. Vast landscapes were relatively empty of humans.

It was in the context of this historic anomaly that America created national reserves, tentatively first in Yosemite in 1864, most notably at Yellowstone in 1872, and then broadly with immense forest reserves, largely uninhabited, beginning in 1891. The premise of the parks was that this was true wilderness, prelapsarian nature. That American Indians had visited the sites mattered little because the indigenes, it was held, were part of the natural order, dissolving into its mountains and forests like salt into the ocean. By the time intellectuals inspected the lands they found only scattered, seemingly inconsequential remnant populations. The wilderness still had the grace of Creation upon it, and for the more secular naturalists it served the role that the ideal frictionless surface did for physicists. Once reserves were established, all that remained was to regulate humanity and humanity's technology, to preserve the park "from fire and ax," as the organic legislation typically put it. Nature would perpetuate itself forever.

The first reserve was Yosemite Valley and the Mariposa Big Trees in the Sierra Nevada of remote California. The granite-walled Valley had a monumentality that could rival any wonder of the ancient world; the sequoias formed a sacred grove that stood to Europe's pitiful offerings as the Mississippi River did to the Seine. That Frederick Law Olmsted, America's premier landscape architect, campaigned on Yosemite's behalf and served on the first advisory commission neatly conflates the reserve's social role. As Central Park transplanted nature to New York City, so at Yosemite the national culture was transplanted to the wilderness. Equally to the point, the land was public, unclaimed by patent. In 1864, Congress ceded the land to California as a park in perpetuity. In 1905 the state returned the sites to join the larger penumbra of parks, Sequoia and General Grant, that had grown like a winter coat around it.[82]

"The Mariposa stands as the Creator fashioned it," declared Thomas Starr King in 1860, "unprofaned, except by fire." In fact, the fires were everywhere. The open vistas of Yosemite Valley were the product of centuries of annual aboriginal burning. The Big Trees were burned almost as frequently, again by indigenes, or where they failed, by lightning. Some of the largest trees had their tops blasted away by bolts; almost all had blackened cavities excavated by repeated surface fires. The marvelous architecture of the groves—their vast columns and open understories, the patches of gloomy grotto and stained glass light, the "cathedral" effect that sprang so universally to the minds of observers— was the result of regular fire.[83]

Although educated visitors saw it otherwise, fire, far from profaning the sequoia, was its means of survival. The clustering so characteristic of Big Trees reflected the history of their formative fires. The geometry of the groves traced the phoenixlike immolation of old trees. Seedling survival was greatest on the sites most intensely burned. Those trees best survived that sprouted in the thick ash beds of fallen giants, enriched in the liberated nutrients, purged of competition, spared for a few precarious years the inevitable grass fires that would follow. Later, impervious to surface burns, the sequoia could absorb the fires that cleaned out its conifer competitors. The history of the groves—their origin, their survival, their decay—was a history of fire. Their universal fire scars were not merely the badge of survival but the means. Their fire-sculpted caverns recorded their history as surely as if they had been chiseled onto black stone stelae.

But early settlers, and certainly early conservationists, saw it otherwise. They identified the endless fires with the broken remnants of sullen indigenes who still lurked on the margins; or with the shepherds, often Basques, who herded their flocks up the Sierra as their kin once had the Pyrenees; or with malevolent miners indifferent to all except bare outcrops; or with fraudent land speculators and timber thieves. They saw, in brief, the sources of fire emanating from a debauched humanity; saw in those fires the pollution of the grove's moral ecology; saw blasphemy. And the idealists among them moved to stop it. When Gifford Pinchot visited the sequoia groves in 1891, he pondered "these highly decorative but equally undesirable fires" that "bulked large in the minds of the Kaweah colonists, most of whom were Eastern tenderfeet." One of them informed Pinchot that "they had saved the Big Trees from burning up twenty-nine times in the last five years." To this Pinchot asked wryly who had saved them "during the remaining three or four thousand years of their age?"[84]

But the true text was revealed, not ironic. Fire belonged on the altar, not excavating basal cavities in the cathedral's pillars. When the U.S. cavalry first assumed responsibility for America's major parks, in 1886, it brought still more rigorous fire control to the Sierra sequoias, driving off invading shepherds and rounding up vagrant tourists like so many hostiles. Fire protection became official policy, and fire suppression a dogma. So impressive was the military presence that the National Academy of Sciences, inquiring into the status of the national forests, proposed in 1896 that forestry be taught at West Point and the Army oversee the nation's forest reserves as well as its parks. Fire and trespass, both intertwined, were the principal threats, and against both the military's force and moral presence were ideal. The transfer of authority to the National Park Service in 1916 changed little; the civilians retained their campaign hats, riding breeches, epaulets, and the standing order to suppress fire.[85]

Nature was less impressed than tourists, however. By the early 1920s the groves themselves were changing a great deal. Debris built up around the trunks of the Big Trees, and the cathedral's aisles were overgrown with sugar pine and white fir. Fires no longer washed through the groves like spring freshets, scouring away the biotic grime. If a fire were to enter now, it would no longer singe away the grasses and scrub but attack the Big Trees themselves. Now they had the fuel to burn through the bark, race up the trunks, and perhaps sear the canopy. Fire has become the poison, not the antidote. Fire protection seemed more urgent than ever. A 1906 experiment in which a controlled burn was conducted to reduce fuels in General Grant National Park led nowhere. Even advocates of "light" burning, like Colonel John White, superintendent of Sequoia National Park in the early 1920s, declined to reintroduce fire into the groves themselves. Instead, crews selectively thinned and hauled away excess fuels. That, too, failed.[86]

By the 1960s the groves were a shambles. Sequoias were dying, sequoia reproduction was nonexistent, Big Trees were invisible amid the throng of congregating conifers, and the cathedral groves were a forest explosion awaiting a spark. The Leopold Report (1963) cited the debauched Sierra forests ("no longer resembling their primeval counterparts") as part of its inquiry into the status of the national parks. Those parks should be, in the report's memorable phrase, "vignettes of Primitive America." And they should include fire, preferably natural but where natural fire was no longer possible, controlled burns that would "restore natural fire regimes to the maximum extent possible so that ecosystems can function essentially unimpaired by human interference." The National Park Service directed its research to those ends. The sequoia groves moved, once more, to center stage of American environmentalism.[87]

Test burns commenced in 1964. After national policy liberated fire in late 1967, at least in principle, Sequoia–Kings Canyon National Park began to free it in practice. The parks embraced more than the Big Trees, and evolved a pharmacopeia of practices. In upper-elevation forests, natural fires were allowed to burn under a set of guidelines, a "prescription." The much-disturbed ponderosa pine forests were underburned. In the sequoia groves themselves, crews began to pile and spot burn. Flames again licked the trunks of the Big Trees until public protest prompted a special panel of inquiry, the Christensen Committee, which published its results in 1987.

What was the model for the wild? Museums, zoos, farms, gardens—all were rejected as paradigms. The committee took as its text the most basic question posed by the Leopold Report: "Is it possible that the primitive open forest could be restored, at least on a local scale? And if so, how? We cannot offer an answer." Twenty-five years later, it was possible to frame at least a partial reply: restore fire. But that begged an even deeper question. What was fire?

Two conceptions—two fires—competed. One held that fire was natural, that lightning-kindled fire was philosophically and ecologically the only legitimate means of park burning, and that the appropriate goal was to "restore" such fire to its proper place in the pantheon of wilderness-ruling processes, much as parks needed to restore wolves, free-running streams, and grizzly bears. Intervene otherwise and you imposed a cultural order on a natural one. You blasphemed the grove. Amid the sequoias, nature should be the ultimate authority, and natural fire the expression of its providence. Remove fire suppression. Let nature run its course.

The competing conception accepted the end but not the means. The biota had changed too much, the reserve was too small a shard of the ancient landscape to survive by itself. Lightning could not start enough fires; and fires that did start would burn with ruinous savagery. However ideologically pure the argument for disengagement, the public would not tolerate the obliteration of the park's charismatic megaflora. Better prepare the site first. Better burn under controlled conditions. Better approximate the natural order with some compromised fire than destroy it with a prophetic, devouring one. Even here, however, although controlled burning could substitute under prescribed conditions, it derived its legitimacy from lightning fire. The ultimate goal was to restore "natural" fire.[88]

The Christensen Committee accepted the compromise. "In the best of all possible worlds," it concluded, the parks "would be sufficiently large that we could adopt a 'let it be' strategy for their preservation and maintenance." But they were not, and the last, best hope was for humans to emulate the natural order as fully as possible, to compensate for humanity's unwanted interventions with careful counterforce. The reality, the committee argued, was that those parks were "tiny islands in a sea of development and urbanization."[89]

But compromise did not end irony. The groves had grown up under a regimen of anthropogenic fire, whether from defiance, tolerance, or necessity. No Big Tree predated the presence of humans. Had the fires that nurtured them derived from lightning or from people? *Sequoia gigantea* was a relic from an otherwise vanished world. Had it survived against all odds? Or had human-caused fires held off its extinction for thousands of years? Again, there was no resolution, only the belief that humans had to be excluded, or admitted under strict, penitential prescriptions, and the determination to keep the flame-toughened Big Trees alive.

A year later, fires in Yellowstone National Park restated the debate in more apocalyptic terms. The conflagrations that swept 45 percent of America's first national park and largest biosphere reserve were an environmental epiphany that revealed with Pentecostal clarity the differing conceptions, both flawed, by which Europe and America viewed preservationist fire. In Europe, critics of the status quo argued that fire had a place within the cultural landscape. In America, dissidents lectured that humans had a role within natural biotas.

Americans had difficulty understanding or even seeing European fire. A country that abounded in vacant lands, that originated the idea of national parks, that had made wilderness preservation a national obsession, and that was pummeled, sometimes massively, by lightning fires simply did not see fires that were embedded within an agricultural landscape. The European experience with fire seemed so contrived that it was meaningless and so slight that it was trivial. And where attempts to transfer European-style fire suppression succeeded administratively, they often failed environmentally.

The removal of fire had proved as powerful ecologically as its introduction. Many fire-dependent species threatened to disappear with the fast-ebbing fires. With wilderness as a counteremblem, American fire scientists increasingly accepted the perspective that naturally caused fire had as much standing in wildlands as black-footed ferrets and buffalo. But wilderness ideology went further. It argued that *only* lightning fire was legitimate, and that places like Yellowstone were large enough to restore a natural regime. A Europe that could not conceive of fire outside a human landscape had nothing to teach America. On the contrary, only America housed the saving remnants of an elect nature, and from its experiences would come the salvation of European nature. Fire, Americans insisted, belonged in the reserves.

The Yellowstone fires blasted the exclusiveness of that presumption. If it was impossible to preserve nature without fire, it was increasingly apparent that it was impossible to preserve fire regimes without humans. Parks and nature preserves changed in the absence of anthropogenic fire. Lightning fires did not occur with the same regimen that fire history indicated had preceded the park's establishment; and they did not interact with the landscape in the same ways as other fire-catalyzed technologies. Even Yellowstone's immense size and symbolism proved inadequate to the task of perpetuating a wholly "natural" regime sustained by exclusively natural processes. Besides, the park's borders were a porous membrane of osmotic policy. The decision about what fires to accept or fight was, in the end, a cultural one, so that burns that were wildfires outside the park became "natural" once they entered.[90]

There was no dissent from the proposition that fire had a place in wilderness. But a growing cadre of critics began to appreciate what was obvious to Europeans, that there were other sources of fire than lightning. To a new generation of critics it appeared that the only alternative to bulimic binges of fire-feast and fire-famine was to replicate something like the indigenous fire practices. It was necessary for humans to burn. But that was tantamount to stating that the reserve had been fashioned by people, that it was not truly and purely wild, and that wilderness was more a state of mind than a state of nature.

This went beyond what most observers were willing to accept. They could not admit the prevalence, and possibly the indispensability, of aboriginal fire. Their quarrel with wilderness orthodoxy was over means, not ends. They were more likely to insist that reserves were biotic islands and that island biology was distinctive. Intervention might be necessary but only because the processes and species that had once roamed across and beyond them could no longer do so. They were likely to argue that the appropriate solution was to expand the size of the reserves and so reduce the perceived necessity for intervention of any kind. If the reserve was no longer an island, it would no longer be subject to island dynamics.

In most sites, compromises resulted that permitted controlled burning, however sub rosa. Some went under the rubric of scientific experiments. The most ingenious, however, was the invention of the oxymoronic "prescribed natural fire" by which a fire could be both natural and managed. A lightning-kindled fire could burn if it did so under an approved prescription monitored by wilderness custodians. It was a modernist riddle, like Gödel's proof, Russell's paradox, or *Star Trek*'s prime directive. If fire could not be avoided, neither could humanity's responsibility for it.

Slowly, backing into the future, both Americans and Europeans began to converge on the common ground of anthropogenic fire. Americans found they had to reconnect fire with people; Europeans, people with fire.

(iii)

There were practical reasons for these differences. America's parks were largely located in an unpopulated public domain, while Europe had to carve them out of landscapes that were already overstocked with humans and likely to remain so. Not only the character of the land but its control was at risk. Nature reserves propagated most easily and on the largest scale in Canada, Australia, and Siberia, more reluctantly in the great game reserves of pastoral Africa, and least successfully in countries that lacked the institutional apparatus to oversee them such as colonies formerly established under Portugal or Spain or densely populated landscapes like India, China, or, indeed, Europe itself.

So it is no surprise that reserves were poorly understood by indigenes or often accepted sullenly as little more than an imposition of the state. If the United States had difficulty mastering locals who were, after all, its own citizens, how much more troublesome did it prove to colonial powers like the British, French, and Dutch who tried to impose an alien order on resentful populations of Ghonds, Xhosas, Zulus, Nagas, Maasi, Ceylonese, Javanese, Merinas, and other tribes beyond their reckoning, much less their power to convert. European advocates could see nature protection as an expression of noblesse oblige, like endowing museums and opera houses; Americans could envision reserves as monuments to a national creation myth, the reconciliation of Old World civilization and New World wilderness; but indigenes, often displaced by the creation of reserves, saw them simply as a resource denied them.

Most reserves were in fact established as wildlife preserves, many based on royal reserves that the new rulers inherited. Others were established to limit the slaughter of big game. The practice merged easily with schemes for setting aside vast forest tracts for commercial exploitation and climatic amelioration. Later, science claimed its tithe, and argued for "strict" nature reserves that had to be kept inviolate. Eventually bowdlerized versions of the American national park concept percolated through Europe's imperium. But unlike the American scene, there could be little pretense that these lands were uninhabited, or that they existed uncontaminated from the Creation. Primitive, they were; pristine, they were not. The arguments over proper means and ends would not reside solely among the administrators, but between them and the local populations. Those natives would have to be regulated, and where possible removed.[91]

Still, advocates for reserves had a compelling case. The industrial capitalism that European expansion had stimulated and on whose tiger's back European imperialists rode was reconstructing (or dismantling) landscapes wholesale and brushed aside the traditional mores that had previously ensured some nature protection. Industrial foresters felled old groves as eagerly as Caesar hacked down druidic sites in Gaul, and for similar reasons. If any vestiges of old nature were to survive, new institutions were essential; new rationales, grounded in markets and science, had to be promulgated; new sacred sites had to supersede those cleared by global capitalism. Even in Europe there were movements to preserve monuments of nature or preferred landscapes from industrial vandalism.

But what frequently began as efforts to preserve big game for hunting, or scenic wonders for public spectacle, evolved into more sophisticated justifications and more varied kinds of reserves. The American concept of a national park traveled well, easily adapting to assorted landscapes and societies. The American concept of wilderness, however, did not. It required two conditions that were little replicated elsewhere: vacant land and a cultural agar in which "wilderness" values could grow like yeast. Instead, Europe found equivalent values in modern science. "Strict" nature reserves could be promoted as "models of nature," as laboratories for scientific research, natural analogues of the botanical gardens that the colonial powers routinely established to assist in their identification and relocation of useful species. The Soviet Union's *zapovedniki,* "inviolable" reserves from which all human activities save science were excluded, thus resembled the network of colonial botanical gardens that orbited around Kew Gardens and the Jardin des Plantes. The goals of science, it was held, transcended national borders, cultural definitions, or the unsavory politics of imperialism.[92]

The dominant international effort centered on Africa. In 1900, seven European powers passed resolutions to encourage the protection of that continent's fabled megafauna. Little came of it. In 1913, Switzerland convened an International Conference for the Protection of Nature, to which sixteen nations sent delegations. The First World War soon terminated discussions. Meanwhile, on the American example two national parks were created in Africa—Albert National Park in the Belgian Congo in 1925, and Kruger National Park in South Africa in 1926. The Swiss proposal was also revived under the direction of P. G. van Tienhoven, operating through the medium of scientific associations. In 1928 an International Office for the Protection of Nature was established within the International Union of Biological Sciences. In 1931, van Tienhoven organized an International Congress for the Protection of Nature. Its focus was Africa. Nature protection had, it seemed, become a new white man's burden. In 1933 the colonial powers met in London, as they had in Berlin in 1885, but this time to partition responsibilities for African nature protection.[93]

The London Conference for the Protection of African Fauna and Flora made it clear that national parks, on the American example, were only one approach to nature preservation. The values of nature reserves were several, and their circumstances many. No single model was sufficient. Intellectual Europe was interested in untrammeled nature as a source of information as well as inspiration, and imperial Europe was reluctant (and unable) to war against natives to enforce a total ban on subsistance hunting, ceremonial visits, and pastoral rights of passage. These were issues it had often failed to resolve with its own peasantry. Accordingly a spectrum of reserves was envisioned, some "strict," some accommodating. (That same year the United States established its first national park for primarily biological values, the Everglades.) The Pan-American Union met in 1940 and ratified a document that reaffirmed the provisions of the London Convention.[94]

As the most far-flung colonial presence, the British empire offered the easiest medium for internationalizing reserves. It appeared that Britain's "empire of nature," as John MacKenzie has termed its constellation of hunting preserves, might become a postwar commonwealth of nature preserves. But it was the Swiss who revived the agenda in 1947, after the Second World War and Indian independence, and who suggested its terms. By now the United Nations offered more neutral political cover, and in 1948 Julian Huxley, director-general of UNESCO, brought together 18 governments, 7 international organizations, and 109 national nature protection organizations who collectively adopted a constitution for what, after 1956, became the International Union for the Conservation of Nature and Natural Resources (IUCN). Its preamble argued that reserves existed for "social, educational and cultural reasons." They were also, proponents argued, good financial investments, sure to encourage jet-age tourism. Most notably, Europe's nineteenth-century scramble for African colonies became a scramble for African preserves. The Serengeti and Mount Kenya became as symbolically important as Fashoda and Khartoum had a century before.[95]

Between 1962 and 1972 the two dominant instruments—national parks and scientific reserves—achieved an institutional maturity. In 1962 the United States hosted the First World Conference on National Parks. A second followed in 1968. Meanwhile the United Nations established its Environment Program (UNEP) and UNESCO inaugurated the Man and the Biosphere Program (MAB), which proposed a network of strict reserves for scientific research. In 1972, the centennial of Yellowstone National Park, UNEP sponsored a Conference on the Human Environment; a Second World Conference on National Parks was held (at Yellowstone); and UNESCO drafted a Convention Concerning the Protection of the World Cultural and Natural Heritage which affirmed that Africa's wildlife, the Grand Canyon, Mount Everest, and other monuments and unique expressions of nature were the common heritage of all humanity, much like Antarctica, the deep ocean floor, the Moon, and planets. While sovereignty resided with individual nations, European ideals had found, it seemed, a global consensus. Protected groves proliferated—wildlife refuges, national parks, biosphere reserves, historic sites, and reserves of many kinds for many purposes. Ironically it was Europe that had few reserved landscapes, and those few were small and long-cultivated.[96]

The friction between colonizer and indigene inevitably led to flame. To natives, fire belonged to the land as much as wind and rain, and was as necessary to human occupation as spears and water. To most officials bent on guarding the grove—the majority of them foresters or influenced by forestry's precepts—such fires were incendiarism. The chronic burning reinforced their belief that fires were destructive and reflected unenlightened superstition, that anthropogenic fire was a political not an ecological act. Poaching, agricultural encroachment, illegal harvesting of flowers and trees, surreptitious grazing—all were violations, desecrations really, of the grove. But nearly every such act was accompanied by fire, and many required fire, so that the contest over reservations became, most visibly, contests for the control of fire.

The appeal to fire protection derived from the assumption that natural ignition was trivial, that anthropogenic fires perverted indigenous biotas, and that where fire seemed to coexist with ecosystems it did no more than cull them. The belief assumed that biotas resisted fire the way tough pines resist a beetle attack; they pumped out ecological sap to repel the infection. Constant fires bent the biota the way seawinds blew the canopy of a Monterey pine into branching banners. Remove those fires and nature would straighten, fill out, and flourish. Pure nature was green, not red, and never black.

Nothing seemed more obvious than that fire protection, preferably fire exclusion, was mandatory for nature reserves. Yet fires still came. In many landscapes lightning was not a negligible ignition source, and as anthropogenic fires pulled out, lightning fires moved in. They were fought. If fire was bad, then the source of the fire did not matter. Besides, the alternative was politically as well as ecologically unthinkable, because if natural fire was accepted, the case against *anthropogenic* fire disintegrated. And if anthropogenic fire was sanctioned, the cause of nature preservation seemingly lost its raison d'être. The specter of blackened land had been a powerful image on behalf of conservation. To spare lands from gun, ax, and fire had been the prime argument for reservations. If the guardians then clearcut, hunted, and burned, their rule had no legitimacy. *Quis custodiet ipsos custodes?*

However difficult the task, removing fire had the moral status of clearing out malaria or tsetse flies, or excluding those hunting safaris that, bristling with high-powered rifles, mowed through Africa's megafauna like a scythe. Certainly this assumption reflected the fire experience of those European states, all of them from temperate Europe, that by the nineteenth century had become colonial powers. If nature was to be manipulated, gardening was the appropriate means. If nature was to be protected, artifice had to be removed, or had to disguise itself into apparent artlessness, or had to be sent to guard the frontier. Fire there might be, but only if tended on the altar or stationed at the gates.

There were a few exceptions to such reasoning and considerable compromising in practice. America had its prescribed natural fire; colonial Africa and Asia, their early burn. Officials practiced "early burning" by burning outward from firebreaks around the reserves or burning patches in critical places so that early-season fires were kept well under control and later-season wildfires would not spread into the reserves. In effect, colonial officials seized the indigenous fire for themselves, much as they took over big-game hunting. Those with the greatest experience in the field recognized the indispensability of this arrangement. Colonel James Stevenson-Hamilton, who for fifty years oversaw the evolution of the Sabi game reserve (later, Kruger National Park) in South Africa, bluntly stated that "in a sanctuary for wild life" it was "essential to burn old long grass, but this must be done methodically." Since most of the actual burning was done by indigenes under European direction, there were continuities with the past.[97]

This of course was never enough to satisfy fire fundamentalists. Fire remained a stigma of the primitive, like the persistence of leprosy or famine. It might endure for a while, but only until education and enlightened institutions could complete the reformation that imperialism had begun. Early burning was a hybrid practice, an old means directed to new ends, the corruption of a platonic ideal by vulgar matter. The sooner it was discarded, the better. Even Stevenson-Hamilton's stature could not prevail against Europe's fire orthodoxies, and in the post–World War II era Kruger National Park inaugurated an ill-fated attempt to exclude fire altogether (the experiment was a disaster, and one the park soon recanted). In 1954 the park was divided into 400 burning blocks (2,500 to 5,000 hectares each) and a burning program installed in which a third was burned each year in the spring after 50 mm of rain had fallen. But there were still problems, some philosophical, some practical.[98]

The results did not replicate what officials believed the "natural" condition should be, so in 1975 the park modified the program to allow a greater range of burning by season and type of savanna. Still, mandatory burning by wind-driven fires during prolonged droughts degraded forage and biodiversity. Another policy adjustment was thus promulgated in 1980 to accommodate the tidal pull, on the order of decades, of wet and dry spells. Wet periods produced more fuels, hotter fires, a rapid recovery; dry periods, fewer combustibles, weaker fires, and a feeble restoration. The preferred season of burning, too, shifted toward that favored by lightning. Notch by notch, the park ratcheted its anthropogenic fire practices to replicate a natural fire regime. In 1990 the old mosaic of burning blocks was replaced by 88 burn units in the hope that bigger patches would allow a more variable pattern of fire spread. Then in 1994, six years after the Yellowstone fiasco, Kruger adopted a policy of laissez-faire burning in which anthropogenic fires were, where possible, suppressed and lightning fires allowed to burn. The park, in effect, accepted the legitimacy of fire but not the legitimacy of human administration over it. In September 1996 they achieved a Yellowstone-like fire complex when dry lightning burned a fifth of the park.[99]

The science was there to argue that the old order of metronomic burning was not sustainable. But the science was not there to argue natural regulation. Nor did geography. Nor did history. The policy, as Winston Trollope noted, "is not based on any practical examples from elsewhere in the savannas of Africa but rather on the basic and sincere belief that if a natural area is large enough, as the Kruger National Park is assumed to be, the ecosystem will function normally in response to natural variations in the environment." Kruger was twice the size of Yellowstone and by the logic of ecological scaling the Transvaal could, it seemed, succeed where the Northern Rockies had failed. In fact, the landscapes of Kruger had not known such conditions, except ephemerally, for a hundred millennia, perhaps a thousand. The fact that the park was laced with roads, surrounded by fences, pocked with artificial watering holes to enhance and concentrate wildlife argued that some intervention was necessary. Instead, the administrators of Kruger, like those at Yellowstone, opted to remove themselves as an ecological agent.[100]

Or, more properly, they sought to remove their moral agency. Every fire choice they had made had suffered some problems for which the guardians could be held accountable. There was no way to abolish fire or to avoid humanity's ignorance regarding a contingent world. Nature would ever change; science would always lag; and officials could only hope to understand the past, never anticipate the future. There was no standard by which to reconcile, for fire, the veld's history, geography, and ideology. The outcome was that anthropogenic fire remained at best a necessary evil, not a necessary good or a viable hybrid of European and indigenous practices. Deferring the problem to lightning removed park officials not only from liability but from irony. Whatever happened was the manifestation of nature's will, the providence of an omniscient ecology.

It is unlikely that such a scheme can survive, and bizarre that the attempt should be made. Since the time of *Homo erectus,* hominids have been the agency of evolution's fire. That humans might abdicate that role was comparable to elephants deciding not to strip the bark from acacias or lions electing to stop hunting antelope. In the end, Africa's Big Animals are the cognate of America's Big Trees. Kruger cannot avoid fire and humans cannot avoid the imperative to assume responsibility for those fires. The park preserved more from the Pleistocene than charismatic megafauna with overgrown tusks and nocturnal roars: within such landscapes lay the hearth of humanity. It was incredible that humans might consider extinguishing it.

Whatever their origins those reserves *did* check a wave of wastage and extinctions; they did help to translate Europe's unhappy experience with island encounters into a model of sacred grove suitable for an industrializing Earth. But however attractive industrial society found preindustrial landscapes, few were not culturally shaped, and they could no more survive in the absence of their contriving culture than a Romanesque church could repair itself. The reserves were, in truth, artifacts of cultural decisions, anomalous landscapes on a planet that saw humans fill and overfill every niche they could reach. By their presence those reserves demanded a new code for human conduct. They seemingly argued for a policy of aggressive nonintervention: officials should guard the perimeter and let the interior seek its own ineffable equilibrium.

But fire, as always, complicated this supposition. Fires kindled by nature, arson, or accident demanded a response; fires removed by policy demanded retribution. There was a fire tithe owed most landscapes, and if humans did not pay it, nature would extort it by force or punish the biota for withholding. There was, it seemed, no escape from fire and the necessity to manage it.

True island parks were not spared either: fire came even to the Galápagos archipelago. If anywhere epitomized the power of island biogeography, it was here, islands not inhabited until discovered by Spanish explorers in 1535. These islands so piqued the curiosity of Charles Darwin that they came to exemplify the saga as well as the facts of evolution by natural selection. The islands had flightless cormorants, marine iguanas, Darwin's celebrated finches, and the giant land tortoises from which the archipelago derived its name. Visited by transient mariners, pirates, and whalers, the Galápagos were annexed by Ecuador in 1832. There was some formal settlement, here and there throughout the archipelago. In 1959, Ecuador declared all remaining uncolonized lands as a national park, and later, with United Nations sanction, a World Heritage site.

There were plenty of ecological disturbances, some deliberate, most a clumsy trampling of the indigenous biota. The native fauna, particularly the tortoises, had been hunted, exotics introduced, even patches of agriculture attempted. There were fires, too. The islands straddled the upper sweep of the cold Humboldt Current; they were dry, though periodically subject to bouts of heavy rains during El Niño episodes that irrigated the mountains into swaths of fine combustibles. The mechanics of Pacific weather meant that the same Southern Oscillation which brought droughts and fire to Indonesia carried rain and fire to the Galápagos. Whether fires were more intense than in the past, they were certainly more intensively scrutinized as the Galápagos moved to the inner circle of environmental icons. The United States has even dispatched fire specialists to assist with suppression.

The crisis came when a fire discovered on April 12, 1994, apparently ignited by lightning, burned national park lands on Isabela Island. The Isabela tortoise had to compete with goats, dogs, and pigs, but fire could mobilize sentiment in ways that slow attrition from exotics could not. Wildfire that threatened biodiversity had become the demon poster child of international environmentalism. The spectacle of the tortoise ponderously trying to flee from flames galvanized a response. Ecuador dispatched crews, park rangers, the Army's firefighting corps, members of the Galápagos National Institute, Forest and Wildlife Institute, and civil defense. The fires burned stubbornly and thoroughly and spread with insidious effects through subterranean tunnels. More dramatically, special crews prepared for the evacuation of the threatened tortoises. With techniques pioneered during the 1985 fires, two-man teams intended to lash each tortoise to a pole and carry it to the shore, where it could reside within an incombustible pen of rocks until the danger passed. Meanwhile, ten tortoises were shuttled by helicopter and donkeys to rocky sanctuary near Puerto Villamil. By the time the fire ceased on June 6, it had burned roughly 40 square kilometers, surrounded by 40 kilometers of fireline built by bulldozer and chainsaw.[101]

If the mechanics of fire ecology in the Galápagos was not well understood, the dynamics of fire threats to island biotas was only too evident. A German observer reported that the fires had originated as a local protest to the park's prohibition against the exploitation of sea cucumbers. Having exhausted local stocks of groupers and lobsters, rapacious fishermen, many recently emigrated from the mainland, had seized on sea cucumbers. When the park moved to stop the harvest within its boundaries, protesting fishermen threatened the Galápagos National Park Service and for several days held the Charles Darwin Research Station hostage. If they were not allowed access, the protesters claimed they would introduce cats and dogs, kill the tortoises, and burn whole islands. The fire on Isabela was enough, as it successfully distracted the authorities. But it did not deceive environmentalist chroniclers. Clearly humans, through their malevolent ally, fire, had broken into the sanctuary and profaned the sacred idols. If fire could not be removed from the reserve, then the treasures of the reserve had to be removed from fire.[102]

The deeper lesson was that even an island was no sanctuary from fire.

(iv)

Nor was Europe exempt. Like many other colonial concepts, nature protection rebounded from the periphery to metropolitan Europe. The intellectual and political problems lost nothing in the transfer. Europe's conceptions were drawn from its cultural experience; its paradigm of a wildlife refuge was a zoo or farm, and its model custodian the gamekeeper or the *Jägermeister*. The most valued scenes were those shaped by art. What role had fire in such places? Intellectuals had not wanted fire in the creation of those scenes, and now saw no reason to rekindle it for their preservation. Germany banned burning in nature reserves altogether. National parks forbade it. Biosphere reserves excluded it. *Zapovedniki* abolished it by decree. Europe's nature enthusiasts had campaigned strenuously to deny native-set fire to reserves in Africa, North and South America, and Asia; they could hardly encourage them in Europe proper. Most of Germany's nature reserves were in private hands, for example, though subject to strict public regulation. If fire was prohibited on private holdings, it could not easily be encouraged in public parks.

Yet paradoxically the unfired landscape tended either to decay or to erupt in wildfire. Industrialization refashioned Europe as fully as it did other environments. Sites that had once held agricultural fire saw it disappear along with hand scythes and draft oxen; sites that once knew controlled burns experienced wildfire. That its environment had been long domesticated did not affect the outcome: Europe's traditional landscapes were as much threatened as those of Africa or South America. Fire appeared where it wasn't wanted, and vanished where it was needed.

Nature preserves suffered twice, once because of the loss of traditional processes, and once again because of their size, dominated by considerations of island biogeography. More often than not, both worked to eliminate fire. Sweden saw the bubbling biodiversity of its tiny parks plummet in the absence of the traditional disturbances that had previously stirred them. Norway, France, and the Netherlands discovered that they had to burn heath, however reluctantly, to preserve even vestiges of once vast moors. Denmark had to import specialists from Finland to fire the Draved Forest when it arranged for experiments to understand its swiddened past. Spain's Doña Park burned from wildfire. Henry Makowski noted how wildfires that occur in reserves showed "time after time, how positive the effect of fire can be on the scenery and the maintenance of certain animal and plant species." Surveying the meadows of the Harz Mountains, Reinhold Tüxen observed that the old techniques were no longer feasible and that the "economic treatments of earlier times" no longer applied, and concluded that among the options "only fire remains." But he doubted it would happen.[103]

In truth, postwar Europe was more obsessed with excluding fire than with reintroducing it. While it might be necessary to cultivate (literally) some species or other—the black heath hen, mountain meadows—the psychological barrier was seemingly impenetrable. The pure reserve had two paradigms: the sacred grove and the uninhabited island. There seemed no place for free-burning fire in either. Regardless, fires came.

In 1990, wildfire broke out at Mount Athos, a prong of the Chalcidice Peninsula extending into the north Aegean and a holy mountain of Eastern Orthodoxy. The autonomy of Athos was nearly complete. It was inhabited solely by monasteries, administered as a monastic district separate from the Greek state, and a sacred grove abstracted from human manipulation since A.D. 960. But in August, after a long drought, strong winds, the absence of roads, and lush (now desiccated) fuels combined to drive fire across 1,500 hectares. The fire burned for two weeks.

Ironically, the absence of human artifice meant the absence of effective control. High winds and rough seas grounded the CL-215s that were the backbone of Greece's aerial fire-suppression program. On August 24, Greece requested assistance from Germany. A C-160 Transall military transport carried helibuckets, firefighters, and a coordinating team, while four giant CH-53 military helicopters flew south. Before the aerial operations ceased on August 30 the helicopters—the heaviest in the German armed forces—had dropped some 1.72 million liters of water.[104]

For more than a millenium Mount Athos had stood inviolate, had survived the Turkish conquest and Greek wars of independence, and had even evaded the Nazi invasion of 1941. But it could not avoid fire. So long as Athos had trees and scrub and sun, fire would reappear like a spectral visitation to remind the faithful and frighten the feckless.

Neither could fire be avoided by that archipelago of nature sanctuaries that speckled the European landscape like biotic atolls. The drought of 1976 recycled wildfire to a western Europe that thought it knew better.

"Especially serious," wrote Peter Moore for *Nature,* were those fires that affected Britain's National Nature Reserves. On the Hartland Moor reserve in Dorset, on the Thursley Common in Surrey, the Glasson Moss in Cumbria, the Dyfi Estuary in Wales, fires threatened irreplaceable fauna and the flora. True, heath was a habitat "basically maintained by fire"; raised bogs experienced major burns from time to time, as documented in their soil profiles; and "many such fires are known to be started deliberately by local farmers who often believe it to be a sensible land practice in such areas, though often for purely superstitious reasons."[105]

But the 1976 outbreak was different, and its fires intolerable—large, deep-burning, and particularly traumatic because they occurred in a fragmented landscape, vulnerable to any shock. Other reserves on raised bogs were fired recurrently, sometimes even annually. None of this, however, the Nature Conservancy Council should accept in "mature, self-sustaining ecosystems," of which Britain had too few. Since the 1940s, England and Wales had lost 30 percent of their heather moors, and Scotland 11 percent. So long as pathways traversed reserves, people—and fire—had entry. So long as drought recurred, mown firebreaks and plowed perimeters were inadequate to prevent fire from spreading through organic soils. The reserves suffered the biotic vulnerability of islands without experiencing their true isolation.[106]

The circumstances at Glasson Moss and Borth Bog seemed especially melancholy, the quality of the site having deteriorated markedly after peripheral drainage and a bad burn in 1969. To prevent a recurrence, it was suggested, "there is a case for considering the construction of wide, water-filled ditches around the reserve boundaries." The reserves would become literal islands. The philosophy of European nature preservation had come full circle.[107]

CONTINENTS

The colonization of Europe was a prelude to Europe's colonization of other continents. Perhaps more than any of its other creation stories, the *Aeneid* is a paradigm of that process. The *Odyssey* was a struggle to return home; the *Aeneid*, the relocation and rededication of that home to distant lands. Revealingly, the founding of Rome became a saga of transferred fires. Before he fled the flames of sacked Troy, Aeneas snatched the fillets that held "Vesta's power, and her undying fire." Fires recur with every renewed action, on the shores of strange lands, in the vision of the Latin seer who foretells the immolation of Lavinia, in the funeral pyres that precede the final confrontation between Aeneas and Turnus, in the similes that describe that epic contest, in the reconsecration of the altar fires. The *Aeneid* is a story of allegorical renewal through the relocation of the vestal fire. From its origins, European colonization meant carrying the torch from the ancestral homeland to a new world. As Europe surged beyond its continental borders, this act became literally true.[1]

Except for Russia, expansion was by sea. Ships carried Europe's biota, as selected for travel, in their holds—a portmanteau biota, Alfred Crosby has described it. They also carried fire, carefully nurtured on sand and brick in the galley and preserved in flint-steel kits. Outright colonization was rare, and often discouraged. Voyagers wanted trade or plunder; for either, they preferred the shelter of islands, or ports protected by naval gunpowder. Where ports were lacking, they built them. Even Tenochtitlán fell to a shipborne siege from brigantines sailing Lake Texcoco. Peninsular Goa survived when Albuquerque lifted a countersiege through seapower.[2]

Those who ventured onto the continents, all whose lands were well populated, were conquistadores, buccaneers, missionaries, rebels, religious dissidents, transients, and refugees of one kind or another. They were not the basis for permanent colonization. Rather trade, conversion, plunder, slaves, or plantations, the usual institutions of contact, all had a continuing connection with the indigenes, and it was not until the native peoples of the Americas and Australia died in legions that thought was given to replacement by African slaves, indentured servants, transported convicts, soldiers, and more political and religious dissidents. The origins of the outposts that became colonies were as eccentric as their produce, commonly dominated by the drugs of the day, from sugar to tobacco to caffeine-laden coffee, tea, and cacao. Colonial factories and plantations clung to the littoral like tree sloths.

Most outposts in Asia and Africa remained there. Whatever political power they acquired, Europeans continued to be a minority population, and their beasts and plants exotics. Some naturalized; most did not. Instead they relied on indigenous labor (and indigenous armies) to remake the indigenous landscape even when redirected by steam transport, capitalist economies, and Enlightenment ideas. At the height of its rule, the British raj held India with only 75,000 Britons. Similarly small populations of Spaniards and Portuguese oversaw the Americas.

Even in North America, Australia, and the far southwestern wedge of Africa where European colonists dominated demographics, movement inland was slow. The Dutch Cape Colony, founded in 1652, took a century to expand beyond the Cape Mountains, and the Great Trek did not occur until the 1830s, and then under the impress of competition from the English settlements of 1820. Discovered in 1501, Brazil remained a littoral society, the far-ranging São Paulo *bandeirantes* excepted. But they were raiding parties, not settlers; permanent movement into the *sertão* did not follow until diamond and gold rushes of the latter eighteenth century, and the colonization of Amazonia not until the latter twentieth. Almost 300 years passed between the time John Cabot sighted North America for England and British descendants breached the Appalachian Mountains in sufficient numbers to create the state of Kentucky. Not until the early nineteenth century did European settlements like swarming bees suddenly hive across whole continents.

Nothing akin to the shock wave that swept discovered islands occurred on the continents. History explains part of that delay, but the geography of scale explains some of that history. Continents were less dominated by endemics, could repopulate species more readily, and could more easily absorb disturbances. Not only were some lands less alien, but many like North America and Siberia had biotas analogous, even related, to European ones. If only in myth, it was possible for a single fire to consume an island. This was not possible on continents. Except for Australia, those continents were, after all, larger than Europe.

Fires and fire practices behaved much like their vectors. On islands they could breed like exotic rabbits, overwhelming everything. On continents, they encountered too many indigenous fires and too many fire-tempered landscapes to impose their own or burn unchecked across the scene. European fire practices had to adapt, just as European agriculture and architecture did. A Tudor manor house planted amid a eucalypt savanna was not only ineffective; it was ridiculous. The introduced fires hybridized, assimilated, and achieved new equilibriums with native fires. At a minimum, European fire practices naturalized as fully as starlings, barley, and anopheles mosquitoes. The landscape filled with fires of diverse pedigrees and compositions. There were European fires, creole fires, mestizo fires, indigenous fires, natural fires. The contest between peoples, the conflict over land, was expressed in, and frequently fought by, control over fire.

CARRYING THE FIRE:
EUROPE EXPANDS

In the beginning, thought the philosopher John Locke, all the world was like America. But whether or not America and the other parts of the inhabited world were prelapsarian in a theological sense, their environments were no tabula rasa. All were inhabited to the fullest extent allowed by indigenous technologies. All knew anthropogenic fire.

In those lands most readily changed, European fires transferred or fused with indigenous sources to establish the dominant fire regimes. In those less easily transformed, Europeans sought to suppress the native fires. The outcome was a palimpsest, with past texts wholly or partly erased, and new texts superimposed with greater or lesser legibility. Eventually the impact of industrialization, particularly of fossil fallows and fossil-fuel combustion, imposed its own transcendent logic everywhere, on Europe no less than on other lands. Until then, control over lands meant control over fire.

(i)

Not all the continents were equally vulnerable to European colonization. Some collapsed; some merged, some repulsed. Those continents most susceptible to megafauna extinctions on first human contact were those most vulnerable to wholesale reformations upon contact with Europe. In a sense, they had never fully restocked from the Holocene holocaust. Some continents became effectively vacant, to be filled by Europeans, European-transported servants and slaves, and European plants and beasts. The Americas and Australia were thus resettled by Europeans, some 50 million of whom emigrated overseas between 1820 and 1930. Other populations resisted better, and even grew so greatly under European rule that they far outnumbered and ultimately expelled their European overlords. So it went in Africa and Asia. Siberia and pockets of southern Africa were awkward exceptions.

The needs of contact and colonization were different. For plantations or trading factories, Europe preferred environments different from those it possessed, notably the tropics, which produced goods like spices that Europe could not manufacture. For its colonies, however, Europe required lands akin to what it had, or sought the means by which to remake those lands into familiar forms. It was easiest to transfer the torch to environments similar to those Europe had previously colonized, to sites already reworked by ax, hoe, and fire, to places readily stripped of indigenous peoples, plants, and animals, and to landscapes over which Europe possessed a clear biotic advantage.

The geography of successful colonies was thus far from arbitrary. Europe colonized the tropics poorly and clumsily, better able to dismantle than to reassemble the pieces. Conversely, Europe expanded briskly into the four cognates of the Mediterranean that it found in Chile, California, Australia, and the Cape of Good Hope. It quickly translated its institutions and agriculture into temperate forests and grasslands like those it had known in central Europe— to woodlands and prairies of North America, the bosques and pampas of South America, the grassy paddocks and savannas of extratropical Australia. It expanded into boreal landscapes like Siberia's taiga and North America's dark conifers about as readily as it had into Finland. These were all environments for which Europeans had a preadapted technology. In most instances, pioneering Europeans possessed a domesticated biota like grazers that the indigenes lacked, and where the resident biota was unsatisfactory for one reason or another Europe created formal gardens, sponsored scientific surveys, and endowed acclimatization societies to search out suitable candidates for emigration or judicial transportation. Once colonization became serious, the indigenous biota, including its peoples, were often disassembled wholesale through disease, war, hunting, trapping, clearing, and grazing. And once relatively emptied, the resulting biotic vacuum soon sucked in whatever flotsam and jetsam were available from its surroundings and whatever had crawled or flown into the stalls and ballast of the European ark.

All these European technologies, however, depended on cotrol over fire. A proper fire was an essential catalyst; an improper one, a threat. Thus landscapes subject to anthropogenic fire were especially attractive and unusually susceptible to European settlement. Many landscapes, already softened by anthropogenic fire, could be plucked from the forge and hammered by European technology into new forms. Open, parklike scenes suggested to explorers the artifice of agriculture, so fully did they intimate the "champion fields" of England (a supposition sometimes correct, sometimes not). Open woodlands resulted from burning, not livestock grazing, but they were typically among the first sites seized by colonists. Parks, prairies, and savannas molded by fire hunting in the Americas and Australia were instantly receptive to grazing by domesticated livestock. In words repeated in continent after continent, J. C. Byrne bombastically declaimed that, even as the natives passed away, they had "performed their allotted task; and the fires of the dark child of the forest have cleared the soil, the hills and the valleys of the superabundant scrub and timber that covered the country and presented a bar to its occupation." It was as though Providence had, through the practices of the natives, prepared the way for their European successors.[3]

Other landscapes, however, burned in ways that Europeans considered reckless and hostile, and they sought to contain those fire practices. In Australia, Governor William Bligh worried that the ceaseless "fires made by the natives are apt to communicate to the dried grass and underwood, and to spread in such a manner as to endanger every thing that cannot bear a severe scorching." In New England Thomas Morton noted the habit of the natives "to set fire of the Country in all places where they come; and to burne it, twize a yeare, vixe at the Springe, and the fall of the leafe." While this routine fire clearing "makes the Country very beautiful, and commodious," it also threatened farms and pastures and compelled the new settlers to ignite their own protective backfires. Dutch officials at Cape Town worried that East India Company residents might imitate their Khoi-Khoi herders and spread fire instead of manure, putting official gardens and (perhaps more tellingly) a fixed social order at risk. In 1687, regulations prescribed a "severe scourging" for a first fire offense and death by hanging for a second. In lands over which Europeans nominally ruled but never colonized by repopulating, indigenous fires were dampened but never extinguished, persisting as an instrument of ecological protest and a potent reminder of how tenuous European control was.[4]

(ii)

Just as there were preferred fire landscapes, so there were also preferred fire practices. Perhaps the closest cognate was fire-fallow agriculture. As in Europe felling, burning, and planting were often a prelude to permanent fields, but until pioneering passed into sedentary society, some form of swidden was prominent.

Since swidden, broadly conceived, was also the agriculture of most indigenous peoples, the transfer was relatively simple. A landscape once swiddened was a landscape readily reswiddened. Among the colonized continents, Australia lacked agriculture as Europeans understood that concept, adopting a fire-catalyzed foraging-and-hunting surrogate—"fire-stick farming," in Rhys Jones's phrase. So British swidden was a novelty. But in the Americas fire-fallow agriculture on the European model blended readily with American Indian and African technologies, while deforming it by the addition of livestock. And in Asia, particularly, swidden evolved into a syncretic agroforestry.[5]

By the time of European contact, agriculture was all over the Americas. Mesoamerica boasted one major center of agricultural dissemination; South

America, at least one other. Still, there were, as in Europe, excluded environments and landscapes that could not readily be broken without domesticated fauna or imported pyrophytes. The boreal forest resisted stubbornly; so did the Great Basin and Mojave Deserts. California followed an Australian model, "cultivating" with firesticks instead of digging sticks. Wildlife could not prune as ruthlessly as overgrazing livestock, so fallow in the Americas and Australia selected different pathways of succession and their woodlands were thinned rather than removed. The absence of drainage technologies kept much of the landscape immune from routine farming and burning. Yet there were niches of farming even in the desert Southwest, assisted by irrigation works, and in the Great Plains, along river bottoms. Virtually nowhere was unaffected by anthropogenic burning, and many landscapes like the tallgrass prairie and the mixed woodlands and savannas of the Southeast were almost certainly sustained by anthropogenic fire.

In the humid regions of what became the southern United States, swidden had arrived early, persisted long, and seeped northward centuries before European contact. But as in Europe, swidden was only part of a matrix of fired landscapes. Other sites, perhaps once slashed and burned, were maintained in grass or mixed scrub for hunting, gathering, defense, travel, and probably aesthetics. While the bottoms of the Tennessee Valley were burned for cultivation, for example, the drier uplands were fired for hunting, chestnut gathering, berry cultivation, and a dozen other purposes. In California the need for reeds and twigs for baskets led to the creation of vast groves of fire-pruned brush. On the Texas plains, Cabeza de Vaca told how the natives "go about with a firebrand, setting fire to the plains and timber so as to drive off the mosquitoes, and also to get lizards and similar things which they eat, to come out of the soil. In the same manner they kill deer, encircling them with fires, and they do it also to deprive the animals of pasture, compelling them to go for food where the Indians went."[6]

But similar stories abound for every American environment, or more generally for virtually every landscape occupied by humans. America's indigenes exploited fire exactly like their economic equivalents throughout the globe, and to similar effect. The fire geography of pre-Columbian America divided between the chronically wet and chronically dry lands, and the critical climatic fact was the way in which one could, for a time, become the other. With fire it was possible to reshape the pieces of the landscape mosaic and rearrange them into new pictures. Probably the intensity of manipulation was much the same in America as in Europe or India or China or any other landscape remade by agriculture. By the time of European contact, fire-fallow agriculture was well established, and not readily distinguished from what most of Europe had long known and what many Europeans still practiced. In much of the Americas, agriculture had existed for as long as it had in Europe. The two continents, both rebounding from an ice-scoured Pleistocene, probably have a similar history of human-driven reclamations.

Yet there were important differences. In some landscapes, fire was opportunistic, having more the character of a snare trap than a great surround. New England boasted a notoriously temperate climate in which virtually every month had the same level of precipitation. There was no strict fire season, only climatic envelopes in the spring and fall into which fire could be inserted, and episodic droughts and hurricane-induced blowdowns that allowed for more eruptive burns. There were pockets of dense shade forest, almost immovable without the leverage of swidden. But underburning was routine along the pine and heath coastal plains and amid blueberries; fire-fallow cultivation for maize was endemic; pine-oak and chestnut-oak forests were regularly burned; and upland prairies used for fire hunting dappled the woods. Even around Lake Champlain in the Adirondacks, far removed from swidden-dominated agriculture, Peter Kalm, one of Linnaeus's apostles, reported from his 1748–51 travels that one of the "chief reasons" for the decrease in the "vast fir [conifer] forests of white, black and red varieties, which formerly had been still more extensive," was aboriginal burning, specifically the "numerous fires which happen every year in the woods through the carelessness of the Indians, who frequently make great fires when they are hunting, which spread over the fir woods when everything is dry. ("Carelessness" was also the epithet flung at European peasants who used fire for the same purposes.) So even in New England, where the evidence is complex, Europeans moved from one temperate climate to another, settling in a land already baked in an anthropogenic hearth, and experiencing less ecological angst than had their ancestors in adapting a Mediterranean agriculture to central Europe. On routinely burned lands the transfer of the torch caused barely a flicker.[7]

The more critical differences were demographic—the catastrophic collapse of pre-Columbian peoples and the equally explosive introduction of livestock. Epidemics swept the continent, one depopulating it, another refilling it with cattle, pigs, sheep, horses, goats, donkeys, as well as émigré Europeans. It was as though, following the Black Death, Mongol hordes had punched into Europe proper and encamped with their herds. There was little opportunity for recovery. The amount of forest already cleared and the prairies ripe with fire-flushed grasses invited rather than repelled newcomers. Farmers reclaimed old swidden plots; graziers ran herds onto grassy hunting grounds; and pioneers burned to promote berries and protect structures from surrounding wildfires, and soon adopted fire hunting with devastating enthusiasm. Without fire-greased lubrication, those ecological gears would soon freeze up. In fact, that is what happened eventually, as woods sprang up and scrub overtook fields and partly camouflaged those ancient, anthropogenic landscapes.

In the end that was precisely the point of permanent colonization. Fixed properties and sedentary societies—the European ideal—frowned on free-burning fire. That was also why the New England colonies sputtered so long, showed so little dynamism. Full-blown colonization needed to expand, not merely exchange. It needed first-contact fires, not circulating swidden. Obsessed with field rotation and manuring, the Palatine Germans who settled in Pennsylvania sent down roots and remained where they were. But the more untrammeled colonists of New Sweden, as Terry Jordan and Matti Kaups have documented, transferred the pioneering technologies of boreal Europe. The Finnish colonization of interior Scandinavia came to North America.[8]

Its New World outpost began in 1638 when Sweden was a major power. Located along the Delaware River, the trading colony never became large and in 1655 the Dutch took it over, succeeded by the English in 1666. At the time of cession the colony's population was estimated at 400, though immigration continued. A large fraction apparently consisted of ethnic Finns, some from Finland proper, many from the Finnmark of Swedish Dalarna. Over the next century they were joined by Welsh, English, Dutch, and especially German and Scotch-Irish. The indigenous tribes, too, contributed. Out of this syncretic stew emerged the fundamental practices of pioneering, the means by which, in something like a century, the American backwoods frontier breached the Appalachians like a ruptured dam and spilled out to the Great Plains and splashed to the Pacific Northwest.

Land use orbited around fire-fallow farming, hunting, trapping, foraging, and stock raising. Swidden was nothing if not adaptable, and it was not difficult to choose from among the spectrum of techniques those that could best adjust to the nuances of new landscapes. Inevitably, the émigrés transferred their fire technologies, nucleated around swidden, to the pine barrens and the mixed forests of the middle Atlantic region, both of them cognates of European biotas and certainly milder than boreal Finland. New conifer forests became *huuhta,* mixed deciduous forests, *kaski.* With the exception of livestock, moreover, the dynamics of Finnish agriculture were not very different from those of the native tribes, generically known as Delawares. Undoubtedly the indigenes were a source of instruction if not inspiration. Swidden and fire hunting were both obvious sources of transfer. All the reasons that boreal Europeans had to burn, their emigrants to the New World had also, and with greater opportunities.[9]

The big differences between the newcomers and the indigenes were the colonists' small herds and the incentive among the European émigrés to move to new lands; with the collapse of native resistance and the recession of competing European powers in the New World, that is exactly what became available. The backwoods frontier exploded westward. The transmuting flame began remaking the landscape, much as it had in Finland and central Sweden, as it was doing in Russia and the settlement wedge that drove across Siberia.

The dominance of European colonists in America meant the dominance of a European-based pioneering, the triumph of adapted European fire practices. But where demographics were different, so was the pedigree of the prevailing fire. Excellent examples of swidden adaptations show striking contrasts between South America and South Asia.

In Brazil the generic *queimada* was a hybrid of Portuguese, African, and indigenous practices. It took the form of swidden, pastoral burning, firing for hunting and foraging, and wholesale cleaning. Some of western Amazonia was chronically wet and some of the northeast relentlessly dry, but most of Brazil experienced seasonal fluctuations ideal for burning. And burned it was. In the dry season, *queimadas* lit up fallowing forest, grass-scrub *cerrado,* fields of every description. The uncertainty of land tenure, the restlessness of a violent frontier swept by repeated mining rushes, the presence of invasive weeds and leaf-cutting ants ready to seize any site older than a few years, and the sheer biotic inertia of a landscape prepared by long centuries of swidden, all argued for the torch. Nothing, it seemed, was done without fire.

Almost without exception the spectacle dismayed European explorers. Enlightenment savants echoed Alexander von Humboldt that fire-singed deforestation deprived future generations of both wood and water. José Vieira Couto condemned the "barbarous agriculture" of the typical Brazilian peasant, armed "with a broadaxe in one hand and a firebrand in the other." Everything European savants detested about fire-fallow agriculture thrived in Brazil with exaggerated exuberance. The "horrific burnings" not only devastated nature's riches but encouraged a society of "sloth and ignorance," shiftless "vagabonds" little different from the "savages" from whom they learned their practices, ever yearning for the next woods. One fire led to another, the violence roving the countryside like the torches of a lynch mob.[10]

Still, the fires were a marvel, as exotic as anacondas. An émigré Italian scientist, Lourenco Granato, confessed that the fire "is terrible, but it attracts us. . . . Really, how beautiful is the fire of a great burn. . . . It is distressing for some, in truth; for others it is a grandiose spectacle." For others, too, it was a source of scientific curiosity. Under the patronage of the count of Luxemburg, Auguste de Saint-Hilaire toured the major Brazilian provinces from 1816 to 1822 in a Humboldtean reconnaissance of its natural history. Searching for the source of the São Francisco River, he pondered the prevalence of the fires (*todo o Brasil*), marveled how the Brazilians continued their use with such "strange perseverance," ritually condemned the practice, and then sought its origins.[11]

According to many Brazilian tribes, a great conflagration had long ago seared the world. The ground itself held the evidence. Dig virtually anywhere and you strike charcoal, a kind of lithic litter. More apparent to observers like Saint-Hilaire was the testimony of the ubiquitous *queimadas* that kindled every pasture, cleansed every agricultural field, opened fallowed forests to farms, exposed outcrops to miners, and swept gardens like a kitchen broom. Although the Portuguese imposed a new political regime, African slaves supplied a new source of labor, and a global market rewired nature's economy to fit the trophic flows of capital, Brazil's fire practices had evolved from and still bore the imprint of the native Brazilians—*o modelo indigena,* concluded Saint-Hilaire. Bananas, sugar, and rice had replaced traditional root crops; cattle had replaced deer and jaguars; and foraging for gold and diamonds substituted for the gathering of medicinal plants and foodstuffs; but the patterns of burning endured. Just as the Portuguese had exploited indigenes as slaves, so they had adapted native fire practices. The result was a fire mixture as complex as Brazil's racial composition.[12]

In India and Burma the imperial British were forced to a more unsettling conclusion. The problem began with teak, rapidly stripped from accessible lands; or more precisely, the crisis was that the teak failed to regenerate. Inspectors cited browsers, competition with other species, and near-annual fires as causes. Professional forestry and reserves were proposed as solutions. But neither could ensure regeneration or control the "wild" hill tribes who lived in virtual symbiosis with the teak. In 1856, Dietrich Brandis became forest officer for Pegu, and in 1864 he was named inspector-general for the newly created Indian Forest Service. Between 1856 and 1870 he and his colleagues found a solution in *taungya.*[13]

The term translates roughly as "hill crop," and the system that evolved was an adaptation of traditional swidden. Brandis has been credited with originating the concept, and he must have recalled central European precedents like *Waldfeldbau* and *Hackwaldbetrieß,* fire-fallow systems of Europe's own hill tribes. Just as these had adapted to the needs of forestry, so could those of Burma and India. All that was needed was to plant teak among the crops; merchantable timber would grow instead of jungle fallow; hill tribes could integrate into the larger market instead of resisting it. Still, the graft did not always take. By 1906 the experiment withered away as a major controversy over appropriate fire policy preoccupied India's imperial foresters. Formal fire protection had become uneconomical, ineffective, and inimical to teak regeneration, and despite official misgivings the conservator of forests for Burma began to withdraw it. By 1920 efforts were under way to revive *taungya.*

In the meantime, the malaise had spread elsewhere in British India and infected other valued species, notably sal, a good industrial surrogate for teak and like it preferring to grow in throngs, not in the isolation typical of most tropical trees. It was also hardened against fire, of which the British saw all too much after they acquired prime sites following the Bhutan war in 1865. Across the province, once-prime sal forests had been "gutted by fire" and were reduced, in the words of a British forester, to a "sea of savannah grasses from 6 to 16 feet high." Probably the observation applied to industrially cut and burned forests, not indigenous ones. In most monsoonal forests, near-annual fires passed over the surface like the near-annual floods of the great rivers, leaving ash instead of silt.[14]

Inevitably the first task of the Forest Department, E. O. Shebbeare recalled, "was fire-protection." Forests were reserved, their access restricted; tracts were fire-quarantined with firebreaks, roads, and rivers; and patrols discouraged incendiarists and swatted out fires. Without the annual fire-floods, saplings and coppice flourished. But so did the rest of the jungle, and soon the evergreen undergrowth suppressed the sal. The failure to regenerate was universal. Some foresters argued for weeding, some (reluctantly) for the restoration of selective burning. Both came too late. Weeds were too vigorous and entrenched to hack away, the jungle too shaded and moist to support fire. Experiments planting sal in mounds failed because of browsing by pigs and rats. Experiments that shaded the sal with grass "hats" (an admittedly "comical sight") failed, too, perhaps from chagrin. By 1914 it "looked indeed as though the disappearance of sal from Bengal forests was only a matter of years."[15]

In desperation, foresters attempted to sow sal on lands swiddened by villagers of the Rabha tribe. Among the rice, cotton, maize, and sesame, young saplings soon thrust upward. Meanwhile, exhaustive experiments by the forest botanist at Dehra Dun concluded that sal needed a seedbed free of humus, lots of overhead sunlight, and some protection from frost and the long desiccation of the dry season, the latter irrelevant in Bengal. These were exactly the conditions provided by Rabha swidden—in fact, exactly the circumstances that had produced the sal forest originally. "This method"—another variant of *taungya*— "as then arrived at as it were by accident, we have followed with only minor modifications ever since." By 1932 it had become a "universal prescription."[16]

The medication included fire. Since all the "existing sal forests sprang up among almost annual fires," foresters sought a suitable fire regime. "It must be admitted," Shebbeare wrote, "that our belief in fire is based more on what we feel than on what we know, but the fact remains that aboriginal villagers, who know more than we do, are strongly in favour of burning." Since villagers provided the labor and integrated sal into their swidden cycles—since the whole system depended on their consent—their sentiments counted. European concepts of fire norms had to yield to traditional practices. In Assam proper, burning resolved the problem of sal regeneration, and in Burma it assisted in the restoration of teak. Eventually analogues appeared in the guise of agroforestry in Dutch Indonesia, British Kenya and Nigeria, Thailand, the Philippines, and elsewhere, with pine, eucalypt, and *Gmelina* as the cultivated trees.[17]

In summarizing the experience, Shebbeare strove to make clear "that *taungya* was adopted in Bengal with the idea, not of introducing an improvement, but of averting a catastrophe." This was not how British foresters and imperial officialdom wanted to restructure the monsoonal forest. But they had neither the wisdom nor the strength to impose their radically conceived new order. It was an open question whether the villagers had adapted to a global timber market or the imperial market had adjusted to the implacable persistence of village life. In truth, both occurred. In the end the British had no alternative to the indigenous fires, could not coerce a biota that with almost Gandhian resolve refused to accept the imperial fire tax. Even so, the British did not carry the torch so much as they left the natives to hold their own. They accepted the light and averted their eyes from the flames.[18]

(iii)

But farming was only half of European agriculture. The other half, herding, was a propellant for expansion. Even more than migratory swidden, first-contact pastoralism had to move. The proliferating herds required a succession of new pastures; and herders, unlike swiddeners, could carry their larder with them. Pioneer herding had led the Neolithic vanguard into Europe; more than any other influence, the herds had undermined the closed fortress of central Europe's forests. In the Americas and Australia exotic herding—or the animals themselves, a good fraction of which ran wild—exploded over landscapes with even greater force. Fire and hoof stimulated changes beyond what either alone could have managed.

The impact of Europe's livestock measured the scale of its colonization. The most rapid expansion by European settlers occurred on those continents that had no indigenous counterforce to pastoralism. It was most profound in Australia and the Americas, which lacked livestock except in the Andean pastures browsed by llamas and alpacas. By contrast, Africa and Asia had abundant domesticates, had little use for Europe's feeble stock, and in fact held the original gene pools from which many of Europe's domestic fauna had descended. Eurasia in particular became a faunal source for American and Australian sinks.

Still, no landscape was exactly right for alien grazers. Most could be made usable with fire, however, so pastoral pioneering and burning became inseparable. The outcome varied according to whether the prevailing climate was dry or wet. In arid landscapes pastoralism often led to overgrazing and destroyed the conditions that made fire possible; and when used to force nutrient flushes from the degrading land, fires became more frenetic and grazing more intense, until fuels degenerated into brush or eroded into dust in a spiral that would ultimately extinguish fire altogether. By contrast, in humid landscapes regular burning was essential to fight back the pressures toward fallow woods and brush. Routine fires rebuilt the biotic dikes that kept the restless woods from swamping the prairie. With mixed grazers and browsers the grasses could be maintained for years, perhaps indefinitely. More typically, grazing cropped the weedy herbage that grew on abandoned swidden (in fact, that forced abandonment) and pushed the system into woody fallow. Thus in forest landscapes fire could effect change, but not perpetuate it; the woods returned. In prairie landscapes fire could sustain the status quo, but not fundamentally alter its structure; the grasses persisted. When fire interacted with livestock, however, its power to change biomes and enforce those changes increased immeasurably.

Fire, fallow, and fauna created the agricultural triangle of Europe's ecological colonization beyond the seas. Controlled burning demanded controlled grazing, and woodland grazing often required successful swidden. For European émigrés, cutting, grazing, and burning were the instruments of pioneering. But like a three-legged stool, the system could easily become unbalanced. That is what the critics who advocated an environmental reformation saw happen all too often and why they condemned the promiscuous use of fire as the ecological equivalent of selling indulgences and denounced the pastoral fire triangle as an unholy trinity.

Even more forcefully than fire and ax, fire and hoof drove expansion. Some lands were overwhelmed by European livestock, some found an equilibrium between the alien and the indigenous, and some resisted the intrusion. The vigor with which livestock filled landscapes depended on what, if any, resistance was offered. The impact was greatest in those continents empty of domesticates; it was as though the introduced megafauna replaced their Pleistocene predecessors, eliminated previously. Even so, those earlier vacated niches had been filled, by and large, by humans, and until that land was again emptied, there was scant place for newcomers and their servant species. The depopulation of indigenous Australians and Americans and of ungulate herds like bison preceded a repopulation by livestock.

The Americas were notably receptive to the most elaborate of Europe's pastoral institutions, those of Spain. The great march of the Mesta's flocks and herds across reconquered Iberia was an eerie prelude to their sprawl across conquered Latin America. Spain's ambition was to seize the wealth and labor of the New World through rule of the existing order, not by imposing a wholly novel one. New Spain wanted a division of labor more than a division of land. But labor plummeted with the collapse of the native population, and the land's ecological tapestry unraveled as quickly as the social fabric. Once-tended landscapes emptied and fell to ruin, while exotic livestock fed on the grasses and vines that grew in the cracks. Sheep, cattle, and goats filled the void, gorged

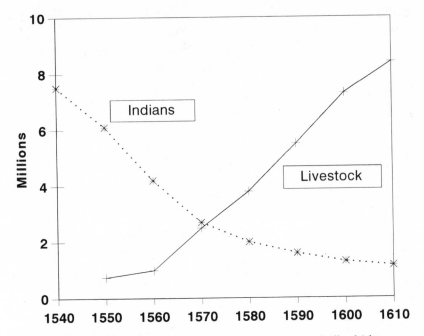

Changing populations in central Mexico. As indigenous humans declined (along
with the landscape they tended), the biotic vacuum was filled with livestock, roughly
ordered along the same principles as in Spain. A similar scenario played out in North
and South America and in Australia; all of these landscapes had been previously
emptied of megafaunal grazers and browsers during their original human colonization. (Data from Gibson 1966)

on a land going to seed, and began to trample and browse the Mexican plateau
into something like the Spanish *meseta*.[19]

Along with livestock, institutions and herding practices also disembarked
from the galleons. Soon there were roundups, lariats, and *rancherías*. Expeditions into the interior marched with flocks of swine, sheep, and cattle, not to
mention horses, just as they had during the Reconquest. The monarchy even
founded a Mexican Mesta. Missions became internal foci for the dispersion of
exotic fauna and for training indigenous peoples in the techniques of herding.
Latin America became as indelibly associated with livestock as Iberia. Increasingly native farms became Spanish haciendas, and a composite landscape of
field and woods evolved into a vast rangeland.[20]

Some places experienced more fire, some less. In the more arid landscapes
of the Mexican plateau, flocks could strip the land into near desert, leaving
whirlwinds of biotic debris. Even worse was Chile, whose mediterranean-

climate regions were crushed by livestock, its aboriginal fires pounded into dust and scrub. Offshore sediments from Mesoamerica show that charcoal levels reached a maximum during the fifty years prior to the Conquest. Then a demographic collapse brought an end to wholesale swidden and grassland fire hunting; and while cattle percolated into grassy clearings and savannas, sustained by regular dry-season burning, the amount of biomass burned declined and has not today restored itself. In Argentina, imported cattle and horses displaced indigenous rheas and capybaras, and brought associated weeds that were no more constrained than their affiliated sheep, cattle, conquistadores, and gauchos.[21]

The lands became a biotic sink until, as Alfred Crosby notes, "only one quarter of the plants growing wild on the pampa by the 1920s were natives." Pampa prairies evolved into pampa paddocks; fire herding with torch and lariat replaced fire hunting by firestick and bolo; and introduced fires, gorging on the newly feral fuels as lasciviously as the proliferating stock, propagated with the abandon of artichoke and giant thistle. What had once helped groom the pampas now disheveled them. The "sight of smoke in the distance," W. H. Hudson recalled, "would cause every man who saw it to mount his horse and fly to the danger-spot where an attempt would be made to stop the fire."[22]

In North America, free-ranging pastoralism was also predicated on an open, or emptying, landscape. The displacement of native peoples, gathering momentum during the nineteenth century, created an ecological void that soon filled with the herds and herding practices of the Europeans who repopulated the lands. The English, Dutch, and French contributed; so, since they served as herders and came from herding cultures, did African slaves. Herders from Britain's Celtic frontiers—the Scotch-Irish, in particular—added their distinctive stock to the broth. In places, indigenous tribes adopted pastoralism as well, first for the horse, then for sheep and cattle. All of them, through routine burning, kept the pastoral stew simmering.[23]

Long-established burning by pre-Columbian peoples had splashed the landscape with grassy openings, carved prairie "barrens" out of woods, rejuvenated canebrakes in wetlands, and kept the understory of most upland forests open, more a savanna than a woodland. Without fire the forest would close in, but routine burning could keep the forest at bay. Local transhumance and droving to markets spread pastoralism (and pastoral burning) beyond the split-rail fences of settlements. The great arc of southern pinelands—its milder climate allowing for year-round use as range, its soils impoverished by row-crop farming, its surface roughage thinned into grasses and forbs by regular fires—provided a corridor through which cattle and swine, in particular, fingered like beads of water around pine needles. Even after the first torch had passed, the pine barrens continued to burn. Beyond its plowed fields the South became notorious for its endemic woods burning, without which its pastoral economy would implode.[24]

Thus the transfer of fire was double, from Europe to North America and from American Indian to European. But differences were as pronounced as similarities. It was possible to direct livestock in ways not imaginable with wildlife; it was possible to drove great herds long distances and, where confined, to overgraze. If American herders became pastoral backwoodsmen, little encumbered by social institutions, so too their herds and flocks ranged beyond the ecological conventions of Europe's gardened landscape. In America, the stone walls had fallen, the hedgerows cleared away. The village infield no longer held the outfield in close orbit: European herders took for their outfield most of the continent.

The conquest of North America, like the reconquest of Iberia, created, for a time, a great biotic vacuum, and into it rushed the anomalous pastoralism of Iberia. For the Great Plains and much of the western basins, the apparatus of Spanish herding informed a beef bonanza that blew over the prairies like a thunderstorm and crushed them like hail. Even the Cordillera became the home for a relocated transhumance, with the Cascades replacing the Pyrenees and the Sierra Nevada of California replacing the looming sierras of Granada. The transfer of Iberian pastoralism was as powerful an influence on American fire history as the transfer of Finnish swidden. For roughly twenty years after the Civil War, great herds of sheep and cattle swarmed over the western ranges.

The cattle drovers' hearth was southern and central Texas. By the late 1860s, Indian resistance, rekindled during the war, ended; the buffalo, the longhorn's natural competitor, was shot out as well; and the railroads and refrigeration cars linked remote pastures with urban markets. The timing of the great droves was critical. The long-ranging herds needed fresh grass, and until spring fodder was established, had to feed on old grasses. But if the herds depended on grass, the grass depended on fire. One solution satisfied all needs: to burn in advance of the plodding herds. If that did not happen, fresh grass was lacking and old grass posed a threat from wildfire. Thus contracts for pasture in the Flint Hills of Kansas, for example, not only required burning but specified the times it should be done.[25]

These conditions could not always be met, however, and they could not, in any event, persist. So long as the range was open, herds could meander among burned and unburned sites, just as bison and pronghorn had before them. But as herd sizes swelled, as fences interrupted the mobility of free-ranging herd and flock, as plowed fields multiplied, and as the sheer ecological weight of milling livestock crushed the range, the ancient linkage between fire and pastoralism, predicated on mobility, broke down. On fenced lands, wildfire threatened winter forage; and on a closed range, controlled burning limited the size of herds, or if access was not restricted, could lead to ruinous overgrazing. In the arid West the blows of the immense herds pummeled the native grasses to a pulp. Mesquite, juniper, sagebrush, chaparral—woody weeds that were inimical to grazers and immune to fire without their interstitial grasses—took over range after range. Worse, by the time livestock populations had diminished significantly, pyrophytes like cheatgrass and Russian thistle had invaded, perverting the biota into a more frequent fire regime that yielded abundant fire but little forage. Their own excesses, both economic and ecological, doomed the environmental conditions that had made the cross-continental droves possible, and with them, the herds.[26]

Along the Cordillera another Iberian pastoral regime installed itself. Shepherds, often Basque, drove flocks up and down the western mountains much as they had in the Cordillera Cantábrica, and it was possible to track their spring ascents and especially their autumn descents by the smoke that rose behind them like clouds of loosened dust. "Hooved locusts" is how John Muir described the flocks in the Sierra Nevada. Their numbers were immense—sheep, not cattle, led the pastoral invasion of most of the American West, as they had much of Latin America, Australia, and South Africa. Elsewhere in California and the Southwest, New Spain's herding frontier relied on trained mission neophytes. But in the post–Civil War era, shepherds tended to be as alien as their flocks, which descended over the western landscape like a toxic cloud.[27]

The fires, thought Muir, did ten times the damage of logging. The seasonal burning flooded adjacent basins like the Willamette Valley of Oregon and the Great Valley of California with smoke. U.S. Geological Survey parties had to shut down mapping operations along the Cascades because of the lingering pall. While sheep cropped understories and trampled soils, and defiled native landscapes with banal indifference, it was smoke that signaled their lethal progress. Mingled with the effluent of settler fires, those clouds of smoke smothered the lowlands. A story in the *Oregonian* read: "We read about Egyptian darkness, but it is smoke, Josephine smoke—smoke in the morning, at noon and at night. Meet a neighbor, it is smoke; parting from one, it is smoke . . . we live in the days of smoke. It is smoke, smoke, smoke!"[28]

It was one thing to have transhumance linked with a village economy, another to lash it to national and global markets. Small flocks integrated into local markets had swollen into a literal "plague of sheep," Motolinia said of Mexico; and fires that in Iberia had dotted mountain slopes like small cottages now sprawled, it seemed, like open-pit mines across whole ranges. Like cattle, horses, and donkeys that so often went feral, pastoralism itself had run wild. But whereas it was difficult to attack pastoralism per se and to track the powerful political and economic interests it often represented, it was easy to denounce fires and to trace the billowing plumes of a polluting pastoralism. The quarrel over herding often expressed itself in a debate over fire.[29]

COUNTER FIRE:
EUROPE CONTAINS

Where it could, Europe installed its own fire practices, and where it could not, it co-opted indigenous forms. Where those strategies failed—and wherever it determined that existing fire regimes were unacceptable—Europe sought to suppress the encountered fires. In principle fire control and fire use were not opposing practices, though European authorities acted as though they were, and where Europe could not accept indigenous fire uses, it argued for fire control. Europe's agents would unpick all those diverse fires by which indigenes had stitched their landscape into an environmental quilt. Sovereignty over land demanded sovereignty over fire.

There was nothing extraordinary in this proposition. It was precisely how Europe's elites viewed fire in Europe, and how they related to the peasantry that exploited fire to wrest meat, fiber, and grain from the land. The firefights that raged between metropole and colony were often little different except in intensity from those between city and country. For both, modernization meant fire suppression. It is one of the great facts of environmental history that this chore fell to foresters. The precepts of fire protection were among the most common texts of forestry. They soon acquired an imperial gloss.

(i)

Imperial forestry evolved into one of the mightiest institutions of colonial rule, economic modernization, and scientific inquiry, and became generally the leading instrument of conservation. European forestry and steam-powered industrialization came to resemble binary suns around which the colonial exploitation of natural resources revolved. The prevailing policies toward fire were those that foresters laid down and enforced.

The distinction between colonies that possessed forestry and those that did not was nearly as great as the difference between those that saw their indigenes increase in number and those whose lands were emptied of natives. Imperial powers that established overseas empires before the Enlightenment, such as Spain and Portugal, generally lacked forestry, itself an Englightenment invention. By the time a forestry school, staffed with German professors, was established in Madrid in 1833 along with trained inspectors (Cuerpo de Ingenieros de Montes), Spain had lost most of its American possessions. Those imperial powers that came later included forestry among the transferred institutions. For Britain, France, Germany, and the Netherlands foresters were as vital as infantry colonels, civil engineers, and professional administrators. "The Forester," Sir David Hutchins proudly proclaimed, was "a soldier of the State, and something more."[30]

That "something more" was a transnational culture of environmental engineering. Cadres of foresters moved from Sierra Leone to Cape Colony to Indochina to the Yukon Territory, much as mining, civil, and military engineers did. An educated elite, foresters served as explorers and surveyors, even ethnographers, in what became a grand reconnaissance of global forests; Humboldtean explorers became Humboldtean engineers. Proconsuls, they ruled over vast areas of "public" or "crown" lands created, sometimes by coercion, out of a swamp of communal holdings. Professionals, they shared universal values that transcended their separate nationalities.

Imperial forestry was a composite. Germany contributed the prescriptions of silviculture, France the belief in the directive power of the state, and Britain a colonial context intimately connected to industrialization. Germans remained the great forest agronomists, as concerned with botany as with economics. Yet although George Ludwig Hartig himself had helped create the Prussian Forest Service, it was France with its Colbertian commitment to *dirigisme* that made forestry an instrument of broad state policy, and that most highlighted the relentless competition between local interests and national goals. The process also ensured that forestry would funnel its timber revenues into government coffers. Those goals soon dispatched French foresters to the Maghreb, West Africa, Indochina, and Madagascar.

But it was Britain ironically that made forestry a major imperial institution— Britain, itself almost bare of woodlands; Britain, the epitome of laissez-faire market capitalism, so often hostile to forestry's distant planning horizon; Britain, so nationalistic, so poorly endowed with public land, and so suspicious of idealistic philosophies. It was Britain that created the exemplar of the transnational forester, endowed immense colonial landscapes for Crown rule as forests and nature reserves, and promoted the virtues of forests for reasons of public health and climatic stability. The expansion of Europe created demands no single nation could satisfy; a cadre of globe-spanning foresters, loyal to the tenets of forestry, was one response. When in 1875, at the recommendation of Sir Dietrich Brandis, Britain trained its imperial foresters at the École Nationale des Eaux et Forêts in Nancy under mixed German and French staff, it distilled the European origins of international forestry, like maple sap boiled into sugar.

In less than a century forestry would dissipate that founding dynamism. In time forestry would become obsessed with the training of technicians, would merge seamlessly into a general curriculum of agricultural and vocational schooling. As decades passed, forestry would come to resemble other behemoths of state bureaucracy. In time, as Europe shed its colonies, forestry would lose the zealotry of its transnational mission. But during its heroic age, forestry's graduates were broadly trained, literate and politically astute, and fanatically motivated emissaries of science and reason. Foresters sought to rationalize the landscapes they encountered, whether those lands were shaped by wind and flood, peasant agriculture, or aboriginal foraging. They were doers, practitioners, not theoreticians: they translated ideas by transplanting institutions. That foresters became the prime repository for fire knowledge and the dominant instrument of fire management was an event of not only political but emotional power. Forestry became the romance of land management. Firefighting became the romance of forestry.

The environments foresters encountered were different from those they had known in Europe. It was not obvious how a tour of Germany and Austria, as the one Brandis conducted in 1890, or of France, like that Major Frederic Bailey led in 1887, prepared students for the monsoonal teak forests of Burma or the dense savanna of Ghana. Hutchins warned: "Often, what is right in European Forestry is wrong in Extra-tropical Forestry. In European Forestry the main controlling factor is light; in Extra-tropical Forestry it is moisture." Book learning without practical apprenticeship in particular locales could be disastrous. But forestry's principles, founded on biological and economic sciences, were assumed to be universal. Nature did not obey one set of rules in the Western Ghats and the fynbos of the Cape Mountains and another in the Buchenwald and Alpes-Maritimes. The trickier question was similarly "reducing," by legal and practical means, the population of indigenes and their traditional usage.[31]

For this, foresters carried in their rucksacks the historical experiences of Europe with its parables of forest destruction and rehabilitation. Long after forestry had segregated itself from the vert and venison of medieval hunting grounds and the estates of the privileged classes, it had to assert its validity as an economic asset. And it had to fight relentlessly against agricultural encroachment and traditional rights of access, pleading that it—and the forests under its care—promoted a larger public good than folk foraging. Not only timber but the larger "forest influences" of stable watersheds and climatic amelioration that well-managed woodlands conveyed were, for foresters, a compelling brief for positing broader goals than peasant agriculture and for demanding the application of state power. Few would dispute, observed E. P. Stebbing, "that these unchecked fires sweeping the countryside are one of the causes in parts—and perhaps of considerable parts—of Africa for the increasing desiccation of climate, the decrease in water supplies, using the term in its widest significance, and in various forms of erosion now making their blatant and evident or insidious and scarcely perceptible appearance." Similar scenes were no less evident in the Blue Mountains of New South Wales, the denuded slopes of the Rockies, and the scoured sierras of the Andes.[32]

But the evidence lay as close as Europe itself. It is not too much to say of Europe proper that it was being recolonized by a vastly liberated and more far-flung economy, nor that it was subject to its own consolidating "empires," as, for example, Germany and Italy amalgamated smaller states into larger wholes.

The collision between village economies and global-edged markets scattered environmental debris to all sides, like chips from a hewn log. *Brandwirtschaft* broke down in the Black Forest because of imported tannic acid from South America. Terraced fields in Greece became irrelevant with imported wheat from North America. As traditional lands lost their defining purposes, they lost their traditional constraints as well. The tempo of change was too rapid, its scale too vast for indigenous control; market forces for deforestation moved faster than social countermeasures for reforestation. Forest devastation followed, and then came soil erosion, catchments thrown into turmoil, mountain torrents, and climatic deterioration, notably drought and desiccation. Ignorant peasants and village communes could not see these larger issues, nor resist them. But educated foresters could, and the state, and perhaps only the state, could impose the necessary order. And what was politically improvident for a European nation-state to do on itself could be done on a colony. In fact, it could even be encouraged under the guise of civilizing heathen and barbarous landscapes.

Someone had to assume responsibility. That foresters sought and clamored for that responsibility meant that the environmental Others that Europe encountered were viewed through forestry's dazzling prism. The tree became the emblem of environmental health, deforestation the paradigm of land abuse, forest reproduction the prognosis of future wealth, and forest humus the deposited capital of nature's economy. For foresters trees determined the structure of the whole environment. Increase tree canopy and you increase shade, and so moisture, and thus build up humus, encourage water retention, suppress undesirable understory species, and hold ripe soils. Reverse that process and losses rather than improvements accumulated. The land spiraled into decay. That had been the understood experience of central Europe, and that was the received academic science behind the administration of immense forest reserves.

But the lands of Europe's swelling colonies were often different. Many landscapes were grasslands or savannas, many forests existed as woody fallow for swidden, timber was secondary to innumerable plants and animals used for hunting and foraging, and fire, far from inhibiting the system, was what kept nudging it along. Imperial foresters, however, were given jurisdiction over *land,* not just woods. The cornucopia of traditional forest foods they dismissed as "minor products." Wildlife, other than royal game like tigers or elephants broken to obedience, was vermin. Grasslands they saw as denuded forests, as corridors for wandering pastoralists, and as fuses for fire. Shifting cultivation they declared as the forest's implacable enemy. Traditional users were wanton destroyers of timber, no better than bark beetles or blister rust. The talismanic tree trumped all other species and uses. Forestry proposed a new appraisal for land and new standards of land practice, not only for reasons of political economy but out of its own heartwood values. What national politics had made difficult in Europe, colonial politics made possible overseas.

The Code Colbert was an ideal, if poorly realized. "I know of no modern system of Forest Exploitation, based on modern Forest Science," wrote John Croumbie Brown in 1883, "in which I cannot trace its influence." The orgy of deforestation that followed the French Revolution was the Code's dark twin, an environmental Reign of Terror that foresters knew had not only deconstructed the woodlands of revolutionary France but was actively overthrowing those environmentally corrupt *ancien régimes* that had characterized the distant lands that Europe's imperial outreach now made into colonies. In both cases fire loomed everywhere, a syndrome of apparent landscape breakdown. Arson was an omnipresent fear; the distinction between arson and accident, irrelevant. In the case of remote colonies, foresters often could not see the forest for the fires.[33]

(ii)

That Great Britain became a global power in forestry is one of the extraordinary sagas of forest history, and one of its grandest anomalies. Britain had long cleared its own woodlands and those of lands, like Ireland, it had newly recolonized. During the agricultural revolution it had sought to reclaim wastelands for farms, not woods. The timber frontier that rippled through boreal Europe began with the deep stones of British capital tossed into the Baltic. The memory of Norman-imposed royal forests still festered. Britain harbored no tradition of professional forestry. Not until 1887 when private subscriptions endowed a forestry chair at the University of Edinburgh, did academic forestry appear, and not until 1905, when the imperial forestry school transferred to Oxford, was there any serious forestry education available in the Home Islands. Forest cadets with classroom training in Britain still did their field apprenticeship in Germany or France. Not from any internal momentum but solely from the prod of expansion did Britain cultivate forestry. Forestry was an artifact of empire, and an essential tool of imperial rule.

The empire centered in India. After the loss of all the American colonies except Canada, that imperium spread in protective shells around that Indian core and along the routes that trafficked to India. It was logical then that Britain's imperial fascination with forestry should begin there as well. Its origins were several, and not initially the product of foresters. Pre-British India hosted examples of forest conservation, from sacred groves to the enshrinement of teak as a royal tree to the caste-like regulation of forest uses. Soon after the British East India Company consolidated its rule in three presidencies—Madras, Bengal, and Bombay—tree-planting experiments sprouted like seedlings, only to wither in the deep litter of company bureaucracy. Curiously, commercial arguments to regulate the teak trade, in particular, failed repeatedly. It was obvious to even the most obtuse observer that the wild exploitation of mature teak by commercial contractors was wrecking valuable woodlands. But company policy promoted agriculture, which also expanded at the expense of woods; and waste was not a compelling cause for reform.

An inquiry from the Royal Navy over the security of teak was, however. The query prompted the Court of Directors in 1805 to sponsor a Forest Committee, which led in 1806 to the appointment of Captain Watson (of the Police Service) as conservator of forests and a declaration that teak, as a royal tree, belonged to the British East India Company. Conservator Watson soon installed a timber monopoly and proceeded to alienate landowners and merchants between Malabar and Travancore; in 1823 the outcry was sufficient to have him removed and his office abolished. Meanwhile, often through superintendents of botanical gardens, there were attempts to cultivate teak plantations. The Indian Navy Board tried again in 1831 to reinstate forest conservancy. But until the railroad redefined the geography of India, logging was restricted by access to timber-floating streams or proximity to major markets. And conversion of woodlands to agriculture—with the substitution of sedentary farmers for migratory pastoralists and *jhum* swiddeners—was considered an "improvement," not a liability. Commercial and military counterarguments failed.[34]

In the end, it was not timber but the forest that mattered, not the traffic in logged woods but the ecological aura surrounding woodlands. What proved compelling was the putative role of forests in regulating soils, water, and climate, and through these effects their impact on agriculture and human health. Deforestation, reformers declaimed, was biotic bloodletting that led to a deteriorated environment given to erosion, floods, droughts, climatic degeneration, and diseases. It was an argument popularized by Alexander von Humboldt, and one argued zealously by the East India Company Medical Corps. Over and again, Company surgeons diagnosed the diseases of deforestation and prescribed forest protection as a prophylactic and reforestation as a restorative. William Roxburgh in Madras and Bengal, Ronald Martin in Calcutta, Donald Butter in Oudh, Alexander Gibson in Bombay, and Edward Balfour and Hugh Cleghorn in Madras—all these surgeons had trained in natural history and many oversaw botanical gardens; all absorbed from their Hippocratic education a perceived link between environmental conditions and public health and became convinced of an insidious connection between denudation and drought (and hence famine and its associated illnesses); all argued for reforestation to restore emaciated ecosystems to health. There was the evidence of St. Helena and Barbados, French evidence from the Alps and ruined tropical isles, the accumulating records of a global reconnaissance by Humboldtean geographers, and their own experiences in India. Roxburgh suggested a link between the great drought of 1791 and land changes, particularly deforestation. In 1824, Bishop Heber added the Siwaliks to the register of ruin.[35]

But reforestation struck at the agricultural expansion that had informed Company policy. Reformation thus required drought, the experience of decades of unregulated logging, and famine (1837–39) before its logic became irresistible even to revenue officers. In 1847 the Court of Directors ordered its presidencies to transmit information on the impact of deforestation on desiccation as a matter of "strong practical bearing on the welfare of mankind" and of course vital to the Company's accounts. "Forest conservancy," as the British liked to call it, soon followed. In 1847 the Bombay presidency appointed Dr. Alexander Gibson as conservator of forests. At least in principle, India's forests were a public good that had to be administered as a public institution and if necessary through public compulsion. However radiant the symbolism, however, the practical consequences at this time were trivial.[36]

Once unleashed, reform was not easily contained. No less than imperial expansion, it had it own dynamic. The three Burmese wars trace in almost dialectic syllogisms the forest policy that evolved.

The First Burmese War (1826) put the Tenasserim teak forests under British rule, and these forests, subjected to rapacious commercial exploitation, were cut out by 1850. To this thesis, the Second War (1852–53), which surrendered the Pegu teak forests to Britain, proposed an antithesis. The example of the Tenasserim forests would not, Lord Dalhousie determined, be repeated for the Pegu teak. Instead, the royal forests were transferred from the Burmese crown to the British, and over them Britain appointed another Company surgeon, Dr. John McClelland. McClelland submitted a report in 1854 critical of the private logging conducted by contractors on the Crown forests. The response by Governor-General Dalhousie was the 1855 Charter of the Indian Forests, which proposed for India's woodlands the kind of rationalization that Dalhousie was pursuing for Indian government, society, and economy through the introduction of telegraphs, railroads, revenue settlements, and rule of law. The larger Dalhousiean program had to wait until Britain suppressed the revolt of 1857 and India became a Crown colony (and an empire in 1884). So, too, forest conservancy had to move beyond Company control and its college of surgeons. In 1856, Dietrich Brandis was appointed superintendent of forests for Pegu. By the time the Third Burmese War (1885) brought Upper Burma to British rule a full-blown forestry department was prepared to oversee its woods.[37]

Whether or not the modern era began with Brandis's appointment, the legend of Indian forestry holds that it did, and the symbolism suggests that the myth has merit. Brandis was a German, the son of philosophy professors, educated at Bonn and Göttingen, a botanist cum forester, a practical Humboldtean, and a gifted, even inspirational, administrator. The surgeons and naturalists who preceded him had little formal training in forestry. They were talented amateurs, shrewd observers willing to study indigenous practices and to identify the sinews that connected India's environmental skeleton to Britain's muscular economy, and often political moralists, as much in the tradition of the English parson-naturalist as the aristocrat-adventurer. They looked to other parts of the burgeoning empire for examples. By contrast, Brandis knew academic forestry and understood the systems of continental forestry. While no ideologue—as his insights into the possibilities of *taungya* demonstrate—he brought rigor to conviction. Forests became more than botanical gardens. The pedigree of the Imperial Indian Forest Service properly traces to him. And for his labors Brandis earned a knighthood.[38]

Sir Dietrich Brandis quickly elaborated the principles of a full-fledged forestry department. He surveyed the land, organized a bureaucracy (skimpy as it was), and arranged for the protection of existing woods and the improvement by silviculture of new stock. Within a year he had added the forests of Tenasserim and Martaban. In 1862 the Government of India detailed him on special assignment to help develop a forest administration for other provinces along the lines of Pegu. A long-delayed appointment in Madras of a conservator of forests (Dr. Hugh Cleghorn, another former Company surgeon) followed. In 1865 the Indian Forest Act formally inaugurated the imperial forest service. Unsurprisingly, Dietrich Brandis became its first inspector-general.

The Forest Act was flawed, unable to impose a common order over all of British India and unable to distinguish precisely what constituted a "forest." Before land could be reserved, all rights, private or communal, that were vested in it had to be recorded through "forest settlements" that specified exactly who had what rights to what uses on the land. Land that did not have rights invested in some person or body of persons reverted to the state. The British soon discovered that Indian customary law was as overgrown and opaque as Hindu theology. So forest protection on the British model first required the introduction of a new legal regime. Foresters were, in effect, instructed to help rationalize the Indian landscape along European lines.[39]

A series of amended acts followed. The most important were the Indian Forest Act VII of 1878, the Burma Forest Act of 1881, the Madras Forest Act of 1882, and the Upper Burma Forest Regulation of 1890; additional legislation brought other, still-fugitive states into conformity. The legislation also designated several categories of forest, of which two were fundamental. "Reserved forests" were lands for which the state had completely settled the question of rights of use and which was granted the highest level of defense. "Protected forests" were lands for which rights were not fully settled and to which the state offered a lesser degree of guardianship. In 1894 the Indian National Forest Policy sought to integrate forestry better with agriculture and reiterated that state forests existed "to promote the general welfare" primarily through "the preservation of the climate and physical conditions of the country" and secondarily "to fulfill the needs of the people." It recommended that forests serve not only as timber holdings but as "fuel fodder reserves" to assist graziers and villagers during times of distress. The specter of drought persisted.[40]

Even in its 1865 avatar this was an ambitious agenda. Britain proposed to install a program of forest management on a subcontinent fourteen times its own size, a population at least an order of magnitude greater than Britain's, and a civilization vastly more complex and convoluted. Scientific forestry—and there was no political legitimacy to any other kind—required trained staff, which Britain, much less India, lacked. Although Brandis arranged for a corps of Britons to study at French and German forestry schools, this would take several years, so he succeeded in hiring two German professionals, Wilhelm Schlich and Berthold Ribbentrop, as his deputies. When Brandis retired, Schlich replaced him, and when Schlich retired, Ribbentrop succeeded him. They were the trinity of Indian forestry—Brandis, the revered organizer, the administrative genius; Schlich, the academic and writer, founding editor of *The Indian Forester,* author of the magisterial *Manual of Forestry,* organizer of forestry education; Ribbentrop, the supreme field man, who said of himself that he "always" would be "one of those forest officers . . . to whom the pruning knife and the rifle, and I might perhaps be allowed to add questions of practical forest treatment and administration, come more handy than the pen."[41]

In 1875 the Indian Forest Service began to educate its British staff at Nancy. To help train a subordinate Indian staff, a forest school was established at Dehra Dun in 1878. In 1884, apparently in response to objections by British nationalists, the school transferred to Cooper's Hill College for Indian Engineering, and in 1905 to Oxford University. Full training continued to require an inspection of Continental forests, forestry's answer to the Grand Tour. While small in number, the corps permeated the service, much as graduates of *grandes écoles* did the French civil service. In time the effect seeped back to Britain itself. Schlich, like Brandis knighted, ended his career holding the forestry chair at the University of Edinburgh.[42]

There were two tasks then, one to rationalize the legal and political regime, and the other to rationalize the growth and use of the forests. Inevitably the two converged. There would be no systematic exploitation or protection of the forests until the question of rights and responsibilities was clarified. But legal rights of access meant nothing without the means of making the forest biologically accessible. To an India awash in savannas, seral jungles, swiddened hills, ancient pastoralists, and the pyric metronome of the Asian monsoon, accessibility mean fire. Time and again these two tasks converged, like thematic Ganges and Brahmaputra Rivers, on the vexatious delta of Indian fire.

Regarding the primacy of fire, all parties concurred. Writing in 1928, E. O. Shebbeare recalled that the "pioneers" of Indian forestry saw fire as "their chief, almost their only enemy." Brandis agreed and, at the first Indian forestry conference, "fire conservancy" was addressed as "the first task of the Forest Department in most provinces of the empire." "There is no possible doubt," Brandis concluded, as to fire protection's "immense value and importance"; there was "no measure which equals fire conservancy in importance."[43]

His successors and the chroniclers of Indian forestry seconded that sentiment. Ribbentrop, in particular, returned to the problem as a hunter might stalk a rogue tiger. "In all classes [of forest] fire-protection is unquestionably a *sine qua non* to complete success." In *Forestry in British India* (1900), he confessed that he returned to fire protection "more frequently than of any other subject" and voiced "no hesitation in doing so." When he wrote his encyclopedic (and misnamed) *Brief History of Forestry,* Bernhard Fernow observed of India that its "fire scourge" was "still the greatest problem" faced by foresters. "I was warned in my first few months of service," E. P. Stebbing recalled, "that in fire protection work no slips were permissible and no slackness; that these orders were not those of a local Government but came down from the Central Government and that no mercy was shown to the backslider."[44]

But Indians were no less passionate. Without fire most Indian forests were unusable. Foresters fought swidden and pastoralism, not only for their competition with high forest, but because those practices were wholly dependent on fire, which the natives seemingly cast to the winds. Stebbing recalled that in every province "the officers of the Department had to commence the work of introducing fire conservancy for the protection of the forests in the face of an actively hostile population more or less supported by the district officials, and especially the Indian officials, who quite frankly regarded the new policy of fire conservancy as an oppression of the people." Captain J. C. Doveton of the Central Provinces argued that fire conservancy was necessary only because "nearly the whole body of the population in the vicinity of the forest tracts have, or imagine they have, a personal interest in the creation of forest fire."[45]

Maddeningly, the burning went on over and again as new fuels presented themselves. The occasions for burning were innumerable, the reasons endless. So too the issue of fire conservancy rekindled annually. An exasperated Ribbentrop recalled how "in the early days" there was "a most marvellous, now almost incredible, apathy and disbelief in the destructiveness of forest fires." These, "in certain provinces almost general, conflagrations," Ribbentrop asserted, were "the chief reason of the barren character of so many of our Indian Hill ranges, and are more closely connected with distress and famine than is usually supposed."[46]

Indians saw the issue otherwise, for without fire the land was even more worthless to them. British India's fire suppression policy, observed Pt. Govind Ballabh Pant (later home minister of India), was "a source of widespread hardship and the opinion of all classes of people seems to be unanimous on this point." When indigenes—pastoralists, farmers, hunters, aboriginal foragers, even forest guards—protested this, in their view, most unjust because most unwise and impossible edict, they did so through fire. Civil unrest flared into arson, sometimes openly as in Kumaon, along the Himalayan foothills, in 1921, most often sub rosa, a guerrilla war of biotic insurgency.[47]

The British fought back. Fire season, Ribbentrop wrote, "is the most trying part of a forester's life, from the Divisional Officer down to the lowest Fire-Guard, and nobody who has not lived through it has any conception of the hardships it entails." Let Ribbentrop—the forester more at ease with pruner and rifle than pen—describe the annual ritual:

> The work begins comparatively early in the season with the cutting of grass, herbs and bushes over miles upon miles of fire-lines, and even at this early period the work has to be constantly inspected to see that it is thoroughly done. When this material has become dry enough to burn, a most anxious and responsible time begins, for it has to be burned without causing damage to the neighboring forests, chiefly at night when the dew has moistened the standing grass and when sparks can be more easily seen. This work becomes more and more dangerous as the season advances, and as the surrounding jungle gets drier and more inflammable. It is at night only that the work can be safely done, and night after night the fire-gangs have to be at work. Then comes a short period of comparative ease, when the fire-lines are finished and the surrounding country is not as yet ablaze. Soon, however, the sky is red at night with grass-fires and fires in private and unprotected forests, and clouds of smoke wreath the horizon in the day time. Now everybody has to be on the alert, the surrounding jungle has to be burned outward when fires from outside approach the fire-protected forests and the belt of safety is not sufficiently wide. In spite of every precaution, the fire is sometimes carried into a protected forest area by the wind and then a fight begins, and compartment after compartment is defended till the fire has been got under. Such a fight is often very protracted, and what that means under the blazing sun of April and May, followed by a stifling night, can only be imagined by people who have lived in the tropic plains of India and can be realized only by actual experience. It is needless to say with what sense of delight the forest officer out here greets the first showers of the monsoon and sees his fire-traces covered with green sprouts of new vegetation.

Even to fight fire required fire.[48]

But was it worth it? No officer at first thought it possible, and no native thought it desirable, to exclude fire. But the brash empire builders of the British regime believed the attempt necessary. Without fire control nothing was secure, either by way of protection or improvement. With it, regeneration flourished, humus built up, and even villagers (so Ribbentrop hoped) could see the wisdom of reform. In reality, the British raj controlled only a scattering of select sites, like hilltop fortresses. The remainder of the countryside continued to burn regardless of silvicultural theories and ardent firefights. And in time, well before they surrendered political rule over India, the British compromised with local fire practices or turned over fire entirely to local peoples.

India was not only the first but the most powerful paradigm. Cyprus established a forest department on the Indian model in 1879, followed by a cascade of others throughout the empire, from Trinidad to Hong Kong; and especially in Africa—in Kenya, Uganda, Rhodesia, Ghana, Nigeria, Sierra Leone—forestry spread like a contagion. Cape Colony was particularly keen for afforestation and the suppression of veld fires in the belief that this would increase rainfall and the effectiveness of mountain catchments. And so it went. The Imperial Indian Forest Service, as Sir William Schlich—honored as the Master of British Forestry—observed, had sent agents to the Federated Malay States, New Zealand, Australia, South Africa, the West Indies, Sudan, Cyprus, even back to Britain, a path he himself had taken. Everywhere the British planted the flag, they transplanted state forestry, as much a part of the colonial apparatus as a postal service and military cantonments. Forestry helped rationalize landscapes according to the principles of a global political economy and helped integrate far-flung biotas into an imperial web of science. Planetary ecology was reconstructed according not only to the trophic flows of capitalism but to the food chains of formal knowledge that linked periphery with center.[49]

Even America felt the reach of Britain's forest imperium. Franklin Hough, first director of the Bureau of Forestry (created in 1876), began his labors with an encyclopedic survey of European forestry, assisted by correspondence with Dietrich Brandis. Aspiring American foresters passed through the same regimen as imperial cadets, studied at Nancy, read Schlich's *Manual,* conducted a similar Grand Tour of Continental sites, and absorbed the same Continental precepts. America's first forestry professor, Carl Schenk, came from Germany; its first professional forester, Bernhard Fernow, was a graduate of the Prussian Forest Service; the first chief of the U.S. Forest Service, Gifford Pinchot, spent a semester at Nancy, and then corresponded vigorously with Brandis about organizing a forestry department and suitable policies; his successor (and founding dean of the Yale School of Forestry, endowed by the Pinchot family), Henry Graves, passed through essentially the same curriculum as the proconsuls of the Indian Forest Service.

America tended to receive European exemplars through an imperial filter, at first British, and after World War I, more often French. Germany was too gardened to serve as a model for America, too lacking in raw public lands. America's silviculture had to be preadapted to colonial circumstances, grafted onto tougher rootstock. Britain's imperial forestry did exactly this. But the Nancy connection, and Britain's withdrawal to Cooper's Hill (which prohibited American students), gradually brought Americans closer to France. France, Gifford Pinchot believed, had "the more valuable instruction and more useful example for the American forester," and this was "especially true in its [forestry's] application to the French colonies, where many of the conditions approximate those with which American foresters find themselves obliged to deal." Then, with the United States at war with Germany, a general repudiation of German culture followed. American foresters formed an engineering brigade, worked shoulder to shoulder with French colleagues, and became convinced that imperial France was a suitable model. They admired French rigor, the enshrinement of the Code Colbert, and the efficiency with which the French colonial foresters attacked fire.[50]

The great difference was that American foresters had to deal with vacated, public lands, and hence with "natural" processes; British and French foresters, with the ineradicable natives. Of course America's public forests were never entirely vacant, and even small numbers of users (notably pastoralists) were endlessly vexatious and relentlessly hostile. In the South, where forests were imposed after settlement and onto semi-abandoned lands, the rural landscape seethed with woods burning that would make a Ghond proud. Still, the question of how to install a first-order forestry department where none existed was strikingly similar to the European colonial experience. America, too, was a forestry colony. When a committee of the National Academy of Sciences inspected the western forest reserves in 1896, it recommended that the experience of British India was worthy of considered emulation.[51]

Not surprisingly, the principals of that review—Gifford Pinchot and Charles Sargent, in particular—had corresponded freely with Brandis, who wrote for the *London Times* that the spectacle of forest devastation in the United States was "without parallel in history." Pinchot described how Schlich had urged on him the necessity for national forests and then dispatched him "with his blessing" on "my pilgrimage to Sir Dietrich Brandis." By "any standard of achievement," Pinchot regarded Brandis as the "first of living foresters," a man who had accomplished "what I might have a hand in doing in America." Brandis, in turn, dispatched Pinchot to Nancy. In 1905, President Theodore Roosevelt sent Brandis an autographed picture with the inscription, "In high appreciation of the work of Sir Dietrich Brandis for the cause of forestry in the United States." Later, there arrived a silver vase with the inscription, "To Sir Dietrich Brandis, Father of American Forestry." Among the subscribers were Pinchot, Schenk, Graves, Theodore Woolsey, Overton Price, and others from that heroic age.[52]

More than any other power Britain helped institutionalize an international culture of forestry. If British capital was busy stripping the world's forests, British foresters were equally busy trying to protect or restock them.

Forest bureaucracies created records, printed journals, sponsored research, and held symposia. In England (1920), Canada (1923), Australia (1928), South Africa (1935), and England again (1947), Britain sponsored imperial conferences that explicitly identified forestry as an organ of geopolitics, even as they reinforced the transnational values that often put British foresters in closer sympathy with French and German colleagues than with their own countrymen on matters of land use. Here experiences could be shared, data exchanged, and techniques standardized. The larger colonies published journals that enjoyed wide circulation, and helped to propagate forest science, establish a canon of forestry administration, and regularize woodland management across the globe. International forestry congresses, modeled on those of geology, geography, and other sciences, widened forestry's gyre still further. Knowledge built up like stacks of railway sleepers, though, unhappily, forestry's rate of learning never exceeded the forests' rate of removal.

Imperial foresters often enjoyed the social standing attained by other savants and entrepeneurs of empire. They were proconsuls, emissaries of a ruling class, often knighted for their services. They circulated through British society much as did the members of the Royal Geographic Society or the superintendents of botanical gardens. Peripatetic scholars amassed an impressive forest literature, all the more astounding when compared with the preceding poverty of preimperial Britain. John Croumbie Brown, for example, poured out a stream of books on forestry from France to Finland, from South Africa to Scotland. Prominent conservators transferred from colony to colony; major centers like India dispatched deputies to review and advise fledgling forestry in Mauritius, Victoria, Nigeria, wherever needed; and special inspectors wrote book after book about their collective experiences.

Consider the case of Sir David E. Hutchins. A graduate of the imperial curriculum at Nancy, Hutchins served in India, then became conservator of forests for South Africa and later for British East Africa, advised the Cyprus Forest Department, toured and lectured the Australian colonies, and scorned pleas for special consideration from lands remote and curious. There were principles to systematic forestry, and to violate them was not only a mistake but a breach of trust. Just as a global economy needed uniform banking laws, so a global forestry had to accept common systems of silviculture. Certainly this was true for fires. "Forest fires, which are such a curse in most of the wild forests of warm countries," Hutchins lectured, "give little trouble when once the forest becomes organized and cultivated." The example of the Esterel Forest in southern France was suitable for the Central Provinces of India, which was usable for Victoria, Tasmania, Cape Colony, wherever. The principles behind *systematic organization*—the critical element—were identical. "What foreigners can do in Southern Europe, or Englishmen can do in India and South Africa, Englishmen can do in Australia," Hutchins proclaimed to skeptical Aussies, "if only the matter is put squarely to them!"[53]

There was more than direct rule involved. Unlike France, its principal rival in imperial forestry, Britain promoted control by local peoples (for reasons of economy as much as noblesse oblige), labored to train them to proper standards, and made some concessions to native lore. (French foresters in West Africa, for example, did not address the natives in their own language even if they knew it. In the same way they sought to impose French silviculture and to make the woods serve French industry. The British, with no national forestry to speak of, were more cosmopolitan, more tolerant of local idiosyncracies, and often more willing to study or adapt native practices.) When the French left, they took forestry with them, as they took everything portable. When the British left, their arboreal grafts typically held and continued to yield fruit; institutions survived.[54]

Curiously, these institutions survived better in dispossessed colonies than in the Home Islands. As the colonies slipped away, so did the justification for imperial forestry. Without that larger compulsory vision, British forestry reverted to gardening, the global adventure abandoned to the study of English oak and Scots pine. At the end of the nineteenth century, it was impossible to study forestry without being enmeshed in the vast web of imperial British forest science and practice. Names like Brandis, Schlich, Ribbentrop, and Hutchins, and later R. S. Troup and H. C. Champion were as well known to international forestry as Joseph Banks and Joseph Hooker to botanists or James Clerk Maxwell and Lord Kelvin to physicists. By the end of the twentieth century, British forestry had so imploded that its experiences barely filled the Home Islands, and its legacy was lodged in microfilm stuffed into wooden, schoolboy lockers in the hallways and boiler basement of Oxford's moldering forestry institute.

(iii)

There was no avoiding fire. Introduced fire broke some landscapes, and native fire was liberated by the fracturing of others. But fire was everyplace, and everywhere it became a ready index by which to record changes in land use, for any alteration of fuels or fire-catalyzed technologies was quickly expressed in restructured fire regimes—or in a chaos of wildfires and arson. For imperial foresters, free-burning fire was the most emphatic of the instruments by which to measure the extent of environmental damage and to judge their success at rehabilitation. Forestry began with fire protection. When E. P. Stebbing, formerly of the Indian Forest Service, now forestry professor at Edinburgh, visited West Africa in 1934, he observed that even the "savannah forest" was "fully capable of being reconstituted [into] high forest by the two agencies of closure and strict fire protection."[55]

There were lessons among the legacies. Despite its early euphoria, imperial forestry could no more impose an alien silviculture than Europe could an alien language, arts, or laws. Natural reproduction was more important than artificial, indigenous processes more powerful than introduced ones. Nowhere was this truer than with fire. Where native peoples demanded access to fire and imperial foresters demanded its expulsion, clashes were unavoidable, and compromises inevitable. In short order the principles of fire conservancy became a dogma of British—indeed, of European—environmental policy. In what is surely one of the most paradoxical outcomes of European expansion, some of the most pyrophobic peoples on the planet assumed control over some of the Earth's most pyrophilic biotas.

In forestry, as in so many other colonial matters, there were two paradigms for contact. In one, the indigenous biota and peoples persisted; in the other, colonizers had a more or less clear field. The best documented examples, one at either end of the spectrum, are those from British India and America. For each, foresters faced the skepticism of colleagues and the outright hostility of indigenes or nature. For each they created a model of fire protection—for India, "fire conservancy," and for America, "systematic fire protection." The first was predicated on the existence of isolated forests, the second on the ability to install an outright alternative to folk fire use. Both became paradigms, then parables, then creation stories. But wherever the encounter occurred, its shock waves, like the tremors of an earthquake, were heard as well as felt. Fire control became a matter of public debate, a subject of political as well as scientific discourse.

No one believed that fire protection in India was possible when, in 1863, Brandis asked Colonel G. F. Pearson of the Central Provinces to try it. Pearson shrewdly selected the Bori Forest, a near-island grove of teak surrounded by cliffs on one side and a river on the other, and for the next two years his youthful corps succeeded in barring fire. They were wet years, and fire returned savagely when the rainy season subsequently shortened. But foresters had seen the lesson they wanted to see; and when the Indian Forest Act was enacted after Bori's two-year trial period, the Forest Department had in fire conservancy a means of enforcement while, in the Act, fire control had a means of expansion. Despite universal protest by natives, fire conservancy became the norm. By 1880–81 the Indian Forest Service had reduced some 28,500 square kilometers to formal fire protection; by 1885–86, roughly 41,500 square kilometers; and by 1900–1901, that figure had doubled to 89,000 square kilometers.[56]

Fire conservancy's critics did not go gently into that colonial night. Field men soon joined natives in protest. A dissenting creed—that fire abolition was impossible, that fire control only built up fuels for fires that must inevitably follow, and that fire exclusion exacted unacceptable ecological costs, particularly for forest regeneration—found converts. Only the most valued blocks were spared fire, and this at the cost of protective burning all around them. In some locales, foresters discovered to their chagrin that native guards were the largest source of fire, this because their preemptive protective burns were the only means to shield the core forests. Worse, where more or less successful, fire exclusion retarded regeneration in teak, sal, pine, and bamboo, precisely the species most valued commercially. In 1907, Burma withdrew fire protection from its reserves. By 1926, "early burning" acquired the imprimatur of the *Indian Forest Manual*. While imperial foresters never liked the practice, they recognized that if they were going to cultivate native species with the aid of native guards, they would have to adapt native burning as well. The best way to counter indigenous fires was to impose their own.

The American controversy erupted half a century later than the one in India; in fact, fire protection achieved its bureaucratic victory at the time fire conservancy was surrendering in Burma. But conditions were different in America. Its colonizing folk were the great incendiarists on private lands, and having sequestered the natives onto reservations, immense public lands were relatively vacant of people, though plastered with lightning ignitions. A developing nation, the United States used fire to smelt the rough ore of its wild landscape into agricultural bullion. So vicious were many fires—so fatal to settlers themselves—that the need for fire control became an argument for forestry.

Forestry replied in kind. "Like the question of slavery," Gifford Pinchot insisted in 1898, "the question of forest fires may be shelved for some time, at enormous cost in the end, but sooner or later it must be met." His successor, Henry Graves, confirmed that fire control was "the fundamental obligation of the Forest Service and takes precedence over all other duties and activities." Fire prevention, he lectured, was 90 percent of American forestry. His successor, William Greeley, downgraded that figure to 75 percent, but always insisted that "smoke in the woods" was the "yardstick of progress" in forestry. With epic drama, a fire-addicted folk was about to close with a fire-loathing forestry.[57]

The climax came in the summer of 1910. Drought-powered conflagrations raged throughout the West, with a 1.3 million-hectare epicenter in the Northern Rockies. The Forest Service, having inherited the national forests only in 1905, moved to fight the fires. Between 78 and 85 firefighters died in the attempt, the portentous origin of America's national archives in fire control. The experience traumatized the Service. Two of its future chiefs personally weathered the firestorms, and not until the 1910 generation—a cadre composed largely of young men—passed out of the Service would it seriously consider an alternative to aggressive suppression.

But that was exactly what critics proposed, almost as the Big Blowup was sweeping Montana and Idaho into its maelstrom of flame. "Light burning" it was called. Its agenda was to adapt frontier fire practices (what the poet Joaquin Miller called the "Indian way") to the public forests, to continue the tradition of lightly burning the surface as a means to inoculate the woods against the fuel buildup that stoked holocaust fires. To foresters the idea was sacrilege ("Paiute forestry," Graves sniffed); to firefighters lamenting the loss of brave comrades, the proposal smelled of treason. When in 1910 the secretary of the interior, Richard Ballinger (victor in a political brouhaha that had ousted Pinchot earlier in the year), suggested that light burning might be an alternative to fire control, the Service saw itself under assault. It fought light burning to the death. In 1914, Coert duBois published a treatise on "systematic fire protection" that underwrote the conceptual counterattack, and in 1923, after several years of inconclusive trials, a forestry panel declared light burning anathema. Systematic fire protection became an American exemplar, the New World's answer to the Bori Forest.

But there was more. The same August that witnessed the Big Blowup in the Rockies and the Big Protest by light burners, the philosopher of pragmatism, William James, published his final essay. A pacifist, James was alarmed by the militarism he saw proliferating to all sides, and wanted to find a "moral equivalent of war" in the same sense that one could speak of a mechanical equivalent of heat. He urged a national conscription of youths to sublimate their martial energies in a war against the forces of nature. Firefighting embodied that sentiment perfectly. The heroic age of American forestry marched to war against fire, and in some significant ways never returned.[58]

In the end, compromises were necessary. Removing people had not removed fire; lightning seized the vacated landscapes and pummeled them with ignitions. Overgrazing destroyed the grassy understories that made light fires possible; suppression worsened fuel accumulation and arrangement; and after a grace period, fires returned larger and more vicious than before. Critics of suppression thus argued with ever greater force and with the authoritative evidence of a deteriorating landscape. Agencies searched desperately for some way to restore fire. By the 1970s "prescribed fire" became an accepted practice in American forestry, and within two decades, an obsession.[59]

Early burning, light burning—equivalents appeared everywhere. Opinions varied, as in good conscience they could. Fire science was confused, contradictory, lost amid the particularities of place and practice. In the absence of controlled and replicable experiments, a kind of scientific scholasticism flourished, filling the desperate need for information with theory, analogy, logic, anecdote, and prejudice. In 1993, Norman Christensen likened the literature of fire ecology to "holy scripture" in that one could, it seemed, find whatever meaning one wanted to seek. A century earlier the issues often seemed clearer only because there were fewer texts for forest dialecticians to reconcile. When Jan Smuts asked South Africa's leading fire authority, John C. Phillips, to produce a "Ten Commandments of Burning," Phillips's preliminary list looked closer to a score, and was on its way to being a hundred. Smuts lost interest. With or without science, decisions had to be made.[60]

And so they were, usually on the basis of a politics that pitted folk practitioners and field operatives against a bureaucratic elite, the appointed mandarins of the environment who believed that fire was alien to the natural forest and its presence an artifact of human misconduct. With fire protection native forests could stabilize, planted woods multiply, and humus ripen. With forest augmentation would come climatic amelioration and improvement in the soils. Surface fires were likened, in Hutchins's ascerbic appraisal, to "burning the carpets to save the house." Ultimately, the surest means of fire protection was through proper silviculture, the full-scale conversion of the forest into a state that would not burn. The first requirement of forest management then was fire control, and the only real questions about fire administration were ones of proper organization and sufficient will. Perhaps it was to be expected. They were alien rulers; confronted with a bewildering diversity of burning and always worried about revenues and insurrection, they moved to suppress what was unusual and threatening. Native fires headed the list.[61]

There was always dissent, even within the ranks of Europeans. Those closest to the ground were more wont to tolerate fire or to argue for the adaptation of indigenous fire practices. In general, sympathy for controlled burning varied in direct proportion to one's proximity to fire in the field. The more remote the observer, the more skeptical of fire's values; the more distant the experience, the more European the education, the less willing was an official to accept or promote indigenous fire practices. Again, there were exceptions. In trying to characterize the African savanna, T. F. Chipp, deputy director of Kew Gardens, once argued that the "annual grass fires" that swept "over extensive areas of country for many decades, must now be considered in the light of a natural factor."[62]

But this was impossible for any forest officer to accept. It meant that fire, which corroded his soils and shriveled his waters, and in the case of West Africa might be pulling Sahara sands into the dry vacuum of its convective columns, was not only beyond his control but had, perhaps, to be encouraged. Such an argument defeated the whole environmentalist agenda of forestry, the assertion that it was something more than colonial plundering, and it challenged the ethos (not to say, mythos) of imperial forestry, the missionary élan that sent privileged youths overseas to convert heathen landscapes.

Ultimately, compromise was exactly what occurred. When it ended, the fire geography of the Earth before and after Europe's imperial expansion was as different as its political geography. The experience not only restructured fire regimes, but reconstituted the meaning of fire ecology itself. Nature's economy acquired a scale commensurate with a global market. Nutrients cycled through new pathways, energy flowed through new circuitry. When guano from a Pacific island could fertilize English wheat fields, when insects, weeds, cultigens, livestock, and peoples could be added (or subtracted) en masse, when wool and autos could be exchanged between Britain and New Zealand, and coal and copra between France and Tahiti, when Pennsylvanian hydrocarbons could substitute for Patagonia's woody fallow, the Earthly ecology of fire had changed on an epic order.

Even more novel was the power of institutions and information. What foresters learned in Burma could influence Uganda, and Canadian experiences with fire could transfer to Australia. Anthropogenic fire no longer responded to "local" circumstances, but shared in a global flow of published science, traveler accounts, and magazine lithographs. The example of the Bori Forest could affect fire regimes in Belize; the light-burning controversy in California could influence fire protection in the jarrah forests of Manjimup. As powerfully as railroads and steamships, institutions could reshape landscapes. Forestry above all could apply and withhold fire according to criteria that were often far removed from the site under consideration; officials could restructure fire regimes they had never seen; and ideas could shape fire-forged landscapes as powerfully as torches and grazers.

In the end, few of forestry's claims were substantiated as more than half-truths. In not a few places trees became weeds, transpiring away the waters they were intended to preserve, crowding and shading out the biodiversity they were supposed to enhance, replacing lush prairies and dappled savannas with opaque brush. Afforestation sent its taproots into irony as often as hardpan. But there was no doubting the conviction of foresters, or the force of their impact; and eventually the backwash returned to Europe itself. In the post–World War II period, Europe found that it too was being reconstituted, that fire was not a problem it had formerly solved and permanently discarded, and that it had to learn (or relearn) from its former colonies the art and science of fire management. Those institutions originally established to project European influence outward now served to receive the unexpected reply.

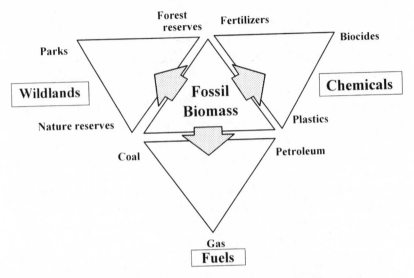

Europe's industrial fire triangle. Fossil fallow and industrial combustion have re-structured pyrotechnologies and land use. Compare with figure on p. 35.

FIRE IN THE ASHES:
EUROPE REKINDLES

Europe's journey outward ended with a return home. The last of the continents that Europe restructured was itself, and it did so with a pervasiveness not witnessed in a millennium. There were several transcendent causes—the impact of the war and its aftermath, the diffusion of industrialization to every village and isle, and the spread of a combustion economy based on coal, oil, and gas. The direct impact of fossil fuels was to restructure the dynamics of Europe's pyrotechnologies and those ecosystems dependent on them. The indirect, and most profound, consequence was to reconfigure the geography of fire altogether.

The production of fossil hydrocarbons traces precisely the contours of modernist fire. Fossil fuel substituted for biomass; fossil fallow abolished the rough diversity of agricultural woods and brush and replaced them with urban enclosure and the industrial fallow of parks and nature preserves. Formerly, productivity and progress had been limited by the source of inputs. Except briefly, it was not possible to take out more than could be replaced. But with fossil biomass, the source was, for practical purposes, unlimited. Although different regions felt the consequences of this conversion at different times and rates, change came to them all, and as the new pyrotechnologies spread it seemed possible to replace fire once and for all with the controlled chemistry of industrial combustion and to abolish flame and smoke permanently from field and forest.

Something quite different occurred. Fire returned. Some places had too much fire, others too little. The first postwar wildfires were an expected outcome of social breakdown, a new verse to an old song. But they did not cease, particularly throughout the Mediterranean, instead metamorphosing like drug-resistant bacteria into more virulent forms. Worse, fires that had once illuminated landscapes like the boreal biota were snuffed out. Not its sources but its sinks established limitations on the natural economy of industrial fire. There was plenty to burn or distill; there were fewer ecological markets in which to dump the manufactured by-products and effluent. Collectively those fire-quakes were the tremors of an environmental tectonics perhaps more profound than any since the Neolithic revolution.

(i)

In August 1949, fires broke out in the Landes, much as they had in 1919 after the First World War. The larger context had indeed repeated itself—drought, a pyrophytic flora, a forest weakly tended during the lengthy war. Some 500 fires burned 47,293 hectares and killed 82 people, including 25 army personnel and 54 firefighters and civilians. Military analogies abounded, as incendiaries were portrayed as saboteurs and the firefight as a theater of war.[63]

Then the denunciations poured forth. Residents said the cause was the resinous woods, gone feral during the war; officials blamed careless or pyromaniacal locals. But all expected that with a return to normalcy the wildfires would be driven back to their cages. Instead, following a hiatus, fires began to reclaim more and more of southern France, especially the southeast, until the region became notorious as the Red Belt. In 1971, fire officials floated the idea for a Project Prometheus that would systematically address the problem, part of a larger scheme for the Conservation of the Mediterranean Forest. In 1974 and again in 1975 the *Revue Forestière Française* devoted special issues to *les incendies des forêts,* and returned, as the fires did, again in 1990. By then the fires had become a seasonal plague, like some kind of arboreal yellow fever; and tourists, not shepherds, were dying in the flames.[64]

The return of wildfire was perplexing. Postwar France had rebuilt its economy and after withdrawing from colonial wars in Indochina and Algeria was enjoying considerable prosperity and political stability. But that was precisely the agency of environmental destabilization. The postwar economy was built on industry and services, not agriculture, and it corroded the rural landscape. The "desertion" of the countryside, set into motion a century before, now removed not only the "surplus" rural population but its core. Ruralites emigrated to the city; urbanites fled, at least seasonally, to the near countryside. Many long-tended landscapes were left to the very old, the very young, the exurban, and the sightseer. If not truly empty, they were emptied of the fussy hands and busy hoofs that had so long shaped them. Tourists replaced transhumant herds, skiers the charcoalers of ages past. Conifer plantations spread across ancient hillsides of heather and abandoned terraces. The fuels were rough, the fires constant, and the ability to combat them insufficient. The old rural order of fire control by close cropping, browsing, and *petit feu* was unraveling; a new one, based on air tankers and firetrucks (internal combustion engines all), foresters, and prescribed burning had not woven a surrogate. Wildfire replaced controlled fire, blotching the littoral like a biotic rash.

Still, modern France was better equipped than the rest of the Mediterranean. There were differentials distinguishable between north and south, east and west, largely according to demographic pressures. There was more fire in the northwest, less in the southeast. Where traditional use intensified, biofuels disappeared into domestic stoves and herds. But in the new landscapes created by rural migration to cities, shrinking populations of livestock, and a combustion economy based on fossil fuels (or atomic power) instead of biomass, fuels proliferated. Fires found something to burn and someone to set them.

The greater the disintegration of rural landscapes, the more rabid the fires. Arson became as endemic as malaria had in previous centuries. Some incendiarism was simply the despair of economically dispossessed groups, some was a more direct expression of political protest, but much of it was not really arson at all but old practices no longer confined within their former place. The ancient European identification of fire with disorder seemed confirmed. Northern Spain and southern France now burned as Corsica and Sardinia traditionally did. Italy saw fire spill through the Apeninnes. Greece erupted into episodic flame as human populations poured into Athens and Thessaloniki and floral populations exploded in the countryside; major outbreaks of fire occurred, with uncanny fidelity, in association with political elections. Here, as elsewhere, only massive agricultural subsidies prevented a complete collapse. By 1990 wildfire had become epidemic. Roughly 90 percent of Europe's total fire load spiraled around the Mediterranean, a black hole of flame.

This new fire genie could not be coaxed back into the old lamps. This was a different kind of fire problem than any the Mediterranean had known since farmers and herders first colonized it. The scene more resembled that in North America or Australia, and Mediterranean Europe turned to those lands rather than its own past for help. From Canada it bought CL-215 air tankers; from America, it borrowed fire behavior models, concepts of fire ecology, and strategies for aggressive suppression. For a while the scene looked like an institu-

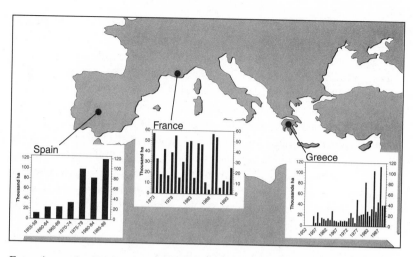

Europe's new fire frontier: the postwar Mediterranean. The unravelling of traditional agriculture (along with deliberate afforestation and rural depopulations) have encouraged a proliferation of fuels, reflected in rising wildfires. Most of Spain's fires flourished in the northwest, where fuels were greatest. Greece exhibited a rising tide of fire; spikes of burning coincided with social unrest, notably during elections. France was more successful in suppressing its revolutionary fires, though whether it could maintain that posture without reintroducing controlled burning or whether wildfires would eventually overwhelm land use (on an Algerian model) was unclear. (Data from FAO and *International Forest Fire News*; University of Wisconsin Cartographic Lab)

tional colonization in reverse with the indigenes—this time increasingly restive European farmers—as the source of contention. Even France, which of course had resisted the most emphatically, soon had CL-215s flying the Côte d'Azur and spoke, *mirabile dictu,* about the virtues of controlled burning.[65]

On all levels of government new institutions emerged. Under FAO/European Economic Community auspices fire seminars were held in Warsaw (1981), Valencia (1988), Athens (1992), and Shushenskoye (1996). The University of Coimbra (Portugal), incredibly, sponsored international symposia, once in 1990 and again in 1994. The major Mediterranean nations worked to consolidate their fire ecology research under the aegis of Sylva Mediterranea. The Mediterranean Agronomic Institute of Chania (Crete) endowed a modern wildland fire science laboratory and training center. And scorched nations themselves established, often for the first time, dedicated fire services to counter the threat. France, Spain, and Italy to impressive effect, Greece to a lesser degree, even Turkey, fielded increasingly sophisticated firefighting forces.[66]

But, as with Europe's colonies, a solution lay with reforms in land use, not with attempted suppression. No organization could cope after-the-fact with such a fire scene, or with the economic earthquake that shook the land. Until genuine surrogates were found for old practices, or until the violent juxtaposition of old and new ceased, the fires could continue. In 1993 Greece suffered its worst fire season on record, 2,417 fires (1,100 is average), with 47,000 hectares of forests burned and 11 farmers dead on the island of Ikaria. Germany sent helicopters, Canada dispatched planes, and the Greek Army formed a smokejumper unit.[67]

And 1994 became for Spain—the country with the most progressive of Mediterranean programs—an *annus horribilis*. In excess of 17,000 wildfires burned 405,000 hectares and killed 31 persons, among them 22 firefighters including a helicopter crew from Russia. Only 67 fires accounted for 74 percent of the burned area, some of them lightning-kindled in the mountains of Aragón, Cataluña, and Valencia. At its height, ICONA mobilized 20,000 firefighters and 210 aircraft; sent out special fire brigades to oversee the largest fires and conduct backfiring; and exploited infrared sensors, computer simulation models of fire behavior, and tapped NOAA satellite imagery.[68]

But the fires roared on, their causes greater than their counterforces. These fires would not be hoed and spaded away or vanish with the suppression of rural arson or political terrorism. They were the fire and sword of a new Reconquest that promised to remake the landscape as thoroughly as had the old.

(ii)

The fire and sword of World War II had swept over Germany from both west and east. By the war's *Götterdämmerung,* aerial firebombing had devastated its industrial cities, and the firestorms at Hamburg, Kassel, and Dresden had become for the Allies' Strategic Bombing Survey trial runs for a future thermonuclear war. But forests too were savagely burned, sometimes deliberately in an attempt to divert manpower, often as an inevitable consequence of fighting. Overcutting and understaffing had added to the destruction. Not least the horrors of the Holocaust branded public memory with a record of hideous fire. Disorder—social, natural, moral—seemed to swirl together in a final conflagration. The postwar artist, Anselm Kiefer, kept the embers alive in paintings that put flame into wooden halls, conifer forests, and charred books made of wood, emblems of Germany's ancient cultural attachment to the forest, all threatened by uncontrolled fire.[69]

The unsettled conditions that accompanied the war's end only aggravated the fire scene. Germany was divided east and west, ruled under military occupation, its economy a shambles. The close cultivation that had traditionally contained fire was impossible; in 1946 and especially in 1947 large fires raged. Then reconstruction began in earnest. Both Germanies, for much the same reasons but with somewhat different methods, sought to control fire and restore forests. West Germany saw the problem more as a question of restoring normalcy, at which point fire could be weeded out of the garden. With a national average of 25 meters of road per hectare, access was easy and fuel complexes broken. East Germany, with more pinelands, more military reservations subject to recurring, accidental fires, an obsession with arson as an antisocial act, and Soviet exemplars of aerial firefighting, developed a more eccentric but specific firefighting apparatus. Revealingly, East Germany produced the only forest-fire textbook written in the postwar era. For both Germanies, however, fire retired to its traditional levels. For both, any fire over 100 hectares qualified as a *Waldbrandkatastrophe*.[70]

So the fires that struck in 1975 and again in 1976 came with the shock of a thunderbolt. Everything went wrong. There had been too much cutting during the war, too much planting in its aftermath. The sand plains of Lower Saxony (Niedersachsen) swayed with young pine afforestations, dense and low. Peasant usage was trivial, even for firewood; the "clean stick" forestry that had once replaced it was impossible in an age of escalating labor costs; small woody material had lost its market and stayed on the land; and postwar silviculture had emphasized restored production, not consumption. A windstorm flattened 100,000 hectares in 1972. Then, in 1975, came drought. Sparks found ready tinder, few natural breaks, and little effective resistance from fire brigades.

There had been scant preparation. The views of senior forester Ehrenfried Liebeneiner were typical. When he received the Karl-Abertz Forestry Prize, he recalled his military service in World War II at the Augustów Forest of Poland. There, in 1942, a fire broke out in dense surface thinnings and threatened the wooden houses of workers. "Polish girls who had been planting pines nearby," he recalled fondly, "went barefoot against the wind toward the firefront and extinguished it with branches. This picture of happy and barefeet children of nature attacking the fire is still clearly in my eyes." There it remained. Under his direction in 1959 and 1968, illustrated leaflets were distributed to foresters and brigades with instructions on firefighting, practically the only training they received. Illustrations showed brave firemen, heads bent against the wind, branches and shovels lowered like the lances of Teutonic knights, charging the head of the fire. Apparently Liebeneiner's vision was in the eyes of many German foresters, who approached the *Waldbrandkatastrophe* with barefoot élan and city firetrucks arrayed like pine boughs.[71]

On August 10, 1975, the critical fire broke out in Südheide Nature Reserve. It quickly overwhelmed local brigades of volunteers and led to a regional declaration of emergency. Other fire brigades rushed to help, though the overly subdivided (and politically jealous) German *Länder* meant that no single state could muster a sufficient force and no truly national response could be coordinated among them. Typically for central Europe, fire prevention was the responsibility of the forestry department, and firefighting was generally handled by urban fire brigades. Untypically, this fire quickly exceeded the capabilities of local fire suppression forces. There was not enough water. The crews were poorly trained for such fires. At one point a brigade from Hamburg was cut off by fast-moving flames, abandoned their equipment, and were saved only by a dramatic helicopter rescue. For its part, the public was mesmerized by graphic images of burned deer and frightened rabbits. Later, in an elaborate public ceremony, a memorial stone was erected in commemoration of the disaster. In the end 8,200 hectares burned.[72]

Greater than the actual damages was the shock—the specter of incompetence, the surprise of restored flame. Even as drought and fire continued the next year, spreading to Brittany heaths and British moors, and as wind leveled more Niedersachsen woods and insects moved in to feast on the dead forest, West Germany determined to squelch a revival. The public response was traditional: lessen the hazards and improve the attack forces. Special legislation for fire protection and disaster response followed in 1978. Even before that, ministerial orders sought to reorganize the landscape. The fires had resulted from unusual conditions, an aftertremor of the war. It was enough to reform silvicultural practices in ways that would break up the indefensible sweeps of pineries. Foresters would, according to the mandated regime, install a system of firebreaks, mix up the forest age classes, and encourage some less flammable hardwoods. Still, changes in markets, usage, and labor costs also ensured that some fires would occur.[73]

For these it was necessary to improve technology and organization. A modern radio communication was established. Steps were taken to allow coordination among *Länder* in the event of similar outbreaks. And experiments were launched in aerial firefighting using helicopter buckets and converted C-160 Transalls as air tankers. The helibuckets were successful, and have been shipped elsewhere in Europe during large fires. The air tanker concept died. Its bizarre successor was a scheme to string explosive cord through very large fire hoses. The resulting blast would blow out flames and saturate fuels. A test conducted outside Berlin succeeded in temporarily extinguishing a windrow of burning Christmas trees, although skeptics thought drizzle from leaden rainclouds probably contributed more to the flames' suppression.[74]

But if the device was flawed, the instinct behind it was true. The fundamental concern was to restore a proper order to the forests, and if traditional agriculture could not furnish suitable tools, then industry would. Pumps, helibuckets, and fire engines would replace sheep, axes, and spruce boughs. East Germany, with more fires but poorer technology, held longer to traditional fire expertise, much as it retained a greater proportion of traditional forest usage. With reunification, however, that knowledge vanished quickly. Revealingly, the experiment with exploding hoses took place in Brandenburg, one of the new *Länder* created by unification, on a site that had previously concentrated much of the former German Democratic Republic's fire expertise. The episode reconfirmed the fire precepts of central Europe: that the social regime determined the regimen of nature, that eruptive fire was an unhappy mixture of social friction and political percussion, and that flame-based technologies could, and should, be replaced by less dangerous devices.

But the story was never quite that simple. In the face of immense odds, Germany had retained its forests. It had satisfied the central European ideal that 25 to 33 percent of the land should be wooded. Despite demographic pressures inherent in one of the most densely populated regions of the world, despite an eighteenth-century legacy that had driven its forests to the wall, despite extraordinary economic changes and two world wars, and despite changes in species composition and soil profiles, the forests had endured. Inevitably they would be compared with forests in other parts of the world, and as Germany's population became more urban and better educated, Germans would see the *Wald* as something more than beams and pulp, and, in select circles, fire as something other than primitive wastage. In particular, there was the perplexing example of the United States.

In the postwar era, America had established the technological standards for wildland firefighting. With war-surplus equipment, it had pioneered mechanized fire suppression and aerial attack; and on its vast public lands, it routinely marshaled legions of firefighters for prolonged campaigns. But amid the extravaganza there were dissenting voices and disparate values. The concept (soon to become an ideology) of wilderness insisted that lightning fires belonged in wildlands, that controlled burning could substitute where necessary for natural ignition, and that the social order in parks and nature preserves, at least, should emulate the natural order. In 1962 the privately endowed Tall Timbers Research Station in Florida inaugurated annual fire ecology conferences that soon attracted researchers and practitioners from around the world. Its premises were that fire was natural, that prescribed fire could be a benign tool of nature management, and that categorical fire exclusion was a mistake. In the southern United States, moreover, even industrial pine forests began to practice controlled underburning to reduce fuels.[75]

Gradually European foresters learned of these developments. In 1973 a group of European fire scientists attended that year's Tall Timbers fire ecology conference. Incredibly, this was the first time that fire specialists from around Europe had met specifically to discuss fire. Their range of concerns was broad, from stubble burning to slash burning; but a particularly vexing question was the status of fire in nature reserves. Behind that concern was the degree to which fire might be tolerated on sites for which it was historically important. Certainly many sites faced extinction in the absence of the syncopated cutting, grazing, and burning that had created them. Even mowing and chemicals were not sufficient surrogates. Perhaps fire was not intrinsically evil, perhaps fire's damages, like Paracelsus's definition of poison, lay with the dosage. Perhaps the fundamental problem was not ecological but psychological, the reflexive horror with which postwar central Europe saw fire.[76]

For all this Europeans from every region had plenty of precedents, ample ranks of dissenters of their own. Among Germans, Conrad and Müller had argued in the 1920s that surface fires (*Bodenfeuer*) could be a "friend to the forester" and had shaped the marvelous pineries of the Balkans. Geographers and scholars of land use recognized the indispensable role of fire in preindustrial agriculture, and wondered how those traditional landscapes could survive the extirpation of fire. But each time that contrary opinions had flared, they had been swatted down by those who actually administered the programs. So they had, too, in America during the 1920s and 1930s. In the postwar period, however, American critics rose like a choir. Western Europe heard.[77]

A spark glimmered at the University of Freiburg. Forestry dean Jean-Pierre Vité, whose family owned a house in Texas, encouraged further study of this exotic question, and in 1974–75 a graduate student, Johann Goldammer, studied at Tall Timbers. His diploma thesis, delivered in 1976, was a theoretical study of fire ecology and management (it apparently introduced the term *Feuerökologie* into German). Within a year the indefatigable Goldammer was conducting the first experimental "prescribed fire" in Germany in decades, and was arranging for a European fire ecology symposium on the Tall Timbers model. Many of the conferees had participated in the 1973 Florida session, and there were two token Americans; but this was an opportunity for central Europeans to consolidate their knowledge. Along with the proceedings, Goldammer rewrote and published his thesis. The Freiburg fire symposia became a recurrent affair. And Goldammer became a missionary for fire ecology.[78]

Like most prophets, he was better received outside his native country. Officials were deeply suspicious of fire, more worried about another *Waldbrandkatastrophe* than about the subtle values of controlled burning. Intensive regulation of forests made fire introduction difficult, and nature reserves categorically refused to allow it; even scientific experimentation was sometimes denied. The forest crisis in central Europe—the notorious dieback—was perceived as a product of introduced industrial pollutants, not the removal of traditional practices. With chemical surrogates and fossil fuels available, foresters attacked fallow (and the fire with which it was inextricably linked) with the zeal with which Bauhaus architects had removed ornamentation. The forest faculty at Freiburg refused to accept fire in its curriculum. Still, under FAO and European Economic Commission auspices more fire seminars were held. Goldammer carried his campaign to Indonesia under Germany's forestry aid mission and edited for FAO its biannual periodical, *International Forest Fire News.*

What finally gave fire an institutional presence was the specter of a universal holocaust, the Niedersachsen *Waldbrandkatastrophe* expanded to a global scale. In 1982, Paul Crutzen and John Birks published a scenario of a thermonuclear war in which high-altitude detonations kindled massive forest fires that spread an immense pall of smoke, a "twilight at noon." Fire and war, combustion and atmospheric contamination—the proposal for a "nuclear winter" captured perfectly the fear of NATO-stockpiled Pershing and Cruise missiles, alarm over air pollution, and the deep suspicion of wildfire. Wildland fire became an object of serious scientific investigation.[79]

But as research deepened, and as the topic of climate change—a global warming instead of a global cooling—implicated biomass burning in the tropics, the need for better knowledge of fire ecology became undeniable. Atmospheric chemistry Europe knew; fire ecology it did not, not even in temperate and boreal forests. The prophetic Goldammer found an audience. He received an appointment with the Max Planck Institute for Chemistry, established a fire ecology research unit in Freiburg, attracted students, organized symposia, issued declarations, arranged for European seminars, and became the most widely traveled fire scientist in history.

The global fire community had found in Johann-Georg Goldammer a successor to Dietrich Brandis. That Brandis had begun as a botanist and then trained in forestry, while Goldammer had begun as a forester and become an ecologist, was symbolic of a century's change in fire philosophy. Through his furious pursuit of fire across the globe, Goldammer succeeded in restoring, however tenuously, a central fire to *Mitteleuropa*. In 1996, with Goldammer as lead referent, the Alfred Toepfer Academy for Nature Protection sponsored the first German workshop on the role of fire in nature reserves.

(iii)

For boreal Europe the crisis was, increasingly, the fire that wasn't there. At the end of World War II, Finland had been savaged with burning, and the relocation of refugees from Soviet-confiscated Karelia had inspired a vigorous if temporary revival of classic forest swidden. Neutral Sweden, however, had not only escaped war damage but boomed during the conflict (with a 20 percent increase in GDP), and saw its economy accelerate afterward as its intact factories and forests fed the postwar reconstruction of central Europe. In place of wartime wildfires it adapted agricultural burning to forestry.

But if Sweden was more successful than most of Europe in accommodating traditional fire, it soon proved more ruthless than most in expunging it. Its more fully prescribed social order dictated a more fully cultivated natural order. There

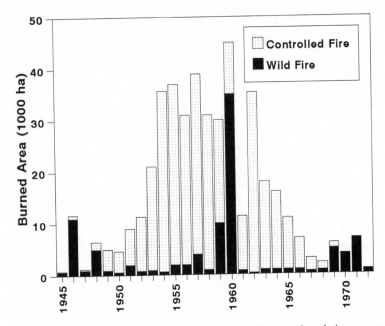

Finnish fire: controlled burning revives, then collapses. But note the relative proportions of controlled fires to wildfires. The real fire budget of Europe is measured not in its wildfires but in the loss of its agricultural burning. (Data from Siren 1973)

was no place in a social democratic state for fire. By the mid-1980s Sweden—a state synonymous with statistics, the founder of the modern census—no longer kept figures on fire. Forest fires had, according to official opinion, vanished into the past along with rune stones and boat burials. There was little evidence of it, and less need for it. That, paradoxically, was exactly the problem.[80]

The future might have gone differently. For a while Swedish forestry pioneered an imaginative technique that adapted *svedjebruk* to the needs of saw-timber logging. Throughout the pineries of Norrland, foresters left mature seed trees standing, then burned off the logging slash beneath them according to regular procedures. In the purged ash beds, the pine regenerated magnificently. Without fire, in fact, practical silviculturalists discovered that pine often did poorly, that other species would replace it, or that, in dense raw humus, little regeneration of any kind occurred. The great forests of Scots pine, they knew, had sprouted after fires, many after forest swidden. They needed a surrogate practice of controlled burning, and found it in *hyggesbränning*. For Norrland—for the Swedish timber industry now that the old-growth forests had been cut—*hyggesbränning* had, according to advocates, "extraordinary meaning."[81]

As a silvicultural technique, *hyggesbränning* began with experiments in 1921 along the Malå River under the direction of Joel Wretlind. They continued for twenty-five years as Wretlind published major reports, turned the Malå region into a demonstration area, conducted tours, and even directed a training film. If the outcome was as much art as science, that was after all the general state of Nordic silviculture. But the experiments were far from haphazard. They sought, factor by factor, to reduce the uncertainty surrounding Scots pine regeneration and growth, to identify prime sites and good times for burning, and to concoct adequate tools and techniques for control. They built on classic boreal-forest science, such as the 1918 studies of Henrik Hesselman. That workers started fires with birch-bark torches and contained the flames with pine boughs only emphasized the continuity between a farmed past and a forested future. And if natural methods were exploited, the goal was unequivocally social: to bring the land into "full production."[82]

Hyggesbränning also served to limit the wildfires that so often gorged on untreated logging slash. A state-sponsored committee on forest fires, convened during the war years, even accepted it in principle. The practice was deliberate and specific, and if hazardous, it was a well-calculated risk. The surrounding landscape, moreover, was increasingly a web of roads and bristled with fire lookouts. As production swelled after the war, so did the area committed to *hyggesbränning*. Recovered from its shock, Finland followed suit. By the early 1960s, controlled burning for boreal forestry was common, and despite silvicultural skepticism from central Europe, generally accepted. Then it collapsed.[83]

The reasons were many. The pioneering generation had passed away, and with them a lifetime of close experience. There were difficulties with the technique—failures when pushed beyond its prescriptions, wildfires from careless escapes. The fundamental reason, however, was the changing character of Swedish society. Steadily, Sweden's population was becoming increasingly urban. The Social Democrats who reigned in the Riksdag wanted full production, scientific methods, and a nature that sustained, rather than threatened, Swedish society. *Hyggesbränning* seemed an archaic and dangerous folk practice out of step with the sleek modernism and universality that had become a state goal. Compared with the green revolution that was sweeping silviculture, *hyggesbränning* appeared wasteful and incapable of sustaining the full production that was the ambition of Sweden's political economy, or of ensuring the security, both physical and social, that was the obsession of Sweden's political philosophy.

Instead, to ensure a maximum and predictable harvest, commercial forestry dominated land use. (Less than 2 percent of Sweden's land is in nature reserves, and these are in widely scattered patches and not of high commercial value.) Further, revisions in the forest law prescribed more and more minutely the type of commercial forestry that Sweden would tolerate. Draining, scarifying (plowing), mechanical planting and harvesting, chemical fertilizers and pesticides—all the extra-ecological wealth of coal- and petroleum-derived products and combustion power superseded fire and fallow. Forest law prohibited more than four cubic meters of dead wood per hectare. Mile after mile of Swedish forest presented the eerie spectacle of woods without snags, stumps, or downed logs. There was little left to burn. Fire lookouts came down. Fire faded away, and the country became a vast tree farm. Fallow was an embarrassment, the ecological equivalent of ranks of unemployed workers in nature's economy. It would be brought into production, assimilated into the nurturing institutions of a welfare state. Once the conditions that encouraged it were removed, fire would, like violent crime and other antisocial behavior, cease. Not since 1933 had Sweden experienced a national fire emergency.

But a sense of ecological emergency began to fester. Its origins were partly ideological, partly environmental. Swedish environmentalism was almost wholly preoccupied with the protection of humans from the hazards around them. It was a subset of Swedish social philosophy, obsessed with questions of security and equity. The environment existed solely to serve human needs, and those needs derived from social relationships. A secure society would produce a stable environment, and a just society would produce an ecologically righteous environment. The one would mirror the other. Equally, an unbalanced environment could not sustain a balanced society. Sweden moved to eliminate toxins, carcinogens, food contaminants, floods, bark beetles, allelopathic shrubs, and of course fires.

Nature's economy, however, did not operate on the same principles as Swedish society's. Too often the outcome of environmental engineering was to homogenize the biota, to abolish all the oddities and eccentricities, the intricate niches, and the unpredictable events inherent in a less socialized nature. For this reformation, while forestry furnished the means, a vision of society proposed the idealized end. Eventually the process leveled once-mosaicked landscapes and abraded away boreal biodiversity. Foresters had mistaken social demand for natural productivity.

The drive to restructure society to a classless norm had its counterpart in biotic homogenization. Sweden's duo-culture of Scots pine and Norway spruce had replaced mottled forest mosaics, culled away older trees, and generally substituted biomass for biodiversity. Ecologists estimate that some 200 species of plants and animals may be at risk in the boreal forest, an astonishing figure granted the relatively low number of species characteristic of the biota. Among them is *Melanophila acuminata*, a beetle equipped with an infrared-sensing organ that allows it to seek out fresh burns. Not only species but whole landscapes threatened to disappear. Mires, meadows, heath, old fields, grazed *utmark*, free-flowing rivers and lakes, offshore archipelagoes, old *svedjor*, virtually all went to support forestry on which, in turn, so much of Sweden's export income and labor structure depended. But even where forestry did not intrude, agriculture was receding under the stress of market forces. Only subsidies kept something like traditional fields in existence. And even before Sweden joined the European Union, subsidies were inevitably diminishing and the prevalence of old-cultivated landscapes with them. Certainly there was little occasion for labor-intensive *brännodling*.[84]

Even preserved sites often failed from fragmentation and the elimination of sustaining anthropogenic practices. Dalby Söderskog National Park, outside Lund, suffered a loss of 41 percent of its species between 1925 and 1970, almost 1 percent a year, thanks to biotic isolation and the abolition of disturbances. Ängsö National Park, early established (1909) to preserve a meadow landscape, saw that environment revert to weeds and invasive trees once officials removed the farmers (and their fires) who had created and tended the fields. Swedish environmental protection had meant removing land from industrial production, not tending it for its own goals. It meant eradicating disturbances, not recreating them. Certainly it did not mean that reserved lands should be deliberately burned.[85]

Ideology mattered. It was embarrassing for a country so long considered a model of social relations to suffer accusations of ecological abuse. Sweden could hardly criticize poor forestry elsewhere and its accompanying social costs—in Brazil or Russia, for example—while open to charges of poor environmental care itself. Threatened boycotts by Green parties, notably in Germany, could apply to Sweden as to the Third World. Sweden's concept of environmental protection was to protect society from nature, not nature from society. Where it saw environmental threats, they took the form of outside pollutants (acid rain, radioactive fallout) that were themselves of anthropogenic origin. Neutral Sweden could not imagine itself, as others could, as a source of ecological problems. Was not the land clothed in useful trees? Were not waste and disturbances eliminated? Clearly, Sweden found itself alienated from the intellectual excitement of ecological philosophies. Clearly, too, environmental ideas could have social consequences. Ignoring them was bad politics, and bad business.

Rectifying the problem was not easy, however. Sweden had lost its prime chance to establish nature reserves. Other than Muddus National Park (preserved by a quirk of geology that prevented easy logging), sites were scattered and small, often no larger than urban parks. There was little that could be considered natural, and for many environments there was little meaning in anything other than cultural landscapes. But both needed fire. Looking primarily to North America for ideas and inspiration, a forest science group at the University of Umeå began to scrutinize fire ecology, recover the fire history of the boreal forest, adapt the Canadian forest fire prediction system, and even conduct small experimental burns. At one point they persuaded the state forestry service to leave intact a burned hillside at Åtmyrliden in Norrland so that they could study the postfire recovery process. They poked among the burned snags and fallen logs like archaeologists excavating Iron Age ruins.[86]

Still, nature reserves were few, forestry vast, and the future of land use uncertain. The environment had ideas of its own. So did the global economy for wood fiber. So did the integration of Europe. As competition intensified over wood products, Sweden would have to fight for market share with pulp from Portugal and sawtimber from Siberia. Yet its labor costs were high and conifer growth in Norrland agonizingly slow. And as agricultural subsidies lessened, more farmland would pass into forestry or other uses, a process certain to accelerate with entry into the European Union. By 1990, Swedish forestry was harvesting only 60 to 70 percent of the annual increment growth.

There would, in brief, be more fuel. Eventually there would be more fire. The question was whether fire would come accidentally or deliberately. The Finns reached into the past, saw controlled burning as part of their heritage, like tar barrels and bark bread, and planned some cautious fire reintroductions to northern nature reserves and perhaps to forestry. The Swedes had struggled to look to a future based on more universalist principles. They knew that to reform fire was to reform society, not an easy choice. Where prescribed fire was an issue, advocates often found it easier to point to North American exemplars than to their own long legacy of folk use.

But whatever model they chose, they could no longer pretend that fire was expungeable, or that the attempt to eradicate it came without costs.[87]

(iv)

If any place seemed immune to fire, it was England. Overcast England had little opportunity for fire, and overcrowded England had little tolerance for it. Even wartime firebombing had confined itself to London and Coventry, and fire ecology to the study of burned-out basements and newly vacant lots. The dramatic postwar reforms of British politics led to greater not lesser control over fire practices. New legislation regulated the burning of rough pasture—for Scotland, the Hill Farming Act (1946), and for England and Wales, the Heather and Grass-burning Regulations (1949). In 1947, Parliament effectively nationalized the British fire services, which exercised jurisdiction not only for urban fire but for wildfires on any land. While foresters and landowners had responsibility for prevention and assisted with planning, actual fire suppression fell to the county brigades organized under the Fire Services Act. Surely, fire would become inconsequential.

But other postwar reforms countered these effects. The industrialization of agriculture took some marginal land out of production and broke the ever-more-tightly-wound mainspring of mixed farming. Forestry sopped up much of the spillage by planting on sites unsuitable for modern farming. Between 1947 and 1991 afforestation increased from 724,000 hectares to 2,141,000 hectares. This rapid stocking of (primarily) conifers placed extensive planta-tions at risk to fire through their early years. Still, the primary sources of fire were railroads and agricultural burning, and further legislation and lawsuits reduced the railroad threat to nil. That left farming, and with more intensive husbandry the prospects were for further reductions in fire use. Surprisingly, perhaps, just the opposite occurred. Farmers found themselves with vast fields of unused straw, perhaps as much as 7.5 million tons. To remove it they burned.[88]

Many factors led to the liberation of straw. But behind them was the break-down in the intricate integration of livestock with field crops, and behind that, the exploitation of fossil hydrocarbons for energy and chemicals. Artificial fer-tilizers reduced the need for manure, tractors replaced draft animals, and the economics of rapid transport and international trade argued against the use of herds and flocks on small farms. The animals no longer needed so much straw for feed or bedding, and farmers no longer required straw for building or fuel. No one in Britain's industrial cities demanded straw for any reason. The straw remained on the fields. Certainly the economics of burning it in situ was favor-able; and, so many farmers believed, was the ecology. Field burning, after all, dated back to the Neolithic.[89]

Experiments tended to agree. In fields planted to winter wheat, spring cere-als, barley, sugar beets, and potatoes, straw burning had negligible effects on yields, and some positive results in controlling weeds. The alternative prac-tice, plowing the straw under, depressed yields and often fed soil organisms, sometimes with deleterious results. In effect, the practice substituted internal combustion for open burning and replaced one fuel (straw) by applying another (petrol). Since all the sites had adequate inorganic nutrients, the potential for fire to stimulate growth in nutrient-poor sites was not tested. Rather, applica-tion of artificial fertilizers was the single most significant practice found to affect yields, and increasingly manure was less usable, and more expensive, than arti-ficial fertilizers. Straw-burning farmers felt vindicated.

The controversy, however, was not about a practice per se but its context. Britain was urban, and its rural scene steadily more exurban. England was one of the most densely populated countries on the planet. Smoke was a blasted nuisance, escaped fires distressingly common, burned hedgerows and a black-ened countryside a bloody disappointment for weekend recreationists, and the spectacle of postmodern Britain setting its fields on fire an embarrassment, like New Age revivals of druidic rituals. An urbanized public, its arguments increasingly emotional, became obsessed with the prospect of massive fire mortality among birds, mice, and rabbits. In October 1972, *The Times* editorialized that "straw burning probably did more to alienate general sympathy from modern farming than any other issue for years, including intensive methods of animal production."[90]

In 1984 the British National Farmers Union responded with a voluntary Straw Burning Code that sought to reduce nuisance smoke and escaped burns. Fires would back into the wind; there would be no burning on Sundays and bank holiday Mondays; fire brigades would be notified in advance; and so on. A year later, researchers tested compliance by monitoring the infrared channel on NOAA weather satellites (their conclusion: the code was working). Still, too much had changed in the English garden. The landscape was crossed with powerlines and gaslines, both emblems of industrial combustion and both vulnerable to wildfires. The motoring public wanted access to the countryside, and didn't want it dressed in mourning. Recreationists replaced railroads as a source of ignition.[91]

More profoundly, the public could see fire only through a smoked glass, darkly. It saw flame in terms of IRA firebombs, fires terrorizing subways and high-rises, and continental-sized fires burning Brazilian rainforests. Besides, fire made good political theater. Natural fires were anthropomorphized, and urban fires naturalized. Environmentalists believed they could not condemn savanna burning in Africa and the fire-clearing of rainforest in Brazil, Indonesia, and Malaysia if Britain burned in its own backyard. They sought the abolition of fire with the zeal that nineteenth-century activists had campaigned for the abolition of slavery and the prevention of cruelty to animals. Postimperial Britain badgered fire-flushed developing countries like an environmental nanny. Inevitably, the pyrophobia affected moor management in Britain, for if burning was bad for stubble, then why should be it good for *Calluna* and *Molinia?* While "technically satisfactory," E. R. Bullen concluded, the practice of straw burning was probably doomed. "In a situation where, until recently, all fires were bad fires the psychology of fire has necessarily an important influence on mankind's thinking."[92]

That observation was wrong in its evidence but right in its conclusion. All fires had not been bad fires "until recently"; quite the reverse. And mankind had not so reasoned, only temperate Europe, and then principally its urban elites. Britain was applying to itself a logic that it had tried, with wildly mixed results, to apply in its fire-prone colonies. Now fire came full circle. The Britain that kept the home fires burning during the war wanted nothing to do with fire outside that hearth. Its imperial experiences with fire Great Britain shed as rapidly as it did its empire. While the postwar economy made fire plausible, the postmodern garden declared it anathema. The controversy ended with the abolition of straw burning.

(v)

If Britain withdrew inward, shrinking to its insular hearth, the Soviet Union marched outward, projecting its newly amassed firepower. Between Stalin's Great Purge and the Great Patriotic War, the USSR had passed through the flames. Its rapid if lopsided industrialization gave it mechanical tools for fire control; its ideological commitment to science made fire research not merely possible but mandatory; and the Cold War (and renewed hostility with China) endowed Siberia with geopolitical interest. The Soviet Union needed its Siberian forests, demanded control over dissident landscapes, and wanted a clear sky in what had become an aerial frontier for nuclear-laden bombers and ICBMs. If Stalin's proposed Great Transformation of Nature would reconfigure the Soviet relationship to steppe and taiga, and to the fires that inhabited them, the Cold War helped determine the character of that reconstruction.

An immense taiga and a sparse population meant that fire control could only develop by aircraft. In 1921, a year after Lenin's Executive Committee passed its special act regarding "The Struggle with Forest Fires," a forestry conference heard recommendations for the use of airplanes and tethered balloons. Experimental flights for forestry continued haphazardly throughout the 1920s. In 1926 an attempt at Leningrad to use a plane for aerial reconnaissance failed ignominiously when the pilot promptly flew to Estonia and defected.[93]

A new attempt began in 1931 when Aeroflot furnished an aircraft to a research program under S. P. Rumyantsev and G. G. Samoilovich of the Leningrad Forestry Academy. The flight of July 7 in Nizhni Novgorod (Gorky after 1932) is considered the effective beginning of aerial fire protection. The next year operational flights were organized for southern Karelia and the northern Leningrad oblast, and in 1933 the program transferred to the All-Union Scientific Research Institute of Agriculture and Forestry Aviation. The program expanded into Komi and Gorky oblasts, and tenuously into the central Urals and Far East. By 1935 experiments had created a new profession, the pilot-observer, and had established the organizational principles for aerial fire patrols that would underlie all its future evolution. In 1936 a newly constituted All-Union Trust of Forest Aviation absorbed the program. For the first time a base was established in Siberia, at Irkutsk.

The original task was primarily observational. The pilot-observer could sight fires even in remote lands, then report their location. Observation of course did not lead to extinction. But the early euphoria inspired a host of airborne suppression ideas. In its extreme form it was hoped that aircraft, equipped with appropriate technologies, could extinguish fires by themselves. They could drop explosives to build fireline, bomb fire fronts with water and chemicals, and patrol smoldering edges. This proved chimerical, but elements of the scheme did reach experimental trials. A. V. Funikov in the steppes and A. M. Simsky, V. F. Stepanov, V. G. Nesterov, and N. P. Kurbatsky in the taiga proposed means of dropping chemicals and water from aircraft. Dry chemicals could be sprayed over grass fires, but in forest cover sprayed water drifted too widely; besides, the aircraft had little load capacity. Other experiments attempted to drop explosives and chemicals in glass ampoules (a kind of reverse Molotov cocktail), again with few positive results. Exploding fire extinguishers only scattered embers, sometimes to a distance of 300 meters. It was quickly apparent that only firefighters could fight fire. In 1934, Georgy Aleksandrovich Mokeev proposed the aerial delivery of firefighters by parachute. Two years later the scheme was tested outside Semonovsky.[94]

It was a pivotal idea for a pivotal year. The All-Union Trust for Forest Aviation, organized in February 1936, marks the onset of institutional permanency for aerial fire protection. The next year, under the direction of Mokeev, a smokejumper training school was established at the dacha of the Russian artist Borisov, outside Krasnoborsk. It was an audacious scheme. The only aircraft available were PO-2 planes. In order to jump, it was necessary to step outside the cockpit and stand on the wing until the pilot—without benefit of windshield, fumbling with topographic maps and joystick—signaled to leap. There were no radios. There was no protective equipment by which to descend safely through the forest canopy. There were no handtools. The aircraft could carry only one smokejumper at a time. The "parachute-fireman" landed near the closest village, rallied the populace to assist, marched back to the site of the fire, and after the fire was out, often with local guides to assist him, commenced his return to the base. He would walk where paths were present, ride if a horse was available, ford streams on pole rafts, and fend for himself until he returned to the base. In 1937 there were seventeen smokejumpers for all the USSR, one a woman.[95]

Boldly the system felt its way deeper into the taiga. New bases were established at Tyumen, along the Urals, Alma-Ata, in Krasnoyarsk, at Khabarovsk. Their effectiveness was minimal, but their symbolism vast, and out of their experiences and legends evolved the phenomenal postwar expansion of fire protection. Miraculously, Avialesookhrana—the aerial forest protection service—survived the war. Nazi Germany's invasion in 1941 posed a greater crisis than taiga fires, for most of its pilots and jumpers were immediately inducted into the Red Army, some within a day of the invasion. Primorye oblast celebrated the inaugural flight for aerial fire protection on June 21; the next day, with the Wehrmacht's invasion, the program ended. A few bases managed to appeal the order, and saved some select figures for training and administration. But the amount of land under protection quickly shrank, planes left for the front, and the able-bodied were quickly drafted into the military. Of 120 pilots, pilot-observers, and smokejumpers inducted, only 20 returned after the war. The burden of the program fell instead to women. For the duration of the war they served as pilots, observers, and firefighters. Their numbers were not large, but they kept aerial firefighting on life support. Those men who survived, like chief pilot-observer V. V. Podolsky, gave continuity to a decade's experience, and on them Avialesookhrana would rebuild in the postwar era.

In 1949 a reorganization transferred Avialesookhrana into the apparatus of the Civil Aviation Administration. Surplus military aircraft and demobilized paratroopers allowed an intensification of patrols where bases existed—mostly in the boreal forests of European Russia—and an expansion where they had not, largely in Siberia and the Far East. The Irkutsk base, now equipped with smokejumpers, not merely observers, hived off cloned centers in Yakutsk and Krasnoyarsk. Around 1950 the service adopted the Nesterov index and adjusted its patrols to forecast fire danger. There were further experiments, inconclusive, with chemicals and explosives in which fires were literally bombed. But the major reforms followed technological improvements—radio communications, new parachute designs, protective clothing that allowed for jumping into wooded areas, and above all an abundant, reliable aircraft capable of transporting a squad of smokejumpers. The venerable Antonov-2 did just that, so it became possible to attack fires without the assistance of conscripted villagers. In 1955, Avialesookhrana experimented with the MI-4 helicopter for carrying water and personnel. In 1957 the Central Air Base at Pushkino organized advanced training courses.[96]

As Soviet industry further mechanized, so did firefighting. As more of Siberia and the Far East felt the ax, so more of their fires experienced the counterforce of shovel and bough. Fire control assisted ethnic nationalities dependent on reindeer by preserving lichen woodlands ("deer pastures"), and thus allowing herds to multiply. It helped bind disparate landscapes to a common Soviet purpose. Fire suppression, for example, was seen as a means of containing the strict nature reserves, *zapovedniki,* that were otherwise left outside the command economy. Aerial fire control was to the taiga what the tractor-plow was to the steppes, part of a socialist revolution of nature's economy. The paramilitary character of aerial fire control, in particular, perfectly suited the Soviet system. What ended World War II with a staff of 200, by 1990 boasted 8,500 aerial firefighters. When, during the 1972 fires in European Russia, 1,100 Siberian smokejumpers were rushed to the firelines around Moscow, Avialesookhrana glowed with pride. The periphery had literally saved the center. A grateful (and frightened) center replied with a major investment of rubles.[97]

Fire suppression suited the style of the neo-Stalinist Brezhnev era. Every aspect of Soviet fire felt the state's rekindled (if somber) interest. Controlled burning was banned; a national fire prevention symbol (a moose fleeing flames) was promoted; fire sciences escalated; and the investment in fire suppression swelled as grandly as hydroelectric schemes and the Baikal-Amur Railway. Fire control promised security. It relied on the same equipment needed to hold restive satellites in Eastern Europe or to invade unruly neighbors like Afghanistan. It promoted a paramilitary institution. It silenced ecological dissent. The Brezhnev era saw fire as a problem and responded as it knew best.

But effectiveness required more than political edicts, sheer size, and a national fire-prevention logo. Several technological innovations made Avialesookhrana, by the mid-1970s, into a major presence in the taiga. Both smaller and larger helicopters became available. The MI-2 allowed for rapid reconnaissance and small deliveries of men and equipment; the MI-8, however, became a workhorse. It could transport whole crews, sling motorized pumps and helibuckets of water, and deposit firefighters directly on site, even in difficult terrain, through a sophisticated rappelling system. By 1970 60 percent of aerial operations depended on helicopters; by 1990, 75 percent; and that number was limited only by the availability of aircraft. In the aftermath of the 1972 fires, too, Avialesookhrana acquired mechanized ground equipment, some of which it integrated with aerial forces in places of high hazard, and some of which it transported with the aid of heavy helicopters. There were experiments with airborne infrared detection systems and field trials to artificially induce rainfall over large fires, to counter dry lightning with wet thunderstorms. Perhaps most critically the long experiments with explosives culminated in an explosive cord, powerful and portable, with which to construct firelines. Now it became possible for small numbers of firefighters to build long corridors of fireline through scrub, forests overgrown with roots, rocky hillsides, any terrain in the taiga. With dramatic suddenness burned area began to plummet.[98]

Even as it placed more and more land under its protection, even as wandering survey parties and defective locomotives kindled more fires, the actual area burned shrank, and in some cases imploded. In 1936 the Arkhangelsk fire center had protected 6.4 million hectares, of which 98,000 hectares burned. In 1985 it protected 44 million hectares, of which 643 burned. In 1946 each fire reported by the Urals fire center averaged 1,292 hectares; by 1980, 1.33 hectares. Sadly, such statistics are deceptive, even corrupt. The boreal forest is notoriously sensitive to large, episodic events that are cruel to the statistical averages beloved by Soviet planners. Probably 10 percent of the reported fires accounted for 90 percent of the burned area, and 10 percent of fire years, those experiencing drought, nurtured the big fires. By 1990, moreover, like the rest of the Soviet system, fire protection reeked with bogus production figures. The rule of thumb was that each reporting site reduced the dimensions of a fire by a half to a full order of magnitude. A 1,000 hectare fire in northern Buryat ASSR might be reported to Ulan-Ude as 500 hectares, and to Moscow as 100 hectares.[99]

But there is no question that the size of burned area did diminish dramatically. A first-order fire suppression system—and the one fielded by the mid-1970s was first-rate—can dramatically reduce fires. The profile of fire diminution is similar to that characteristic of the other industrialized nations with boreal forests—comparable to Sweden, Finland, Canada, and the United States. What the Soviets did in Siberia, Americans who were outfitted with similar technologies and purposes achieved in Alaska. The problem is that those initial gains become progressively more difficult to sustain, economically and ecologically.

For most countries the mounting resistance had to do with the problem of diminishing returns and, as they begin to assess the ecological consequences of fire suppression, problems of biodiversity and fuel buildup. At some point they realize that, for wildlands, suppression is a necessary but not a sufficient program of fire management. All this was no less true for the USSR. But the Soviet system had political burdens the others lacked. Aerial fire suppression was, in the final analysis, a political institution, an expression of the state's geopolitical will. It responded to the political ecology of a totalitarian regime. When the Soviet state imploded, beginning in August 1991, so did the apparatus of fire control.

Before that collapse, the Soviet Union had the largest wildland firefighting system in the world. But its scientific apparatus was no less impressive. In the prewar period most expertise clustered around Leningrad, particularly at the Forestry Academy. In 1931, Professor M. E. Tkachenko introduced the term "forest pyrology" (*lesoi pirology*) to embrace the full range of fire-related topics, this within a collection of edited papers on wildland fire. Through various forestry institutes (the Central Scientific Research Forestry Institute in Leningrad, under the dual leadership of Professors Serebrennikov and Matreninsky, was especially important), fire sciences developed throughout the 1930s, survived Stalin's purges, and with surprisingly cosmopolitan curiosity explored all aspects of fire behavior, ecology, control, and use. Forest fires became, further, a subject for the Soviet Academy of Sciences.

Interest was theoretical as well as practical. The primary techniques were statistical (as in the United States and Canada): attempts to determine more precisely just when, where, and under what conditions fires started and spread, and what biotic changes they induced. The ultimate objective was practical, the better control of wildfire. Scholars began, in brief, to translate folk knowledge into a scientific format. In 1937, Serebrennikov and Metreninsky, on behalf of the forest research institutes, published a popular textbook on fire science and control. But the war destroyed, literally, the Serebrennikov School, both of whose leaders died during the siege of Leningrad.[100]

Still fire science survived the assault. The school's two major students, I. S. Melekhov and V. G. Nesterov, persisted and completed their theses after the war; and research, like industry, began to move beyond the Urals. Nesterov amalgamated wartime firefighting, offensive and defensive, into a 1944 text, *Forest Fire Control,* and later (1949) invented a simple index for estimating fire danger, still in use forty years later. Melekhov soon established his credentials as the "founder of Russian forest pyrology." His 1947 text, *The Nature of Forests and Forest Fires,* went well beyond fireline technologies, and was in fact far more sophisticated and inclusive than comparable works in the West.[101]

The postwar reconstruction built on its prewar precedents. In 1949 the Leningrad Forest Institute created a special Forest Fire Protection Department, headed by N. P. Kurbatsky. The department quickly rebuilt the Serebrennikov legacy into a major research endeavor. Among its members was the indefatigable Mokeev, endlessly experimenting with fire control technologies. That same year the Far Eastern Scientific Forestry Research Institute in Khabarovsk commenced systematic studies on fire behavior and danger rating and on fire control technology. Its leader, Dr. A. M. Starodumov, was, like his counterparts, keenly interested in developments in the West, particularly North America, and personally translated the dominant American text, Kenneth Davis's *Forest Fire: Control and Use.* In 1959 the Soviet Academy of Sciences established the V. N. Sukachev Institute for Forest Science in Krasnoyarsk. There it dedicated a Forest Fire Research Laboratory and recruited Kurbatsky to direct it. The history of postwar fire research is largely the record of these three institutions.

They took on specialties, some peculiar to the geography of their regions, some the result of history and personality. Leningrad concentrated on forest pyrology in European Russia and specialized in aerial operations, including detection and weather modification. The Krasnoyarsk laboratory studied the fire ecology of Siberia, but also pioneered research in fire fundamentals and became, as much as any place, the locus for national models. The Khabarovsk institute focused on the unusual conditions of the Far East, adopting as specialities the modeling of fire spread and fire danger prediction. The Academy, moreover, sponsored research through its regular programs in forestry and ecology. In sum, the expansion of aerial fire control demanded an expansion in knowledge, not only technical but ecological. Besides, the Communist Party was committed ideologically to science. Where one went, so did the other.

Then came the fires of 1972. Clearly, if suppression was to improve, it required better science as well as more aircraft. A December 1972 resolution strengthened the power of Goskomles (the State Forestry Commission), increased its funding, added chairs of forestry to educational institutes, published new training manuals, and called for a major investment in research, reaching out to previously untapped institutes dedicated to space science and civil defense. The outcome, as one veteran recalled, was a veritable "explosion" of fire science.[102]

All the existing research institutes expanded, and new ones were added, much as Avialesookhrana spun a denser web of secondary and tertiary fire bases. Firefighting equipment was developed in affiliation with the Krasnoyarsk and

Khabarovsk laboratories, with special attention given to converting agricultural and military machinery. (Leningrad kept its own experts in-house, focusing on aircraft and pumps.) At the Siberian Technological Institute, Professor G. N. Dorrer investigated fire spread models; under Professor A. M. Grishin the physics department at Tomsk University developed comprehensive mathematical models of fire behavior; and the Soviet Academy of Sciences sponsored fire ecology research in the Urals, western Siberia, Yakutsk, and Arkhangelsk. At Khabarovsk, H. P. Telitsyn propagated a series of fire spread models that leaped across the taiga like the crown fires they characterized. Publications increased threefold over the previous decade. They did not peak until the advent of perestroika in 1986.[103]

Charismatic, indefatigable, the deputy chair of Goskomles' fire committee, Kurbatsky was everywhere, and under his direction there began a series of annual fire symposia (biennial after 1976). As a sustained exercise, only the Tall Timbers fire ecology conferences rivaled it, the former ending as the latter gathered momentum. But the Tall Timbers conferences—so important in consolidating fire knowledge around the planet—said not a word about the Soviet Union. And Soviet science, while knowledgeable about Western developments, could not reply for itself. Because the proceedings were published in the USSR, there were few copies printed; because they were in Russian, they were little read outside the Soviet Union; and because they dealt with forest fires, there was little incentive to translate them into English, the dominant language of international combustion. Within the Soviet Union the conferences were grand events, eagerly anticipated, fondly remembered. Outside the USSR the proceedings went unread and uncited.[104]

As fast as it flared, even faster did the flame die out. By the time *perestroika* confirmed the stagnation of the Soviet economy, publications had fallen to the level of the 1950s. A system that had reached institutional saturation now began to senesce. After the August revolution of 1991, fire institutes fell like root-burned snags in the wind. When, in 1993, Johann Goldammer convened a symposium in Krasnoyarsk on the Fire Ecology of Northern Eurasia, an attempt to tear down the barriers that had isolated Russian fire science, weeds had overgrown the "academic campus" of the Sukachev Institute, researchers worked with little (or no) salary, and technicians spent their summer afternoons tending potato patches along the high banks of the Yenisei River. In the euphoria of contact, there was a promise of some Western aid, but Western Europe had little institutional fire research outside the Mediterranean, the United States had spent two decades downsizing its own Cold War–inflated fire research programs, and the Canadian Forest Service was collapsing its investment in fire science with unseemly haste. The West could talk but not pay much for the privilege. Both Melekhov and Kurbatsky died the same year, 1994. An era died with them.[105]

By the last half of the 1980s, as the Soviet Union creaked and shuddered to its collapse, three fires triangulated the empire's fire status—the fire that was seen, the fire that was hidden, and the fire no one allowed or discussed, the one that mattered most.

The fire and meltdown at the Chernobyl nuclear plant in April 1986 mesmerized the West, and its nuclear smoke cloud, charged with radioactive debris, confirmed Western Europe's worst fears about fire. Unable to deny the event, the Soviet Union allowed remarkably full coverage by the media under the principle of glasnost. But the radiation flareup was only the beginning. The fires came later.

The contaminated landscape surrounding Chernobyl was evacuated—100,000 people in all—and other forests farther north, also laced with radionuclides, were cleared as monitoring crews discovered them. The effect was the same as creating nature reserves. When humans quit tending the landscape, the fuels went feral; and when controlled fire ceased, lightning and accidental ignitions moved in. Aggressive fire control was difficult, if not impossible, due to radioactivity. During the summer drought of 1992, fires outside Gomel in Belarus burned through contaminated woods and two evacuated villages, and then continued directly into the Chernobyl abandoned zone. The fires reentrained still-active radionuclides, particularly cesium-137, lodged in the soil and forest litter, and cast them into the atmosphere once again. The aerosol levels of radioactive cesium increased tenfold. The Bryansk region experienced 135 fires. Another round of wildfires broke out in 1996. Still, these were surface fires, not crown fires, whose convective columns could have lofted the resident radionuclides into the stratosphere. What the original fire at the nuclear plant had not loosed, subsequent forest fires promised to do for it.[106]

By then, however, the Soviet Union had disintegrated, and its capacity for command-style fire suppression fell with it. Fire in 1992 spread like a pall throughout European Russia, including Moscow, and like its 1972 precedessor it unnerved the successors of the commissars. There was a similar promise of more money for fire control and research funds for the Chernobyl cleanup. The reconstituted Russian Forest Service and its counterparts in Belarus and Ukraine moved, warily, to combat fires in and around sites deemed unsafe for human habitation. The prospects were poor; but by such perverse means, the Chernobyl catastrophe confirmed the iconography, if not the logic, of European fire control.

While Western Europe, fascinated and horrified, kept watch over Chernobyl, it missed completely the far vaster biotic meltdown that savaged Transbaikalia less than a year later in May 1987. The full extent of the holocaust is unknown even today, glasnost or not, Soviet Union or not. Only a fluke—that a fragment of the vast complex seared Manchuria at a time when China had foreign aid missions on the ground—alerted Western fire scientists that anything had occurred.

When the Great Black Dragon fire broke loose, there were Canadian fire specialists on the scene. There was no denying the fire's presence. It burned a million-hectare swath through the Hinggan Forest, killed hundreds when it swept through railway towns, and became the subject of intense scrutiny by Western observers; even Harrison Salisbury toured the scene. "The forest bequeathed to me a sense of deep foreboding," he wrote. "I felt as if I were participating in an inquest on the fate of the earth. . . . Never had a story so affected me." There were hints that other fires had burned north of the Amur River, and as scientists in the United States and Canada began to collect satellite maps of the China fire, they discovered large burns in Chita, Buryatia, Amur, and southern Yakutia. Further investigation through satellite imagery steadily enlarged estimates of the area burned. By 1994 the best guess was 12 to 14 million hectares. The complex was more than a dozen times the size of the Great Black Dragon fire, and probably twenty-five to thirty times the size of the next year's 1988 Yellowstone complex that so impressed the American media and on which the United States expended more than $130 million in failed suppression efforts.[107]

The Soviets denied that anything unusual happened, certainly that anything occurred beyond their control. Official reports admit to 860 fires and a burned area of 92,000 hectares (or according to a later task force report, 290,000 hectares). One reason for the evasion is that forestry officials considered only those strictly forested lands that burned, ignoring the immense grasslands and pine savannas that are characteristic of the region. This of course was in addition to the bureaucratic reflex to downgrade the numbers. The error between official reports and satellite evidence is at least two orders of magnitude. Unofficially, fire scientists in Chita province admit that 5 to 6 million hectares burned in that province alone. Officially the Soviet Academy of Sciences declined to mount any formal expeditions to investigate the fires on the Orwellian theory that it could not study what did not occur. There would be no formal record, no smoking snag, no trail of incriminating ash.[108]

The grounds exist, however, for a plausible reconstruction. Probably the villagers of Transbaikalia were spring-burning their fields, as they have always done, as the Siberian indigenes had before them. Unfortunately, decrees after the 1972 fires made the practice illegal. It had to be done, yet it could not be regulated by fire officials, could not be integrated with the apparatus for fire control, and could not be informed by fire weather forecasts. The taiga was dry; the fires spread from field to forest; and then the notorious *burya,* the dry wind that sweeps south like a spring torrent, hit the flames. The dynamics of big fires known to the Siberian taiga from time immemorial rushed into force. The fires exploded. Probably hundreds of surface fires scrambled into the

The great transformation of nature: the USSR as firepower. (a) Early aerial firefighting crew, Siberia. (Avialesookhrana) (b) Painting by V. N. Dovrovolsky (1980), commemorating the 1977 firefight in the Urals. (Fire Museum Yekaterinberg, by permission of V. N. Dobrovolsky) (c) Wildland fire statistics, Russia, 1947–1991. Fire suppression became particularly effective in the late 1960s, especially after the government committed major resources following the 1972 fires around Moscow. But suppression could not contain fires for long, and a resemblance of success was maintained only by manipulating the statistical record—by transferring land from "protected" to "unprotected" categories and by ignoring the immense fires of 1987. (Data from Korovin, 1996)

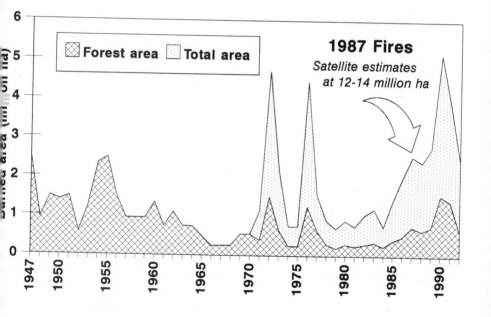

crowns, hillsides erupted into flame like matchboxes, and grass fires bolted across steppes and savannas with the speed of galloping horses. Probably, too, the ubiquitous wooden villages were swept into the maelstrom. Control efforts collapsed, as they had to. No force could withstand such a conflagration, which moved with the implacability of a hurricane. Not until the winds subsided did the wildfires slow, and not until the summer rains did the smoke end. While the West remained transfixed by Chernobyl or read the ashes of the Black Dragon Fire like tea leaves for what it hinted at Deng Xiaoping's China, probably the largest wildland fire on the Earth in the last fifty years, possibly the last seventy—likely the largest since the Siberian fires of 1915—vanished into the aerosols of a global atmosphere and left no greater record than the campfires of sable-trapping *promyshlenniki*.[109]

The official response was the reflex of a command society. The director of the Chita fire center was removed. A task force silently inquired into the disaster, and recommended more planes, more firefighters, more bulldozer-equipped tanks, as if this were an uprising in Budapest or Prague, not the Transbaikalian taiga. Records were expunged from the archives. When Mikhail Gorbachev celebrated the 70th anniversary of the Bolshevik Revolution five months later and used that platform to declare the necessity to recover history, neither he nor forestry officials was prepared to include the 1987 holocaust.

But internally Avialesookhrana, or Goskomles, or the serious *nomenklatura* could not deny what had occurred. Wildfire returned, and could not be suppressed by sheer mechanical strength; nor could the taiga be intimidated by ukases from the Supreme Soviet, or insurrection stilled by a Brezhnev Doctrine for socialist nature. If the 1972 fires announced the start of a new round of adventurism, the 1987 fires wrote its sad conclusion; they did to the fire establishment what the failed invasion of Afghanistan did to the Soviet military. *Perestroika* had come to the taiga. A command economy had to relearn Bacon's dictum that nature to be commanded must be obeyed.

The catastrophe's causes were many; some inevitable. But critical to the debacle was the dissociation between traditional burning and modern fire suppression. In its larger contours the problem was European. To it, however, the Soviet Union imparted its own distinctive character. Officially, fire use had no place in Soviet silviculture. Even slash burning fell under suspicion during the Stalinist purges, although it continued out of necessity, as agricultural burning did, away from official inspectors. Even in the era of perestroika, there remained what one Avialesookhrana official called the "psychological problem" attendant to any controlled burn. One center director recalled how he had been grilled for two hours by the KGB in the name of state security for igniting a backfire in a desperate effort to control a wildfire raging on the Kola Peninsula. That the Soviet military maintained its primary submarine base at Murmansk nearby made the act more visible than had it occurred in the Verkhoyansk Mountains, but it was smarter to let such a fire go and lie about its final size than to combat it with counterfires. Under such a regime, controlled burning could be considered a prima facie act of sabotage or at a minimum an expression of antisocialist behavior.[110]

The suspicion extended even to science. Certainly there was curiosity among fire ecologists. No one could study the taiga without awareness of fire's role in shaping its structure and dynamics. Many researchers could recall from their own past or that of their parents the common practices of spring burning, firing for berries and honey production, burning to flush pasture and assist hunting. But such technologies were primitive, unworthy of a state founded on scientific socialism. Still, the facts were there, and there were massive forest die-offs from moth infestations—sites badly in need of sanitization and fuel reduction. And beginning in the 1960s there was the curious example of the United States, loudly arguing in print the case for prescribed fire although doing little enough in the field.

The Krasnoyarsk laboratory became a center for inquiry, the ever-curious Kurbatsky granting it his imprimatur. Fire ecologist V. V. Furyaev experimented in the mid-1960s with burning in the defoliated forests, and later with underburning in pine plantations. Meanwhile, arguing from the example of postfire regeneration by pine, on the evidence of poor restocking in thick humus, on the value of surface fires in larch, and by the example of the underburning practiced by herders in Tuva, S. V. Belov proposed a concerted program of controlled burning. In the 1973 Krasnoyarsk symposium he called the prospect "alluring," but admitted, as did others, the "psychological barrier" that blocked its acceptance. Even the case for "clean-burn" backfiring had to be argued with dialectical care. When Furyaev sought to publish extracts from American experiments in prescribed fire, including burning in sequoia groves, he was denied permission on the grounds that the ideas were illogical, that they were possibly even expressions of CIA-instigated disinformation.[111]

Eventually the Academicians forced the issue into a formal hearing. They presented their case, while forestry and fire officials to a man refused to accept it; and the panel ruled in favor of fire exclusion. By now the 1972 fires had strengthened fire suppression's political standing: Moscow wanted the fires ended and was not interested in the subtle dialectics of fire ecology. By official edict the state banned burning. The proposal was revived at the 1978 Krasnoyarsk symposium, this time disguised as a means of fuel reduction and hence of fire control. But the *apparat* remained unmoved. Nothing happened. Even experimentation was silenced.[112]

Still, the facts of Siberian fire ecology could not be decreed null and void. A handful of researchers defied the ban and continued to burn and gather data—forestry's equivalent to the dissident artists and writers who secretly painted and circulated manuscripts underground. But even where it evaded punishment, *samizdat* science was denied support. There was no funding and no outlet for publication. When the ban was finally lifted after the 1987 debacle, these studies, evolved out of folk practice, became a basis for reconstruction. Like Russian Orthodox churches seized by the Bolshevik state and then, after the August revolution, reconsecrated, that preserved knowledge could help rebuild a new fire regime.

By then, however, fire suppression had acquired the violent disjunction between theory and practice so characteristic of Soviet society at large. Designed along paramilitary lines, fire suppression dominated nature's economy as the military-industrial complex did the state economy. Gargantuan in one dimension, absent in others, this institutional and technological unevenness made a consistent program of fire management difficult. At just the time when the United States had begun redirecting its cold war on fire to mixed purposes, the Soviet Union had concentrated on the one task it could do best, the one that combined an ideology of maximum production with an ideology of technology. A balanced reconciliation was awkward, aptly illustrated when Avialesookhrana sought to assist with fuel-reduction burning around villages in south Krasnoyarsk oblast. Hovering a meter above the ground in giant MI-8 helicopters, crewmen tossed wooden matches out the opened door.[113]

After the August revolution of 1991 the system spiraled rapidly inward. Staffing fell to the levels of the 1960s. In the new Russia the taiga, no less than society, had to convert to a market economy. Aviation gas—the sine qua non of aerial protection—now had a hard currency market outside Russia. So did the taiga. Fires increased, their full magnitude hidden because the area under formal protection shrank, and it was those areas no longer subject to any systematic fire control that racked up the greatest burning. No longer did Avialesookhrana protect "deer pastures." No longer could fire control keep pace with logging slash. Skeptics believed that Russia might become a boreal Brazil, a global scandal in mismanaged fire.

Then wildfire again struck Moscow and spared Avialesookhrana from systemic failure. In 1992, drought-propelled wildfires once more surrounded Moscow, frightened the authorities, inspired another emergency committee, and led to new funding, mostly for the development of firefighting technologies like air tankers. All of that added a new verse to an old refrain. More significant for the future was the progressive integration of the Russian fire establishment into a global community. The United States and Russia arranged for study tours, exchanges of personnel, a mutual aid treaty across the Bering Strait. Russian scientists participated in international symposia, and the FAO/ECE scheduled its 1996 fire seminar for Shushenskoye. As concern mounted over global climate changes, it became obvious that Russia held the largest carbon stocks on the planet. No calculus of global fire could ignore Russia, but neither could Russia profitably ignore the fire practices—or fire philosophy—of the rest of the world.[114]

It could no longer tolerate the "peculiar psychology" that had informed its official fire policies. If it was not prepared to encourage fire, as the Americans believed necessary, neither could it pretend to garden it away, as Europeans insisted, or elect to suppress it, as it had attempted in its authoritarian past. It could not eradicate fire through a technological pogrom, or banish it to internal exile, or subvert it through infiltration. It knew more than it admitted about fire, and had a better basis for management than it perhaps wished to concede. But whatever unique resolution it would concoct, Russia could not deny fire; and no inventory of planetary fire could ignore Russia. However much its status as a thermonuclear superpower plummeted, its standing as a natural firepower went ballistic.

PLANETS

A world war fought on its soil and the postwar loss of empire did little to diminish Europe's influence on global fire. In 1987, excluding the USSR, Europe contributed only 0.3 percent of the global biomass burned, and 90 percent of that was concentrated in Spain, Portugal, Italy, and Greece. Yet Europe remained omnipresent, if no longer omnipotent, throughout the planet. If, as a consideration of its authority, one includes the Neo-Europes and the power of Western science, then the European hegemony was greater than in the floodtide of imperialism.

Like the heat within a fire, the transfer of European ideas, machines, practices, and institutions took several forms. Some spread by conduction, from direct contact with European fire specialists or Europe-sponsored programs. Much came from secondary sources, Europe's former colonies, now reradiating their influence as major centers of fire protection and fire science. If Europe's fire practices and values were lost in the conversions, nonetheless the fire establishments of Australia, Canada, Russia, and the United States, for example, bore closer resemblance to Europe than to other civilizations. And then there was a kind of global convection by means of Europe's obsession with fire-induced atmospheric changes and the changing climate of world opinion those concerns affected.

The end result was to install Europe's vestal fire as a global standard.

Conduction:
The European Connection

Through national aid programs, scientific education, international institutions like the United Nations, and contacts with former colonies, Europe connected to much of the world, and influenced conceptions about fire and fire practices. A portion of the contact involved fire practices directly, but most followed indirectly through ideas about proper agriculture, forestry, and nature conservation, all of which determined how countries should think about fire and how they should apply and withhold it. Knowledge and technology flowed from Europe outward like heat transferred along an iron rod held at one end over a flame. Anyone picking up that rod felt the impact of Europe's distant vestal fire.

Colonial contacts were rarely severed completely. France held the most fiercely to its possessions, to a relict *presence Française*. Throughout its retained possessions and particularly throughout Francophone Africa, France continued to instruct as much in fire practices as in the enunciation of nasal vowels. A major research program centered in the Ivory Coast. Meanwhile, the class ranking of Peninsular Spanish above South American creole asserted itself in fire. Why Latin America should look to Spain for guidance was puzzling, but that is what happened. So while fire scientists studied in the United States, administrators (and even field personnel) often trained in Spain, and Spain published a special fire newsletter. Britain had little to offer its former possessions once it lay down the burden of imperial forestry. With money from the Ford Foundation, the Commonwealth Forestry Institute microfilmed its entire holdings and sent the collection to the now-developing countries mostly in Africa as a kind of intellectual dowry. More important, the Commonwealth countries communicated among themselves, so that there was an exchange of expertise between the English-speaking nations like Canada, New Zealand, Australia, and (even after it left) South Africa. What would happen with the states of the former USSR was unclear. Certainly units of Avialesookhrana—fire centers at Minsk, Kiev, and Alma-Ata, for example—communicated freely with their old colleagues.

More important, however, were foreign aid programs, some national, some under the auspices of the United Nations. Germany, for example, proud of its forest heritage, sponsored forestry missions to Mali and Indonesia and elsewhere which included programs in fire management. Typically, aid programs brought with them equipment manufactured by the sponsoring nation, further incentive to use firefighting hardware, which in turn influenced the software of fire policy. For the Third World, particularly for the nonaligned nations, the United Nations became a neutral source of expertise. But the Food and Agriculture Organization, which had responsibility for fire, was heavily staffed by west Europeans. So was the U.N. Environment Program, UNESCO's Man and the Biosphere Program, and the International Union for the Conservation of Nature. So, too, were the major institutions of transnational science like the International Union of Forest Research Organizations, the Scientific Committee on Problems of the Environment, and the International Geosphere-Biosphere Program, all of which oversaw fire research.

Like the heated iron bar, the flow of information went one way, from Europe

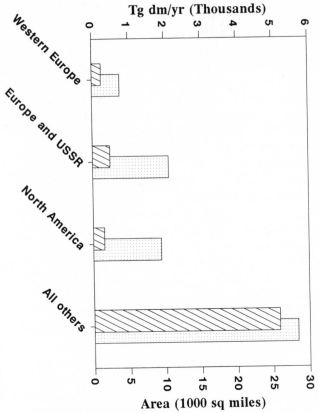

Europe and the world.
(a) Biomass burning.
(b) Fossil-fuel burning. Europe's contribution remains relatively small, and mostly focused along its Mediterranean perimeter. Interestingly, North America has a higher proportion of "lost" fires, reflecting the abrupt collapse of agricultural burning in Canada and the United States. While Europe accelerates its combustion of fossil fuels, its relative contribution to world effluence is shrinking. That France has committed so heavily to nuclear power has also helped shrink Europe's combustion load. (Data from Andreae 1991 and Turner II et al. 1990)

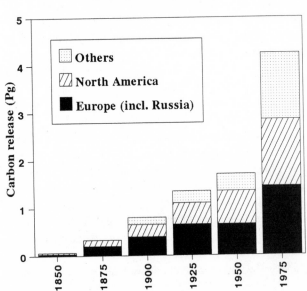

outward. Finns, Germans, Britons, and French traveled to Asia, Africa, and Latin America to educate in modern fire practices, but Senegalese, Bolivians, and Thais did not go to Europe to reciprocate. The FAO's lexicon, *Wildland Fire Management Terminology,* included English, Spanish, French, and Italian, and planned an expansion to include Portuguese and Russian, all European languages and the languages of former European colonies. In association with the European Economic Commission, FAO has sponsored fire seminars in Poland, Spain, Greece, and Russia. Between 1970 and 1989, FAO's field program, headed by a Dane, oversaw 66 projects—24 in Africa, 20 in Asia, 17 in Latin America, and 5 in Europe and the Middle East. Among major enterprises were the "modern fire control project" in India (1988–93); two regional fire studies, one for the Mediterranean countries, and one for Central America and the Caribbean; and sponsorship of the biannual *International Forest Fire News.* Inevitably the arrangement propagated European ideas and norms. In 1995, FAO proposed to drop fire data from its inventories. "Sustainable development" was the watchword; more directly social measurements should take precedence over more removed environmental ones.[1]

As concern over global environmental change accelerated, fire control became as vigorous a topic for environmental agendas as arms control had been earlier for geopolitics. By the 1990s, motivated particularly by the specter of climatic change, there commenced a grand reconnaissance of the Earth as a fire planet. For too long Americans and Soviets had forced an ideological polarity that made either system distasteful to many neutrals. Europeans could fill that intellectual void, and did. That western Europe, at least, was prosperous argued for the success of its ideas regarding land use and forestry, no less than banking and manufacturing. Reconnaissance required comparisons for understanding; for many, Europe supplied that norm. Like the Olympic torch carried from Greece to Montreal or Seoul, Europe's vestal fire was transported to congregations around the world.

RADIATION:
THE NEO-EUROPES

But over the centuries, that vestal flame had died down, or even been banked in the ash. Large portions of the world—Africa, for example—might accept the European norm officially but were unable to transplant it outside policy statements. It remained decorative, like a logo, or an English garden outside a Kenya bungalow. More significant were the Neo-Europes, which became independent centers of fire experience and fire expertise. More lightly populated, more endowed with abundant wildland fire, they became secondary sources

for propagation, radiating heat not only around them but back to the informing firefront itself.

The English-speaking Neo-Europes—the United States, Canada, Australia,
and South Africa—dominated the scene, and because of them English remained
the language of fire science. Its postwar apartheid policies isolated South Africa
politically, but apart from French researchers in West Africa, South African
scientists were practically the only on-site source of fire research in the continent. Besides, the mediterranean climate of the Cape linked its ecological
dynamics with those in California, southern Europe, and Australia, all major
foci for fire research. Whether or not the scientists themselves participated in
international symposia, their English-published studies could. In the 1980s it
was calculated that South Africa accounted for 80 percent of Africa's electrical power generation. Something like that figure certainly applies to the geography of the continent's fire sciences.[2]

Globally, the United States became during the postwar period as supreme
in wildland fire as in economics, military power, the arts, science, and higher
education. Particularly with the Soviet Union closed, anyone wishing to see
modern fire control or to study the frontiers of fire science traveled to America. By the early 1960s the U.S. Forest Service oversaw three dedicated fire
laboratories; had successfully converted surplus military trucks, jeeps, planes,
and helicopters to firefighting; fielded a rapid deployment force of trained fire
crews; and campaigned against fires with a logistical power greater than that
available to the military of many Third World nations. Canada and Australia,
good allies both, looked to the United States for models, and with thoughtful
adaptations found them.[3]

Yet the American model was flawed, and all parties knew it. Canada had
long cultivated fire science within its own institutions and pursued fire control from its own imperatives. It could, moreover, share in the expertise of
the Commonwealth, as interested in Australia, Britain, or New Zealand as in
America. It adopted the best of the American system, adapted what did not
quite fit, invented alternatives where possible, and followed the logic of its
own needs. Without surplus military aircraft, it created the CL-215 air tanker,
the only plane designed specifically for aerial firefighting. Shunning the American fire-danger rating system, it devised its own, which eventually spread
throughout the circumpolar boreal nations. Uneasy with the boom-and-bust
economy of American science and suspicious of the American passion for
lab-based formulas, as though prescribed fire were literally a pharmaceutical, Canada organized a fire research program with a sophisticated balance
between field and laboratory. Still, there was much in common. The Canadian Interagency Fire Center in Winnipeg was modeled on the National Inter-

agency Fire Center at Boise, Idaho. Fire councils spanned the borders. A mutual aid treaty sent American resources north and Canadian south during emergencies. Between them America and Canada soon established a North American bloc that represented the best in high-tech fire control. And in countries where Americans were politically unacceptable as fire advisers, Canadians sometimes served as surrogates.[4]

Australia, too, studied the American model warily. It liked the concept of cooperative fire protection, admired the strength of American fire science, and beginning in 1952 arranged for regular fire study tours between the two nations under FAO auspices. But its fire experts shielded their collective eyes against the dazzling spectacle of aerial attack, and insisted that controlled burning, not fire suppression, was the essence of a truly Australian strategy for bushfire protection. Adrift between Britain and America, postwar Australia set about reinventing itself. How it would cope with bushfire was part of that enterprise. Accordingly, Australia devised its own fire-danger rating meter, experimented with controlled burning, investigated eucalypt fire ecology and Aboriginal fire history, and mustered an institutional structure for bushfire fighting with volunteer brigades.[5]

Even America came to doubt its postwar course. Since 1908 American fire officers had had access to virtually unlimited emergency funds with which to fight fires. The American system wove its institutional patterns around that abundance like ribbons on a maypole. That funding—the sheer plentitude of money for firefighting—was what powered the expansion of fire suppression, what awed foreign observers, and what finally isolated the American model as an international standard. What most of the world wanted was American affluence and American firepower (or Canadian air tankers), not American ideals. In compromise the United States forged mutual asssistance pacts with Canada, Mexico, and Russia; sent advisers to Brazil, trainers to Argentina, Chile, and the Pacific Trust Islands; hosted sessions to train Latin American instructors; and dispatched fire specialists to wildfires in the Dominican Republic, Costa Rica, the Galápagos Islands, and Ghana.

But as it grew to question its role as a global policeman, the United States had equal reason to question its capacity as a global fireman. Criticism of ever-more-powerful fire control built like a thunderstorm. In many landscapes, controlled fire was a benign alternative; in nature preserves, it was often a necessity. Increasingly what the American fire community wanted to do was spread its hard-won gospel of fire management—of mixed fire control and use—but it found few takers. Outside of Canada, Australia, and Russia, most of the world lacked the unpopulated public lands that were the prime cause for and obsession of the evolved American system. Most nations had lands filled with people; most wrestled with questions of agricultural or pastoral burning; and many were infected with European ideals of fire exclusion. Regardless, the American presence was undeniable, and if viewed through very different cultural prisms, it was nonetheless studied and where possible its most photogenic expressions were avidly copied.[6]

Collectively, the Neo-Europes had much in common, and were both an accessory and a counterweight to European fire traditions. Where they collectively differed from Europe was in the need each felt to accommodate indigenous fire, whether from native peoples or nature, although the struggle was long and fiercely fought. Where they differed from each other was in the nature of that accommodation, the specific geographic and cultural concessions that underlay their compromises with European norms. Australia arrived at an acceptable system first, by the early 1960s; America, South Africa, and Canada, not until the early 1970s. Where all of them, except South Africa, differed from the rest of the world was over the presence of public, vacant land that would not be converted to agriculture and for which, other considerations aside, fire could never be cultivated away. The Neo-Europes could not be Europes, did not wish to be Europes, and had to design appropriate fire practices just as they had to devise distinctive political institutions and invent unique creation stories.

Still, there was one other firepower in addition to the Big Four. The Soviet Union west of the Urals belonged with Europe, but east of the Urals it resembled a Neo-Europe. The experiences of fire protection in Siberia and the Far East became a paradigm for other Soviet allies. As much as America, the Soviet Union became a secondary source of modified European fire ideas and practices. It exported aerial firefighting to China and Mongolia, as well as, in less dramatic forms, to Poland and East Germany. Soviet fire specialists even advised Cuba on aerial reconnaissance, and at one point traveled to Vietnam to do feasibility studies. In terms of sheer landmass the Soviet system, in its various forms, was more widespread than the North American and Australian systems combined. Mongolia had more smokejumpers than the United States. China added fire protection to the curriculum of the national forestry school in Harbin.[7]

What the Soviet model lacked was the kind of formal debate and compromise that had characterized the Big Four, along with the capacity to move outside the larger Soviet bloc. Just when the others were accepting controlled burning, at least in principle, the 1972 fires pushed the Soviet Union into the Brezhnevian doctrine that the more that is forbidden the better, and banned even traditional burning. Suppression was mandated from Moscow; control was imposed by edict. A reconciliation between taiga and settlers was yet to come.

Even so, détente opened, briefly, a window on the West. Both Canadian and American delegations inspected the Soviet system in 1976. Then the invasion of Afghanistan shut down contacts. Instead, advisers and exchanges moved to affiliated fire protection systems, notably China and Mongolia, which suffered large fires between 1986 and 1990. Within the USSR, fire protection developed in isolation, its technological evolution as distinctive as Australian marsupials. Not until a Soviet delegation toured the United States in 1990 were contacts revived. When Americans reciprocated a year later, it was on the eve of the August revolution; and as exchanges elaborated, the Soviet Union collapsed, and left most of its fire establishment in the rubble. How it would rebuild was not apparent. What the newly independent states like Belarus, Ukraine, and Kazakhstan—all of which had inherited aerial fire centers—would do was unknown. But it was unlikely that they could shed their legacy of fire control any more than they could escape the ruble zone or the railway net and gas pipelines that still bound them to the Russian Federation.[8]

Nor could the world easily escape Europe's influence, even when it was reradiated secondarily. More powerful yet was the pervasive presence of Western science. Whatever was or was not done, the world increasingly understood fire and fire practices through the medium of modern science. As international environmentalism demonstrated, properly publicized science could influence policy. The ancient European quarrel between those who used fire in the field and those who condemned it from the cities was about to become global.

CONVECTION:
BLACK DEATH, HEAT DEATH

And a flame slender as the hepaticas,
Blood-root, and violets so soon to be now.
But the black spread like black death on the ground,
And I think the sky darkened with a cloud
Like winter and evening coming on together.
　　　　　　　　—Robert Frost, "The Bonfire"

In the 1980s, fire became an emblem of global environmental havoc. The meanings it had for Europe were extended over the Earth. Modern science furnished the mechanism; the atmosphere, the medium; and international environmentalism, the message. Air replaced soil as a universal index of ecological health. Europe's crisis in air quality, brought on by abusive combustion, appeared to foreshadow climatic disruptions that would punish the planet. Unwarranted burning would convert the Earth into a crockpot. Violently or subtlely, quickly or slowly, by flame or by soot, through outright incineration or through strangulation from poisonous emissions, fire would catalyze the long-dreaded heat death of the Earth.

With the atmosphere, fire found a milieu in which every act of combustion contributed to a common cauldron. No matter how remote, how small, how traditional, how horrific the fire; no matter whether coal, petroleum, gas, lignite, wood, or stubble was the fuel; no matter if it burned in automobiles, furnaces, or trash cans, or on street corners, sugar cane fields, wilderness mountains, wetlands, larch forests, or tropical savannas, the effluents mingled indiscriminately in the all-encircling air. A fire anywhere contributed to atmospheric contamination everywhere. The alliance between atmospheric sciences and environmentalism lofted fire into the sky, and that act of intellectual convection promised to lead to political conventions to regulate, if not suppress, the originating combustion.

The dichotomy between the two great forms of combustion had become undeniable. When fossil hydrocarbons were first exhumed, they were a European eccentricity. But they soon penetrated every aspect of economic life, and hence of ecological dynamics. They powered new pathways for energy, reconfigured the circulation of nutrients, designed the schematics for industrial metabolism, and substituted for the biochemicals essential for agriculture. They seemingly transcended the closing circle of ecological necessity. No longer was energy restricted to what coppiced woods could grow or to the vagaries of the oat harvest for draft animals. No longer was fertilizer dependent on manure or guano, or weed control on hoes and harrows. The purgative and renewing fire retreated into tractors and to factories for the production of pesticides, herbicides, and artificial fertilizers. No longer need agriculture pay the tithe of fallowed fields; and the industrial fallow of parks and reserves came with prohibitions. Clearly internal combustion was replacing open burning.

But not completely, and perhaps not quickly enough, and certainly not without costs. By 1990, as measured by atmospheric emissions, biomass burning accounted for at least 40 percent of global combustion. To those who saw any smoke as a pollutant, any combustion effluents as atmospherically degenerative, any loss of biologically stored carbon as both wasteful and destructive, that burning was intolerable. As newly emergent markets in China, India, Brazil, and elsewhere rapidly scaled up their consumption of fossil hydrocarbons, it seemed self-evident that the air could be cleaned only by controlling fire. That conclusion became more forceful as it became apparent that like open burning, industrial combustion also liberated its effluents into the atmosphere. The composite outcome was a convective column of greenhouse gases, acid rain, toxins, smog, ozone, and a cocktail of other chemicals noxious to human and biotic health that towered into global consciousness. Even more, those emissions threatened to unhinge a climatic regime that had been stable for more or less 6,000 years.[9]

The targeting of fire as a villain, however, was a peculiarly European obsession. Probably its demonization began with the publication of the nuclear winter concept in 1982. Immense, thermonuclear-war-kindled firestorms—the memory of Hamburg, Dresden, Hiroshima, and Tokyo mingled with fears of Europe as a battlefield for World War III—would send their convective columns, powerful as hurricanes, through the troposphere and spread soot in a colossal pall over the Northern Hemisphere. Eventually that dark cloud would reach the Southern Hemisphere. Agriculture would fail. Ecosystems would die. The prospects for postwar recovery would collapse. Most of the Earth would resemble the dead-forest landscapes of Bohemia. On the killed woods new fires would gorge, prolonging the havoc.[10]

It was a bold idea, synchronizing with then-fashionable forecasts of a coming ice age, fears of NATO Pershing and Cruise missiles, Green alarms over Germany's puzzling forest dieback, and the emergence of atmospheric chemistry as a maturing science. Quickly, the scientific community rallied to investigate and politicians funneled funding. The euphoria, however, passed as rapidly as a struck match; within a few years the idea had died. But the vivid linkage of fire with environmental destruction through the medium of the atmosphere endured. It soon found common cause with other environmentalist concerns such as the destruction of the Brazilian rainforest through fire-assisted clearing and combustion-catalyzed acid deposition. Later, it was joined by the specter of Kuwait oil fires, by theories regarding the parboiled extinction of the dinosaurs through global conflagrations ignited by extraterrestrial firesticks, and before the intellectual ashes of nuclear winter had cooled by the prospect of a greenhouse summer.[11]

In this scenario slow combustion replaced fast, and the reckless release of greenhouse gases would inevitably lead to global warming, perhaps to climatic perversions sufficient to render the Earth into a fascimile of hellish Venus. In 1988, fires blanketed Amazonia with smoke clouds the size of western Europe, wildfires leaped through 45 percent of Yellowstone National Park utterly indifferent to control efforts, and a NASA scientist proclaimed that the Earth had already crossed the threshold of the greenhouse effect. Soon, fires fed by urban bush burned though major cities like Sydney, Australia, and Oakland, Santa Barbara, and Los Angeles, California, and along Europe's Mediterranean rim. Atmospheric science moved from nuclear winter to greenhouse summer as easily as a maple tree shedding old leaves and sprouting new ones. In the politics of Big Science, climate became as powerful a talisman as cancer.

What remained constant was the telegenic imagery of diabolical fire, an iconography that satisfied proponents of control and dismayed their critics.

Unsurprisingly, Europeans tended to be most adamant about the hazards of fire. Biomass burning was to ecological health what smoking tobacco was to human health. For the Earth one might as well burn garbage in the streets as stubble in the fields or swidden plots in the forest. Certainly fire became prominent, even if it did so as political theater, as photogenic spectacle, as an image by which to animate activist concerns of all sorts. Pyrophobes argued the need for a convention on greenhouse gases that would do for climate warming what the Montreal Convention did for protecting the ozone layer. Open fires would go the way of CFC-propellant spray cans.

And yet there were, as always, dissenters. They wanted better distinctions between good fires and bad, wanted to discriminate between land-clearing fires which added carbon to the atmosphere and regular burning which simply recycled it, demanded equal time for fire's virtues as a benevolent tool of land management and a necessary process in nature preservation, and protested the exploitation of images in place of arguments. They urged controlled burning as a device for forest health, and thereby for carbon sequestration. They noted that most quasi-natural landscapes suffered from too little fire, or improper fire, not from too much fire. They documented examples of biodiversity lost through fire exclusion. They insisted that savanna burning be segregated from cooking fires, that the competition between industrial combustion and traditional fire be made explicit, that colleagues (if not the public) recognize that fossil-fuel combustion occurred outside an ecological context, indifferent to season and place and species, while biomass burning took place within ecosystems long programmed to accommodate it. They argued that the pyrophobes were spreading a pall of misinformation as damaging as the smoke cloud forecast by the nuclear winter scenario.

But fire ecology tended to be local, and atmospheric chemistry global. The latter carried the field. Mostly, fire critics tended to be from Europe and knew fire from laboratories and factories. Increasingly they worked for space agencies like NASA and ESA and saw fire through the instruments of remote sensing. Most fire skeptics tended to come from Neo-Europes and knew fire through ecological fieldwork. Town and country, center and periphery, theoretician and practitioner—the old fault lines were reactivated even within the scientific community. That fire reentered Europe's consciousness was a surprise, and that it became an object of serious inquiry by a web of Big Science institutions and international field campaigns from South Africa to Siberia was a marvel. That, in the end, European authorities condemned it as destructive to the existing order was only too predictable. Putative social values would smother fire like a fog of halogens.[12]

Probably fire would survive in places where industrial combustion could not reach, and on sites where, out of ecological necessity, there was no real alternative for nature preservation. Elsewhere, fire would recede for reasons of convenience or compulsion. What Europe had failed to impose directly on land, it appeared on the verge of imposing through the air. Even far-distant fires felt the draft. In some places it was sufficient to blow out the flame; others survived, but flickered precariously in the wind.

EPILOGUE
Beyond the Realm of Fire

Beyond the reaches of sea and land and air and space lay the realms of fire.
—Arthur C. Clarke, *2001*

What was Europe? As the second millennium approached its end, Europe had no ready answer. The European Union struggled with the most mundane questions, each caught like flies in webs of spidery institutions and encased in bureaucratic cocoons. Its eastern frontier was, once again, a kaleidoscope of ethnic hostilities and evanescent nationalities. The Mediterranean revived rivalries that dated back to the Bronze Age. How far to the east should Europe extend? How far to the south? How could it govern amid a babble of languages, landscapes that extended from Mediterranean maquis to boreal bogs, and a geopolitical tradition that sought to limit the supremacy of any one country, that insisted on a balance of power that left its political landscape preternaturally fragmented? What, for that matter, was the relationship between the European Union and historic Europe?

Its fires shared these uncertainties. Yet there were defining features that had shaped European fire, few by themselves definitive, yet together compelling. Europe was a geographic diamond, boreal and mediterranean along one axis, maritime and continental along another, the center stubbornly temperate. Europe's was a landscape worked since Neolithic times by mixed agriculture, a biotic mosaic of fields and pastures, crops and herds in metastable equilibrium. It was demographically dense, with few places spared from intensive human artifice. It was a people—many peoples, rivals to one another—that expanded aggressively to other seas and lands. Europe was the inventor of modern science, the developer of the industrial revolution, the exemplar for the wholesale exploitation of fossil hydrocarbons. All this made Europe's fire unique, and allowed European fire, more than any other, to influence the planet. If Europe's was not a normative fire for the Earth, it came as close as any was likely to get. Europe had become, as it had always seen itself, the keeper of the vestal flame.

There is a saying common to many European peoples—one of the universal truths about fire and one of its greatest epigrams—that fire makes a good servant but a bad master. That Europe should state its connection to fire in terms of social relations is wholly fitting. Europe's fire was a fire contained within and subordinated to European society. It was not merely that fire was anthropomorphized, but that it had a niche in the hierarchical order of society and needed to be kept in its place. From that encasing society fire drew its standing, strength, and meaning. It belonged in the hearth, on the altar, within the furnace, or if brought to fields and pastures, it was to be kept on halter or within fences. It was the domesticated fire, the Olympic torch, the Ivan Kupalo bonfire, the Midsummer blaze on the hilltop. Its social context, not its natural heritage, defined it.

In his Allegory of the Cave, Plato had proposed that fire encouraged false visions, that it substituted the shadows of things for the things themselves. How apt it is that a critique of fire, even if symbolic, should be at the core of a founding tract in European political philosophy, one that predicated a rigid social order! That was the prescribed fire of Europe's ruling intelligentsia. If they could find substitutes for the corrupting and fickle fire, they would, as they had found substitutes for so much else of nature. So, paradoxically, they remade a world of genuine shadows into the virtual shadows of human artifice. Echoing Plato, Gaston Bachelard wondered if fire-induced reverie replaced rational analysis altogether.[1]

Other peoples—the Neo-Europes among them—have endowed their sacred fire with other meanings. Eventually Americans recanted their effort to rekindle Europe's vesta, and turned instead to nature's fire. The wilderness fire became the defining flame from which all others derived and to which all others referred for meaning. (An American forester, H. H. Chapman, once restated the European epigram to read that fire was the best of friends and the worst of enemies, proposing an equality of standing, suggesting fire could be seen as a worthy Other, whether as rival or comrade.) Australians saw in fire the manifestation of an ineffable bush that, in strenuous and sometimes awful ways, defined them.

And so it goes. Each such meaning was culturally constructed, of course, but not every culture referred fire explicitly to a social setting. Europe's did. Humans ruled, fire served. Servants might use fire (and did widely in field and forge), but masters determined the proper purpose and prescriptions. The domesticated fire thrived only in those habitats society created for it. Fire by itself—fire outside its prescribed place—was a freak of nature, an outlaw, a feral sheepdog, a page torn from a book and blown by the wind. A fire outside the ordained social order was beyond ken, beyond redemption, beyond any social significance.

The metareality was culture. Over and again Europe had discovered surrogates for most of nature and had reduced the rest to artifice. It had made earth from sea and turned land into lake. It had converted woods to heath, and moor to forest. It had created soils from sand and seaweed, drained marshes into paddocks, raised hills from slag, spewed clouds from smokestacks, and shaped rivers, even the mighty Rhine, into chemical canals. Modernization had accelerated rather than slowed the process. Europe's contemporary ecology was the metabolism of its industry. Industrialization substituted for gardening as silica, molecule by molecule, replaces lignin in petrified wood; the original grain remained.

Its intellectuals believed that fire was no different from the waters, soils, trees, and creatures that Europe had domesticated in its own image. Fire served only at society's pleasure, and by implication it could thrive wherever humans contrived habitats for it. Europe came to believe that it could, in principle, exist without fire; many accepted that Europe's industrial garden would be better rid of it. Equally, Europe (and its Neo-Europes) took fire far outside its indigenous realms.

Europe's quest had carried fire beyond its natural geography, past the physics and chemistry of combustion, past the ecology of free-burning flame, beyond what anyone—Plato, Pliny, Theophrastus, Linnaeus, Brandis—could have imagined. Europe's fire had gone to the Greenland ice sheet and across the white wastes of Antarctica; had voyaged, on space ships, beyond the atmosphere; had traveled to the abiotic Moon and red Mars. Europe had mechanized combustion into electricity and abandoned it, here and there, for nuclear power. It had substituted gas and coal for the hearth, condemned wood smoke as a pollutant and carcinogen, burned its fields with diesel tractors, and fired its pastures with petroleum-derived fertilizers. It was no longer possible to imagine, as Heraclitus could, a world informed by fire. In the end Europe would, it seemed, transcend the realm of fire altogether.

This was an illusion, as perhaps Europe was. If Europe could transcend fire, even temporarily, then it was also true that fire transcended Europe. It existed beyond the imagination of mortals and beyond the moral universe of humans. Europe could never tame or suppress nature completely; it could never hope to abolish fire on a planet heaped with combustibles and marinated in oxygen. Paradoxically, the more Europe committed to fossil hydrocarbons the more natural, wild, or accidental fires would flourish. Yet the belief persisted that the full control of free-burning fire was a suitable means, and fire's exclusion a worthy ideal.

The world was stranger for this loss, not more brilliant, and more dangerous for the demonization of fire, not more secure. Nothing about fire had been easy. It was a flickering mirror that radiated back the face and hand of its holder; it was humanity's pyric double. If, as Plato insisted, its flames distorted, they also transformed what was otherwise unusable, and if their light was imperfect, they also illuminated what was otherwise unseen. If fire could not unshackle an imperfect humanity from itself, it had, for long centuries, defined that creature in ways nothing else could. It had even defined Europe. Whatever ignorance inevitably remained, it was hard to see how extinguishing the fire could illuminate the cave any better. In truth, it was never really possible.

In September 1991, hikers in the Ötztaler Alps discovered the body of a man protruding through glacial ice. Quick-frozen he had survived through 5,300 years, a mummy from the Neolithic, from the era of agricultural colonization that had so stamped Europe's history. Painstakingly, forensic scientists reconstructed the story of the ice man's last minutes. There was a blow to the head. He had staggered and dropped his quiver. Lurching forward, he had parted with bow, ax, backpack, a birch-bark satchel. Then he had moved on. To the last, clutching it as to life itself, surrendering it only as he fell, he held to a birch-bark vial of embers. But even as the fire went out, as death rushed upward in his fall, he wore around his waist another satchel that held the tinder and flints for its rekindling.[2]

So too Europe's folk had held fire for a long time, almost to the end. Prehistoric Europe had flourished by capturing fire and historic Europe had tended it to suit Europe's purposes. It had configured fire much as it had shaped stone into house and temple, and herded cattle for milk and meat. To controlled fire Europe owed much of its existence; in the vestal fire Europe found an emblem of self-identity; and with the transforming fire it discovered a medium of historic preservation. The most enduring of Europe's artifacts and archives are those burned shards that fire has transmuted into incorruptible carbon— charred kernels of einkorn, fired strata of ancient Troys, landnam charcoal in bog and moor, black carbon in farmed soils, and industrial soot in acid lakes. They would outlive pyramids and amphitheaters, museum parchments and papyrus rolls, iron axes and steel muskets, kraft-paper books and computer disks. Europe was possible because of fire, and its history would longest survive, paradoxically, where fire had worked.

Yet the relationship was, in the end, unequal. For all its postmodern technological deconstructions of fire, for all the arrogance of its sublimation of Vesta into pure symbol, for all its evasions before the mirroring flame—the truth was that Europe could not survive without controlled combustion, but that fire could exist without Europe. However far Europe moved or sought to move beyond the realm of fire, fire would persist. The Earth willed it. Together with the crows and wolves, fire would pick Europe's bones, even if unlike the others it would also preserve them, through geologic time if necessary. It would be there long after the vestal flame had expired or escaped.

After Europe there would still be fire.

NOTES

1. For a concise, neatly illustrated summary of European geology, see Autran (1992: 9–33). A fuller, and for the geologically literate, more leisurely tour is Ager (1980). Selectively useful are Cloud (1988) and, especially for its illustrations, Andrews (1991).

2. The geoscience texts cited above outline major climatic events. For the more recent eras, see Flohn and Fantechi, eds. (1984). Somewhat old-fashioned but very useful, particularly for its attention to matters of interest to fire behavior like local winds, is Kendrew (1961). Also insightful is Taylor (1936: 68–88). For fire history, the geography of vegetation is a better guide to provinces than climate alone.

3. See Hsü (1983), and Andrews (1991: 96–97).

4. For winds, see Vélez (1993: 16) and McCutchan (1977: 1–11).

5. The case for fire as a regulator, or index, for past oxygen contents is forcibly conveyed in Lovelock (1979, esp. pp. 70–72).

6. Unpublished experiments from the Intermountain Fire Sciences Laboratory reaffirm the role of fuel attributes, especially moisture. For more specific studies of paleofire and the evolution of the atmosphere, see Robinson (1989:

223–240); Cope and Chaloner (1980: 647–648; 1985: 257–277).

7. As guides to the general evolution of life, see Gould (1993), and Cox and Moore (1993). An excellent introduction to European paleoecology is Huntley and Webb, eds. (1988), especially chapters on Europe by William A. Watts (pp. 155–192) and Brian Huntley (pp. 341–383).

8. An excellent introduction is available in Roberts (1989). Details for each of Europe's fire provinces are given in the separate regional histories.

9. Hough (1926) exhaustively surveys the technology of fire starting, including natural processes; see especially pp. 84–85. Rossotti (1993: 21–32) explains the chemistry of ignition, industrial as well as natural. For natural fermentation, see Viosca, Jr. (1931: 439–442) and Chistjakov et al. (1983: 259–272). Volcanoes routinely start fires during eruptions, but these are local effects and are often overtaken by lava flows or ash falls; for a study of such a landscape, however, see Vogl (1969: 4–60).

There is little doubt, however, that lightning has been and continues to be the commanding source of natural ignition. Probably the best summaries are still those of Komarek (1968a: 5–41; 1968b: 169–197; and 1974: 421–427).

For a complementary inquiry for North America, see Taylor (1974: 455–482). While these studies center on North America, they have obvious allusions for other, similar landscapes, including Europe. Komarek (1972: 473–511) developed this prospect for Africa, and others have elaborated on the possibilities (also in Africa), but there has been little research for Europe with the exception of the Finns and, curiously, the Swedes; see Granström (1993: 737–744). Among this dispersed literature, see Kailidis and Markalas (1979), Seurre (1923: 439–443), and Keränen (1929: 3–8).

10. See, in addition to the references in note 9, Le Houerou (1973: 244–245) for Italy; Trabaud (1994: 553) for France; Vasquez and Moreno (1994: 649) for Spain; Kailidis and Markalas (1979) for Greece. For Finland, see Keränen (1929: 3–8). For the French fire, see International Forest Fire News (1990: 6); for the Moscow fires, unpublished reports from Avialesookhrana (1972), with film footage of firefighting available at the fire museum in Yekaterinburg; for Austria, International Forest Fire News 2 (1989: 3). A brief summary is contained in Economic Commission for Europe and FAO, "Forest Fire Statistics, 1985–1988," ECE/TIM/51.

Overall the statistical accounting of fire, both wild and controlled, is wretched.

11. See van der Ven (1973: 21).

12. The best introduction to paleofire is still Komarek (1972: 219–240). A contemporary update is Clark and Robinson (1993: 193–214). Good papers on technique include Harris (1958: 447–453) and (1981: 47–58); Patterson et al. (1987: 3–23); Teichmuller and Teichmuller (1968: 347–418). The ongoing debate about the character of fusinite is summarized in Scott (1989: 443–475). A fascinating case study, in which Car-

boniferous fire ecology eerily mimics that of today, is Arens (1991: 279–288). A good summary of the case for fire at the Cretaceous-Tertiary boundary is Anders et al. (1992: 485–492). A map of the critical sampled sites (mostly iridium, but charcoal too) is available in Gould, ed. (1993: 166).

13. The experiments are described in Harris (1958: 447–453; 1981: 47–58). The case for analogy is found in Komarek (1972) and Arens (1991).

TORCH

1. The best summary of the evidence for very early fire possession is Bellomo (1990). The oldest, and probably most controversial site, is described in Gowlett et al. (1981), and among the replies, Isaac (1982). For a surer, but later date, see Brain and Sillen (1988). A good survey is available in Clark and Harris (1985).

Syntheses of varying utility include Oakley (1961); Clark and Harris (1985); and Perles (1977), which thoroughly treats the European, especially French, archaeological record; for an English digest, see Perles (1981). Useful in tracking sites is Whitehouse and Whitehouse (1975) and Lambert and the Diagram Group (1987).

2. Several outstanding studies ponder the meaning of humanity's possession of fire. The most recent is Goudsblom (1992), a wonderful meditation on the character of humanity's species monopoly from the perspective of a widely read sociologist; a summary is available in Goudsblom (1986). Many of Carl Sauer's works address the question of anthropogenic fire; what they lack in technical rigor, they more than make up for with insight; see Sauer (1975 and 1972). Also mandatory are essays by Komarek (1965 and 1967). For general

background still useful is Pfeiffer (1972). Consider also Tylor (1964).

3. The tarsier as fire fondler is described in Komarek (1967: 153–154); the chimps, in Brink (1957). Stories about raptors seizing and redistributing fire are common in fire myths in Australia, Africa, and the Americas; confirmation comes by personal communication from Henry Lewis.

4. On the parade of hominids through Europe: for a substantial narrative, see Cunliffe, ed. (1994); for graphic aids, see Lambert and Diagram Group (1987) and Whitehouse and Whitehouse (1975).

5. Sauer (1956: 55). For aboriginal analogues, see Lewis and Ferguson (1988); Lewis (1973); and Blackburn and Anderson, eds. (1993), which is full of detail about pre-European Californians; Stewart (1956); Pyne (1991, 1982, and 1995). In fact, the documentation on aboriginal burning is so enormous that it is difficult to absorb en masse: it only requires that someone look for it. An impressive sampling is available in H. H. Bartlett (1956). An inquiry into why anthropologists have ignored this phenomenon is given in Stewart (1963).

6. Bandelier, ed. (1973: 92–93). Reference to Artemis from Hough (1926: 199).

7. For Virginia Indians, see Harriot (1972), especially the drawings by John White. For California Indians, see Blackburn and Anderson, eds. (1993) and Lewis (1973). For Plains tribes, see Higgins (1986).

8. For an introduction to fire-assisted changes during the Mesolithic, consult Mellars (1976); Simmons and Tooley, eds. (1981: esp. 82–124); and as a prelude, Roberts (1989: 93). Specific consequences are discussed in the five regional fire histories.

9. The classic summary of the vanishing megafauna is Martin and Klein, eds. (1984). A fascinating inquiry into

the consequences of these losses for fire is Schüle (1990).

10. My account of domestication follows closely Sauer (1972). The classic organization of agricultural origins into "hearths" is Vavilov (1949–50).

11. Several studies examine the question of fire in agricultural origins, particularly the Near East grass and grazer complex. For a review article, see Lewis (1972). An eccentric but useful linguistic analysis that attempts to derive a common pyric origin for domestication is available in Forni (1984). See also Komarek's ever-enlightening essays (1965 and 1967).

12. For a good introduction to the concept and its connotations, see Conklin (1954). For Bartlett's ascerbic evaluation, see Bartlett (1955–61: II, 511).

13. The phrase comes from Jones (1969). For a summary of Aboriginal fire practices, see Pyne (1991), which also includes a brief sketch of Australia's California cognate. A more recent summation of prehistoric California life is Blackburn and Anderson, eds. (1993). Brazilian fire practices are poorly studied; for an introduction to anthropogenic fire on the *cerrado,* see Anderson and Posey (1991).

14. The fascinating story of Europe's Neolithic is the subject of many works and innumerable speculations. Valuable guides are Roberts (1989) and Cunliffe, ed. (1994). A good synopsis that places the European experience in a larger context is Grigg (1974).

The scholarly literature is grounded in archaeology, which brings an odd mixture of exceedingly detailed artifactual accounts and speculative ideologies. Among accounts that achieve a working balance, see Bogucki (1988), Whittle (1985), Jarman et al., eds. (1982), and Clark (1977). For a concise summary of agricultural origins, grounded in both archaeology and biology, see Zohary and

Hopf (1988). For fauna, see Clutton-Brock (1987).

15. The swidden cycle varied enormously. The fifty-year model derives from detailed studies in Bohemia as described by Soudsky and Pavlu (1972). But many, many variants existed—some in forests, some in coppice, some in peat, some in single-year fallow fields of weeds. The separate regional histories will provide details.

16. For a handy overview, see Grigg (1974). Interestingly fire ceremonies display the same pattern.

17. The horse has its own literature. A concise summary is available in Clutton-Brock (1987: 80–90). For a fascinating study that synthesizes Neolithic agriculture, the horse, population movements, and languages, see Mallory (1989).

18. See Crosby (1986: 145–170).

19. Corrigan, ed. (1965: 143).

20. Quoted in Smith and Gnudi (1966: xxvii).

21. See Wertime and Wertime, eds. (1982), especially Conophagos (1982: 181–192).

22. A survey of fire warfare is sketched in Pyne (1982: 390–403). Useful references include Stockholm International Peace Research Institute (1975); Fisher (1946); and Partington (1961).

23. I am indebted to Barnes (1996) for alerting me to several references in the *Iliad* that I had missed. On fire warfare in Gaul, see citations in Brown (1883b: 2).

24. Good surveys of fire-starting apparatus are available in Hough (1926); Davidson (1947); and Lagercrantz (1954).

25. Hough (1926: 86). Lagercrantz (1954) reproduces several photographs of ancient fire-starting devices still known in Norrland, Sweden.

26. Lagercrantz (1954: 78).

27. Hough (1926: 123–126); Goudsblom (1992: 170–172); Beaver (1985).

28. The question of fire's social control under such conditions is one of many important issues that inform Goudsblom's fascinating monograph, *Fire and Civilization*. I am indebted to the author for forcing me to consider the topic in contexts outside my preferred habitat.

HEARTH

1. The story of the Serbian experiment is given in Goudsblom (1992: 70–71) and Vitruvius quoted (1992: 114); Weber (1976: 16); Tacitus (1970: 115).

I am indebted to Johan Goudsblom for alerting me to the significance of Europe's urban fire history.

2. Medieval England example from Jones (1981: 33).

3. Gibbon (1963: 703); Juvenal from Goudsblom (1992: 114).

4. Fustel de Coulanges quoted in Goudsblom (1992: 111).

5. The reference on wooden shingles comes from Pliny by way of Robinson (1977: 384).

6. For fire protection in ancient Rome, see Robinson (1977) and Rainbird (1986).

7. Plutarch (1932: 651).

8. See Goudsblom (1992: 114–115); Tacitus (1989: 362–363).

9. Tacitus (1989: 364).

10. See Robinson (1977) and Rainbird (1986).

11. All quotations regarding the London fire are taken from Cowie (1970: 59, 66, 71, 80–81, 108, 117–118).

12. Goudsblom (1992: 149–150); Jones et al. (1984); Frost and Jones (1989).

13. Weber (1976: 16).

14. Hawthorne (1843).

15. Bachelard (1964: 7).

16. The fullest (and undoubtedly the dullest) compendium of fire mythology is Frazer (1974). A companion compendium is Edsman (1950).

17. Egyptian and Canaanite references from Laughlin (1975: 97–100, 156–157). Old Testament sources from Deutoronomy 12:31, 18:21; II Kings 16:3, 21:6; Jeremiah 19:5; Genesis 22:6; Gibil references in Laughlin (1975: 176–177). An overview is given in Hough (1926: 126–144, 182–183). For a detailed study of the Priestly sacred fire, see Morgenstern (1963), which offers an explanation different from Laughlin's.

18. For Agni and the hearth fire, see Nagy (1990: 85–121, 143–180). An annotated version of the Nadab and Abihu story is available in Laughlin (1975: 125–140). For the Zoroastrian fire rites, see Modi (1937: 199–230).

19. My reading relies heavily on Laughlin (1975: 2–44). Other citations: Ezekial reference from Laughlin, p. 60; Psalm 29:7; and Laughlin quote (1975: 245). For the Philistines and their contribution to Hebrew fire rites, see Jones (1972: 343–350).

20. Laughlin (1975: 66–142); Leviticus 6:1–6.

21. Sources for this analysis include Laughlin (1975: passim) and Goudsblom (1992: 72–94). See Vergil, *Aeneid,* Book XI, for an elaborate series of ceremonial fires.

22. Baal quote from Laughlin (1975: 156).

23. Bachelard (1964: 14); Burnet (1928: esp. 130–168), with Diogenes quoted on page 147. A thorough if discursive survey of the evolution of fire philosophy is found in Gregory (1934).

24. Bachelard (1964: 7).

25. Sources on the Pythagoreans and the central fire come from Burnet (1928: 296–297). For Plato see Rouse, trans. (1956: 315–316).

26. Lucretius (1951: 47).

27. Good summaries exist in Gregory (1934: 43, 45). For Theophrastus, see Coutant, trans. (1972: 2).

28. John Donne: "An Anatomie of the World." Gregory (1934: 62, 65); Boerhaave quoted in Bachelard (1964: 60).

29. See Faraday (1957).

30. Bachelard (1964: 9). Bachelard suggests that fire induces a poetic reverie that makes its rational analysis impossible, and then proves just that thesis by his own hallucinogenic scholarship. The psychological (especially psychoanalytical) discussion of fire is fatuous, at best; for another sample, see Grinstein (1952: 416–420), or Sigmund Freud's own convoluted inquiry in Freud (1950: 288).

31. The best source on fire ceremonials is Frazer (1923a: I, 269–300). A useful (and competent) abbreviation is available in Frazer (1923b: 638–641). An obsessively thorough encyclopedia of Germanic fire rites is Freudenthal (1931).

32. Quoted in Frazer (1923a: I, 202).

33. Ibid., p. 269.

34. The synod is discussed ibid., p. 270; Goudsblom (1992: 135).

35. Wilde (1887: 214).

36. Frazer (1923a: I, 329–331).

37. Frazer (1923a: II, 20); for the cat fires, II, 39. For an alternative interpretation of fire ceremony origins, one that agrees more closely with my own, see Freudenthal (1931: 216).

38. Frazer (1885). For a fuller elaboration, see Frazer (1923a: II). Vergil, *Aeneid,* Book II, lines 297–299, and Book III, lines 283–286. For familial rites and the hearth, especially the dangers of reckless fire-lending, see Freudenthal (1931: 7, 55–68).

39. See "The King and the Hearth: Six Studies of Sacral Vocabulary Relating to the Fireplace," in Nagy (1990: 143–180); quotes, pp. 170, 144.

40. Nagy (1990: 195–196); Frazer (1923b: 159–161).

41. Beard (1980).

42. Dumézil (1970: 311), but see the entire chapter from which the observation comes, "The Fires of Public Worship," pp. 311–326. On Nero, Tacitus (1989: 361). The episode occurred during a ceremonial pilgrimage Nero made of the Capitoline gods before departing on a tour of the eastern empire; shaken at Vesta's shrine, he canceled the trip, and soon afterward Rome, including the shrine, burned in the great conflagration, perhaps started on Nero's orders.

ETERNAL FLAME: FIRE IN MEDITERRANEAN EUROPE

1. Provencal proverb quoted from Bartlett (1955: I, 340).

2. The literature on the Mediterranean biota is vast. What follows are good introductions that include fire ecology. See Mooney et al., tech. coords. (1977); Conrad and Oechel, tech. coords. (1981); diCastri and Mooney, eds. (1973); diCastri et al., eds. (1981); *Ecologia Mediterranean* 13 (4), special issue on fire (1987); Goldammer and Jenkins, eds. (1990); and *Proceedings Tall Timbers Fire Ecology Conference,* vol. 13 (Tallahassee, 1974), passim; Trabaud and Prodon, eds. (1993); Gomez-Campo, ed. (1985); UNESCO (1977); Keeley (1984). An excellent introduction is available in Le Houerou (1981).

The scientific literature is enormous, though often repetitive and so specific as to resist any generalization. Most of the older literature is in French; Spanish, to a lesser extent Italian, and still in its beginnings, Portuguese, scientists are adding to it. Summaries of Spanish fire ecology are available in "La Restauracion de la Vegetacion en los Montes Españoles," *Ecolo-*

gia, Fuera de Series, 1 (1990); *Cuadernos de Ecologia Aplicada* 1 (Los Incendios Forestales) (1976); ICONA (1985); Viegas, ed. (1988 and 1990). Good cross sections of the French literature appear in special issues of forestry journals; see, for example, "Les incendies de forêts," *Revue Forestière Française* (numero special 1975), pp. 260–550, and "Espaces Forestiers et Incendies, *Revue Forestière Française* (numero special 1990) and *Forêt Méditerranéenne* 14 (2) (1993). The best guide is the general bibliography published by the International Association of Wildland Fire.

Historical works should begin with the classic Semple (1931); a modern update that integrates ancient texts with archaeology is available in Smith (1979). Other introductions include the forceful Thirgood (1981); Hughes (1975 and 1994); Meiggs (1982); and Braudel (1972), whose scope far exceeds its title, see particularly "Part One: The Role of the Environment." Shorter but extremely valuable essays include Heichelheim (1956: 165–182) and Darby (1956: 183–216).

To place Mediterranean agriculture in a larger context, see Grigg (1974: esp. 123–152). A delightful introduction to the regional natural history is Attenborough (1978).

3. See Le Houerou (1981: 479–521, esp. 486), and Trabaud (1981b: 523). For the origin of "pyrophyte," see Trabaud (1987: 27).

4. Columella, cited in Rackham (1986: 184).

5. See, for example, Smith (1972).

6. Percentages of cultivation from Le Houerou (1981: 486).

7. See Smith (1979: passim); Lelle and Gold (1994: 118–126).

8. Xenophon, *Economics* XV III: 2; Vergil, *Georgics* I: 84–93; Lucan, from Smith (1979: 296); contemporary wheat

stubble burning from Henry Lewis, personal communication; Cato, Columella, and Palladius from White (1970: 142).

9. Homer and Vassus quoted in Liacos (1973: 69–70); Pliny quoted in White (1970: 141).

10. Vergil, *Aeneid,* trans. by T. H. Delabere-May, 10 405–411; Silius Italicus quoted in Pounds (1973: 145).

11. Richardson (1901: 183).

12. Homer quoted in Semple (1931: 290); Pyrennes fire, from Thirgood (1981: 67); Thucydides quoted in Liacos (1973: 67); Vergil, *Aeneid* XII, p. 325; Lucretius (1951: 209).

13. Theophrastus (*De Igne:* 16).

14. Brown (1883a: 105 fn).

15. Plato, *Critias,* quoted in Darby (1956: 185); Gibbon (1963: 15).

16. Marsh (1965: 11–12).

17. Gibbon (1963: 703).

18. Quoted in Hughes (1994: 146).

19. Macrobius quoted from Thirgood (1981: 69).

20. General surveys of Mediterranean transhumance include Semple (1931: 297–341) and Braudel (1972: I, 85–102); Braudel quote from p. 94. On European transhumance, generally, see Rafiullah (1966); Evans (1940); Arbos (1923); Davies (1941).

21. Cato quoted from Thirgood (1981: 31); Tomaselli (1977: 34).

22. Fernow (1907: 279).

23. On the Mesta, see Klein (1920); Braudel (1972: I, 91–95); Smith (1979); Manderscheid (1980). For an ecological analysis that avoids the usual clichés, see Ruiz and Ruiz (1987), and for a contemporary survey by the same authors (1984). Other useful studies on Iberian pastoralism include Ruiz and Gonzales-Bernaldez (1982–83); Marañon (1988); Bunting and Rego (1988); Garcia and Poll (1979); MacKay (1977); Bishko (1958: 47–69).

24. Braudel (1972: I, 89–91).

25. My description relies heavily on Kish (1954). See also Marino (1988).

26. Kish (1954: 303).

27. Leone and Saracino (1990: A.13, esp. 2).

28. Ibid., pp. 6–7.

29. Quoted in Braudel (1972: I, 301).

30. Kipling (1992: 326–327); Woolsey (1917: v).

31. The most thorough review of agricultural burning is Sigaut (1975).

32. Smith (1979: esp. 257–271; 1972: 397–407). For a summary of regional botany, see Wright and Wanstall (1977: 24–33). A monograph on the medieval grazing and forest regime is available in Sclafert (1959).

33. See Kuhnholtz-Lordat (1938); Trabaud (1981a: 451) and Delabraze and Valette (1981: 475); Robertson (1977: 284).

34. For a case study, see Merriman (1976).

35. See, variously, Trabaud (1981a: 451); Le Houerou (1981: 525) and Trabaud (1981b: 523–526); Amouric (1992: 68). Lentheric (1895: 334) suggests that the culprits were the Saracens, while the other authors finger the insurgent locals.

36. See Amouric (1992: 15–23), quote from p. 29; also, Guiny (1877: 513). One of the earliest references is in de Ribbé (1865: v).

37. There are many descriptions available. A very nice one, however, is found in Braudel (1972: I, 143).

38. The text, with commentary, is reproduced in English in Brown (1883b). For a summary of the code, see Glacken (1967: 491–494) and Fernow (1907: 192–194), and for its setting in French history, see Pincetl (1993); for the laws, see Woolsey (1917), quote from p. 5.

39. For an excellent English summary of French forestry in 1887, see Bailey (1887a: 341–355, 389–402, 439–450, 489–501, 537–545).

40. Bailey (1887b: 251).

41. Ibid., p. 444.

42. Quotes from Fernandez (1897: 3); Woolsey and Greeley (1920: 284).

43. Bailey (1887b: 245–256, 293–304); quote from p. 250.

44. Ibid., p. 298. See also Fernandez (1897: 1–8).

45. See Woolsey and Greeley (1920: 4).

46. Fernandez (1897: 7); Woolsey and Greeley (1920: 276).

47. Bailey (1887b: 294); Fernandez (1897: 7, 6).

48. See Guiny (1877: 513–527). The syndicates are described in Amouric (1992) and Seigue (1972). The interwar years saw an outpouring of French fire studies. For a useful sampling, see Jourdan (1930); Joubert (1923 and 1929); R. D. and S. L. (1937); Salvador (1922); Pallu (1931); Coffin (1931 and 1932); Ducamp (1932); Negre (1924); Barbey (1924); and Flahault (1924).

49. Fernandez (1897: 4); Bailey (1887b: 294–295, 293, 298–299); Woolsey and Greeley (1920: 287).

50. Hutchins (1916: 45); Bailey (1887a: 494–495).

51. For an introduction to Corsican natural history, see Cardona and Contandriopoulos (1979); and for land use history, Smith (1979), Girod-Genet (1912), and Surier (1912). A good English survey of the forest fire scene is given in Woolsey and Greeley (1920) and Woolsey, Jr. (1917).

52. See Smith (1979: 32–35).

53. Woolsey and Greeley (1920: 112, 154); de Ribbé (1865: 32).

54. Woolsey and Greeley (1920: 133, 154); Woolsey, Jr. (1917: 8).

55. Woolsey and Greeley (1920: 154–155); Woolsey, Jr. (1917: 130–133).

56. See Associated Press, July 31, 1989, for information on the fires. Probably the best source for tracking the fire scene in recent years is *International Forest Fire News,* biannually issued through the U.N.'s FAO.

57. My basic sources for French North Africa are Boudy (1948), especially vol. 1, pp. 230–269, for Algerian Forest Service and pp. 629–684 for fire history; Kuhnholtz-Lordat (1938); and Woolsey and Greeley (1920). For a general (if slanted) background on the larger environmental history, see Thirgood (1987b and 1981). Murphy (1951) outlines the classic arguments for anthropogenic destruction of the landscape.

58. Rosenblum (1986: 145); and Horne (1977: 23).

59. Bailey (1987a: 542); Woolsey and Greeley (1920: 56).

60. See de Ribbé (1866).

61. For an early comparison between France and Algeria, see de Ribbé (1865: 32–36 and passim); Woolsey and Greeley (1920: 4, 90).

62. Lefebvre (1882).

63. Woolsey, Jr. (1917: 7).

64. See the appendix, ibid., for a translation of the entire Algerian Code of 1903.

65. Quoted ibid., pp. 51–52.

66. Woolsey and Greeley (1920: 101).

67. A good description is available in Woolsey, Jr. (1917: 10–45).

68. French fire statistics cited in Boudy (1948: I, 631); quotes, pp. 629, 684.

69. On this incendiary warfare, see Le Houerou (1973: 245).

70. Mayle (1991: 123).

71. Kuhnholtz-Lordat (1938).

72. On the natural history of the islands, see Greuter (1979); Attenborough (1978); Cardona and Contandriopoulos (1979). Good introductions to the history of their environmental problems are available in Giavelli and Rossi (1990) and Vernicos (1990).

73. Cherry (1981).

74. Cardona and Contandriopoulos (1979: 141); Greuter (1979: 89).

75. Vernicos (1990: 153); Tomaselli (1977: 34); Tennant (1885: 97).

76. See Tennant (1885: 296, 102, 96, 80).

77. Le Lannou (1941: 174–180, 221). On fires in contemporary Italy, see Leone and Saracino (1990: A.13) and Cesti (1988).

78. My primary source for Cypriot forest history is Thirgood (1987b), supplemented as indicated for particular items.

79. Bricogne (1877); Montrichard (1874: quote on p. 39).

80. Baker (1879: 333).

81. Ibid., and Dobbs (1885).

82. On the dimensions of the national goat herd, see Thirgood (1981: 125); Thistleton-Dyer, quoted in Hutchins (1909: 28).

83. Baker (1879: 336).

84. Baker, quoted in Thirgood (1987b: 113); Madon quoted in Thirgood (1987b: 128).

85. Geddes quoted in Dunbar (1983: 111).

86. G. H. (1926: 249–250).

87. Madon (1881: 36, 46).

88. Ibid., pp. 35, 46. See also Madon (1930: esp. 1–5).

89. Madon quoted in Thirgood (1987b: 99).

90. Madon (1881: 38).

91. Hutchins (1909: 30–31).

92. Ibid., p. 28; Le Houerou (1981: 500).

93. Chapman, "Foreword," in Thirgood (1987b: xiii).

94. Troup quoted in Thirgood (1987b: 150).

95. Quote from Thirgood (1981: 139).

96. Murdoch (1959: 61).

97. Macmillan quoted in Lapping (1985: 336).

98. Quote from Thirgood (1987b: 279).

99. War-related statistics, ibid., p. 275; other statistics from Cyprus Forestry Department (1991).

100. For statistics, see Thirgood (1981: 146); for assessment of fire's role, see Chapman, in Thirgood (1987b: xiii); Thirgood (1987b: 267).

101. Cicero, *De Natura Deorum* II: 60.

102. See Caesar, Pearl trans. (1962: 103, 198–199), and Tacitus (1970: 123).

103. See Le Houerou (1981: 513–514).

104. Ibid., p. 517. The story is retold endlessly in all the major fire symposia and land use conferences of recent decades. Good examples are Economic Commission for Europe et al., *Seminar on Forest Fire Prevention, Land Use and People* (Athens, 1992); *Proceedings, International Conference on Forest Fire Research* (University of Coimbra, 1990), and *2nd International Conference on Forest Fire Research,* 2 vols. (University of Coimbra, 1994). From time to time forestry periodicals have published special issues on the fire question; see, for example, *Forêt Méditerranéenne* 14, no. 2 (1993), and "Espaces forestiers et incendies," *Revue forestière française,* numero special 1990. A typical summary is Chautrand (1972).

CONTROLLED COMBUSTION:
FIRE IN CENTRAL EUROPE

1. Iversen (1973: 28). Except where indicated, I follow Iversen's account closely, regretting only that I must abbreviate his extraordinary and delightful book to the point of parody.

Other general works that I have found useful for central Europe include Huntley and Webb III (1988), Jordan (1988), and Birks et al., eds. (1988), esp. Ammann (pp. 289–299), Küster (pp. 301–310), and Vad Odgaard (pp. 311–319).

2. Iversen (1973: 61–62).

3. See ibid., pp. 88–90. For the original experiment, see Steensberg (1979).

A tidy capitulation complete with photos is given in Steensberg (1993: 200–210).

4. Caesar, Pearl trans. (1962: 103).

5. Iversen (1973: 97).

6. Ibid., pp. 85–86; for a recent critique, see Graumlich (1993). For overview of early human changes, see the excellent essay by Behre (1988).

7. See Clark et al. (1989). For recent studies from the Alps, see Wick (1994). For the etymology of Switzerland, see Schneiter (1970: 52).

8. See Glacken (1967: 309).

9. Cited in Postan, ed. (1966: 134).

10. Quoted in Darby (1956: 199). This is a marvelous essay, and I have followed its general outline closely.

11. Quoted in Bloch (1966: 213).

12. Figures from Braudel (1990: II, 263–264).

13. Malouet and Gilbert quoted, respectively, ibid., pp. 238, 353–354.

14. For descriptions of paring and burning, see Steensberg (1993: 155–185); Sigaut (1975); Montag (1990); Bringeus (1963); Fenton (1985: 102); Gailey and Fenton, eds. (1970). Allusion to Tatars from "Treatment of Waste Lands in the Low Countries" (1893: 361–363). For a contemporary French critique not given in Sigaut, see Marsaux (1848: 324–325). A summary of France's agricultural revolution is available in Clout, ed. (1977), esp. Sutton (pp. 247–300) and Clout (pp. 407–446).

15. See Marshall (1970: 145–152); Darby (1936a: 455); Young (1970: 197–199, 108–109, 218).

16. Turbilly quoted in Kuhnholtz-Lordat (1938: 155).

17. For heath fires, see Montag (1990: 55–60); Sigaut (1975); see also Great Britain fire history. For the Brittany fires, see Gloaguen (1990); Roze (1993); Clement and Touffet (1981). For Jutland law, see Steensberg (1993: 122). A useful summary of heath fires in eighteenth-century northern Germany is found in Delfs (1993). I'm grateful to Peter Lex, Forstmeister, Lüneberger Heide, for bringing this to my attention.

18. I have relied heavily on three sources: Steensberg (1993: 176–181); Thorpe (1957: 87–121); and Olwig (1977). Dates from Thorpe (1957: 92–93).

19. Quote from Olwig (1977: 114).

20. Thorpe (1957: 98, 87).

21. A concise summary of the origins is available in Schacke (1951: 45–54). Schacke quotes Winston Churchill, who urged a similar society for Scotland: "Here is surely a cause for which the Fiery Cross should blaze."

22. See Olwig (1977: 266–276), for the early arguments, and p. 386 for Holst's motto.

23. Ibid., p. 308, for the final figures, and p. 379 for quote.

24. Steensberg (1993: 178).

25. Ibid., p. 181.

26. Olwig (1977: 396–400).

27. Hutchins (1916: 393). A good survey of how silva was integrated with the reclaimed lands of central Europe is Bechmann (1990).

28. An interesting survey of forest swidden around Europe (and compared with India and South Africa) is available in Brown (1883a). Brown disapproved of the practice, but appreciated its great breadth and went to Finland in large part to learn about a practice that, for much of Europe, had faded into history.

29. I follow closely Steensberg (1993). Useful companions are Kuhnholtz-Lordat (1938 and 1958). The Polish example is summarized on pp. 127–129, and comes from a study by Lewicka (1972). See also and Podolak (1972). A description of transhumance is available in Davies (1941: 165).

30. Steensberg (1993: 134–142). Steensberg derives his data from a monograph published by F. L. Hlubeck in

1846, and a more recent thesis (unpublished) by Hans Frühwald in 1987.

31. *Brandwirtschaft* in the Black Forest is treated carefully in Steensberg (1993: 146–151) and Montag (1990: 10–38). The grand summary, however, remains Schneiter (1970).

32. Banfield cited in Darby (1956: 200); Vogelmann quoted in Goldammer 1993: 2); Hutchins (1892: 62). Also useful for a concise overview is Thirgood (1989).

33. Quotes from Sigaut (1975: 24–25, 29, 23–24).

34. Sigaut (1975: 23–24); Steensberg (1993: 151–152; Kuhnholtz-Lordat (1938: 167–169; Fisher (1897: 267–271).

35. Brown (1883b: 94–99).

36. See Montag (1990: 41).

37. For alpine fire practices in general, see Steensberg (1993: 142–146).

38. For alpine pastoralism, see Davies (1941: 155–168) and Evans (1940: 172–180).

39. Lauder quoted in Brown (1883a: 94).

40. See, for example, Blache (1923); Garde général des forêts (1850). For persistence, see Krüger (1951). Includes photos.

41. See Hutchins (1909: 23–24).

42. Fernow (1907: 8–45); Young (1979). An excellent summary of nineteenth-century forestry is available in Franklin Hough (1887), submitted to the State Department.

43. Fernow (1907: 45).

44. Ibid., p. 22; Hutchins (1892: 35–36).

45. Fernow (1907: 22); Hutchins (1892: 54).

46. Brown (1883b: 12–13). A synopsis of the Code and its context, also based on Brown's compilation, is available in Glacken (1967: 491–497).

47. For a translation of the 1661 report, see Brown (1883b: 13–20); quotes from pp. 19–20.

48. Ibid., p. 48.

49. The story is told in many places. See Fernow (1907: 200–203). A much fuller treatment, with considerable silvicultural and technical detail, is found in Woolsey and Greeley (1920: 169–205). For a spirited account by a contemporary observer, see Marsh (1965: 398–436). For a British forester's perspective, see Bailey (1887a: 449–450). Fernow and Woolsey disagree frequently on dates and statistics. In general, where I could not find an authoritative French source, I have accepted Woolsey's figures.

50. Vandal reference from Dubos (1980: 99).

51. Woolsey and Greeley (1920: 169).

52. Ibid., pp. 203–204; Lafforgue (1914). Related fire studies include Ruffault (1924); Muel (1900); Anon., "Continental Notes: France" (1924); and Bailey (1887a).

53. Woolsey and Greeley (1920: 204–205, 275–276).

54. Ibid., p. 276.

55. Moir (1881: 2).

56. Marsh (1965: 329).

57. Fernow (1907: 206–207); Woolsey and Greeley (1920: 142–145).

58. Such stories constitute the folklore of forestry. See, for example, Woolsey and Greeley (1920), Marsh (1965), Glacken (1967), and "Notes on the Influence of Forests on the Storage and Regulation of the Water Supply," *Indian Forest Service*, Bulletin 9 (1906).

59. For the role of föhn winds in torrents, see Brown (1880: 13–14). For a meteorological treatment, see Kendrew (1961: 337–338).

60. Pinchot and Woolsey quotes taken from Woolsey, Jr. (1917: viii, xiii).

61. Lockert (1991: 13–41). The best distillation of German fire lore at the end of the century is Gerding (1899).

62. Lockert (1991: 13–14). For the 1982 fire statistics, see Von Badenberg (1893). Large fires are frequent news

items in forestry journals of the time. As a sample, consider Bachmann (1892); Brofinger (1905); and Anon., "Große Waldbrände in Bayern" (1909).

63. Lockert (1991: 15–19). See K. M. Müller (1931), D. M. Müller (1932); Conrad (1925); Meinecke (1927). The orthodox view of free-burning fire is contained in manuals like Weck (1950).

64. Lockert (1991: 13–14); Hutchins (1892: 104).

65. Dubos (1980: 49).

66. For the reference to the rules of Knut, see Freudenthal (1931; 11).

67. Quotes from Steensberg (1993: 181).

68. A thumbnail sketch of World War II as a fire war is given in Pyne (1982: 394–395). The torching of German nature preserves comes from Schama (1995: 73).

69. See Tüxen (1973: 7–13).

70. Makowski (1973: 15–17).

WILD HEARTH:
FIRE IN BOREAL EUROPE

1. Quoted in Jones (1977: 15); Kuusi et al., eds. (1977: 99).

2. There are many good surveys of the boreal environment. An excellent summary is The Plant Cover of Sweden, Acta Phytogeographica Suecica 50 (Uppsala, 1965). Still the best distillation of fire history and ecology is Wein and MacLean, eds. (1983). More recent reviews of statistics are Stocks (1991) and Goldammer and Furyaev, eds. (1996). Classics in regional fire ecology include Zackrisson (1977); Uggla (1973) and (1958); Siren (1973); Koh (1975); Viro (1969). For a survey of fire risk at a time when fire was still a threat, see Kinnman (1936). For the curious story of allelopathic plants and fire, see Zackrisson and Nilsson (1989).

3. For Sodankylä, see Franssila

(1959); for Ulvinsalon, Haapanen and Siitonen (1978); for Muddus, Engelmark (1987 and 1981), and Uggla (1958).

4. Granström (1991 and 1993).

5. See Zackrisson (1977, 1980, 1978, 1979); Segerström et al. (1994); Bradshaw and Zackrisson (1990); and Linder (1992). For an excellent profile of regional fire traits, see Schimmel (1993). A study on the character of the varves is available in Renberg (1976).

6. For information about the Magnus brothers and their place in humanistic learning, I have relied heavily on the fascinating study by Johannesson (1991). References from the Historia come from the most recent Swedish edition, Historia om de Nordiska Folken (1982).

7. Olaus Magnus (1982: 34, 424, 102). See also p. 279: iron-bearing mountains especially attract lightning, with all its risks.

8. Elephant allusion, ibid., p. 104.

9. Ibid., p. 543.

10. Ibid., pp. 571–573.

11. Ibid., pp. 84, 581–583.

12. For Lapp (Saami) history, see Aronsson (1991) and Collinder (1949). The classic accounts of the Lapps and landscape fire are L. L. Laestadius (1824); Petrus Laestadius (1833); and Fellman (1906). A good summary, with English translations of the critical passages is available in Massa (1987). A useful introduction to Lapland ecology is Epstein (1984). Also helpful for assessing the history of this most adaptable people are Hansegård (1978) and Beach (1981).

13. Quotes from Massa (1987: 238, 235–240). See also Campbell (1982: 234–236); Bylund (1974); and for another (earlier) view of the conflict, Högstroöm (1747: 253); and for Lapp retaliatory burning, Ehrenmalm as quoted in Högbom (1934: 37). For colonization in general, see Segerström (1990); Bylund (1956); Frödin (1952);

Rudberg (1957); Bodvall (1959). For a comparable study of northern Finland, see Tegengren (1952); and for a sparsely populated site, Hicks (1976).

14. Fellman quoted from Massa (1987: 238).

15. See, by way of comparison, Huttunen and Tolonen (1972), and Welinder (1975).

16. Tolonen and Kukkonen (1989); quote from p. 64.

17. See Huttunen (1980). This is a superb study, which I have followed closely. An earlier version is Huttunen and Tolonen (1975). Excellent supporting studies are available in a series of contributions by M. Tolonen (1985a,b, 1980, 1978a,b,c). For complementary studies, see K. Tolonen (1978, 1987, 1983).

18. Quoted from Huttunen (1980: 25, 35).

19. Tweedie (1913: 281–282).

20. My description derives from Berglund, ed. (1991).

21. Ibid., p. 434; the authors note that "Sweden's national agricultural policy has without doubt been a crucial factor, perhaps the most crucial." For a diagrammatic summary of six millennia of change, see the chapter "Landscape-ecological Aspects of Long-term Changes in the Ystad Area," pp. 405–424. Page 418 includes a summary of charcoal dust.

22. Olaus Magnus (1982: 571–573).

23. See Mead (1981: 67, 88, 133, and passim), esp. pp. 200–205 for urban reforms and their relationship to fire.

24. Quotes from Mead (1981: 201).

25. Oinonen (1967). See also Oinonen (1968).

26. Oinonen (1967: 19).

27. For a brief description of *saeter*, see Davies (1941: 166–167).

28. See Grotenfelt (1899).

29. Soininen (1959: 154).

30. Bennett (1792: 35–49).

31. Bureus cited in Steensberg (1993: 175).

The literature on Scandinavian swidden is large. Two excellent points of departure are Soininen (1959) and Montelius (1953). Also recommended, although not in English, are the entries under "Svedjebruk" in *Kulturhistorisk Lexikon För Nordisk Medeltid*, vol. 17 (Rosenkilde og Bagger). *Suomen Antropologi* 4 (1987), Special Issue on Swidden Cultivation, is indispensable both for its translations of Finnish sources and a relatively comprehensive bibliography, particularly useful for eighteenth-century sources. Again, Steensberg (1993: 107–123). A recent anthology (with English summaries) is available in Larsson (1995).

For a detailed description of a *svedje*, complete with photographs, see Bannbers (1934). To place the practice within the larger spectrum of Finnish agriculture, see Soininen (1974), which has an English summary and captions. To place Finnish pioneering in a larger context, see Jordan and Kaups (1989). This, in turn, builds on Vilkuna (1953), which establishes the transfer to the New Sweden colony. The two outstanding summaries of swidden recorded as it was disappearing are Grotenfelt (1899) and Heikinheimo (1915), the first by an agonomist and the second by a forester, both critics. A popular review of the impact of these practices (and others) is available in Linkola (1988) and Tvengsberg (1988).

For the Finnish colonizations of interior Sweden, see Brogberg (1988), which contains an English summary. Other studies focus on particular regions. See, for example, Hicks (1976 and 1988); Wallerström (1984); Frödin (1952), esp. pp. 38–56; Isaksson (1967), esp. pp. 351–352; Campbell (1982); Falk (1921); Bromander (1902).

For regional studies of swidden, see Lars J. Larsson (1989); Byberg (1928);

Bylund (1956); Westin (1930); Jirlow (1969); Larsson (1979–80); Kardell et al. (1980); Lööw (1985); Weimarck (1979); Myrdal and Söderberg (1991); and Nellbeck (1953).

Not to be forgotten are some of the classic studies from the eighteenth century, including Faggot (1750); Gadd (1753–54); Bennett (1792).

An interesting discussion (in English) on *svedjebruk* is Brown (1883a), which includes comparisons with other lands, notably India.

32. Reference to Charles IX from Montelius (1953: 45); etymology of Sweden from Schneiter (1970: 49).

33. The Bishop Agardt quotation is from "Sverige från skövling till odling," p. 22.

34. Moberg (1975).

35. Mead (1968: 184). For a detailed description of the actual process of re-colonization, see Smeds (1960).

36. Biographical information from Blunt (1971). Landscape description from Linnaeus, as quoted in Blunt (1971: 15). Other useful studies include Frängsmyr, ed. (1983) and Worster (1979: 26–56).

37. Linnaeus to the Governor of Umeå, 1734, quoted in Blunt (1971). Linnaeus's travels are published as follows, allowing for two English translations: Carl von Linné, *Linné i Dalarna,* edited anthology by Bertil Gullander (1980); Marie Åsberg and William T. Stearn, "Linnaeus's Öland and Gotland Journey 1741," *Biol. J. Linn. Soc.* 5 (1973): 1–107; Carl Linnaeus, *A Tour in Lapland* (reprint 1971): Carl Linnaeus, *Skånska Resa,* Carl-Otto von Sydow, ed. (1959); Carl Linnaeus, *Wästgöta Resa* (1928).

38. Åsberg and Stearn (1973: 20).

39. Linnaeus (1971: 199).

40. References for structural fires from Linnaeus (1959: 284); Åsberg and Stearn (1973: 120, 59).

41. Åsberg and Stearn (1973: 20). See Broberg (1978).

42. Linnaeus (1971: 112–114).

43. Åsberg and Stearn (1973: 93); Linnaeus (1928: 274).

44. A good synopsis of all three activities, as they were manifest in Småland, is given in Käll (1989) and Lans-Olof Larsson (1989). See also Linder (1992), and for an eighteenth-century critique, Kudenshöld (1753). Potash production served a useful housekeeping function in that it burned scraps and debris left from other activities or gathered from otherwise useless woods. For a description of saltpeter production, see Linnaeus (1959: 120–121) and for potash (1959: 429–430).

45. Kaila (1931); Åström (1988); and for a detailed description of the process by Linnaeus in an English translation from his Skåne travels, see Weimarck (1968: 17–20); and for the Swedish, Linnaeus (1959: 86–87). For a nice summary of tar production on Gotland, see Kardell (1988).

46. Linnaeus, quoted by Weimarck (1968: 19).

47. From Linnaeus, *Skånska Resa,* as quoted in Weimark (1968: 17–20).

48. Krook quoted in Weimarck (1968: 48); for pastoralism, see Davies (1941: 166–167).

49. Linnaeus (1959: 54).

50. Quote from Åsberg and Stearn (1973: 71). For references on heath, see Malmer (1965); Damman (1957); Malström (1952); Romel (1952); Sjöbeck (1933). The latter reproduces a photograph of heath burning (p. 93). For meadows, see Sjörs (1949).

51. The figures derive from Malström (1952), but a more accessible source, which also beautifully reproduces his maps, is available in Nilsson, ed. (1990: 18–19). This is also my source for the Mästocka fires.

52. My discussion relies heavily on

Bringeus (1963), which comes with an extensive English summary, and on Steensberg (1993: 171-176).

53. Linnaeus (1928: 106-107, 114-115; 1959: 272, 319).

54. Arrhenius (1862: III, 248).

55. Grotenfelt (1899: 275-276).

56. See, for example, Bringeus (1963: 158-159). The critics are well represented. A good example is G. B. (1862). An excellent survey from a sympathetic observer is Stenius (1742). Stenius avoids blanket condemnation for keen discrimination among various soils and practices, nicely complementing the Linnaean literature. For contemporary studies after the advent of English paring and burning, see Lindau (1849) and Tham (1817).

57. Quotes from Åsberg and Stearn (1973: 32); Linnaeus (1959: 516-517). I have, however, followed the excellent summary of the controversy, complete with English translation in Weimarck (1968: 45-48).

58. Cited in Weimarck (1968: 45).

59. Ibid., p. 47.

60. Ibid.

61. See Geertz (1963).

62. Linnaeus quote from Weimarck (1968: 47).

63. Linnaeus (1959: 433-434; 77).

64. For Enlightenment concepts of natural history, see Worster (1979).

65. See Dahl (1961) and for Finland, Jones (1977: 89-94) and Mead (1981: 154-156). For Faggot on fire, see Faggot (1750).

66. For a good summary see Blunt (1971: 183-192). For the transition to a new style of exploration, see Goetzmann (1986).

67. Lagerlöf (1990). To place this in a literary setting, see Albulin (1989: 158-167).

68. For an overview of the economic revolution, see Heckscher (1954) and Mead (1981).

69. Höger quoted in Weimarck (1968: 4); Lagerlöf (1990: II, 145).

70. Heckscher (1954: 226); Östlund (1993: 1).

71. Heckscher (1954: 227-228); Östlund (1993: 4-5). See also Faberberg (1972); Gaunitz (1984); Bjorklund (1984). For a global context, see Tucker and Richards, eds. (1983) and Richards and Tucker, eds. (1988).

72. Fernow (1907: 250-259).

73. Falkman (1852: 46, 114-143, 145).

74. See Mead (1968: 115-117); the von Berg quotations are from Heikinheimo (1987: 200). For an excellent overview of Finnish forestry, consult Raumolin (1984). A good digest is found in Fernow (1907: 235-242). A detailed summary (in English) of Finnish forestry and legislation up to 1883 is Brown (1883a), esp. pp. 209-221. For a self-criticism of swidden from the Finns, see Blomqvist (1888).

75. See Brown (1883a: 209-221).

76. Grotenfelt (1899) and Heikinheimo (1915).

77. For the committee reports, see *Underdånigt betänkande och förslag anqående åtqärder för befrämjande af en förbättrad skoqshushållninq* (Stockholm, 1856); *Underdånigt Betänkande och förslag anqåwnde Skogsförhållandena i Norrland och åtgärder för östadkommande af en förbättrad skogshushöllning derstädes* (Stockholm, 1871).

78. Lagerlöf (1990: II, 145-150).

79. See, for example, Falkman (1852: 85), for a description of Sweden, and for Finland, Blomqvist (1888: 6-9); quote on "fire as friend" from p. 8.

80. The account squares with that from Brown (1883a: 18). "To extinguish forest fires there are adopted the usual plans for beating with boughs the fire advancing in the grass, cutting lanes, across which the fire may be unable to

spread, and burning a small portion of forest in advance of the conflagration, keeping the new fire under control and extinguishing it when a small space has been cleared."

81. Lagerlöf (1990: II, 154–159). For a Finnish account of a wildfire, see Topelius (1875: 89–90).

82. For a popular survey of the 1888 fires, see Ett Ögonvittne [an eyewitness], *Norrland brinner! En beskrifning öfner eldsvådorna i Sundsvall, Umeå m. fl. Ställen* (Stockholm, 1888). Pictures of Umeå after the burn are available in Västerbottens Museum (n.d.: 12).

83. For statistics, see Högbom (1934: 5–9, passim); Wahlgren (1914: 388). For the relative contributions of different national models, see Skogsbrandsläckningskommittén (1946: 136–141). Germany's influence dates to I. Ad. Ström, Sweden's first forester. See, for example, his passages on fire in Ström (1830: 288–294).

84. Probably the best summary is Skogsbrandsläckningskommittén (1946), which summarizes fire suppression at its height, before the postwar green revolution hit forestry, and which also includes a comprehensive bibliography of Swedish fire literature up to 1944 and so supersedes its predecessors. Apart from sources already cited, three useful cross sections of the forest fire establishment prompted by the 1913 season are Dybeck (1915); Lundberg (1915); Dencker (1914). Probably the development of fire lookout towers best characterizes the infrastructure for fire protection. See Humble (1914).

85. Basic surveys of *hyggesbränning* include Viro (1969); Arnborg (1949); Uggla (1957); Wretlind (1932 and 1948). For context, see Uggla (1957: 171–190); and Siren (1973: 191–210).

86. See Viro (1969: 7–10); Eneroth (1928); Wibeck (1911). Quote on Lind, from Arnborg (1949: 31).

87. Viro (1969: 11–12); Wretlind (1948: 5). For Wretlind's understanding of the ecology of fire, see his earlier studies (1932 and 1934).

88. Arnborg (1949). Statistical data courtesy of Anders Granström.

89. Viro (1969: 11–13).

90. Lagerlöf (1990: II, 202–203).

91. Ibid., pp. 228–229.

92. Ibid., pp. 240–242.

93. Ibid., pp. 231–232.

94. Bernes and Grundsten, eds. (1992: 138).

95. Nilsson, ed. (1990: 100).

96. A good description of the legal regime, and its consequences, is Stjernquist (1976).

97. Sources for lake acidification and liming are Renberg et al. (1993a,b) and Bernes and Grundsten, eds. (1992: 84–89). For a good comparison, see Rosenqvist (1978).

98. The best summary is Wik (1992), which consists of eight published short papers in addition to a comprehensive introduction. For a Finnish equivalent, see Oldfield et al. (1980).

FLAMING FRONT:
FIRE IN EURASIAN EUROPE

1. Quoted from Frierson (unpubl. 1993a: 1). I am most grateful to Professor Frierson for making available to me drafts of several unpublished essays on the subject of fire in Russia. They exposed for me a historical lode that I did not know and could not have found on my own. In sharing this information, Professor Frierson has shown a generosity that goes far beyond the bounds of collegial courtesy, and I am extremely appreciative.

2. Haxthausen (1968: I, xv).

3. For an introduction to climate and geography, see Borisov (1965); Kendrew (1961); and Gregory (1968: 163–231).

4. A good survey of climate-driven factors behind large fires is Valendik (1990).

5. The best introductions to Russian fire ecology are Wein and MacLean, eds. (1983), esp. chapters 2, 5, 12–14, and Goldammer and Furyaev, eds. (1996). An excellent statistical profile of fire in the early 1990s is given in Korovin (1993). Other useful publications include Antonovski et al. (1992); Furyaev (1992); Gromtsev (1993); and Shcherbakov (1979).

6. Frierson (unpubl., 1993b: 8); Cochrane (1970: I, 247).

7. Frierson (unpubl., 1993b: 11). The Novgorodian worship of Perun is recorded in Baron, ed. and trans. (1967: 93); Ibn-Dustah quoted from Smith (1959: 51). A detailed examination of ancient fire lore is available in Gimbutas (1967). For the contemporary survival of fire rites, see Milovsky (1993).

8. This passage paraphrases or quotes from Frierson (unpubl., 1993b: 22, 34).

9. See Frierson (ibid., pp. 12–13); Billington (1966: 23–24).

10. Frierson (1993b: 11–13); Billington (1966: 24–25); Payne (1958: 30).

11. Payne (1958: 84).

12. Bakunin quote from Billington (1966: 25).

13. Billington (1966: 25); Massie (1980: 64–66).

14. For the early history, see Portal (1969); Sulimirski (1970); and especially enlightening for its geographic detail, Gregory (1968: 78–162). Napoleon quoted in de Ségur (1971: 316).

15. Red Square reference from Billington (1966: 23).

16. My account follows closely the excellent description given by Linnard (1970: 192–197).

17. Linnard (1970: 192–197).

18. Figures on beekeeping are from Kurbatsky and Telitsyn (1994: 27–28).

19. For a simple schema see French

(1983a). Also excellent but not so clear for an understanding of fire-fuels relations is Pallot and Shaw (1990: 113–114).

20. See Pallot and Shaw (1990: 113–114); Smith (1959: 47–118, esp. 74–75); Pallas cited in Sigaut (1975: 113–114). On Russian agriculture, see Smith (1959); Davies (1952); Gregory (1968: 232–294); French (1964, 1963, 1983b,c; and Michael Confino's study (and map), as recapitulated in Braudel (1988: I, 354–357); Semonov (1893); Postan, ed. (1966); French (1983b,c). For a detailed study of the advent of three-field system in Belarus, see French (1969). For evolution (and overlap) of systems, see Alayev et al. (1990).

21. Pallot and Shaw (1990: 119–131).

22. Ibid., pp. 117–119.

23. Citations from the Novgorod Chronicle are from Sofronov and Vakurov (1981: 12–13); see also Michell and Forbes, trans. (1970: passim). Dobell (1830: I, 14).

24. D'Auteroche (1770: 42–43, 44).

25. Wright (1902: II, 303); Fletcher (1591: 19); Scott (1854: 66); Hill (1970: II, 37).

26. Hill (1970: II, 38); Rappoport (1913: 93); Isaev quoted in Frierson (unpubl., 1993a: 1); Hapgood (1970: 128).

27. Brandes (1889: 37).

28. Lansdell (1970: I, 253–263).

29. Kiachta story in Hill (1970: II,37).

30. Erman (1848: I, 88).

31. Scott (1854: 67).

32. Weber (1968: I, 238–239, 314–315); quote about Peter from Massie (1980: 375).

33. Juel quoted from Massie (1980: 376); Morley (1866: 230).

34. Morley (1866: 230).

35. Keller (1971: 204).

36. Massie (1980: 85).

37. Ibid., pp. 90–91; Lamb (1948: 76–77).

38. For Charles XII, see Massie

(1980: 443–446, and elsewhere). Nesterov's text was translated into English by D. I. Lalkow in 1946–47 and filed in typescript at Canada's Petawawa Forestry Research Institute. For the passages on military fire, see Nesterov (1947: 204–208).

39. My account follows closely de Ségur (1971: 311).

40. Ibid., pp. 312–315.

41. Ibid., pp. 316–317.

42. For the Moscow fire of 1812, see Bremner (1839: II, 42–44, which weighs the principal sources.

43. Kamchatka reference from Dmytryshyn et al., eds. (1986: 9). Buryat prophecy in Erman (1848: I, 157), and Eden (1890, 112).

44. Haxthausen (1968: I, 191).

45. An excellent distillation of pre-Russian Siberia is available in Forsyth (1991: 69–91). For a massive (but ideologically skewed) survey, see Levin and Potapov, eds. (1961).

46. Bell (1966: 53).

47. Ibid., pp. 103–104, 107, 192.

48. Dawson, ed. (1980: 8, 12, 14); Spuler (1972: 72–73).

49. Adams (1870: 276.)

50. Bell (1966: 67); Donner (1933: 66); Lindgren (1930: 529, 532). See also Lindgren (1935: 230). For hunting, see Ravenstein (1861: 353). For swidden, see Bell (1966: 68).

51. The story of the Khabarovsk Evenki is in a letter to Stephen Pyne from H. P. Telitsyn, reporting on Karavanov (1994). For the coexistence that developed between new and old peoples, see Lindgren (1938: 605–621).

52. For the analogy, see Lewis and Ferguson (1988: 57–77); Lewis (1977 and 1982).

53. Sources for Evenki burning are in Kurbatsky and Telitsyn (1994: 27).

54. For Ainu and Koryak, see Czaplicka (1914: 221, 44–45, 265); for Gilyaks, see Czaplicka (1914: 44–45) and Eden (1890: 184); for Yukaghir, Jochelson (1926: 150–151); and for the Altai tribes, Chadwick and Zhirmunsky (1969: 168–169).

For an interesting summary of fire mythology and rites for the former steppe peoples, see Holmberg (1927: IV, 449–456). Most tribes accept the origins of fire from lightning, but all seem to show powerful influences from Indo-European lore, probably through Iran.

55. Reference to the chronicles from Portal (1969: 42). For a succinct overview of the historical significance of the region, see McNeill (1964).

56. Excellent summaries are available in Stebelsky (1983a,b) and Shaw (1983).

57. For climate, see Kovda (1961).

58. For description of agricultural systems, see Pallot and Shaw (1990: 112–135) and Kovda (1961). Quotes from Price (1912: 117); Bremner (1839: 379); Swinton (1792: 492).

59. Pallas (1803: I, 200, 312); D'Auteroche (1770: 106–107); Perry (1716); on fallow firing, Adrianovsky (1883: 83), which comes courtesy of Cathy A. Frierson; on town sites, see Smith (1959: 85).

60. Price (1912: 50).

61. The best summary of these fascinating events is Armstrong (1975); quote from p. 216.

62. I have relied heavily on the essays contained in Wood, ed. (1991), especially those by Dmytryshyn, Collins, and Goryushkin. The jacket cover partly reproduces "The Siberian Boundary Post," which originally appeared in Kennan (1891). A fascinating summary of primary documents is Dmytryshyn, et al., eds. (1985). Other classic sources in English on Siberian expansion include Fisher (1943); Kerner (1946); Gibson (1969). An interesting synopsis is Bassin (1988).

63. Bell (1966: 61); Howard (1893: 33).

64. Howard (1893: 27–28); Dobell (1830: I, 253–254); Cochrane (1970: 395–396).

65. Kennan (1910: 87); Collins (1860: 268); Atkinson (1858: 301).

66. Wright and Digby (1913: 159); Haviland (1971: 10); Chekhov (1967: 5, 18–19); Gerrare (1903: 162); Wenyon (1971: 111).

67. Chekhov (1959: 272; 1967: 19).

68. Nansen (1914: 167–168, 326–327).

69. Shirov (1966: 17).

70. For sample accounts of fire mining, see Collins (1860: 124) and (1962: 152). For the diamond rush, see Mowat (1970: 132–133). The practices of course are ancient, and similar techniques were used in Alaska and Northwest Canada with similar results.

71. Wright (1902: II, 304); Fraser (1903: 186); Stadling (1901: 30–31); Gerrare (1903: 102); Wright and Digby (1913: 167). For a general overview, see Drew (1959).

72. Shostakovitch (1925: 365).

73. Nansen (1914: 327, 389, 332).

74. Ibid., pp. 389, 392.

75. Ibid., p. 332.

76. For wildfires see, for example, Eden (1890: 111–112). Examples from Arseniev (1941: 172–174, 190–191). The latter gives a classic description of a large forest fire in the Far East.

77. Arseniev (1941: 305); Erman (1848: I, 459).

78. Dimensions of the *izba* hearth from Frierson (unpubl., 1993b: 22).

79. The "forest people and farming people" reference comes from Frierson (unpubl., 1993a: 5).

80. See Pallot and Shaw (1990: 112–135).

81. D'Auteroche (1770: 235).

82. On swamp reclamation, see French (1964). Peter Pallas described denshiring in Sigaut (1975: 113, 114). Deforestation is outlined in French (1983b: 23–43, esp. 38–41).

83. See Stebelsky (1983a); Gregory (1968: 285–286).

84. Frierson (unpubl., 1993a: 2).

85. Ibid., pp. 1–2.

86. Ibid., p. 6.

87. Pinchot (1967: 44–45).

88. An excellent summary exists in French (1983b: 23–44); the figure cited is from p. 36.

89. My source for the *yasak* and fire comes from Furyaev in an unpublished essay commissioned by myself; he cites as his source, *Russian Historical Library,* Archeographic Commission, vol. 5, 1676–1700 (St. Petersburg, 1842), p. 5. Steller cited in Gibson (1969: 197). Erman (1848: I, 429). For the ecology of fur and fire, see Johnson et al. (1995).

90. On Russian pig iron production, see Portal (1969: 17). Quotes on wood consumed and village firefighting from Erman (1848: I, 181–182, 219). See also Brown (1884).

91. The best source, though erroneous in details, is Fernow (1907: 217–242). I have supplemented this outline with essays produced under contract with Dr. V. V. Furyaev, Sukachev Institute of Wood and Forestry, Krasnoyarsk, listed collectively as Furyaev (1993). Among these studies are "On the History of Russian Forest Law and Forest Management in the 13th–17th Centuries," "The Forestry History in Russia from the 18th to the Mid-19th Century," and "Historical References to Forest Laws in Russia Concerning Forest Fire Protection," for which Dr. Furyaev's primary source is Shelgunov (1857).

Peter the Great's fire code is in Furyaev (1993: 1).

92. Quote from Anna in Nesterov (1947: 76); Furyaev, "Historical Refer-

ences," pp. 1–2; Fernow (1907: 223–224, 228–229).

93. Furyaev, "Historical References," pp. 2–3.

94. Furyaev, "Historical References," pp. 1 (on Arnold), 4–5; Fernow (1907: 223–224). Feodor Arnold (1819–1902) graduated from the Forest Institute in 1839, then traveled to forestry's hearth in western Europe for three years before returning to dominate Russian forestry. He helped found new institutes, codified regulations, lectured at the Forest Institute and Agricultural Academy, founded a journal, translated critical works from French and German sources, directed the Forest Department in the Ministry of Appanages, and wrote manuals, texts, and two fundamental histories, one a history of forestry in Russia, France, and Germany, and the other a three-volume survey of the Russian forest (1893–1899). Virtually every forester of note was influenced by Arnold. See Furyaev, "Forestry History in Russia," pp. 3–4; Fernow (1907: 230–231).

95. Furyaev, "Historical References," pp. 4–6; Fernow (1907: 229).

96. Furyaev, "Historical References," pp. 5–6.

97. Furyaev, "Historical References," p. 7; Fernow (1907: 230).

98. Murchison and Olanion quoted in Furyaev, "Miscellaneous Essays," p. 11.

99. Good summaries exist in French (1983b: 30, 36–41); Lodijensky (1901). Fernow (1907: 224).

100. For the evolution of forest commissions and regulations, see French (1983: 38–39) and Fernow (1907: 224–228). For literature on forest protection, see V. V. Furyaev, "On the History of Studies of Forest Fires in Russia" (1992d). For a note about the embassy to Nancy, see Bailey (1887a: 341).

101. Estimates of forest land are from Lodijensky (1901: 319).

102. French (1983b: 37–39); statistics on industrial production from Dmytryshyn (1971: 21).

103. Fernow (1907: 218, 242).

104. Nat (1902), trans. by Jim Toppin (1994); report given at the April 1, 1902, meeting of the Moscow Forest Society. Unless otherwise specified, all subsequent quotations come from this fascinating treatise.

105. Kurbatsky and Telitsyn (1994: 4).

106. Quotes from Baxter and Atkins (1976: 22–23, 152, 53), which reproduce in English translation Kulik (1927) and Suslov (1927), the latter of which summarizes the data of the first ethnographer to the region. Two other Russian reports, translated into English, are available in Shapley (1960) and Krinov (1960). Another popular version is Stoneley (1977).

107. Baxter and Atkins (1976: 64, 70).

108. See Bereschchnoy and Drapkina (1964); Kurbatsky (1964); Vasiliev (1973).

109. Sources include Sofronov and Vakurov (1981: 12–14); Nesterov (1947: 75–76); Michell and Forbes, trans. (1970: 160, 193).

110. Furyaev, "Miscellaneous Essays," pp. 1–3, 10–12.

111. Shostakovitch (1925: 365–371). See also Furyaev, "On the History of Fires and Fire Prevention in the Forests of the Middle Regions of the Left Bank of the Volga River and Siberia," unpubl. essay, p. 5.

112. Shostakovitch (1925: 365).

113. Ibid., pp. 368–370; Sofronov and Vakurov (1981: 15).

114. Erman (1848: I, 429).

115. Chekhov (1959: 306).

116. Strogy (1911: 1), trans. by Jim Toppin. Unless otherwise specified, subsequent quotations come from this study, pp. 1–15.

117. Ibid., p. 10.

118. Wright and Digby (1913: 184–185).

119. Strogy (1911: 15, 11).

120. Kurbatsky and Telitsyn (1994: 4–6).

121. Ibid., p. 5; Furyaev, "On the History of Fires and Fire Prevention," p. 4.

122. The provisions of the act are explained in Anon., "50th Anniversary of Aerial Forest Protection, Tyumen Oblast" (unpubl. manuscript, 1981), p. 1.

123. Sofronov and Vakurov (1981: 16); Furyaev, "On the History of Fires and Fire Prevention," p. 1.

124. See Billington (1966: 25, 482, 638, note 43).

125. Source for fire research history, Kurbatsky and Telitsyn (1994: 4–13).

126. Ibid.

127. Sofronov and Vakurov (1981: 16).

128. See Shcherbakov (1977).

129. For the 1972 fires, see Sofronov and Vakurov (1981: 3–4); Furyaev, "On the History of Fires and Fire Prevention," pp. 1–2; Denisov (1979); reports from files of Avialesookhrana.

130. Furyaev, (1992b: 1–3); Denisov (1979).

SPOT FIRE:
FIRE IN ATLANTIC EUROPE

1. Harris (1981).

2. The Scottish fires are described in Thompson (1971: 51–52).

3. For good popular summaries, see Vincent (1990: esp. 183–214); Roberts (1989: 143–144); Simmons (1988: 105–116). The best technical digest is in Walker and West, eds. (1970), especially Smith (1970); Simmons et al. (1981); Simmons (1968, 1995); Dimbleby (1961); Tallis and Switsur (1983, 1990). The dissenting view is available in Bennett et al. (1990) and a measure of skepticism in Moore (1996).

Many relevant essays on British landscape history exist in Birks et al., eds. (1988). For prehistory see Edwards (1988) and O'Connell et al. (1988). See also Turner (1964) and Dimbleby (1984).

Other standard works pertinent to any understanding of landscape evolution (hence fire history) include Hoskins (1955); Godwin (1975); Tanley (1939); and for a concise précis, Pennington (1969). Interesting for its fire skepticism is Rackham (1986). A rather full review of fire ecology in the British context is contained in Tubbs (1968), esp. pp. 185–188, 224–229.

4. De la Pryme quoted in Smith (1970: 82). An excellent discussion of peat formation is available in Moore (1975).

5. For an introduction to aboriginal fire practices, see Pyne (1991: 85–104, 121–150). Sample studies from different biogeographic regions include Blackburn and Anderson, eds. (1993: esp. 55–174); Lewis and Ferguson (1988: 57–77); Anderson and Posey (1991); and Balée (1992: 185–197).

6. Defoe quoted in East (1951: 477).

7. Ibid.

8. For examples, see Pottle, ed. (1961: 155); MacDermot (1911: 252).

9. Domesday estimates from Hinde (1985: 12–13).

10. For commoners' rights, see Hinde (1985: 56), and for the Afran Valley, pp. 212–213. See also Anderson (1967: II, 507); MacDermot (1911: 274–275); and *Manwood's Treatise of the Forest Law,* 4th ed. (1717). The 1607 statute is described in Rackham (1986: 320–321).

11. Elgee (1912: 33–35, 44–46). For an introduction to pastoralism, see Bailey and Bailey (1994); Walton (1919–20); Rafiullah (1966: 32–34); and Jordan (1981: esp. 25–38). Useful studies are available in Birks et al., eds. (1988); Hughes and Huntley (1988: 91–110);

Dodgshon (1988: 139–152); and Chambers et al., (1988: 333–348).

12. Radley (1965: 1255); Anderson (1967: I, 239, 349); Miller (1961: 164).

13. Anderson (1967: I, 493, 507–508, 659); Fisher (1907: IV, 645); Staffordshire quote from Rymer (1976: 172); White (1924: 32).

14. Anderson (1967: II, 351); White (1924: 31).

15. Anderson (1967: I, 307).

16. See Sauer (1968: 96), for examples of real and symbolic burning in Iceland. Darby (1976: 167); Anderson (1967: 143–144, 510).

17. Young (1970: 145–152); Anderson (1967: I, 343).

18. On the origins of the practice, see Dodgshon and Jewell (1970). See also Lucas (1970) and Fenton (1970). A good digest is available in Steensberg (1993: 158–165).

19. Quoted in Fenton (1985: 84).

20. Marshall (1970: 145–152); Darby (1936a: 455); Young (1970: 197–199, 208–209).

21. For a brief, ecologically informed (but partisan) summary of the Clearances, see McIntosh et al. (1994). A more thorough summary is available in MacPherson (1959).

22. Anderson (1967: II, 507); Prebble (1963: 77); Ritchie (1920); Anderson (1967: 347).

23. Anderson (1967: I, 507–508).

24. Quoted in E. G. R. Taylor (1936: 377). See Young (1970: 481) for examples of how potential fuels were utilized to other ends.

25. For the 1830 incendiarism, see Wells (1985); Hobsbawm and Rudé (1968); and Wakefield (1831).

26. See Tubbs (1968: 225).

27. Dallas quoted in Tubbs (1968: 225).

28. Quotes from Great Britain Board of Agriculture and Fisheries, Committee on Inquiry on Grouse Disease (1911: I,

394–395). My account follows closely from this source, especially the chapter by Lord Lovat, pp. 392–413, as well as the study by Wallace (1917).

A summary of recent research is given in Budiansky (1995: 208–218). The criticism of too much fire is really a critique of too many too-small fires.

29. Wallace (1917: 7); Great Britain Board . . . (1911: 399).

30. Great Britain Board . . . (1911: 399, 401, 403).

31. See Kayll (1966); Tubbs (1968: 139–140); Miller (1961).

32. An excellent summary of competing fire practices in the postwar period is given in Ward (1972). Good surveys, from a conservation perspective, are also available in Smith and Atherden (1985); Usher and Thompson (1993).

33. Fernow (1907: 308).

34. Quote from Hutchins (1892: 35).

35. Lloyd George quoted from Hinde (1985: 17). Basic books on British forestry include James (1981); Rackham (1980); Anderson (1967). A good digest of the latter is provided in Matthews (1983).

36. Le Sueur (1925: 170); Simmons (1988: 113); Anderson (1967: II, 507–508).

37. Le Sueur (1925: 170–176, esp. p. 170). See also Law (1925).

38. Quotes from Anderson (1967: II, 228–229, 483).

39. See forestry periodicals such as the *Journal of the Forestry Commission, Forestry, Scottish Forestry,* and Forestry Commission Bulletin No. 14, *Forestry Practice* (many editions), and Forestry Commission, "Forest Fires," Leaflet No. 9; *Journal of the Forestry Commission* 13 (March 1934): 9–29; Anon., "58th Annual Excursion—Northumberland," *Scottish Forestry* 9 (1955): 120; Rodger (1935:20); Long (1936: 195).

40. Stephen Haden-Guest et al., eds. (1956: 259).

41. A good summary (and the source of the quotes) is McVean (1959).

42. For a digest of forest fire protection in the postwar era, see Aldhous and Scott (1993).

43. Recall the famous ballad:

"At Boolevogue as the
   sun was setting
O'er the bright May
   meadows of Shelmalier,
A rebel hand set the
   heather blazing
And brought the neighbors
   from far and near."

44. Brad (1947: 187). Other sources for the bracken invasion include Lousley (1946: 6–7; 1947); Rymer (1976).

45. Rymer (1976: 152).

46. Ibid.; Brad (1947).

47. Lousley (1947).

48. Quote from Evans (1957: 71); see also Arensberg and Kimball, as cited by Arnold (1994: 155).

49. Figures from Mitchell (1976: 93–96). See also Vincent (1990: 206–207).

50. There are numerous studies of Irish colonization on a regional basis which, taken collectively, give a reasonable survey of the Irish landnam: O'Connell et al. (1988); Morrison (1959); Dodson and Bradshaw (1987); Hannon and Bradshaw (1989); Jelicic and O'Connell (1992); Mitchell (1990); O'Connell and Doyle (1990); Dodson (1990); and Mitchell (1988). A good summary is also available in Mitchell (1976: 114–134).

51. For a careful (and sympathetic) summary of Irish pastoralism, see Evans (1957: 27–38). Quote from O'Brien and O'Brien (1972: 44).

52. O'Brien and O'Brien (1972: 64); Spenser quoted from Jordan (1981: 8).

53. For fire ceremonies, see Frazer (1923b) and Evans (1957: 272–277). Boate quoted in Lucas (1970: 100).

54. Evans (1957: 121); Lucas (1970: 101, 106).

55. An interesting analysis of reclamation is available in Connell (1950). For an evocation of the fuel crisis, see Mitchell (1976: 208).

56. For a sketch, see Evans (1957: 146–148). A detailed survey is available in Lucas (1970).

57. Evans (1957: 147); Mitchell (1976: 209).

58. Wilde quoted in Evans (1957: 295).

59. Howitz (1886). For an overview of forest history, seen from the perspective of the Scots pine, see Bradshaw and Browne (1987).

60. For the Shetlands, see Bennett et al. (1992) and Johansen (1975). For the Faeroes, see also Johansen (1971) and West (1972: 5).

61. Quoted in Billington (1974: 60).

62. Arnor quoted in Palsson and Edwards, trans. (1978: 60).

63. See Faegri (1944); Vorren (1986); Kaland (1986). A summary of a more interior Norse landnam is given in Hafsten (1965). Some outstanding contributions are also available in Birks et al., eds. (1988), especially Austad, pp. 11–29; Kvamme, pp. 349–368; Nilssen, "Development of the Cultural Landscape in the Lofoten Area, North Norway," pp. 369–380; and Moe et al., "The Halne Area, Hardangarvidda: Use of a High Mountain Area during 5000 Years: An Interdisciplinary Case Study," pp. 429–462. Indispensable to any study of fire history and Norse colonization is Thorarinsson (1944). A thorough overview of the archaeological (and some of the biogeography) behind Norse colonization is Bigelow, ed. (1991).

64. See Vorren (1986: 17). My account is a much abridged summary of this fascinating article.

65. An excellent summary is available in Kaland (1986). Also useful but dated is Vorren (1979). For a more

recent study of coastal heath fire ecology, see Braathe (1973).

66. See Rafiullah (1966: 34–35).

67. Bennett et al. (1992); Johansen (1975).

68 For the Faeroes, see Johansen (1975) and (1971), and West (1972: 5).

69. A good distillation of early human and natural history is Sauer (1968: 86–96). See also Ashwell and Jackson (1970) for the deforestation chronicle.

70. Thorarinsson (1944: 192–203, 213–214 [English summary]).

71. Quoted in Jones (1986: 183–184).

72. The most succinct survey is Fredskild (1988). For more technical studies, see Fredskild (1978, 1973, and 1967); Pedersen (1972); and Iversen (1952–53).

73. See Fredskild (1988); Pedersen (1972); and Sadler (1991). For a succinct comparison with other Norse islands, see Fredskild (1978: 37–38).

74. For New World sites see Magnusson (1973: 144–147).

75. A good introduction to this curious biota is Sunding (1979).

76. See Bramwell (1976) and Parsons (1981). For exotics, see Kunkel (1976).

77. On the Guanches, see Schwidetzky (1976), and for a spirited analysis of them as the "pickets deployed in front trenches" held by all the indigenes encountered by far-ranging Europeans, see Crosby (1986: 71–103).

78. For the pines, see Parsons (1981: 254–255).

79. Ibid., pp. 259–262.

80. Ibid., p. 263.

81. Ibid., pp. 265–266.

82. Ibid., pp. 268–269.

83. For the story of Zarco, see Duncan (1972: 7–8), and of the fire, Crone, ed. and trans. (1937: 9). For the original Portuguese, see Ferreira (1959: 166).

84. Quotes from Crone, ed. and trans. (1937: 9), Valentim Fernandes, cited in Ferreira (1959: 166–167). Ferreira has

gathered all the known sources (pp. 165–177), and with his conclusions I agree.

85. Crone, ed. (1937: 9).

86. Story from Lewis (1994: 950–951).

87. The rabbits are described in Crosby (1986: 75). An excellent overview of the Madeiran landscape and land use is available in Smith (1968).

88. See Smith (1968: 4); Callender and Henshall (1968: 19).

89. Smith (1968: 23).

90. Parsons (1981: 254, 268–271).

91. The principal documents have been translated into English by the Translation Service of New Zealand's Department of Internal Affairs under the title "Report on the Forest Fire on the Island of La Gomera in September 1984," a copy of which is stored at the Forest Research Institute Library, Rotorua. The quotations are from pp. 6 and 16.

92. Ciesla (1994: 71).

93. My principal sources are Sauer (1969: 79, 115, 183, 227, 244); Andagoya quotation from p. 244. See also Beard (1949); Las Casas (1992); Oviedo (1959), quotation from p. 41. The Oviedo reference to maize comes from Sauer (1969: 242). Sauer's study is vituperative, even by the standards of the Columbus revisionism. But he is one of few scholars (for a long time the only one) to examine the geographic evidence and consequences, including fire.

94. Las Casas (1992: 27–28, 47, 73, 126).

95. Sauer (1969: 295).

ISLANDS

1. Holdgate (1966).

2. Darwin (1958: 370). The figures for indigenous and alien flora are from Renvoize (1979) and D. M. Moore (1979). Consider also Holdgate (1966),

which includes a table of impacts for the principal islands in the southern Atlantic, southwestern Pacific, and Indian Oceans.

3. The originator of the concept, William Goetzmann, describes his ideas in *New Lands, New Men: The United States and the Second Great Age of Discovery* (Viking, 1986). A distillation and extrapolation is available in Pyne (1993). A wonderfully stimulating, if sometimes opaque, inquiry on some environmental consequences of the era is Grove (1995).

4. My presentation of both St. Helena and Mauritius follows the impressive scholarship of Grove (1995), adjusted to the themes of this book. Quotation from Correa, as cited in Grove (1995: 96).

5. Quoted in Wallace (1902: 296); Governor Roberts quoted in Grove (1995: 115). Indeed that book thoroughly elaborates the whole saga of the "desiccation discourse." A distilled version is available in Grove (1994).

6. Quoted in Grove (1995: 304).

7. I follow closely, though with eccentricities of interpretation, the work of Grove (1995). A detailed review of forestry debates is available in Brouard (1963).

8. Grove (1995: 251).

9. Various quotes, ibid., pp. 181, 185–186, 196, Bernardin quote from Brouard (1963: 20).

10. Poivre quoted from Grove (1995: 202); governor quote from Toussaint (1997: 33); Bernardin quote from Brouard (1963: 23).

11. Poivre quoted from Grove (1995: 204).

12. Cited in Thompson (1881: 235). See also Thompson (1881, both sections). Figures come from p. 235.

13. See Brouard (1963: 35–38).

14. Gleadow (1904: 55).

15. Ibid., pp. 55–57.

16. *Annual Report of the Forest Department for 1948* (1949: 5); *Annual Report . . . 1949* (1950: 9); *Annual Report . . . 1948,* p. 5; *Annual*

Report . . . 1957 (1958: 6).

17. Banks quoted in Grove (1988: 26).

18. Wharton, ed. (1968: 238).

19. The ethnic terminology for the Pre-Columbian peoples is confusing. Traditionally, residents of the Greater Antilles were known as Arawaks, and the residents of the Lesser as Caribs. Linguists have argued that they should be known, respectively, as Tainos and Island Caribs. Since cultural groups can differ from linguistic groups, and since much of the evidence needed to classify the peoples more precisely disappeared with European contact—since, moreover, the differences if any in fire practices among these groups is trivial—I will use Taino and Island Carib, in accordance with the usage in Rouse (1986: 108–117).

20. See Sauer (1969) and Watts (1987). For two visions of the ecological encounter, see Crosby (1986) and Grove (1995). An outstandingly detailed description of environmental change on Martinique is given in Kimber (1988). Also useful is Harris (1965) and the long-standard Beard (1949).

21. Different dates given for earliest occupation. Kimber (1988) cites 5,000 years B.P. (p. 76); Rouse (1986) 5000 B.C. (p. 108); *International Forest Fire News* 3 (July 1990): 5.

22. Colt cited in Watts (1987: 166); for Raynal, see Kimber (1988: 190).

23. A full account is given in Grove (1995: 264–308).

24. Ibid., pp. 266, 293–296.

25. See Beard (1949: 30–31).

26. The indispensable reference is Bartlett (1955–61; 3 vols.), and my observations derive from reading his extensive comments, with more intensive research on selective topics. See, in particular, Bartlett (1957b: 44–45) and the classic summary of the two systems given in Geertz (1963).

27. Bartlett (1957a: 44–45).

28. For the fire ecology of the tropics, see Mueller-Dombois (1983) and Goldammer, ed. (1990).

29. Bartlett (1955–61: II, 511); Conklin (1954: 133–142); Geertz (1963).

30. Boomgaard (1988); quote and debate over origins of teak, p. 61.

31. Ibid., p. 71.

32. Ibid., pp. 73–81; de Vriese references on p. 61, and note 3. See also Spalteholz (1928: 698).

33. Spalteholz (1928: 697–698).

34. Ibid., pp. 698, 701.

35. Strugnell (1932: 39–40); Spalteholz (1928: 700).

36. Potter (1988: 130).

37. duBois (1929: 24).

38. Ibid.

39. See Burger (1924 and 1930).

40. Nibbering (1988).

41. For an introduction to contemporary Indonesian fires, see Davis (1984); Goldammer and Seibert (1990); and ongoing reports in *International Forest Fire News*.

42. For dating sequences, see Rouse (1986: 19–42).

43. Cook, quoted in Bartlett (1955–61: III, 173–175); Beaglehole, ed. (1962: II, 50); Bartlett (1955–61: I, 25).

44. McClone (1983: 11).

45. Many sources exist on the environmental impact of Polynesian colonization. The best synopsis is McClone (1983), on which I rely heavily. Other useful sources include Stevens et al. (1988); Davidson (1984: esp. 38–43); *New Zealand Journal of Ecology* 12 (Supplement) (1989), which brings together a rich assortment of studies; Cumberland (1962); Molloy (1977). For the moa, see Anderson (1989 and, in abbreviated form, 1984); that 1984 volume also contains two complementary studies, by Cassels and by Trotter and McCulloch. For a general survey of biological history, see Kuschel, ed. (1975), which includes two essays on human ecology in particular, by Green and Salmon. An account of Maori fire origin myths is given in Hough (1926: 162–164). Two popular but useful surveys of fire history, viewed from a forester's perspective, are Cooper (1989) and Farrow (1993).

46. See Stevens et al. (1988: 103).

47. See Davidson (1984: 39), for evidence of precontact fires. McClone (1983: 23). On pioneering species, see Stevens et al. (1988: 108).

48. McClone (1983: 18–20). The same points are made in Stevens et al. (1988: 118–120).

49. Darwin (1962: 422–423).

50. Davidson (1984: 39).

51. A good popular account of Easter Island's degradation is given in Ponting (1991: 1–7); and for a more thorough survey, Jennings (1979).

52. Darwin (1962: 424).

53. Druett (1983: 41).

54. Fairburn, cited in Trussell (1982: 37); on field burning, Druett (1983: 41); quotation on pioneering burns, cited in Arnold (1994: 21); Tau-tha (1886: 555); B. Moore (1969: 52). Moore gives very precise descriptions of the conversion process.

55. Acland (1980: 65); Butler (1964: 56); and Acland quoted in McLean (1992: 6).

56. Barker (1973: 194–199). Descriptions of other bushfires are found in McLean (1992: 45–48).

57. Guthrie-Smith (1969) describes in careful detail how fire and weeds could interact; quote from p. 272.

58. Baughan poem from O'Sullivan, ed. (1970: 4–5).

59. See Roche (1987 and 1991). Vogel quote from Wynn (1979); fire quote from Allsop, ed. (1964: 29). For the United Fire Brigades' Association, see Arnold (1994: 243–246).

60. For an exhaustive summary of the fires, see Arnold (1994).

61. Quote from Tau-tha (1886: 555).

Poem fragment from "Gorse Burning," in Woodhouse, ed. (1950: 89).

62. Department of Forestry (1919: 6).

63. Ellis (1921: 3–4 and 1922: 8).

64. State Forest Service (1946: 15). Another account, with photos, is available in McLean (1992: 86–88).

65. For an assessment of fire and erosion as it appeared on the eve of postwar reforms, see Cumberland (1944).

66. For a good summary of high country land use and futures, see K. F. O'Connor (1982).

67. For the disestablishment story, see Roche (1991) and Birchfield and Grant (1993).

68. A mandatory study for prehistoric fires is Burney (1986). For the composition of Pleistocene fauna, see Dewar (1984). An excellent summary of Madagascar's natural history, though somewhat dated, is available in Battistini and Richard-Vindard, eds. (1972).

69. Sources for the story of the *afotroa* are given in Battistini and Verin (1972: 324). The story of the renewed charcoal influx is a continual theme throughout Burney (1986).

70. See Dewar (1984: 575–587).

71. A good summary of missionary activity and subsequent geopolitical maneuvering between Britain and France is given in M. Brown (1979).

72. Quotations are all derived from Bartlett (1955–61), indispensable as always: Copland, vol. I, p. 150; Ellis, vol. I, pp. 179–180; Moss, Vol. I, p. 429.

73. Quotations are again derived from Bartlett (1955–61): Catat, vol. I, pp. 115–116; Charon, vol. I, pp. 122–123; Durand, vol. I, p. 174; S.-V. Duruy, vol. I, pp. 176–177.

74. Bartlett (1955–61: I, 442–444).

75. Perrier de la Bathie (1927: esp. Appendix II); and Humbert (1927). Both published later, summary studies: Perrier de la Bathie (1936) and Humbert (1959).

76. Rauh (1979); Griveaud and Albignac (1972); and for the original arguments, Humbert (1927: 13–15, 77–78).

77. Stratton (1964: 148, and passim).

78. Marcuse (1914: 267).

79. Bartlett (1955–61: I, 47); Rauh (1979: 418); Griveaud and Ablignac (1972: 739).

80. See Chauvet (1972: 191–199, esp. 196).

81. *The British Empire Forestry Conference* proceedings (1920), p. 68.

82. On Yosemite, in particular, see Runte (1987: 28–31); and Sax (1980: 17–26). Also essential reading: Nash (1982), a marvelous book that includes a small passage on Yosemite (pp. 105–107), but more importantly synopsizes the cultural context of American parks and wilderness; and Schama (1995: 185–201), which offers a wonderful meditation on the Big Trees as sacred grove and nationalist symbol.

83. King (1962: 32). Sequoia ecology has a rich literature. See Harvey et al. (1980); a good bibliography is available in "Fire Management Plan: Sequoia and Kings Canyon National Parks" (November 1991, revision: 121–126). For a survey of native Californian fire practices, see Wickstrom (1987), and Blackburn and Anderson, eds. (1993).

84. Pinchot (1972: 44).

85. See National Academy of Sciences (1897: 5, 17–18).

86. Wells (1906). An overview of fire programs is sketched in Bancroft et al. (1985).

87. Leopold et al. (1963: 28–45). Excerpts of the report were widely reproduced. See also Christensen et al. (1987: ii).

88. For summaries of the debates, see Bancroft et al. (1985) and Christensen et al. (1987). The Sierra parks became, along with Everglades, the premier centers for fire management in the national parks system, not least because of their

passion for debating the philosophy behind their practices.

89. Ibid., p. 32.

90. A good summary of the dissenting perspective for management is available in Bonnicksen and Stone (1982). A more theoretical critique is available in Pyne (1995: 238–255). For a summary of the literature, see Despain et al. (1994).

91. The British were the most active reservers. For an account of wildlife reservations, see MacKenzie (1988). For a survey of the controversies surrounding African reserves, see Anderson and Grove, eds. (1987). For the dissemination of the national park idea, see Burnett and Harrington (1994), and Nash (1982: 342–378).

92. For Russia and the context of nature reserves, see Wiener (1988). For the role of botanical gardens, see Grove (1995).

93. I rely heavily on Nash (1982: 354–360).

94. Nash (1982: 360–361), which provides an excellent introduction to the international wilderness and park movement. Also fundamental is Hayden (1942).

95. Nash (1982: 363).

96. See Elliott, ed. (1974); UNESCO (1971); and UNESCO (1972).

97. Stevenson-Hamilton (1937).

98. See van Wilgen et al. (1990: esp. 207–209); Trollope et al. (unpubl.), copy courtesy of senior author; and van Wyk (1971).

99. For a tidy summary of changing fire programs, see Trollope et al. (unpubl.: 2–3).

100. Ibid., p. 7.

101. Nowak (1994: 651); Izurieta (1995); Marquez et al. (1995); Wikelski (1996).

102. Makowski (1973: 15–17).

103. Ibid., p. 16; Tüxen (1973). For the interesting case of the Netherlands, see van der Ven (1973).

104. For information see *International Forest Fire News* 4 (December 1990): 4–7.

105. P. D. Moore (1976: 112–113).

106. Statistics on moors from Usher and Thompson (1993: 70).

107. Moore (1976: 113).

Continents

1. Vergil (1961: Book II, lines 297–299).

2. Crosby (1986: 89).

3. J. C. Byrne, quoted in Hallam (1979: 76).

4. Bligh (1792: 49); Morton (1632: 52–54); Bands (1977: 248–249).

5. R. Jones (1968–70: 224–228).

6. See Blackburn and Anderson, eds. (1993); Bandelier (1973: 92–93).

7. Kalm (1972: 374). For New England, see Pyne (1982: 45–65); Patterson et al. (1987) and Patterson and Sassaman (1988). For the obligatory dissenting view, see Russell (1983). Russell assumes that the burden of proof rests with those who argue in favor of burning, while evidence from every corner of the world argues against those who, like herself, dispute aboriginal burning. In fact, there is plenty of evidence to support the case for anthropogenic fire regimes of many kinds in New England.

8. This argument is developed with relentless detail in Jordan and Kaups (1989). I accept their thesis, but have modified it to trace fire practices rather than log cabin styles and fencing. For the story of New Sweden, see also Johnson (1911), Wuorinen (1938), and the lavishly illustrated Ruhnbro, ed. (1988).

9. For New Sweden fire hunting, see Holm (1702: 133–134). and Lindestrom (1979: 149).

10. Quotes from Dean (1995: 138–139).

11. Saint-Hilaire (1975: 75 and 1833: II, 133–134). Saint-Hilaire conducted a series of expeditions on a Linnaean model to most of the regions of the Brazil; the Coleção Reconquista do Brasil has reproduced the lot in Portuguese translation.

12. Ibid., p. 27.

13. The literature on *taungya,* both its science and mythology, is large. A synopsis is available in Jordan et al., eds. (1992). See, in particular, Takeda, "Origins of Taungya," pp. 18–31. Two other general sources worth inspecting are Stebbing (1922) and Troup (1928).

14. Shebbeare (1932: 20).

15. Ibid., pp. 24, 22.

16. Ibid., p. 25

17. Ibid., pp. 30, 32.

18. Ibid., pp. 33.

19. Gibson (1966: 152–153); Melville (1994); O'Hara et al. (1994).

20. See Melville (1994) and Klein (1920).

21. For Chile, see Bahre (1979). On offshore charcoal deposits, see Suman (1991).

22. Crosby (1986: 160–161); Hudson (1918: 68–69).

23. An excellent, if overly clipped synopsis of American pastoralism and its origins is Jordan (1981).

24. See, for example, Jordan (1981: 37, 57, 61, 85, 106–107). For an overview of southern fire history, see Pyne (1982: 143–160.)

25. For an introduction to the Flint Hills, see Anderson (1964) and Reichman (1987). The literature is quite large and detailed.

26. The spread of brush over the public lands of the West is a pervasive topic in the ecological literature. From the perspective of fire, a good starting place is Wright and Bailey (1982). Updates are abundant in government-sponsored research publications, for example, McArthur et al., compilers (1990).

27. Muir (1911).

28. Muir (1897); *Oregonian* quoted in Morris (1934: 324).

29. Quoted in Melville (1994: vi).

30. Hutchins (1916: 142). On Spanish forestry, see Manderscheid (1980: esp. 65–80) and Fernow (1907: 300–305).

31. Hutchins (1916: 138). See also Baden-Powell (1899).

32. Stebbing (1941: 140).

33. Brown (1883: iii).

34. The two standard works are Ribbentrop (1989), with a commentary by Ajay S. Rawat, and Stebbing (1922). Recent additions include Rawat, ed. (1993); Rawat (1991); Lal (1992); Grove (1995), which details the intellectual and institutional context of pre-Brandis forestry.

35. A richly detailed analysis of these events is given in Grove (1995: 380–473).

36. Quoted in Grove (1995: 437).

37. A good synopsis of the origins and issues surrounding British imperial forestry, contrasting India with Africa, is available in Stebbing (1941).

38. For Brandis, see Stebbing (1922), Ribbentrop (1989), and Hesmer (1975).

39. For details, see Ribbentrop (1989), Stebbing (1922), and Baden-Powell (1899).

40. Quoted in Ribbentrop (1989: 18).

41. Ribbentrop (1989: 151).

42. Synopsis given in Ribbentrop (1989: 175–185).

43. Shebbeare (1928: 1); Brandis (1872).

44. Ribbentrop (1989: 145, 149); Fernow (1907: 321); Stebbing (1941: 140).

45. Stebbing (1922: II, 542); Doveton (1875: 5).

46. Ribbentrop (1989: 127).

47. Pant quoted by Rawat, in Ribbentrop (1989: 21). For civil unrest and incendiarism, see Gadgil and Guha (1993), and Guha (1991).

48. Ribbentrop (1989: 130–131).

49. Schlich in *Proceedings, The British Empire Forestry Conference* (London, 1920), p. 67.

50. Pinchot, in Woolsey and Greeley (1920: vi); see Woolsey's own comments in the introduction and on p. 1.

51. National Academy of Sciences (1897: 245–256).

52. Pinchot (1972: 7), and for evaluations of Brandis, pp. 7–72, passim; for correspondence in connection with the NAS committee, pp. 106–107. See also Hesmer (1975: 327–385), and for quotations, pp. 327 and 385.

53. Hutchins (1916: 33, 43).

54. Stebbing (1937: 58).

55. Ibid., p. 7.

56. For an overview of the controversy, see Pyne (1994). The best documentation is found in the early forest conferences (1871–72, and 1875), and in the pages of the *Indian Forester.*

57. The light-burning controversy has been told in several forms. A concise summary (and a source for my quotations) is Pyne (1994). Fuller versions are available in Pyne (1982: 100–125), and for California's debates, Clar (1959).

58. James (1967), 1910 essay.

59. See Pyne (1982), and for an update, Pyne (1995: 183–237).

60. Christensen quoted in Ackerman (1993: 23); Smuts in Phillips (1971: 3–4).

61. Hutchins (1916: 28).

62. Chipp quoted in Stebbing (1937: 8).

63. For the 1949 fires, see Cremieu-Alcan (1992), and Dujas and Traimond (1992).

64. The relevant special volumes of *Revue Forestière Française* are 26 (1974), 27 (1975), and 42 (1990). See also the special issue of *Forêt Méditerranéenne* 14, no. 2 (1993).

65. For good summaries of the scene, see the conference proceedings listed

under note 66. A tidy précis from the perspective of a geographer is Clout (1983).

66. Viegas, ed. (1990 and 1994). The best index of the unfolding story are the archival volumes of *International Forest Fire News.*

67. Dimitrakopoulos (1994).

68. Vélez (1995).

69. For a fascinating analysis of Kiefer's art and its cultural context, see Schama (1995: esp. 120–134).

70. See Mißbach (1972). See pages 9–14 for statistics on postwar fires. For an overview of German fire protection in the mid-1970s, see Goldammer (1982), Piesnack (1982), Lockert (1991).

71. Liebeneiner (1959, 1963, and 1979); I'm grateful to J. G. Goldammer for sending me the first and last items, and for providing a translation of the latter.

72. An official account of the incident is available in "Die Waldbrandkatastrophe in Niedersachsen," Reihe B, DST-Beiträge zum Kommunalrecht, Heft 2 (Deutscher Städtetag, 1976). A general account (in English) is available in Otto (1982), and in German, Otto (1978). See also Otto (1985), Liebeneiner (1978), and Eißmann (1978). A detailed journalistic account of the fire is available in Luttermann (1981). I am also indebted to J. G. Goldammer for observations regarding the fire that he sent me in a letter of June 20, 1995.

73. The drought-propelled fires of 1976 inspired several scientific studies. See P. D. Moore (1976), Glouaguen (1990), Roze (1993), and Clement and Touffet (1981). For an excellent summary of the resulting organization as it applies to what is generally recognized as the best fire district in Germany, see Lex (1988). I'm grateful to Forstdirektor Lex for supplying this document.

74. For photos of the experiment,

see the promotional brochure "The Answer to a Burning Global Problem: The WAGNER 2RS System," Wagner Alarm-und Sicherungssysteme, and Soppa (1995).

75. For the American context, see Pyne (1982 and 1995: esp. 203–213).

76. See *Proceedings, Tall Timbers Fire Ecology Conference*, vol. 13 (Tall Timbers Research Station, 1973).

77. Conrad (1925), Müller (1931), and Meinecke (1927).

78. *VW-Symposium "Feuerökologie"*, Part 1: Symposions-Beiträge, Part 2: Johann Georg Goldammer, *Feuerökologie und Feuer-Management* (Freiburg im Breisgau, 1978).

79. Crutzen and Birks (1982).

80. A popular review of Swedish fire history with an emphasis on the contemporary status is available in Pyne (1995: 76–94).

81. Wretlind (1948: 5).

82. Ibid. This book is a summary of Wretlind's research. Two large preliminary studies are useful for tracing the evolution of the idea and practice: Wretlind (1932 and 1934).

83. See Skogsbrandsläcknings-kommittén (1946).

84. See Bernes and Grundsten, eds. (1992: 8–9, 66–63); for beetle, see Ehnström (1991: 47–52). For good background studies, see Angelstam (1992 and 1993).

85. Dalby Söderskog statistics were collected from posted information at the park.

86. For a sample of the Umeå group's efforts, see the special issue (*Tänd eld på skogen!*) of *Skog & Forskning* 4 (1991). Two recent theses deal directly or indirectly with fire: Östlund (1993) and Schimmel (1993).

87. For an introduction to the Finland experiments, see Ruuhijärvi (1986).

88. See Aldhous and Scott (1993).

89. For good summaries of the controversy, see Bullen (1974); U.K. Ministry of Agriculture, Fisheries and Food (1984); Pierce (1982); and Wilton (1985).

90. Quoted in Bullen (1974: 233).

91. Muirhead and Cracknell (1985).

92. Bullen (1974: 233).

93. My sources for the history of aerial fire protection are several, some published, most from unpublished talks given at the various aerial fire centers under Avialesookhrana for the 50th anniversary celebration in 1981. I am grateful to Nicolai Andreev, Eduard Davydenko, and Alexei Shcherbakov and the various regional centers themselves for making copies available. In particular, I have relied on the following (in Russian): "Report Dedicated to the 50th Anniversary of Aerial Fire Protection [Urals Aerial Fire Center]"; A. P. Butskikh and P. N. Pryakhi, "Brief Historical Summary to Honor the 50th Anniversary of the Aerial Forest Protection [Central Air Base]"; "Summary for 50th Anniversary of Aerial Fire Protection, July, 1981 [Irkutsk Aerial Fire Center]"; "Summary History [Yakutsk Aerial Fire Center]"; "Report Given at the Celebratory Meeting Dedicated to the 50th Anniversary of the Northern Base (Arkhangelsk) of Aerial Forest Protection"; "Northern Base of Aerial Protection of Forests, 50th Anniversary [Arkhangelsk Aerial Fire Center]"; "50th Anniversary of Aerial Forest Protection, Tyumen Oblast [Tyumen Aerial Fire Center]"; V. I. Skvoretsky, "Report, The Organization and Development of the Western-Siberian Base for Aerial Forest Protection [Alma-Ata Aerial Fire Center]."

Published sources include Nesterov, trans. Lalkow (1947); Serebrennikov and Matreninsky (1937); Melekhov (1939, 1947, and 1948); Davydenko and

Butskikh (1984); Artsybashev (1984); *Avialesookhrana* [booklet] (Moscow, 1989); *The Russian Forest and Its Protection* (Moscow, 1986).

The story of the defecting pilot comes from "Report Given at the Celebratory Meeting Dedicated to the 50th Anniversary of the Northern Base (Arkhangelsk) of Aerial Forest Protection," courtesy Avialesookhrana, pp. 2–3.

94. See Nesterov (1947: 203); Butskikh and Pryakhi, "Brief Historical Summary," p. 3; Serebrennikov and Matreninsky (1937), which includes photos and the drop footprints for retardant; Kurbatsky and Telitsyn (1994: 12–13). Mokeev later published a book on the subject (1950).

95. Details from "Report Given at the Celebratory Meeting (Arkhangelsk)," p. 6, and Davydenko and Butskikh, (1984: 9); for the Primorye episode, see Kurbatsky and Telitsyn (1994: 26).

96. See "Report Given at the Celebratory Meeting (Arkhangelsk)," pp. 8–9.

97. Information on *zapovedniki* from Douglas Weiner, letter to author.

98. The history of technological developments is scattered throughout the 50th anniversary reports. For a description of infrared sensing and artificial rainfall, see Artsybashev (1984: 140–151).

99. Statistics from "Report Given at the Celebratory Meeting (Arkhagelsk)," p. 14; "Report Dedicated to the 50th Anniversary of Aerial Forest Protection [Urals]," p. 3. Observations on the corruption of statistics come from discussions with personnel of Avialesookhrana, especially at the Central Air Base.

Several authors have attempted to estimate the annual burned area. See Krankina (1993); Shvidenko and Nilsson (1994); and Stocks (1991).

In October 1994 I attended a NATO Scientific Workshop on the geologic records for burning in which two scientific groups from the Russian Federation contributed posters. One estimated the annual burned area at 1 million hectares, the other at 5 million. Probably a third of the country has no formal protection. Until better means of reconnaissance exist, there is little reason to place much confidence in reported statistics.

100. There are numerous scattered sources for a history of Soviet fire science, not least the record of publications themselves. However, I am relying most heavily on an extended historical study that I commissioned from Kurbatsky and Telitsyn (1994).

Other published sources in English include Artsybashev (1984) and Nesterov (1947). The Krasnoyarsk fire symposia include English abstracts, which provide a good index of what was studied, when, and by whom.

101. Melekhov (1947); Serebrennikov and Matreninsky (1937).

102. Quote from Kurbatsky and Telitsyn (1994: 30).

103. For some of the publications, see Grishin (1992); Dorrer (1989); Sannikov (1973); and Shcherbakov (1979).

104. For the publications of the conferences, see the Bibliography for listings under Kurbatsky, ed.

105. See Kurbatsky and Telitsyn (1994: 28–42) for a detailed summary of regional fire research efforts and the collapse that resulted. I attended the 1993 Krasnoyarsk symposium, and speak from that experience. For an obituary of Kurbatsky, see Furyaev and Tsvetkov (1994).

106. See Dusha-Gudym (1992 and 1994).

107. For the Great Black Dragon fire, see Cahoon, Jr., et al. (1991) and White and Rush (1990); quote from Salisbury (1989: 159–160). For estimates of the Transbaikalia fires (and composite satellite imagery), see Cahoon, Jr. et al. (1994).

108. In July 1993, I arranged to visit

the scene of the fires through contacts with Avialesookhrana. The trip was carefully crafted to prevent me from seeing any of the major sites, or to talk with anyone in a position to describe them. A copy of the task force report was carefully edited to remove all portions of the text save the recommendations, and additionally deleted the names of the group's members. Nonetheless, I was able to gather some data and interview some observers. Not least, the pattern of denial, coupled with the undeniable evidence of satellite imagery, began to shape the contours of what probably occurred.

109. This is my best guess as to what occurred. If the CIA releases, as it has promised, its more sophisticated satellite images, or if Russia chooses to release (or conduct) its own internal investigations, a truer picture will emerge.

110. See Nesterov (1947: 86–89) for slash. The story of the Kola fire is from conversations with P. Popov, July 1991.

111. My primary source is an extended essay which I commissioned from V. V. Furyaev on "The Use of Fire in National Practice in Russia: Experience" (unpubl., 1993). Some of the principal publications related to this topic (all in Russian) are: Furyaev (1966); Valendik et al. (1979, appendix 3); Kurbatsky (1962: esp. 65–71); Sofronov and Vakurov (1981); Belov (1973); Vasilenko (1970).

112. The story of the hearing is based on personal conversations with V. V. Furyaev.

113. The story of the dissident researchers comes from conversations with Russian scientists in Chita. The account of the helicopters comes from Nicolas Kolev, Avialesookhrana director for the Krasnoyarsk aerial fire center.

114. The best summary of developments is contained in *International Forest Fire News,* beginning with the January 1992 issue.

PLANETS

1. See Troensegaard (1990).

2. For South Africa, see Van Wilgen et al. (1990). Two larger syntheses nicely flank it: Booysen and Tainton, eds. (1984) and "Fire in Africa," *Proceedings, Tall Timbers Fire Ecology Conference,* vol. 11 (1971).

3. For the United States, see Pyne (1982 and 1995), especially "Initial Attack" and "Coldtrailing" (1995: 183–237).

4. Canadian fire history desperately needs a historian. A thumbnail sketch is available in Pyne et al. (1996: 657–667). Some beginning source materials on fire ecology include Wein and Maclean, eds. (1983); Stocks (1991); Johnson (1992). For human fire history see Lewis and Ferguson (1988); Barnes (1987); Van Wagner (1988); White (1985); Murphy (1985). For contemporary fire management, consult Stocks and Simard (1993); Day et al. (1984); Van Wagner (1984). Very valuable too are Canadian contributions to (or sponsorship of) fire symposia, including the biennial forest and fire meteorology conferences. Especially useful is Alexander and Bisgrove, eds. (1990).

5. The best source for Australia's history is Pyne (1991). Two other standard references are Luke and McArthur (1978) and Gill et al., eds. (1981).

6. See, for example, Perkins and Roby (1987); Beall (1987); Dittmer (1987); Taft and Mutch (1987); and Sorensen (1979).

7. Information on the dissemination of the Soviet system comes from conversations with Avialesookhrana and select published and unpublished works. For Mongolia, see Dietrich (1990).

8. See Moody (1976). Johann Goldammer and I traveled in July and August 1991, the U.S. Forest Service

delegation two months later; between the two trips, the August revolution occurred.

9. Estimate from Andreae (1991).

10. The originating study was Crutzen and Birks (1982). Its successors developed into a minor industry. As a sample, see Harwell (1984) and Ehrlich et al. (1984).

11. For an excellent summary of the state of the sciences in 1989, see Levine, ed. (1991).

12. The best digest of evolving campaigns is given in *International Forest Fire News*. The scheme has included Canada, Brazil, South Africa, Russia, and has plans for Southeast Asia. An outline of fire's role within the IGBP is available in Prinn (1991).

NOTES: EPILOGUE

1. Bachelard (1964: 2–3).
2. Spindler (1993: 84).

GLOSSARY

abatis Defensive obstacle formed by felled trees with sharpened branches facing the enemy.

aeolian loess Wind-blown deposits of loamy, unstratified material typically associated with the peripheries of glaciated lands.

ager (Latin) Cultivated field.

alang-alang (Tagalog) General term used in Philippines and Indonesia for grasslands dominated by the genus *Imperata.*

allelopathy The suppression of growth of one plant species by another due to the release of toxic substances.

anticyclone System of winds that rotates about a center of high atmospheric pressure clockwise in the northern hemisphere and counterclockwise in the southern.

autarky Policy of establishing a self-sufficient and independent national economy.

Avialesookhrana (Russian) Aerial forest protection service.

bandeirantes (Portuguese) Mestizo groups that flourished around São Paulo, Brazil, and specialized in long-range raiding and slaving.

Belgorod line Defensive perimeter begun in the sixteenth century along southern Russia, from Belgorod to Simbirsk.

Beltane The first day of May in the old Scottish calendar; the May Day Festival, characterized by hilltop bonfires.

blanket bog Organic soil that completely covers a site.

Brandwirtschaft (German) General term for swidden agricultural practices, particularly where the fallow involves woods.

brännodling (Swedish) General term for fire-fallow agriculture practices, particularly where organic soils are involved. For the woodland equivalent, see **svedjebruk.**

broadcast burning Controlled burning in which the flaming front is allowed to propagate over large areas.

byre Cow barn.

Cacique (Spanish, from Arawak) Local chieftain.

Calluna Genus of low shrubs, including the common heather *(Calluna vulgaris).*

cambium The thin living layer of cells in trees between the heartwood and the bark.

cañada (Spanish) Cattle path; also, ravine.

cerrado (Portuguese) The varied grasslands of central Brazil, akin to the American prairie.

CFC Chlorofluorocarbons.

corvée (French) Labor exacted in lieu of taxes by public authorities.

counterfire Generic expression for any fire set in opposition to a wildfire; alternatives: backfire, burning out.

currach A large coracle (a round boat covered with hides) with a keel.

devonshiring *See* **paring and burning.**

dirigisme (French) State planning or control.

duff Partly decayed organic matter on the forest floor.

ECE European Economic Commission, an institution within the United Nations.

écoubuage (French) Swidden agriculture in organic soils; *see also* **paring and burning**

ENSO El Niño–Southern Oscillation; the large-scale, irregular shifting of winds and moisture between the eastern and western Pacific in response to changing ocean temperatures.

ESA European Space Agency.

epicormic Growing from a dominant bud exposed to light and air.

eustatic Relating to or characterized by worldwide change of sea level.

FAO Food and Agriculture Organization, an institution within the United Nations whose responsibilities include forestry.

fjäll (Swedish) High barren field or moor, typically above the treeline; English cognate, *fell.*

flashover The explosive growth of a fire when it becomes heated to the flash point or when smoldering material is suddenly brought into contact with oxygen.

Föhn (German) Warm, downslope wind; originally applied in Switzerland.

forb An herb other than grass.

Forstmeister (German) Head forestry official or ranger.

fusain Fossil charcoal.

fynbos (Dutch) General term applied to the Mediterranean-climate brushlands around the Cape of Good Hope.

Greek fire An incendiary, liquid composition used in warfare by the Byzantine Greeks.

hetman A Cossack leader.

huuhta (Finnish) Swidden cultivation in old-growth forests; first-contact conversion of old woods to agriculture.

hyggesburning (Swedish) A system of controlled burning in logged pine to reduce slash and encourage regeneration.

ICONA (Spanish) Acronym for Instituto Nacional para la Conservacion de la Naturaleza, which includes the Spanish Forestry Service and has responsibility for wildland and forest fire protection.

Imperata Genus of tropical grasses, including *alang-alang.*

infield Cultivated plots.

izba (Russian) Peasant's house.

jhum (India) Eastern Indian term for forest swidden.

kaski (Finnish) Swidden cultivation in second-growth forests, often birch; successor to *huuhta* cultivation.

kyttlandsbruk (Swedish) Swidden cultivation in organic soils.

ladang (Malay) Local term for swidden cultivation.

lande (French) Moor or heath. Also, *Landes* the southwest section of France once dominated by heath-like vegetation.

Länder (German) Individual provinces or states federated into Germany.

landnam (Danish) Old Norse term for first-contact swidden.

latifundium (Latin; pl. -a) A great landed estate with primitive agriculture and labor often in a state of partial servitude.

laterite Residual product of rock decay that is red in color and has a high content in the oxides of iron and hydroxide of aluminum.

lay Arable land used temporarily for haying or grazing

ling Heath plant, particularly *Calluna vulgaris.* Also, *ljung* (Swedish).

maquis (French) Generic term for the

brushlands growing in Mediterranean-climate Europe.

mare nostrum (Latin) A common Roman expression for the Mediterranean Sea; literally, "our sea."

marl Loose or crumbling earthy deposit that contains a substantial amount of calcium carbonate and is used especially as a fertilizer for soils deficient in lime.

meseta (Spanish) Central plateau of Spain.

Mesta (Spanish) Common expression for El Honrado Concejo de la Mesta de Pastores, the royally charted monopoly in wool that organized shepherds and through them much of the Spanish landscape.

mor Forest humus that forms a layer of largely organic matter abruptly distinct from the mineral soil beneath.

mull Friable forest humus that forms a layer of mixed organic matter and mineral soil and merges gradually into the mineral soil beneath.

oblast (Russian) Political subdivision of a republic in the USSR.

orrery An apparatus showing the relative positions and motions of bodies in the solar system by balls moved by wheelwork.

paludification The process of coverting to organic soils, particularly in marshlands.

pannage Food for swine in a forest; the legal right or privilege of pasturing swine in the woods.

paring and burning Swidden cultivation in organic soils; also, devonshiring and denshiring in honor of the British site where the practice became best developed.

petit feu (French) Controlled burns in fields or wood plantations, typically conducted by foresters.

plantain Any of a genus (*Plantago*) of short-stemmed elliptic-leaved herbs with spikes of minute greenish flowers.

playa (Spanish) Beach; often applied in English to dry lake beds.

podocarp Plant of the genus *Podocarpus,* a genus of evergreen trees in the southern hemisphere having pulpy fruit and one hard seed.

podzol (From Russian) Any of a group of zonal soils that develop in a moist climate, especially under coniferous or mixed forest and have an organic mat and a thin organic-mineral layer above a light gray leached layer resting on a dark illuvial horizon enriched with amorphous clay.

polder (Dutch) Tract of low land reclaimed from a body of water.

promyshlennik (Russian) Fur trapper and trader.

prytaneum (Latin, from Greek) A public building or hall in an ancient Greek city, containing the sacred hearth and serving as the place of meeting and dining for officials and sometimes for state visitors.

Pteridium Genus of ferns, including bracken (*Pteridium aquilinum*).

pyrophyte Plants showing exceptional adaptations for fire, often promoting more intense or frequent fires.

queimada (Portuguese) A controlled burn, typically agricultural; generic expression for such fires in Brazil.

rayonnement (French) Radiance; often used by intellectuals to describe the spread of French culture.

reboisement (French) Reforestation.

repoblación forestal (Spanish) Reforestation program begun under Franco regime.

Reutberge (German) A system of swidden cultivation, especially as used in the Schwarzwald.

rick A stack (as of hay) in the open air.

resin tapping Collecting resin from pines; also, turpentining.

saeter (Norwegian) Pasture high in the mountains of Norway and Sweden where herds are kept in summer and butter and cheese made; the hut associated with such pastures.

saltus (Latin) Rough pasture.

samizdat (Russian) System in the USSR in which government-suppressed literature is clandestinely printed and distributed.

sartage, essartage (French) Felling, often associated with agricultural clearing.

sawah (Malay) Wet or irrigated rice field.

scleromorphic Pertaining to plants having small, hard-coated leaves, typically adapted to semi- or seasonally arid climates. Alternative expression, **sclerophylly.**

shieling Summer pasture in the mountains.

silva (Latin) Woods.

skerry Rocky isle, or reef.

shifting cultivation Alternative expression for swidden; a system of farming in which the cultivated plots move around a landscape.

sukhovei (Russian) A dry, desert wind from the region of the Caspian Sea.

svedjebruk (Swedish) Customary pattern of forest swidden. Individual plots known as *svedja* (pl.), so gives rise to numerous compound words.

swidden (Originally Norse) Generic term for fire-fallow cultivation, particularly those involving woodlands as part of the fallow cycle.

taiga (Russian) Moist subarctic coniferous forest that begins where the tundra ends, typically dominated by spruces and firs.

taungya (Karen) System of agroforestry in which traditional swidden is integrated with trees commercially valued as timber.

tavy (Malagasy) Forest swidden typical of Madagascar.

transhumance Seasonal movement of livestock and especially sheep between mountain and lowland pastures.

trophic Of or relating to nutrition.

tussock A hummock in marsh bound together by plant roots; the grasses or sedge that grow in tussocks.

utmark (Swedish) Agricultural outfield.

varve Pair of layers of alternately finer and coarser silt or clay believed to comprise an annual cycle of deposition in a body of still water.

viverrid Any of a family of carnivorous mammals that are rarely larger than a domestic cat but are long, slender, and like a weasel in build with short, more or less retractile claws and rounded feet.

Waldbrandriegel (German) One of several systems of firebreaks used particularly with pine plantations, in which noncombustibles are planted in the firebreaks.

Waldfeldbau (German) A system of swidden in which fields and woods rotate.

Wallace Line Hypothetical boundary separating the characteristic Asian flora and fauna from those of Australasia and forming the common boundary of the Australian and Asian biogeographic regions.

windrow Row of cut vegetation (as grain or wood) set for drying.

yasak (Russian) An annual fur tax, usually in sable.

zalezh' (Russian) First-contact swidden.

zapovednik (Russian) Part of a system of strict nature reserves, akin to a biosphere reserve.

BIBLIOGRAPHY

Ackerman, Jennifer. "Carrying the Torch." *Nature Conservancy* 43 (1993): 16–23.

Acland, J. B. A. "Sheep Farming in New Zealand." *Tussock Grassland and Mountain Lands Institute Review* 39 (1980): 65.

Adams, Arthur. *Travels of a Naturalist in Japan and Manchurin.* London: Hurst and Blackett, 1870.

Adrianovsky, A. "Ob'iasnenie kollektsii po udobreniiu." *Izvestiia imperatorskogo obshchestva liubitelei estestvoznaniia, antropologii i etnografii* 44, no. 2 (1883).

Ager, Derek V. *The Geology of Europe.* New York: John Wiley, 1980.

Alayev, E. B., et al. "The Russian Plain." In *The Earth as Transformed by Human Action,* edited by B. L. Turner II et al., pp. 543–560. Cambridge: Cambridge University Press, 1990.

Albulin, Ingemar. *A History of Swedish Literature.* Uddevalla: Swedish Institute, 1989.

Aldhous, J. R., and A. H. A. Scott. "Forest Fire Protection in the UK: Experience in the Period 1950–1990." *Commonwealth Forestry Review* 72 (1993): 39–47.

Allsop, F., ed. *New Zealand Forestry.* Wellington: Government Printer, 1964.

Alexander, M. E., and G. F. Bisgrove, eds. *The Art and Science of Fire Management.* Edmonton: Northern Forestry Centre, 1990.

Amouric, Henri. *Le Feu à l'épreuve du temps.* Narration, 1992.

Anders, Edward, et al. "Major Wildfires at the Cretaceous-Tertiary Boundary." In *Global Biomass Burning,* edited by Joel S. Levine, pp. 485–492. Cambridge: MIT Press, 1991.

Anderson, Anthony B., and Darrell A. Posey. "Reflorestamento Indigena." *Ciência Hoje* (December 1991): 6–12.

Anderson, Atholl. *Prodigious Birds.* Cambridge: Cambridge University Press, 1989.

———. "The Extinction of the Moa in Southern New Zealand." In *Quaternary Extinctions,* edited by Paul S. Martin and Richard G. Klein, pp. 741–767. Tucson: University of Arizona Press, 1984.

Anderson, David, and Richard Grove, eds. *Conservation in Africa: People, Policies, and Practice.* Cambridge: Cambridge University Press, 1987.

Anderson, Kling. "Burning Flint Hills Bluestem Ranges." *Proceedings, Tall Timbers Fire Ecology Conference,* vol. 3, pp. 89–103. Tallahassee: Tall Timbers Research Station, 1964.

Anderson, Mark. *A History of Scottish Forestry.* 2 vols. Nelson, 1967.

Andreae, Meinrat O. "Biomass Burning: Its History, Use, and Distribution and Its Impact on Environmental Quality and Global Climate." In *Global Biomass Burning*, edited by Joel S. Levine, pp. 3–22. Cambridge: MIT Press, 1991.

Andrews, Michael Alford. *The Birth of Europe*. London: BBC Books, 1991.

Angelstam, Per. "Conservation of Communities: The Importance of Edges, Surroundings and Landscape Mosaic Structure." In *Ecological Principles of Nature Conservation*, edited by Lennart Hansson. New York: Elsevier Applied Science, 1992.

————. "The Ghost of Lost Forest Past: Natural Disturbance Regimes as a Basis for Reconstruction of Biologically Diverse Forests in Europe." Unpublished manuscript, 1993.

Annual Report of the Forest Department for 1948. Port Louis, 1949.

Annual Report of the Forest Department for 1949. Port Louis, 1950.

Annual Report of the Forest Department for 1957. Port Louis, 1958.

Anon. "Austria. Forest Fires Statistics for 1988." *International Forest Fire News* 2 (1989): 3.

Anon. "Continental Notes: France." *Transactions of Royal Scottish Arboricultural Society* 39 (1924): 134–137.

Anon. "Große Waldbrände in Bayern." *Forstwissenschaftliches Centralblatt* 53 (1909): 605–606.

Anon. "50th Anniversary of Aerial Forest Protection, Tyumen Oblast [Tyumen Aerial Fire Center]" [in Russian]. Unpublished manuscript, 1981.

Anon. "58th Annual Excursion: Northumberland." *Scottish Forestry* 9 (1955): 120.

Anon. "Northern Base of Aerial Protection of Forests, 50th Anniversary [Arkhangelsk Aerial Fire Center]" [in Russian]. Unpublished report, 1981.

Anon. "Notes on the Influence of Forests on the Storage and Regulation of Water Supply." *Indian Forest Service*, Bulletin 9 (1906).

Anon. "Report Dedicated to the 50th Anniversary of Aerial Fire Protection [Urals Aerial Fire Center]" [in Russian]. Unpublished report, 1981.

Anon. "Report Given at the Celebratory Meeting Dedicated to the 50th Anniversary of the Northern Base (Arkhangelsk) of Aerial Forest Protection" [in Russian]. Unpublished report, 1981.

Anon. "Summary History [Yakutsk Aerial Fire Center]" [in Russian]. Unpublished report, 1981.

Anon. "Summary for 50th Anniversary of Aerial Forest Protection, July 1981 [Irkutsk Aerial Fire Center]" [in Russian]. Unpublished report, 1981.

Anon. "Treatment of Waste Lands in the Low Countries." *Indian Forester* 19 (1893): 361–363.

Anon. *Underdånigt betänkande och förslag, angående åtgärder för befrämjande af en förbättrad skogsförhållandena*. Stockholm, 1856.

Anon. *Underdånigt Betänkande och förslag, angåwnde Skogsförhållandena i Norrland och åtgärder för östadkommande af en förbättrad skogshushållning derstädes*. Stockholm, 1871.

Antonovski, M. Ya., et al. "A Spatial Model of Long-Term Forest Fire Dynamics and Its Applications to Forests in Western Siberia." In *A Systems Analysis of the Global Forest*, edited by Herman H. Shugart et al., pp. 373–403. Cambridge: Cambridge University Press, 1992.

Arbos, P. "The Geography of Pastoral Life with European Examples." *Geographical Review* 13 (1923): 559–575.

Arens, Nan Crystal. "Wildfire in the Paleozoic: Preliminary Results of a Case Study in the Fire Ecology of a Pennsylvanian Floodplain Forest, Joggins, Nova Scotia, Canada." In *Fire and the Environment: Ecological and Cultural Perspectives: Proceedings of an International Symposium,* edited by Stephen C. Nodvin and Thomas A. Waldrop, pp. 279–288. General Technical Report SE-69. U.S. Forest Service, 1991.

Armstrong, Terence. *Yermak's Campaign in Siberia.* London: Hakluyt Society, 1975.

Arnborg, Tore. *Från svedjebruk till hyggesbrännings.* Särtryck ur Norrlands Skogsvårdsförbunds Exkursionsprogram 1949. Stockholm, 1949.

Arnold, Rollo. *New Zealand's Burning: The Settler's World in the Mid 1880s.* Wellington: Victoria University Press, 1994.

Aronsson, Kjell-Åke. *Forest Reindeer Herding A.D. 1–1800.* Archaeology and Environment, 10. Umeå: Department of Archeology, University of Umeå, 1991.

Arrhenius, J. *Handbok i Svenska Jordbruket.* Vol. 3. Uppsala, 1862.

Areseniev, V. K. *Dersu the Trapper.* New York: Dutton, 1941.

Artsybashev, E. S. *Forest Fires and Their Control.* Russian Translations Series, 15. Rotterdam: A. A. Balkema, 1984.

Åsberg, Marie, and William T. Stearn. "Linnaeus's Öland and Gotland Journey 1741." *Biological Journal of the Linnaean Society.* 5 (1973): 1–107.

Ashwell, Ian Y., and Edgar Jackson. "The Sagas as Evidence of Early Deforestation in Iceland." *Canadian Geographer* 14 (1970): 148–166.

Åström, Sven-Erik. *From Tar to Timber: Studies in Northeast European Forest Exploitation and Foreign Trade, 1660–1860.* Commentationes Humanarum Litterarum, 85. Helsinki: Societas Scientiarum Fennica, 1988.

Atkinson, Thomas W. *Oriental and Western Siberia.* New York: Harper and Bros., 1858.

Attenborough, David. *The First Eden: The Mediterranean World and Man.* Boston: Little, Brown, 1978.

Austad, Ingvild. "Tree Pollarding in Western Norway." In *The Cultural Landscape: Past, Present and Future,* edited by Hilary H. Birks et al., pp. 11–29. Cambridge: Cambridge University Press, 1988.

Autran, A. "Introduction to the Geology of Western and Sourthern Europe." In *Geology and the Environment in Western Europe,* edited by G. Innes Lumsden and Editorial Board of the Directors of the Western European Geological Surveys, pp. 9–33. Oxford: Clarendon Press, 1992.

Avialesookhrana. Unpublished reports on 1972 fires [in Russian]. Pushkino, 1972.

Avialesookhrana. Statistics and unpublished reports [in Russian]. Pushkino, 1989.

Bachelard, Gaston. *The Psychoanalysis of Fire,* translated by Alan C. M. Ross. Boston: Beacon Press, 1964.

Bachmann. "Große Waldbrand am 27. Juli 1892 in Bosen." *Zeitschrift für Forst- und Jagdwesen* 24 (1892): 776–779.

Baden-Powell, B. H. *Village Communities in India.* New York: Charles Scribner's Sons, 1899.

Bahre, Conrad. *Destruction of the Natural Vegetation of North-Central Chile.* University of California Publications in Geography, 23. Berkeley: University of California Press, 1979.

Bailey, Arthur W., and Patricia G. Bailey. "The Traditions of Our Ancestors Influence Rangeland Tradition." *Rangelands* 14 (1994): 29–32.

Bailey, Major Frederick. "Forestry in France." *Indian Forester* 13 (1887a): 341–355, 389–407, 439–450, 489–501, 537–545.

————. "A Forest Tour in Provence and the Cevennes." *Indian Forester* 13 (1887b): 245–256, 293–304.

Baker, Samuel. *Cyprus As I Saw It in 1879.* London: Macmillan and Co., 1879.

Balée, William. "Indigenous History and Amazonian Biodiversity." In *Changing Tropical Forests,* edited by Harold K. Steen and Richard P. Tucker, pp. 185–197. Durham: Forest History Society, 1992.

Bancroft, Larry, et al. "Evolution of the Natural Fire Management Program at Sequoia and Kings Canyon National Park." In *Proceedings, Symposium and Workshop on Fire,* edited by James E. Lotan, et al., pp. 174–180. General Technical Report INT-182. U.S. Forest Service, 1985.

Bandelier, Adolf, ed. *The Journey of Alvar Nuñez Cabeza de Vaca . . . 1528–1536,* translated by Fanny Bandelier. New York: AMS Press, 1973 (reprint).

Bands, D. P. "Prescribed Burning in Cape Fynbos Catchments." In *Proceedings of the Symposium on the Environmental Consequences of Fire and Fuel Management in Mediterranean Ecosystems,* edited by Harold A. Mooney and C. Eugene Conrad, pp. 245–256. General Technical Report WO-3. U.S. Forest Service, 1977.

Bannbers, Ola. "Skogen Brukas. Svedjebruksbilder från Västerdalarna." In *Svenskas Kulturbilder,* edited by Sigurd Erixon and Sigurd Wallin. Ny Följd, Först Bandet, Del I & II. Stockholm, 1934.

Barbey, A. "Après l'incendie." *Revue des eaux et forêts* 62 (1924): 553–560.

Barker, Lady. *Station Life in New Zealand.* Auckland: Golden Press, 1973 (reprint of 1883 edition).

Barnes, Chip. "Epic Fire." Unpublished essay. 1996.

Barnes, Michael. *Killer in the Bush: The Great Fires of Northeastern Ontario.* Erin, Ontario: Boston Mills Press, 1987.

Baron, Samuel H., ed. and trans. *The Travels of Olearius in Seventeenth-Century Russia.* Palo Alto: Stanford University Press, 1967.

Bartlett, Harley Harris. *Fire in Relation to Primitive Agriculture and Grazing in the Tropics: Annotated Bibliography.* 3 vols. Ann Arbor: University of Michigan Botanical Gardens, 1955–61.

————. "Fire, Primitive Agriculture, and Grazing in the Tropics." In *Man's Role in Changing the Face, of the Earth,* vol. 1, edited by William L. Thomas, Jr., pp. 692–720. Chicago: University of Chicago Press, 1956.

————. "Possible Separate Origin and Evolution of the *ladang* and *sawah* Types of Tropical Agriculture." *Ninth Pacific Science Congress of the Pacific Science Association* (1957a): 45–46.

————. "Some Words Used in Connection with Primitive Agriculture in Southeast Asia." *Ninth Pacific Science Congress of the Pacific Science Association* (1957b): 44–45.

Bassin, Mark. "Expansion and Colonialism on the Eastern Frontier: Views of Siberia and the Far East in Pre-Petrine Russia." *Journal of Historical Geography* 14 (1988): 3–21.

Battistini, R., and G. Richard-Vindard, eds. *Biogeography and Ecology in Madagascar.* The Hague: Dr. W. Junk Publ., 1972.

Battistini, R., and P. Verin. "Man and the Environment in Madagascar." In *Biogeography and Ecology in Madagascar,* edited by R. Battistini and G. Richard-Vindard, pp. 324–356. The Hague: Dr. W. Junk Publ., 1972.

Baxter, John, and Thomas Atkins. *The Fire Came By.* New York: Doubleday, 1976.

Beach, Hugh. *Reindeer-Herd Management in Transition: The Case of Tuorpon Saameby in Northern Sweden*. Uppsala, 1981.

Beaglehole, J. C., ed. *The Endeavour Journal of Joseph Banks, 1768–1711*. 2 vols. 2d edition. Sydney: Trustees of the Public Library of New South Wales, 1962.

Beall, Ben. "Wildland and Fire Training in the Western Pacific." *Fire Management Notes* 48 (1987): 10–12.

Beard, J. S. *The Natural Vegetation of the Windward and Leeward Islands*. Oxford Forestry Memoirs, 21. Oxford: Clarendon Press, 1949.

Beard, M. "The Sexual Status of the Vestal Virgins." *Journal of Roman Studies* 70 (1980): 12–27.

Beaver, Patrick. *The Match Makers*. London: Henry Mellard, 1985.

Bechmann, Roland. *Trees and Man: The Forest in the Middle Ages*, translated by Katharyn Dunham. New York: Paragon House, 1990.

Behre, Karl-Ernst. "The Role of Man in European Vegetation History." In *Vegetation History*, edited by B. Huntley and T. Webb III, pp. 633–671. Boston: Kluwer Academic Publ., 1988.

Bell, John. *A Journey from St. Petersburg to Pekin, 1719–22*, edited by J. S. Stevenson. New York: Barnes and Noble, 1966.

Bellomo, Randy. "Methods for Documenting Unequivocal Evidence of Humanly Controlled Fire at Early Pleistocene Archaeological Sites in East Africa: The Role of Actualistic Studies." Ph.D. dissertation, University of Wisconsin-Milwaukee, 1990.

Belov, S. V. "A Managed Forest Fire: The Means of Regeneration of Pineries and Larch Forests in the Taiga Zone." In *Combustion and Fires in the Forest*, edited by N. P. Kurbatsky et al., pp. 213–222 [in Russian]. Krasnoyarsk: Academy of Sciences of the USSR, 1973.

Bennett, K. D., et al. "Fire and Man in Post-Glacial Woodlands of Eastern England." *Journal of Archaeological Science* 17 (1990): 635–642.

———. "Holocene History of Environment, Vegetation and Human Settlement on Catta Ness, Lunnasting, Shetland." *Journal of Ecology* 80 (1992): 241–273.

Bennett, Stephan. "Kortt underrättelse om det savolaeiska svedjebruket på torra marker." *Ny Journal uti Hushållningen*. Stockholm: 1792.

Bereschchnoy, V. G., and G. I. Drapkina. "Izuchenie anomal'nogo prirosta lesa v raione padeniia Tungusskogo meteorita." *Meteoritika* 24 (1964): 162–169.

Berglund, B. E., ed. *The Cultural Landscape during 6000 Years in Southern Sweden: The Ystad Project*. Ecological Bulletins, 41: 11–28. Copenhagen: 1991.

Bernes, Claes, and Claes Grundsten, eds. *The Environment*. National Atlas of Sweden, 1992.

Bigelow, Gerald E., ed. *The Norse of the North Atlantic*. Acta Archaeologica, 61. Copenhagen, 1991.

Billington, James H. *The Icon and the Axe*. New York: Knopf, 1966.

Billington, Ray Allen. *Westward Expansion*. 4th edition New York: Macmillan, 1974.

Birchfield, Reg J., and Ian F. Grant. *Out of the Woods*. Wellington: GP Publications, 1993.

Birks, Hilary H., et al., eds. *The Cultural Landscape: Past, Present and Future*. Cambridge: Cambridge University Press, 1988.

Bishko, Charles Julian. "The Castilian as Plainsman: The Medieval Ranching Frontier in La Mancha and Extremadura." In *The New World Looks at Its History*, edited by Archibald R. Lewis and Thomas F. McGann. Austin: University of Texas Press, 1958.

Bjorklund, Jorgen. "From the Gulf of Bothnia to the White Sea: Direct Swedish Invest-ment in the Sawmill Industry of Tsarist Russia." In *History of Sustained-Yield Forestry: A Symposium,* edited by Harold K. Steen, pp. 47–69. Durham: Forest His-tory Society, 1984.

Blache, Jules. "L'Essartage: Ancienne practique culturale dans les Alpes Dauphinoises." *Revue géographie alpin* 11 (1923): 553–575.

Blackburn, Thomas C., and Kat Anderson, eds. *Before the Wilderness: Environment Management by Native Californians.* Menlo Park: Ballena Press, 1993.

Bligh, Captain William. *A Voyage to the South Sea.* London, 1792.

Bloch, Marc. *French Rural History,* translated by Janet Sondheimer. Berkeley: Uni-versity of California Press, 1966.

Blomqvist, A. G. *Om Skogseld.* Helsingfors, 1888.

Blunt, Wilfred. *The Compleat Naturalist: A Life of Linnaeus.* New York: Viking Press, 1971.

Bobrick, Benson. *East of the Sun: The Epic Conquest and Tragic History of Siberia.* New York: Poseidon Press, 1992.

Bodvall, Gunnar. "Bodland i norra Hälsingland (Bodland in North Hälsingland. Stud-ies of the Part Played by Land Clearance in the Expansion of the Permanently Set-tled Area up to 1850)." *Geographica* 36 (Uppsala, 1959).

Bogucki, Peter. *Forest Farmers and Stockholders: Early Agriculture and Its Conse-quences in North-Central Europe.* Cambridge: Cambridge University Press, 1988.

Bonnicksen, T. M., and E. C. Stone, "Managing Vegetation Within U.S. National Parks: A Policy Analysis." *Environmental Management* 6 (1982): 109–122.

Boomgaard, Peter. "Forests and Forestry in Colonial Java: 1677–1942." In *Changing Tropical Forests,* edited by John Dargavel et al., pp. 59–87. Canberra: Australian National University, 1988.

Booysen, Peter de V., and Neil M. Tainton, eds. *Ecological Effects of Fire in South African Ecosystems.* Ecological Studies, 48. Heidelberg: Springer-Verlag, 1984.

Borisov, A. A. *Climates of the U.S.S.R.,* edited by Cyril A. Halstead. Chicago: Aldine Publishing Co., 1965.

Boudy, P. *Économie Forestière Nord-Africaine.* 4 vols. Paris: Editions Larose, 1948.

Braathe, Peder. "Prescribed Burning in Norway: Effects on Soil and Regeneration." *Pro-ceedings, Tall Timbers Fire Ecology Conference,* vol. 13, pp. 211–222. Tallahassee: Tall Timbers Research Station, 1973.

Brad, K. W. "Bracken Control—Artificial and Natural. *Grass and Forage Science* 2 (1947): 181–189.

Bradshaw, Richard H. W., and Philip Brown. "Changing Patterns in the Post-Glacial Distribution of *Pinus sylvestris* in Ireland." *Journal of Biogeography* 14 (1987): 237–248.

Bradshaw, Richard H. W., and Olle Zackrisson. "A Two Thousand Year History of a Northern Swedish Boreal Forest Stand." *Journal of Vegetation Science* 1 (1990): 519–528.

Brain, C. K., and A. Sillen. "Evidence from the Swartkrans Cave for the Earliest Use of Fire." *Nature* 336 (1988): 464–466.

Bramwell, David. "The Endemic Flora of the Canary Islands: Distribution, Relation-ships and Phytogeography." In *Biogeography and Ecology in the Canary Islands,* edited by G. Kunkel, pp. 207–240. The Hague: Dr. W. Junk, 1976.

Brandes, Dr. Georg. *Impressions of Russia,* translated by Samuel C. Eastman. London: Walter Scott, 1889.

Brandis, Dietrich. "Memorandum No. 263." *Forest Conference of 1875.* Simla, 1872.

Braudel, Fernard. *The Identity of France.* 2 vols. Translated by Sian Reynolds. New York: Harper and Row, 1988–90.

————. *The Mediterranean and the Mediterranean World in the Age of Phillip II.* 2 vols. Translated by Sian Reynolds. New York: Harper and Row, 1972.

Bremner, Robert. *Excursions in the Interior of Russia.* 2 vols. London: Henry Colburn, 1839.

Bricogne. "Les forêts de l'empire Ottoman." *Revue des eaux et forêts* (1877): 273–289.

Bringeus, Nils-Arvid. *Brännodling: En historik-ethnologisk undersökning.* Skrifter från folklisvsarkivet i Lund. Utgivne genom sällkskpet folkkultur, 6. Lund, 1963.

Brink, A. S. "The Spontaneous Fire-Controlling Reactions of Two Chimpanzee Smoking Addicts." *South African Journal of Science* 53 (1957): 241–247.

Broberg, Gunnar. *Carl von Linné Om jämviktgen i naturen.* Stockholm: Bokförlaget CARMINA, 1978.

Brofinger. "Der große Brand am 15–16 August 1904 in den Staatswaldungen des flg. forstamtes Bodenwöhr." *Forstwissenschaftliches Centralblatt* 49 (1905): 253–261.

Brogberg, Richard. *Finsk invandring till mellersta Sverige.* Svenska Lansmål och Svenskt Folkliv. B. 68. Uppsala: Almqvist & Wiksell, 1988.

Bromander, C. V. "Svedjebruket på Finnskogen." *Svenska turistföreningens årsskrift* (1902): 259–296.

Brouard, N. R. *A History of Woods and Forests in Mauritius.* Port-Louis: Government Printer, 1963.

Brown, John Croumbie. *Finland: Its Forests and Forest Management.* Edinburgh: Oliver and Boyd, 1883a.

————. *Forestry in the Mining Districts of the Ural Mountains in Eastern Russia.* Edinburgh: Oliver and Boyd, 1884.

————. *French Forest Ordinance of 1669.* Edinburgh: Oliver and Boyd, 1883b.

————. *Reboisement in France.* London: H. S. King, 1880.

Brown, Mervyn. *Madagascar Rediscovered: A History from Early Times to Independence.* Hamden, Conn.: Archon Books, 1979.

Budiansky, Stephen. *Nature's Keepers: The New Science of Nature Management.* New York: Free Press, 1995.

Bullen, E. R. "Burning Cereal Crop Residues in England." *Proceedings, Tall Timbers Fire Ecology Conference,* vol. 13, pp. 223–235. Tallahassee: Tall Timbers Research Station, 1974.

Bunting, Stephen C., and Francisco C. Rego. "Human Impact on Portugal's Vegetation." *Rangelands* 10 (1988): 251–255.

Burger, Dr. D. "Brand in gebergtebosch" [Forest Fires in Mountain tracts with a Dry Monsoon]. *Tectona* 21 (1930): 405.

————. "Voorwaarden, waaraan plantensoorten moeten voldoen voor gebruik bij boschbrandbestrijding of Java" [Conditions to Which Plants Have to Obey If Used for Firefighting Purposes in Java's Forests]. *Tectona* 17 (1924): 462–481.

Burnet, John. *Early Greek Philosophers.* 4th edition. London: Adam and Charles Black, 1928.

Burnett, G. W., and Lisa M. Butler Harrington. "Early National Park Adoption in Sub-Saharan Africa." *Society and Natural Resources* 7 (1994): 155–168.

Burney, David Allen. "Late Quaternary Environmental Dynamics of Madagascar." Ph.D. dissertation, Duke University, 1986.

Butler, Samuel. *A First Year in Canterbury Setttlement.* Auckland: Blackwood and Janet Paul, 1964.

Butskikh, A. P., and P. N. Pryakhi, "Brief Historical Summary to Honor the 50th Anniversary of Aerial Forest Protection [Central Air Base]" [in Russian]. Unpublished, 1981.

Byberg, A. T. "Värmlämdskt svedjebruk vid tiden omkring år 1860." *Fataburen* (1928): 165–175.

Bylund, Erik. "Kollisionen mellan svenskt och lapskt näringsfang." In *Samenes og sameiområdenes rettslige stilling historisk belyst,* edited by Knut Bergsland, pp. 108–123. Oslo: Universitetsforlaget, 1974.

———. "Koloniseringen av Pite Lappmark T.O.M. år 1867." *Geographica.* Skrifter från Uppsala Universitets Geografiska Institution, 30. Uppsala, 1956.

Caesar, Julius. *Caesar's Gallic War,* translated by Joseph Pearl. Woodbury, N.Y.: Barron's Educational Series, 1962.

Cahoon, Donald R., Jr., et al. "Satellite Analysis of the Severe 1987 Forest Fires in Northern China and Southeastern Siberia." *Journal of Geophysical Research* 99 (1994): 18627–18638.

———. "The Great Chinese Fire of 1987: A View from Space." In *Global Biomass Burning,* edited by Joel S. Levine, pp. 61–66. Cambridge: MIT Press, 1991.

Callender, Jennifer M., and Janet D. Henshall. "The Land Use of Faial in the Azores." In *Four Island Studies.* Bude, Cornwall: Geographical Publications Ltd., 1968.

Campbell, Åke. *Från vildmark till bygd.* Umeå: Två Forläffare Bokförlag, 1982 (facsimile edition).

Cardona, M. A., and J. Contandriopoulos. "Endemism and Evolution in the Islands of the Western Mediterranean." In *Plants and Islands,* edited by D. Bramwell, pp. 133–169. New York: Academic Press, 1979.

Cassels, Richard. "Faunal Extinction and Prehistoric Man in New Zealand and the Pacific Islands." In *Quaternary Extinctions,* edited by Paul S. Martin and Richard G. Klein, pp. 741–767. Tucson: University of Arizona Press, 1984.

Cesti, Giancarlo. "Forest Fires in Italy." *Suid-Afrikaanse Bosboutydskrif* 145 (1988): 47–58.

Chadwick, Nora K., and Victor Zhirmunsky. *Oral Epics of Central Asia.* Cambridge: Cambridge University Press, 1969.

Chambers, F. M., et al. "Development of the Late-Prehistoric Cultural Landscape in Upland Ardudwy, North-west Wales." In *The Cultural Landscape: Past, Present and Future,* edited by Hilary H. Birks et al., pp. 333–348. Cambridge: Cambridge University Press, 1988.

Chautrand, L. "Les incendies de forêt en Provence-Côte d'Azur." *Bulletin technique d'information* (Ministère-de-l'agriculture) 268 (1972): 405–413.

Chauvet, B. "The Forests of Madagascar." In *Biogeography and Ecology in Madagascar,* edited by R. Battistini and G. Richard-Vindard, pp. 191–199. The Hague: Dr. W. Junk, 1972.

Chekhov, Anton. "On Siberia." In *The Unknown Chekhov,* translated by Avrahm Yarmolinsky. London, 1959.

———. *The Island: A Journey to Sakhalin,* translated by Luba and Michael Terpak. New York: Washington Square Press, 1967.

Cherry, John F. "Pattern and Process in the Earliest Colonization of the Mediterranean Islands." *Proceedings of the Prehistoric Society* 47 (1981): 41–68.

Chistjakov, V. I., et al. "Measures for Fire Prevention on Peat Deposits." In *The Role of Fire in Northern Circumpolar Ecosystems,* edited by Ross Wein and David Maclean, pp. 259–272. New York: John Wiley and Sons, 1983.

Christensen, Norman L., et al. "Final Report: Review of Fire Management Program for Sequoia–Mixed Conifer Forests of Yosemite, Sequoia and Kings Canyon National Parks." Unpublished report, Sequoia–Kings Canyon National Parks, February 27, 1987.

Ciesla, Bill. "Fires in Europe." *Wildfire* 3 (September 1994): 71.

Clar, Raymond. *California Government and Forestry.* 2 vols. Sacramento: California Division of Forestry, 1959–67.

Clark, Grahame. *World Prehistory in New Perspective.* 3d edition. Cambridge: Cambridge University Press, 1977.

Clark, J. D., and J. W. K. Harris. "Fire and Its Roles in Early Hominid Lifeways." *The African-Archaeological Review* 3 (1985): 3–27.

Clark, J. S., and J. Robinson. "Paleoecology of Fire." In *Fire in the Environment: The Ecological, Atmospheric, and Climatic Importance of Vegetation Fires,* edited by P. J. Crutzen and J. G. Goldammer, pp. 193–214. New York: John Wiley and Sons, 1993.

Clark, J. S., et al. "Post-Glacial Fire, Vegetation, and Human History of the Northern Alpine Forelands, South-Western Germany." *Journal of Ecology* 77 (1989): 897–925.

Clement, B., and J. Touffet. "Vegetation Dynamics in Brittany Heathlands after Fire." *Vegetatio* 46 (1981): 157–166.

Cloud, Preston. *Oasis in Space: Earth History from the Beginning.* New York: Norton, 1988.

Clout, Hugh. *The Massif Central.* 2d edition. Oxford: Oxford University Press, 1983.

Clout, Hugh, ed. *Themes in Historical Geography of France.* New York: Academic Press, 1977.

Clutton-Brock, Juliet. *A Natural History of Domesticated Mammals.* Austin: University of Texas Press, 1987.

Cochrane, John. *Narrative of a Pedestrian Journey through Russia and Siberian Tartary.* 2 vols. New York: Arno Press, 1970 (reprint).

Coffin, Emm. "Les incendies de forêts dans le département du Var." *Bulletin du comité des forêts* 48 (1931): 658–663.

———. "Les incendies de forêts: Une Organization de défense." *Bulletin du comité des forêts* 50 (1932): 82–92.

Collinder, Bjorn. *The Lapps.* Princeton: Princeton University Press, 1949.

Collins, David N. "Subjugation and Settlement in Seventeenth- and Eighteenth-Century Siberia." In *The History of Siberia,* edited by Alan Wood, pp. 37–56. New York: Routledge, 1991.

Collins, Perry. *Siberian Journey down the Amur to the Pacific, 1856–1857,* edited by Charles Vevier. Madison: University of Wisconsin Press, 1962.

———. *A Voyage down the Amur.* New York: D. Appleton and Co., 1860.

Conklin, Harold C. "An Ethnological Approach to Shifting Agriculture." *Transactions, New York Academy of Science* 17 (1954): 133–142.

Connell, K. H. "The Colonization of Waste Land in Ireland, 1780–1845." *Economic History* 3 (1950): 44–71.

Conophagos, Constantine. "Smelting Practice at Ancient Laurion (Greece)." In *Early Pyrotechnology: The Evolution of the First Fire-Using Industries,* edited by Theodore A. Wertime and Steven F. Wertime, pp. 181–192. Washington, D.C.: Smithsonian Institution Press, 1982.

Conrad, A. "Das Bodenfeuer als Freund des Forstmannes." *Forstliche Wochenschrift Silva* 13 (1925): 139–141.

Conrad, C. Eugene, and Walter C. Oechel, eds. *Proceedings of the Symposium on Dynamics and Management of Mediterranean-Type Ecosystems.* General Technical Report PSW-58. U.S. Forest Service, 1981.

Cooper, Neill. "History of Fires and Legislation: Fires Within and Outside Forests; Costs, Statistics, Overall Causes." *Prevent Rural Fires Convention,* pp. 10–17. Wellington: Ministry of Forestry, 1989.

Cope, M. J., and W. G. Chaloner. "Fossil Charcoal as Evidence of Past Atmospheric Composition." *Nature* (February 14, 1980): 647–648.

———. "Wildfire: An Interaction of Biological and Physical Processes." In *Geological Factors and the Evolution of Plants,* edited by Bruce H. Tiffney, pp. 257–177. New Haven: Yale University Press, 1985.

Corrigan, Robert W., ed. *Aeschylus.* New York: Dell Publishing Co., 1965.

Coutant, Victor, trans. *Theophrastus De Igne.* Assen, Netherlands: Royal Vangorcum Ltd., 1971.

Cowie, Leonard W. *Plague and Fire: London, 1665–1666.* East Sussex: Wayland Publishers, 1970.

Cox, C. Barry, and Peter D. Moore. *Biogeography: An Ecological and Evolutionary Approach.* 5th edition. Oxford: Blackwell Scientific, 1993.

Cremieu-Alcan, Philippe. "Août 1949: La forêt landaise en feu." In *Le feu à la maison, par les bois et dans le champs,* edited by Andrée Corvol. pp. 53–57. Cahier d'Études, 1992.

Crone, G. R., ed. and trans. *The Voyages of Cadamosto.* London: Hakluyt Society, 1937.

Crosby, Alfred. *Ecological Imperialism: The Biological Expansion of Europe, 900–1900.* Cambridge: Cambridge University Press, 1986.

Crutzen, P. J., and J. W. Birks. "The Atmosphere after a Nuclear War: Twilight at Noon." *Ambio* 11 (1982): 115–125.

Cumberland, Kenneth B. "Climatic Change or Cultural Interference?" In *Land and Livelihood: Geographical Essays in Honour of George Jobberns,* edited by M. McCaskill, pp. 88–142. New Zealand Geographical Society, 1962.

———. *Soil Erosion in New Zealand.* Wellington: Soils Conservation and Rivers Control Council, 1944.

Cunliffe, Barry, ed. *The Oxford Illustrated Prehistory of Europe.* Oxford: Oxford University Press, 1994.

Cyprus Forestry Department. "Data on Fires Occurred in the Main State Forests during the Decade 1981–1990." Unpublished report to Chania Workshop, 1991.

Czaplicka, M. A. *Aboriginal Siberia: A Study in Social Anthropology.* Oxford: Oxford University Press, 1914.

Dahl, Sven, "Strip Fields and Enclosure in Sweden. *Scandinavian Economic History Review* 9 (1961): 56–67.

Damman, A. W. H. "The South-Swedish Calluna-Heath and Its Relation to the Calluneto-Genistetum." *Botaniska Notiser* 110 (1957): 363–398.

Darby, H. C. "The Clearing of the Woodland in Europe." In *Man's Role in Changing the Face of the Earth,* vol. 1, edited by William L. Thomas, Jr., pp. 183–216. Chicago: University of Chicago Press, 1956.

———. "The Draining of the Fens, A.D. 1600–1800." In *An Historical Geography of*

England before A.D. 1800, edited by H. C. Darby, pp. 444–464. Cambridge: Cambridge University Press, 1936a.

———. "The Economic Geography of England, A.D. 1000–1250." In *An Historical Geography of England Before A.D. 1800,* edited by H. C. Darby pp. 165–229. Cambridge: Cambridge University Press, 1936b.

Darby, H. C., ed. *A New Historical Geography of England After 1600.* Cambridge: Cambridge University Press, 1976.

Darwin, Charles. *The Origin of Species.* New York: New American Library, 1958.

———. *The Voyage of the Beagle,* edited by Leonard Engel. New York: Anchor Books, 1962 (reprint).

D'Auteroche, M. l'Abbe Chappe. *A Journey into Siberia.* London, 1770.

Davidson, D. S. "Fire-Making in Australia." *American Anthropologist* 49 (1947): 426–437.

Davidson, Janet. *The Prehistory of New Zeland.* Auckland: Longman Paul Ltd., 1984.

Davies, Elwyn. "The Patterns of Transhumance in Europe," *Geography* 26 (1941): 155–168.

Davis, R. W. "Russia in the Early Middle Ages." *Economic History Review* 13 (1952): 116–127.

Davis, J. B. "Burning Another Empire." *Fire Management Notes* 45 (1984): 12–17.

Davydenko, E. P., and A. P. Butskikh. *Aerial Fireman* [in Russian]. Moscow: Lesnaya Promyshlennost, 1984.

Dawson, Christopher, ed. *The Mongol Mission.* New York: Sheed and Ward, 1980.

Day, D. L., et al. *Keeping the Flame: Fire Management in the Canadian Park Service.* Proceedings of the 1990 Interior West Fire Council, Annual Meeting and Workshop. Information Report NOR-X-309. Edmonton: Northern Forestry Center, 1994.

Dean, Warren. *With Broadaxe and Firebrand: The Destruction of the Brazilian Atlantic Forest.* Berkeley: University of California Press, 1995.

Delabraze, Pierre, and Jean Ch. Valette. "The Use of Fire in Siviculture." In *Proceedings of the Symposium on Dynamics and Management of Mediterranean-Type Ecosystems,* edited by C. Eugene Conrad and Walter C. Oechel, pp. 475–482. General Technical Report PSW-58. U.S. Forest Service, 1981.

Delfs, Jürgen. "Waldbrände im 18. Jahrhundert." *Kreirkalender* (1993).

Dencker, S. S. *Om släckning af skogseld, moss- och ljunbrand.* Landskrona, 1914.

Denisov, A. K. "Forest Fires in the Woodland of Middle Zavolgie in 1921 and 1922 and Their Lessons." In *Combustion and Fire in the Forest* [in Russian], edited by N. P. Kurbatsky, pp. 16–26. Krasnoyarsk, 1979.

Department of Forestry. *State Forestry: Report for the Year Ended 31st March, 1919.* Wellington, 1919.

Despain, D., et al. *A Bibliography and Directory of the Yellowstone Fires of 1988.* 2d edition. Fairfield: International Association of Wildland Fire, 1994.

Dewar, Robert E. "Extinctions in Madagascar: The Loss of Subfossil Fauna." In *Quaternary Extinctions,* edited by Paul S. Martin and Richard G. Klein, pp. 574–593. Tucson: University of Arizona Press, 1984.

diCastri, Francesco, and Harold Mooney, eds. *Mediterranean-Type Ecosystems: Origin and Structure.* Berlin: Springer-Verlag, 1973.

diCastri, Francesco, et al., eds. *Mediterranean-Type Shrublands.* Ecosystems of the World, 11. Elsevier, 1981.

Dietrich, John H. "Project Report. Long Term Rehabilitation of Fire-Stricken Areas,

Mongolian Peoples Republic. Fire Operations and Statistical Reporting," FAO FO:MON/87/004 (FAO, 1990).

Dimbleby, G. W. "Anthropogenic Changes from Neolithic through Medieval Times." *New Phytologist* 89 (1984): 57–74.

———. "The Ancient Forest of Blackamore." *Antiquity* 35 (1961): 123–128.

Dimitrakopoulos, Alexander P. "The 1993 Forest Fire Season in Greece." *International Forest Fire News* 10 (1994): 11–12.

Dittmer, Ken. "Chilean Fire Course." *Fire Management Notes* 47 (1987): 6.

Dmytryshyn, Basil. "The Administrative Apparatus of the Russian Colony in Siberia and Northern Asia, 1581–1700." In *The History of Siberia,* edited by Alan Wood, pp. 17–36. New York: Routledge, 1991.

Dmytryshyn, Basil. *USSR: A Concise History.* 2d edition. New York: Scribners, 1971.

Dmytryshyn, Basil, et al., eds. and trans. "An Account by the Cossack Piatidesiantnik, Vladimir Atlasov, Concerning His Expedition to Kamchatka in 1697." In *Russian Penetration of the North Pacific Ocean, 1700–1799,* vol. 2. Portland: Oregon Historical Society Press, 1986.

———. *Russia's Conquest of Siberia, 1558–1700: A Documentary Record.* Portland: Oregon State Historical Society, 1985.

Dobbs, E. D. "Cyprus." *Indian Forester* 11 (1885): 54–56.

Dobell, Peter. *Travels in Kamtchatka and Siberia.* 2 vols. London: Henry Colburn and Richard Bentley, 1830.

Dodgshon, Robert A. "The Ecological Basis of Highland Peasant Farming, 1500–1800 A.D." In *The Cultural Landscape: Past, Present and Future,* edited by Hilary H. Birks et al., pp. 139–151. Cambridge: Cambridge University Press, 1988.

Dodgshon, R. A., and C. A. Jewell. "Paring and Burning and Related Practices with Particular Reference to the South-Western Counties of England." In *The Spade in Northern and Atlantic Europe,* edited by Alan Gailey and Alexander Fenton, pp. 74–87. Belfast: Ulster Folk Museum, 1970.

Dodson, J. R. "The Holocene Vegetation of a Prehistorically Inhabited Valley, Dingle Peninsula, Co. Kerry." *Proceedings Royal Irish Academy* 90B (1990): 151–174.

Dodson, John R., and Richard H. W. Bradshaw. "A History of Vegetation and Fire, 6600 B.C. to Present, County Sligo, Western Ireland." *Boreas* 16 (1987): 113–123.

Donner, Kai. *Ethnological Notes about the Yenisey-Ostyak.* Soumalis-ugrilaisen Seuran Toimituksia, 66. Helsinki, 1933.

Dorrer, G. A. "Theory of Forest Fire Spread as a Wave Process." Ph.D. thesis. Krasnoyarsk: Siberian Technological University, 1989.

Doveton, Capt. J. C. *Forest Conference of 1875.* Simla, 1875.

Drew, Ronald F. "The Emergence of an Agricultural Policy for Siberia in the XVII and XVIII Centuries." *Agricultural History* 33 (1959): 29–39.

Druett, Joan. *Exotic Intruders.* Auckland: Heinemann, 1983.

duBois, Coert. "Forest Fire Protection in Java." *Forest Worker* (1929): 24.

Dubos, René. *The Wooing of Earth.* New York: Scribner, 1980.

Ducamp, Roger. "Au pays des incendies." *Revue des eaux et forêts* 70 (1932): 380–393.

Dujas, Jean-Michel, and Bernard Traimond. "Le choix du coupable: L'incendie dans les Landes de Gascogne." In *Le feu à la maison, par les bois et dans le champs,* edited by Andrée Corvol, pp. 60–61. Cahier d'Études, 1992.

Dumézil, Georges. *Archaic Roman Religion,* translated by Philip Krapp. 2 vols. Chicago: University of Chicago Press, 1970.

Dunbar, G. S. "The Forests of Cyprus under British Stewardship." *Scottish Geographical Magazine* 99 (1983): 111.

Duncan, T. Bentley. *Atlantic Islands: Madeira, the Azores and the Cape Verdes in Seventeenth-Century Commerce and Navigation.* Chicago: University of Chicago Press, 1972.

Dusha-Gudym, Sergei I. "Forest Fires on the Areas Contaminated by Radionuclides from the Chernobyl Nuclear Power Plant Accident." *International Forest Fire News* 7 (1992): 18–19.

———. "News from the Forest Fire Situation in the Radioactively Contaminated Regions." *International Forest Fire News* 10 (1994): 4–6.

Dybeck, W. "Synpunkter vid skogsbrandförsäkringsfragans ordnande i Sverige." *Skogsvårdföreningens tidskrift* (1915): 401–442.

East, W. G. "England in the Eighteenth Century." In *An Historical Geography of England before A.D. 1800,* edited by H. C. Darby, pp. 465–528. Cambridge: Cambridge University Press, 1951.

Ecologia Mediterranean 13, no. 4 (1987) [special issue on fire].

Economic Commission for Europe and FAO. "Forest Fire Statistics, 1985–1988." ECE/TIM/51.

Economic Commission for Europe, et al. *Seminar on Forest Fire Prevention, Land Use and People.* Athens: Ministry of Agriculture, 1992.

Eden, Charles. *Frozen Asia.* London, 1890.

Edsman, Carl-Martin. *Ignis Divinus: Le feu comme moyen de rajeunissement et d'immortalité: Contes legends, mythes et rites.* Skrifter Utgivna av Vetenskaps-Societeten i Lund, 34. Lund, 1950.

Edwards, Kevin J. "The Hunter-Gatherer/Agricultural Transition and the Pollen Record in the British Isles." In *The Cultural Landscape: Past, Present and Future,* edited by Hilary H. Birks et al., pp. 255–266. Cambridge: Cambridge University Press, 1988.

Ehnström, Bengt. "Många insekter gynnas." *Skog & Forskning* 4 (1991): 47–52.

Ehrlich, Paul, et al. *The Cold and the Dark.* New York: Norton, 1984.

Eißmann, Helmut. "Der Waldbrand im Veldensteiner Forst 1976." *Allgemeine Forstzeitschrift* 33 (1978): 250–252.

Elgee, Frank. *The Moorlands of North-eastern Yorkshire.* London, 1912.

Elliott, Hugh, ed. *Second World Conference on National Parks.* Morges, Switzerland: International Union for Conservation of Nature and Natural Resources, 1974.

Ellis, L. MacIntosh. *State Forest Service: Report for the Year Ended 31st March, 1921.* Wellington, 1921.

———. *State Forest Service: Report for the Year Ended 31st March, 1922.* Wellington, 1922.

Eneroth, O. "Bidrag till kännedomen om hyggesbränningens inverkan på marken." In *Festskrift utgiven med anledning av skogshögskolans 100-års jubileum 1828–1928,* pp. 429–500. Stockholm, 1928.

Engelmark, Ola. "Forest Fire History and Successional Patterns in Muddus National Park, Northern Sweden." Ph.D. thesis, University of Umeå, 1987.

———. "Forest History of Muddus National Park, N. Sweden." *Wahlenbergia* 7 (1981): 33–38.

Epstein, D. M. "Reindeer Herding and Ecology in Finnish Lapland." *Geojournal* 8 (1984): 159–169.

Erman, Adolph. *Travels in Siberia.* 2 vols. London: Longman, Brown, Green, and Longmans, 1848.

"Espaces Forestiers et Incendies." *Revue forestière française* (1990) [special issue].

Evans, E. Estyn. *Irish Folk Ways.* London, 1957.

———. "Transhumance in Europe." *Geography* 25 (1940): 172–180.

Faberberg, Bengt. "The Transfer of Peasant Forest to Sawmill Companies in Northern
Sweden." *Scandinavian Economic History Review* 21 (1972): 164–191.

Faegri, K. "On the Introduction of Agriculture in Western Norway." *Geologiska föreningens i Stockholm förhandlingan* 66 (1944): 449–462.

Faggot, J. "Afhandling om svedjande samt utväg til hushållning med skogar." *Kung-
ligs Svenska Vetenskapsakademins Handlingar.* Stockholm, 1750.

Falk, Erik. "Finnarna i Värmland intill 1600-talets slut." *En bok om Värmland av Värm-
länningar* 3 (1921): 229–284.

Falkman, Ludwig. *Om Svenskas skogarnas nuwarande tillstand och deras inflytande
på landets framtid.* Stockholm, 1852.

Faraday, Michael. *The Chemical History of a Candle.* New York: Crowell, 1957 (reprint).

Farrow, R. G. "Rural Fire in New Zealand: A Look at Our Past History, Current State
and Future Needs." Presented to 64th Annual Conference of the Institution of Fire
Engineers (New Zealand Branch). Hamilton, August 1993.

Fellman, Jacob. *Anteckningar under min vistelse i.* Del 1. Helsinki, 1906.

Fenton, Alexander. "Paring and Burning and the Cutting of Turf and Peat in Scotland."
In *The Spade in Northern and Atlantic Europe,* edited by Alan Gailey and Alexander Fenton, pp. 155–193. Belfast: Ulster Folk Museum, 1970.

———. *The Shape of the Past: Two Essays in Scottish Ethnology.* Edinburgh: J. Donald, 1985.

Fernandez, E. E. "Forest of L'Esterel and Fire Conservancy in France." *Appendix Series
of The Indian Forester,* part 1, pp. 1–8. 1897.

Fernow, Bernhard. *A Brief History of Forestry in Europe, the United States, and Other
Countries.* Toronto: University of Toronto Press, 1907.

Ferreira, Padre Manuel Juvenal Pita. *O Arquipélago da Madeira Terra do Senhor Infante.*
Funchal, 1959.

Fisher, George J. B. *Incendiary Warfare.* London: McGraw-Hill, 1946.

Fisher, Raymond H. *The Russian Fur Trade, 1550–1700.* Berkeley: University of California Press, 1943.

Fisher, W. R. *Dr. Schlich's Manual of Forestry.* Forest Protection, vol. 4. London: Brad-
bury, Agnew and Co., 1907.

———. "Forestry in the Ardennes." *Indian Forester* 23 (1897): 267–271.

Flahault, Ch. "Incendies de forêts." *Revue de botanique appliquée and d'agriculture
coloniale.* Bulletin 32 (1924): 241–247.

Fletcher, Giles. *Of the Russe Commonwealth.* 1591.

Flohn, Hermann, and Roberto Fantechi, eds. *The Climate of Europe: Past, Present and
Future.* Boston: D. Reidel Pub. Co., 1984.

Forestry Commission (Great Britain). Bulletin 14. London: Forestry Commission.

———. "Forest Fires." Leaflet 9. London: Forestry Commission.

Forêt Méditerranéenne 14, no. 2 (1993) [special issue].

Forni, G. "From Pyrophytic to Domesticated Plants: The Palaeontological-Linguistic
Evidence for a Unitary Theory on the Origin of Plant and Animal Domestication."

In *Plants and Ancient Man: Studies in Palaeoethnobotany*, edited by W. Van Zeist and W. A. Casparie, pp. 131–139. Rotterdam: A. A. Balkema, 1984.

Forsyth, James. "The Siberian Native Peoples Before and After the Russian Conquest. In *The History of Siberia*, edited by Alan Wood, pp. 69–91. New York: Routledge, 1991.

Frängsmyr, Tore, ed. *Linnaeus: The Man and His Work.* Berkeley: University of California Press, 1983.

Franssila, Matti. "Kulovaaran ja säätekijöiden välisestä riippuvuudesta." *Acta Forestalia Fennica* 67 (1959): 1–26.

Fraser, John Foster. *The Real Siberia.* New York: Cassell and Company, 1903.

Frazer, Sir James G. *Balder the Beautiful: The Fire-Festivals of Europe and the Doctrine of the External Soul.* 2 vols. New York: Macmillan and Co., 1923a.

———. *The Golden Bough.* New York: Macmillan and Co., 1923b.

———. *Myths of the Origin of Fire.* New York: Hacker Art Books, 1974.

———. "The Prytaneum, the Temple of Vesta, the Vestals, Perpetual Fires." *Journal of Philology* 14 (1885): 145–172.

Fredskild, Bent. "Agriculture in a Marginal Area: South Greenland from the Norse Landnam (985 A.D.) to the Present (1985 A.D.)." In *The Cultural Landscape: Past, Present and Future,* edited by Hilary H. Birks et al., pp. 381–393. Cambridge: Cambridge University Press, 1988.

———. "Palaeobotanical Investigations at Sermermiut, Jakobshavn, West Greenland." *Meddelelser om Grønland* 178, no. 4 (1967).

———. "Palaeobotanical Investigations of Some Peat Deposits of Norse Age at Qagssiarssuk, South Greenland." *Meddelelser om Grønland* 204, no. 5 (Copenhagen, 1978).

———. "Studies in the Vegetational History of Greenland." *Meddelelser om Grønland* 198, no. 4, (1973).

French, R. A. "Bebrujsk and Its Neighbourhood in the Early Seventeenth Century." *Journal of Byelorussian Studies* 2 (1969): 29–56.

———. "Introduction." In *Studies in Russian Historical Geography,* vol. 1, edited by James H. Bater and R. A. French, pp. 18–19. New York: Academic Press, 1983a.

———. "Russians and the Forest." In *Studies in Russian Historical Geography,* vol. 1, edited by James H. Bater and R. A. French, pp. 23–44. New York: Academic Press, 1983b.

———. "The Introduction of the Three-field Agricultural System." In *Studies in Russian Historical Geography,* vol. 1, edited by James H. Bater and R. A. French, pp. 65–81. New York: Academic Press, 1983c.

———. "The Making of the Russian Landscape." *Advancement of Science* 20 (1963): 44–56.

———. "The Reclamation of Swamp in Pre-Revolutionary Russia." *Institute of British Geographers, Transactions and Papers* 334 (1964): 175–188.

Freud, Sigmund. "The Acquisition and Control over Fire." In *Collected Papers,* vol. 5, p. 288. London, 1950.

Freudenthal, Herbert. *Das Feuer im Deutschen Glauben und Brauch.* Berlin and Leipzig: Walter de Gruyter and Co., 1931.

Frierson, Cathy A. "Flames and Conflagration in the Daily Life of the Peasants of European Russia in the Nineteenth Century." Unpublished manuscript, 1993a.

———. "The Semiotics of Fire in the Daily Life of the Peasants of European Russia in the Nineteenth Century." Unpublished manuscript, 1993b.

Frödin, John. *Skogar och myrar i norra Sverige i deras funktioner som betesmark och slåtter.* Institutet för Sammilignende Kulturforskning Serie B: Skrifter 46. Oslo, 1952.

Frost, L. E., and E. L. Jones. "The Fire Gap and the Greater Durability of Nineteenth-century Cities." *Planning Perspectives* 4 (1989): 333–347.

Furyaev, V. V. "Historical References to Forest Laws in Russia Concerning Forest Fire Protection." Unpublished manuscript, 1992a.

———. "Miscellaneous Essays." Unpublished manuscript, 1993.

———. *Moth-Damaged Forests of the Taiga Zone and Their Burning-out* [in Russian], Moscow, 1966.

———. "On the History of Fires and Fire Prevention in the Forests of the Middle Regions of the Left Bank of the Volga River and Siberia." Unpublished manuscript, 1992b.

———. "On the History of Russian Forest Law and Forest Management in the 13th–17th Centuries." Unpublished manuscript, 1992c.

———. "On The History of Studies of Forest Fires in Russia." Unpublished manuscript, 1992d.

———. "The Forestry History in Russia from the 18th to the Mid-19th Century." Unpublished manuscript, 1992e.

———. "The Role of Fires in Forest Formation Process." Unpublished manuscript, 1992f.

———. "The Use of Fire in National Practice in Russia: Experience." Unpublished manuscript, 1993.

Furyaev, Valentin, and Peter Tsvetkov. "In Memoria [*sic*] of N. P. Kurbatsky." *International Forest Fire News* 11 (1994): 30.

Gadd, Pehr Adrian. *Ovaldige tankar om jordens svedande och kyttande i Finland I–II.* Turku, 1753–54.

Gadgil, Madhav, and Ramachandra Guha. *This Fissured Land: An Ecological History of India.* Berkeley: University of California Press, 1993.

Gailey, Alan, and Alexander Fenton, eds. *The Spade in Northern and Atlantic Europe.* Belfast: Ulster Folk Museum, 1970.

Garcia, Antonio Abellan, and Anna Olivera Poll. "La transhumancia por ferrocarril en España." *Estudios Geograficos* 40 (1979): 385–413.

Garde général des forêts. "De l'essartage dans les Ardennes." *Annales forestières* (1850): 238–241.

Gaunitz, Sven. "Resources Exploitation on the North Swedish Timber Frontier in the Nineteenth and the Beginning of the Twentieth Centries." In *History of Sustained-Yield Forestry: A Symposium,* edited by Harold K. Steen, pp. 134–144. Durham: Forest History Society, 1984.

G. B. "Om bränning af jord wid odling." *Läsning för folket* 2 (1862): 68–74.

Geertz, Clifford. *Agricultural Involution: The Processes of Ecological Change in Indonesia.* Berkeley: University of California Press, 1963.

Gerding, L. *Die Wald-, Heide-, und Moorbrände.* Neudamm, 1899.

Gerrare, Wirt. *Greater Russia.* New York: Macmillan, 1903.

G. H. "Forestry in Cyprus." *Empire Forestry Journal* 5 (1926): 249–250.

Giavelli, Giovanni, and Orazio Rossi. "Rational Management of Small Mediterranean Islands: Ecological Demographic Evaluations." In *Sustainable Development and Environmental Management of Small Islands,* edited by W. Beller et al., 119–140. Man and the Biosphere Series, 5. New York: Parthenon Publ. Group, 1990.

Gibbon, Edward. *The Decline and Fall of the Roman Empire*. New York: Dell Publishing Corp., 1963 (abridged).

Gibson, Charles. *Spain in America*. New York: Harper Torchbooks, 1966.

Gibson, J. R. *Feeding the Russian Fur Trade*. Madison: University of Wisconsin Press, 1969.

Gill, A. M., et al., eds. *Fire and the Australian Biota*. Canberra: Australian Academy of Sciences, 1981.

Gimbutas, Marija. "Ancient Slavic Religion: A Synopsis." In *Ancient Slavic Religion: Essays in Honor of Roman Jakobson*. Vol. 1. Paris, 1967.

Girod-Genet, Lucien. "Le régime pastoral de la Corse." *Bulletin trimestriel, Société forestière de Franche-Comté et des provinces de l'est* 11 (1912): 600–613.

Glacken, Clarence J. *Traces on the Rhodian Shore*. Berkeley: University of California Press, 1967.

Gleadow, Frank. *Report on the Forests of Mauritius with a Preliminary Working Plan*. 1904.

Gloaguen, J. C. "Post-burn Succesion on Brittany Heathlands." *Journal of Vegetation Science* 1 (1990): 147–152.

Godwin, Harry. *The History of the British Flora*, 2d edition. Cambridge: Cambridge University Press, 1975.

Goetzmann, William, H. *New Lands, New Men: America and the Second Great Age of Discovery*. New York: Viking, 1986.

Goldammer, Johann Georg. *Feuerökologie und Feuer-Management*. Part 2 of *VW-Symposium "Feuerökologie."* Freiburg im Breisgau: Freiberger Waldschutz-Abhandlungen, 1978.

———. "Forest Fire Problems in the Federal Republic of Germany." In *Forest Fire Prevention and Control*, edited by T. van Nao, pp. 143–147. The Hague: Martinus Nijhoff and Dr. W. Junk, 1982.

———. "The Multi-Faceted Aspects of Forest Fires." *Disaster Management* 5 (1993): 2.

Goldammer, J. G., ed. *Fire in the Tropical Biota*. Ecological Studies, 84. Berlin: Springer-Verlag, 1990.

Goldammer, J. G., and V. V. Furyaev, eds. *Fires in the Ecosystems of Boreal Eurasia*. Kluwer, 1996.

Goldammer, J. G., and M. J. Jenkins, eds. *Fire in Ecosystem Dynamics: Mediterranean and Northern Perspectives*. The Hague: SPB Academic Publishing, 1990.

Goldammer, J. G., and B. Seibert. "The Impact of Droughts and Forest Fires on Tropical Lowland Rain Forest of East Kalimantan." In *Fire in the Tropical Biota*, edited by J. G. Goldammer, pp. 11–31. Berlin: Springer-Verlag, 1990.

Gomez-Campo, C., ed. *Plant Conservation in the Mediterranean Area*. The Hague: Dr. W. Junk Publishers, 1985.

Goryushkin, Leonid M. "Migration, Settlement and the Rural Economy of Siberia, 1861–1914." In *The History of Siberia*, edited by Alan Wood, pp. 140–157. New York: Routledge, 1991.

Goudsblom, Johan. *Fire and Civilization*. London: Penguin Books, 1992.

———. "The Human Monopoly on the Use of Fire: Its Origins and Conditions." *Human Evolution* 1 (1986): 517–523.

Gould, Stephen Jay, ed. *The Book of Life*. London: Ebury Hutchinson, 1993.

Gowlett, J. A. J., et al. "Early Archaeological Sites, Hominid Remains and Traces of Fire from Chesowanja, Kenya." *Nature* 294 (1981): 125–129.

Granström, Anders. "Elden och des följeväxter i södra Sverige." *Skog & Forskning* 4 (1991): 22–27.

———. "Spatial and Temporal Variation in Lightning Ignitions in Sweden." *Journal of Vegetation Science* 4 (1993): 737–744.

Graumlich, Lisa J. "High Resolution Pollen Analysis Provides New Perspective on Catastrophic Elm Decline." *Trends in Ecology and Evolution* 8 (1993): 387–388.

Great Britain Board of Agriculture and Fisheries, Committee on Inquiry on Grouse Disease. *The Grouse in Health and in Disease.* London, 1911.

Green, R. C. "Adaptation and Change in Maori Culture." In *Biogeography and Ecology of New Zealand,* edited by G. Kuschel, pp. 591–641. The Hague: Dr. W. Junk, 1975.

Gregory, James S. *Russian Land, Soviet People.* New York: Pegasus, 1968.

Gregory, Joshua C. *Combustion from Heracleitos to Lavoisier.* London: Edward Arnold & Co., 1934.

Greuter, Werner. "The Origins and Evolution of Island Floras as Exemplified by the Aegean Archipelago." In *Plants and Islands,* edited by D. Bramwell, pp. 87–106. New York: Academic Press, 1979.

Grigg, D. B. *The Agricultural Systems of the World: An Evolutionary Approach.* Cambridge: Cambridge University Press, 1974.

Grinstein, Alexander. "Stages in the Development of Control over Fire." *International Journal of Psychoanalysis* 33 (1952): 416–420.

Grishin, A. M. *Mathematical Modeling of Forest Fires and New Methods of Fire Control* [in Russian]. Novosibirsk, 1992.

Griveaud, P., and Albignac, R. "The Problems of Nature Conservation in Madagascar." In *Biogeography and Ecology in Madagascar,* edited by R. Battistini and G. Richard-Vindard, pp. 727–740. The Hague: Dr. W. Junk, 1972.

Gromtsev, A. N. "Pattern of Occurrence of Fires in Spontaneous Forests of Northwestern Taiga Landscapes." *Russian Journal of Ecology* 24 (1993): 161–164.

Grotenfelt Gösta. *Det primitiva jodbrukets metoder in Finland under den historiska tiden* [Methods of Primitive Agriculture in Finland during Historical Times]. Helsinki, 1899.

Grove, Richard H. "A Historical Review of Early Institutional and Conservationist Responses to Fears of Artificially Induced Global Climate Change: The Deforestation-Desiccation Discourse, 1500–1860." *Chemosphere* 29 (1994): 1001–1014.

———. "Conservation and Colonialism: The Evolution of Environmental Attitudes and Conservation Policies on St. Helena, Mauritius and in Western India 1660–1854." In *Changing Tropical Forests,* edited by John Dargavel et al., pp. 19–46. Canberra: Centre for Resource and Environment Studies, Australian National University, 1988.

———. *Green Imperialism: Colonial Expansion, Tropical Island Edens, and the Origins of Environmentalism, 1600–1860.* Cambridge: Cambridge University Press, 1995.

Guha, Ramachandra. *The Unquiet Woods.* Delhi: Oxford University Press, 1991.

Guiny, A. du. "Incendies des forêts des Maures et de L'Esterel en 1877." *Revue des eaux et forêts* 16 (1877): 513–527.

Guthrie-Smith, H. *Tutira: The Story of a New Zealand Sheep Station.* 4th edition. Wellington: A. H. & A. W. Reed, 1969.

Haapanen, Antii, and Siitonen, Pertti. "Kulojen Esiintymien Ulvinsalon Luonnonpuistossa." *Silva Fennica* 12, no. 3 (1978): 187–200.

Haden-Guest, Stephen, et al., eds. *A World Geography of Forest Resources.* New York: Ronald Press, for the American Geographical Society, 1956.

Hafsten, Ulf. "Vegetational History and Land Occupation in Valldalen in the Sub-alpine Region of Central South Norway Traced by Pollen Analysis and Radiocarbon Measurements." *Årbok for Universitetet i Bergen,* Mat. Naturv. Serie, 3 (1965).

Hallam, Sylvia. *Fire and Hearth: A Study of Aboriginal Usage and European Usurpation in South-western Australia.* Canberra: Australian Institute of Aboriginal Studies, 1979.

Hannon, Gina E., and Richard H. W. Bradshaw. "Recent Vegetation Dynamics of Two Connemara Lake Islands, Western Ireland." *Journal of Biogeography* 16 (1989): 75–81.

Hansegård, Nils-Erik. "The Transition of Jukkasjärvi Lapps from Nomadism to Settled Life and Farming." *Studia Ethnographica Upsaliensa* 39 (1978).

Hapgood, Isabel F. *Russian Rambles.* New York: Arno Press, 1970 (reprint).

Harriot, Thomas. *A Briefe and True Report of the New Found Land of Virginia.* New York: Dover Publications, 1972 (reprint of 1590 Theodor de Bry edition).

Harris, David R. *Plants, Animals, and Man in the Outer Leeward Islands, West Indies: An Ecological Study of Antigua, Barbuda, and Anguilla.* Berkeley: University of California Press, 1965.

Harris, T. M. "Burnt Ferns from the English Wealden." *Proceedings of the Geological Association* 92 (1981): 47–58.

———. "Forest Fire in the Mesozoic." *Journal of Ecology* 46 (1958): 447–453.

Harvey, H. Thomas, et al. *Giant Sequoia Ecology: Fire and Reproduction.* Scientific Monograph Series, 12. U.S. National Park Sevice, 1980.

Harwell, Mark A. *Nuclear Winter: The Human and Environmental Consequences of Nuclear War.* New York: Springer-Verlag, 1984.

Haviland, Maud D. *A Summer on the Yenisey, 1914.* New York, 1971 (reprint).

Hawthorne, Nathaniel. "Fire-Worship." December 1843.

Haxthausen, Baron August von. *The Russian Empire.* 2 vols. New York: De Capo Press, 1968 (reprint).

Hayden, Sherman Strong. *The International Protection of Wild Life.* New York: Columbia University Press, 1942.

Heckscher, Eli F. *An Economic History of Sweden,* translated by Göran Ohlin. Cambridge: Harvard University Press, 1954.

Heichelheim, Fritz M. "Effects of Classical Antiquity on the Land." In *Man's Role in Changing the Face of the Earth,* vol. 1, edited by William L. Thomas, Jr., pp. 165–182. Chicago: University of Chicago Press, 1956.

Heikinheimo, Olli. *Kaskeamisen vaikutus Suomen metsiin* [The Impact of Swidden Cultivation on Forests in Finland]. Helsinki, 1915. Extracts in *Suomen Antropologi* 4 (1987): 200.

Hesmer, Herbert. *Leben und Werk von Dietrich Brandis, 1824–1907.* Abhandlungen der Rheinisch-Westfälischen Akademie der Wissenschaften, 58. Opland: Westdeutscher Verlag, 1975.

Hicks, Sheila. "Pollen Analysis and Archaelogy in Kuusamo, North-east Finland, an Area of Marginal Human Interference." *Transactions of the Institute of British Geographers* 1 (1976): 189–207.

———. "The Representation of Different Farming Practices in Pollen Diagrams from

Northern Finland." In *The Cultural Landscape: Past, Present and Future,* edited by Hilary H. Birks et al., pp. 189–207. Cambridge: Cambridge University Press, 1988.

Higgins, Kenneth. "Interpretation and Compendium of Historical Fire Accounts in the Northern Great Plains." *Resource Publication* 161 U.S. Fish and Wildlife Service, 1986.

Hill, S. S. *Travels in Siberia.* 2 vols. New York: Arno Press, 1970 (reprint).

Hinde, Thomas. *Forests of Britain.* London, 1985.

Hobsbawn, E. J., and G. Rudé. *Captain Swing.* New York: Pantheon Books, 1968.

Högbom, A. G. *Om skogseldar förr och nu.* Uppsala: Almqvist & Wiksell, 1934.

Högstroöm, Pehr. *Beskrifning Öfver Sweriges Lapmarker 1747.* Två Förläffare Bokförlag (facsimile edition).

Holdgate, M. W. "The Influence of Introduced Species on the Ecosystems of Temperate Oceanic Islands." International Union for the Conservation of Nature and Natural Resources. *Proceedings, 10th Meeting* (1966): 157–176.

Holm, Thomas. *Kort beskrifning om provincien Nya Sverige uti America, som nu förjden af Engelske kalles Pensylvania.* Stockholm: J. H. Werner, 1702.

Holmberg, Uno. *The Mythology of All Races.* Finno-Ugric, Siberian, vol. 4. Boston: Archaeological Institute of America, 1927.

Horne, Alistair. *A Savage War of Peace.* New York: Viking Press, 1977.

Hoskins, W. G. *The Making of the English Landscape.* London: Penguin, 1955.

Hough, Franklin. *Forestry in Europe: Reports from the Consuls of the United States.* Washington, D.C.: Government Printing Office, 1887.

Hough, Walter. *Fires as an Agent in Human Culture.* U.S. National Museum, Bulletin 139 (1926).

Howard, B. Douglas. *Life with Trans-Siberian Savages.* New York and London: Longmans, Green, 1893.

Howitz, D. "The Re-Afforesting of Waste Lands in Ireland, and the Application of Forestry to the Remedy of the Destructive Torrents and Floods of the Catchment Basins of the Chief Rivers of Ireland." *Indian Forester* 12 (1886): 271–273.

Hsü, Kenneth. *The Mediterranean Was a Desert.* Princeton: Princeton University Press, 1983.

Hudson, W. H. *Far Away and Long Ago: A History of My Early Life.* New York: E. P. Dutton, 1918.

Hughes, J. Donald. *Ecology in Ancient Civilizations.* Albuquerque: University of New Mexico Press, 1975.

———. *Pan's Travail: Environmental Problems of the Ancient Greeks and Romans.* Baltimore: Johns Hopkins University Press, 1994.

Hughes, Jo, and Brian Huntley. "Upland Hay Meadows in Britain: Their Vegetation, Management and Future." In *The Cultural Landscape: Past, Present and Future,* edited by Hilary H. Birks et al., pp. 91–110. Cambridge: Cambridge University Press, 1988.

Humbert, Henri. "La destruction d'une flore insulaire par le feu: Principaux aspects de la vegetation à Madagascar." *Mémoires de l'Académie Malagache,* fasc. V (1927).

———. "Origines présumées et affinités de la flore de Madagascar." *Mémoires de l'Institut Scientifique de Madagascar* Series B, 9 (1959): 149–187.

Humble, O. Hj. "Brandtornssystem för Jämtlands län." *Norlands skogsvårdförbunds tidskrift* 1 (1914): 27–31.

———. "Om brandtorn i de norrländska skogarna." *Skogsvårdföreningens tidskrift* (1907): 12–17.

Huntley, B., and T. Webb III, eds. *Vegetation History.* Boston: Kluwer Academic Publishers, 1988.

Hutchins, D. E. *A Discussion of Australian Forestry.* Perth, 1916.

———. *Journal of a Forest Tour.* Cape Town, 1892.

———. *Report on Cyprus Forestry.* London, 1909.

Huttunen, Pertti. "Early Land Use, Especially the Slash-and-Burn Cultivation in the Commune of Lammi, Southern Finland, Interpreted Mainly Using Pollen and Charcoal Analyses." *Acta Botanica Fennica* 113 (1980): 25–35.

Huttunen, Pertti, and Kimmo Tolonen. "Human Influence in the History of Lake Lovojärvi, S. Finland." *Finsk Museum* (1975): 68–117.

Huttunen, Pertti, and Mirjami Tolonen. "Pollen-Analytical Studies of Prehistoric Agriculture in Northern Ångermanland." *Early Norrland* 1 (1972): 9–34.

ICONA. *Estudios sobre Prevención y Efectos Ecologicos de los Incendios Forestales.* Madrid: Servicio de Publicaciones Agrarias, 1985.

"Les incendies de forêts." *Revue Forestière française* (1975) [special issue].

Isaac, Glynn. "Early Hominids and Fire at Chesowanja, Kenya." *Nature* 296 (1982): 876.

Isaksson, Olov. *Byställma och bystadga: Organisationsformer i övre Norrlands kustbyar.* Skytteanska Samfundet, 1967.

Iversen, Johs. "Origin of the Flora of Western Greenland in the Light of Pollen Analysis." *Oikos* 2 (1952–53): 85–103.

———. *The Development of Denmark's Nature since the Last Glacial,* translated by Michael Robson. DGU V. Series, 7-C. Copenhagen, 1973.

Izurieta, V. Lcdo. Arturo. Letter to Editor. *Wildfire* 4 (1) (1995): 46–47.

James, N. D. G. *A History of English Forestry.* Oxford: Basil Blackwood, 1981.

James, William. "On the Moral Equivalent of War." In *The Writings of William James,* edited by James J. McDermott, pp. 663–669. New York: Modern Library, 1967.

Jarman, M. R., et al., eds. *Early European Agriculture: Its Foundations and Development.* Cambridge: Cambridge University Press, 1982.

Jelicic, Ljubica, and Michael O'Connell. "History of Vegetation and Land Use from 3200 B.P. to the Present in the North-West Burren, a Karstic Region of Western Ireland." *Vegetation History and Archaebotany* 1 (1992): 119–140.

Jennings, J. D. *The Prehistory of Polynesia.* Cambridge: Harvard University Press, 1979.

Jirlow, Ragnar. "Från seedjande till plogbruk: Drag ur Upplands jordbrukshistoria." *Uppland Årsbok* (1969): 45–74.

Jochelson, Waldemar. *The Yukaghir and the Yukaghirized Tungus.* Publications of Jesup North Pacific Expedition, 9. New York, 1926.

Johannesson, Kurt. *The Renaissance of the Goths in Sixteenth-Century Sweden,* translated by James Larson. Berkeley: University of California Press, 1991.

Johansen, Johannes. "A Palaeobotanical Study Indicating a Previking Settlement in Ijornuvik, Faroe Islands." *Fródskaparrit* 19 (1971): 147–157.

———. "Pollen Diagrams from the Shetland and Faroe Islands." *New Phytologist* 75 (1975): 369–387.

Johnson, Amandus. *The Swedish Settlements on the Delaware, 1638–1664.* 2 vols. Philadelphia, 1911.

Johnson, Edward. *Fire and Vegetation Dynamics.* Cambridge: Cambridge University Press, 1992.

Johnson, W. N., et al. "The Relationship of Wildland Fire to Lynx and Marten Populations and Habitat in Interior Alaska. Final Report." Galena, Alaska: U.S. Fish and Wildlife Service, 1995.

Jones, Allen H. "The Philistines and the Hearth: Their Journey to the Levant." *Journal of Near Eastern Studies* 31 (1972): 343–350.

Jones, E. L. *The European Miracle.* Cambridge: Cambridge University Press, 1981.

Jones, E. L., S. Porter, and M. Turner. "Gazetteer of English Urban Fire Disasters." *Historical Geography Series* 13. Norwich: Geo Books, 1984.

Jones, Gwyn. *The Norse Atlantic Saga.* 2d edition. Oxford: Oxford University Press, 1986.

Jones, Michael. *Finland: Daughter of the Sea.* Folkestone: Dawson, 1977. Hamden, Conn.: Anchor Books.

Jones, Rhys. "Fire-Stick Farming." *Australian Natural History* 16 (1969): 224–228.

Jordan, Carl F., et al., eds. *Taungya: Forest Plantations with Agriculture in Southeast Asia.* Wallingford: CAB International, 1992.

Jordan, Terry G. *The European Culture Area: A Systematic Geography.* 2d edition, New York: Harper and Row, 1988.

———. *Trails to Texas: Southern Roots of Western Cattle Ranching.* Lincoln: University of Nebraska Press, 1981.

Jordan, Terry G., and Matti Kaups. *The American Backwoods Frontier: An Ethnic and Ecological Interpretation.* Baltimore: Johns Hopkins University Press, 1989.

Joubert, A. "Comment diminuer les incendies de forêts." *Revue des eaux et forêts* 61 (1923): 256–262.

———. "Les quatre incendies de la forêt de Valbonne." *Revue des eaux et forêts* 67 (1929): 534–540.

Jourdan, Alfred. "Les incendies de forêt." *Mémoires de l'Académie d'Aix-en-Provence* 21 (1930): 71–86.

Kaila, E. E. "Tervapolton Leviäminen Suomessa 1700-luvun Puolimaissa" [Tar-burning in Finland in the Middle of the 18th Century]. *Silva Fennica* 21 (1931).

Kailidis, D. S., and S. Markalas. "Forest and Range Fires Caused by Lightning in Greece." *Deltion, Idruma Dasikon Ereunon, Greece* 99 (1979).

Kaland, Peter Emil. "The Origin and Management of Norwegian Coastal Heaths as Reflected by Pollen Analysis." In *Anthropogenic Indicators in Pollen Diagrams,* edited by Karl-Ernst Behre, pp. 19–36. Rotterdam: A. A. Balkema, 1986.

Käll, John. "Tjära och beck i Sunnerbo—ett extraknäck." In *Skogen och Smålänningen,* edited by Olof Nordström et al., pp. 100–114. Historiska föreningens i Kronobergs Län skriftserie, 6. SmpTRYCK AB, 1989.

Kalm, Pehr. *Peter Kalm's Travels in North America, the English Edition of 1770, revised from the original Swedish and edited by Adolph B. Benson with a translation of new material from Kalm's diary notes.* New York: Imprint Society, 1972.

Karavanov, K. P. "Update on the Existing Ecological Condition and a Forecast of Environmental Impacts Expected from the Development of the Khakandja Gold-Silver Deposit" [in Russian]. Report on Project No. 2/9. Far Eastern Affiliation of the Russian Academy of Sciences. Unpublished report, 1994.

Kardell, Lars. *Hall-Hangvar: En gotlänsk skog och dess historia.* Avdelningen för Landskapsvard rapport 39. Swedish University of Agricultural Sciences, 1988.

Kardell, Lars, et al. *Svedjebruk förr och nu.* Avdelningen för Landskapsvard rapport 20 (1980).

Kayll, A. J. "Some Characteristics of Heath Fires in North-East Scotland." *Journal of Applied Ecology* 3 (1966): 29–40.

Keeley, Jon K. *Bibliographies on Chaparral and the Fire Ecology of Other Mediterranean Systems.* Report 58, Davis: California Water Resources Center, University of California, 1984.

Keller, Boris A. "The Steppe and Forest Steppe of European Russia." In *World Vegetation Types,* edited by S. R. Eyre, p. 204. New York: Macmillan, 1971.

Kendrew, W. G. *The Climates of the Continents.* 5th edition. Oxford: Oxford University Press, 1961.

Kennan, George. *Siberia and the Exile System.* New York: Century Co., 1891.

———. *Tent Life in Siberia.* New York: G. P. Putnam's Sons, 1910.

Keränen, Dr. J. "Blitzschlag als Zünder der Waldbrände im Nördlichen Finnland." *Acta Forestalia Fennica* 34 (1929): 3–8.

Kerner, R. J. *The Urge to the Sea: The Role of Rivers, Portages, Ostrogs, Monasteries, and Furs.* Berkeley: University of California Press, 1946.

Kimber, Clarissa Therese. *Martinique Revisited: The Changing Plant Geographies of a West Indian Island.* College Station: Texas A&M University Press, 1988.

King, Thomas Starr. *A Vacation Among the Sierras: Yosemite in 1860,* edited by John A. Hussey. San Francisco: Book Club of California, 1962.

Kinnman, Gunno. "Skogseldsrisken och Väderleken." *Svenska skogsvårdsföreningens tidskrift* 32 (1936): 481–512.

Kipling, Rudyard. "In the Rukh." In *The Jungle Books,* edited by W. W. Robson. Oxford: Oxford University Press, 1992.

Kish, George. "Transhumance in Southern Italy." *Papers of the Michigan Academy of Science, Arts, and Letters* 39 (1954): 301–307.

Klein, Julian. *The Mesta: A Study in Spanish Economic History, 1275–1836.* Cambridge: Harvard University Press, 1920.

Koh, Elmar. "Studier över skogsbränder och skenhälla i älvdalskogarna" [A Study of Fires and Hard Pan in the Forests of Ålvdalen]. With English summary. *Sveriges skogsvårdsförbunds tidskrift* (1975): 300–336.

Komarek, E. V. "Ancient Fires." *Proceedings, Tall Timbers Fire Ecology Conference,* vol. 12, pp. 219–240. Tallahassee: Tall Timbers Research Station, 1972.

———. "Fire Ecology—Grasslands and Man." *Proceedings, Tall Timbers Fire Ecology Conference,* vol. 4, pp. 169–220. Tallahassee: Tall Timbers Research Station, 1965.

———. "Fire—and the Ecology of Man." *Proceedings, Tall Timbers Fire Ecology Conference,* vol. 6, pp. 143–170. Tallahassee: Tall Timbers Research Station, 1967.

——— "Introduction to Lightning Ecology." *Proceedings, Tall Timbers Fire Ecology Conference,* vol. 13, pp. 421–427. Tallahassee: Tall Timbers Research Station, 1974.

———. "Lightning and Fire Ecology in Africa." *Proceedings, Tall Timbers Fire Ecology Conference,* vol. 11, pp. 473–511. Tallahassee: Tall Timbers Research Station, 1972.

———. "Lightning and Lightning Fires as Ecological Forces." *Proceedings, Tall Timbers Fire Ecology Conference,* vol. 8, pp. 169–197. Tallahassee: Tall Timbers Research Station, 1968b.

———. "The Nature of Lightning Fires." *Proceedings, Tall Timbers Fire Ecology Conference,* vol. 7, pp. 5–41. Tallahassee: Tall Timbers Research Station, 1968a.

Komité (dertill i nåder förordnad Komité). *Underdånigt Betänkande och Förslag, angående Skogsförhållandena i Norrland och åtgärder för östadkommande af en förbättrad skogshushållning derstädes.* Stockholm: Iwar Haeggströms, 1871.

Korovin, G. N. "The Structure of the Russian Forests Wildlife." Paper delivered at the Conference on Fire in the Forests of Boreal Eurasia, Krasnoyarsk, 1993.

Kovda, V. A. "Land Use Development in the Arid Regions of the Russian Plain, the Caucasus and Central Asia." In *A History of Land Use in Arid Regions,* edited by L. Dudley Stamp, pp. 183–185. Paris: UNESCO, 1961.

Kowaeska-Lewicka, *see* Lewicka, Anna.

Krankina, Olga N. "Forest Fires in the Former Soviet Union: Past, Present, and Future Greenhouse Gas Contributions to the Atmosphere." In *Carbon Cycling in the Boreal Forest and Sub-Arctic Ecosystems,* edited by Ted S. Vinson and Tatyana P. Kochugina, pp. 179–186. EPA/600R-93/084. U.S. Environmental Protection Agency, 1993.

Krinov, E. L. "Commentary on Kulik's 'The Tunguska Meteorite.'" In *Source Book in Astronomy 1990–1950,* edited by Harlow Shapley, pp. 79–81. Cambridge: Harvard University Press, 1960.

Krüger, Fritz. "Cosas y Palabras del Noroeste Iberico. I. Un sistema de cultivo arcaico: la quema del monte." *Nueva Revista de Filologia Hispanica* 4, no. 3 (1951): 231–253.

Kudenshöld, N. "Om aske-bränning i skogen af förruttnade träd." Stockholm, 1753.

Kuhnholtz-Lordat, Georges. *L'Écran vert.* Paris: Éditions du Museum, 1958.

———. *La Terre incendiée.* Nîmes: Éditions de la Maisson Carreo, 1938.

Kulik, L. A. "The Problem of the Impact Area of the Tunguska Meteorite of 1908" [in Russian]. *Doklady Akad. Nauk SSSR* (A), 23 (1927): 399–402.

Kunkel, Günther. "Notes on the Introduced Elements in the Canary Islands' Flora." In *Biogeography and Ecology in the Canary Islands,* edited by G. Kunkel, pp. 207–240. The Hague: Dr. W. Junk, 1976.

Kurbatsky, N. P. "The Forest Fire in the Region of the Tunguska Event of 1908" [in Russian]. *Meteoritika* 24 (1964).

———. *Technique and Practice of Forest Fire Suppresion* [in Russian]. Moscow: Nauka, 1962.

Kurbatsky, N. P., ed. *Combustion and Fires in the Forest* [in Russian]. Krasnoyarsk, 1973.

———. *Combustion and Fires in the Forest* [in Russian]. 3 vols. Krasnoyarsk, 1979.

———. *Problems in Forest Pyrology* [in Russian]. Krasnoyarsk, 1975.

———. *Questions in Forest Pyrology* [in Russian]. Krasnoyarsk, 1970.

Kurbatsky, N. P., and H. P. Telitsyn. "Essays on the History of the Development of the Theory and Practice of Forest Fire Control and Use in Russia." Unpublished manuscript, 1994.

Kuschel, G., ed. *Biogeography and Ecology of New Zealand.* Monographiae Biologicae, 27. The Hague: Dr. W. Junk, 1975.

Kuusi, Mati, et al., eds. *Finnish Folk Poetry-Epics.* Finnish Literature Society, 1977.

Kvamme, Mons. "Pollen Analytical Studies of Mountain Summer-Farming in Western Norway." In *The Cultural Landscape: Past, Present and Future,* edited by Hilary H. Birks et al., pp. 349–368. Cambridge: Cambridge University Press, 1988.

"La Restauracion de la Vegetacion en los Montes Españoles." *Ecologia,* Fuera de Series, 1 (1990) [special issue].

Laestadius, L. L. *Om Möjligheten och fördelen af allmänna uppodlingar i Lappmarken.* Stockholm, 1824.

Laestadius, Petrus. *Foortsättning af journalen öfver missions-resor i Lappmarken, innefattande åren 1828–1832.* Stockholm, 1833.

Lafforgue, G. "Les incendies dans les forêts de pins maritimes." *Pins et résineux* 20 (March 1914): 34–36.

Lagercrantz, Sture. *African Methods of Fire-Making.* Studia Ethnographica Upsaliensia, 10. Uppsala, 1954.

Lagerlöf, Selma. *The Further Adventures of Nils,* translated by Velma Swanston Howard. London: Puffin Books, 1993.

————. *The Wonderful Adventures of Nils,* translated by Velma Swanston Howard. London: Puffin Books, 1990.

Lal, J. B. *India's Forests: Myth and Reality,* 2d ed. Dehra Dun: Nataraj Publishers, 1992.

Lamb, Harold. *The City and the Tsar.* Garden City: Doubleday, 1948.

Lambert, David, and the Diagram Group. *The Field Guide to Early Man.* New York: Facts on File, 1987.

Lane-Poole, C. E. "Transcript of Evidence Given before the Royal Commission, 1 April 1939." In *Report of the Royal Commission . . . ,* edited by Leonard E. B. Stretton (1939).

Lansdell, Henry. *Through Sibera.* 2 vols. New York: Arno Press, 1970 (reprint).

Lapping, Brian. *End of Empire.* New York: St. Martin's Press, 1985.

Larsson, Bo. *Svedjebruk och röjningsbränning i Norden-terminologi, datering, metoder.* Skrifter om skogs—oc lantbrukshistoria, 7. Stockholm: Nordiska museet, 1995.

Larsson, Lars J. "Svedjebruk i Värend och Sunnerbo." In *Skogen och Smålänningen,* edited by Olof Nordström, et al., pp. 61–99. Historiska föreningens in Kronobergs län skriftseries, 6. SmpTRYCK AB, 1989.

————. "Svedjebruket i Smaland." *Kronobergsboken* (1979–1980): 65–77.

Larsson, Lars-Olof. "Skogstillgang, skogsprodukter och sagar i Kronobergs län." In *Skogen och Smålänningen,* edited by Olof Nordström, et al., pp. 115–201. Historiska föreningens i Kronobergs län skriftserie, 6. SmpTRYCK AB, 1989.

Las Casas, Bartolomé de. *The Destruction of the Indies: A Brief Account,* translated by Herma Briffault. Baltimore: Johns Hopkins University Press, 1992.

Laughlin, John Charles Hugh. "A Study of the Motif of Holy Fire in the Old Testament." Ph.D. dissertation, Southern Baptist Theological Seminary, Louisville, Kentucky, 1975.

Law, F. W. "Some Apects of Forest Protection." *Transactions of the Royal Scottish Arboricultural Society* 39 (1925): 140–149.

Lefebvre, Henri. "Les incendies de forêts en Algerie: Les incendies de forêts en 1881 dans l'arrondissement de Philippeville." *Revue des eaux et forêts* 21 (1882): 49–70.

Le Houerou, Henri Noel. "Impact of Man and His Animals on Mediterranean Vegetation." In *Mediterranean-Type Shrublands,* edited by Francesco diCastri et al. Ecosystems of the World, vol. 11, pp. 479–521. New York: Elsevier, 1981.

————. "Fire and Vegetation in the Mediterranean Basisn." In *Proceedings, Tall Timbers Fire Ecology Conference,* vol. 13, pp. 237–277. Tallahassee: Tall Timbers Research Station, 1973.

Le Lannou, Maurice. *Pâtres et paysans de la Sardaigne.* Tours: Arroult et Cie, Maitres Imprimeurs, 1941.

Lelle, Mark A., and Michael A. Gold. "Agroforestry Systems for Temperate Climates: Lessons from Roman Italy." *Forest and Conservation History* 38 (1994): 118–126.

Lentheric, Charles. *The Riviera: Ancient and Modern,* translated by Charles West. London: T. Fisher Unwin, 1895.

Leone, Vittorio, and Antonio Saracino. "Arson and Forest Fire Industry: The State of the Art in Italy." *Proceedings, 1st Conference on Forest Fire Research.* Coimbra: Universidade de Coimbra, 1990.

Leopold, A. Starker, et al. "Study of Wildlife Problems in National Parks." *Transactions, North American Wildlife Natural Resources Conference* 28 (1963): 28–48.

Le Sueur, A. D. C. "Woodland Fires." *Journal of the Land Agents' Society* 24 (1925): 170–176.

Levin, M. G., and L. P. Potapov, eds. *The Peoples of Siberia.* Chicago: University of Chicago Press, 1961.

Levine, Joel S., ed. *Global Biomass Burning.* Cambridge: MIT Press, 1991.

Lewicka, Anna. "Brandwirtschaft und brandordnung, im 19. und 20. Jahrhundert in den polnischen Karpaten." In *Getreidebau in Ost- und Mitteleurope,* edited by I. Ballassa. Budapest, 1972.

Lewis, Henry T. "A Time for Burning." Occasional Publication, 17. Boreal Institute for Northern Studies, University of Alberta, 1982.

———. "Management Fires vs. Corrective Fires in Northern Australia: An Analogue for Environmental Change." *Chemosphere* 29 (1994): 949–963.

———. "Maskuta: The Ecology of Indian Fires in Northern Alberta." *Western Canadian Journal of Anthropology* 7 (1977): 15–52.

———. *Patterns of Indian Burning in California: Ecology and Ethnohistory.* Ballena Press Anthropological Papers, 1. Ballena Press, 1973. Reprinted in *Before the Wilderness,* edited by Thomas Blackburn and Kat Anderson. Menlo Park: Ballena Press, 1993.

———. "The Role of Fire in the Domestication of Plants and Animals in Southwest Asia: A Hypothesis." *Man* 7 (1972): 195–222.

Lewis, Henry T., and Teresa Ferguson. "Yards, Corridors, and Mosaics: How to Burn a Boreal Forest." *Human Ecology* 16 (1988): 57–77.

Lex, Peter. "Organisational, Technical and Silvicultural Measures for Forest Fire Prevention and Suppression in the Lüneburg Administrative Region." Unpublished, 1988.

Liacos, L. G. "Present Studies and History of Burning in Greece." *Proceedings, Tall Timbers Fire Ecology Conference,* vol. 13, pp. 65–96. Tallahassee: Tall Timbers Research Station, 1973.

Liebeneiner, Ehrenfried. "Der Forst—und Holzwirt." Jg. 34, Heft Nr. 12 vom. (June 25, 1979).

———. "Der große Waldbrand bei Lutterloh 1976." *Allgemeine Forstzeitschrift* 33, no. 11 (1978): 238–241.

———. "Waldbrandbekämpfung." *Allegemeine Forstzeitschrift* 18, no 31 (1963): 485–487.

———. "Waldbrand-Fibel." *Allgemeine Forstzeitschrift* 14, no. 31 (1959): 554–555.

Lindau, Conrad. *Om brännodlingester ny method eller praktisk anwisning huru ödemarker med ringea arbestforstnad och utan gösel tunna pa tid göras frustbärande.* Stockholm, 1849.

Linder, Per. "Bränning av pottaska skapade nya skogar." *Skogen* 12 (1992): 36–39.

———. "Jämtgaveln: En studie av brandhistorik, kulturpaverkan och urskogsvärden i ett mellannorrlänskt skogsområde." Länsstyrelsen i Västernorrlands Län, 3 (1988).

Lindestrom, Peter. *Geographicae Americae: with an account of the Delaware Indi-*

ans: based on surveys and notes made in 1654–1656. New York: Arno Press, 1979 (reprint).

Lindgren, Ethel John. "An Example of Culture Contact without Conflict: Reindeer Tungus and Cossacks of Northwestern Manchuria." *American Anthropologist* 40 (1938): 605–621.

———. "North-Western Manchuria and the Reindeer Tungus." *Geographical Journal* 75 (1930): 529–532.

———. "The Reindeer Tungus of Manchuria." *Journal of the Royal Central Asian Society* 22 (1935): 230.

Linkola, Martti. "Skogen som finländskt kulturlandskap." *Nord Nytt* 33/34 (1988): 71–80.

Linnaeus, Carl. *A Tour of Lapland.* New York: Arno Press, 1971 (reprint).

———. *Skånska Resa,* edited by Carl-Otto von Sydow. Stockholm: Wahlström and Widstrand, 1959.

———. *Wästgöta Resa.* Göteborg: Thulin and Ohlson Antikvariak Bokhandel, 1928.

Linnard, William. "Terms and Techniques in Shifting Cultivation in Russia." *Tools and Tillage* 1 (1970): 192–197.

Linné, Carl von. *Linné i Dalarna,* edited by Bertil Gullander. Forum, 1980.

Lockert, Andreas. *Entwicklung der Waldbrandsituation unter der Feuerschutzpolitik seit dem 19. Jarhundert in Deutschland.* Thesis, Forestry School, Albert-Ludwigs-Universität, Freiburg, 1991.

Lodijensky, J. N. "Forests of Russia." In *Russia: Its Industries and Trade,* edited by J. N. Lodijensky, pp. 316–324. St. Petersburg, 1901.

Lööw, Kjell. *Svedjefinnar—om 1600-talets finska invandring i Gävleborges lan.* Läns museet i Gaäveleborgs län, Rapport 1985:1 (1985).

Lousley, J. Edward. "Bracken on Bombed Sites." *School Nature Study* 41 (1946): 6–7.

———. "The Flora of Bombed Sites in the City of London in 1944." *Report of the Botanical Society and Exchange Club of the British Isles* 12 (1947): 875–883.

Lovelock, J. E. *Gaia.* Oxford: Oxford University Press, 1979.

Lucas, A. T. "Paring and Burning in Ireland: A Preliminary Survey." In *The Spade in Northern and Atlantic Europe,* edited by Alan Gailey and Alexander Fenton, pp. 99–147. Belfast: Ulster Folk Museum, 1970.

Lucretius. *On the Nature of the Universe,* translated by R. E. Latham. New York: Penguin, 1951.

Luke, R. H., and A. G. McArthur. *Bushfires in Australia.* Canberra: Australian Government Printing Service, 1978.

Lundberg, Gustaf. "Om skogseld, dess förbyggande och bekämpande." *Skogsvårdföreningens tidskrift* (1915): 114–156.

Luttermann, Klaus. *Die große Waldbrandkatastrophe.* Berlin: efb-Verlag, 1981.

MacDermot, Edward T. *Manwood's Treatise of the Forest Law.* 4th edition. London, 1717.

———. *The History of the Forest of Exmoor.* London: Barnicott & Pearce, Taunton, 1911.

MacKay, Angus. *Spain in the Middle Ages: From Frontier to Empire, 1000–1500.* New York: St. Martin's Press, 1977.

MacKenzie, John M. *The Empire of Nature: Hunting, Conservation, and British Imperialism.* Manchester: Manchester University Press, 1988.

MacPherson, A. "Land Use Problems in the Hill Areas of Scotland." *Geographical Essays in Memory of Alan G. Ogilvie,* edited by Ronald Miller and J. Wreford Watson. New York: Thomas Nelson and Sons, 1959.

Madon, P. G. "Forest Conservancy in the Island of Cyprus." Nicosia: Government Printing Office, 1930 (reprint).

————. "The Preservation of the Forests of the Island of Cyprus." Enc. No. 2 in Cyprus No. 366 (1881).

Magnus, Olaus. *Historia om de Nordiska Folken.* Mälmo: Gidlunds förlag, 1982.

Magnusson, Magnus. *Viking Expansion Westwards.* New York: Henry C. Walck, 1973.

Makowski, Henry. "Problems of Using Fire in Nature Reserves." *Proceedings, Tall Timbers Fire Ecology Conference,* vol. 13, pp. 15–17. Tallahassee: Tall Timbers Research Station, 1973.

Mallory, J. P. *In Search of the Indo-Europeans.* London: Thames and Hudson, 1989.

Malmer, Nils. "The South-Western Dwarf Shrub Heaths. In *The Plant Cover of Sweden.* Acta Phytogeographica Suecica, 50. Uppsala, 1965.

Malström, Carl. "Hallands skogar genom tiderna." In *Natur i Halland,* edited by Carl Skottsberg and Kai Curry-Lindahl. Göteborg, 1952.

Manderscheid, Erich Bauer. *Los Montes de España en la Historia.* Madrid: Ministerio de Agricultura, 1980.

Marañon, Teodoro. "Agro-Sylvo-Pastoral Systems in the Iberian Peninsula: *Dehasas* and *Monados.*" *Rangelands* 10 (1988): 255–258.

Marcuse, Walter D. *Through Western Madagascar in Quest of the Golden Bean.* London, 1914.

Marino, John A. *Pastoral Economics in the Kingdom of Naples.* Baltimore: Johns Hopkins University Press, 1988.

Marquez, C., et al. "The Fire of 1994 and Herpetofauna of Southern Isabela." *Noticias de Galápagos* 54 (1995): 8–10.

Marsaux, Ch. "Sur la combustion des gazons." *Annales forestières* (1848): 324–325.

Marsh, George Perkins. *Man and Nature,* edited by David Lowenthal. Cambridge: Harvard University Press, 1965.

Marshall, William. *Rural Economy of the West of England.* 2 vols. New York: A. M. Kelley, 1970 (reprint).

Martin, Paul S., and Richard G. Klein, eds. *Quaternary Extinctions: A Prehistoric Revolution.* Tucson: University of Arizona Press, 1984.

Massa, Ilmo. "Pasture Burn-Clearing as a Method of Colonization in Northern Fennoscandia." *Suomen Antropologi* 4 (1987): 235–239.

Massie, Robert K. *Peter the Great.* New York: Ballantine, 1980.

Matthews, J. D. "Forestry." *Proceedings of the Royal Society of Edinburgh.* Two Hundred Years of the Biological Sciences in Scotland (1983): 141–170.

Mayle, Peter. *Toujours Provence.* New York: Alfred Knopf, 1991.

McArthur, E. Durant, et al., compilers. *Proceedings, Symposium on Cheatgrass Invasion, Shrub Die-Off, and Other Aspects of Shrub Biology and Management.* General Technical Report INT-276. U.S. Forest Service, 1990.

McClone, M. S. "Polynesian Deforestation of New Zealand: A Preliminary Synthesis." *Archaeology in Oceania* 18 (1983): 11–25.

McCutchan, Morris H. "Climatic Features as a Fire Determinant." In *Proceedings of the Symposium on the Environmental Consequences of Fire and Fuel Management in Mediterranean Ecosystems,* edited by Harold A. Mooney et al. General Technical Report WO-3. U.S. Forest Service, 1977.

McIntosh, Alastair, et al. "Reclaiming the Scottish Highlands: Clearance, Conflict, and Crofting." *The Ecologist* 24 (1994): 64–70.

McLean, Gavin. *New Zealand Tragedies: Fires and Firefighting.* Wellington: Grantham House, 1992.

McNeill, William H. *Europe's Steppe Frontier, 1500–1800.* Chicago: University of Chicago Press, 1964.

McVean, D. N. "Muir Burning and Conservation." *Scottish Agriculture* 39 (1959): 79–82.

Mead, W. R. *An Historical Geography of Scandinavia.* New York: Academic Press, 1981.

———. *Finland.* New York: Frederick A. Praeger, 1968.

Meiggs, Russell. *Trees and Timber in the Ancient Mediterranean World* Oxford: Oxford University Press, 1982.

Meinecke, Dr. Th. "Heidebrennen." *Der Deutsche Forstwirt* 9 (1927): 601–602, 605–606.

Melekhov, I. S. *The Effect of Fires on Forests* [in Russian]. Moscow and Leningrad, 1948.

———. *The Nature of Forests and Forest Fires* [in Russian]. Arkhangelsk, 1947.

———. *Study of Forest Fires in Northern Forests* [in Russian]. Arkhangelsk: AITI, 1939.

Mellars, Paul. "Fire Ecology, Animal Populations and Man: A Study of Some Ecological Relationships in Prehistory." *Proceedings of the Prehistoric Society* 42 (1976): 15–45.

Melville, Elinor G. K. *A Plague of Sheep: Environmental Consequences of the Conquest of Mexico.* Cambridge: Cambridge University Press, 1994.

Merriman, John M. "The Norman Fires of 1830: Incendiaries and Fear in Rural France." *French Historical Studies* 9 (1976): 451–466.

Michell, Robert, and Nevill Forbes, trans. *The Chronicle of Novgorod, 1016–1471.* Hattiesburg, Miss.: Academic International, 1970.

Miller, G. R. "Land Use in the Scottish Highlands. VII. The Management of Heather Moors." *Advancement of Science* 21 (1961): 163–189.

Millot, Professor J. "In Conclusion." In *Biogeography and Ecology in Madagascar,* edited by R. Battistini and G. Richard-Vindard, pp. 741–756. The Hague: Dr. W. Junk Publ., 1972.

Milovsky, Alexander S. "The Death of Winter." *Natural History* 99 (1993): 34–39.

Mißbach, Karl. *Waldbrand: Berhütung und Bekämpfung.* Berlin: VEB Deutscher Landwirtschafts-Verlag, 1972.

Mitchell, F. J. G. "The Impact of Grazing and Human Disturbance on the Dynamics of Woodland in S.W. Ireland." *Journal of Vegetation Science* 1 (1990): 245–254.

———. "The Vegetational History of the Killarney Oakwoods, SW Ireland: Evidence from Fine Spatial Resolution Pollen Analysis." *Journal of Ecology* 76 (1988): 415–435.

Mitchell, Frank. *The Irish Landscape.* London: Collins, 1976.

Mitchell, T. L. *Journal of an Expedition into the Interior of Tropical Australia.* New York: Greenwood Press, 1969 (reprint).

Moberg, Vilhelm. "Svedjegubban." In *Berättelser ur min levnad.* Stockholm: Aldus, 1975.

Modi, Jivanji Jamshedji. *The Religious Ceremonies and Customs of the Parsees.* 2d edition. Bombay, 1937.

Moe, Dagfinn, et al. "The Halne Area, Hardangarvidda: Use of a High Mountain Area during 5000 Years—An Interdisciplinary Case Study." In *The Cultural Landscape:*

Past, Present, and Future, edited by Hilary H. Birks et al., pp. 429–462. Cambridge: Cambridge University Press, 1988.

Moir, E. McA. *Report of a Visit to the Torrent Regions of the Hautes and Basses Alpes, and Also to Mount Faron, Toulon.* Calcutta, 1881.

Mokeev, G. A. *Aerial Protection of Forests* [in Russian]. Moscow, 1950.

Molloy, B. P. J. "The Fire History." In "Cass: History and Science in the Cass District, Canterbury, New Zealand," edited by C. J. Burrows, pp. 157–188. Canterbury: Department of Botany, University of Canterbury, 1977.

Montag, Susanne. *Brandrodungsformen zum zwecke der landwirtschaftlichen zwischennutzung in den Wäldern Europas.* Thesis, Albert-Ludwigs-Universität. Freiburg, 1990.

Montelius, Sigvard. "The Burning of Forest Land for the Cultivation of Crops." *Geografiska Annaler* 35 (1953): 41–54.

Montrichard, G. de "L'île de Chypre." *Revue des eaux et forêts, annales forestières* 13 (1874): 33–42.

Moody, William D. "Technical Report, U.S.-U.S.S.R. Technical Exchange Program. Smokejumping—Rapelling. October 1976." Unpublished report, U.S. Forest Service, 1976.

Mooney, Harold A., et al., eds. *Proceedings of the Symposium on the Environmental Consequences of Fire and Fuel Management in Mediterranean Ecosystems.* General Technical Report WO-3. U.S. Forest Service, 1977.

Moore, Briscoe. *From Forest to Farm.* London: Pelham Books, 1969.

Moore, D. M. "Origins of Temperate Island Floras." In *Plants and Islands,* edited by D. Bramwell, pp. 69–85. New York: Academic Press, 1979.

Moore, Peter D. "Fire on Heathland." *Nature* 264 (November 11, 1976): 112–113.

———. "Hunting Ground for Farmers." *Nature* 382 (August 1996): 675–676.

———. "Origin of Blanket Mires." *Nature* 256 (July 1975): 267–269.

Morgenstern, Julian. *The Fire Upon the Altar.* Chicago: Quadrangle Books, 1963.

Morley, Henry. *Sketches of Russian Life Before and During the Emancipation of the Serfs.* London, 1866.

Morris, William G. "Forest Fires in Oregon and Washington." *Oregon Historical Quarterly* 35 (1934): 313–339.

Morrison, M. E. S. "Evidence and Interpretation of 'Landnam' in the North-East of Ireland." *Botaniska Notiser* 112 (1959): 185–204.

Morton, Thomas. *New English Canaan.* London, 1632.

Mowat, Farley. *The Siberians.* New York: Bantam Books, 1970.

Muel, E. "Les incendies dans les forêts de pin maritime." *Revue des eaux et forêts* 39 (1900): 340–341.

Mueller-Dombois, Dr. Dieter. "Fire in Tropical Ecosystems." In *Fire Regimes and Ecosystem Properties,* edited by H. A. Hooney et al., pp. 137–146. General Technical Report WO-26. U.S. Forest Service, 1981.

Muir, John. *My First Summer in the Sierra.* Boston and New York: Houghton Mifflin, 1911.

———. "The American Forests." *Atlantic Monthly* 80 (August 1897): 145–157.

Muirhead, K., and A. P. Cracknell. "Straw Burning of Great Britain Detected by AVHRR." *International Journal of Remote Sensing* 6 (1985): 827–833.

Müller, D. M. "Die Bedeutung von Waldbränden für Ausbau und Verjüngung europäischer Urwälder." *Allgemeine Forst- und Jagd-Zeitung* 108 (1932): 108–113.

Müller, Karl M. *Aufbau, Wuchs und Verjüngung der südosteuropäischen Urwälder.* Hannover, 1929.

———. "Zur Frage der 'Brandtheorie.'" *Allgemeine Forst- und Jagd-Zeitung* 107 (1931): 305–312.

Murdoch, Captain A. G. "Mastering a Menace." *American Forest* 65 (1959): 38–39, 57–59, 61.

Murphy, Peter. *History of Forest and Prairie Fire Control Policy in Alberta.* Edmonton: Alberta Energy and Natural Resources Ministry, 1985.

Murphy, Rhoads. "The Decline of North Africa since the Roman Occupation: Climatic or Human?" *Annals of the Association of American Geographers* 41 (1951): 116–132.

Myrdal, Janken, and Johan Söderberg. *Kontinujitetens dynamik: Agrar ekonomi i 1500-talets Sverige.* Stockholm, 1991.

Nagy, Gregory. *Greek Mythology and Poetics.* Ithaca: Cornell University Press, 1990.

Nansen, Fridtjof. *Through Siberia: The Land of the Future.* London: Heinemann, 1914.

Nash, Roderick. *Wilderness and the American Mind.* 3d edition. New Haven: Yale University Press, 1982.

Nat, S. T. *Forest Fires and Countermeasures against Them* [in Russian]. Moscow, 1902.

National Academy of Sciences. *Report of the Committee Appointed by the National Academy of Sciences Upon the Inauguration of a Forest Policy for the Forested Lands of the United States to the Secretary of the Interior.* Washington, D.C.: Government Printing Office, 1897.

Negre, M. "Les incendies de forêts dans les montagnes des Cevennes." *Revue des eaux et forêts* 62 (1924): 414–421.

Nellbeck, Roland. *Några drag ur Svenske skogsvårdhistoria.* Unpublished manuscript, 1953.

Nesterov, V. G. "Forest Fire Control," translated by D. I. Lalkow. Canadian Forestry Service. Unpublished manuscript, 1947.

Nibbering, Jan Willem. "Forest Degradation and Reforestation in a Highland Area in Java." In *Changing Tropical Forests,* edited by John Dargavel et al., pp. 155–177. Canberra: Australian National University, 1988.

Nilssen, Eilif J. "Development of the Cultural Landscape in the Lofoten Area, North Norway." In *The Cultural Landscape: Past, Present and Future,* edited by Hilary H. Birks et al., pp. 369–380. Cambridge: Cambridge University Press, 1988.

Nilsson, Nils-Erik, ed. *The Forests.* National Atlas of Sweden, 1990.

Nowak, Rachel. "Fire Threatens Galápagos Tortoises." *Science* 264 (April 29, 1994): 651.

Oakley, Kenneth P. "On Man's Use of Fire, with Comments on Tool-Making and Hunting." In *Social Life of Early Man,* edited by Sherwood L. Washburn, 176–193. Chicago: University of Chicago Press, 1961.

O'Brien, Maire, and Conor Cruise O'Brien. *A Concise History of Ireland.* New York: Beekman House, 1972.

O'Connell, C. A., and G. J. Doyle. "Local Vegetation History of a Pine Woodland on Clonfinane Bog, County Tipperary." In *Ecology and Conservation of Irish Peatlands,* edited by G. J. Doyle, pp. 23–40. Dublin, 1990.

O'Connell, Michael, et al. "Post-glacial Landscape Evolution in Connemara, Western Ireland with Particular Reference to Woodland History." In *The Cultural Landscape: Past, Present and Future,* edited by Hilary H. Birks et al., pp. 267–287. Cambridge: Cambridge University Press, 1988.

O'Connor, K. F. "The Implications of Past Exploitation and Current Developments to the Conservation of South Island Tussock Grasslands." *New Zealand Journal of Ecology* 5 (1982): 97–107.

Ögonvittne, Ett. *Norrland brinner! En beskrifning öfner eldsvådorna i Sundsvall, Umeå m. fl. Ställen.* Stockholm, 1888.

O'Hara, S. L., et al. "On the Arid Margin: The Relationship between Climate, Humans and the Environment. A Review of Evidence from the Highlands of Central Mexico." *Chemosphere* 29 (1994): 965–981.

Oinonen, Eino. "The Correlation between the Size of Finnish Bracken (*Pteridium aquilinum* (l.) Kuhn.) Clones and Certain Periods of Site History." *Acta Forestalia Fennica* 83 (1967): 1–51.

———. "The Size of *Lycopodium clavatum* L. and *L. annotinum* L. Stands as Compared to that of *L. Complanatum* L. and *Pteridium aquilium* (L.) Kuhn Stands, the Age of the Tree Stand, and the Dates of Fire, on the Site," *Acta Forestalia Fennica* 87 (1968): 1–53.

Oldfield, F., et al. "History of Particulate Atmospheric Pollution from Magnetic Measurements in Dating Finnish Peat Profile." *Ambio* 10 (1980): 185–188.

Olwig, Kenneth. "The Morphology of a Symbolic Landscape: A Geosophical Case Study of the Transformation of Denmark's Jutland Heaths Circa 1750–1950." Ph.D. dissertation, University of Minnesota, 1977.

Orkneyinga Saga, translated by Hermann Pálsson and Paul Edwards. New York: Penguin Books, 1978.

Östlund, Lars. *Exploitation and Structural Changes in the North Swedish Boreal Forest, 1800–1992.* Dissertations in Forest Vegetation Ecology, 4. Umeå: University of Umeå, 1993.

O'Sullivan, Vincent, ed. *An Anthology of Twentieth Century New Zealand Poetry.* Oxford: Oxford University Press, 1970.

Otto, H. J. "Measures to Reduce Forest Fire Hazards and Restoration of Damaged Areas in Lower Saxony." In *Forest Fire Prevention and Control,* edited by T. van Nao, pp. 173–179. The Hague: Martinus Nijhoff and Dr. W. Junk, 1982.

———. "Sylviculture According to Site Conditions as Method of Forest Protection." *Journal of Applied Entomology* 99 (1985): 190–198.

———. "Zur Waldbrandsituation in Niedersachsen." *VW-Symposium "Feurökologie,"* vol. 1, pp. 5–27. Freiburg, 1978.

Oviedo y Valdés, Gonzalo Fernández de. *Natural History of the West Indies,* translated and edited by Sterling A. Stoudemire. Studies in the Romance Languages and Literatures, 32. University of North Carolina Press, 1959.

Pallas, P. S. *Travels through the Southern Provinces of the Russian Empire in the Years 1793 and 1794.* 2 vols. London, 1803.

Pallot, Juliet, and Denis J. B. Shaw. *Landscape and Settlement in Romanov Russia, 1613–1917.* Oxford: Clarendon Press, 1990.

Pallu, Roger. "La Protection des Forêts contre l'incendie en France." *Congrès international du bois et de la sylviculture* (1931): 549–559.

Pálsson, Hermann, and Paul Edwards, trans. *Orkneyinga Saga.* New York: Penguin Books, 1978.

Parsons, James J. "Human Influences on the Pine and Laurel Forests of the Canary Islands." *Geographical Review* 71 (1981): 253–271.

Partington, J. P. *History of Greek Fire and Gunpowder.* Cambridge: Cambridge University Press, 1961.

Patterson, W. A., and K. E. Sassaman. "Indian Fires in the Prehistory of New England." In *Holocene Human Ecology in Northeastern North America,* edited by G. P. Nicholas, pp. 107–135. New York: Plenum Press, 1988.

Patterson, W. A., et al. "Microscopic Charcoal as a Fossil Indicator of Fire." *Quarternary Science Review* 6 (1987): 3–23.

Payne, Robert. *The Holy Fire: The Story of the Fathers of the Eastern Church.* London: Skeffington, 1958.

Pedersen, Anfred. "Adventitious Plants and Cultivated Plants in Greenland." *Meddelelser om Gronland* 178, no. 7 (1972).

Pennington, Winifred. *The History of British Vegetation.* London: English Universities Press, 1969.

Perkins, James H., and George A. Roby. "Fire Managment Training in International Forestry." *Fire Management Notes* 48, no. 1 (1987): 18–20.

Perles, Catherine. "Hearth and Home in the Old Stone Age." *Natural History* 90 (1981): 38–41.

———. *Préhistoire du feu.* Paris: Masson, 1977.

Perrier de la Bathie, H. *Biogéographie des plantes de Madagascar.* Paris: Société d'éditions géographiques, maritimes et coloniales, 1936.

———. *Le Tsaratanana, l'Ankaratra et l'Andringitra.* Mémoires de l'Académie Malgache, fasc. III (1927).

Perry, Captain John. *The State of Russia under the Present Czar.* London, 1716.

Pfeiffer, John. *The Emergence of Man.* 2d edition. New York: Harper and Row, 1972.

Phillips, John C. "Fire in Africa: A Brief Re-Survey." *Proceedings, Tall Timbers Fire Ecology Conference,* vol. 11, pp. 3–4. Tallahassee: Tall Timbers Research Station, 1971.

Pierce, R. T. R. "Why Farmers Burn Straw." *Span* (February 25, 1982).

Piesnack, J. "Forest Fire Prevention and Control in the German Democratic Republic." In *Forest Fire Prevention and Control,* edited by T. van Nao, pp. 97–99. The Hague: Martinus Nijhoff and Dr. W. Junk, 1982.

Pincetl, Stephanie. "Some Origins of French Environmentalism." *Forest and Conservation History* 37 (1993): 80–89.

Pinchot, Gifford. *Breaking New Ground.* Seattle: University of Washington Press, 1972 (reprint).

———. *The Fight for Conservation.* Seattle: University of Washington Press, 1967.

Plutarch. *The Lives of the Noble Grecians and Romans,* translated by John Dryden. New York: Modern Library, 1932.

Podolak, Jan. "Alte Rodungsverfahren und Brandwirtschaft in der Slowakei." In *Getreidebau in Ost- und Mitteleurope,* edited by I. Ballassa, pp. 143–177. Budapest, 1972.

Ponting, Clive. *A Green History of the World.* New York: St Martin's Press, 1991.

Portal, Roger. *The Slavs,* translated by Patrick Evans. London: Weidenfeld and Nicolson, 1969.

Postan, M. M., ed. *The Cambridge Economic History of Europe.* Vol. 1. *The Agrarian Life of the Middle Ages.* 2d edition Cambridge: Cambridge University Press, 1966.

Potter, Lesley. "Indigenes and Colonisers: Dutch Forest Policy in South and East Borneo (Kalimantan)." In *Changing Tropical Forests,* edited by John Dargavel et al., pp. 127–154. Canberra: Australian National University, 1988.

Pottle, Frederick, ed. *Boswell's Journal of a Tour to the Hebrides with Samuel Johnson, 1773.* New York: McGraw-Hill, 1961.

Pounds, Norman J. G. *An Historical Geography of Europe 450 BC–AD 1330.* Cambridge: Cambridge University Press, 1973.

Prebble, John. *The Highland Clearances.* New York: Penguin, 1963.

Price, M. P. *Siberia.* Methuen: London, 1912.

Prinn, Ronald G. "Biomass Burning Studies and the International Global Atmospheric Chemistry (IGAC) Project," In *Global Biomass Burning,* edited by Joel S. Levine, pp. 22–28. Cambridge: MIT Press, 1991.

Pyne, Stephen J. *Burning Bush: A Fire History of Australia.* New York: Henry Holt, 1991.

———. *Fire in America: A Cultural History of Wildland and Rural Fire.* Princeton: Princeton University Press, 1982. (Paperback ed., Seattle: University of Washington Press, 1997.)

———. "Nataraja: India's Cycle of Fire." *Environmental History Review* 18 (1994): 1–20.

———. "Space: The Third Great Age of Discovery." In *Space: Discovery and Exploration,* edited by Martin J. Collins and Sylvia K. Kraemer, pp. 14–65. New York: Hugh Lauter Levin Associates, Inc., 1993.

———. *World Fire: The Culture of Fire on Earth.* New York: Henry Holt, 1995. (Paperback ed., Seattle: University of Washington Press, 1997.)

Pyne, Stephen J., Patricia L. Andrews, and Richard D. Laven. *Introduction to Wildland Fire.* 2d ed. New York: Wiley, 1996.

Rackham, Oliver. *Ancient Woodland: Its History, Vegetation and Uses in England.* Edward Arnold, 1980.

———. *The History of the Countryside.* London, 1986.

Radley, J. "Significance of Major Moorland fires." *Nature* 205 (1965): 1255.

Rafiullah, S. M. *The Geography of Transhumance.* Aligarh: Department of Geography, Aligarh Muslim University, 1966.

Rainbird, J. S. "The Fire Stations of Imperial Rome." *Papers of the British School at Rome* 54 (1986): 147–169.

Rappoport, A. S. *Home Life in Russia.* London: Methuen and Co., 1913.

Rauh, Werner. "Problems of Biological Conservation in Madagascar." In *Plants and Islands,* edited by D. Bramwell, pp. 405–421. New York: Academic Press, 1979.

Raumolin, Jussi. "The Formation of the Sustained Yield Forestry System in Finland." In *History of Sustained-Yield Forestry: a Symposium,* edited by Harold K. Steen, 155–169. Durham: Forest History Society, 1984.

Ravenstein, E. G. *The Russians on the Amur.* London: Trübner and Co., 1861.

Rawat, Ajay S. *History of Forestry in India.* New Delhi: Indus Publishing, 1991.

Rawat, Ajay S., ed. *Indian Forestry: A Perspective.* New Delhi: Indus Publishing, 1993.

R. D. and S. L. "Les incendies de l'automne 1936 en Provence." *La Nature* (1937): 322.

Reichman, O. J. *Konza Prairie.* Lawrence: University of Kansas Press, 1987.

Renberg, Ingemar. "Annually Laminated Sediments in Lake Rudetjärn, Medelpad Province, North Sweden." *Geologiska föreningens* 98 (1976): 355–360.

Renberg, Ingemar, et al. "Prehistoric Increases in the pH of Acid-Sensitive Swedish Lakes Caused by Land-Use Changes." *Nature* 362 (April 29, 1993a): 824–826.

———. "A Temporal Perspective of Lake Acidification in Sweden." *Ambio* 22 (1993b): 264–271.

Renvoize, S. A. "The Origins of Indian Ocean Island Floras." In *Plants and Islands,* edited by D. Bramwell, pp. 107–129. New York: Academic Press, 1979.

Ribbé, Charles de. *Des incendies de forêts dans la region des Maures et de l'Esterel.* Paris 1865.

————. "La question des incendies de forêts dans l'Algérie et dans les Maures de la Provence." *Revue agricole et forestière de Provence* (1866).

Ribbentrop, Berthold. *Forestry in British India.* New Delhi: Indus Publishing, 1989 (reprint of 1901 edition).

Richards, John F., and Richard P. Tucker, eds. *World Deforestation in the Twentieth Century.* Durham: Duke University Press, 1988.

Richardson, R. B. "The Church as a Protector of Forests." *The Nation* (September 5, 1901): 183.

Ritchie, James. *The Influence of Man on Animal Life in Scotland.* Cambridge: Cambridge University Press, 1920.

Roberston, Jane M. S. "Land Use Planning of the French Mediterranean Region." In *Proceedings of the Symposium on the Environmental Consequences of Fire and Fuel Management in Mediterranean Ecosystems,* edited by Harold A. Mooney, et al., pp. 283–288. General Technical Report WO-3. U.S. Forest Service, 1977.

Roberts, Neil. *The Holocene: An Environmental History.* Oxford: Blackwell, 1989.

Robinson, J. M. "Phanerozoic O_2 Variation, Fire and Terrestrial Ecology." *Global Planet* (1989): 223–240.

Robinson, Olivia. "Fire Prevention at Rome." *Revue internationale des droits de l'antiquité* 3 (1977): 377–388.

Roche, M. M. *Forest Policy in New Zealand: An Historical Geography, 1840–1919.* Palmerston North: Dumore Press, 1987.

————. *History of Forestry.* Wellington: New Zealand Forestry Corporation Ltd., 1991.

Rodger, Sir Alexander. "Recent Forest Fires." *Journal of the Forestry Commission* 14 (March 1935): 20.

Romel, Lars-Gunnar. "Heden." In *Natur i Halland,* edited by Carl Skottsberg and Kai Curry-Lindahl, pp. 331–347. Göteborg, 1952.

Rosenblum, Mort. *Mission to Civilize.* New York: Harcourt Brace Jovanovich, 1986.

Rosenqvist, I. Th. "Alternative Sources for Acidification of River Water in Norway." *Science of the Total Environment* 10 (1978): 39–49.

Rossotti, Hazel. *Fire.* Oxford: Oxford University Press, 1993.

Rouse, Irving. *Migrations in Prehistory.* New Haven: Yale University Press, 1986.

Rouse, W. H. D., trans. *Great Dialogues of Plato.* New York: Mentor Books, 1956.

Roze, Francoise. "Plant Recolonisation after Fire in Brittany Littoral Heathlands." *Acta Ecologica* 14 (1993): 529–538.

Rudberg, Sten. "Ödemarkerna och den perifera bebyggelsen i Inre Nordsverige" [Unsettled Areas and Frontier Settlement Areas in Inner Northern Sweden]. *Geographica* 33. Uppsala, 1957.

Ruffault, Pierre. "Measures de protection contre l'incendie dans deux forêts particulières de la Gironde." *Revue des eaux et forêts* 62 (1924): 563–574.

Ruhnbro, Rune, ed. *Det Nya Sverige i landet Amerika.* Wiken, 1988.

Ruiz, J. P., and F. Gonzales-Bernaldez. "Landscape Perception by Its Traditional Users: The Ideal Landscape of Madrid Livestock Raisers." *Landscape Planning* 9 (1982–83): 279–297.

Ruiz, M., and J. P. Ruiz. "Ecological History of Transhumance in Spain." *Biological Conservation* 37 (1987): 73–86.

————. "Environmental Perception, Livestock Management and Rural Crisis in Sierra de Guadarrama (Madrid, Spain)." *Acta biol. mont.* 4 (1984): 455–466.

Runte, Alfred. *National Parks: The American Experience.* 2d edition. Lincoln: University of Nebraska Press, 1987.

Russell, E. W. B. "Indian-set Fires in the Forests of the Northeastern United States." *Ecology* 64 (1983): 78–88.

Ruuhijärvi, Rauno, et al. "Some Consequences of Using Prescribed Burning in Forestry." *Lammi Notes* 13 (1986): 1–5.

Rymer, L. "The History and Ethnobotany of Bracken." *Botanical Journal of the Linnaean Society* 73 (1976): 151–176.

Sadler, Jon. "Beetles, Boats, and Biogeography: Insect Invaders of the North Atlantic." In *The Norse of the North Atlantic,* edited by Gerald Bigelow, pp. 207–209. Copenhagen: Munksgaard, 1991.

Saint-Hilaire, Auguste de. *Viagem as nascentes do Rio São Francisco,* translated by Regina Regis-Junqueira. Coleção Reconquista do Brasil, vol. 7. São Paulo: Universidade de São Paulo, 1975.

————. *Voyage dans le District des Diamans et sur le littoral du Brésil.* 2 vols. Paris, 1833.

Salisbury, Harrison. *The Great Black Dragon Fire.* Boston: Little, Brown, 1989.

Salmon, J. T. "The Influence of Man on the Biota." In *Biogeography and Ecology of New Zealand,* edited by G. Kuschel, pp. 643–661. The Hague: Dr. W. Junk, 1975.

Salvador, J. "Considerations sur les incendies de forêts dans le massif de l'Esterel." *Revue des eaux et forêts* 60 (1922): 226–238.

Sannikov, S. N. "Forest Fires as the Evolutionary/Ecological Conditions for Reproduction of Pine Populations in the Ural Part of Siberia." In *Burning and Fires in Forests,* pp. 236–277 [in Russian]. Krasnoyarsk, 1973.

Sauer, Carl O. "Man's Dominance by Use of Fire." *Geoscience and Man* 10 (1975): 1–13.

————. *Northern Mists.* Berkeley: University of California Press, 1968.

————. *Seeds, Spades, Hearths and Herds.* Cambridge: MIT Press, 1972.

————. "The Agency of Man on the Earth." In *Man's Role in Changing the Face of the Earth,* vol. 1, edited by William L. Thomas, Jr., pp. 49–69. Chicago: University of Chicago Press, 1956.

————. *The Early Spanish Main.* Berkeley: University of California Press, 1969.

Sax, Joseph L. *Mountains without Handrails.* Ann Arbor: University of Michigan Press, 1980.

Schacke, Dirk. "The Danish Heath Society." *Scottish Geographical Magazine* 67 (1951): 45–54.

Schama, Simon. *Landscape and Memory.* New York: Knopf, 1995.

Schimmel, Johnny. *On Fire: Fire Behavior, Fuel Succession and Vegetation Response to Fire in the Swedish Boreal Forest.* Dissertations in Forest Vegetation Ecology, 5. Umeå: University of Umeå, 1993.

Schneiter, Fritz. *Agrargeschichte der Brandwirtschaft.* Forschungen zur geschichtlichen Landeskunde der Steiermark, 25. Graz, 1970.

Schüle, W. "Landscapes and Climate in Prehistory: Interactions of Wildlife, Man, and Fire." In *Fire in the Tropical Biota: Ecosystem Processes and Global Challenges,* edited by J. G. Goldammer, pp. 273–318. Heidelberg: Springer-Verlag, 1990.

Schwidetzky, Ilse. "The Prehispanic Population of the Canary Islands." In *Biogeography and Ecology in the Canary Islands,* edited by G. Kunkel, pp. 15–36. The Hague: Dr. W. Junk, 1976.

Sclafert, Thérèse. *Cultures en Haute-Provence: Déboisements et pâturages au Moyen Âge.* S.E.V.P.E.N., 1959.

Scott, A. C. "Observations on the Nature and Origin of Fusain." *International Journal of Coal Petrology* 12 (1989): 443–475.

Scott, Charles Henry. *The Baltic, the Black Sea, and the Crimea.* London: Richard Bentley, 1854.

Segerström, Ulf. "The Natural Holocene Vegetation Development and the Introduction of Agriculture in Northern Norrland, Sweden." Ph.D. dissertation, Sveriges Lantbruksuniversitet, Umeå, 1990.

Segerström, Ulf, et al. "Disturbance History of a Swamp Forest Refuge in Northern Sweden." *Biological Conservation* 68 (1994): 189–196.

Ségur, Count Philip de. "The Burning of Moscow." In *Russia under Western Eyes,* edited by Anthony Cross, pp. 311–317. New York, 1971.

Seigue, A. "Les incendies de la forêt méditerranéene. Historique, essay prospectif." *Bulletin technique d'information* (Ministre de l'agriculture) 268 (1972): 415–423.

Semonov, D. P. "Cultivation of the Soil." In *Industries of Russia,* vol. 3, edited by J. M. Crawford, pp. 74–92. St. Petersburg, 1893.

Semple, Ellen Churchill. *The Geography of the Mediterranean Region: Its Relation to Ancient History.* New York: Henry Holt and Co., 1931.

Sequoia–Kings Canyon National Parks. "Fire Management Plan: Sequoia and Kings Canyon National Parks." November 1991.

Serebrennikov, P. P., and V. V. Matreninsky. *Forest Fires and Their Control.* Moscow, 1937.

Seurre. "Role de l'électricité atmosphérique dans les incendies de forêts." *Bulletin du comité des forêts* 20 (1923): 439–443.

Shapley, Harlow. *Source Book in Astronomy, 1900–1950.* Cambridge: Harvard University Press, 1960.

Shaw, Denis J. B. "Southern Frontiers of Muscovy, 1550–1700." In *Studies in Russian Historical Geography,* vol. 1, edited by James H. Bater and R. A. French, pp. 117–142. New York: Academic Press, 1983.

Shcherbakov, I. P. *Forest Fires in Yakutia and Their Influence on the Nature of Forests.* Novosibirsk: Nauka, 1979.

———. "Forest Vegetation in Burned and Logged Areas of Yakutsk." In *North American Forest Lands at Latitudes North of 60 Degrees.* Proceedings of a Symposium. Fairbanks: University of Alaska et al., 1977.

Shebbeare, E. O. "Fire Protection and Fire Control in India." *Third British Forestry Conference,* pp. 1–5. Canberra, 1928.

———. "Sal taungyas in Bengal." *Empire Forestry Journal* 11 (1932): 22–33.

Shelgunov, N. *The History of Russian Forest Legislation* [in Russian]. St. Petersburg, 1857.

Shirov, S. M. *Social Organization of the Northern Tungus.* Oosterhout, Netherlands: Anthropological Publications, 1966.

Shostakovitch, V. B. "Forest Conflagrations in Siberia, with Special Reference to the Fires of 1915." *Journal of Forestry* 23 (1925): 365–371.

Shvidenko, Anatoly, and Sten Nilsson. "What Do We Know About the Siberian Forests?" *Ambio* 23 (1994): 396–404.

Sigaut, François. *L'Agriculture et le feu: Role et place du feu dans les techniques de pré-
paration du champ de l'ancienne agriculture européenne.* Paris: Mouton & Co., 1975.
Simmons, I. G. "Evidence for Vegetation Changes Associated with Mesolithic Man in
Britain." In *The Domestication and Exploitation of Plants and Animals,* edited by
Peter J. Ucko and G. W. Dimbleby, pp. 111–119. Chicago: University of Chicago
Press, 1968.
———. "The Earliest Cultural Landscape of England." *Environmental Review* 12 (1988):
105–116.
———. "The History of the Early Human Environment." In *Moorland Monuments,*
edited by B. Vyner. London: CBA Research Report 101, 1995, pp. 5–15.
Simmons, I. G., and J. B. Innes. "Prehistoric Charcoal in Peat Profiles at North Gill,
North Yorkshire Moors, England" *Journal of Archaeological Science* 23 (1996):
193–197.
Simmons, I. G., et al. "The Mesolithic." In *The Environment in British Prehistory,* edited
by Ian Simmons and Michael Tooley, pp. 82–124. London: Duckworth, 1981.
Simmons, I. G., and M. J. Tooley, eds. *The Environment in British Prehistory.* London:
Duckworth, 1981.
Siren, Gustav. "Some Remarks on Fire Ecology in Finnish Forestry." *Proceedings, Tall
Timbers Fire Ecology Conference,* vol. 13, pp. 191–210. Tallahassee: Tall Timbers
Research Station, 1973.
Sjöbeck, Marten. "Den försvinnande ljungheden." *Svenska Turistföreningens Årsskrift*
(1933): 84–103.
Sjörs, Hugo. "Slatterängar i grangärde Finnmark [English summary: Meadows in
Grangärde Finnmark, SW. Dalarna, Sweden]." *Acta Phytogeographica Suecica* 34
(1949).
Skog & Forskning 4 (1991): "Tänd eld på skogen!" [special issue].
Skogsbrandsläckningskommittén. "Utlatande rörande metoder och materiel vid skogs-
brandsläckande." *Statens off. utredn. 1946.* Stockholm, 1946.
Skvoretsky, V. I. "Report: The Organization and Development of the Western-Siberian
Base for Aerial Forest Protection [Alma-Ata Aerial Fire Center]" [in Russian]. Unpub-
lished report, 1981.
Smeds, Helmer. "Post War Land Clearance and Pioneering Activities in Finland." *Fen-
nia* 83 (Helsinki, 1960).
Smith, A. G. "The Influence of Mesolithic and Neolithic Man on British Vegetation: A
Discussion." In *Studies in the Vegetation History of the British Isles,* edited by D.
Walker and R. G. West, pp. 81–96. Cambridge: Cambridge University Press, 1970.
Smith, Catherine Delano. "Late Neolithic Settlement, Land-Use, and *Garigue* in the
Montpellier Region, France." *Man* 7 (1972): 397–407.
———. "The Land Use of Eastern Madeira." In *Four Island Studies.* Bude, England:
Geographical Publications Ltd., 1968.
———. *Western Mediterranean Europe.* New York: Academic Press, 1979.
Smith, Cyril Stanley, and Martha Teach Gnudi. *The Pirotechnia of Vannoccio Biringuc-
cio.* Cambridge: MIT Press, 1966 (reprint).
Smith, R. E. F. *Peasant Farming in Muscovy.* Cambridge: Cambridge University Press,
1958.
———. *The Origins of Farming in Russia.* Paris: Mouton and Co., 1959.
Smith, Richard T., and Margaret A. Atherden. "Recent Vegetative Change and the Man-
agement of Ilkley Moor, West Yorkshire." In *The Biogeographical Impact of Land-*

Use Change: Collected Essays, edited by Richard T. Smith, pp. 39–50. Biogeography Study Group, 1985.

Sofronov, M. A., and A. D. Vakurov. *Fire in the Forest* [in Russian]. Novosibirsk, 1981.

Soininen, Arvo M. "Burn-beating as the Technical Basis of Colonisation in Finland in the 16th and 17th Centuries." *Scandinavian Economic History Review* 7 (1959): 150–166.

———. *Vanha Maataloutemma.* Helsinki, 1974.

Soppa, Rainer. "Neue Methoden der Waldbrandbekämpfung." *Algemeine Forstzeitschrift* 50 (1995): 654–655.

Sorensen, James. "Seventeen Years of Progress Through International Cooperation, 1962–1978." U.S. Forest Service, 1979.

Soudsky, B., and I. Pavlu. "The Linear Pottery Culture Settlement Patterns of Central Europe." In *Man, Settlement, and Urbanism,* edited by P. J. Ucko et al., pp. 317–328. London: Duckworth, 1972.

Spalteholz, C. O. R. "Forestry in the Dutch East Indies." *Journal of Forestry* 26 (1928): 697–701.

Spindler, Konrad. *The Man in the Ice,* translated by Ewald Osers. London: Phoenix Books, 1993.

Spuler, Bertold. *History of the Mongols: Based on Eastern and Western Accounts of the Thirteenth and Fourteenth Centuries,* translated by Helga and Stuart Drummond. Berkeley: University of California Press, 1972.

Stadling, J. *Through Siberia,* edited by F. H. H. Guillemard. Westminister: Archibald Constable and Co., 1901.

State Forest Service. *Annual Report of the Director of Forestry for the Year Ended 31st March 1946.* Wellington, 1946.

Stebbing, E. P. "Forestry in Africa." *Empire Forestry Journal* 2 (1941): 126–144.

———. *The Forests of India.* 3 vols. London: John Lane, The Bodley Head, 1922.

———. *The Forests of West Africa and the Sahara.* London: W. and R. Chambers, 1937.

Stebelsky, I. "Agriculture and Soil Erosion in the European Forest-Steppe." In *Studies in Russian Historical Geography,* vol. 1, edited by James H. Bater and R. A. French, pp. 45–63. New York: Academic Press, 1983a.

———. "The Frontier in Central Asia." In *Studies in Russian Historical Geography,* vol. 1, edited by James H. Bater and R. A. French, pp. 143–173. New York: Academic Press, 1983b.

Steensberg, Axel. *Draved: An Experiment in Stone Age Agriculture: Burning, Sowing and Harvesting.* Copenhagen: National Museum, 1979.

———. *Fire Clearance Husbandry: Traditional Techniques Throughout the World.* Herning: Poul Kristensen, 1993.

Stenius, Jacob. *Kort underrättelse om kärr och mossor samt deras nyttjande.* Stockholm, 1742.

Stevens, Graeme, et al. *Prehistoric New Zealand.* Auckland: Reed Books, 1988.

Stevenson-Hamilton, Col. James. *South African Eden: From Sabi Game Reserve to Kruger National Park.* London, 1937.

Stewart, Omer C. "Barriers to Understanding the Influence of Use of Fire by Aborigines on Vegetation." *Proceedings, Tall Timbers Fire Ecology Conference,* vol. 2, pp. 117–126. Tallahassee: Tall Timbers Research Station, 1963.

———. "Fire as the First Great Force Employed by Man." In *Man's Role in Chang-*

ing the Face of the Earth, vol. 1, edited by William L. Thomas, Jr., pp. 115–133. Chicago: University of Chicago Press, 1956.

Stjernquist, Per. *Laws in the Forests: A Study of Public Direction of Swedish Private Forestry.* Act. Reg. Societatis Humaniorum Litterarum Lundensis, 69. Lund, 1976.

Stockholm International Peace Research Institute. *Incendiary Weapons.* Cambridge: MIT Press, 1975.

Stocks, Brian J. "The Extent and Impact of Forest Fires in Northern Circumpolar Countries." In *Global Biomass Burning,* edited by Joel S. Levine, pp. 197–208. Cambridge: MIT Press, 1991.

Stocks, B. J., and A. J. Simard. "Forest Fire Management in Canada." *Disaster Management* 5 (1993): 21–27.

Stoneley, Jack. *Cauldron of Hell: Tunguska.* New York: Simon and Schuster, 1977.

Stratton, Arthur. *The Great Red Island.* New York: Scribners, 1964.

Strogy, Alxander A. *The Siberian Forests* [in Russian]. St. Petersburg, 1911.

Ström, I. Ad. *Handbok för skogshushållare.* Stockholm, 1830.

Strugnell, E. J. "The Teak Forests of Java." *Empire Forestry Journal* 11 (1932): 39–40.

Sulimirski, Tadeusz. *Prehistoric Russia: An Outline.* New York: Humanities Press, 1970.

Suman, Daniel O. "A Five-Century Sedimentary Geochronology of Biomass Burning in Nicaragua and Central America. In *Global Biomass Burning,* edited by Joel S. Levine, pp. 512–518. Cambridge: MIT Press, 1991.

Sunding, Per. "Origins of the Macaronesian Flora." In *Plants and Islands,* edited by D. Bramwell, pp. 13–40. New York: Academic Press, 1979.

Suomen Antropologi 4 (1987) [special issue on swidden].

Surier, A. "Pour la forêt Corse." *Pins et Résineux* 51 (1912): 36.

Suslov, I. M. "In Search of the Great Meteorite of 1908" [in Russian]. *Mirovedenie* 16 (1927): 13–18.

"Svedjebruk." In *Kulturhistorisk Lexikon För Nordisk Medeltid,* vol. 17 (Rosenkilde og Bagger).

Swedish Phytogeographical Society. *The Plant Cover of Sweden.* Acta Phytogeographica Suecica, 50 [special issue]. Uppsala, 1965.

Swinton, A. *Travels into Norway, Denmark, and Russia.* London, 1792.

Tacitus. *The Agricola and the Germania,* revised, translated by H. Mattingly. London: Penguin Books, 1970.

———. *The Annals of Imperial Rome,* revised edition, translated by Michael Grant. London: Penguin Books, 1989.

Taft, Julia V., and Robert W. Mutch. "International Wildfire Emergencies: Management in the 21st Century." In *Proceedings of the Symposium on Wildland Fire 2000,* edited by James B. Davis and Robert E. Martin. pp. 155–163. General Technical Report PSW-101. U.S. Forest Service, 1987.

Takeda, Shinya. "Origins of Taungya." In *Taungya: Forest Plantations with Agriculture in Southeast Asia,* edited by Carl F. Jordan, et al., pp. 18–31. Wallingford: CAB International, 1992.

Tallis, J. H., and V. R. Switsur. "Forest and Moorland in the South Peninne Uplands in the Mid-Flandrian Period. I. Macrofossil Evidence of the Former Forest Cover." *Journal of Ecology* 71 (1983): 585–600.

———. "II. The Hillslope Forests." *Journal of Ecology* 78 (1990): 857–883.

Tanley, A. G. *The British Islands and Their Vegetation.* Cambridge: Cambridge University Press, 1939.

Tau-tha. "Three Months' Privilege Leave to New Zealand." *Indian Forester* 12 (1886): 555.

Taylor, Alan R. "Ecological Aspects of Lightning in Forests." *Proceedings, Tall Timbers Fire Ecology Conference,* vol. 13, pp. 455–482. Tallahassee: Tall Timbers Research Station, 1974.

Taylor, E. G. R. "Camden's England." In *An Historical Geography of England before A.D. 1800,* edited by H. C. Darby, pp. 354–386. Cambridge: Cambridge University Press, 1936.

Taylor, Griffith. *Environment and Nation: Geographical Factors in the Cultural and Political History of Europe.* Toronto: University of Toronto Press, 1936.

Tegengren, Helmer, "En Utdöd Lappkultur i Kemi Lappmark: Studier i Nordfinlands Kolonisationshistoria." *Acta Academiae Aboensis Humaniora* 19. (Åbo, 1952).

Teichmuller, M., and R. Teichmuller. "Cainzoic and Mesozoic Coal Deposits in Germany." *13th Inter-University Geology Conference,* pp. 347–418. American Elsevier, 1968.

Tennant, Robert. *Sardinia and Its Resources.* London, 1885.

Tham, P. "Om odling at gamla masslupna ängar genom bränning." *Kongl. Svenska Lantbruks–Academiens Annaler* 5 (1817): 218–286.

Thirgood, J. V. "The Barbary Forests and Forest Lands, Environmental Destruction and the Vicissitudes of History." *Journal of World Forest Resources Management* 2 (1987a): 137–184.

———. *Cyprus: A Chronicle of Its Forests, Land, and People.* Vancouver: University of British Columbia Press, 1987b.

———. *Man and the Mediterranean Forest: A History of Resource Depletion.* New York: Academic Press, 1981.

———. "Man's Impact on the Forests of Europe." *Journal of World Forest Resources Management* 4 (1989): 127–167.

Thompson, Donald A. "Lightning Fires in Galloway, June 1970." *Scottish Forestry* 25 (1971): 51–52.

Thompson, R. "Report on the Forests of Mauritius." *Indian Forester* 6 (1881): 223–241, 287–288.

Thorarinsson, Sigurdur. "II. Svedjning På Island i forna tider." *Tefrokronologiska Studier På Island,* 26 (1944).

Thorpe, H. "A Special Case of Health Reclamation in the Alheden District of Jutland, 1700–1955." *Institute of British Geographers* 23 (1957): 87–121.

Tolonen, Kimmo. "Effects of Prehistoric Man on Finnish Lakes." *Bolski Archivum Hydrobiologii* 25 (1978): 419–421.

———. "Natural History of Raised Bogs and Forest Vegetation in the Lammi Area, Southern Finland Studied by Stratigraphical Methods." *Annales Academiae Scientiarium Fennicae,* Series A, no. 144 (1987).

———. "The Post-Glacial Fire Record." In *The Role of Fire in Northern Circumpolar Ecosystems,* edited by Ross Wein and David Maclean, pp. 21–45. New York: John Wiley and Sons, 1983.

Tolonen, Mirjami. "Comments to the Paper: 'On Vohtenkellarinsuo, a Bog in Paimio, SW Finland with a Cultural Origin.'" *Bulletin, Geological Society of Finland* 56 (1985a): 227–230.

———. "Palaeoecological Record of Local Fire History from a Peat Deposit in SW Finland." *Annales Botanici Fennici* 22 (1985b): 15–21.

———. "Palaeoecology of Annually Laminated Sediments in Lake Ahvenainen, S. Finland. I. Pollen and Charcoal Analyses and Their Relation to Human Impact." *Annales Botanici Fennici* 15 (1978a): 177–208.

———. "Palaeoecology of Annually Laminated Sediments in Lake Ahvenainen, S. Finland. II. Comparison of Dating Methods." *Annales Botanici Fennici* 15 (1978b): 209–222.

———. "Palaeoecology of Annually Laminated Sediments in Lake Ahvenainen, S. Finland. III. Human Influence in the Lake Development." *Annales Botanici Fennici* 15 (1978c): 223–240.

———. "Postglacial Pollen Stratigraphy of Lake Lamminjärvi, S. Finland." *Annales Botanici Fennici* 17 (1980): 15–25.

———. "The History of Agriculture in Sääksmäki Traced by Pollen Analysis." *Annales Botanici Fennici* 15 (1978d): 47–54.

Tolonen, Mirjami, and Ilka Kukkonen. "Postglacial Landscape Development in the Lower Reaches of the River Paimionjoki, SW Finland." *Annales Botanici Fennici* 26 (1989): 53–85.

Tomaselli, R. "Degradation of the Mediterranean Maquis." In UNESCO, *Mediterranean Forests and Maquis: Ecology, Conservation, and Management.* MAB Technical Notes, 2. Strasbourg: Council of Europe, 1977.

Topelius, Zachris. "Skogselden." *Boken om vårt land.* Helsinki, 1875

Toussaint, Auguste *History of Mauritius,* translated by W. E. F. Ward. London: Macmillan, 1977.

Trabaud, Loius. "Dynamics after Fire of Sclerophyllous Plant Communities in the Mediterranean Basin." *Ecologia Mediterranea* 13 (1987): 25–37.

———. "Effects of Past and Present Fire on the Vegetation of the French Mediterranean Region." In *Proceedings of the Symposium on Dynamics and Management of Mediterranean-Type Ecosystems,* edited by C. Eugene Conrad and Walter C. Oechel, pp. 450–457. General Technical Report PSW-58. U.S. Forest Service, 1981a.

———. "Man and Fire: Impacts on Mediterranean Vegetation." In *Mediterranean-Type Shrublands,* edited by Francesco diCastri, et al. Ecosystems of the World, vol. 11, pp. 523–526. New York: Elsevier, 1981b..

———. "Wildland Fire Cycles and History in Central Southern France." In *Proceedings, 2nd International Conference on Forest Fire Research,* vol. II. Coimbra: University of Coimbra, 1994.

Trabaud, L., and R. Prodon, eds. *Fire in Mediterranean Ecosystems.* Ecosystem Research, Report 5. Brussels: European Economic Commission, 1993.

Troensegaard, Jan. "FAO's Role in Forest Fire Protection: An Overview of Activities 1970–1989." *Unasylva* 162, no. 41 (1990): 17–20.

Trollope, W. S. W., et al. "A Structured versus a *Laissez Faire* Approach to Controlled Burning in the Kruger National Park in South Africa." Unpublished manuscript.

Trotter, Michael, M., and Beverley McCulloch. "Moas, Men, and Middens." In *Quaternary Extinctions,* edited by Paul S. Martin and Richard G. Klein, pp. 708–727. Tucson: University of Arizona Press, 1984.

Troup, R. S. *Silvicultural Systems.* London, 1928.

Trussell, Denys. "History in an Antipodean Garden." *Ecologist* 12 (1982): (37).

Tubbs, Colin R. *The New Forest: An Ecological History.* London: Newton Abbot, David & Charles, 1968.

Tucker, Richard P., and J. F. Richards, eds. *Global Deforestation and the Nineteenth-Century World Economy.* Durham: Duke Press Policy Studies, 1983.

Turner, Judith. "The Anthropogenic Factor in Vegetational History." *New Phytologist* 63 (1964): 73–89.

Tüxen, Reinhold. "The Use of Fire in Nature Conservation?" *Proceedings, Tall Timbers Fire Ecology Conference,* vol. 13, pp. 7–13. Tallahassee: Tall Timbers Research Station, 1973.

Tvengsberg, Per Martin. "Finnskogen brukes." *Nord Nytt* 33/34 (1988): 59–70.

Tweedie, Mrs. Alec. *Through Finland in Carts.* New York: Thomas Nelson & Sons, 1913.

Tylor, Edward B. *Researches into the Early History of Mankind and the Development of Civilization,* edited and abridged by Paul Bohannan. Chicago: University of Chicago Press, 1964.

Uggla, Evald. *Ecological Effects of Fire on North Swedish Forests.* Uppsala, 1958.

———. "Fire Ecology in Swedish Forests." *Proceedings, Tall Timbers Fire Ecology Conference,* vol. 13, pp. 171–190. Tallahassee: Tall Timbers Research Station, 1973.

———. "Mark- och luftemperarurer vid hyggesbränning." *Norrlands skoqsvå rdsförbunds tidskrift* 4 (1957): 443–500.

———. "Skogsbrandfält i Muddus Nationalpark." *Acta Phytogeographica Suecica* 41 (1958).

U.K. Ministry of Agriculture, Fisheries and Food. *Straw Disposal and Utilisation: A Review of Knowledge* (July 1984).

UNESCO. *Convention Concerning the Protection of the World Cultural and Natural Heritage.* Paris, 1972.

———. *MAB: Final Report.* Paris, 1971.

———. *Mediterranean Forests and Maquis: Ecology, Conservation, and Management.* MAB Technical Notes, 2. Brussels: Council of Europe, 1977.

Usher, M. B., and D. B. A. Thompson. "Variation in the Upland Heathlands of Great Britain: Conservation Importance." *Biological Conservation* 66 (1993): 69–81.

Valendik, E. N. *The Struggle with Big Forest Fires* [in Russian]. Novosibirsk: Nauka, 1990.

Valendik, E. N., et al. *Large Forest Fires* [in Russian]. Moscow: Nauka, 1979.

van der Ven, J. A. "Nature Management in The Netherlands and Its Financial Consequences with Special Attention to the Role of Fire." *Proceedings, Tall Timbers Fire Ecology Conference,* vol. 13, pp. 19–37. Tallahassee: Tall Timbers Research Station, 1973.

Van Wagner, C. E. "Forest Fire Research in the Canadian Forestry Service." Petawawa, Ontario: Petawawa National Forestry Institute, 1984.

———. "The Historical Pattern of Annual Burned Area in Canada." *Forestry Chronicle* 64 (1988): 182–185.

van Wilgen, B. W., et al. "Fire Management in Southern Africa: Some Examples of Current Objectives, Practices, and Problems." In *Fire in the Tropical Biota,* edited by J. G. Goldammer, pp. 179–215. Berlin: Springer-Verlag, 1990.

van Wyck, P. "Veld Burnings in the Kruger National Park: An Interim Report of Some Aspects of Research." In *Proceedings, Tall Timbers Fire Ecology Conference,* vol. 11, pp. 9–31. Tallahassee: Tall Timbers Research Station,

Vasilenko, A. V. "On the Problem of Studying the Process of Burning under Burning-off in Larch Forests." VNIILM 52. Moscow, 1970.

Vasiliev, N. V. "The Effects of Fire Caused by the Tunguska Meteorite on the Forest" [in Russian]. In N. P. Kurbatsky, ed., *Combustion and Fire in Forests* (1973): 223–227.

Vasquez, A., and J. M. Moreno. "Spatial Pattern of Lightning and Human Caused Fires in Spain." In *Proceedings, 2nd International Conference on Forest Fire Research,* vol. 2, pp. 649–650. Coimbra: Universidade de Coimbra, 1994.

Västerbottens Museum. *Historien om Umeå.* Umeå: Västerbottens Museet, n.d.

Vavilov, N. I. "The Origin, Variation, Immunity and Breeding of Cultivated Plants," translated by K. Starr Chester. *Chronica Botanica* 13 (1949–50).

Vélez, Ricardo. "High Intensity Forest Fires in the Mediterranean Basin: Natural and Socio-economic Causes." *Disaster Management* 5 (1993): 16–20.

———. "The 1994 Forest Fire Season." *International Forest Fire News* 12 (1995): 12–13.

Vergil. *The Aeneid,* translated by T. H. Delabere-May. New York: Bantam Books, 1961.

Vernicos, Nicolas. "The Islands of Greece." In *Sustainable Development and Environmental Management of Small Islands,* edited by W. Beller et al., pp. 141–168. Man and the Biosphere Series, 5. New York: Parthenon Publ. Group, 1990.

Viegas, Domingos Xavier, ed. *Jornadas Cientificas sobre Incendios Florestais.* Coimbra: University of Coimbra, 1988.

———. *1st International Conference on Forest Fire Research.* 2 vols. Coimbra: University of Coimbra, 1990.

———. *2nd International Conference on Forest Fire Research.* 2 vols. Coimbra: University of Coimbra, 1994.

Vilkuna, Kustaa. "Varpå Beror den Finske Svedjebondens Kolonisationsfömaga." *Värmland Förr och Nu* 51 (1953): 9–20.

Vincent, Peter. *The Biogeography of the British Isles: An Introduction.* London: Routledge, 1990.

Viosca, Percy, Jr. "Spontaneous Combustion in the Marshes of Southern Louisiana." *Ecology* 12 (1931): 439–442.

Viro, P. J. "Prescribed Burning in Forestry." *Communicationes Instituti Forestalis Fenniae* 67 (1969).

Vogl, Richard J. "The Role of Fire in the Evolution of the Hawaiian Flora and Vegetation." In *Proceedings, Tall Timbers Fire Ecology Conference,* vol. 9, pp. 5–60. Tallahassee: Tall Timbers Research Station, 1969.

Von Badenberg. "Große Waldbrand in der Osbserförsterei Christianstadt am 31. August 1892." *Zeitschrift für Forst- und Jagdwesen* 25 (1893): 359–360.

Vorren, Karl-Dag. "Anthropogenic Influence on the Natural Vegetation in Coastal North Norway during the Holocene: Development of Farming and Pastures." *Norwegian Archaeological Review* 12 (1979): 1–21.

———. "The Impact of Early Agriculture on the Vegetation of Northern Norway: A Discussion of Anthropogenic Indicators in Biostratigraphical Data." In *Anthropogenic Indicators in Pollen Diagrams,* edited by Karl-Ernst Behre, pp. 1–18. Rotterdam: A. A. Balkema, 1986.

Wakefield, Edward Gibbon. *Swing Unmasked or, The Causes of Rural Incendiarism.* London, 1831.

Wahlgren, A. *Skogsskötsel.* Stockholm, 1914.

Walker, D., and R. G. West, eds. *Studies in the Vegetational History of the British Isles.* London: Cambridge University Press, 1970.

Wallace, Alfred. *Island Life,* 3d edition. London: Macmillan and Co., 1902.

Wallace, Robert. *Heather and Moor Burning for Grouse and Sheep.* Edinburgh, 1917.

Wallerström, Thomas. "Odlingsspår i skogsmark–om svedjande i Råneå och Töre socknar i arkeologisk belysning." *Norbotten.* Norbottens Museum Årsbok (1984): 21–51.

Walton, C. L. "Transhumance and Its Survival in Great Britain." *The Geographical Teacher* 10 (1919–20): 103–106.

Ward, S. D. "Controlled Burning of Heather, Grass, and Gorse." *Nature in Wales* 13 (1972): 24–32.

Watts, David. *The West Indies: Patterns of Development, Culture and Environmental Change since 1492.* Cambridge: Cambridge University Press, 1987.

Weber, Eugen. *Peasants into Frenchmen: The Modernization of Rural France, 1870–1914.* Palo Alto: Stanford University Press, 1976.

Weber, Friedrich Christian. *The Present State of Russia.* 2 vols. London: Frank Cass & Co., Inc., 1968.

Weck, Johannes. *Waldbrand: Seine Vorbeugung und Bekämpfung.* Stuttgart: W. Kuhlammer Verlag, 1950.

Weimarck, Gunhild. "Svedjebruket i Södra Scerige." *Bygd och natur 60 Årsbok,* 1979: 37–56.

———. *Ulfshult: Investigations Concerning the Use of Soil and Forest in Ulfshult, Parish of Örkened, during the Last 250 Years.* Acta Universitatis Lundensis, sectio II, no. 6. Lund, 1968.

Wein, Ross W., and David A. MacLean, eds. *The Role of Fire in Northern Circumpolar Ecosystems.* SCOPE, 18. New York: John Wiley and Sons, 1983.

Welinder, Stig. "Prehistoric Agriculture in Eastern Middle Sweden." *Acta Archaeologica Lundensia.* Series in 8 Minore, no. 4. Lund, 1975.

Wells, A. J. "Helping the Sierra Sequoias." *Sunset Magazine* 16 (1906): 280–283.

Wells, Roger. "Rural Rebels in Southern England in the 1830s." In *Artisans, Peasants and Proletarians, 1760–1860,* edited by C. Emsley and J. Walvin, pp. 124–165. London: Croom Helm, 1985.

Wenyon, Charles. *Across Siberia on the Great Post Road.* New York: Arno Press, 1971 (reprint).

Wertime, Theodore A., and Steven F. Wertime, eds. *Early Pyrotechnology: The Evolution of the First Fire-Using Industries.* Washington, D.C.: Smithsonian Institution Press, 1982.

West, John F. *Faroe: The Emergence of a Nation.* London: C. Hurst and Co., 1972.

Westin, Josef. *Kultergeografiska Studier Inom Nätra-, Näske-, och Utbyåarnas Flodområden samt Angrånsande Kusttrakter.* Meddelanden från Lunds Universitets Geografiska Institution. Avhandlingar II. Lund: Carl Bloms Boktryckebi, 1930.

Wharton, Captain W. J. L., ed. *Captain Cook's Journal during His First Voyage Round the World.* . . . London, 1893; facsimile ed., Libraries Board of South Australia, 1968.

White, Cliff. *Wildland Fires in Banff National Park, 1880–1980.* Occasional Paper, 3. Ottawa: Parks Canada, 1985.

White, Gilbert. *The Natural History of Selborne.* London: Arrowsmith, 1924.

White, K. D. *Roman Farming.* London: Thames and Hudson, 1970.

White, R. S., and M. F. Rush. "The Jiagedaqui Fire Management Project (JAIPRO): An Example of International Assistance." In *The Art and Science of Fire Management,* edited by M. E. Alexander and G. F. Bisgrove, pp. 287–296. Information Report NOR-X-309. Edmonton: Northern Forestry Center, 1990.

Whitehouse, David, and Ruth Whitehouse. *Archaeological Atlas of the World.* London: Thames and Hudson, 1975.

Whittle, Alasdair. *Neolithic Europe: A Survey.* Cambridge: Cambridge University Press, 1985.

Wibeck, Evard. "Om ljungbränning för skogskultur." *Meddlanden från statens skogsvörsöksanstalt* 8 (1911): 7–94.

Wick, Lucia. "Early-Holocene Reforestation and Vegetation Change at a Lake Near the Alpine Forest Limit: Laga Basso (2250 m asl), Northern Italy." In *Festschrift Gerhard Lang,* edited by A. F. Lotter and B. Ammann, pp. 555–563. *Dissertationes Botanicae* 234 (1994).

Wickstrom, C. Kristina Roper. *Issues Concerning Native American Use of Fire: A Literature Review.* Yosemite Research Center, Publications in Anthropology, 6. Yosemite National Park, 1987.

Wiener, Douglas. *Models of Nature: Ecology, Conservation, and Cultural Revolution in Soviet Russia.* Bloomington: Indiana University Press, 1988.

Wik, Maria. *Environmental Records of Carbonaceous Fly-Ash Particles from Fossil-fuel Combustion.* Ph.D. dissertation, University of Umeå, 1992.

Wikelski, Martin. "Setting a World Heritage Ablaze: The 1994 Fire in the Galápagos." *International Forest Fire News* 14 (1996): 8–11.

Wilde, Lady. *Ancient Legends, Mystic Charms, and Superstitions of Ireland.* 2 vols. London, 1887.

Wilton, B. "Straw: Burn or Incorporate?" *Span* (January 28, 1985).

Wood, Alan, ed. *The History of Siberia.* New York: Routledge, 1991.

Woodhouse, A. E., ed. *New Zealand Farm and Station Verse, 1850–1950.* Auckland: Whitcombe & Tombs Ltd, 1950.

Woolsey, Theodore S., Jr. *French Forests and Forestry: Tunisia, Algeria, Corsica.* New York: John Wiley and Sons, 1917.

Woolsey, Theodore S., Jr., and William B. Greeley. *Studies in French Forestry.* New York: John Wiley and Sons, 1920.

Worster, Donald. *Nature's Economy: The Roots of Ecology.* Garden City: Anchor Books, 1979.

Wretlind, J. E. "Naturbetingelserna för de nordsvenska järnpodsoleråde moränmarkernas tall-hadar och mossrika skogssamhällen." *Svenska skossvardsföreningens tidskrift* (1934): 329–390.

———. *Nordsvensk hyggesbränning.* Stockholm: Truckeri AB Thule, 1948.

———. "Om hyggesbränningarna inom Malå revir." *Norlands skogsvårdsrörbunds tidskrift* (1932): 243–331.

Wright, George Frederick. *Asiatic Russia.* 2 vols. New York, 1902.

Wright, Henry A., and Arthur W. Bailey. *Fire Ecology: United States and Southern Canada.* New York: Wiley-Interscience, 1982.

Wright, L. W., and P. J. Wanstall. *The Vegetation of Mediterranean France: A Review.* Occasional Papers, 9. London: Department of Geography, University of London, 1977.

Wright, Richardson L., and Bassett Digby. *Through Siberia: An Empire in the Making.* New York: McBride, Nast, and Co., 1913.

Wuorinen, John H. *The Finns on the Delaware, 1638–1655.* New York: Columbia University Press, 1938.

Wynn, G. "Pioneers, Politicians and the Conservation of Forests in Early New Zealand." *Journal of Historical Geography* 5 (1979): 171–188.

Young, Charles R. *The Royal Forests of Medieval England.* Philadelphia: University of Pennsylvania Press, 1979.

Young, Reverend Arthur. *General View of the Agriculture of the County of Sussex.* New York: A. M. Kelley, 1970 (reprint).

Zackrisson, Olle. "Dendroekologisks metoder at spara tidigara kulturinflytandei den norrlänska barrskogen." *Fornvännen* 74 (1979): 259–268.

———. "Forest Fire History: Ecological Significance and Dating Problems in the North Swedish Boreal Forest." In *Proceedings of the Fire History Workshop,* edited by Marvin A. Stokes and John H. Dieterich, pp. 120–123. General Technical Report RM-81. U.S. Forest Service, 1980.

———. "Influence of Forest Fires on the North Swedish Boreal Forest." *Oikos* 29 (1977): 22–32.

———. "Skogsvegetationen vid stranden av Storvindeln under 200 år." *Svensk Botanisk Tidskrift* 72 (1978): 205–226.

Zackrisson, Olle, and Marie-Charlotte Nilsson. "Allelopati och dess betydelse po scårföryngråde skogsmarker." *Skogsfakta* 59 (1989).

Zohary, Daniel, and Maria Hopf. *Domestication of Plants in the Old World.* Oxford: Clarendon Press, 1988.

INDEX

Abihu, 62, 395
Abolin, R. I., 332
Aboriginal fire, 29, 299–301, 350, 388, 451. *See also* Fire hunting
Abraham, 61–62
L'Academie Malgache, 440
Achilles, 45
Acidification (Swedish lakes), 271–273
Acland, J. B. A., 430
Adams, Arthur, 298
Adolphus, Gustavus, 72
Aegean islands, 127–128
Aeneid, 45, 55, 63, 89, 90, 397; as fire allegory, 463
Aerial fire protection, 517–531
Afforestation, 185, 324, 361, 499, 502; Britain, 364–366; Canaries, 390; Central Europe, 195–187, 190–201; fire protection for, 199–201; India, 486; Ireland, 373; Madeira, 389; Russia, 325. *See also* Reforestation
Africa, 3, 10–12, 17–18, 30, 97, 156, 292, 360, 383, 385, 401, 410, 417, 436, 441, 444, 453–454, 456, 460, 464–465, 467, 471, 474, 477, 482, 491, 498, 517, 533. *See also* North Africa; South Africa; West Africa
Ager, 35, 86–88, 96, 104, 108–109, 158, 161, 166, 176, 180, 203. *See also* Agricultural fire; Saltus; Silva
Agricultural fire, 25, 31–41, 287, 460; boreal Europe, 242–254; Britain, 348–352, 356–357, 367, 514–516; central Europe, 147–209 *passim*; as ceremony, 242–254; colonization of

steppes, 301–303; ecology of, 87–88; fire-fallow systems, 34–37, 158–166 *passim;* France, 108, 164, 167–170; Mediterranean Europe, 86–95; New Zealand, 430–434; and pastoralism, 88–91; and reclamation of Europe, 32–41; Russia, 276, 281–287, 309–311; and transfer of European practices, 467–474. *See also* Agricultural revolution; Pastoral fires; Swidden
Agricultural revolution, 346, 351, 359; Britain, 351; 356; central Europe, 166–184; and forestry, 187–188; Ireland, 372–373; problems with, 187–188; Russia, 312–318; Sweden, 252–253. *See also* Agricultural fire; Paring and burning
Agroforestry, 473. *See also Taungya*
Ainu, 299–300
Air tankers, 506, 538. *See also* CL-215
Alang-alang, 420, 424
Alaska, 20, 126, 521
Alexander I (tsar), 293, 321
Alexander the Great, 76
Alexis (tsar), 279
Alfonso V of Aragon, 103
Alfonso X of Castile, 99
Algeria, 107, 135–136, 440, 501, 503; fire history; 120–125
Algerian Forest Service, 122–125
Alheden, Denmark, 172–173
Alps, 11–12, 14, 103, 106, 112, 149, 158, 162–163, 177, 182–183, 194, 373, 377, 485; fire protection for, 195–196; origin of term, 182

Weyerhaeuser Environmental Books

William Cronon, Editor

Weyerhaeuser Environmental Books explore human relationships with natural environments in all their variety and complexity. They seek to cast new light on the ways that natural systems affect human communities, the ways that people affect the environments of which they are a part, and the ways that different cultural conceptions of nature profoundly shape our sense of the world around us.

The Natural History of Puget Sound Country by Arthur R. Kruckeberg

Forest Dreams, Forest Nightmares: The Paradox of Old Growth in the Inland West by Nancy Langston

Landscapes of Promise: The Oregon Story, 1800–1940 by William G. Robbins

Weyerhaeuser Environmental Classics

The Great Columbia Plain: A Historical Geography, 1805–1910 by D. W. Meinig

Mountain Gloom and Mountain Glory: The Development of the Aesthetics of the Infinite by Marjorie Hope Nicolson

Cycle of Fire by Stephen J. Pyne

World Fire: The Culture of Fire on Earth

Vestal Fire: An Environmental History, Told through Fire, of Europe and Europe's Encounter with the World

Fire in America: A Cultural History of Wildland and Rural Fire

Burning Bush: A Fire History of Australia

The Ice: A Journey to Antarctica

VESTAL FIRE

*An Environmental History,
Told through Fire, of Europe and
Europe's Encounter with the World*

Stephen J. Pyne

Foreword by William Cronon

"*Vestal Fire* is Stephen Pyne's masterpiece. In it, he offers nothing less than a retelling of all of European history from a vantage point no other historian has ever adopted so consistently before: that of the fire which in Pyne's view burns at the very heart of Western civilization. Fire, he argues, was pivotal throughout the long process of creating Europe as we know it today: employed by early European peoples to clear the continent for agriculture, present always in the march of armies and empires, contained but never fully controlled in the rise of a new urban-industrial order, and fundamental to Europe's eventual colonial expansion to the far corners of the planet."—William Cronon

Stephen Pyne has been described as having a consciousness "composed of equal parts historian, ecologist, philosopher, critic, poet, and sociologist." Here he takes the reader on a journey through time, exploring the terrain of Europe and the uses and abuses of these lands as well as, through migration and conquest, many parts of the rest of the world. Whether he is discussing the Mediterranean region, Russia, Scandinavia, the British Isles, central Europe, or colonized islands; whether he is considering the impact of agriculture, forestry, or Enlightenment thinking, the author brings an unmatched insight to his subject.

Vestal Fire takes its title from Vesta, Roman goddess of the hearth and keeper of the sacred fire on Mount Olympus. But the book's title also suggests the strengths and limita-